DIALECTICS

THE LOGIC OF MARXISM, AND ITS CRITICS — *AN ESSAY IN EXPLORATION*

BY

T. A. JACKSON

" I beseech you, in the bowels of Christ—believe it possible you may be mistaken ! "—OLIVER CROMWELL.

" Even a little humour is permissible if it be not overdone."
—FRED CASEY.

" The slogan is not to flinch in the struggle."—F. ENGELS.

LONDON

LAWRENCE AND WISHART LTD

FIRST PUBLISHED IN 1936

MADE AND PRINTED IN GREAT BRITAIN BY TONBRIDGE PRINTERS LTD
PEACH HALL WORKS TONBRIDGE KENT

CONTENTS

PROLOGUE

THIS essay is an attempt to clear the ground for a better and fuller appreciation of that which gives Marxism its living unity—namely, the Dialectical Materialist *Method*. Its special feature is that it seeks to show what this method *is* by means of an examination of what it *did* in the hands of Marx and Engels. It considers the Dialectical Materialist Method *in action* in the theoretical practice of these its first elaborators, and following them (so far as falls within its purpose) that of their disciples, Lenin and Stalin.

No pretence is made that this essay is in any way final or authoritative. Very much to the contrary : it is in every respect an *essay*, a venture—an attempt at a provisional exploration of a field which no British Marxist has hitherto attempted on anything but a most perfunctory scale. It is therefore liable to all the faults and mischances necessarily attending such provisional essays. None the less it *is—an attempt* ! If its demerits—whatever they may be—provoke others better qualified to cover the ground in a more worthy manner it will have more than served its purpose.

This essay has been rendered necessary by two things. The first is the appalling state of Marxist studies in England, as evidenced by the quality of all but a very few of the works purporting to treat of Marx and Marxism which have appeared in Britain in recent years ; the second is the fact of the existence of a cleavage in the Marxist camp represented by the conflict—carried at times to the pitch of actual combat in arms—between the Communists on the one side and the Social-Democrats and their allies upon the other.

No Marxist can view this conflict without concern : no Marxist who takes his Marxism seriously can treat it as a mere *personal* squabble, arising from " faults on both sides," which could be composed by the exercise of tact and patience. What is at stake in this conflict is the basic significance of Marxism itself, and upon such an issue no Marxist can do other than choose his side and help to fight the issue, theoretical

9

and practical, to a finish.   Full frankness is far more likely to produce union and agreement than any " diplomacy."

As long ago as April, 1920, Stalin spoke of this cleavage in Marxism in these words :

" There are two groups of Marxists.   Both are working under the flag of Marxism and consider themselves genuine Marxists.   Nevertheless they are far from being identical.   More than that.   A complete gulf divides them, for their respective methods of work are diametrically opposed to each other.

" The first group usually confines itself to the superficial recognition of Marxism—to solemnly proclaiming it.   Unable or not willing to study *the essence* of Marxism, unable or not willing to apply it in practical life, it transforms the living revolutionary propositions of Marxism into dead, meaningless formulas.   It bases its activities, not on experience, not on the results of practical work, but on quotations from Marx.   It takes its guiding lines and directives not from an analysis of living reality, but from analogies and historical parallels.   Discrepancy between word and deed—such is the principal disease from which this group suffers. . . . The name of this group is, in Russia, Menshevism ; in Europe, Opportunism.

" The second group, on the other hand, transfers the centre of gravity of the question from the superficial recognition of Marxism to its realisation, to its application in practical life.   Indicating the path and means of realising Marxism for various situations, changing the path and means when the situation changes—this is what this group concentrates on mainly.   It takes its directives and its guiding lines not from historical analogies and parallels, but from the study of surrounding conditions.   In its activities it relies not on quotations and aphorisms, but on practical experiences, testing every step it takes by experience, learning from its mistakes and teaching others to build a new life.   This . . . explains why in the activities of this group there are no discrepancies between word and deed, and why the teachings of Marx fully preserve their living, revolutionary force. . . . The name of this group is Bolshevism —Communism."—STALIN: *Lenin*, pp. 5-6.

Disregarding as irrelevant the objection that might be urged that Stalin, being a partisan in the dispute, is no more than any man " a judge in his own cause," we affirm that the issue is ultimately as Stalin here states it.

" Marxism " is either a mere abstract opinion, having only an incidental connection with the practical realities of life and struggle—in which case there is no need for a " Marxist " to feel responsible for squaring his theory with his practice— or, alternatively, the Marxist world-conception is primarily a *theory of action*, one derived so intimately from the facts of life and struggle that he who declares himself a Marxist thereby takes upon himself the responsibility for *living* Marxism as well as preaching it.

. . . . .

But before Marxism can be *lived* it must be *understood* : before it can be wielded as a weapon it must be *grasped*. And in order that a grasp of the essential logic of Marxism may become widespread in Britain it is before all things necessary to clear away the whole fabric of misconceptions and misrepresentations which stand as a blanket-veil between the ordinary British worker and Marxist understanding.

Although there have been " Marxists " of sorts in Britain since before the death of Marx, the working-class movement in Britain has never been consciously or purposefully Marxist. At best it has been *adulterated* by such " Marxism " as has been available, and this, the native-British " Marxism," has in turn, " like the dyer's hand," been " subdued to that it works in."

Nothing evidences this better than the quality of the literature produced by native British Marxists. Apart from a score of works, all of recent date, in which an attempt is made to elucidate current problems by the aid of Marxist theory, this native British Marxist literature consists almost wholly of works purporting to " explain " Marxist theory *in* the *abstract*, in terms suited to the (presumably *infantile*) understanding of the plain man.

No objection is here raised to simplification *as such*. On the contrary, no work could be more useful than that of presenting Marxism in such a way as can easily be assimilated by the ordinary man. What calls for protest is the fact that those who in Britain set out to " simplify " Marx commonly begin by reducing him to a *simpleton*, and those who offer to " explain " him are as a rule primarily concerned only to *explain him away*.

We take the ground here that Marx and Engels (and this

applies also to Lenin and Stalin) are their own best expounders :
that to attempt to " simplify " that which they have already
made as simple as it is humanly possible to make it, cannot
fail to result in a distortion of their plain sense and a misrepresentation of their clearly-presented meaning.   Not
" simplification " but *amplification* and, above all, *application*
is what Marxism needs in Britain.

.   .   .   .   .

As usually presented to the English-speaking world by
its popular expositors, literary and oratorical, " Marxism "
is a loosely aggregated bundle of separate and distinct
" theories " which have no connection with each other
beyond the fortuitous fact that they all originated with
the one man, Karl Marx.   Resolved thus into a jumble of
" theories "—of Value, of Capital, of Crises, of History, of
Class-War, of Revolution, and so on—each theory being
presented as quite separate and self-contained—Marxism
becomes an Old Curiosity Shop in which political amateurs
and literary *dilettanti* can rummage for decorative oddments,
just as they rummage in the Caledonian Market for old china,
pewter plates, and bawdy prints.

In this way it has become quite a tradition in Britain for
men to pose as " Marxists " on the strength of wearing a
" Marxist " feather in the hair, or fig leaf on their intellectual
nakedness.   Nobody laughs in Britain to hear of " Marxists "
who are also Christians, Theosophists, Spiritualists, or even
Thomists—men who contrive to divide their allegiance
between Karl Marx and the Blessed Saint Thomas Aquinas,
even as others, with equal solemnity, seek to effect a synthesis
between the philosophies of Marxism and of the Herr Doktor
Sigmund Freud.

This eclectic-opportunist trick of disrupting the living unity
of Marxism into a rubbish-heap of incompatible fragments
has in Britain received high academic approval.   Here, for
instance, are the words of the learned Professor of Political
Science in the University of London :

" The essence of Marx's work lies not in any special
economic doctrine so much as in the *spirit* by which this
total accomplishment was performed. . . .

" Marxism as a social philosophy can be most usefully
resolved into *four distinct parts*.   It is first and foremost
a *philosophy of history* . . . it is a *theory of social development* intended to guide the party of which he was a

leader. **Marx** in the third place outlined a *tactic*. . . .
He was, finally, an *economic theorist*.

" For Marx himself, of course, none of these aspects
is properly separable from any other. They form a
logical whole, the unity of which he would have passion-
ately defended. It is, however, possible to reject the
validity of his economic system, while accepting the
large outlines of his social theory."—Professor H. J.
LASKI : *Communism*, pp. 22–26.

That this may fairly be taken as representative of what
passes for " Marxism " in Britain is evidenced by the fact
that Professor Laski has, without in any way modifying the
opinion above cited, taken of late to calling himself a
" Marxist." As such he has been welcomed with acclaim
into the " Marxist " camp, even to the extent of being chosen
as the chief speaker at the function organised by the (*Marxist*)
National Council of Labour Colleges to commemorate the
fiftieth anniversary of the death of Karl Marx.

Professor Laski exhibits, in the quotation given above, a
characteristic common to the whole British school of " explainers " of Marx. *He takes it calmly for granted that he
understands Marxism far better than Marx understood it
himself !* Marx, he argues, would have " defended passion-
ately " *the logical unity* of his theoretical system. But herein,
according to Professor Laski, Karl Marx was self-deluded.
Marxism, he affirms, *can* be " separated " into parts capable
of being considered in complete isolation. So, we might
retort, is Professor Laski capable of being " separated " from
his head, his lights, or his liver ! But in that case he would
cease to be Professor Laski. And in like manner a Marxism
disrupted is not Marxism, but a mangled corpse.

Professor Laski, however, sins in thoroughly respectable
company. Here is a choice specimen of what has passed in
Britain for a critical evaluation of Marxist doctrine :

" There are two remarkable inconsistencies between
the general sociological position taken up by Marx and
Engels and their persistent assertion of the economic
basis of history. . . . In the first place they agreed
that . . . ' the whole world, natural, historical, intellectual, is represented as a process, i.e., as in constant
motion, change, transformation, development.' If that
be true, is it conceivable that every department of life—
—' natural, historical, intellectual ' (by the way, a very
slipshod division)—is *chained* to economics and cannot

attain an independent development and existence of its own ? In the second place, Marx's insistence that each epoch has its own characteristic law of development is inconsistent with the assertion that economic considerations are the prime movers in historic evolution."— J. RAMSAY MACDONALD : *Socialism and Society*, p. 42.

This passage, so sublime in its owlish stupidity, so ludicrous in its spurious profundity, is truly characteristic of Ramsay MacDonald ; but, as is apparent from its family likeness to the quotation from Professor Laski, it is none the less characteristic of the whole " British " school of Marxian interpretation.

That MacDonald, of all men living or dead, should accuse *anybody* (let alone Engels !) of " slipshod " thought or speech is MacDonaldite *in excelsis*. It should not, however, prevent us from noting that in failing to perceive any reason for the allocation of the phenomena of universal development into just those departments—of Nature, of History, and of the Thought-process in itself—MacDonald follows the fashion of his school in treating as of no account the fundamental dialectical *method* whereby the conclusions of Marx and Engels were reached.

Similarly MacDonald, faced with an affirmation that the entire universe is in constant *movement*, finds a " contradiction " between that affirmation and the assertion that history has an " economic basis." Why ? Because this latter assertion, to MacDonald (and his school), means that " every department of life " (who said " slipshod " ?) " is *chained* to economics."

Since to Marx the term " economics " denotes a *movement*— " the sum and total of human productive activity—with its objective outcome "—and was therefore " a department of life " (in the MacDonaldite sense)—to talk of mankind's non-economic activities being " chained " to their economic ones is as illuminating as to speak of a man being " chained " to his own feet or bowels. To resent the fact that the life activities of men in their social inter-relations are, however various, all interdependent, is, in effect, to demand a physiology in which digestion goes on without intestines and is quite " independent " of food or feeding.

Likewise MacDonald sees in the assertion that historic epochs have differing laws of development a contradiction to the assertion that in historical evolution economic determinants are primary. Why ? To Marx epochs are distinguishable each from each precisely by means of differences, progressively developed, in the economic constitution of society. For MacDonald, on the other hand, as for the true-blue British school of economists, " economic laws " are part of the *fixed and immutable* order of Nature, and can no more *change* than the lions in Trafalgar Square can lay eggs.

In short, MacDonald herein places himself critically on a par with that soldier in the British force sent in 1919 to overthrow the Soviet regime who was given a pot of caviare as part of his loot. " This here *jam*," said he, " tastes *fishy* ! " MacDonald complains of Marx's doctrine that it is neither metaphysical, eclectic, nor idealist, but *Dialectical* and *Materialist*.

. . . . .

A significant change has overtaken the attitude of the British intelligentsia towards Marx and Marxism—a change not unconnected with the continuance of the world depression and the failure of every effort to overthrow the (*Marxist*) Communist regime in the U.S.S.R. Marx is now by general consent admitted to the ranks of the very greatest intellects of all time, while Dialectical Materialism—the *method* and *world-conception* of Marx and Marxism—is beginning to be discussed, for the truly " British " reason that it is " the official (!) philosophy " of the U.S.S.R.

It would therefore seem to be timely to direct attention to the essential *unity* of Marxism and to its validity as a guide to action. As against all the critics, belittlers, revisers and explainers of Marx, we affirm, and seek herein to prove, that in the fifty years and more which have elapsed since Marx died events have so completely vindicated his standpoint, his method, and his main conclusions that his doctrine is, in general, *truer to-day than when it was first formulated*.

This is, we affirm, not only true objectively in the sense that developments have in fact made actual the situations and inter-relations which Marx and Engels had the genius to foresee and to predict, but true also subjectively, in the sense that the working-class in Britain, and with it its allies in the ranks of the intelligentsia and the progressive middle and upper classes, are better prepared, theoretically, to *begin* to comprehend Marxist theory than they were in Marx's own lifetime—than they ever have been at any time previous to this time present.

That consideration has determined the form of this essay

as well as its substance. As to the latter, it will be perceived that, far from making any attempt to carry Marxist theory *beyond* the point at which Marx left it, the main, virtually the sole, purpose of this essay, is to demonstrate the point at which Marxist theory *began*.

The respects in which, for instance, Lenin, and following Lenin, Stalin, have extended and amplified Marxist theory are dealt with herein only so far as is necessary to establish their essential connection with the basic presuppositions and method of Marx and Engels themselves.

For that reason the earlier chapters of this essay are devoted to an attempt to elucidate, with the aid of Marx's *Theses on Feuerbach*—herein taken as the seminal form of Marxian Theory—the whole philosophical and political-theoretical background from which Marxism took its rise. That this entails what will seem, at first glance, to be a highly disconnected survey of the *incidentals* of the Marxist world-conception, is a circumstance which was unavoidable. It has the methodological advantage of presenting Marxism in its embryonic phases as a preliminary to, and as an elucidation of, the theory in its fully matured form.

The continuity of the earlier chapters, and more or less of the whole work, is, furthermore, interrupted by frequent digressions in which the objections and mis-presentations of the would-be " simplifiers " of Marx are disposed of. This was necessary to the purpose of the essay—since it is precisely the efforts of these " simplifiers " which constitute to-day the chief obstacle to the general understanding and acceptance of Marx's theory and practice. To those who find these " interruptions " of the argument an annoyance sympathy is extended, but no apology. To such readers I offer a hint borrowed from Heine :

> " If you who read become tired of the ' stupid ' stuff herein, just think of what a dreary time I must have had in writing it ! I would recommend you, on the whole, once in a while to skip half a dozen leaves, for in that way you will arrive much sooner at the end."
> —HEINE : *The Baths of Lucca*, Chap. IX.

For readers with stouter stomachs, and a better comprehension of the purpose in view, we note that after the survey of the *Theses on Feuerbach* the essay deals in succession with the relations between the Marxist conceptions of Nature and of History ; and between those of History and of Revolution in general and the Proletarian Revolution in particular. Here again the purpose is *not* to advance any new or original speculations, but, on the contrary, to explore the route by which Marx and Engels reached the conceptions for which they are famous. Superficially these chapters might seem to be guilty of the rashness of challenging comparison with (particularly) Engels' classic expositions, *Ludwig Feuerbach* and *Anti-Dühring*. A more careful reading will show that they are designed expressly to enable a reader to *begin* the reading of those masterpieces (and with them every work of Marx and of Lenin—particularly the latter's *Materialism and Empirio-Criticism*) with a fuller and a better comprehension of their purpose than has hitherto commonly been brought to their study in Britain.

In the culminating chapter four selected " man-handlers " of the Marxist Dialectic are critically examined at full length. This is done in order to complete the exposition by demonstrating, in sequence with the preceding chapters, the general connection between the Marxist conception of understanding (its subjective Dialectics) and its conceptions of Nature, History, and Revolution (its objective Dialectics). The four victims chosen for this special treatment have been so selected because they are typical of the main trends of divergence from the true line of Marxist advance observable in the Marxist movement in Britain to-day.

No apology is offered for the *manner* of this criticism :

> " It's *war* we're in ; not *politics* !
> It's *systems* wrastling now, not *parties*.
> And vict'ry in the end'll fix
> Where longest will and truest heart is ! "
> —LOWELL.

The author has been far too occupied with the problem of attaining accuracy to find time to study politeness.

For the translations from Marx, Engels, and Heine for which no page references are given the author accepts full responsibility. Those from Marx, Engels, Lenin, and Stalin which have page references are taken from the editions published by Messrs. Martin Lawrence (who were good

B

enough to place at the author's disposal advance copies of
their more recent issues), except, of course, in the cases of
Marx's *Capital* (Vol. I, Sonnenschein edition ; Vols. II and
III, Kerr's edition) Engels' *Socialism Utopian and Scientific*
and his *Condition of the Working Class in England in* 1844
(Allen and Unwin). I have also to thank Messrs. Martin
Lawrence for many acts of help and encouragement; and
those comrades who have looked over the MSS. and the
proofs and made helpful suggestions deserve a public ack-
nowledgement likewise. Neither of these comrades is to be
blamed for any faults found herein; on the contrary, the
reader has them to thank for the fact that there are not
many more.

CHAPTER I

THE MAKING OF MARXISM

" Not criticism but revolution is the motive force of history."
                                    MARX-ENGELS : *German Ideology.*

MARXISM considered as an objective fact is a social *movement.*

It is a movement which takes the historical form of a revolutionary class struggle—that of the proletariat, the class of those who live wholly or mainly by the sale of their power to labour.

This struggle is simultaneously one *against* something, namely capitalism, and *for* something, namely Socialism and Communism. More specifically, it is a struggle to wrest the power of mastery and control in society—the State power—from the capitalist class, in order that the proletariat (aided by its allies) becoming the ruling class in its turn may effect the transformation of Human Society from one organised primarily for the production of commodities (of things to sell) into one organised basically for the production of things to satisfy the needs and desires of the people who co-operate to produce them.

Marxism is thus a movement in which theory and practice form a synthetic whole. It can be defined in respect of the objective at which it aims as the theory and practice of the revolutionary struggle of the proletariat (*a*) for the conquest of State power, (*b*) for the maintenance of the revolutionary dictatorship of the proletariat through a period of revolution until, (*c*) by the economic and social reconstruction of society, class divisions (and with them class struggles and the dictatorial State power historically begotten by class struggles), have been eliminated in consequence of the removal of that which caused their rise and development.

Discriminating in this definition between the end and the means—the process whereby the end is reached—we note that :

    A. The ultimate end envisaged by Marxism is a classless
        society in which State power—the power wielded by
        a ruling class in constraint and coercion of all rival
        classes—no longer exists. This does not mean that
        what is envisaged is a condition of planless anarchy.

It means that " when the State for the first time becomes truly the instrument of all members of society alike " it ceases to be *coercive*, and therefore ceases to be a " State." " The *government* of persons will be replaced by the *administration* of things." (ENGELS.) The revolutionary class struggle waged by Marxism is, therefore, waged as a means to the end of abolishing all class struggles, and all possibility of their arising. Only so can the Marxian theory and practice of revolutionary class struggle be rightly evaluated.

B. The means proposed for the attainment of this end are not arbitrary empirical formulae, capable of application piecemeal as separate and self-contained " reforms." The means envisaged are those of an historically developing process of struggle in which the ultimate end is attained only through a series of historical stages, each of which has its special distinguishing form of development. Thus, the whole process may be divided into (1) The development of the revolutionary proletarian struggle ; (2) The open and conscious struggle for State power ; (3) The enforcement of the proletarian dictatorship (*a*) against would-be counter-revolutionaries ; and (*b*) for the economic transformation of society ; (4) The outcome of the dictatorship in its own replacement by a classless society.

It will be obvious at a glance that this conception derives its force as a whole, and in its parts, from a specific historical conception of Human Society, its nature and mode of development. It pre-supposes, for instance, the existence of class divisions and their developing struggles ; and therein it pre-supposes that these classes had a specific historical origin ; but will, ultimately, be brought to an end by a continuance of the historical process. Equally it presupposes that the course of development of these struggles is influenced by the purposive and conscious action of men as individuals and in their class combinations.

All this presupposes a specific world-conception in which the historical process of Human Society forms a detail in a general whole. And this world-conception, in turn, presupposes a specific theory of knowledge, its nature, origin, and mode of unification—in a word, a *logic*.

The term by which this Marxian world-conception and

its specifically distinguishing *logic* is known is " DIALECTICAL MATERIALISM."

SOME PRELIMINARY CONSIDERATIONS

The founders of Marxism, Karl Marx and Frederick Engels, did not write a textbook on logical method. This has been advanced as a reason for treating their work as unfinished and supplementing it by more " up-to-date " methods.

The unanswerable reply to all such strictures was given by Lenin. Asked by a supercilious intellectual, " What book did Marx or Engels write on Dialectical Materialism ? " Lenin replied with the counter question, " *What book did Marx or Engels write that was* NOT *on Dialectical Materialism ?* "

Since in this essay we seek to extract the logic of Dialectical Materialism from its actual practical use by Marx and Engels, and that not only in their expositions of theory but in their actual revolutionary practice, we shall, while touching upon all the more familiar aspects of Marxism—its conception of political procedure, of History, of Revolution as the out-come of the Historical process, and of the universe generally —do so only so far as they concern our immediate purpose, the exposition of its *logical method*. This restriction of our scope is convenient,—but it has also a no less real incon-venience arising from the organic unity of Marxism as a whole. The distinction of the method from its results can be made only tentatively, and relatively.

Provisionally, then, we begin with an attempt at definitions —remembering that " from a scientific standpoint all definitions are of little value, but do no harm provided their inevitable deficiencies are not forgotten " (ENGELS).

By MATERIALISM we mean any world-conception or mode of thinking which treats thoughts, ideas, concepts, as " *mind pictures* "—as the reflection in human consciousness of a real, material world, existing outside us whose existence is inde-pendent of our consciousness or will.

By IDEALISM we mean any world-conception or way of thinking which treats thoughts, ideas, etc., as *other than* reflections of a *material* world—other than the consequence of, and *reliable pictures* of the world of material things.

By MATTER we mean that which we apprehend by means of our senses, the substance of material things ; anything and everything which, extended in space, offers in greater or less degree resistance to pressure, and manifests movements perceptible by the senses.

" Matter is a philosophic category which refers to the objective reality given to man in his sensations—a reality which is copied, photographed, and reflected by our sensations but which exists independently of them."
—LENIN : *Materialism* (p. 102).

" Matter is that which, acting upon our sense organs, produces sensation ; matter is the objective reality, given to us in sensation."—LENIN : *Materialism* (p. 116).

By METAPHYSICS we mean any way of thinking which supposes that *behind* the " physical " qualities we perceive in material things—including our own bodies and brains and their workings—there is another " something " which is *not* " physical " (meaning not " bodily," i.e. *not* " material "). The Greek word " *Meta*," meaning " beyond," gives the clue to the meaning of " meta-physics."

By DIALECTIC we mean that which partakes of the nature of a " discussion in *dialogue*," in which the Truth is reached by the clash of opposite opinions. Applied to Nature a " Dialectical " conception is one that views all Nature as in process of development in consequence of its inherent interactions or *antagonisms*. Applied to thought and reasoning, *Dialectical* method treats all things and all concepts as *products* of a process, as each a *new* thing brought into being by the inter-action of things *different* from itself ; as things therefore which, being in existence, at once become themselves *foci* of further action and reaction from which *newer* things and formations result.

" To the metaphysician things and their mental reflexes, ideas, are isolated ;—are to be considered one after the other and apart from each other, are objects of investigation, fixed, rigid, given once and for all. . . .

" *Dialectics*, on the other hand, comprehends things and their representations, ideas, in their *essential connections*, their concatenation, motion, origin, and ending."—ENGELS : *Socialism*, pp. 31, 34.

Dialectical Materialism is therefore that sort of Materialism (*a*) which has been freed from Metaphysical and Idealist suppositions ; (*b*) which treats the world of Nature (including men) as in constant process of developing transformation ; and (*c*) which therefore manages its thinking in a correspondingly developing way—proceeding to view all things from the contrasted aspects of their many-sidedness, their unity-in-diversity, and their developmental sequences, external and internal.

Marx and Engels themselves are an illustration of their own dialectical mode of reasoning.

They are known to us as the founders of the theory upon which the whole modern Socialist and Communist movement bases (more or less clearly and consistently) its practice.

In that sense Marxism, " the science of the revolutionary proletarian struggle," is a *cause* of the modern Socialist and Communist movement.

But Marx and Engels were not *born* Marxists ; neither did they *invent* the proletariat or its struggles. What they did was to give to a relatively blind and instinctive struggle the theory which converted it into a *conscious* struggle with a specific plan and purpose.

And Marx and Engels learned how to do this, acquired their own distinctive theory, as a result of participating in the proletarian, Socialist and Communist movement of their own day. Marx and Engels transformed first themselves and thereafter the revolutionary proletarian struggle by practical participation therein. *They acquired their dialectical theory in the course of, and with the aid of, their dialectical practice.* Thus Marxism is at one and the same time a *cause* and a *consequence* of the revolutionary proletarian struggle.

The writings of Marx and Engels placed in chronological order illustrate this. They fall into three main groups.

(1) Works connected with the revolutionary struggles of the period of 1843–51.

(2) Works of theoretical preparation for further struggles : the critical analysis of the existing order.

(3) Works connected with the First International and the revival of the revolutionary proletarian struggle from 1864 onwards. After Marx's death in 1883 Engels carried on the work of developing the re-establishment of the International.

In each of these groups their writings are pre-eminently *practical*. That is to say they deal with questions and problems arising in and from the actual prosecution of the revolutionary struggle. Marx's most famous and least obviously utilitarian work, *Capital*, was, for instance, written with a profoundly practical intent and purpose. He analysed the workings of Capitalism in order the better to be able to carry on the struggle for its overthrow. Even in the most limited sense of the word " practical," the works of Marx and Engels are noteworthy in that *all of them are*

controversial. Capital itself is a " critique " of the classic
political economy of the time. The *Communist Manifesto,*
the next best known (*by name !*) of the works of Marx and
Engels, is, as its name avows, a *party* manifesto. The best
known work of Marx's earlier period, the *Poverty of Philosophy,*
is a polemic against Proudhon. The best known work of
his later period, the *Civil War in France*, is a passionate
polemic in defence of the Commune and against its exterminators—again a *party* manifesto. The best known (by
repute) work of Engels is his *Herr Eugene Dühring's Revolution
in Science* (the *Anti-Dühring*). In fact, the only seeming
exception in the whole of the works of Marx and Engels are
Marx's pamphlet *Wage-Labour and Capital* and Engels'
Ludwig Feuerbach, and each of these is specifically and
categorically propaganda and written with general polemical
intent.

Yet another practical aspect of the writings of Marx and
Engels must be noted. Even if we put aside the works in
which the polemic is against the bourgeois order, rather than
any specific defender thereof, the whole of the writings of
Marx and Engels are directed to the end of clarifying the
theory and bettering the practice of the revolutionary
proletarian struggle, and most of them, in whole or in part,
are directed against *confusionists within the ranks of the
movement itself*.

Those who avow, as do the followers of Kautsky, and
their British imitators, that Lenin was the "inventor" of
the polemical practice of "creating dissension within the
camp" of the "united" Socialist and Labour movement,
are either plain liars or are totally ignorant of the actual work
of Marx and Engels.

For our purpose the earlier period, that which was a
formative period for Marx and Engels themselves and for
their Dialectical Materialism, is of paramount importance.
In this period they conducted polemics against Utopianism
in Britain, Germany and France. Specifically, they wrote
polemics against the " German " (or " true ") Socialists,
against " Bruno Bauer & Co.," against Feuerbach, against
Max Stirner, and against Proudhon. Engels' later polemic
against Dühring was a parallel struggle, as were Marx and
Engels' polemic wars with Bakuninism and the Anarchists.
So, likewise, was Lenin's polemic against Menshevism,
against the Empirio-Critics, and against the Second International and Kautsky. Each is a repetition of the earlier

controversy in a new historical setting. The fundamental similarity of the issues in each case is remarkable.

Since the earlier controversy is less well known, and since it was in the earlier struggle that Marx and Engels " found " themselves, we give it first and fuller consideration.

.   .   .   .

Critics and revisers of Marxism always begin with Marx's and Engels' intellectual dependence upon the philosophy of Hegel. They forget that for every deed, as for every man, there is both a father and a mother. Every deed requires not only a *doer*, with the *will* to do, but the *object* upon which the deed is executed. Every thought requires not only a thinker, but the object of his thought. That Marx and Engels took their departure *from Hegel* is as undoubted as it is important. But what is of infinitely greater importance is the fact that what they took from Hegel was—*their departure*.

That they retained all their lives a fondness for (as Marx himself called it) " coquetting with Hegelian terminology " is true. So do piously brought-up Atheists retain a fondness for " coquetting " with quotations from Scripture. When it is remembered that the Hegelian philosophy remained during the whole period up to 1850 the official philosophy of the Prussian State universities, and that therefore its turns of phrase were the " correct thing " in the serious literature of the day, it will be self-evident why Marx and Engels derived so much zest from using " official " language for revolutionary ends.

Marx and Engels, as university students, made the acquaintance of the Hegelian philosophy just when the " school " it had founded was breaking up into a " Right " and a " Left " wing. Of these schools all that here need be said is that the " Right " clung rigidly to Hegel's *system*— his formal panorama of the universal process—and along with it his *absolute* Idealism, while the " Left," led brilliantly by LUDWIG FEUERBACH (1804–1872), laid its chief emphasis upon Hegel's *method*, his dialectic, and sought with varying degrees of success to free it from mysticism and idealism. Marx and Engels, after having been powerfully influenced by Feuerbach, moved beyond him and evolved a standpoint and a method in which Hegel:—

" was not simply put aside. On the contrary, one started out from his revolutionary side . . . from the *Dialectical method*."—ENGELS : *Feuerbach*, p. 53.

The Hegelian method was " Pelmanised " for its followers in the " sacramental formula " (as Marx called it) "Negation of the Negation." Both Marx and Engels used the phrase— it was an instance of their " coquetting with Hegelian terminology "—with telling effect. Since the phrase is a scandal and an abomination to all bourgeoisdom to this day, and is made a chief count in the indictment against Marx by several of his recent critics, we may profitably give it a little attention.

Terrifying though this phrase may sound, mystifying to the last degree as it becomes in the hands of an idealist, this formula is none the less capable of a simple and, what is more, an illuminating explanation. Light begins to break through the mystery as soon as it is seen (*a*) that it summarises the *conclusion* of a *logical* operation ; (*b*) that it is preceded by a process whose formula is in turn that of Spinoza, " all determination is *negation*."

What does this latter phrase mean ? What it *says* : that all *distinguishing* of things in thought is a de-*term*-ination, a setting of limits to *that which* the " thing " *is*. Or, otherwise stated, all distinguishing of things is an *act* of mentally *separating* a thing from that which it is *not*. Thus all " determination," which is *particularisation*, consists in " negating " or breaking up an undifferentiated *generalisation*.

Furthermore, the process of discriminating one *particular* thing from a general mass is simultaneously a process of distinguishing the *counter*-particularity of that *from which* it is distinguished. Hence (and it is here that Hegel's real contribution *begins*, all the foregoing being common to him and his predecessors)—hence a *full* comprehension of the thing involves comprehending it simultaneously in two opposite ways, namely, as *distinct from* and, at the same time, as *one with* that from which it is distinguished. Hence all logic consists in the performance, with due circumspection, of this operation of *negating* unity by resolving it into multiplicity (Analysis) and *re-creating* it by distinguishing the unity persisting in the multiplicity (Synthesis).

Now it is to be observed that all the text-books on Logic come precisely to this conclusion—that all knowledge is *relative* in the sense that a thing simply cannot be understood from itself alone. To *know* a thing is to distinguish in it the respects in which it is like, and those in which it is unlike, all other things. By grouping these degrees and kinds of likeness and unlikeness in a series of gradations we reach the logical unity of the Universe of Things. Only when we can distinguish in one and the same thing the whole series of its likenesses and differences in their graded inter-relation, from the most uniquely particular to the most comprehensively universal, do we truly *know* that thing. Only when we can do the same for *all* things both separately and in conjunction will we truly *know* the universe in its two-fold character of Unity in Multiplicity and Multiplicity in Unity.

But, if all this is to be found in all the logic books, what was it that Hegel *added*? Two things:

Firstly, being an *Idealist*, Hegel interpreted the canon of the Identity of Being and Thinking as meaning that the logical *activity* of conjoined analysis and synthesis is the *true essence* of the *Universal Unity*—the universe as a whole.

Secondly, Hegel, perceiving that a thing *understood* was *qualitatively* a totally different thing from the same thing *not* understood, saw that *for us* the logical process of understanding did in fact *create new things*!

Combining these two principles synthetically into one, Hegel reached his famous conception of the Universe as in process of perpetual self-creation by means of the logical operation of discriminating itself into This and *not*-This (Affirmation and Negation; Thesis and Antithesis) and re-establishing its unity in a new developed synthesis (the Negated Negation).

As he stands Hegel is, taken at his face value, such a farrago of incomprehensibility that it is obvious that he cannot simply be so taken.

This Marx and Engels saw (along with a few hundred thousand others). But what Marx and Engels were alone in seeing was that, precisely because of the masterly logical consistency with which Hegel had proceeded from his Idealist starting point, his method only needed turning inside out (or right side up) to become an equally consistent and thoroughgoing method for materialism. Take the two points described above:

Hegel started with the axiom of the " identity " (i.e., the complete reciprocal co-relation) of Being and Thinking. Agreed! says the materialist, provided you recognise that Thinking reflects Being and *not vice versa*. Hegel affirmed that the logical process was an *activity*. Agreed! says the materialist, provided you recognise that it is the *subjective form of appearance of an objective activity*, that of a material brain and sense-organs functioning in a living flesh-and-blood human being in a material universe, all of which are pre-supposed in all possible *acts* of thinking, feeling, or willing.

Hegel affirmed that the general form, or " law," of the logical process was a movement from " absolutely " *undifferentiated* unity to "absolutely " *differentiated* unity. Granted, says the materialist—provided that you recognise that what is being differentiated is (*a*) on the one side the objective material universe, and (*b*) on the other side its reflection in human consciousness.

Hegel affirmed that the self-movement of the Universal whole constantly begot, by means of the integrating inter-action of its differentiated details, a connected and pro-gressive *series of new forms*. Granted, says the materialist, provided you concede that these new forms are forms and modes of *material* existence, and that one of the material activities in this process of perpetual creation is that of men themselves.

Thus it was that Hegelianism, the completest and most systematic Negation of Materialism ever developed, begot its own Negation in Dialectical Materialism.

. . . . .

What this revolutionising of the Hegelian method led to in detail at the hands of Marx and Engels it is our purpose to inquire. By a superlatively happy chance we are able to begin our examination at a point where this transformation of the Hegelian method is in actual process of accomplish-ment.

Hunting in 1888 among Marx's papers, Engels lit upon a notebook in which in the spring of 1845 Marx had jotted down for later elaboration eleven notes (or " theses ") on Feuerbach. They are, as Engels said when he published them as an Appendix to his *Ludwig Feuerbach*, " invaluable as the first document in which is deposited the brilliant germ of the new world outlook."

They are rough notes only, and so abbreviated as to be, in places, very hard to render into English. But they are literally " invaluable " for our purpose since they show us Dialectical Materialism almost in the act of getting born. We shall, therefore, first of all set out these *Theses on Feuerbach* in full, and then examine them in detail in succeed-ing chapters.

MARX'S THESES ON FEUERBACH

*** The translation here given is that given as an Appendix in the Martin Lawrence edition of ENGELS' *Ludwig Feuerbach*. Words and phrases added in square brackets are added by the present author as an aid to elucidation.

I

The chief defect of all hitherto existing materialism—that of Feuerbach included—is that the object, reality, sensuousness * [i.e., that which is apprehended by the senses] is conceived only in the form of the *object* or *contemplation*, but not as *human sensuous activity*, *practice*, not subjectively. Thus it happened that the *active* side, in opposition to materialism, was developed by idealism—but only abstractly, since, of course, idealism does not know [recognise] real sensuous activity as such. Feuerbach wants sensuous objects, really differentiated from the thought objects, but he does not conceive human activity itself as activity *through objects*. Consequently, in the *Essence of Christianity*, he regards the theoretical attitude as the only genuinely human attitude, while practice is conceived and fixed only in its " dirty Jew " [i.e., " alien," " outsider "] form of appearance. Hence he does not grasp the significance of " revolutionary," of practical-critical, activity.

II

The question whether objective truth can be attributed to [attained by] human thinking is not a question of theory, but is a practical question. In practice man must prove the truth—i.e., the reality and power, the " this-sidedness " of his thinking. The dispute over the reality or non-reality of thinking which is isolated from practice is a purely scholastic question.

III

The materialist doctrine that men are products of circumstances and upbringing, and that, therefore, changed men are

---

* *Sensuousness* : *Not* " addiction to fornication and kindred pursuits." *Sensuous reality* is, in the terminology of Kant and his successors, that side of reality *as perceived*, which is opposite to its *rational form—object or contemplation* (German : *Ansehauung*).

the products of other circumstances and changed upbringing, forgets that circumstances are changed precisely by men, and that the educator must himself be educated. Hence this doctrine necessarily arrives at dividing society into two parts, of which one towers above Society (in Robert Owen, for example).

The coincidence of the changing of circumstances and of human activity can only be conceived and rationally understood as revolutionising practice.

IV

Feuerbach starts out from the fact of religious self-alienation, the duplication of the world into a religious-imaginary world and a real one. His work consists in the dissolution of the religious world into its secular basis. He overlooks the fact that after completing this work the chief thing still remains to be done. For the fact that the secular foundation lifts itself above itself and establishes itself in the clouds as an independent realm is only to be explained by the self-cleavage and self-contradictoriness of this secular basis. The latter must itself, therefore, first be understood in its contradiction, and then by the removal of the contradiction be revolutionised in practice. Thus, for instance, once the earthly family is discovered to be the secret of the holy family, the former must then itself be theoretically criticised and radically changed in practice.

V

Feuerbach, not satisfied with *abstract thinking*, appeals to *sensuous contemplation*, but he does not conceive sensuousness as a practical, human—sensuous activity.

VI

Feuerbach resolves religion into its human essence [content]. But this human essence is no abstraction inherent in each single individual. In its reality it is the *ensemble* [concatenation ; synthetic aggregation] of the social relations.

Feuerbach, who does not attempt the criticism [i.e. critical analysis and evaluation] of this real essence, is consequently compelled :

   (1) To abstract from the historical process and to fix the religious sentiment as something for itself and to presuppose an abstract—*isolated*—human individual.

(2) The human essence, therefore, can with him be comprehended only as " genus "—as a dumb internal generality which merely *naturally* unites the many individuals.

VII

Feuerbach, consequently, does not see that the " religious sentiment " is itself a *social product*, and that the abstract individual whom he analyses belongs in reality to a particular form of society.

VIII

Social life is essentially *practical*. All the mysteries which seduce theory into mysticism find their rational solution in human practice and in the comprehension of this practice.

IX

The highest point attained by contemplative materialism [*Anschauungs-Materialismus*] is the outlook of single individuals in " civil society."

X

The standpoint of the old materialism is " civil society " ; the standpoint of the new is *human* society or socialised humanity.

XI

The philosophers have only *interpreted* the world in different ways ; the point, however, is to *change* it.

CHAPTER II

MATERIALISM; IDEALISM; AND MATERIALISM

IN his *Necessity of Communism*—a work which seeks to prove that Communism, as Marx understood it, is not in the least "necessary"—Mr. J. Middleton Murry observes, (p. 15):

> "I do not think it would be an exaggeration to say that Marx's *Thesen über Feuerbach*—a bare five hundred words of compressed and pregnant thinking—are completely unknown to the average English Marxist."

Since with Mr. Middleton Murry exaggeration usually bears the same proportion to exactitude as sack did to bread in the diet of Sir John Falstaff—("but one half-pennyworth of bread to this intolerable deal of sack!")—it is necessary to observe that here the "exaggeration" is on the near side of the truth.

For English-speaking Marxists who cannot read German these *Theses* have, until quite recently, been available only in the "translation" ("Bless thee, Bottom! thou art *translated*!") of Engels' *Feuerbach*, published by Kerr & Co., Chicago.

That this work is "unknown" is true only "in the 'Pickwickian' sense." It has in fact been sold in thousands, and two generations of would-be Marxists have studied it diligently. This, however, far from making the *Theses* better understood, has had exactly the contrary effect. In this version, which is inaccurate, "bowdlerised" and generally incomprehensible, the translator has worked the "miracle" which Huxley credited to another writer: "He has made the darkness *opaque*!" Moreover, they are appended to a translation of Engels' *Feuerbach*, which is a scandal made outrageous by an "introduction" in which Engels' argument is first of all falsified, and then brushed aside as "obsolete." In this setting the *Theses* have been, not so much made public as *buried alive*!

Ignorance as to their true meaning has given rise to all sorts of misinterpretations, particularly of the justly famous Eleventh *Thesis*—which in a free translation would run: "The philosophers have changed only the *interpretation* of the world : our job, however, is to change *the world*." Since in the English-speaking world, any and every sort of theorising passes for " philosophy "—(as when Dr. Johnson said, naively, he " had tried hard to be a philosopher, but *cheerfulness* would keep breaking through ! ")—this *Thesis* has been interpreted as indicating Marx's repudiation of *all* theory—*including his own !*—all possibility of arriving at objectively valid generalisations.

Thus Mr. Middleton Murry uses the *Theses on Feuerbach* as a pulpit from which to discourse on the texts : " Every country gets the Communism it *deserves* ! " " In England Communism *must* be English ! " " The only thing not explained by Marxism is Marx itself ! " and so on, denying in effect all but a purely provisional subjective validity to Marx's basic theory. Thus, likewise, each intellectual who sets out to " bring Marx up to date " vindicates his dogmatic repudiation of " Marxian dogma " by quoting Marx's own saying (made on a special occasion and with a specific reference which is, of course, conveniently ignored) : " All I know is that I am no ' Marxist ' ! "

It is, therefore, necessary, as a preliminary to the examination of these *Theses* to discover in what sense Marx repudiated " philosophy."

The Objectivity of Marxist Theory

Marxism is, above all, a " philosophy " of action. So much is generally admitted. It is also, as we shall see, a systematic refutation of all *dogmatism*—the completest refutation thereof the world has hitherto known. But if anything should by now be self-evident, it is the *Marxist* quality of Stalin's saying, " theory without practice is sterile, practice without theory is blind." No sort of beginning can be made in understanding Marxism, unless it is envisaged from the start as embodying the completest attainable *unity of Theory and Practice*.

In a preface addressed to the German working-class movement, then fighting gallantly under conditions of illegality (in 1874), Engels said :

> " Without German philosophy, particularly that of Hegel, German scientific socialism (the only scientific socialism extant) would never have come into existence. Without a sense for theory Scientific Socialism would never have become blood and tissue of the workers. . . .

" It is the specific duty of the leaders to gain an ever clearer understanding of the theoretical problems . . . and constantly to keep in mind that Socialism, having become a science, demands the same treatment as every other science—*it must be studied* "—ENGELS : *Peasant War*, preface to 2nd ed.

Fourteen years later he returned to the same theme :

" In academic circles the old fearless zeal for theory has now disappeared completely along with the classical philosophy. Empty eclecticism and an anxious concern for career and income . . . occupies its place. . . .

" Only among the working class does the German aptitude for *Theory* remain unimpaired . . . The more disinterestedly and ruthlessly science proceeds, the more it finds itself in harmony with the interests and effort of the workers. . . .

" The German working class is *the inheritor of German classical philosophy*."—ENGELS : *Ludwig Feuerbach*, p. 70.

When Marx affirmed that " the philosophers have *only* interpreted the world in different ways " his saying must be itself interpreted *dialectically*.

Up till then philosophy had proceeded on the assumption that the world-order was something fundamentally fixed and immutable : that change, motion, action and reaction were all incidental only, aspects of the fleeting " *un-real* " appearance of things. In countering this assumption with the affirmation, " the point is *to change it*," Marx not only shifted the focus of interest and the criterion of reality from the *inner* world of thought to the *outer* world of things and material activities : he affirmed likewise (by implication) that the " interpretation " of the world must be changed yet again, and this time with the aid of, and in unison with *practice*, to one based upon the fundamental *changeability* of Reality. That Reality could in fact not only *change*, but *be changed by Man*, was the fact affirmed in the Eleventh Thesis. And this, far from being a mere superficial repudiation of all " theory," was the most radical revolution in philosophical theory it was possible to achieve.

    .   .   .   .

Turning now to the *Theses*, we have first to note that they constitute a *series* in three groups ; and that this *series* has a clear affinity with the Hegelian logical progression of Thesis, Antithesis, Synthesis.

The first group, comprising the first three *Theses*, deal

with Feuerbach's materialism " *an sich* "—*as such*,—along with " all hitherto existing materialism."

The second group, comprising *Theses* Four to Seven inclusive, deal with Feuerbach's materialism "*fur sich* "— as it is *for itself*, in its special characteristics, particularly its theory of Religion.

The third group, comprising the remaining four *Theses*, deal with Feuerbach's materialism " *an-und-fur sich* "—from both aspects in synthesis. That is to say, they develop the logical consequences of the examination and present Marx's *dialectical materialist* conclusion from this examination.

MARX AND MATERIALISM

The First *Thesis* has as its implied background and point of departure an historical fact.

The German " Critical " Philosophy (called also the " Transcendental " philosophy), as developed by Kant, Fichte, Schelling, and Hegel and their followers, had, beyond question, secured a complete victory in general academic and public opinion, over the 17th and 18th century Materialism represented in England by Bacon, Hobbes, Locke and their followers, and in France by Descartes, Condillac, Cabanis, D'Alembert, Lamettrie, Laplace, d'Holbach, Diderot, Helvetius, Dupuis, Volney, etc.

Marx begins by affirming that this victory was won because of a radical defect in the *method* of the Materialists in question. He affirms, further, that Feuerbach, in breaking away from Hegel and returning to the materialist standpoint had returned likewise to this defective method.

.   .   .   .   .   .

It speaks volumes for the manner in which Marxism has been understood in Britain, that this recognition that the older materialism had defects has been treated as a repudiation of Materialism itself ; and that this recognition that the Critical philosophy was, *in certain respects*, an advance upon the preceding materialism, has been treated as, *in substance*, an acceptance of an idealistic methodology. Marx and Engels, it is admitted, used the *name* " Materialist "— but this, so we are told, must not be taken seriously. They only " called " their world conception " Materialist " to scandalise the bourgeoisie !

Examples of these endeavours to represent Marx first as repudiating all theory, then as repudiating all Materialism, are as plentiful in Britain as slugs on a damp night. We have a whole school of neo-Dietzgenian " Monists " who claim the name of " Marxism " for an eclectic hodge-podge of Idealism and Materialism joined in unholy matrimony and blessed with the name of " proletarian Monism "—which we are assured is an enormously superior article to *mere* " Historical " Materialism. So, too, we have G. D. H. Cole, who (in *What Marx Really Meant*) invites, with large Oxonian scorn, " all the theological parrots that screech about the Marxian temple " to " squawk " at his assertion that when Marx " wrote ' materialist ' it would be *natural* (!) in our day to write ' realist.' " (" Materialism " *is* such a *horrid* word— don't you think, Mrs. Blenkinsop ?) Marx—so G. D. H. Cole assures us—only " *called* (!) his conception of history ' materialist ' because he was *determined* (!) to mark it off sharply from the metaphysical idealism of Hegel and his followers." 'Tis, you see, a mere matter of *name* that separates Marx from Hegel !

This is precisely the opinion of Max Eastman, in *Marx, Lenin, and Revolution* (a work which many " Marxists " in the sphere of influence of the N.C.L.C. imbibe surreptitiously as a sort of intellectual " bootleg "). Eastman asseverates thus :

> " Marx not only failed to escape from philosophy with his Dialectic Materialism, but he *failed to escape*, in the essence of the matter *from idealistic Philosophy*. . . . That explains why Marx and Engels repudiated with such violence " the materialism of natural science," " the materialism which exists to-day in the minds of naturalists and physicians " calling it ' abstract,' and ' mechanical ' and even ' shallow and vulgar.' *Why should one kind of materialism describe another kind as shallow and vulgar ?* "—EASTMAN : *loc. cit.*, pp. 44–5.

Max Eastman (who will be dealt with more fully later) gives the game away in that last sentence (all the italics are ours). When he is not railing at Marx and Marxian orthodoxy Max Eastman is a poet, of sorts, and an art critic. In his art criticism he has, perforce, to deal with art forms and decorative patterns in which what were vigorous and in-spiriting originals have through mechanical and unintelligent repetition grown conventionalised, stereotyped, devitalised, and debased out of all recognition. They have in the customary phrase been " *vulgarised.*" Max Eastman may, possibly, avoid the word ; he cannot deny that as a term of criticism it has a precise and an objective significance. When Marx and Engels applied it to the 19th century " materialists "—who at best merely "marked time" on the positions won with spirited gallantry by their predecessors, while at the same time affecting to despise them— Marx and Engels used the term " vulgar " in its precise, critical, sense.

Max Eastman is probably too ignorant of the history of Materialism to be aware of this. But ignorance is no excuse for downright *dishonesty*. He gives references to the passages which support, he claims, his allegation that Marx and Engels " repudiated with violence " the materialism, not of *particular materialists*, but of Natural *Science* itself. His first reference (inexactly indicated !) is to the following :

> " The weak points in the *abstract materialism of natural science*, a materialism that excludes history and its process, are at once evident from the abstract and ideological conceptions of its spokesmen, whenever they venture beyond the bounds of their own speciality."— Marx : *Capital,* ch. XV., Vol. I (Sonnenschein ed., p. 367).

The second of Eastman's references is to the following :

> " Here Feuerbach lumps together the materialism that is a general world-outlook resting upon a definite conception of the relation of matter and mind, and the special form in which this world outlook was expressed at a definite stage of historical development, *viz.*, in the eighteenth century. More than that, he confuses it with *the shallow and vulgarised form* in which the materialism of the eighteenth century continues to exist to-day *in the minds of naturalists and physicians*, the form which was preached on their tours in the ' fifties ' by Buchner, Vogt, and Moleschott."—Engels : *Ludwig Feuerbach*, p. 35–6.

It stands clear to demonstration that by the commonest of all sharpers' tricks—that of tearing a phrase from its context—Max Eastman has contrived to exemplify the popular proverb (which proverb, by the way, has a fine *dialectic* quality), that " *the half of a truth is the whole of a lie* ! "

Engels made the Marxian attitude towards this school of " natural-scientific materialism " perfectly clear in the review of Marx's *Critique of Political Economy* he wrote for a London German paper, *Das Volk*, in 1859 :

> ". . . And while those sciences in which the specu-

lative tendency never assumed any kind of importance
came in fashion there was also a recrudescence of the old
metaphysical manner of thinking. . . . Hegel fell into
oblivion ; and there developed the new natural-scientific
materialism which was almost indistinguishable theoretically from that of the eighteenth century, and for the
most part only enjoyed the advantage of having a richer,
natural-scientific material at its disposal, particularly in
chemistry and physiology. The narrow philistine mode
of thought of pre-Kantian times one finds reproduced
even to the most extreme triviality in Buchner and
Vogt ; and even Moleschott, who swears by Feuerbach,
continually runs amok in the most diverting fashion
among the simplest of categories. The lumbering cart-
horse of everyday bourgeois understanding naturally
stopped dead in confusion before the ditch which
separates essence from appearance, cause from effect.
But if one goes gaily hunting over such badly broken
ground as that of abstract thinking, one must not ride
cart-horses."—ENGELS, *loc. cit.* [quoted in *Ludwig
Feuerbach*, Appendix, p. 96.]

Eastman does not even ride a cart-horse ; he rides a
spavined mule which (having " neither pride of ancestry nor
hope of posterity ") continually " bucks " its rider into the
mire.

G. D. H. Cole, to do him justice, has neither the need nor
the inclination to descend to such " Back-of-the-Bowery "
tricks. Cole's efforts to do justice to Marx would, in fact,
be positively pathetic were they not so lugubriously comic.
" Most people," he says, meaning most people who know
nothing whatever about materialism—i.e., most British
university dons !—

" think instinctively [*read :* from force of habit] of
materialism as asserting the supremacy of matter over
mind, or even as denying the existence of mind save as
a derivative quality (!) of matter, whereas no such
doctrine is involved in, or even reconcilable with, the
Materialist Conception of History."—COLE : *loc. cit.*,
p. 15.

That this fairly represents the customary donnish notion
of materialism is only too true. But what a state of things
is here when a man has to go out of his way to prove that
Marx was not guilty of fatuosities that would hardly impose
on the famous swans of St. John's ! To talk of one abstraction

("matter") asserting its "supremacy" over another ("mind") is as rational as supposing a civil war between sweetness and sound, or a duel to the death between a cosine and a syllogism. To talk of "mind" as a "quality" is to betray a quality of mind seldom met with outside Bedlam. Oblivious of all this, Cole, with the air of St. George rescuing the virgin (Marx) from the dragon of misrepresentation, proceeds :

> "What this conception does assert is that *mind* (*!*) as a formative force in History, works by *embodying itself* (*!*) in things, changing their shape and potency, etc. . . . The things that Marx calls 'material' and regards as the agents of social evolution are more and more products of the human mind."—COLE: *ibid.*, pp.15,16.

This asserts nothing less than that "*Mind*" (in the *abstract !*) firstly exists as an entity totally distinct from and independent of "Things" (in the *concrete*), and then by some miracle succeeds in "embodying" itself in these "things," thereby, as the vulgar would put it, "mucking them about no end ! " So G. D. H. Cole contrives to credit Marx with the very "metaphysical" confusion and *absolute* dualism of which the whole of Marxism is a complete refutation !

But—let us be charitable !—G. D. H. Cole "really means " something different ; only, unfortunately, being British and expensively miseducated, he is quite incapable of saying what he means. What he was trying to say had been said for him (had he but known it) in 1888 by—Frederick Engels ! Speaking of the origin of Marxism as a development from Hegelianism, Engels says :

> "The separation from the Hegelian school was here also [i.e., as was the case with Feuerbach] the result of a return to the materialist standpoint. This means that it was resolved to comprehend the real world—Nature and history—just as it presents itself to everyone who approaches it free from preconceived idealistic fancies. It was decided relentlessly to sacrifice every idealistic fancy which could not be brought into harmony with *the facts conceived in their own, and not in a fantastic connection*. AND MATERIALISM MEANS NO MORE THAN THIS. But here the materialistic world outlook was taken really seriously for the first time, and was carried through consistently—at least in its basic features—in all domains of knowledge concerned."—ENGELS : *Ludwig Feuerbach*, p. 53.

This passage—particularly the phrases we have emphasised —would have saved Douglas Cole many flounderings. It would have enabled him to answer his own question, " What *did* Marx *really* mean ? " in three words—*What he said !* But if critics are going to be forced to *read* Marx and Engels, and (worse still !) to *understand* them, before they set out to " explain," " simplify " or " revise " them, what a pruning of publishers' catalogues there will be !

. . . .

In the first *Thesis* Marx neither repudiates materialism nor reproaches Feuerbach for returning to the materialist standpoint. Marx's charge is that, in his manner of breaking away from Hegel, Feuerbach had, in the phrase beloved of German philosophers, been guilty of the error of " emptying out the baby along with the bath-water ! " He had *returned* to the materialist standpoint, but in doing so he had not carried with him the *real*, substantial gains achieved by the Critical philosophy in Idealist *forms*. It was right to discard the Idealist *form* ; it was wrong to throw away along with that form its essentially *materialist* content.

" With reference to the refutation of a philosophical system," says Hegel :

> " it must be purged of the erroneous idea that the system is to be presented as false throughout, and that the true system is just opposed to the false . . . for then this opposite would itself be one-sided. Much rather, *being superior, it must contain the subordinate*.
>
> " Further, the refutation must not come from outside ; that is, it must not proceed from assumptions which lie beyond that system and do not correspond with it."—

—Hegel : *Science of Logic*, Vol. II, pp. 214–15.

Or, in the words in which Comte paraphrased this observation : " One only destroys that which one replaces." Feuerbach had merely contraposed his system to Hegel's. At best he had pointed out a flaw in the Hegelian system, and pointing out that a system has flaws in no way removes the need to use that system for what, flaws notwithstanding, it will still accomplish better than any alternative. To really refute a system it is necessary to devise a means of doing all that it was designed to do, only *doing it better*. Philosophical systems, like everything else in the Universe, do not exist alone. There is, it is true, a Materialist standpoint, and it is the opposite of the Idealist standpoint. But there is no such thing as a *fixed system* of Materialism, any more than there is a fixed system of Idealism. Since the Idealists, each in his order of succession, have all occupied themselves with *material* facts, however idealistically they may have *interpreted* them, the facts remain facts, and *material* facts, despite all the idealistic disguise the system of interpretation may have thrown over them. Conversely the Materialists, each in his turn, have all been concerned with the problem of the relation of Thinking to Being. They have therefore been concerned with Thoughts, Ideas, reasoning—with *mental* operations ; hence it follows that, as was humanly inevitable, every system of Materialism had its *ideal* content—contained, in fact, specific *idealisms*, despite all the efforts of the materialists to reach a *consistently* materialist interpretation of their subject-matter.

Feuerbach broke with the idealist system of Hegel—and that was good. But in returning to the materialism of the eighteenth century he returned to the *idealism* contained therein in solution, which was bad. Yet Feuerbach himself was a means of assisting this *dialectical* development of philosophy, since he has historically this very significance— that (in Hegelian terminology) he was a *moment* in the dialectical transmutation of Hegel's Absolute Idealism into Marx's Dialectical Materialism.

DEVELOPMENT IN MATERIALISM AND IDEALISM

An historical progression in philosophy begins with Bacon (1561–1626), Descartes (1596–1650), and Spinoza (1632–77), and ends with the movement from Kant (1724–1804) to Hegel (1770–1831).

It began as an attempt to reach by consistent and precise reasoning a full understanding of the Natural Universe. It was soon forced to face the need to inquire into the scope and limits of the instrument of understanding itself. It culminated in the Critical philosophy which, after an inquiry into the nature of Reason itself, claimed to have found (Hegel) the true *nature* of the Universe in the Logical process whereby Reason converted perceptions into conceptions, and these in turn into *Universal Understanding*.

Thereafter what had been the *philosophical* movement broke into two mutually repellent movements. On the one side, that of Dialectical Materialism and the positive sciences (whose Materialist practice was all the more dialectic the more its practitioners repudiated Materialism and the dialectic in terms); and on the other side, that of a mob of disintegrating idealisms all steadily degenerating into solipsism, mysticism, and supernaturalism. One movement rose *above* philosophy into positive science; the other sank *below* it into Irrationalism.

.   .   .   .   .

The general issues dividing Materialism and Idealism are described by Engels thus :

"The great basic question of all philosophy, especially of modern philosophy, is that concerning the relation of thinking and being."—ENGELS : *Feuerbach*, p. 30.

This question was not raised idly or by chance. It arose from the fact that *before* philosophy, before any sort of science, among the barbarian and savage ancestors of modern men the belief prevailed that thinking and sensation were not activities of men's bodies, but " of a distinct soul which inhabits the body and leaves it at death " (ENGELS, *ibid.*). Hence the basic question of philosophy was itself an historical product—the outcome of the carrying over of the beliefs of barbarians and savages into Theology, and the dominant position occupied by the theologians in European Society when it had "awakened from the long hibernation of the Middle Ages " (ENGELS) :

"The question : which is primary, Spirit or Nature ? —that question, in relation to the Church, was sharpened into this : ' Did God create the world, or has the world been in existence eternally ? '

"The answers which the philosophers gave to this question split them into two great camps. Those who asserted the primacy of spirit to nature, and, therefore, in the last instance, assumed world creation in some form or another . . . comprised the camp of Idealism. The others, who regarded Nature as primary, belong to the various schools of Materialism.

"*These two expressions, Idealism and Materialism, primarily signify nothing more than this.*"—ENGELS : *Ludwig Feuerbach*, p. 31.

We have emphasised the last sentence in this extract because it is a truth which tends to get pushed out of sight in the development of the secondary and tertiary differences between Idealism and Materialism. Once it is conceded that objective, *material* Nature is historically and logically presupposed in any speculative thinking about Nature or man, or thinking itself—the basic contention of Materialism is admitted. Alternatively, any attempt to deprive Nature of its primacy, and to elevate " spirit," consciousness, or thinking, from the status of something *derived* into something primary over, or *co-primary with*, Nature—all such attempts are Idealisms, in that they deprive Nature of both its objectivity and its materiality.

Engels notes a development of the issue from its above-noted " primary " form :

> " The question of the relation of thinking and being has yet another side : in what relation do our thoughts about the world surrounding us stand to this world itself ? . . . Are we able in our ideas and notions of the real world to produce a correct reflection of reality ? This in philosophical language is called the question of the ' identity of thinking and being.' "—ENGELS : *Ludwig Feuerbach*, p. 31.

In Engels' day it was true to say, as he did, that " the overwhelming majority of philosophers " answered the question whether we are able in our thinking correctly to reflect the reality of the external world, " in the affirmative." To-day, however, the decadence of philosophy is manifest in the fact that the reverse is the case. What passes for " philosophy " to-day, in the majority of cases, takes as its starting point the assumption that our minds are so constituted that we *cannot* in our thinking *correctly reflect* reality ; we can at best, it is alleged, " represent " or " symbolise " it.

This modern movement has arisen from a tendency noted by Engels :

> " Another set of philosophers . . . question the possibility of any cognition (or at least of an exhaustive cognition) of the world. To them among the moderns belong Hume and Kant, and they have played a very important role in philosophical development."—ENGELS, *ibid.*, p. 32.

Herein is revealed yet another *dialectical* aspect of the historical movement of philosophy. HUME (1711–76), from whose " Scepticism " all modern philosophical agnosticism has arisen, and KANT, whom Hume " aroused from dogmatic slumber," between them stimulated the greatest advance made in the whole history of philosophy. Yet, while those who carried their stimulus out to its logical conclusion passed thereby ultimately *beyond* " philosophy " into Dialectical Materialism, those who clung and cling fast to the positions held by Kant and Hume have destroyed philosophy by con-

verting it into a systematic surrender to clericalism, supernaturalism, sophistry and mystery-mongering.

In the earlier stages of its modern development philosophy,
and particularly Materialism, was the dominant intellectual
force in Europe. Materialism, despite what might have been
expected from the prominent position occupied by the Church
and Religion, was so much in line with the prevailing opinion
in politics, morals, and art that BACON, HOBBES, and LOCKE,
with their disciples, dominated the intellectual history of
England in the seventeenth and eighteenth centuries ; while
their French disciples, who developed the materialist side
of the metaphysics of DESCARTES, dominated that of France
all through the eighteenth century.

Yet in a few years this once dominant Materialism found
itself completely supplanted by the Idealist philosophy (of
the so-called " Transcendentalists ") which, originating in
Germany, became little less triumphant in France and in
England than it was in the land of its origin. And this
was no mere swing of the pendulum—no mere alteration
without progress. Since the rise of the German Critical
Philosophy it has been impossible to do without the discriminations it was the first to make ; though, truth to tell,
they are not always used with either precision or understanding. It would be impossible to carry on any sort of
philosophical discussion nowadays without discriminating
between phenomena and noumena, form and content, object
and subject, empirical and speculative (or " theoretical "),
Things-in-themselves and Things-for-us, and so on. And
all this we owe to Kant and the post-Kantian idealists,
who in their turn were swept aside and superseded in less
than a generation after the death of Hegel.

" The proof of the pudding is in the eating." It would
be interesting to see how any of the ultra-modern improvers
upon Marx could account for this development except in
terms of Dialectical Materialism.

.   .   .

Marx's first *Thesis* does more than note the bare fact that
German Idealism made an advance upon Anglo-French
Materialism. It indicates wherein the specific nature of this
advance lay.

To Materialism Nature was allowed to be *active*, but the
rôle of Thought was purely *passive*, limited to receiving what
was " given " in the senses, and to excogitating upon that
which was " given." It was Kantian and post-Kantian

Idealism which elucidated and emphasised the *constructive* rôle played by subjective *activity*—and carried this emphasis to the limit of extravagant exaggeration.

Anglo-French materialism had truly and correctly started with the recognition of the basic fact that the objects of thought existed prior to and were perceived by a thinking subject. But they advanced no further. The thought was *simply* the *effect* produced in us by the activity of the Thing.

Here is how the matter is stated (and very finely) by THOMAS HOBBES :

> " Concerning the thoughts of man. . . . Singly they are every one a ' representation ' or ' appearance ' of some quality, or other accident of a body without us, which is commonly called an ' object.' Which object worketh on the eyes, ears, and other parts of a man's body and by diversity of working, produceth diversity of appearances.
>
> " The original of them all, is that which we call ' sense,' for there is no conception in a man's mind, which hath not at first, totally or by parts, been begotten upon the organs of sense. *The rest are derived from that original.*"—HOBBES : *Leviathan* (1652), Chap. I.

Only a little inspection is needed to reveal the point at which this position laid itself open to idealist attack. Men were conscious of " appearances," which had their origination in the " organs of sense." But men did not, and could not, rest content with these " appearances." They had, as Hobbes affirmed (without fully grasping the force of the affirmation), to be analysed and " valued " in order that rational concepts and judgments might be derived from them. Moreover—and this, curiously enough, it was left for Kant and his fellow-Idealists to point out—each *form* of " appearance " had its material, objective *content*, and it was this *content* rather than the *form* (or " image," as the materialists called it—tending from their passive conception of the thought process to lay chief stress on the *visual* form of the " appearance ") which gave the undeniable evidence of the existence and primacy of objective material reality.

As the question stood with the Materialists, knowledge, originating in the " sensible forms " apparent in sensation, was *derived* thence by means of a " faculty " called " Reason " —but what that faculty was in itself was at once the bone of contention. The Idealists fought for the notion that this was none other than the " soul " of the Theologians, a *super-*

natural faculty whereby man was able to transmute the "illusions of sense" into reliable, and even Eternal, Truths. The Materialists fought for the position that, however mysterious the Reason might be, it was none the less *Natural*. Hence they endeavoured to prove that so-called "general" or "universal" Truths were mere "names of names." The question resolved itself into a battle round the problem : Have we any Ideas independent of Experience ? Locke, following (but independently) in the steps of Hobbes, formulated the aphorism : "There is nothing in the Intellect which was not previously in the Senses." Leibnitz replied : "Except the Intellect itself ! " And soon the disputes of the mediæval schoolmen were reproduced in the fight between the Locke-ian "Sensationalists" and the Leibnitz-ian "Intellectualists."

A comparison with the Middle Ages will help to bring out the dialectic nature of the situation—of this return to the past, but on a higher plane. Anatole France, the master ironist, hits off these mediæval disputes with inimitable (and malicious) skill :

"While the little children played at hopscotch under the Abbey walls our friends the monks devoted themselves to another game equally unprofitable, at which, nevertheless, I joined them—for one must kill time. . . .

"Our game was a game of words which pleased our coarse yet subtle minds, set school fulminating against school, and put all Christendom in an uproar. We formed ourselves into two opposing camps.

"One camp maintained that before there were apples there was The Apple ; that before there were jackanapes there was The Jackanapes ; that before there were lewd and greedy monks there was The Monk, Lewdness, and Greed ; that before there were feet to kick and backsides to be kicked The Kick in The Arse existed from all eternity in the bosom of God.

"The other camp replied that on the contrary apples gave man the idea of The Apple, jackanapes the idea of The Jackanapes, monks the idea of the monk, greed and lewdness, and that the kick in the backside existed only after having been duly given and received.

"The players grew heated and came to fisticuffs. I was an adherent of the second party, which satisfied my reason better, and which was, in fact, condemned by the Council of Soissons."—ANATOLE FRANCE : *Revolt of the Angels.*

With inimitable pungency Anatole France here drives home the fact that what was satisfactory to reason was seldom satisfactory to the Church authorities, and the fact, too, that the basic issues in dispute between Idealists and Materialists—those of the origin of ideas, and their validity as reflections of external reality—were developed forms of issues raised originally within the Church in the course of the development of dogmatic theology and casuistry.

.   .   .   .   .

A parallel dialectical contrast is seen in the Kantian philosophical revolution.

In the first place it is interesting to notice that Kant was roused into action by the crisis in philosophy precipitated by DAVID HUME, and Hume in turn was brought into action by the retort delivered by GEORGE BERKELEY, afterwards Bishop of Cloyne, to the then triumphant Hobbes-Locke Materialism.

BERKELEY (1685–1753) took the ground that man's know-ledge is limited of necessity to sensations—to changes in states of consciousness. " Knowledge " is therefore limited to—*mental facts*. Let it be granted, he argued, if you will, that those changes in our mental states we call sensations are induced in us by some " thing," power, force, or existence, outside ourselves. Even so, *what* warrant have we for saying that this Whatever-it-is is *material* at all ? Since all our knowledge exists in our *minds*, and since it is admitted by Locke and his followers that some part at any rate of the contents of our knowledge—mathematical truths, for example —are " pure " mental constructions, at most derived from these same sensations, which you agree are states of conscious-ness—that is, *mental* facts—by what warrant do you make the leap from the mind, which is *all of which you have experi-ence*, to a world of " Matter " of which you know and can know nothing ?

Again—and here Berkeley hit the metaphysical Materialists shrewdly—you yourselves argue that you *receive sensations* from without. You perceive Qualities of various kinds. How do you excuse yourselves for passing from those *qualities* to a hypothetical substratum, this " Matter " which is, you claim, the *sub-stance* of (that which stands under) the Qualities you perceive ? Mind we know, since it is in the mind that we experience sensation, and in the mind we reason, but what do we know of this " Matter "—this mysterious something hidden behind the qualities perceived in sensation ?

It is well known that " coxcombs vanquish Berkeley with

a grin," and that the sturdy old Tory Dr. Johnson replied to him practically—by kicking a big stone so that it struck against a tree.

In principle Johnson was right—but his very mode of retort proved his inability to reply by argument. Johnson was right in perceiving that, however fine Berkeley's argument might be in theory, nobody could live for an hour by taking Berkeley's argument as a basis for practical procedure. But the theoretical reply came first of all from Hume.

DAVID HUME (1711–76) adopted that most deadly of all logical devices—that of taking the enemy's guns and using them upon him.

Let it be granted, he says in effect, that all that Dr. Berkeley has said about Matter is correct : we know only *qualities* which we perceive as *sensations* ; we know nothing directly of any substratum in which these qualities are supposed to inhere. This substratum may be, as Dr. Berkeley supposes, a Universal Mind of which our minds are parts— but even if this is so, on Berkeley's own showing we *know*, and can *know*, nothing of it.

And by the same process of reasoning—since all we know are *sensations*, some of which seem to be of external, and some of internal origin—by what right does Dr. Berkeley assume to know a *substratum* (i.e., " Mind ") for the one group, while denying all credit to the supposition of a substratum for the other ? " Mind " is just as much an assumption or inference as " Matter." If one goes, the other goes with it ; and much else. Along with it goes *cause* and all the other assumed " universals " in whose favour men have an in-eradicable prejudice. Sensations, Hume granted, have a way of occurring in regular sequences and combinations, and these regularities of occurrence have created in men an all but irresistible disposition to treat the earlier members of a sequence as a *cause* of the later, and to suppose that some *cause* binds together those invariably experienced in con-junction. But, however irresistible, the conviction is but a prejudice.

This was a complete knock-out for Berkeley. But it was a no less complete suicide for Materialism of the metaphysical kind. Hume had blandly lured Berkeley into his parlour and roasted him to a cinder ; but to do so he had burned the House of Philosophy over his own head and reduced himself to ashes along with his victim.

Kant's refutation of Hume's scepticism is well known—*by*

repute. Whether it is so well known in practice may be doubted. We state here only so much of it as concerns our purpose.

Kant agrees that all our knowledge *begins* with experience, and that it necessarily presupposes the existence of external objects. He denies that it *ends* there, since we have knowledge of matters which go beyond all experience. He agrees that this latter kind of knowledge presupposes the former kind :

" For how is it possible that the faculty of cognition should be awakened into exercise otherwise than by means of objects which affect our senses, and partly of themselves produce representations, partly rouse our powers of understanding into activity to compare, to connect, or to separate these, and so to convert the raw material of our sensuous impressions into *a knowledge of objects, which is called experience* ? In respect of time, therefore, no knowledge of ours is antecedent to experience, but begins with it."—KANT : *Critique of Pure Reason,* Everyman ed., p. 24.

But, argues Kant, there is another element in knowledge :

" Though all our knowledge begins with experience, it by no means follows that all arises *out of* experience. For, on the contrary, it is quite possible that our empirical knowledge is a compound of that which we receive through impressions, and *that which the faculty of cognition supplies from itself* (sensuous impressions giving merely the *occasion*), an addition which we cannot distinguish from the original element given by sense, till *long practise* has made us attentive to and skilful in separating it."— KANT : *ibid.*

Prior to Kant the philosophers had been divided into the Materialists, who derived all knowledge from the external world by the two-fold route of Sensation and Reflection upon Sensations, and the Idealists and Sceptics, who had maintained that there were in the Mind *ideas* which could not be so accounted for, *ideas* whose *universality* of scope and *abstract* nature indicated that they were *innate*, were presupposed in all experience.

Kant's historical position is that he negated this antagonism and by a synthesis of the two points of view reached a standpoint which he claimed reconciled them in a higher conception. He agreed that abstract conceptions such as Time, Space, Causality, etc., cannot be resolved into experience *alone* ; on the other hand, they could not (*a priori*

D

though they were in character) be conceived in *absolute* independence of experience. They are, in fact, he claimed, necessary pre-conditions supposed in, and therefore controlling *forms* of, all Experience (as distinct from its " matter " or "content", which was derived from without).

"There are not two *sources* of Knowledge, he argued—on the one side external Objects, and on the other Human Understanding. Knowledge has but *one* source, and that is the *union* of Object and Subject. Thus water is the *union* of oxygen and hydrogen ; but you cannot say that water has two causes, oxygen and hydrogen ; it has only one cause, viz., the union of the two.

" The whole world is to us a series of Phenomena. Are these Appearances the *production of the Mind* to which they appear ; or are they the pure presentation of the things themselves ? Idealism or Realism ? Neither yet both. The Mind and the object *co-operating* produce the appearance or Perception. In their union Perception is effectuated."—G. H. LEWES : *Biog. Hist. of Philosophy*, pp. 546–47.

We cannot here trace out the development of Kant's system in detail. Nor is it necessary. What is of moment to us is the significance of Kant in his actual place in the historical sequence of Philosophy as contrasted with his significance when taken out of that sequence and used as a starting point to-day.

In his own day his effect was enormous. For the time being the Kantian Transcendentalism swept all before it, and Humeian Scepticism (which survives to-day as " Philosophic " agnosticism) and Anglo-French Materialism (called " Realism " by Lewes in the extract above—perhaps as a " tip " for G. D. H. Cole ?) were both swept into the background.

The reason is not hard to discover. As against the Dogmatist, theological and otherwise, Kant's limitation of human inquiry to the things which are within the compass of men's mental grasp was as destructive as the Scepticism of Hume. What mattered in practice was not that Kant, like Hume, affirmed that he knew, and could know, nothing of the things the dogmatist was so cocksure about ; the point lay in his logical demonstration that the dogmatist *didn't know either* !

So far Hume and Kant were at one ; and so far Kant told

on Hume's side as against Berkeley—and all the more so since the plain " common sense " on whose side Berkeley claimed, and not unjustly, to have ranged himself was treated very cavalierly by Kant, to whom the highest order of Truth was that which had been most completely purged of all trace of *empirical* content. That is to say, to Kant, the farther one retreated by the operations of Reason from the empirical prejudices of plain common sense, the nearer one approximated to Absolute Truth. Kant's system, so far as he carried it in his *Critique of Pure Reason*, does, in fact, supply at any rate a *quasi*-scientific basis for Scepticism, and that, too—in the light of his crushing demonstration of the impossibility of any rational proof of the existence of God—for " scepticism " in the limited anti-theological sense.

But on another side Kant's conclusions were as hostile to those of Hume as his primary postulates were in agreement with his.

Hume had argued that, apart from the question whether our senses did or did not deceive us, the human Understanding was a thing so wavering, uncertain, and fickle—so *treacherous*—that no Philosophy could be other than the mere prejudice-begotten opinion of a particular philosopher. Kant, on the contrary, averred and made a giant's stride on the road towards proving that the Understanding, though limited by the conditions of its own nature, was none the less, and because of that nature, *thoroughly to be trusted within those limits*.

Moreover, though Kant agreed with Hume again in the view that no final philosophy (in the sense of a fixed world *scheme*) was possible, he insisted as stoutly as Hobbes, Locke, Hume, D'Holbach, Helvetius, Lammettrie or Diderot upon the right of the Critical Reason to bring anything and everything within its purview :

" Reason must be subject in all its operations to criticism, which must always be permitted to exercise its functions without restraint ; otherwise its interests are imperilled, and its influence obnoxious to suspicion. There is nothing, however useful, however sacred it may be, that can claim exemption from this searching tribunal, which has no respect of persons. The very existence of reason depends upon this freedom ; for the voice of reason is not that of a dictatorial and despotic power, it is rather like the vote of the citizens of a free State, every member of which must have the privilege of giving free expression to his doubts, and possess even the right of *veto*."—KANT : *Critique of Pure Reason*, p. 423.

There are thus two opposite significances to be perceived in Kant even in his first *Critique*—quite apart from the conflicts discernible between it and his later *Critiques* (of *Practical Reason* and *Judgment* respectively). On the one side he told heavily against materialism and anti-religious scepticism (for which the theologians were, and are still, truly grateful). When in his second *Critique* he drew the conclusion that, since we cannot *prove* the existence of God, *therefore* we *must believe*—faith being an " intuition of the Practical Reason ! "—he secured himself and his successors from all official interference by the State.

But, on the other side, all that Kant might say or do could not prevent the movement he had initiated from gathering weight and momentum. Thus the movement initiated by Kant led to Hegel, and Hegel, in turn, through Feuerbach, led to revolutionary Marxism—Dialectical Materialism.

KANT AND THE BOURGEOIS STANDPOINT

It is easy to see this historical significance in Kant now— it was not at all so easy then ; and Kant himself would have been horrified had he known such results were possible. Yet (as Engels notes) this potentiality was perceived as early as 1835 by one man, and that man the inimitable and ill-fated Heinrich Heine (1799–1854). Heine's parallel between Kant and Robespierre is a classic :

" To tell the honest truth, compared with us Germans, you French are moderate and tame ! At best you could only kill a king ; and he had lost his head long before you chopped it off. And over that you must needs make such a drumming and shouting and stamping of feet that all the earth was shaken ! One really does too much honour to Maximilian Robespierre when one compares him to Immanuel Kant.

" Maximilian Robespierre, that great cockney of the Rue Saint-Honoré, had of course his destructive fit when the question of the monarchy came up, and he twitched frightfully enough when his regicidal epilepsy was on him ; but when it became a question of God, he wiped the blood from his hands, and the white froth from his lips, put on his sky-blue Sunday coat with the shining buttons, stuck a nosegay in his bosom and went out to celebrate the Fete of the Supreme Being ! . . .

"But if Immanuel Kant, the great destroyer of the world of thought, went far beyond Maximilian Robespierre in terrorism, he had many points of resemblance which challenge a comparison of the two of them.

"Firstly, we find in both the same inexorable, cutting, prosaic, sober sense of honour and integrity. Then in both of them is the same talent for mistrust—which the one showed towards all thoughts and called ' *criticism*,' while the other applied it to all men and called it ' republican *virtue* ' !

"Also there was made manifest in both, and that in the highest degree, the same *grocer* spirit, the spirit of the common bourgeois ! Nature had intended them to weigh out sugar and coffee, but Destiny decided that they should weigh other things. It placed into the scales of the one a *king* ! And into those of the other— a *god* !

" *And they both gave exact weight !* "—HEINE : *Germany* (1835), *Works*, Vol. V.

Heine's brilliant penetration, revealed rather than concealed by his surface-show of jesting, saw a connection between the standpoint of Kant and that of the bourgeoisie. And saw too that this had a profoundly revolutionary significance. It has a similar significance to-day, though in a dialectically transmuted form.

When men to-day raise the cry of " Back to Kant ! " their practical objective is not to attain a parallel position from which to attempt the revolutionary overthrow of current modes and fashions of thought. Their practical objective is : Back to the Bourgeois Point-of-view ! Wipe out all that has been accomplished *since* Kant.

In itself, detached from its historical setting, Kant's system bristles with contradictions—one set of which provoked the movement which culminated in Hegel's complete revolutionising of the Kantian system.

Another set—his concessions to Hume—gave a starting point for the whole *anti*-rational movement of return to solipsism and supernaturalism fashionable to-day.

"The principal feature of the philosophy of Kant is an attempted reconciliation of Materialism and Idealism, a compromise between the claims of both, a fusion of heterogeneous and contrary philosophic tendencies into one system. When Kant admits that something outside

of us—a thing-in-itself—corresponds to our perceptions he seems to be a Materialist. When he, however, declares this thing-in-itself to be unknowable, transcendent, 'trans-intelligible,' he appears to be an Idealist. Regarding experience as the only source of our knowledge, Kant seems to be turning towards Sensationalism, and by way of Sensationalism under special conditions towards Materialism. Recognising the *a-priority* of space, time, and causality, etc., Kant seems to be turning towards Idealism. Consistent Materialists and consistent Idealists . . . criticise him for this inconsistency."
  —LENIN : *Materialism and Empirio-Criticism*, p. 163.

It was seeking to remove the inconsistencies of Kant from the standpoint of Idealism that led to the movement (*via* Fichte and Schelling) which culminated in Hegel.

.   .   .   .   .

We have devoted so much space to Kant for the reason that Hegel is almost, if not quite, unintelligible except as a development *from* Kant. Since Kant is read in Britain to-day only less than Hegel—who is by general consent unreadable—it is easy for critics, revisers, and " explainers " of Marx to fasten upon certain of his Hegelian turns of phrase and use them to prove (*a*) that Marx never left off being a Hegelian ; and (*b*) that Hegel was " clean daft ! " Which enables the *literati* in question to imply—to put it in workshop English—that " old man Marx was ' potty ' in spots."

The truth is that practically all the things for which these critics denounce Hegel *can be found already, in principle, in Kant.*

When Kant restricted the field of possible knowledge to the subjective forms in which we became aware of the objective world he affirmed a proposition which gave a foundation for Hegel's *aphorism*, " All that is real is rational, all that is rational is real."

Kant, it is true, denied all knowledge of Things-in-themselves : Hegel found the denial inconsistent on two sides—firstly, because, on the principle that experience supplies the material content of all thought-forms, the thought-form Thing-in-itself must have derived from some experience to be valid ; secondly, because that experience was supplied in the phenomena themselves, and in the relation between them and the understanding. As Engels put it, paraphrasing Hegel : " If we know all the qualities of a Thing there is nothing left to discover about the Thing-in-itself save the fact that it exists independently of ourselves."

Hegel thus carried the principle of the identity of Being and Thinking which Kant had accepted in a subjective form over into a completely unified system. If, as Kant held, the laws of the mind's operation gave a true and a reliable representation of reality, then all inconsistency was got rid of if the contrast between Subject and Object was treated as an oppositional contrast between the *This*-side and the *Yonder*-side of *one and the same Reality*.

Kant's principles compelled him, in refuting the Sensationalists (Locke, etc.), to avow that we do not perceive qualities, *as such*, separately ; the whole perceiving consciousness active in perception is modified *as a whole* by the whole of external reality. Hegel treated these *two* " wholes " as the positive and negative aspects of one *developing* whole, and so reached *Absolute* Idealism.

Kant had made the oppositional unity of Object and Subject the pivot of his whole system—but, inconsistently, he had conceived that their union was *active* and result-producing only on *one* side, the side of subjectivity. Hegel removed the inconsistency and built his system on the conception that it was not in the " pure " object or in the " pure " subject that the Truth lay, but in the *active inter-relation* between them, which relation produced a progressive transformation both of subject *and* of object. On the plane of Idealism this conception led straight to mysticism, and through mysticism to the negation of all rational Thought. Transferred, in an inverse form, to the plane of Materialism, this led straight to the Marxian world-conception.

The incidentals of Hegel's logical procedure, so far as they concern Dialectical Materialism, we will deal with as they arise in the course of the argument. Here we need do no more than summarise the results in relation to Marx's First *Thesis on Feuerbach*.

When Marx affirms that " all hitherto existing materialism " conceived objective reality " only in the form of the *object* or *Anschauung*, but not as *human sensuous activity*, *practice*—not subjectively," we see now to what he is alluding.

Idealism had developed the *active* side (of the thought-relation of Object-Subject), but " only abstractly "—only in the sense of developing the general laws of Thought, of logic and dialectics, and marking the specific limitations of human brainwork. The Materialists had never developed, and the Idealists were debarred by their Idealism from developing, the *active* side of actual flesh and blood *human practice through objects.*

It is, when you come to think of it, an amazing thing ; but none the less it is true that as the philosophical game had been played, and that by both sides, any appeal to the actual, objective *practice* of mankind in real life had by general consent been ruled " off-side." The deep-rooted prejudice that saw in the " empirical " understanding—the " practical " Reason of Kant—only a lower, baser, and scarcely reputable poor relation of the lordly " Pure " Reason—which was most lordly and most to be admired when it was most purified from empirical taint—runs all through philosophy until it is exalted into a cardinal principle in the German transcendentalists.

Feuerbach, though he broke with Hegel to the extent of affirming that Nature existed independently of all Thought, retained these prejudices automatically. Theoretical specu- lative reasoning was for him, as for Kant, Fichte, Schelling, and Hegel—and for the matter of that also for the meta- physical materialists—not only the sole means of arriving at Truth, but also that which placed man in a category absolutely different from that of the brutes. At the outset of his *Essence of Christianity* Feuerbach lays down the proposition :

" Religion has its basis in the essential difference [i.e., difference in *essence*] between Man and the brute— *the brutes have no religion. . . .*

" But what is this essential difference between Man and the brute ? The most simple, general, and also the most popular answer to this question is—*consciousness :* but consciousness in the strict sense, for the consciousness implied in the feeling of self as an individual, in dis- crimination by the senses, in the perception and even judgment of outward things according to definite sensible signs, cannot be denied to the brutes. Consciousness in the strictest sense is present only in a being *to whom his species, his essential nature, is an object of thought. . . .* Where there is this higher consciousness there is a capability of science. Science is the cognisance of species. In practical life we have to do with individuals, in science with species. But only a being to whom his own species, his own nature, is an object of thought can make the essential nature of other things or beings an object of thought."—FEUERBACH : *Essence of Christianity* (Geo. Eliot's trans.), pp. 1–2.

All the points made by Marx in his First *Thesis* are illustrated in this passage. " Objects " are conceived and dealt with only as *thought*-objects, only as " species " generalised from the particulars of concrete experience. The *true* nature of these objects is their *abstract* " essence " as distinguished in thought, in the theoretical understanding. Practice is conceived as a fixed opposite of " science," of theoretical understanding. Practice—such as even brutes are capable of—is indeed as necessary to thought as the Jews are and have been to Christian civilisation. But practice, like the Jews, should not be any the better esteemed on that account. Rather the contrary, since the object of philosophising is to attain in thought to the contemplation of an object which, while it is made apparent in practice, is so only under a disguise which it is the business of thought to strip away.

.   .   .   .   .

This leads us straight to the question of the relation between practice and Theory ; between the Truth as it *is* and the Truth as it *only appears to be to us*.

TRUTH AND THE CRITERION OF PRACTICE

Idealism achieved, as we have seen, more than a relative historical ascendency over the Materialism of the seventeenth and eighteenth centuries. It achieved a positive advance in that, particularly at the hands of Hegel, it destroyed for ever all the theoretical proofs that had from time to time been advanced in favour of this or that system of Absolute and final Truth.

"Truth, the cognition of which is the business of philosophy, became in the hands of Hegel no longer an aggregate of finished dogmatic statements which, once discovered, had merely to be learned by heart. Truth lay now in the *process of cognition itself*, in the long historical development of science, which mounts from lower to ever higher levels of knowledge without ever reaching, by discovering so-called absolute Truth, a point at which it can proceed no further, and where it would have nothing more to do but to fold its hands and admire the absolute Truth to which it had attained."— ENGELS : *Ludwig Feuerbach*, p. 21.

This fact—that Truth is progressively unfolded, that all Truths attained and attainable by mankind are contingent, provisional, and relative—is one given much verbal homage nowadays.

We "are all 'Relativists' now "—though, truth to tell, those who make most of their Relativism do so in a most obnoxiously *absolute* fashion. What, therefore, falls due for notice here is, *first*, the fact that Idealism only won this ground from metaphysical materialism in a negative sense— and promptly relapsed into the error it had overcome !— *second*, that the reaping of the gains won in the prolonged intellectual struggle was made possible only by the return to the materialist standpoint and the *criterion* of *practice*. This return has been made fully and consistently by Dialectical Materialism, and by it alone.

. . . . .

The second *Thesis on Feuerbach* formulates this criterion in classic form. Whereas the idealists from Kant to Hegel had applied—and, as against the dogmatists and meta-physical materialists, had applied successfully—the criterion of practice only in its theoretical form of a Critical methodological procedure, Marx boldly traverses the whole Transcendentalist assumption by an appeal to *actual objective practice*—" practice through objects."

Whether a given thought or a body of knowledge has at any moment objective Truth is a question that can never be settled by abstract argumentation. Kant had shown, and Hegel had built a method out of his showing, that abstract Thought carried to absolute conclusions, apart from practice, proved to theoretical demonstration mutually destructive and opposite Truths. The mediæval schoolmen had pro-pounded conundrums like the famous query " How many angels can dance upon the point of a needle ? " and had persuaded themselves that they had reached a solution which at any rate made for edification. Earlier the Eleatic school of Greek philosophers had proved logically that motion did not, and could not, occur—since it was possible only on the supposition that a body was and was not at one and the same time in a given place.

Yet while the philosophers had been " proving " all these things the human race had gone on existing, and in order to exist had gone on working and producing. The experimental sciences, too, despite the handicap of much lumber carried over from theology and metaphysics, had in their laboratory practice achieved concrete and definite results. These results might be, as the speculative philosophers alleged, *merely* contingent, *merely* provisional, *merely* relative truths. Yet that they were *truths*—and *absolutely* true within their limits —continued and unfailing successes in applying them in practice proved to demonstration.

This fact, in view of recent tendencies among the British and American intelligentsia, needs to be underlined.

Let us return for a moment to Kant's famous " unknowable " *Thing-in-itself*. Kant's demonstration that human knowledge is conditioned by the nature of human faculties, and the quantity and quality of human experience, has been revived with a new " twist " on it—to imply that either no Truth at all is attainable by mankind, or alternatively that any affirmation can be made into a " Truth," if only enough people can be persuaded to assert it often enough. (The " onlie begetter " of this latter theory was the Bellman in the *Hunting of the Snark*—" *What I tell you three times is true !* ")

Dealing with the Humeian-Kantian " agnosticism " developed from the speculative doubt " as to possibility of any cognition (or at any rate of an exhaustive cognition) of the world," Engels says :

" The most telling refutation of this, as of all philosophical fancies, is *practice*, viz., *experiment and industry*. If we are able to prove the correctness of our conception of a natural process by making it for ourselves, bringing it into being out of its conditions, and using it for our own purposes into the bargain, then there is an end of the Kantian incomprehensible ' thing-in-itself.' The chemical substances produced in the bodies of plants and animals remained just such ' things-in-themselves ' until organic chemistry began to produce them one after another, whereupon the ' thing-in-itself ' became a ' thing-for-us,' as, for instance, alizarin, the colouring matter of the madder, which we no longer trouble to grow in the madder roots of the field, but produce much more cheaply and simply from coal tar. For three hundred years the Copernican solar system was a hypothesis. . . . But when Leverrier, by means of the data provided by this system, not only deduced the necessity of the existence of an unknown planet, but also calculated the position in the heavens which this planet must necessarily occupy, and when Galle really found this planet the Copernican system was proved."—ENGELS : *Ludwig Feuerbach*, pp. 32–33.

Truth, in short, is not a mysterious and immutable essence hidden " behind the veil " or " beyond phenomena." On the contrary, modern experimental scientific and industrial practice is continually, as Engels indicates, enlarging the extent and complexity of the known phenomena of the Universe and the number of uses to which this knowledge can be put. And, in so doing, experimental and industrial practice is continually converting what were yesterday, so to speak, deemed " unknowable " *noumena* into " phenomena " *known*, and reduced to practical comprehension. That which Hegel proved theoretically is proved practically with every advance of knowledge—namely, *the Relative Knowability of the so-called " Unknowable."*

As a recital of facts Engels' statement cited above (it was written in 1888) is to-day a commonplace, which might be extended into volumes. But the materialist implications of these commonplaces, far from being generally conceded, are often either denied or sought to be explained away.

In their eagerness for the refutation of Materialism, an eagerness which has social-historical roots, and has also, directly or indirectly, a political motivisation, whole schools of open or camouflaged Idealists have sought to evade or misrepresent this Criterion of Practice. Thus, for instance, we get the whole school of Pragmatists, whose formula is " a belief is true if it works." This at first glance seems to correspond to the demands of the Marxian formula of which it is a parody—that the Truth of Thought is proved in practice.

But an examination of the Pragmatists' actual procedure, especially in the service of religious apologetics, reveals that with them it has an exactly opposite meaning, namely—that one can *make a false belief " true " by keeping on believing in it !* Applied to belief in Christianity, for example, it emerges as the doctrine that Christianity is " proved " to be true " for *you* " if you find " *in practice* " that (like " Guinness ") it is " *good for you*." Two things are hereby made clear : (1) For the Pragmatists Truth is merely a subjective moral " valuation " of *beliefs*, as " good " or " bad." (2) " Practice " with the Pragmatists is synonymous with a wilful self-blinding—a total negation of *objective* practice.

All the " modernist " systems are like Pragmatism in their insistence that " Truth," the " Universe " and " Objective Reality " are actually *different* for each and every man ;

which is only a roundabout, card-sharper's way of asserting that neither Truth nor the Universe of Material Reality have, or can have, any *objective* existence.

This, since these " philosophers " are still forced to live in a material world—and the world has yet to hear of a " philosopher " refusing to eat his dinner on the ground that " Matter does not exist ! "—means nothing less than that the whole aim of subjectivist idealist philosophy to-day is to proclaim an absolute rupture between Theory and Practice. Since Marxism is in a certain sense " relativist," it is necessary here to mark off sharply the distinction between the " relativism " of Dialectical Materialism and that of the *subjectivists*.

RELATIVITY, ABSOLUTE AND RELATIVE

Every formulation of the Truth made by mankind is of necessity a statement of the Truth *as it appears* to the formulator. So much is self-evident. A man's knowledge, however much it may be genuine *knowledge*, is still only *human* knowledge. It is at best only so much of the Truth as a man in the then existing conditions can attain.

So far, then, only *relative* Truth is attainable by man— relative in quantity as compared with what was known generally yesterday, and that which will, most likely, be known to-morrow ; and relative in quality since the significance even of what is thoroughly known depends upon its connection with other things not so thoroughly (or, possibly, *at all*) well known. Moreover, it is the Truth of a *relation*— that between Men and Things, and Things among themselves as viewed from the standpoint of Mankind.

But does this mean that human knowledge is *absolutely relative* ? That the Truth attained by man is as a whole and in all its details *not at all truly True* ? That it has only such " Truth " as is possessed by a mirage, an imagination, a dream vision—that of a fictional substitute for, or symbol of, Reality ?

A whole group of related schools contend to-day that this is the case.

Let us take a concrete instance.

To all appearances the sun rises daily in the east and, after ascending to its meridian, sinks daily in the west. Taking appearances at their face value we would say, " As true as that the sun will rise in the morning."

But this truth is admittedly that of the appearance only.

We know now that the *apparent* movement of the sun is due to the *real* movement of the earth.

Is the first statement, then, *absolutely false* ? No, it records a true experience, truly observed ; moreover, its content is valid—the sun *does* change its position daily and in a regular way measured from any fixed point *on the earth's surface*. Given the earth's surface as a point of view, and the essence of the observation the *changing relation* between the two objects (the observer and the sun) is a fact *absolute* within that relation.

But *only* so within those limits. To an observer on the moon both the earth and the sun would seem to move around *it*. Here too the content, change of relative position, would be correctly apprehended—but there would be a failure in each case to establish a harmony between these correctly apprehended objective facts and other facts which demonstrate that their form of appearance—their phenomenal mode of presentation—was capable of misinterpretation.

From yet another point of view—that of an observer on the surface of the sun—the movements of the earth would be similarly apprehended correctly as to content, but inversely as to form. From the point of view of the " fixed " stars the sun and the solar system with it are moving as one group in a definite direction. From the point of view of the earth the sun is fixed.

All these statements considered abstractly—as *absolutely-absolute* are false ; all are only relatively *true*, but their relativity is *not absolute* since they are all of *absolute* validity within their relation, which is a *persisting* relation and *so far* absolute. The relative therefore is only *relatively* relative.

Relativity is *true*, but *only relatively so*, and the problem of practice is to distinguish in every percept, and every concept, conclusion, and judgment, the respects in which it possesses absoluteness of truth, and the relative truth of appearance only.

So much being provisionally clear, let us test this conclusion by a scrutiny into the case as presented by those " modernist " tendencies it is convenient to lump together under the umbrella-name of " Pragmatists."

Firstly, as to this name. Its root or dictionary meaning is that of something laid down by arbitrary decree. Its modern use was brought into fashion by the American WILLIAM JAMES, the psychologist, who in his *Varieties of Religious Experience* advanced the notion that, in matters of Faith and Morals, one can *make* a belief " true " by contriving to believe it hard enough ; that, therefore, a belief was " true " for you if it proved " salutary," if it " made for righteousness." The successors, imitators, and refiners upon James have sought (*a*) to reduce all knowledge to the status of " belief " ; and (*b*) to apply to all beliefs the " pragmatic sanction " invented by James as an artifice of religious apologetics.

It will be seen that for the plain man it will be a convenient (" salutary ") aid to the identification of Pragmatism if we remember that, as has been said above, the soul of Pragmatism was enunciated by the immortal Bellman : " What I tell you three times is true." (Moreover, for the Pragmatist every " Snark " turns out to be a " Boojum ! ")

The ultra-Left (or is it the infra-Right ?) of the school is occupied by the " Solipsists " (*sol* = sole, only ; *ipsi* = I, myself)—those who argue (carrying Berkeley's position to the limit) that nothing exists except in one's own mind, *and one may have dreamed even that* !

At bottom, it will be perceived, the school constitutes a retreat to Humeian-Kantian scepticism. But it is not only that. We have seen already that Hume, and, despite the ambiguities in his system as a whole, Kant likewise, told in their day heavily on the side of anti-supernaturalism and anti-clericalism. But their doctrine, as we have seen, had an opposite significance—that of discrediting all the seeming certainties attained by human thinking. And it is this, the *reactionary*, side of Humeian-Kantian scepticism which is developed in these " modernist " schools, as is evidenced by the enthusiasm with which their arguments are taken up and adapted to the service of religious apologetics.

Philosophically the *trick* by means of which these schools attain such plausibility as they possess consists in juggling with the two senses of the term " sensation." This in common usage may mean either the act and fact of becoming aware of a particular object or external happening, or it may mean the subjective pleasure-pain, attraction-repulsion reaction induced in consciousness by sensation in its primary sense.

Thus by these schools all subjective activity is reduced to that of fixing " values " upon experienced phenomena and classifying them as " good " or " bad," " salutary " and " insalutary," and so on. Furthermore, much as these schools insist upon the *absolute* relativity of experienced phenomena, their whole case depends upon the postulate of the relative *absoluteness* of the subjective *ego*. If, as with the *ultras*, this *ego* is conceived as necessarily distinct and different in each and every man, the solipsist conclusion—that there are as many *universes* as there are men—is reached. If, as with the moderates, the *ego* is conceived as like-natured in all men, the door is flung wide open for the return of the Dogmatic Theology of the mediæval schoolmen.

Whether it be interpreted as a parallel phenomenon or as a practical consequence, the fact remains that the rise of the Pragmatic-subjectivist schools has coincided with a rapid growth in the number of recruits to the Catholic Church from among the intelligentsia. Catholicism is, in fact, " quite the mode."

The Marxian canon laid down in the Second *Thesis* is thus highly apposite. Let us apply it.

To Pragmatism, as to all idealism, *material reality*, as such, does not exist : its current slogan is that " modern science has *proved* (!) that matter does not exist." This does not mean that any " philosopher " refuses to eat his dinner on the ground that dinners " don't exist, really." It means that he complies with the custom of eating because he finds the result " salutary ! "—and, in most cases, highly so !

Very good. Now let the pragmatist explain why in every language the same terms are applied to the valuation of food, and its consumption, as to conduct in society. The pragmatist, like his neighbour, not only " likes " to do certain things ; he " likes " mutton. He not only " loves " his neighbour (as himself ?), he " loves " roast goose ! He finds Christianity " salutary," and, acting on medical advice, finds that the same term may be applied to a regulated diet, and an occasional dose of Epsom salts. At bottom the concrete evidence of language points—and that irresistibly—to the fact that valuation is an operation which has no other explanation save in terms of actual practice in a really existent world of objective *materiality*. Only in a world of real flesh and blood men, faced with the need to grapple physically and mentally with actual material things, have these discriminations any meaning.

And, what is more, only in such a world can there arise those very variations in and contradictory modes of *valuation* upon which the pragmatist relies for his case.

Take an example. A worker in a factory is set to gauge steel balls for use in ball-bearings. These must be of the *right* size or they are of no use. What is the *right* size ? It is recognised that, in practice, *absolute* accuracy is unattainable, but it is possible, and the gauger does in fact, by the use of upper and lower-limit gauges, sort out as " right " those that do not vary beyond a prescribed limit—in this case one of the 10,000th part of an inch plus or minus.

Another worker, a scientific instrument maker, may be set to produce a result accurate within limits of a 100,000th plus or minus. Another, in another factory, may be allowed limits as wide as 1000th. In wood-working factories limits of one thirty-second of an inch would be " fine " limits ; by engineering standards they would be " coarse." And so on.

Now observe firstly—*absolute* accuracy is recognised to be in practice unattainable. Does that mean that no sort of accuracy, no approximation to accuracy, is attainable at all ? As is self-evident in the examples given above, *absolute* accuracy is, like the Euclidean line or point, an *abstraction* reached by the mind by the mental elimination of variations which in practice can be eliminated only more or less.

Absolute accuracy being then unattainable—except conceptually—does this mean that nothing is attained but *error* ?

By metaphysical standards that which is not " True " is " False " ; that which is not " False " is " True." Let it be so. Will it be argued, when, as is often proved in practice, accuracy can be attained (as in giant telescope reflectors) to within limits of *one* hundred-millionth part of an inch, that no sort of accuracy is attainable ? Put it, if you will, that any given thing is accurate " only " to an extent. Equally true it is that the said thing is *false only* to an extent. *Why do the Pragmatists and Subjectivists fasten upon the one 100,000,000th in an inch of falsity and treat as non-existent the 99,999,999 parts in each inch of accuracy ?*

Their motive is, in the actual social relations in which they arise and argue, clearly apparent. Directly or indirectly, or both, they are concerned to find weapons with which to combat the rising forces of revolution at whose head stands Dialectical Materialism.

Their excuse is that it is " contradictory," and therefore " illogical," to say that a thing can be both True and False, exact and inexact, at one and the same time. Be it so ; but let it be observed firstly that this is an objection, not to the facts or to the practice, but wholly and solely to the *terminology* in which those facts are stated. Secondly, be it observed that the " Hegelianism " involved in the coexistence of

E

opposites (true and false, etc.) is not of theoretical but of practical origin. The gauger aforesaid does use " opposite " gauges, and in practice approximations to accuracy are attainable in no other way. It is not the fault of Hegel that a navigator achieves accuracy in his reckoning by using *three* chronometers. (If he used only *one* he would be at the mercy of its temporary or permanent aberrations ; if only *two*, he would be unable to determine which had varied ; by using *three* he gets a reliable *mean*.)

These things arise, and that inevitably, from the *practical* basis of the discrimination between Theory and Practice, Subject and Object. And the whole subjectivist argument is an endeavour to smuggle in, by logical sleight of hand, a complete divorce of Theory from Practice, and a return to the sophistication and mystery-mongering that that divorce makes possible.

For, be it reiterated—all thinking is that of *men*, in a *real* world. That we are forced by the nature of human understanding to make abstractions from Reality in order to provide ourselves with theoretical standards of measurement and appraisal does not in the least make the objective world any the less objective, material, or real ; or make our abstractions any the less abstract. " First Principles," so called, are in fact better described as Final Abstractions. And our theoretical practice in making and using abstractions finds its justification, or its condemnation, in and so far as we can or cannot use them in practice *to achieve objective results*.

That this seems to assert no more than is asserted in the pragmatist saying—" a belief is true if it works "—only the more vindicates the Dialectical Materialist standpoint. In actual life and practice the Pragmatists prove that what they mean is that " any argument is good enough to use against a Materialist if *only you can* ' get away with it ! ' "

In sum :—

> " The distinction between subjectivism (scepticism, sophistry, etc,) and dialectics, among other things, lies in this, that in (' objective ') dialectics the distinction between the relative and the absolute is itself relative. For objective dialectics the absolute is also to be found in the relative. For subjectivism and sophistry the relative is only relative and excludes the absolute."—LENIN : *Materialism*, etc., p. 324.

In real practical life, as in experimental science and industry this fact is well understood, and the criterion of practice is constantly applied. Because in England it is customary to express the boiling point of water as " 212 degrees," while in France it is expressed as " 100 degrees," and in Poland and parts of Russia as " 80 degrees," nobody supposes, therefore, the fact that water boils is called in question, or that there is any doubt as to the temperature at which, at the sea-level, water will boil. All that is proved is that three different conventional modes of expressing one and the same fact have become habitual in as many areas. Thus the variety in the expressions only emphasises the more strikingly the singleness of the objective fact to which they bear united testimony. All together testify to the fact that water can be made to boil, and that this phenomenon occurs invariably in a set of circumstances known with such precision that the result can be produced whenever the means are at hand for establishing the necessary preconditions.

This has immense consequences for theory—since it bears directly upon the cardinal problem of philosophy, the test of Truth. It has a significance no less profound for human practice, since if theory be established thus as the summing-up and generalisation of the Truths established by practice, Theory can then be made the starting point for further practice.

" Philosophy " in the broad, non-restrictive sense of the systematic search for Truth and the co-ordination of the verified results of the search—the union of Theory and Practice—thus ceases to be a toy, a parlour game, a means of private entertainment, a choice of fashionable intellectual wear—and becomes an instrument of revolutionary struggle, a weapon of war.

MATERIALISM *and* MATERIALISM

Taking the first two *Theses* in conjunction we get a good preliminary view of the manner in which Marx's Dialectical Materialism was marked off from any and every sort of Idealism on the one side, and from the " older," the pre-Kantian Materialism on the other.

Marx's separation from Idealism is clear : an objective, material world *does* exist (as commonsense says it does), and what is more, the actual objective practice of mankind proves that really, dependable (and therein *verified*) knowledge of this external, material world is not only attainable but is, in fact, attained, and that increasingly.

Human practice, however, subjective as well as objective,

theorectical as well as practical, at the same time proved
that Truth was to be found in a direction quite different
from that in which the older Materialists had sought it.
The Truth attainable by human thinking was not that of an
abstract absolute truth such as would exist for a being freed
from human passions and limitations. Such a " Truth " was
unthinkable ; and worthless, could it ever be divined. The
Truth to which mankind can attain is that of the *developing
synthesis* of relations within which man " lives, moves, and
has his being." It is a *relative* Truth, since it is the Truth of
a set of inter-relations and inter-actions viewed from *within*
those relations. It is relative again in *quantity* : it is always
being added to, and always capable of further addition.
Qualitatively, however, it is relatively *absolute* ; that is to
say, though it may not be the whole of the Truth, it is truly
true, so far as it extends.

It is in this *dialectical* combination of the " opposites,"
Theory and Practice, Absoluteness and Relativity, Per-
sistence and Variability, Stability and Growth, that the
Dialectical Materialist epistcmology [conception of knowledge]
makes its first departure from the older, pre-Kantian
Materialism.

The chief weakness of that materialism, namely, that it
treated the concept of a thing as *the same as* the object of
which it was a reflection, and therefore failed to discriminate
between the "*this*-sidedness " and the "*yonder*-sidedness " of
reality, and failed to conceive thought-activity as a subjective practice which derived its point and significance from the
fact that it was the reciprocal reflex of an objective *activity*—
this weakness was indicated in the First *Thesis*.

The correlative of the fact that Thought-activity is the
reflex form of objective activity was the theme of the Second
Thesis. If thoughts, ideas, etc., are *reflections* of external
reality, the question arises : Have we any criterion by which
the *Truth* of the reflection can be tested ? As we have seen,
the answer is—*the criterion of practice*.

But employing the criterion of practice brings us directly
into contact with the *Dialectical* character of both external
reality and its thought-reflex. The *practice* to which we
turn is the activity of men *through objects*, an activity which
not only changes those objects, and modifies their inter-
relation, but changes likewise the quantity and quality of
Truth available for the use of mankind.

This brings out the second weakness of the older materialism

—its inability to bring within its compass any process of an *historical*, or dialectical, character :—

"The Materialism of the last century was pre-dominantly *mechanical*, because, at that time, of all natural sciences, mechanics, and indeed only the mechanics of solid bodies—celestial and terrestrial—in short, the mechanics of gravity, had come to any definite conclusions. . . . As the animal was to Descartes, so was man a machine to the materialism of the eighteenth century. This exclusive application of the standards of mechanics to processes of a chemical and organic nature —in which processes, it is true, the laws of mechanics are also valid, but are pushed into the background by other and higher laws—constitutes a specific, but at that time inevitable, limitation of classical French materialism.

"The second specific limitation of this materialism lay in its inability to comprehend the universe as a process—as matter developing in an historical process. . . . Nature, it was known, was in constant motion. But, according to the ideas of that time, this motion turned eternally in a circle and therefore never moved from the spot ; it produced the same results over and over again."—ENGELS : *Ludwig Feuerbach,* pp. 36–7.

This weakness was especially apparent when the Materialists turned their attention to the problems of society—of politics and morals. This fact is the theme of the Third *Thesis.*

.   .   .   .   .   .

While, as we have seen, Philosophy on its Idealist side had made progress in developing the theory of cognition, its Materialist wing had not simply marked time. On the contrary, while Idealism, despite its progressive achieve-ment, was doomed, because it was Idealist, to end in a rehabilitation of camouflaged Theology (i.e., Metaphysics) and ultimately in a return to supernaturalist mysticism and the abandonment of Philosophy, Materialism was developing in the opposite direction :

"The French enlightenment of the eighteenth century, particularly French materialism, was not only a struggle against the existing political institutions, as well as the existing religion and theology, but was quite as much an open, outspoken struggle against the metaphysics of the seventeenth century and against all metaphysics. . . . . Philosophy was set up in opposition to metaphysics ; just as Feuerbach, when he first came out decidedly against Hegel, placed *sober philosophy* in opposition to *intoxicated speculation.*"—MARX-ENGELS : *The Holy Family.*

Materialistic philosophy, in both England and France, developed on two sides. One side developed from metaphysics, through the transition stage of " Natural Philosophy," into the positive sciences (astronomy, geology, physics, chemistry, etc.), each of which, as soon as it took rank definitely as a specific science, declared its final independence of all philosophising *a priori.* On the other side, materialistic philosophy developed into the systematised materialist critique of the theory of the " Soul "—out of which emerged " psychology "—of the so-called " moral sense " in man and of the political and civil institutions of society. On this side French Materialism, though it took its rise directly from the English materialism of HOBBES and LOCKE, far outdistanced its tutors.

" The man who ruined the theoretical credit of the metaphysics of the seventeenth century and of all metaphysics was PIERRE BAYLE [1647–1706]. His weapon was scepticism, forged out of the magical formulae of metaphysics itself. . . . Just as Feuerbach, by combating speculative theology, was driven further to combating speculative philosophy, precisely because he recognised speculation to be the best support of theology—because he had to drive the theologians back from pseudo-science to crude, repellant faith— so religious doubt forced Bayle into doubting the metaphysics which supported this faith."—MARX-ENGELS : *The Holy Family.*

Following the impetus given by Bayle, three physicians developed the Materialist conception of man on its physical side. The physician LEROY took the Cartesian notion that animals were " animated machines," and applied it to men. Later LAMETTRIE (1709–51), in his " *Man a Machine,*" worked out the same conception which :

" . . . . declared the soul to be a mode [i.e., *aspect*] of the body and ideas to be *mechanical motions.*"—MARX-ENGELS, *ibid.*

The physician CABANIS (1757–1808) completed this development in his " *Physical Basis of the Moral Nature of Man.*" Cabanis was the author of the axiom usually attributed to Moleschott, who only quoted it with approval—" the function of the brain is to generate thought as the function of the liver is to secrete bile, or the kidneys urine."

Working more or less parallel with these avowedly "mechanistic" physiologists were the *critical* Materialists and their allies, who were concerned with moral and social questions. Here the development begins with LOCKE and his Sensationalist Theory of Knowledge.

> " The whole wealth of metaphysics now [early eight-eenth century] consisted in nothing but thought entities and heavenly things, at precisely the time when real entities and earthly things began to concentrate all attention upon themselves. Metaphysics had become stale. . . .
>
> " In addition to the negative refutation of the theology and metaphysics of the seventeenth century, a positive anti-metaphysical system was needed. A book was required which would systematise the practical activities of the time and give them a theoretical foundation. LOCKE's *Essay Concerning the Human Understanding* came from the other side of the Channel as if at call. . . . Locke gave a basis to the philosophy of *bon sens*, of commonsense ; that . . . there is no philosophy other than that of the normal human senses and the under-standing based on them.
>
> " CONDILLAC . . . proved that the French were right in rejecting metaphysics as being a mere figment of the imagination and of theological prejudices. . . . He gave an exposition of Locke's ideas and proved that not only the soul, but the senses, not only the art of creating ideas, but also the art of sensuous perception are matters of experience and habit. The entire development of man, therefore, depends upon upbringing and external circumstances. . . ."
>
> " HELVETIUS, who likewise started out from Locke . . . comprehended it [materialism] at once in its relation to social life Sensuous qualities and egoism, pleasure and enlightened self-interest are the foundations of all morality. The natural equality of human intelligences, the unity between the progress of reason and the progress of industry, the natural goodness of man, the omnipotence of upbringing are the principle features of his system."— MARX-ENGELS : *The Holy Family*.

The affinity between the doctrine here outlined and that accepted by the whole movement of Radicalism, which in

England culminated in Owenite Communism and Chartism, and in France in " critical Utopian Socialism and Communism," is obvious. *Bentham's* " Utilitarianism " was avowedly derived directly from Helvetius, and his celebrated " greatest good of the greatest number " is only an echo (and a perverted one) of the " *general good,*" which, according to the French Materialist school it was the purpose of morality (or " virtue ") to serve.

Its affinity with the doctrine of ROBERT OWEN. " Man's character is made *for* him and not *by* him," is equally apparent, while its claim that all men were *by nature* equal in intellectual endowments—or at any rate equal in *potentiality*—was the basis of the claim to *equality* which was, in one form, the doctrine of the Jacobins of the French Revolution, and in another that of their successors—Baboeuf and his Equalitarian Communism ; and Fourier, Owen, and the Utopian schools.

A few quotations will suffice to demonstrate the similarity of HELVETIUS and OWEN :

" I am convinced that a good education would diffuse light, virtue, and consequently, happiness in Society ; and that the opinion that genius and virtue are merely gifts of nature is a great obstacle to the making of any further progress in the Science of Education. And in this respect is the great favourer of idleness and negligence. . . . Education makes us what we are."— HELVETIUS : *On the Mind,* Essay III, chap. 30.

" Any general character, from the best to the worst, from the most ignorant to the most enlightened, may be given to any community, even to the world at large, by the application of proper means ; which means are to a great extent at the command and under the control of those who have influence in the affairs of men."— ROBERT OWEN : *New View of Society,* Everyman ed., p. 16.

" If citizens could not procure their own private happiness without promoting that of the public, there would then be none vicious but fools."—HELVETIUS : *On the Mind,* Essay II, chap. 22.

" In proportion as man's desire of self-happiness, or his self-love, is directed by true knowledge, those actions will abound which are virtuous and beneficial to man . . . every individual will necessarily endeavour to promote the happiness of every other individual within his sphere of action ; because he must see clearly and without any doubt comprehend such conduct to be the essence of self-interest, or the true cause of self-happiness."—OWEN : *New View of Society*, p. 56.

In short, men, however much they may vary as individuals, are all possessed of a nature in common. The basic tendency of that nature is to seek happiness, and, despite differences of physical capacity, all men can be made most happy by the practice of *virtue*, by that conduct which should and would promote the general happiness if the laws and institutions were correctly based on Natural Law. If men are vicious it is either because they have been mistaught, or because bad laws and obnoxious social arrangements promote vice by causing individual interests to conflict with the general interest of mankind.

Compare now with the passages from HELVETIUS and OWEN (given above), the following :

" In the contradiction between Faith and Love . . . we see the practical, palpable, ground of necessity that we should raise ourselves above the standpoint of Christianity, above the peculiar standpoint of all religion. We have shown that the substance and object of religion is altogether *human ;* we have shown that divine wisdom is human wisdom ; that the secret of theology is anthropology ; that the absolute mind is the so-called finite subjective mind. But religion is not conscious that its elements are human ; on the contrary, it places itself in opposition to the human. . . . *The necessary turning point of history* is therefore the open confession, that the consciousness of God is nothing else than the consciousness of the species ; that man can and should raise himself only above *the limits of his individuality*, and not above the laws, the positive essential conditions of his species ; that there is no other essence which man can think, dream of, imagine, feel, believe in, wish for, love and adore as the *absolute*, than the essence of human nature itself."—FEUERBACH : *Essence of Christianity*, p. 270.

The terminology is vastly different and heavily charged with Hegelianisms, but the substantial content is identical— the prelude to all change is a general change in *belief*, in *opinion* ; the end sought is the identification of the *individual* with the *general* interest—the realisation of the *law* of *human nature*—which law rests upon a something, abstract and immutable, resident in each separate human individual, which makes them all " as one " by Nature.

THE DILEMMA OF MECHANICAL DETERMINISM

In the Third *Thesis* Marx subjects this conception to criticism, and brings out its one-sided static and abstract character.

Preoccupied as they were with their endeavour to reduce all phenomena to terms of a single, all-embracing, Universal Law, the eighteenth-century materialists could not help but commit the logical sin of substituting abstractions for objective reality. They conceived Natural Law, not as a tendency common to a group of facts, by means of which they can be distinguished from other groups of facts, but as something logically antecedent to the facts—something which the facts were " forced " more or less unwillingly to " obey." A progressively unfolding " law," one undergoing a process of cumulative mutation—an " evolutionary " conception as we should call it—was in fact excluded by their method of approach.

It followed therefore that in formulating their criticism of the then established order, the eighteenth-century materialists all pursued the method of first formulating the " Law of Nature " and then proving that this " Law " had been woefully infringed with disastrous consequences. To secure the general well-being and happiness of mankind it was first of all necessary to abolish the bad laws which put a premium upon " vice "—(satisfying individual interest at the expense of the general interest)—and replace them with laws which put a premium upon " virtue "—(seeking self-satisfaction only in such ways as promoted general happiness and well-being). Thereafter, as we have seen in the extracts given, both Helvetius and Owen, with all their respective followers, were convinced that a wisely directed system of Education would make *virtue universal,* and (except for the feeble-minded and the insane) cause *vice* to disappear completely.

Marx, it will be observed, does not fall foul of this theory on the score of its " Utopian " belief in the " perfectibility " of man, or in the progressive amelioration of his lot. Neither does he quarrel with the identification of " virtue " with the gratification of human appetites and impulses in ways consistent with the general interest of society. Nor does he cavil at the conception that since *all men alike* are, subjectively, synthetic *unities* (of sensations, memories of sensations, judgments, and volitions based upon sensations) they are all, therefore, and so far, " naturally " *equal*. All these propositions have a large measure of truth ; but that, however, is of no significance beside the fact that in the conjunction the mechanical materialists gave them they were unusable.

Marx therefore raises the issue that the conception as applied to society in an uncritical form is theoretically unsound and self-stultifying in practice. He impales it upon the horns of a dilemma :

> " The materialist doctrine that men are the products of circumstances and education . . . forgets that circumstances are *changed precisely by men*, and that the Educator *must himself be educated*."—MARX : *Theses on Feuerbach*.

Formulated as a doctrine, the " mechanical " theory affirmed the all-powerfulness of circumstances (including education). Men's characters, and conduct, on this view, were the passive *results*, the mechanical continuations of the activity of circumstances.

But the doctrine was advanced by men who most certainly wanted circumstances changed, and who desired to change education as a means of changing men sufficiently to make them change their circumstances. On one side man was the victim of circumstances : on the other, circumstances were at the mercy of men. The dilemma was complete.

It can be, as Marx indicates, formulated from another angle. The change contemplated was to begin with *a changed education*. Whence was this education to come ? *Who was going to educate the Educator ?*

It was the problem, deemed insoluble by metaphysicians : *Which came first, the hen or the egg ?*

.   .   .   .   .

The Materialists of the eighteenth century were waging a struggle, a struggle against the Grand Monarchy and its clerical " police in cassocks." As against the claims of the Church to possess " revealed Truth " the HOBBES-LOCKE sensationalism, with its denial of all " innate " ideas, provided a deadly weapon, and one that fitted in admirably with the Newtonian astronomy and the mechanistic physiology developed from Cartesian physics. It was not safe to challenge the " Divine Right " of the Monarchy too openly, but if it could be shown, as the Newtonian astronomy did, that the active creative function of God was exhausted in giving the Universe its initial " push off " the plausibility of the conception of the King as a Divine agent was heavily shaken, along with all other alleged examples of miraculous intervention in human affairs. The "Sensationalist" philosophy had resolved the emotions as well as the understanding into "corporeal sensations." All that was left to do to complete the discredit of the Church and the *ancien regime* was to demonstrate that morals, laws, and political authority all took their rise from and had their justification in *public utility*. "*The good of the people is the supreme law.*"

The first move in the struggle was to demonstrate that under the name of morals the priests in all lands had mixed with unimpeachable maxims others of patent absurdity. That wise maxims were found at least as often on the lips of pagan and Oriental priests and sages as on those of Christian priests was clear proof that these latter had no monopoly of even such wisdom as they might possess. On the contrary, the bias of the philosophers led them to " discover " in the Oriental sages a wealth of virtues which to-day strikes us as inexpressibly absurd. It was part of the battle. It helped to clear the ground for the demonstration that such merits as the Christian ethics possessed were common to the entire human race, while the special absurdities of Christian theology, though unique in form, was likewise common to priestcraft and superstition everywhere.

It was necessary to find a theoretical basis for morals, since these were, in the theory of the philosophers the only " natural " and proper basis for law and government—whose function was the administration of the law. This basis was found in *utility*. Governments were established because of the need to regulate social conduct—to reward the virtuous and repress the vicious and anti-social. How had bad institutions grown up ? How had government grown tyrannical and oppressive ? How had it come to be that governments and governing institutions, such as the Church, had encouraged vicious courses—practices which put private advantage in opposition to the public good ? This was the problem.

The priests who, of course, denied that the governments were oppressive had their theory to account for vicious courses—men were compelled by the lusts of the flesh which dimmed the " light of the soul," the promptings of conscience, and the teaching of Scripture. " The heart of man is deceitful above all things and desperately wicked." Helvetius, Owen, and Feuerbach, each in his way, levelled an assault upon the doctrine of the natural depravity of man, seeing in that doctrine one of the chief theoretical supports of the then prevailing order.

HELVETIUS particularly devoted himself to demonstrating that the lusts of the flesh, far from being a cause of corruption, were the mainspring of progress. Hunger led men to produce and devise the arts of manufacture ; the desire and hope of gratification led men to seek the esteem of their fellows and the security and satisfaction that depended thereupon. The love of women inspired men to be courageous and to seek to be publicly so well-esteemed that the most desirable women would be at their disposal. The more enlightened and far-seeing the self-interest, the more private interest would be identified with the public good.

Both Helvetius and Owen base themselves openly on the conviction that men are neither good nor bad by Nature, but soon become corrupt if society is constructed other than in conformity with Natural Law. Helvetius holds that part of the established law—so much as secures property—arises direct from natural law. There are, he says, in addition, other laws, and these are of two sorts :

> " . . . . the one are variable by their nature ; and such are those as regard commerce, taxes, military discipline, etc. These may and ought to change according to times and circumstances. The other, *immutable* by their nature, are only variable from their not being yet carried to perfection."—HELVETIUS : *On Man*, Vol. II, sec. 10, chap. 7.

Ignorance, superstition, the idleness and inattentiveness of legislatures, and the clash of interests produced by conquest, produces a state of law favourable to knaves, who accordingly defend those laws with all their power. The virtuous should, and do, desire the abolition of bad laws, " but the virtuous are few in number, and are not always the most powerful." Helvetius ends on a note of pessimism. His work, " *On Man*," he kept back from publication until after his death in 1771 :

> " It was once my intention to have published this book under a fictitious name, as the only means of reconciling with my own safety the desire I entertained of rendering service to my country. But . . . a change has happened in the circumstances and government of my fellow-citizens. The disorder, which I hoped in some measure to remedy, is become incurable : the prospect of public utility is vanished, and I defer the publication of the work till its author be no more. My country [France] has at length submitted to the yoke of despotism. *She will never again produce any writer of extraordinary*

eminence. It is the characteristic of despotic power to extinguish both genius and virtue."—HELVETIUS : *On Man*, Preface.

" Never prophesy until you know ! " Within a generation after these words were written France was a republic and shaking the whole world to its foundations !

THE EDUCATION OF THE EDUCATOR

Men are by nature neither Good nor Bad. A lone man on an uninhabited island may be wise or unwise—he cannot be *immoral* or moral since his conduct has no social significance. He can neither benefit nor injure others. Only in society is either possible. But whence came society ? The eighteenth-century materialists could only suppose that at some time or another somebody *invented* it ! Thus at bottom the material-ists were driven back to an idealist supposition—society takes its rise in an *idea* which has no discernible material ante-cedents.

Again, if men ultimately learned everything from Nature, and had created Society in accordance with the promptings of Natural Law, how had society ever departed from that Law ? Whence came the " ignorance " which allowed *despotisms* to become established ? Helvetius made two daring guesses : one was " Chance "—an abandonment of the theoretical riddle ! The other was that ignorance was more than mere absence of knowledge—it was positive *misinformation*, administered with corrupt motives by priest-craft and statecraft. The problem was merely shifted : whence originated these sources of evil ? Again there was no solution but the Natural frailty of man. The theory that man is by nature neither *good* nor *bad* was continually driven back to its opposite—Man is by nature *both* good *and* bad, and only chance (or the Devil !) could decide which would prevail.

But, despite the violent rupture between Theory and Practice involved, they refused to accept this form of the priests' theory of the dual nature of man—" half angel, half brute beast ! "

They fell back upon their intellectualist theory of society, and in their practical systems they, as Marx said, " divided Society into two parts, one of which towers above Society." This conceptual division had two opposite concrete applica-tions, from each of which a different school was historically to take its departure.

On one view it was the tyrant, the oppressive ruler, who, with his corrupt supporters and dependants, " towered above society," imposed his will upon it and, by his disturbing influence, set private interests in opposition to the public good. This was a practical surrender of the immutable Natural Law theory of Society, but it had the " pragmatic " advantage of corresponding to the facts. Both Owen and Helvetius traced most of the evils of society to the unequal distribution of wealth and property ; both of them attributed this unequal distribution to bad laws and wrong principles of government. Each traced the origin of the evil to *an intellectual and moral source* ; each therefore looked to an intellectual and moral force for the remedy. Each of them looked for " virtuous " and " enlightened " rulers who would correct the evils produced by the bad ones.

They differed, of course, widely in their respective attitudes to property. Helvetius stood for *individual* property, Owen for *common* property, but they both saw that the property question lay at the root of the social question, and herein both were far in advance of Feuerbach, for whom the property question had hardly risen above the horizon.

Helvetius' attitude to the property question is highly significant—and illustrates in a remarkable way that conceptual division of society into " society " proper and a *super*-social force to which Marx alludes. In one chapter of his work *On Man* Helvetius propounds a series of " the first questions we should ask ourselves when we would establish good laws." The fifth question is :

" If the establishment of despotism in an empire does not destroy all the bonds of social union ? "—HEL-VETIUS : *On Man*, Vol. II, 9, 2.

The sixth question :

" If property can be a long time respected without introducing, *as in England*, a certain equilibrium of power among the different classes of citizens ? "—HELVETIUS : *ibid*.

The tenth question :

" *If the poor have really a country ?* If the man without property owes anything to the country where he possesses nothing ; if the extreme indigent, being always in the pay of the rich and powerful, must not frequently favour their ambition ; and, lastly, if the indigent have not *too many wants to be virtuous* ? "—HELVETIUS : *ibid*.

He goes on to suggest a scheme startling in its " up-to-

date "-ness (!).   He proposes *an equal distribution of the
land* between families, and drives this home in a footnote :

> " On this supposition, to preserve a certain equality
> in the diffusion of property, if a family diminishes, it
> must cede a part of its land to some neighbouring and
> more numerous families.   *Why not ?* "—HELVETIUS :
> *ibid.*

It is a very fine example of the dialectic of history that a
proposal which in 1770 figured as the ultra-Left of revolutionary suggestion should in our own day constitute the main
plank in the programme of neo-Catholic " Distributivism "
and a demagogic bait of Nazi " *Socialism.*"

Helvetius' conception that the " poor " stood in fact
outside society ; that they were the political allies of the
" rich and powerful," who likewise stood outside society at
its opposite pole, gives a splendid example of the bifurcated
conception of society.   It is all the more noteworthy as
including a rudimentary form of the concept of class struggle
—here conceived as a purely destructive and reactionary
force—which Marx and Engels were to make so fruitful.

Owen, in his earlier period, still stood substantially at this
point of view.   We have quoted earlier his declaration that
" any character . . . may be given to any community, even
to the world at large, by applying certain means which are
. . . under the control . . . of those who possess the government of nations."   In his address at New Lanark he, in out-
lining his proposals, emphasised the greatness of the change
his plans would produce.   " *But,*" he says,

> " this change will bear no resemblance to any of the
> revolutions which have hitherto occurred.   These have
> been alone calculated to generate and call forth all the
> evil passions of hatred and revenge ; but that change
> which is now contemplated will effectually eradicate
> every feeling of irritation and ill-will which exists among
> mankind.   The whole proceedings of those who govern
> and instruct the world will be reversed."—OWEN :
> *Address at New Lanark,* January 1st, 1816.

Here the bifurcated conception of society is seen sliding
over into its opposite form.   Those who have discovered the
true " Moral Law " and those who will put it into execution
are here the ones who " tower above " society, with its old
prejudices, ignorances, and vices :

> " Whence, then, have wickedness and misery pro-

ceeded ? I reply. *Solely from the ignorance of our fore-fathers !* [Owen's italics.] It is this ignorance, my friends, that has been, and continues to be, the only cause of all the miseries which men have experienced. This is the evil spirit which has had dominion over the world."—OWEN : *ibid.*

Which is almost in terms identical with Helvetius :

" It is by weakening the stupid veneration of the people for ancient laws and customs that *sovereigns* would be enabled to purge the earth of most of the evils that lay it waste, and be furnished with *the means of securing* the possession of their crowns."—HELVETIUS : *On the Mind,* II, 17.

In fine, on the " mechanical " materialist view society is a *structure.* It may be well designed or ill, well built or not so well. It may need expansion and enlargement or contraction ; or it may need pulling down and rebuilding. One thing it cannot do, and that is *to transform itself in virtue of its own inherent motive forces.* Hence it followed, for those who supposed themselves in possession of a new plan of social organisation, that their standpoint was not that of the concrete society of their day, but one which " towered above " that society and enabled them to penetrate beyond all its delusions to a more perfect conception. That which Mr. Middleton Murry in his ignorance asserts of Marx—that his theory " accounts for everything save Marx himself "—is true, *not* of Marx, but of the Utopians and the Materialists from whom they derived.

And, moreover, worked out into a system, this conceptual division of society into the active and originating *few* and the passive, ignorant, superstition-bound, bribed and corrupted mass has played a big rôle in the intellectual development of Europe and America since the days of the Utopians. Sophisticated with Fichtean egoism, it provides Carlyle's Great-man Theory ; adulterated with Socialism, it begets Bakunism, Fabianism, and Trotskyism. Fused with Kant's Thing-in-itself, it begets Schopenhauer, Stirner-ite Anarchism, and Freudianism. Adulterated with neo-Darwinism, it begets Nietzsche, and finally Fascism !

Once again the historical dialectic works itself out. The practical standpoint of the revolutionary bourgeois Materialism of the eighteenth century provides a theoretical standpoint for the reactionary anti-Materialist bourgeoisie in the twentieth century. In the meanwhile it has given rise, on another side, to Utopian Socialism and revolutionary proletarian Communism.

.   .   .   .   .

How did Marx break through the *impasse* from which the eighteenth-century Materialists and their continuators could not escape ? By a more thoroughgoing, by a *dialectical*, application of materialism.

It was not a question of Men *or* Circumstances ; it was a problem of Circumstanced *Men*. As soon as we turn away from considering Man in the abstract and fix our attention upon any one real man the fact leaps to the notice that included in his circumstances are *other men*.

Thus for each man taken separately circumstances are different. That is the first point. The second is like unto it : circumstances are alike for *all* men at a given time and place only in so far as all are alike dependent upon the existence of organised society, and that in turn is conditioned as to its form and function by the relation between it *as a whole* and objective Nature. Thus for each and every man taken separately " natural " circumstances have a force and a significance in practice quite other than that of Nature in the abstract—Nature in general—the sort of Nature the eighteenth-century materialists sought to formulate in an immutable Law. The same is true of Man himself. For each man taken separately his own powers and potentialities had a practical significance which varied in accordance with his *relation* to his fellow-men, and only through the plexus of *social* relations was he affected by Natural circumstance.

The eighteenth-century Materialists, in keeping with their inherited prejudices, had sought for immutable and permanent Truth ; hence they had abstracted away all the concrete variations which give specific practical importance to phenomena. They overlooked, in their search for certainty, the concrete fact that in real life what men have to deal with are regular *progressions*, dependable modes of *variation*. For the farmer the significant truth is not that the sun preserves its mean distance from the earth, but that, comparing one day with another, *it doesn't*. For the farmer the fact that *wheat* grains *are unchangeably* wheat grains is not the significant fact. What concerns him is that they can be changed into growing wheat which will ripen into a harvest. Not the fixities of variable Nature, but its fluidities : not change in the abstract, but the calculable regularity in change—these are the things that concern men in real life.

So with society. What exists concretely is not abstract society, but a number of concrete societies. These, however they may have arisen, had one feature in common—they were *liable to change*. On the mechanical view this liability to change was an aberration, an abnormality, something to be disregarded when seeking a correct theoretical conception of society. On the dialectical materialist view it was these very changes which were significant, and the problem was to find *in* and *by means of* the changes the *law* of—the observable persistency in—social change.

It was accepted as axiomatic by the eighteenth-century materialists that society existed because it had a utility for men, and that utility was found in the security and opportunity it created for *productive activity*—for the development of arts, crafts, and manufactures. It was not perceived that these very arts, crafts and manufactures were, considered collectively, so many ways in which men in group aggregations did in fact change—and that continually—the significance of Nature for themselves. The sea, which is "unplumb'd salt, estranging" to men at one age, is a highway and a connecting link as soon as they have learned to navigate it. The richly-grown valley bottom, which is a death-trap to a primitive, is a gold-mine to the agriculturist with a plough. And so on.

Moreover, not only did men in their productive activities change Nature both objectively and relatively. They changed *themselves* and their social inter-relations. Not only did the specialisation of crafts—the division of labour—lead to progressive variation in men's activities; it made men more dependent upon each other in exact proportion as it made their experience and the knowledge resulting different for each. *It combined men more closely the more it separated them.* So too production led to *property*. There is no point in "property" apart from production, and no point in government apart from property. And there can be no *private*, or "several," property without social inequalities producing not merely variations, but *antagonisms* of interest—which antagonisms derive their whole significance from the fact that men are *dependent* upon that very society within which these antagonisms are developed.

Thus by the use of the dialectical approach to the problem Marx was able to bring within the materialist conception all the phenomena before which the mechanical approach broke down. There was no need to fall back upon "pure chance," no need to suppose either "natural" vice or "natural" virtue. Nor was there any need to suppose an arbitrary, inexplicable, "intellectual" origin for society, law, or morals, or (and this was *the* point) for progressive *changes* in either. Taken in its broadest aspect, mankind could not live except in society, and society could not exist without productive activity, and productive activity constantly resulted in the changing of Nature, of Society, and of human nature itself. Men cannot live without changing their circumstances ; and in the act of changing their circumstances they changed positively and relatively themselves.

.   .   .   .   .

How does this bear upon the problem of the Great Educator ? And upon the bifurcated conception of society ?

Firstly, let it be observed that, even in the restricted sense of the word education, the schoolmasters' sense, the problem is a social one—having its roots in the political, social, and economic *division of labour* within society. Just as one set of men can only specialise on metal-working on condition that other men simultaneously specialise on food production, clothing production, house production, and so on, so it is clear that men can only specialise on *teaching* in a state of things in which there exists (*a*) the need to be taught, (*b*) the knowledge to impart.

Each of these arises, *dialectically*, from the same source —the social specialisation of status and function, which rests ultimately upon the specialisation of individual activities in social production.

All knowledge is derived ultimately from objective practical experience. But it does not end there. Each specialist is, because he is a specialist, learned only within his specialty. That he may be a specialist he must also be an *ignoramus* with regard to things outside his speciality. Thus arises, *in society* (i.e., not "naturally" in the eighteenth-century sense) the *speciality of generalisation*, that of co-ordinating and systematising the results reached by the practical experience of specialised individuals. Part, and a vital part, of the process of social growth is this "socialisation" of individual achievement. No man in society is limited in his range of knowledge to those facts he has actually discovered for himself. That the specialists in generalisation will themselves be limited to the specific ignorances of their speciality the whole history of philosophy stands to testify ; on the other hand, the growth and accumulation of proved and tested fact and knowledge demonstrate that in real life, out of two ignorances, that of the *practical* and that of the *theoretical* specialist, real knowledge, the union of Theory and Practice, is constantly being produced. " Out of nothing, nothing comes," and the deliverer of new Truths can become such only on condition of producing a new synthesis of the *experience*, practical and theoretical, of mankind. On its *formal* side each new truth is linked with truths, real or seeming, previously possessed by mankind. On its substantial side the new truth is a *truth*, so far as it summarises the verified experience of mankind, and a *new* truth in so far as it presents that experience in a connection never previously observed. Thus the Great Educator is himself *educated* by the totality of the social relations and activity of his time. He is himself an example of the fact that in *changing their circumstances men simultaneously change themselves*.

But the Great Educator, of the kind we are concerned with —the Owen kind—appears as an *antagonist* of the existing order of society. Quite so ! That is to say, to put the same thing in its *obverse* form, he is the *protagonist* of an alternative order—one he often conceives to be the " true " social order from which society has inadvertently deviated. Such a contraposition can only arise in a condition of *crisis*, more or less acute within society—in circumstances in which tension-strains, counter-tendencies, have made themselves apparent within society, and men, conscious of opposing interests, find themselves increasingly forced by their actual life problems into class conflicts.

In such circumstances the new truth cannot help but serve as an expression of *so much of a new social order as has already been pre-formed within the framework of the established order*. This, since it is a *social* order, must exist as a plexus of objective relations between men, with the concomitants thereof, a plexus of emotional reactions to the prevailing order shared in greater or less completeness and intensity by all the members of this group, and a body of *opinion*, more or less co-ordinated, which expresses the point of view of this class.

Thus the Great Educator is (*a*) educated by society ; (*b*) expresses a tendency latent within society which is tending to become dominant therein ; and (*c*) is, even despite himself, the representative of a revolutionary force making for the overthrow of the old order and its replacement by a new one. As such the Great Educator holds up to the old doomed society the sentence of its own extinction. As such, he

" towers above society " as the executioner towers above his victim ; and at the same time, as the spokesman of all that is most vital and progressive in the society of his day, he is more truly representative of society as in fact it is than are the figureheads of the old order, who only in semblance " tower above " society as the, nominally, sole source of Law, Order and Authority. The Great Educator thus does actually *represent* society ; while its official " representatives " merely *mis*-represent it. In short :

" The *coincidence* of change in circumstances and in human activity can be conceived and rationally understood only as *revolutionising practice* "—*i.e.*, only as the outcome of practice which has, in fact, *revolutionised* ; and as, also, the starting point for *consciously* revolutionising practice.

CHAPTER III

RELIGION; HUMANITY; AND HUMANISED RELIGION

" The Criticism of Religion is the beginning of all Criticism."—MARX.

IT is one of those ironies of which history is full that LUDWIG
FEUERBACH (1804–1872), the man whose work acted as an
historical catalytic and brought Marxism into being, is known
to-day, if at all, in Britain almost solely because Marx and
Engels deemed him worth the trouble of controverting. The
general oblivion which has overtaken him reacts upon the
second group into which we have divided Marx's *Theses on
Feuerbach*, and so much so that, as they stand, they are almost
meaningless for British readers. We must therefore preface
our examination with a survey of Feuerbach's *Essence of
Christianity*.

.   .   .   .   .

LUDWIG FEUERBACH'S *Essence of Christianity* appeared in
the year 1841. Engels thus describes the effect it produced :
"While Materialism conceives Nature as the sole
reality, Nature in the Hegelian system represents merely
the 'alienation' of the Absolute Idea—so to say a
degradation of the idea. In all circumstances, thinking
and its thought-product, the idea, is here the primary,
Nature the derived element, which only exists at all by
the condescension of the idea. And in this contradiction
they floundered as well or as ill as they could.

"Then came FEUERBACH'S *Essence of Christianity*.
With one blow it pulverised the contradiction, in that
without circumlocution it placed materialism on the
throne again. Nature exists independently of all philosophy. It is the foundation upon which we human
beings, ourselves products of Nature, have grown up.
Nothing exists outside Nature and Man, and the higher
beings our religious fantasies have created are only the
fantastic reflection of our own essence.

"The spell was broken. The [Hegelian] 'system'
was exploded and cast aside. And the contradiction
shown to exist only in our imagination was dissolved,

87

One must himself have experienced the liberating effect of this book to get an idea of it. Enthusiasm was general,* we all became at once Feuerbachians. How enthusiastically Marx greeted the new conception and how much —in spite of all critical reservations—he was influenced by it one may read in *The Holy Family*."—ENGELS : *Ludwig Feuerbach*, p. 28.

The *Essence of Christianity* is divided into two parts. The first part deals with the " True or Anthropological Essence of Religion," the second with the " False or Theological Essence of Religion." In an introduction the essential natures of man and of religion are discussed.

The essential Nature of Man is his " consciousness of his *species*," his *human* nature. The *content* of this consciousness is found in *feeling*, in emotion :

" What, then, *is* the nature of Man, of which he is conscious, or what constitutes the specific distinction, the *proper humanity* of Man ? Reason, Will, Affection. . . .

" To will, to love, to think, are the highest powers, are the absolute nature of Man, as man, and the basis of his existence. Man exists to think, to love, to will. . . .

" That alone is true, perfect, divine which exists for its own sake. But such is love, such is reason, such is will. The divine trinity in Man, above the individual man, is the unity of reason, love, will. Reason, Will, Love, are not powers which Man possesses, for he is nothing without them, he is what he is only by them ; they are the constituent elements of his nature, which he neither has nor makes, the animating, determining, governing powers—divine absolute powers—to which he can oppose no resistance."—FEUERBACH : *Essence of Christianity*, p. 3.

Having thus demonstrated that " the *absolute* to man is his own nature," and that " the divine nature which is discerned by feeling is in truth, nothing but feeling enraptured, in ecstasy with itself, intoxicated with joy, blissful

---

* *The Essence of Christianity* was first translated into English in 1854 by Marian Evans (" George Eliot "). It had no success, and the publishers lost heavily by it. Some of the unbound sheets were bought (1874) and issued in a new binding by a free-thinking publisher, who took the opportunity to put Marian Evans' better-known pen-name " Geo. Eliot " on the cover. Still it had no great sale. The remainder of the sheets, in another new binding, were issued as a " second edition " in 1881. It had no " liberating effect " in Britain—but then Britain had never " fallen for " Hegel. It was not till after 1865 that a school of (modified) Hegelians appeared in Britain—chiefly in Oxford.

in its own plenitude," Feuerbach turns to the essence of Religion and finds that, whereas " in the perceptions of the senses consciousness of the object is distinguishable from consciousness of self," in religion " consciousness of the object and self-consciousness coincide." Religion is, in fact, the exaltation of man's self-consciousness into an independent existence which, as such, is adored :

> " Such as are a man's thoughts and dispositions, such is his God ; so much worth as a man has, so much and no more has his God. Consciousness of God is self-consciousness, knowledge of God is self-knowledge. By his God thou knowest the man, and by the man his God ; the two are identical."—FEUERBACH : *ibid.*, p. 12.

After an examination of the proposition that the essence of the Divine is the human, Feuerbach concludes :

> " The course of religious development . . . consists specifically in this, that man abstracts more and more from God, and attributes more and more to himself. This is especially apparent in the belief in revelation. That which to a later age, or a cultured people, is given by nature or reason, is to an earlier age, or a yet uncultured people, given by God. . . .
>
> " In relation to the Israelite, the Christian is an *esprit fort*, a freethinker. Thus do things change. What yesterday was still religion is no longer such to-day ; what to-day is atheism will to-morrow be religion."— FEUERBACH : *ibid.*, pp. 31–32.

There is no need to dwell in detail upon the stages whereby Feuerbach applies this conception to the main tenets of Christianity. Two extracts will suffice on this head. The first is from the opening of Part I, and deals with the " true " (i.e., anthropological) essence of Religion :

> " Religion is the disuniting of Man from himself ; he sets God before himself as the antithesis of himself. God is what Man is not—Man is what God is not. . . .
>
> " God and man are extremes : God is the absolutely positive, the sum of all realities ; Man the absolutely negative, comprehending all negations. . . .
>
> " But in religion man contemplates his own latent nature. Hence it must be shown that this antithesis, this differencing of God and Man, with which religion begins, is a differencing of Man with his own nature."— FEUERBACH : *ibid.*, p. 33.

The second extract we take from Part II, which is concerned

with the *false* (i.e., the theological) essence of Religion. Premising that " the essential standpoint of religion is the practical or subjective," Feuerbach argues :

" . . . Therefore to religion the whole, the essential, man is that part of his nature which is practical, which forms resolutions, which acts in accordance with conscious aims . . . which considers the world not in itself, but only in relation to those aims or wants. The consequence is that everything which lies behind the practical consciousness, but which is the essential object of theory —theory in its most original and general sense, that of objective contemplation and experience, of the intellect, of science—is regarded as lying outside Man and Nature, in a special personal being."—FEUERBACH : *Ibid.*, p. 187.

Therefore, argues Feuerbach, it is necessary that we should rise above Christianity, which falsely inverts the true relation between Man and his essential Being, and set man free to " believe in " and " adore " the essence of Human Nature itself. That which men have done unconsciously, and in a topsy-turvy fashion, let them do consciously and right side up. " Man has his highest being, his God, in himself." " The beginning, middle, and end of religion is MAN."

．　　　．　　　．　　　．　　　．

ASPECTS OF FEUERBACH'S CRITIQUE

Feuerbach's approach to the criticism of religion differs radically from that of the eighteenth-century Deists and Humanists. Their concern had been primarily with the rational aspect of Religion—its Theory of the Universe, of Man, and of Morals. They came to conclusions totally destructive of all dogmatic Theology, and all supernaturalist ethics : these emerged as Deism, Pantheism, and, though rarely, in downright Atheism.

This vigorous polemic struggle of the English and French Materialists, Rationalists, and Deists had, as we have seen, powerful reactions upon German philosophy, which owed most of the high toleration with which it was regarded by the State to the fact that it was believed that it would place Theology and Politics (i.e., Clericalism and Kingcraft) upon a securer theoretical foundation. These hopes were doomed to frustration : the little finger of Rehoboam (the critical Dialectic) proved thicker than the loins of Solomon (the metaphysical Age of Reason). Whereas Voltaire and his hosts had chastised Clericalism and Kingcraft with whips
,

Kant, Hegel, and their hosts were destined to chastise them with scorpions.

Feuerbach's immediate point of departure was not Hegel (whose conception of religion was mystico-logical), but the leading German Protestant Theologian SCHLEIERMACHER (1768–1834). Dogmatic Theology, Schleiermacher contended, is not religion : it is the product of reflection upon religion. The irreducible essence of religion is *feeling*—the subjective intuition in which man becomes aware of his complete dependence upon God. Christianity is the realisation in the subjective experience of the Christian of his immediate relation to Christ as Redeemer.

Feuerbach takes from Schleiermacher this conception of subjective emotion as supplying the essence of religion, and accepts, too, the sense of dependence, of need, as its primary content. He differs from him in that, where Schleiermacher had postulated God, Feuerbach, by the method of theoretical analysis, found the *general humanity* of Man. For the Christological antithesis of God and Man resolved into a unity by the mystical function of the God-Man, Feuerbach substituted the antithesis of Man as empirically Individual and *generally* Human, united in the Humanised-Individuality and Individualised Humanity of the Human Family bound together by the philosophical-religion and religious-philosophy of Love to Man.

" Religion is the first form of self-consciousness. Religions are sacred because they are the traditions of the primitive self-consciousness. But that which in religion holds the first place—namely God—is . . . in itself, and according to truth, the second, for it is only the nature of man considered objectively : and that which to religion is the second—namely Man—must therefore *be constituted and declared* the first. Love to Man must be no derivative Love ; it must be original. If human nature is the highest nature to Man, then, practically, the highest and first law must be also the *love of man to man*. *Man to man is God* ; this is the great practical principle ; this is the axis on which revolves the history of the world."—FEUERBACH : *ibid.*, pp. 270–71.

What is remarkable here is not the Atheist *form* of Feuerbach's conclusion, but the substantial religiosity of its *content*. Feuerbach concedes that Religion is *formally* false ; but he holds most stoutly to the conviction that it is *substantially* true. This enables him to find a " materialist "

sense in which all the chief points of the Christian system are
" true."   " The fundamental dogmas of Christianity are
realised wishes of the heart ! "   (Oh, Freud ! how " up to
date " you are !) The dogma of the Resurrection realises the
wish for immortality. Immortality is " true " in the sense
that " while we are, death is not ; where death is, we are
not." Miracles are true in the sense that everything wished
for can be imagined, and every imagination can be imagined
as *real*. The dogma of the Miraculous Conception is the
realisation of a dialectically transmuted wish—alienation
from Nature and from natural functions makes the notion of a
Pure Virgin pleasurable in the highest degree : natural
human feeling makes the thought of a Mother and her Babe
likewise in the highest degree pleasurable ; the two conjoined
give us the concept of the Virgin-Mother. And so on.

All this is as atheistic as you please in form—but it all
carries with it implicitly and explicitly the notion that *the
characteristic religious attitude*—that of penitential abasement,
of sycophantic adoration, alternating with egotistic exaltation
—is something fixed, absolute, and ineradically rooted in
Human Nature.

Feuerbach, in short, comes to a logical conclusion which
is, *in terms*, indistinguishable from that of the eighteenth-
century Deists, Atheists, and Materialists. The difference is
—and it is an immense one—in the practical application,
that Feuerbach translates this conclusion from Rationalism
into Romanticism :

> " The real idealism of Feuerbach becomes evident as
> soon as we come to his philosophy of religion and ethics.
> He by no means wishes to abolish religion : he wants to
> perfect it. Philosophy itself must be absorbed in re-
> ligion. . . ."—ENGELS : *Ludwig Feuerbach*, p. 43.

Compare, for instance, with Feuerbach's " atheistic "
Religion of Man the following samples from eighteenth-
century Deistic Rationalism :

> " The knowledge of a God is not impressed upon us
> by the hand of Nature, for then men would all have the
> same idea ; and no idea is born with us. . . . Whence
> then is this idea derived ? From *feeling* ; and from that
> natural logic which unfolds itself with age, even in the
> rudest of mankind."—VOLTAIRE : *Philosophical Dic-
> tionary* (" God "), 1765.

> " If you have but a village to govern, it *must* have a
> religion. . . . Had it been possible for the human mind

to have devised a religion [a sarcasm to dodge the clerical press censors] what would that religion have been ? Would it not have been . . . that of serving one's neighbour for the love of God instead of butchering him in God's name ? . . . That which should teach a pure morality about which there should never be any dispute ? . . . That which should offer men more encouragements to social virtues than expiations for social crimes ? "—VOLTAIRE : *ibid.* (" Religion ").

" The will of God, just and good, is that the children of the earth should be happy, and enjoy every pleasure compatible with the public welfare. Such is the true worship, that which philosophy should reveal to the world. No other saints would belong to such a religion than the benefactors to humanity . . . none would be rejected as reprobate, but the enemies to society, and the gloomy adversaries to the pleasures."—HELVETIUS : *On Man* (1772), Vol. I, Sec. 1, Chap. 13.

" Every religion is good that teaches Man to be good."—PAINE : *Rights of Man* (1792).

" An endeavour to conciliate mankind, to render their conditions happy, to unite nations that have hitherto been enemies, and to extirpate the horrid practice of war, and break the chains of slavery and oppression is acceptable in [the Great Father's] sight."—PAINE : *ibid.*

" It is not true, then, that the followers of the law of nature are atheists ?' ' No ; it is not true. On the contrary they have stronger and more noble ideas of the Divinity than the greater part of mankind. . . .' ' What is the worship which they render him ? ' ' A worship which consists entirely in action ; in the observation and practice of all the rules which the supreme wisdom has imposed on the motion of every being ; eternal and unalterable rules, which maintain the order of the universe and which, considered in relation to man, com pose the law of Nature.' "—VOLNEY : *The Ruins* (1791).

In *form*, in phrase, FEUERBACH has advanced beyond all these. But whereas the Deists are all moving *from* religion—in the clericalist sense—over to a rational concentration upon the mundane concerns of men and the relations between men in society, Feuerbach's is a movement back from Rationalism into romantic sentimentalism—and *Religion*. " Feuerbach," says Engels,

" . . . does not simply accept mutual relations based

on reciprocal inclination between human beings—such
as sex-love, friendship, compassion, self-sacrifice, etc.—
as what they are in themselves . . . instead, he asserts
that they will come to their full realisation for the first
time, as soon as they are consecrated in the name of
religion ! "—ENGELS : *Feuerbach*, p. 44.

THE OBJECTIVE ROOTS OF RELIGION

In the Fourth *Thesis* Marx deals with the general contention of *The Essence of Christianity*. Feuerbach, starting
from the fact that the world of religion was an imaginary-
fanciful duplication of the *real* world, had found in that fact
the secular basis of all religious imaginings. But suppose it
proved ! Grant that it is true that men's consciousness had,
by a subconscious process which could be laid bare by
philosophical analysis, resolved the content of consciousness
into an antagonism of Religious and Real Worlds. Suppose
this. What then ?

Why *then* there arose the question which Feuerbach did
not ask—*Why had the consciousness of man played just this
trick and no other ?*

From a rational and materialist point of view Feuerbach
compared unfavourably with old Schleiermacher. The
theologian had postulated a *real* God, upon whom man felt
a *real* dependence. Feuerbach, by limiting his inquiry to
an introspective analysis, had got no further than postulating
as the basis for this bifurcation of the unity of experience
into the dualism of Theological Religion the contrast between
man's Empirical individuality and his abstract, general
species—his " humanity." This was simply substituting one
mystification (" Humanity ") for another (" God "). Since on
a consistently materialist view the distinction between a
man's particularity and his generality could only become
real for man on the basis of concrete objective experience, it
was to this *objective* experience that Feuerbach should have
turned for the ultimate secret of the origin of " religious self-
alienation." Obviously, if the " earthly family "—human
society—is that which the heavenly family does but reflect,
there must be a reason why it is reflected, and, furthermore
and especially, a reason why in the religious consciousness the
reflection is taken for the higher reality—while the true reality
is regarded as only a debased, derived, and evanescent copy of
its own reflection. Feuerbach's improvement upon Schleiermacher was, even if his amendments are accepted (and Marx

does not reject them), the sort of improvement which produced a result ten times more mystical and irrational than
its original. Feuerbach had in fact *revealed* the problem, but
had not solved it.

The problem was : Why did reality translate itself in the
mind of man into a duplication of itself and a second, a
" higher " *Religious* " Reality " ? The secret was at Feuerbach's finger's-end. That upon which every man was, is,
and evermore will be " dependent " is—the totality of the
social relations indispensable to his actual existence. In a
word, *society*. When that society contains a contradiction—
when its growth as a whole involves the ripening within
itself of antagonistic movements and counter-movements—
then the conditions are created which find expression in a
bifurcated world-concept, a concept of a religious imaginary
world contraposed as the opposite to and complement of
the everyday " vale of tears."

.   .   .   .   .

Marx had already raised this issue, not in opposition to
Feuerbach, but as an application of his doctrine. In the first
definitely *Socialist* work written by Marx—his articles in the
Franco-German Year Book—which were written between
September and December, 1843, and published in February,
1844, he had demonstrated that the criticism of religion,
though " the beginning of all criticism," was by no means its
end. On the contrary, it led directly to the criticism of the
legal-political-moral basis of the established order of society,
the then-established State. And already, in this article, which
is deliberately expressed in the manner of the Feuerbach school
—(Marx and his partner, Ruge, both being Feuerbachians,
had tried, with only partial success, to secure the co-operation
of Feuerbach himself)—already Marx shows foregleams of a
recognition that " forms of law and of the State cannot be
explained in and from themselves alone, but have their roots
in the *anatomy* of civil society—in political economy " :

" The man who has found in the fantastic reality of
Heaven, where he sought a supernatural being, no more
than his own reflection, will no longer be satisfied to
find only the semblance of himself, only the unhuman,
where he seeks, and must seek, his true reality.

" The basis of irreligious criticism is : Man makes
religion, *religion does not make man*. And, in truth,
religion is consciousness of self and the *self-feeling* of a
man who has either not yet found himself or has lost

himself again.   Also, man is not an abstract being
existing outside the world. Man—that is the world of
men, the State, society. This State, this society, produces religion—an inverted consciousness of the world—
because the world is itself an *inverted world*. Of *this*
world Religion is the general theory, its encyclopædic
compendium, its logic in popular form, its spiritual
point d'honneur, its enthusiasm, its moral sanction, its
solemn complement, its general consolation and justification. It is the fantastic realisation of man, *because* man
possesses no true realisation. The struggle against
religion is therefore, indirectly, the struggle against that
world whose spiritual aroma is religion.

Religious misery is at once the expression of real
misery and a protest against that *real* misery. Religion
is the sigh of the hard-pressed creature, the sentiment
[" heart "] of a heartless world, as it is the soul of soulless
circumstances. *It is the opium of the people.*"—MARX :
On Hegel's Philosophy of Law (1844) [included in *The
Jewish Question*, pub. Martin Lawrence], pp. 13–14.

Here is expounded with masterly wit and pungency just
what Feuerbach had left a riddle. That the demonstration is made from Feuerbach's own premises makes it all the
more completely his " refutation "—in the Hegelian sense.
Here is the beginning, not only of the " theoretical criticism "
of the secular basis of which Religion is the fantastic reflection,
but also of its practical criticism—its " radical " changing in
practice.

Feuerbach had found the " necessary turning point of
history " in the philosophical criticism of religion and its
outcome, the synthesis of religion and philosophy—in Humanised Religion. Marx does far otherwise :

" Religion is an illusory sun which revolves around
man only so long as he does not revolve around himself.
It is, therefore, the task of history to establish the truth
of this life after the *other-world*-liness of truth has disappeared. It is first of all the task of philosophy, in the
service of history, to expose self-alienation in its unholy
forms after the holy form of human self-alienation has
been exposed. *The criticism of heaven* thus transforms
itself into the criticism of earth, the criticism of religion
into the criticism of law, the criticism of theology into
the criticism of politics."—MARX : *ibid.*, p. 14.

Marx, as good as his word, turns to the criticism of law

and politics—with what results we shall see. But he does not limit himself to the advocacy of theoretical criticism, or elaborate a philosophy of reconciliation :

" War against German conditions ? Certainly. They are below the level of history, they are beneath all criticism, but they remain an object of criticism just as the criminal who is below the level of humanity remains an object of attention for the executioner. In the fight against these conditions criticism is not a passion of the brain, it is the brain of passion. It is not an anatomical instrument, it is a weapon. . . .

" Criticism which occupies itself with this situation is criticism in a hand-to-hand fight, and in a hand-to-hand fight it is not a question of whether the opposing party is a noble, worthy or interesting opponent. It is purely one of hitting him. . . .

" In any case, the weapon of criticism certainly cannot supplant the criticism of weapons. Material force must be overthrown, *but theory itself becomes a material force when it takes hold of the masses.* . . .

" The criticism of religion ends with the lesson that man is the highest being for mankind—that is, with the categorical imperative to overturn all conditions in which man is a degraded, enslaved, abandoned, and contemptible creature."—MARX : *ibid.*, pp. 15, 16, 20–21.

Reading " between the lines " an interesting sub-note can be detected in this magnificent opening of the Marxist battle —an urgent plea to Feuerbach to " come over and help us." It was already clear that Germany was approaching its " 1789," and this article made it perfectly plain that its author stood with the group—that of revolutionary Communism— which would do its best to see to it that Germany did not lack its " 10th of August " or its " 1793 " either. Feuerbach, as the one living philosopher to whom the Socialists of all sects could look up with respect, would have been an immensely valuable asset to the revolutionary party.

The appeal failed : Marx and his friend Engels had to go on and turn themselves into leaders as best they could. That they made the effort to win over Feuerbach counts heavily to their credit.

.   .   .   .   .

Why did Feuerbach fail to see the significance of the political movement going on under his very eyes ? Why was it that, as his biographer confesses, politics remained for him a territory whose boundary it was impossible to cross ? Because of the radical defect in his method pointed out by Marx in the fifth, sixth, and seventh *Theses.* " Feuerbach, not satisfied with abstract thinking, appeals to sensuous contemplation "—but the *contemplation* of the *idea*, of Man, of Nature, of what you will, is still only *contemplation*, only operating with an *idea.* What is more, since the *idea* was contemplated wholly in the abstract, in *detachment*, it made no difference, in practice, when Feuerbach insisted to reiteration on the need to exalt the *sensuous* " content " of the idea, above the logical *general* thought-*form.* The sensuous *content* thereby became the " form," and the thought-form was treated as its *content.* Thereby Hegel's idealism was simply translated into metaphysical materialism in Hegelian disguise :

> " He who loves man for the sake of Man, who rises to the love of the species, to *universal love*, adequate to the nature of the species, he is a Christian, is Christ himself. He does what Christ did, what made Christ Christ."—FEUERBACH : *Essence*, p. 269.

It is here made manifest that for Feuerbach man is to be " loved " not for what he is in reality (just as he is " without one plea "), but for what he is by philosophical interpretation, a member of the *genus homo*—not Tom, or Dick, or Harry, but *that* of which Tom, Dick, and Harry are transient, evanescent, superficial, phenomenal presentations only. In real life it is, Feuerbach concedes, Tom, Dick, and Harry who must be dealt with, and this in their concrete particularity. But they become the objects of *universal love* only so far as they are not Tom, not Dick, not Harry, but Man-in-General, who exists, as such, only in the philosophers' brain.

Leaving aside for a moment the sentimental question as to how far it is necessary, or desirable, to embrace mankind within the compass of a " love " that is truly *universal*, and the cognate problem as to how far real universality of love is empirically attainable by man, the fact stares us in the face that in objective reality Humanity-in-General exists only in the aggregation of particular Toms, Dicks, and Harrys of real life and practical conduct. Their *universality* exists only *in*, and by means of, their concrete particularity, and they lose significance as particular specimens only in so far as, in the active practice of social life, they co-operatively create their synthesis in Human Society, in which their particularity is not lost, but specifically determined as part to whole. As against the Individual man, Mankind exists concretely only as Society—as the organised totality of socially inter-related Men. Feuerbach sees men only *in* the *abstract*, in their ghostly semblance—he does not conceive them in their *activity*, their functioning, practical interaction. He *contemplates*, and finds joy in the contemplation of the sensory (" sensual ") pole in the subject-object relation of the *idea*. "He does not conceive *sensuousness* [i.e., that from which the ' sensuous ' element in perception is derived] as—practical human-sensuous activity." He does not realise that a man *feels*—and in this connection thinking is a synthetic complex of specialised feeling—only in so far as he is a plexus of corporeal *activities* in active process of contact with and reaction against external, objective, material reality. Thought is for him still something nobly aloof from " mere " empirical reality. He tries hard to " love " this lowly clay, but his true love is for the lordly *abstract-universal*— " pinnacled dim in the intense inane."

Feuerbach was not the first to mistake abstraction for analysis ; not the first to perform upon himself the subconscious confidence-trick of substituting for the *thing*—the *real* object of thought—the *idea* of the thing. We saw in the preceding chapter how the pre-Kantian materialists all did this, quite naïvely, and thereby gave an opportunity for Idealism to win a theoretical victory over them. This, however, did not prevent the eighteenth-century Materialist movement from being a highly efficient instrument of revolutionary struggle : its limitations were those of its time, and of the class which in England and France fought in the vanguard of the struggle for progress. Nor did the theoretical victory of the German idealists signify that they were, as individuals, or that the class from whose standpoint they spoke *was*, actively or consciously, revolutionary. On the contrary, precisely *because* Germany was economically and politically backward, its intellectuals, the professorial representatives of the bourgeoisie, could take a detached and *abstract general*-critical view of the much more *practical* (and therefore less " pure ") speculations of the English and French champions of the emancipation struggle of the bourgeoisie. And hence, too, their actual theoretical victory over Anglo-French Materialism counted relatively (i.e., in practical relation to the State and clericalism in Germany), at any rate at first, on the side of Reaction as a discrediting of the *revolutionary* emancipation struggle in advance.

This, let us anticipate the course of our argument to observe, does not *contradict,* or falsify, the Marxian Materialist Conception of History. On the contrary a good example of what we may style the " Feuerbach fallacy "—that of substituting for a *thing* in its *actual relations* the *idea* of the thing divorced from those relations—is the trick of supposing that Marx contended that each " country "—considered in the abstract, in the idea—detached from all other countries— develops in a way " determined absolutely " by its rate and degree of " economic " development ; so that a " backward " country must always remain " backward," unless by some miracle its " economic basis " gets up speed of its own volition. That this ghastly burlesque of Marxism was even possible— still more, that it should *actually* have been advanced in all seriousness, most of all, that it should have played the big part it has in the recent history of " Marxism "—all this stands to remind us that, as Voltaire would put it, " we learn from history that men learn nothing from (reading) history." Or, as Engels put it :

> " The materialist conception of history has a lot of ' friends ' nowadays to whom it serves as an excuse for *not* studying history."—ENGELS, letter to *Schmidt,* August 5th, 1890.

On the question which prompted this digression Engels observed :

> " The English Deists and their more consistent successors, the French materialists, were the true philosophers of the bourgeoisie, the French even of the bourgeois revolution. The German petty-bourgeois runs through German philosophy from Kant to Hegel, sometimes positively and sometimes negatively. But the philosophy of every epoch, since it is a definite sphere in the division of labour, has as its presupposition certain intellectual material, handed down to it by its predecessors, from which it takes its start. And that is why economically backward countries can still play first fiddle in philosophy : France in the eighteenth century compared with England (on whose philosophy the French based themselves) and, later, Germany in comparison with both."—ENGELS' letter to *Schmidt,* October 27th, 1890.

.   .   .   .   .

The other respect in which Feuerbach's attitude bears a resemblance to the efforts of the English Deists and French materialists—his attempt to effect a re-orientation of Religion and make Humanity the object of adoration—likewise had an opposite practical political significance from their essentially revolutionary advance. With them the criticism of Religion was, and avowedly so, *a mode of political struggle*. Whether Diderot did actually drink a toast to " the day when the last king shall be strangled in the entrails of the last priest," or whether it was D'Holbach, or another—or their enemies who invented it and fastened it on them— makes no difference to the fact that they *felt* very much like that. Anyway, with them Religion and the State were things that simply could not be discussed separately. With Feuerbach, on the contrary, preoccupation with Religion, and the new philosophically " rationalised " religion of Humanity, was a mode of withdrawing from political struggle, a mode of discrediting such struggles—particularly in consciously revolutionary forms.

It is significant that in France, *after* the failure of the Revolution of 1848 and the butchery of the Parisian proletariat in the Days of June, an exactly parallel development took place, quite independently of Feuerbach, and arising directly from relics left over from eighteenth-century Materialism—by then a spent force. This development was the attempt by AUGUSTE COMTE (1798–1857) to establish a " *Religion of Humanity* "—relics of which still survive.

COMTE, who was directly influenced by ST. SIMON, and at second-hand by FOURIER, published between 1829 and 1842 (i.e., contemporary with Feuerbach's active period), in six successive volumes, what at first he called his *Social Physics*, and later *Sociology*. For this " science " Comte selected as a motto a phrase from the celebrated French theologian, BLAISE PASCAL (1623–62) :

" The whole succession of Man during the long series of ages, should be considered as *One Man*, who continues to live, and who continually learns."

This resolution of all mankind, in all ages, in all their concrete diversity and antagonism, into *One Man* was characteristic of the theological metaphysics of the seventeenth century—especially to a Christian theologian to whom, professionally, " this world is but a fleeting show." That it should have been revived in the nineteenth century by a German and a French philosopher, each of whom was a quasi-" materialist," and the latter of whom spoke categorically in the name of " science," is highly significant. Comte made this one-piece, single-track, conception of the historical development of mankind—of One-Man "Humanity"—the basis of his "science" of Sociology (He invented this latter term, because it enabled him the better to separate mankind from its objective history and treat the development of the sciences eclectically, each in its own separate and self-contained compartment). He describes his "Sociology" as :

> "Representing in a direct and *continuous* manner the mass of the human race, present, past, and *even future*, as constituting, in all aspects, and more and more, whether in space or time, an immense and eternal social *unity*, whose various organs, individual or national, always united by an intimate and *universal solidarity*, inevitably concur, each in its special mode and degree in the fundamental evolution of Humanity—a conception both prime in value and *entirely modern* which must finally form the rational basis of Positive Morality."—
> COMTE : *Course of Positive Philosophy*, Vol. IV.

Here, be it noted in passing, we have the archetype of Mr. Ramsay MacDonald's "biological sociology"—down to and including its "morality" and its smug self-gratification on its own "entire Modernity"! MacDonald, however, derives from Herbert Spencer, whose intellectual pedigree and social position were almost identical with those of Comte, and who, accordingly, spent half a lifetime in indignantly rebutting the quite unfounded assertion that he had "borrowed from" Comte. They were, in fact, history's parody each of the other. Late in 1848 Comte commenced the series of lectures from which the "Religion of Humanity"—(otherwise known as the "Positive Church")—was the positive outcome. He announced himself as opposed to "Royalists, Aristocrats, or Democrats, whether Catholic, Protestant, or Deist," because all these were :—

> "tendencies which . . . really serve to prolong and aggravate our moral anarchy because they hinder the diffusion of that *social sympathy and breadth of view* without which we can never attain fixity of principle and regularity of life."—COMTE : *General View of Positivism*.

He adopted as the slogans of his "Religion" :

> "Reorganisation without God or King by the systematic *worship of humanity*.
>
> "Man's only right is—to do his Duty.
>
> "The Intellect should always be the servant of the heart, and should never be its slave."—COMTE : *ibid.*

Finally he summed up his position in the formula :—
> "All departments of our knowledge are really com-
> ponent parts of one and the same science, the Science
> of Humanity. In social-life Progress should be regarded
> as Order made manifest—as the object of Order—as the
> Development of Order."—Comte : *General View.*

Nothing could be clearer than the similarity between the
attitude of Comte, and that of Feuerbach. Their difference is
equally obvious. Feuerbach retreats from the arena of
political struggles to the more rarified air of philosophy where
he can sentimentalise about Man-in-General in peace.
Comte presses forward into the arena, with a " brand-new "
Scientific-religion and Religious-science which will, he claims,
cure men for ever of the folly of political struggle. That
Comte's worship of " Order," " Science " and " Humanity "
—the first historical form of the doctrine doomed to become
famous as the doctrine of " class-collaboration "—should have
been first preached just when the corpses of the Days of June
had hardly had time to get cold is the best and surest comment
upon it, and upon Feuerbach's " humanised religion."

.   .   .   .   .

In the sixth and seventh *Theses* Marx lays bare the philosophical roots of Feuerbach's fallacy. Feuerbach had turned
the Hegelian logic upon Hegel ; Marx now turns that logic
upon Feuerbach himself, and shows that it is not possible
to reach materialist conclusions by simply using Hegel's
logic *ready-made* upon a materialistic subject-matter. The
logic itself had to be inverted to correspond with the reversal
of the standpoint from which it was used. By shifting his
standpoint, Feuerbach had broken the main-spring of the
Hegelian dialectic ; necessarily he could get from it thereafter
only *metaphysical* results.

The central fallacy involved in all metaphysical reasoning
is—expressed in terms of logic—the complete confusion of
the relations between the categories of Particular and General :
of Unique and   " Universal."

Thus, for instance, if I affirm : "John is a Man " I affirm
that " John " is a particular specimen of the general (or
" universal ") category " Man." I understand *what* " John "
is by subsuming him under (or " identifying him with ")
the wider category " Man."

Metaphysical reasoning proceeds on the tacit or explicit
assumption that the general category " Man " and the

particular category " John " exist independently of each
other : that over and above all the particular " Johns " in
creation (and " Toms," and " Dicks " and " Harrys " and
so on) over and above all particular men, there exists somewhere—and would exist if all the particular men ceased to be,
or had never been—the general category " Man."

Similarly : if a certain quantity of hydrogen and a certain
quantity of oxygen are chemically combined we get as a
result, *neither* oxygen *nor* hydrogen, but *water*. Now, metaphysics holds that in " water," " hydrogen " and " oxygen "
still maintain a *separate* existence. They have been *merely
logically* " subsumed " under the " water " category. Mystically conceived (in absolute metaphysics) this gives the result
that " hydrogen," " oxygen " AND " water " *all* have existed,
and will exist side-by-side *eternally*.

The dialectic method traverses this rigid metaphysic
completely. The category " Man " includes, certainly, all
possible " men." But " Man " and " men," though distinct,
separate, and separable logical categories, are *only* so as
logical discriminations, as *ways of looking* at one and the
same set of facts. " Man " *is*—*all men*, conceived from the
standpoint of their *generality*—that in which *all* men are *alike*.
" Men " is a conception of the same fact—" all men "—but
in respect of their multiplicity, the fact that no two of them
are exactly alike. For dialectics, the particular and the
general, the unique and the universal—for all their *logical*
opposition—exist in fact, *in* and by means of *each other*.
The " Johniness " of John does not exist, cannot possibly be
conceived as existing, apart from his " manniness." We
know " Man " only as the common characteristic of all
particular men ; and each particular man is identifiable,
as a particular, by means of his variation from all other men
—from that generality " Man " by means of which we classify
" all men " in one group.

It is in the recognition of this " identity of all (*logical* pairs
of) *opposites*," and in the further recognition that all
categories form, logically, a series from the Absolutely Universal to the Absolutely Unique—(in each of which opposites
its other is implicit)—that the virtue of Hegel's logic consists.

Thus, for instance : " Water " is, in Hegelian language,
the " identity " of the " opposites " hydrogen and oxygen.
They are " opposites " *logically* in that each *is* what the other
is *not* (the fact that they are in addition, in other respects,
each what the other *also is*, only the better brings out the

difference between dialectics and metaphysics). For dialectics, all discriminations are *relative to* a particular standpoint of discrimination. Thus hydrogen and oxygen are " opposites " but they can and do *unite* to form something which is *not* (and in that sense is " opposite " to) *either* oxygen or hydrogen. Qualitatively considered—i.e., in respect of their distinguishing *qualities—both* the hydrogen and the oxygen have disappeared and been replaced by an entirely *new* combination of qualities. At the same time, quantitatively considered (as so much *substance*), they continue to exist, but in an *altered* form. Thus water is *the same as* hydrogen plus oxygen and also *not the same*. More correctly, it *is* hydrogen and oxygen in a new *relation*—that of synthetic union instead of oppositional separation.

A further example will make the issue clear.

That for which Hegel is best abused—it is about the only thing known about his Logic in Britain generally—is his famous saying : " Being and non-Being are identical." This, for the academic philistine, is the last word in outrageous absurdity ; *and so it is, if it be understood metaphysically* ! As Hegel used it, it gives the key to his whole method.

Logic, says Hegel, differs from all other sciences in this, that it constitutes its own subject-matter. All other sciences presuppose *logic*—since their work is the logical arrangement of their specific subject matter. The only presupposition of logic, on the contrary, is—logic itself ! How then are we to begin ?

What is a *Beginning*—logically considered ?

It is not *something*—not *Being*—since it is only *beginning* ! On the other hand, it is not *nothing*—*non*-Being—since it *is* a beginning. Beginning, therefore, is *not* Being and also *not* non-Being. And at the same time it implies *both*—and the passage of one into the other. It is, in short, a *process of Becoming*, a process in which the categories Being and *non*-Being reveal their common ground.

Let us now translate this into concrete terms. John is— a man. Man is a category in which *all* men (John, and all the *not*-Johns) are conjoined. I begin to distinguish John *from* the not-Johns by observing those things in which he is *not*—*what the other men are*. At the same time the fact that I have to begin upon the process of distinguishing implies—and this is a glaring, staring, undeniable fact—that, apart from his special distinguishing characteristics, John is identical with all the *not*-Johns who comprise the rest of the human race. Thus, logically expressed, John is *understood* when he is most fully conceived as the " identity " of John-in-special and *not-John* (i.e. *all* men) in general.

It is quite simple, really, and profoundly true. Absolutely " pure " Being : the bare logical category Being, since it is " pure " (i.e. emptied of all empirical content) is totally indistinguishable from the " pure " category of " non-Being." It is, in fact, only by means of its particular qualities that any one thing can be distinguished from any other, and the act of distinguishing is simultaneously a positive assertion (that *this* thing is *this*) and a negative one (that *this* is *not that*). Thus all acts of distinguishing in thought are simultaneously acts both of affirmation and negation, and imply, as well as this *opposition*, their synthetic conjunction (i.e. the *likenesses* as well as differences must both equally *exist*, or the one could not be distinguished as *not* the other).

This is all there is to the celebrated mystery of " the identity of Being and non-Being," which only requires to be rescued from the mystification of its Hegelian form to become an invaluable instrument of logical procedure.

As to this mystification. Observe that in logical operations the mystic trinity—affirmation, negation, and negation of negation (or thesis, antithesis, and synthesis; or, as Marx himself said, " in English, position, opposition, composition ")—this mystic trinity is a coexistent relation. When I affirm that " John is a man " I postulate the oppositional contrast between John and *not-*John and their coexistence (the negation of their mutual negation) all *at once*. Certainly as the logical process is worked in my mind I distinguish first one pole, then the other of the *separation* and then their *conjunction*. But all three relations—or better still, the *whole* three-fold relation—*exists* from the beginning and its existence is presupposed in the logical act. Thus those critics of Marx who have supposed that in objective history there appears *first* the thesis, then, later on, the *anti-thesis*, and then, at long last (" pat, like the catastrophe in a comedy ") the synthesis—those who suppose this (and they are many !) have in the first place forgotten to go to Hegel for their Hegelianism and in the second have, in cheerful philosophical illiteracy, converted the *dialectical* process into a metaphysical succession in *formal* (i.e. non-dialectical) *logic* !

For their benefit let us observe that as Hegel himself points out (*Science of Logic*, Vol. II, p. 478), the " Trinitarian " process might just as well, and as correctly, be

described as a " Quadrinitarian " process. *Four* stages might
be discriminated—undifferentiated unity : its differentiation
into (1) positive and (2) negative ; and the restoration of
unity in its differentiated form. If these Hegelophobes will
now consult Kant's *Critique of Pure Reason*—and they usually
laud Kant as much as they abuse Hegel—they will find this
quadrated movement all set out in detail, both in the
" Transcendental Analytic," and the " Transcendental
Dialectic " sections of that immortal work. It would seem
that, in Britain, the primary prerequisite for one who desires
to *correct* Marx in respect of his Hegelianism is a total
ignorance, not only of Hegel, but of the whole history of
philosophical controversy.

Let us return. The relations distinguished in logic all
coexist in the subject-matter. The logical process is therefore,
though it takes time to perform, one which, *according to
Hegel, for whom the logical process was in fact the universal
process, the process of the Universe*, really operated in a *timeless*
order. It only *seemed* to be one of development in time, it
was objectively, *absolutely*, a process beyond, and transcending, time. That, of course, is Hegel's mystification—but its
relics remain in the method of Feuerbach.

Feuerbach sets himself to discover the *essence* of Christianity, and through Christianity, of *religion*, by purely logical
analysis. No absolute objection can be raised against this
procedure *a priori* ; on the contrary, the logical method is
implied in a correct, historical method. In so far as
Christianity *is* a religion, the nature of religion can be found
in it by analysis, as in any other religion. But the logical
method has two obvious pitfalls :—(1) there is the danger of
confounding the particular *form* (Christianity) with the
general (Religion) ; and (2) there is in consequence the danger
of ignoring the fact that, in all its forms, religion is not *only*
religion but one of the many simultaneous activities of mankind. The purely historical method, on the other hand,
carries with it the danger of confounding logical continuity
with simple succession ; and of losing the fundamental
identity in the multiplicity of variation. Both methods must
be used, in dialectical conjunction—as Marx used them—
to produce satisfactory results.

Contemporaneously with Feuerbach, the Hegelian method
was being applied to elucidating the origin of Christianity by
David Frederick STRAUSS, and Bruno BAUER. The former
sought to reduce the history of primitive Christianity to

terms of an antagonism developed between counter-tendencies in the primitive Church in the course of which pious imaginings and counter-imaginings developed memories of an actual Jesus into the Christ of Theology and Christist mythology.

Bauer, attacking the problem on another side, sought to trace the development of Christianity from a non-Christian cult, which historically preceded it ; and found the operative cause of its progression in the purposive and " tendencious " inventions of rival groups within the priesthood of the cult. The final value of these conclusions does not here concern us. The point is that both BAUER and STRAUSS saw that the problem for solution was bound up in the *variations of form* the religion underwent. Feuerbach was concerned with the opposite problem—with the *religion* which persisted through all the variations.

His reply to those who confounded his work with that of Strauss and Bauer is notable :

" The historical critic . . . shows that the Lord's Supper is a rite lineally descended from the ancient cultus of human sacrifice ; that once, instead of bread and wine, real human flesh and blood were partaken. I, on the contrary, take as the object of my analysis and reduction, only the Christian significance of that rite. . . . . I proceed on the assumption that only that significance which a dogma or institution has in Christianity (of course, in ancient Christianity, not in modern) . . . is also the *true* origin of that dogma or institution, in so far as it is Christian."—FEUERBACH : *Essence of Christianity* (Introduction).

Now, it is proper to inquire into what the Lord's Supper meant and means for Christians ; but, to do so, one must give proper significance to the fact that it has meant different things to different men at different times. In fact, the real problem *begins* when it is seen that although the Christian rite is not, in fact, a cannibal feast, it does, in fact, employ the terminology of cannibalism, which terminology *is* deemed sacred and part of the " holy mystery." That the Christian rite is not, *for* Christians, cannibalistic is not a solution : it is the problem itself. What are the Christians doing with a cannibal rite (as it is in *form*) when they are not cannibals ? How, and why, did a cannibal rite secure this place in their esteem ? That which has to be solved is *not* simply the *continuity*—the fact that the emotional attitude of the cannibal to the rite, as such, was substantially identical with the emotional attitude of the Christian to his rite. That what has to be solved is the problem of the continuity *in the* difference ; and the difference *in the* continuity.

Seeing the problem only on its subjective side, Feuerbach, even in despite of his method, implicitly postulated the emotion as *absolute and immutable.* He fell, in spite of himself, into the metaphysical pit and supposed that Religious emotion is (not *relatively,* but) *in itself* a distinct, fixed, ineradicable, emotional entity, a subjective something quite separate from all other emotions. In Marx's words, he was compelled (since he supposed this special *kind* of emotion was the essentially " human " emotion) " to abstract from the historical process and to fix the religious sentiment as something *for itself."*

And since emotion is a subjective fact—to consider the *emotion* in itself, and apart from the individuals in whom it arises, and apart from all its particular historically conditioned modes of manifestation was, in effect, to deny all validity to the historical process. Abstracting away the individual while retaining the specific individual emotion gave as its result—the individual emotion *minus* the individual. Thus Feuerbach, for all his " materialism " landed himself in the absurdly non-dialectical, metaphysical, idealistic position of affirming, virtually, that man's *individual feelings* exist, logically and historically, prior to the conditioning facts and circumstances which make him an individual. Which was the same thing as treating all mankind, in all its historical progression, as One Man, and all history as involving no change, no *progression,* other than the simple unfolding of the faculties of the individual. Feuerbach, that is, " comprehended the human essence only as ' genus ' as a dumb internal generality which merely *naturally* [' by nature,' *a priori*] unites the many individuals [who compose mankind]."—(Marx).

How Feuerbach might have proceeded, even on his own premises, to discover " that the ' religious sentiment ' is itself a *social product* " [and not, as with Feuerbach, *the producer of society*] and " that the abstract individual, whom he analyses, belongs in reality to a particular form of society," Marx himself indicates in a famous passage in *Capital :*

" The religious world is but the reflex of the real world.
And for a society based upon the production of commodities, in which the producers in general enter into

social relations with one another by treating their products as commodities and values, whereby they reduce their individual private labour to the standard of homogeneous human labour—for such a society Christianity with its *cultus* of abstract Man, *more especially in its bourgeois developments, Protestantism, Deism, etc.*, is the most fitting form of religion. . . .

" In the ancient . . . modes of production, we find that the conversion of products into commodities, and therefore the conversion of men into producers of commodities, holds a subordinate place. . . . The ancient organisms of production are, as compared with bourgeois society, extremely simple and transparent. . . . This narrowness is reflected in the ancient worship of Nature and in the other elements of the popular religions. The religious reflex of the real world can then only finally vanish when the practical relations of everyday life offer to man none but perfectly intelligible and reasonable relations . . . to his fellow man and to Nature."— MARX, *Capital*, Vol. I, p. 51.

Marx here tracks down to its hidden origin that mysterious " religious *feeling* "—that " awe," that " reverence," that " something, not ourselves, which makes for righteousness " (Matthew Arnold), that " sense of absolute dependence " (Schleiermacher and Feuerbach), that *fear* alternating with and intensified by *hope*—which is universally recognised to be the subjective root of all religion.

In primitive societies the individual man is conscious of direct dependence upon Nature and its mysterious caprices. As human society develops its productive powers, so mankind collectively imposes its will upon Nature ; and to the extent that it does so successfully Nature ceases to be mysterious, and ceases therefore to be regarded with " awe " —ceases to compel " worship."

But in the very act of subduing Nature mankind has created a new thing, *human society*—the totality of the inter-relations between men—begotten by mankind's collective production-activity, its collective imposition of will upon Nature. Between the individual Man and Nature now intervenes this new thing, no less mysterious, and awe-inspiring : a thing which as production develops historically into *commodity* production grows all the more inexplicable from the individual standpoint, and far more capricious in its alternations of benevolence and malevolence than ever

Nature could be.   Hence, as fast as Religion dies in one form, it is resurrected in another ; and the more specifically commodity-production begets the relations of *competitive individualism* the more inevitably its religious reflex takes the form of the *abstract individual* Man—the " Humanity " of Feuerbach and of the Comteists, the Superman of Nietzsche, the " Life Force " of Bernard Shaw, etc., etc.

As the seventh *Thesis* on Feuerbach affirms : " the *abstract individual* . . . belongs, in reality, to a particular [historically conditioned] *form* of society."

.   .   .   .   .

The mystification induced by the peculiar relations of a commodity-producing society—of which the phenomenon Marx calls the " fetichism of commodities " is an example— can be traced through all the theorising of the bourgeoisie. That " fetichism," that fact that all the relations of bourgeois society appear to be the reverse of what they are—so that bourgeois " order " is an organised anarchy and its anarchy (competition and *crises*) an essential of that order—this fetichism accounts for all the obtuseness of the critics of Marx.   It accounts for the " atomic " sociology which sees in society nothing but individuals in simple juxtaposition. It accounts for their theorising on the problem of cognition.

All the typically bourgeois theories of cognition start with a mass of separate (" individual ") sensations, which the " consciousness " has somehow to build up into comprehension.   Thus arises the school of Ernest Mach which postulates as *primary* facts a mob of " psychological elements." Thus arises the " Fictionalist " school which treats these " units " of sensation as " symbols " with which a " representation " of reality may be constructed.

Just as every-day bourgeois sociologising sees in human society a mere " arrangement " of human atoms, so the typical bourgeois psychologising sees in consciousness a mere " pattern arrangement " of *separate* sensations, which in turn are " ultimate " facts.   So, in like manner, *formal* logic postulates a " logical reason " which merely arranges the materials of perception in a categorical order which it treats thenceforward as a " higher " Reality—(a secret it shares with God !)

The bourgeois theorist, moreover, sees that every concept can be analysed into sensations—visual, auditory, olfactory, savoury and tactual.   His problem thereafter is either to postulate a " faculty " in virtue of which these separate sensations are " organised " into significant combinations, or to dodge the problem by affirming that all these *different* sensations are not different, really, but the same thing— sensation *in the abstract.*

His difficulty is that of his spiritual brother, the economist, who, finding that in large-scale capitalist production a host of men do, in fact, produce to-day much more per head than an equal number did a hundred years ago, attributes the increase to every cause but the right one—the actual, practical *co-operation* in the work-process itself. Since this co-operation involves, as one of its details, *supervision*—and since this supervision is exercised in the *name* of the capitalist owner of the plant, the means, and implements of production, the economist jumps to the conclusion that the increase is due wholly to the capitalist Attributing the whole of economic progress to the " genius " of heaven-sent " captains of industry," he supposes that society is an aggregation of self-contained units, who become a social whole only so far as they are " organised " by governments on the one hand and captains of industry on the other.

He cannot see the obvious fact that *society,* actively engaged upon production is, logically and historically, *pre-supposed* in the specialisation of occupations and crafts *within* society—in the social division of labour—so that the specialisation and the integration of the specialised functions are two co-relative and concomitant phases of one and the same historical progression of the social whole. And exactly in the same way the theorist of cognition cannot see that the physiological differentiation of the sense organs, in, through, and by means of objective practice, has as its co-relative and concomitant the synthetic unity of the understanding which all the senses together, in practice, co-operate to produce.

The act and practice of physically " grasping " a thing, of working upon it with all the sense-organs that can be brought to bear, is the *obverse* of the mental " grasping " which is, when effected, *understanding* a thing. Not being able to conceive this process in its two aspects, external and internal, of simultaneous differentiation and integration, of objective and subjective *practice,* the bourgeois theorist of cognition flounders for ever in the No Man's Land between Subject and Object, Thinking and Being—alternatively prostrating himself before their inexplicable Duality and genuflecting before their inscrutable unity.

It is not therefore to be wondered at that in history as the bourgeoisie conceives it, all *religious* emotions, theories and practices are conceived as existing in a class apart from, and having no necessary connection with, the rest of the practices, theories, and emotions observable in a given society. And this, notwithstanding the glaring fact that the men who provide, in combination, the religious data, are the same men who in the same social union provide other data.

The problem whether there exists any such thing as a specifically "religious" emotion is not a problem of psychology. Similar emotions, or rather, an identical emotionality, can be excited by the most profane things. There is nothing that we to-day regard as "profane"—swearing, drinking, smoking, eating to excess, fornicating—that has not been at some time a specifically *religious* practice. And there is nothing in the love, fear, awe, reverence, dependence, and all the rest of it, that religion is specially supposed to excite that is not aroused, in varying degrees of intensity, by all the incidentals and circumstantials of profane existence. The origin and function of religion must, as Marx indicated, be sought not in *individual* psychology, but *in society* and its historical development.

Feuerbach's failure to perceive this was lamentable. None the less the mode of his failure led—to Marx.

.   .   .   .   .

Falsifications of the Issue

Before passing to the third and last group of the *Theses on Feuerbach*, it is necessary, as part of the vindication of Marx, and Marx-Engels' Marxism, to note how totally Marx' brilliant penetration of the secret of Religion has been mis-"interpreted" by "Marxists."

Feuerbach himself was guilty of a mystification—though not a deliberate one—when he said, "Backwards I am with the materialists, but not *forward*."

It is one of the oldest tricks of Theological controversy to juggle with the ambiguous uses of the terms "Materialism" and "Idealism." In one sense, the proper sense, they denote two opposite attitudes to the question of the relation between Thinking and Being,—they denote two schools of philosophy. In priestly usage, on the contrary, a "materialist" is—a glutton, a drunkard, a sensualist, an anti-social egoist ; while, according to the same authority, an "idealist" is the reverse of all these, a self-sacrificing altruist. And it is in this false, misleading, "priestly" sense that the terms are commonly employed in the public press and by the less reputable type of controversalist.

H

The priests invented this trick for a double purpose. In the first place, on the priestly theory of man—(" the heart of man is deceitful above all things and desperately wicked ")—anyone who did not accept them and their ministrations at their own value, was, of necessity, a man who logically *ought* to have delighted in " fornication and all other deadly sin," all the " sinful lusts of the flesh." In the second place, by fastening this charge upon their materialist opponents, they by implication secured an alibi for themselves.

History bears testimony to the fact that their argument was false in each case. Priests have not *always*, or at all times been altruistic. Not *always*! In fact, never so where the Church and its material possessions have been concerned. On the other hand, the greatest of Materialists—Diderot, Feuerbach himself, Marx, Engels, Lenin, to name no more—have in their private and social lives been conspicuously " idealistic " in the priestly sense of the term.

It was, therefore, doubly unfortunate that Feuerbach should fall into the pitfall dug by the priests, and, in consequence of having (in Engels' phrase) mistaken materialism itself for one of its historically conditioned forms, declare himself in the sense quoted above.

But Feuerbach can be forgiven : he, at least, harmed himself by his error more than anybody else. His confusion on this point helped to keep him back from that practical participation in revolutionary struggle which would have developed his theory in proportion as he unified his practice therewith. Those who cannot be so easily forgiven are the " Marxists " who, in the name of Marx, return to, and labour to re-establish the very fallacies, and false ideologies, he spent his life in refuting.

The practical political application of the Marxian materialist conception of religion is, in present-day society, the complete exclusion of religion from the State apparatus—which includes its exclusion from the curriculum of the State schools. This was expressed in the German Social-Democratic programme in the formula, " Religion shall be declared and treated [i.e., *by the State*] as a private matter " [i.e., as one in which the State, as such, had no standing or concern]. Obviously this involved the disestablishment and disendowment of all State churches and, also, the placing of anti-religious propaganda on an equal footing with religious propaganda. Equally obviously, each of these things is " *atheistic* " in practice—as the priest class is quick to point out.

But, as should be well known by now, the phrase " religion is a private matter," received in the course of time, under the corroding acid of opportunism, a new interpretation. It became a Party injunction that " all discussion of religion or of the churches is, in and by the Party, *verboten* ! "

If this could happen in Germany, even in the lifetime of Engels (much to his furious disgust), better was hardly to be expected from the English-speaking world—the classic breeding-ground of compromise and hypocrisy. In point of fact even the worst the most degenerate Social-Democratic opportunism could do in Germany has been outdistanced from the start in Britain and the U.S.A.

From the latter we may cite the " classic " example of the translation of Engels' *Ludwig Feuerbach* by Austin Lewis, referred to in our first chapter. Engels in the course of his argument refers to the effort of Feuerbach to give his own new meaning to the word " religion," in the conviction that, as in the past, a re-orientation of religion would lead to a reconstruction of society. Engels comments thus :

" Feuerbach's assertion that ' periods of human development are distinguished only by religious changes ' is decidedly false. Great historical turning-points have been *accompanied* by religious changes only so far as the three world religions which have existed up to the present—Buddhism, Christianity, and Islam—are concerned. . . . Even in regard to Christianity, the religious stamp in revolutions of really universal significance is restricted to the first stages of the struggle for the emancipation of the bourgeoisie . . . when the bourgeoisie of the eighteenth century was strong enough to possess an ideology of its own, suited to its own class standpoint, it made its great and conclusive revolution— the French— . . . troubling itself with religion only so far as this stood in its way."—ENGELS : *Feuerbach*, p. 45.

Austin Lewis commenting on this asserts :

" It is evident that this is not entirely true, for, in the English-speaking countries, at all events, not only the bourgeois, but frequently also the proletarian movements *attempt to justify themselves from Scripture* (!). The teachings of the Bible and the Sermon on the Mount are frequently called to the aid of the revolutionary (!) party. Christian Socialists, in the English and American, not the Continental sense of the term, are admitted as such to the International Congress ; and other evidences of *the compatibility of religion with the proletarian movement* (! ! !) can be traced."—Lewis : *loc. cit.*, p. 15.

It is a problem which to " admire "—in the Shakespearian sense—most : the author's incapacity to grasp Engels' meaning or his shameless defence of the most hypocritical opportunism. It is true that, in Britain, Keir Hardie, though the son of sturdy Freethinkers, found it expedient to allege (in election addresses !) that " I learned my Socialism from the New Testament " and " My cause is the cause of God ! " It is also true that such a truculent " revolutionary " as J. Ramsay MacDonald has declared that " Socialism has no more to do with a man's religion than it has with the colour of his hair." But MacDonald also achieved the feat of letting it be believed, in the free-thinking town of Leicester, that he was an " agnostic " ; in Aberavon that he was a sort of Calvinist ; and in Seaham Harbour that he inclined to Methodism. That the British and American Labour movements have on the theoretical side exhibited a theoretical destitution appalling to behold, is only too true ; as also that " Christian " Socialists of the Anglo-American brand have been accepted at Congresses (of the Second International)— it being notorious that part of the intellectual inheritance which the British and American movements have carried over from their bourgeois teachers has been the canon that it is absurd and impossible to seek to reconcile theory and practice.

All this is clear ; as is the fact that *after* their victory the French (like the English) bourgeoisie were quick to drop their anti-religious attitude in order that *religion might be kept alive for the people* ! But these facts, instead of invalidating Engels' argument, only the more sharply *under-score it.* Like the revolutionary French bourgeoisie, the revolutionary proletariat is concerned with religion *only so far as it gets in its way.* To suppose that it is, or can be, any *aid* to the revolutionary proletariat, is to falsify the conception of Marx and Engels at its roots. And that such should be done in the very act of *introducing* a work of Engels to readers in the English language, is a monument of brazen impudence typical of the manner in which " Marxism " has been preached in Britain and the U.S.A.

The same introduction contains a falsification of equal brazenness. Referring to the " natural scientific " materialists of his day—(Buchner, Vogt, Moleschott, etc.)—Engels says :
" The vulgarising pedlars who in Germany in the 'fifties busied themselves with Materialism by no means

overcame the limitations of their teachers. All the advances of natural science which had been made in the meantime served them only as new proofs of the non-existence of a creator of the world : and, in truth, it was quite outside their scope to develop the theory any further."—ENGELS : *Feuerbach*, p. 38.

In his text Austin Lewis substitutes for " a creator " the formula, " the Creator "—*thus making it appear that Engels objected* to Buchner, Vogt, Moleschott and Co., not on the score of their failure to achieve philosophical progress, but *on the score of their atheism* !

Lest the point of this falsification of Engels' plain meaning should be lost, Austin Lewis enlarges upon it in his introduction :

" The 'vulgarising pedlars ' . . . these were the popular materialists—the ' blatant atheists '—who *without scientific knowledge* . . . used every advance of science as a weapon of attack upon the Creator and popular (!) religion. Engels sneers at these as not being scientists at all. . . . Of the same class were the Secularist lectures . . . of whom Bradlaugh and Ingersoll were in every way the best representations."—LEWIS : *loc. cit*, pp. 12–13.

Every assertion here is false—except the pre-eminence given to Bradlaugh and Ingersoll in their category. The " vulgarising pedlars " were *not* " blatant atheists," they *were* men of scientific knowledge, all of them distinguished as such. They did not in the least resemble the secularist lecturers referred to, except in so far as these latter drew a good deal of inspiration from Buchner, Vogt, and Moleschott, and suffered from similar limitations.

They did not, and could not " use " anything to " attack the Creator," since, in terms of their own standpoint, the said " Creator " did not exist and as a non-existence could not be " attacked." Their attack was not upon " popular religion " but upon priestly superstitions. Engels' complaint is, *not* that they attacked superstition, but that they kept the attack still upon the nature-scientific level upon which the eighteenth century materialists had fought their fight : Engels did not deny that, for instance, Buchner's *Force and Matter* contains, in his own words, " richer scientific material " than, for instance, D'Holbach's *System of Nature*. The point was that with richer materials Buchner attempted not *more*, but *less* than D'Holbach had attempted fifty years before. D'Holbach *had* attempted to formulate a science of society in terms of the mechanical materialism of his day. Buchner left the question of a science of society, of history, severely alone—comprising it generally under the head of biological evolution. Engels did not " sneer "—he " handed out a thick ear ! " Finally, the real ground of complaint against Bradlaugh and Ingersoll does not lie on the score of their atheism ;—a man who, like Austin Lewis, is abysmally ignorant of the mighty work of the fighting materialists of the eighteenth century, could, and should be grateful for so much of their work as survived in that of Ingersoll and Bradlaugh. Where they lay wide open to attack was on the side upon which Lewis is *significantly silent*—their petty-bourgeois political hostility to the revolutionary class-struggle of the proletariat.

If the wells of Marxist propaganda have been poisoned, as they have by Austin Lewis—(his "translations" of Engels' *Feuerbach* and of his *Anti-Dühring* have been, failing the ability to read German, all the Anglo-American proletariat knew of those works)—other phenomena peculiar to Britain become clearer. We give two examples.

From a work purporting to expound " Dialectical Materialism " published within the last few years and still persistently advertised, we select the following :

> " If we separate from men and things all thoughts of goodness, power, intelligence, perfection, life, and such like, and *add them all together* to form one thought of complete superiority in all matters, *this thought is God.* . . .
>
> " When we realise that thought is real, and just as objective as anything else, we have *here* (! !) the *explanation* (! ! !) of *why God is a real and very powerful influence* (! ! !) . . . if understanding were more general (!) we should not have the silly quarrel between *Theists* who take God on faith, and Atheists *who deny God also on faith* (! ! !), and Agnostics who say they do not know one way or the other. . . .
>
> " The idea of God is built up just like any other idea, and *therefore we can understand God.* (! ! !) and consequently we are able to explain Him. . . ."—FRED CASEY : *Method in Thinking*, p. 140.

Ramsay MacDonald himself at his highest flight never achieved a finer masterpeice in the art of " with many words making nothing understood," or a more truly " British ' exercise in facing-both-ways-at-once. Fred Casey does not wait for the New Jerusalem to make his lions to lie down with his lambs. Idealism and Materialism : Humeian sceptism, Kantian-transcendentalism ; Theism, Atheism, Agnosticism (and mental *rheumatism*) all repose cheek-by-jowl in this philosophical Irish stew for which Fred Casey alone holds the copyright ! And he calls it " *dialectical materialism.*" !

But Britain can do better than that, even, in the way of improvising startling variations upon the " materialism " of Marx. What Casey does like a bungling amateur (letting the rabbit he is going to " produce " from the hat, drop on its way *to* the hat) Mr. Middleton Murry does with the dash of a professional *virtuoso* :

" Marx's function towards society was to bring it to a knowledge of *its destiny.* (! ! !) He, first among men, achieved a disinterested (! ! !) vision of the cardinal process of modern history. . . .

" We must recognise and be responsive to the values which have been embodied in religion. . . . Those values, objectively (! ! !) distinguished are two : *Spirituality and Disinterestedness*—an impersonal awareness of Eternity, and a personal consecration to ethical passion in Time. Those values were embodied in the living figure of a new Man, the Son of Man, [*he means Karl Marx !*] according to his time.. . . .

" Marx . . . was a man of imagination. And he was more : he was a man of ethical passion. . . . He called to men, *like the great prophet* (! ! !) *before him,* ' Repent ye, for the Kingdom of God is at hand ! ' Was the coming Reign of God, *which Jesus foresaw,* a thing of terror or a thing of joy ? . . . That the *individual* man should make the thing of terror a thing of joy by anticipating the revolution *in his own heart and mind,* was the whole gospel of Jesus. It is the whole gospel *of Marx.* (! ! !) "—J. Middleton Murry : *Necessity of Communism,* pp. 37, 48, 117.

And this cacophany of clotted bosh—this conjuration of the really-truly-true-Truth about the " Message of Marx " into an exercise in subjective acrobatics, to be indulged in by aspirants to personal salvation, like a dose of Moral Epsom Salts, as and when required—*this* comes from the man who, and from the work in which he, reproached us all for our " ignorance " of Marx's *Theses on Feuerbach* !

CHAPTER IV

OUT OF DARKNESS—MORN !

In the first seven *Theses on Feuerbach*, Marx develops his critical standpoint *negatively* : first against " all hitherto existing " Materialism, then against that of Feuerbach in particular—which, since Feuerbach's " materialism " was not consistently materialist, involved, as the preceding criticism had also involved, a critique of Idealism. In the concluding four *Theses* Marx develops his own position *positively*. In them he lays the critical foundations for his *Dialectical Materialism*—a materialism which is all the more thoroughly *materialist* than any preceding materialism, precisely because it is more critically *dialectic* than any of the Idealist elaborators of the dialectical method had contrived to be.

The Atomic Conception of Society

The eighth *Thesis* affirms : " Social life is essentially practical." This point we have already covered incidentally in the discussion of the " mystery " of God and Religion, which is one of the most obvious of those " mysteries which mislead theory into mysticism " and " find their rational solution in human practice, and in the comprehension [understanding] of this practice." But the *Thesis* has an objective as well as a subjective application. It is not only the life of the individual in society, as misinterpreted in his own brain, which finds an explanation, and a rational rectification in practice and the understanding thereof. The objective *life* of Society itself—its life-process—its developing movement and the positive outcome thereof—this, too, is objectively *practical* and loses its mystical disguise when and only when it is so comprehended. The point is of immense importance and needs elaboration.

Human society consists of men standing in relations of association to each other. That is axiomatic. But why do they so stand ? And what follows as a result ?

A mechanical-materialist view would be that there is nothing in society but the men, and that they change only so far as they learn continually as a result of the association, which in turn " just happens." This, as will be seen, is where the matter rested with the eighteenth-century materialists.

But why do men associate ? And is not the association itself, the aggregate, also a *real* thing ? Does not it, too, undergo a process of change analogous to the growth " in wisdom and stature " of the individual humans ? Is it not part of the materialist case that it is his relation to the *society*—the aggregate—into which he is born which *determines* a man's life course ? Evidently there is, in addition to the individual men, the Society itself. That too is *real*—though not tangible and " material." Here, if the reasoner is not on the alert, the Idealism begins to creep in.

One Idealism will be that of supposing that the men would *not naturally* have associated at all ; that they are only kept from flying off and living, Robinson Crusoe fashion, " on their own " by some over-riding force—that of the State ; of the Idea which gave birth to the State ; or of God whose " moral government " is expressed in the " Order " of the external universe, and the Order of human society. The pseudo-" Realist " counter to this : that men are "made " to associate by something in their " Nature "—so that to know the society one needs first to know the *men*—leads back to mysticism and supernaturalism via the " mystery " of the " moral nature of man," or the " mystery " of " Intelligence *per se*."

Both the Idealist and the " Realist " views result in an *atomic* conception of society—that of society as a simple aggregation. Just as the supernaturalist supposes that but for the restraining hand of God all the atoms in the Universe would fly apart and frisk around " on their own," thus causing chaos to " come again," so the Idealist, in one disguise or another, argues that but for some restraining power—the King, the State, the *idea*, the Law, or what you will—men would fly asunder and their association cease to be. The " Realist " view is the same, with the gears in reverse : men are so forced to associate by their " nature " that only a miracle, in the shape of some compelling power from without, would break up their association. These views are " atomic " in that each conceives society as a mechanical aggregation of self-contained unit-atoms ; and conceives further, that neither the atoms nor the aggregate is capable of any fundamental *organic* change. The atoms may be re-arranged virtually at will : but the result will be just the same thing in essence, with only its *shape* altered. The shape may alter but the atoms, except for their surface contacts, will remain the same, whatever is done to them.

.   .   .   .   .

Despite all modernist boasts, and all the " tall-talk " about " evolution " that goes on, these views are anything but " obsolete." On the contrary, every Tory, every Liberal, every non-Marxian Socialist starts fundamentally from this *atomic* conception of society. What is more : under the form of the " very latest " theories of psychology, and of the (fundamentally *solipsist*) theories of knowledge based thereupon this atomic conception of society is (implicitly) postulated as the very basis of the " newest " and " most scientific " outlook upon the world.

In Sidney Hook's *Towards the Understanding of Karl Marx*, for instance, several pages are devoted to establishing the contention that Marx's theory of knowledge differed from that of Engels (who, we learn, misled Lenin). It is, of course, conceded that Engels and Lenin in the course of their practice blundered into accuracy !

Hook's point derives from the first *Thesis on Feuerbach* and the stress laid therein upon the *active* role played by thought, upon the fact that sensations are " forms of practical sensory activity " (Hook). Engels, he claims, was always relapsing into eighteenth-century mechanical materialism, and Lenin, following him, committed the " howler " of treating sensations as " *literal copies of the external world.*" What is wrong with so treating them ? As we have seen, the fault of the eighteenth-century materialists lay in their failure to recognise *consistently* that the mental potentiality of man was an active ingredient in the *sensation* itself : that the sensation was in fact *produced* by the interaction between external and internal *activity*. Locke (to whom Hook refers as holding the position to which, he alleges, Engels and Lenin reverted) *separated knowledge as such completely from sensation by his theory of ideas*. To Locke ideas, the units of knowledge, were *mental* constructions for which the materials were supplied by sensation. Kant attacked Locke's position from one side by demonstrating that there was a *mental* element in *sensation* itself : Cabanis, the French developer of Locke, attacked his position from the opposite side and demonstrated that no gulf could be fixed between sensation and ideation, which was simply *sensation of a more complex order*—sensation " historically " developed. Marx in the

Theses on Feuerbach combines the critical refutation of Lockeian dualism made by Kant and, following him, Hegel, *with that made by Cabanis.*

Let us put the matter bluntly : if sensations do not supply us with a truly reliable " picture " of the external world, or if the term " picture " be cavilled at, with true information about the external world, *what do they supply* ?

Mr. Sidney Hook, in fact, by means of a juggle, seeks to prove that Marx was an Empirio-Critic of the Machian school ; and, as Lenin proved in his classic *Materialism and Empirio-Criticism*, the Machian school is a camouflaged retreat to solipsism, and thence through Sophistry to Supernaturalism. Sidney Hook is entitled to some sympathy, firstly, because he has had an academic training inflicted upon him, and, secondly, because he has the wit to see how abominable a caricature of Marxism was presented by the " orthodox Marxism " of the German Social-Democracy. But that is no excuse for his juggling falsification of emphasising Marx's *dialectic* at the expense of his *Materialism.* He who would grasp the essence of Marx must comprehend *both* the materialism in his Dialectic and the Dialectic in his materialism.

To apply a practical test : we put it to Sidney Hook as a matter of actual, real, life practice—does he believe that a science of society is possible ? If so, why does he say that " to speak of Marxism as an ' objective science ' is to emasculate its class character ? " This says neither more or less than that Marxism is ONLY *subjectively true* ! If Sidney Hook thereafter goes on to applaud Marxism enthusiastically, *this fact notwithstanding*, it stands proved to demonstration that for Sidney Hook *no objective science of society is possible at all, to anybody* ! " Science " becomes—and this is typical of all " up to date " solipsisms—a mere matter of choosing which *fictional representation* of reality happens best to suit one's own personal taste and inclination. " Society " becomes an inexplicable and fortuitous aggregation of individual atoms, capable only of *valuation* in terms of the subjective " class " inclinations of the valuer.

To return to our subject. The life of Society as such is— *objective practice.* Society is not *only* men-in-aggregation : it is men in *active* inter-relation among themselves, and in active, *collective*, practical, reciprocal interaction with Nature. Thus Society is not just Man + man + man. . . . It is Man ×

Man × Man. . . . Over and above the simple aggregation
of men is their objective, practical, interaction, as a result
of which men and circumstances are in constant process of
transformation and re-transformation.   And since men,
individually, are born into not only a natural but a *social*
environment, which includes the *ideas* of their fellow men
so far as these become objective in the actual *practice* of
the teaching, upbringing, propaganda, laws, institutions, and
detailed conduct of these fellow men, men are born into
Society as a going concern—a plexus of objective practice
acting upon and reacted against by every individual.   It is
therefore as impossible to account for the society by examining the nature of the individual—(which by the way is
what the modern solipsists all attempt to do, even more than
did the mechanical materialists)—as it would be to comprehend the nature of the Atlantic from the examination of a
sample bucketful.

We have already, in the course of our inquiry into the
" mystery " of God and Religion, seen how the relations of
bourgeois society, based as they are on free competition in
the production and exchange of commodities, result in the
" fetichistic " inversion of the true objective relations of
society when viewed from the standpoint of the single
individual.   In seeing that we saw, firstly, that the " atomic "
conception of society was a " necessary " (i.e., inevitable,
necessitated) reflex of that social order.   We saw also that,
this notwithstanding, just as it is possible to perceive correctly
the inter-relation of the details of a picture even though the
picture as a whole is upside down, so it is possible, even
within the limits of the bourgeois order, to gain an approximately correct notion of its internal inter-relations.

Here emerges the *dialectical* fact that in turning the theories
typical of the bourgeois order upside down (or, *right* side up),
Marx was able to take over from them many correctly observed
facts, and correctly reached generalisations, just as they had
been able to do with those which preceded them. [Hegel, for
instance, took over from Spinoza much that he found valid :
" to be a philosopher," he said, " it is necessary first of all
to have been a Spinozist."]   So, too, the " atomic " view
contains, in each of its main forms, an element which is
salved from the wreck of " atomism " as a system.   The
conservative, legalistic, theory, that Society was only held
together by the restraining force of the State and its Law
(with God in the background as a reserve for emergencies),

has a validity which holds good for societies based upon commodity production and exploitation. The more these grow towards the acme of free competition, the more the clash of individual interests seems to threaten to disrupt Society into a chaos of discordant atoms. In such circumstances, the State is bound to present itself in its primary aspect of a power " towering above " Society which keeps its disruptive tendencies in check.

But Society does not fly to pieces. It is true that there are, periodically, Revolutions during which the restraining force of the State is in abeyance. But always " order " is restored again, and, though in an altered form, the State is re-established. This vindicates, within limits, the alternative form of the atomic view—the notion that something " mysterious " and " ultimate " in the *nature* of man as an individual, makes him constantly seek association with his fellows, so that though the association is liable to disturbance from the operation of outside forces, or by reason of the " fraility of human nature itself," Society is an immutable fact that cannot be destroyed.

The germ of truth in this view is that, despite all tendencies to the contrary—competition, class-conflicts, civil wars, and revolutions — Society does persist. But it is not any " mysterious " or " mystical " *human nature* that makes it do so. It persists as an objective continuity of *Practice*, caused in turn by the objective practical inter-relation between Mankind (as an aggregate) and Objective Nature. Revolutions not only do not destroy that practical inter-relation, but they are ultimately traceable to it, and its positive, developing outcome. The Dialectical Materialist view, therefore, neither loses the Society in the multiplicity of the individuals, nor the individuals in all their divergent multiplicity in the unity of Society. It is marked off clearly from the mystical-*absolute* view which makes The State and Society interchangeable terms ; and it is equally clearly marked off from the view that poses The State and Society in irreconcilable contra-position. It neither confounds the historical development of mankind with natural history and biology : nor poses it in opposition to them as a form of multiple biography. The Law of Motion of Nature is not simply *continued* in the Law of Motion of Society, and of the individual Man. Society has its own law of motion which is *connected with* that of Nature on the one side and of the individual man on the other, but is *distinct* and *different* from them. It is connected with them *dialectically*, not mechanically.

We shall have occasion to note many examples of the " atomic " sociology and its survival in the " up-to-date " schools ; and note, too, many examples of how " mysteries " which " seduce speculation into mysticism " find " their solution in human practice and in the comprehension of that practice." For the moment we will pass on to the ninth and tenth *Theses*.

THE DIALECTIC CONCEPTION OF SOCIETY

That " the highest point attained by *contemplative* materialism—i.e. materialism which does not understand sensuousness* as practical activity—is the outlook of single individuals in civil society," we have already seen. The term " civil society " is used here since, despite the many differences between the civilisation of the classic (Græco-Roman), the mediæval, and the modern bourgeois periods of history, they have all this much in common : they are based upon the division of labour and property ; they, therefore, exhibit class distinctions and antagonisms and their correlative, the State ; and they all rest ultimately upon exploitation (of slaves, serfs, and wage-labourers respectively). This continuity observable through all these revolutionary transformations gave to the pre-Marxian social philosophers the notion that these characteristics are those of an *immutable* Law of Nature. That it did so is an example of and throws further light upon the persistence of mechanical and atomistic conceptions of Society.

The facts, however, which the atomistic conception could not account for—facts which became embarrassing in their force after the French Revolution and its defeat at the hands of the Holy Alliance, as also in consequence of the Industrial Revolution in Britain and its repercussions on the Continent —the facts of the proletariat and its struggles—are brought within the scope of the materialist outlook in the tenth *Thesis*.

What was the alternative to the standpoint of the single

* *Sensuousness :* In 1845 it was customary to denote Idealism under the term " Spiritualism," and the quality of being idealistic as " spiritual." Contrariwise, materialism was known as " sensualism," and a materialistic writing or argument as " sensuous." Material reality was referred to as " sensuous " reality, in contrast to " spiritual " or " ideal " reality. It was a terminology very popular with Christian apologists, since it enabled them to imply that their opponents were addicted to fornication, etc. A section of the materialist school took them on their own ground and glorified " sensualism " in exactly this latter sense (Swinburne, for example).

individual in civil society ? Was it a retreat from the human standpoint altogether ? A retreat to idealistic Absolutism, either mystical, supernatural, or both ? Not in the least ! It was *an advance* from the standpoint of " civil society " to that of " *human society* or socialised humanity."

Civil society (as it was understood in the eighteenth century), or " civilisation " as we nowadays term it, is neither the first, the only, or the final form of society. " There were brave men before Agamemnon " and there was, in fact, civilisation before that of Greece and Rome. More important, still, there was *society* before there was civilisation, and *history* before " history " begins. Contrariwise : just as civil society itself has run through a whole gamut of changes, so, too, civil society itself will in its ultimate bourgeois form pass and give place to a new and higher form of social organi- sation which will, on the one hand grow out of it, as it itself grew out of all that went before it, and on the other, provide in turn a fresh starting-point for a still newer development. This entails that the method which takes *society* as its stand- point must itself be capable of growth likewise. The dialectic method excludes any notion of " ultimate finality " :

" A system of natural and historical knowledge, em- bracing everything, and *final for all time*, is a contra- diction to the fundamental law of dialectical reasoning. This law, however, by no means excludes—on the contrary, it includes—the idea that the systematic knowledge of the external universe can make giant strides from age to age."—ENGELS : *Anti-Dühring*.

Hence, in abandoning the point of view of the " single individual in civil society," Marx did not endeavour to find a standpoint *absolute in itself*—(which is what Absolutists and so-called " Monists " really attempt to do)—or abandon all hope of real knowledge and certainty (as do the solipsists and Humeans). He found a new and a more satisfactory point of view, one which comprised within itself " the affirmative recognition of the existing stage of things and the recognition likewise of its *negation* "—of the fact that just as this had itself come to be out of that which it was not, so, too, a new order would come to be, in consequence of what it itself had been. In a wider concept which embraced Society as a developing whole, in which civil society, and particularly the bourgeois order, were " *momenta*," transitional phases, of active pro- gression—in this concept, that of *human society* which, otherwise expressed, is that of " associated humanity"—

Marx found the " point of view " for his " new " dialectical materialism.

How *new* it was, and how far-reachingly revolutionary we have already seen in part, and will see still more hereafter. Here it is necessary to dwell somewhat upon the term " associated humanity."

Strictly the term is the equivalent of " human society." That is to say : provided the distinction beloved of the eighteenth century between " natural " and " artificial " man and society be dropped ; and provided, further, that we drop, too, that other eighteenth-century habit of contraposing the " artificiality " of civil society to the " natural humanity " of the " simple savage," then the terms are identical.

The point Marx had to make was that Society, even in its most sophisticated civilisations, is never *absolutely* " artificial." And, likewise, savagery, at its most savage and primitive, is never *absolutely* " natural," never *absolutely* devoid of deliberately adopted artifices. This is a commonplace with the hosts of anthropologists who have grown up *since* Marx wrote these *Theses*. *It was a revolutionary paradox when he wrote them.* The extent of the change worked by Marx can be inferred from the manner in which the anthropologists all fall, almost to a man, into the opposite pit. The eighteenth century made an *absolute* division between savagery and civilisation. It admitted of borderline cases, barbarians who were savages with a veneer of civilisation, or civilised men in process of relapsing into barbarism. It did not admit any organic *connection* between them—any possibility of the one growing out of the other. The anthropologists are so filled with a sense of the *natural growth* of savage societies (called nowadays, for politeness, " primitive " societies) and of the survivals from and analogies therewith they find in civilised societies, that they see nothing but the growth and continuity. Thus, for the anthropologists, primitive society is merely civilisation at a " low " level, civilisation being the *same thing*, only more so.

If the anthropologists were to say that civilised society is simply savagery on a bigger and more complicated scale, they would say the same thing in a more truthful form.

The truth overlooked is that between the various stages of social development there are *radical* differences. Therein the eighteenth-century sociologist was more correct than his twentieth - century brother. But radical differences, *oppositions* even, though there were, the fact remains that the one *did grow out* of the other,—and herein the twentieth century anthropologists are correct in their turn.

The *Dialectical* method of approach alone enables us to see the Continuity *in* and *through* the *Dis*-continuity ; and *vice versa*.

On this point another observation is called for.

Mr. Sidney Hook (who is *not* an anthropologist, but a professor of Philosophy) has, in the introduction to his *Towards the Understanding of Marx*, made the following observation :

> " One cannot be orthodox at any price and a lover of the truth at the same time. This was clearly demonstrated by the tenacity with which ' orthodox ' Marxists [he is referring here to the German Social Democrats chiefly—with a sidelong glance at the American De Leonites] who, in practice, had long since abandoned Marx and Engels, clung *to the latter's* anthropology in the face of the most conclusive findings of modern anthropologists. If the acceptance of Morgan's *out-moded* anthropology is necessary to orthodox Marxism, the author must be damned as a heretic on this point as well. Morgan was a great pioneer anthropologist. But no one to-day can accept his *universal scheme* of social development for the family and other institutions, without intellectual stultification."—HOOK : *loc. cit.*, p. 7.

There are, in this passage, a number of undoubted truths : one cannot love the truth and also be orthodox at any price ; that is why it is saddening to see Sidney Hook, who probably set out with the best of intentions, allowing himself to be intimidated by the anthropological *orthodoxy* current in Yale, Harvard, Columbia, and other academic fortresses of the " defence mechanism " of American imperialism. It *is* " the fashion " to *say* that " Morgan is out-moded." But then it *always has been* " the fashion " to say this ever since Morgan wrote. *And it was for that reason that Engels (with Marx's approval) rallied to Morgan's defence.*

Similarly, it is true to say that the " orthodox " Marxists in question had in practice " long since abandoned Marx and Engels,"—but that is no reason why Hook should abandon *both* Marx *and* Engels under the specious cloak of trying to separate the one from the other and to construct a new " orthodoxy " out of their disrupted ruins.

It is true that the findings of modern anthropologists have,

I

in some respects, and to a degree, modified some conclusions which Morgan deduced from the facts he was the first to collect and attempt to classify. But the real " out-moding " of Morgan current to-day lies, not in *new* facts which have been revealed, but in the interpretation which it is now " fashionable " to place upon those facts. These facts, however, can all be reconciled with Morgan's general conclusions, provided that these are interpreted with intelligent flexibility and not in a rigid, *a priori* fashion.

Finally, it is simply *not true* that Engels took over Morgan's anthropology without critical modification, and thereby separated himself from Marx. In the introduction to his *Origin of the Family, etc.*, Engels says :

" It was no less a person that Karl Marx who had reserved to himself the privilege of displaying the results of Morgan's investigations in connection with his own materialist conception of history. . . . He wished thus to elucidate the full meaning of this conception. . . . He [Morgan] had arrived, in comparing civilisation and barbarism, in the main, at the same results as Marx. . . . My work can only offer a meagre substitute for that which my departed friend was not able to accomplish. But in his copious extracts from Morgan I have critical notes which I herewith reproduce as fully as feasible."—ENGELS : *Origin* : preface (1884).

This, as it stands, is sufficient to do two things. First, it establishes the fact that, in his appraisal of Morgan, Engels, at any rate, believed himself to be working along a line which Marx himself would have followed. Secondly, it proves that Engels is concerned with Morgan's work only so far as it could, and can be, regarded as complementary to Marx's own conception of history. That is to say, Engels (and Marx) were not concerned to defend any of Morgan's conclusions, taken separately, as *final truths* of anthropological science. They were concerned with Morgan, so far, *and only so far*, as he threw, and throws light upon the historical progression of human society—which is, in fact, something with which " orthodox " anthropology is not in the least concerned. Anthropologists, as specialists, treat their subject-matter as a cross-section of society ; of the historical process itself they are completely (and professionally) ignorant.

This radical difference of approach is made clear in Engels' first sentence :

" Morgan was the first to make an attempt at intro-

ducing a logical order into *the history of primeval society*."
—ENGELS, *loc. cit.*, chap. I.

Thus, it is not any special detail in Morgan that Engels
regards as " of faith," but the general fact, unknown to the
eighteenth century, that *primeval times had their history too*.
And that to have proved so much was a revolutionary achievement is proved by the attempt of one of the " very latest "
schools, that of the " Diffusionists," to return to the eighteenth
century point of view and to identify " history " with " artificial " civilisation, tracing all civilisation to *one* centre of
mechanical diffusion, namely, Egypt. Where the eighteenth
century put " God," or the Great Man, the Diffusionists put
" Egypt." And it is as an ally (direct or indirect) of this
reaction that Sidney Hook spurns Morgan and seeks to use
him as a means of discrediting Engels.

The central fact in the Morgan sociology, and that which
gave it revolutionary significance in the eyes of Marx and
Engels, was (as we have seen) its demonstration that *the
Family has a history*—that it is not an ultimate, irreducibly
basic unit upon which the whole structure of society is built,
but something *derived* from previously existing society. The
Family is, that is to say, not a *cause*, or an indispensable
pre-condition of Society, but a *consequence*, a product of
social development, which has undergone transformation
in the course of development, and which will therefore,
and in time, just as surely cease to be as it has come
into being.

The significance of this in the eyes of Marx and Engels
can best be appreciated when it is recognised that in the eyes
of the official law codes of bourgeois society and of its official
moralities (especially clericalist and Catholic), *the Family* is,
along with Private Property and the State, one of the immutable foundation pillars upon which *all* social existence
depends. It was for that reason that the great Utopians
(Fourier particularly) directed their critique of bourgeois
society as much against the Family-institution as against
private property itself.

Morgan's work was of immense significance because it
demonstrated with an immense body of incontestable fact
that, whatever else might be true, the Family was *not*
immutable (since it demonstrably had gone through a process
of change and development) and *not* a pre-condition of Society,
since it was demonstrably an institution of Society, arising
on grounds of social utility, and developing in accordance

with the historical transformation of the *forms* and requirements of that social utility. *It was not the Family which
made Society, but Society which made the Family.* That was
the first central fact in Morgan's work which Marx and Engels
hailed as a triumphant proof of the theory they had reached
by another, an analytical, line of reasoning.

Morgan also demonstrated that the institutions of Property
and of Government (the State) fall likewise into the same
category. They, too, were neither of them mystical *ultimates*
which were " discovered " (with or without supernatural
aid) once and for all. That Property arose originally, not from
any mystical intuition of *absolute Right*, but from simple
utility—simple " use and wont "—that it had, accordingly,
undergone a whole series of historical transformations, that
it was therefore a social institution which society could,
should, and would remodel as and when its convenience
demanded—all this was demonstrated by the work of Lewis
Henry Morgan. Furthermore, Morgan demonstrated, and
that most brilliantly and in the most important (and neglected) part of his *Ancient Society*, that the institutions of
Government (Law and the State), instead of being things
" discovered " once and for all by the more or less legendary
" founders " of civilisation—Solon, Numa, Moses and Co.—
were also the historical products of the actual life-experience
of savages and barbarians. After Morgan's work it ceased
to be possible to treat " savagery " and " barbarism " as
examples of people living " without law " or with " imperfect
laws." Savages were proved to have a far more methodically
regulated (and therefore, in that sense, a far more " artificial ")
social organisation than it was possible for bourgeois-minded
theorists to conceive. The difference between civilisation,
barbarism, and savagery was shown to be a difference, *not*
of degrees of possession of an *absolute* Law, and an *absolute*
civil organisation, but of *forms* of law and of social organisation, which *forms* in turn rested ultimately upon differences
in respective *modes of economic production.*

That is what Morgan proved. That in the course of proving
it he supposed a schematic sequence of development for *all*
human societies everywhere, of a metaphysically mechanical
rigidity—that he failed to allow for possibilities of variation,
of alternative modes of progression which in no way invalidated his main generalisation—that he was (as even Darwin
was) guilty occasionally of positive errors of observation ;—
these things are the merest of incidentals. The fact that

Morgan's main work stands, and that stronger for all subsequant discoveries, is proved by the very practice of those who belittle and disparage him in the very act of appropriating the results he achieved.

Who are they who are most eager to prove Morgan " outmoded " ?

They fall into two camps. Firstly, there are the Catholic " anthropologists " who, finding that this science, like all others, can no longer be denied dogmatically a right to exist, fasten upon this, as upon every other field of knowledge, with no other intent than to find " evidence " of the " eternal truths of the (Catholic) Christian revelation." Secondly there are the bourgeois-empirical, anti-revolutionary schools, whose primary interest is to find in anthropology " evidence " of the *ultimate* and *absolute* " value " of all the chief incidentals of bourgeois society—its competitive individualism, its division of labour, its authoritarian State systems, and so on.

Both schools fall foul of Morgan precisely because of his revolutionary significance. The Catholics are concerned to find " evidence " for the origin of Society in *the Family*, the anti-revolutionary bourgeois empirics are concerned to find " private property " and the " Authoritarian State " at the origin of society. Both have joined hands to defend the myth of *the caveman* as the starting point of the Family, Private Property and The State. This myth in one or other of its variants is the root-form of those types of " anthropological sociology " fashionable in the universities, from the standpoint of which Morgan is " out-moded." That Sidney Hook should mistake this reactionary reversion to the socialphilosophy which Morgan overthrew as an advance upon Morgan's scientific achievements is typical of the theoretical degeneration which has set in among the bourgeois intelligentsia generally, a degeneration which gathers headway and acquires cynical impudence in exact proportion to the intensification of the state of crisis wherein the whole existence of bourgeois society is threatened.

That there may be no room for doubt, here are Engels' words :

" Up to the beginning of the 'sixties, a *history* of the family could not be spoken of. . . . No *historical development* of the family was even recognised. . . .

" The repeated discovery that the original maternal " gens " was a preliminary stage of the paternal " gens " of civilised nations has the same significance for primeval history that Darwin's theory of evolution has for biology, and Marx's theory of surplus value for political economy. Morgan was thereby enabled to sketch the *outline* of a history of the family, showing in bold strokes, at least, the classic stages of development, *so far as the available material will at present permit such a thing.* . . .

"Here and there *some special hypothesis of Morgan has been shaken or even become obsolete.* But in no instance has the new material led to a weakening of his leading propositions."—ENGELS : *Origin,* preface (1891).

From which it is as clear as noonday that neither Engels nor Marx supposed for a moment that Morgan's work gave an immutable law, good for the *whole* field of anthropological data. Such a conception was undialectical ; and anything beyond a broad outline was as impossible in 1874, as in 1884, *and* 1891. What Marx and Engels were concerned with was that Morgan supplied the evidence which proved the conclusion they had reached conjecturally from the analysis of " civil society," namely, that this must have developed historically from an " un-civil " society, which in turn must have undergone a series of historical permutations and transformations. This Morgan definitely proved, and proved so well that he made it possible for a host of pigmies, with not a tithe of his genius, to follow up his clues and create a reputation by " proving " that what Morgan had supposed to be universal was not absolutely so. The point, even if true (and it is not so in every case), is beside the point. Morgan was concerned, as Marx and Engels were concerned, with tracing back the historical process whose *hither* end is historical European civilisation. If there may be found social forms which did not contribute to that main stream, and if these social forms prove, in the end, to be a statistical majority of the varieties discovered, this makes as little difference to the argument as it does to find that an overwhelming majority of anthropoid species did not and could not evolve into Man. One variety able to do so is enough for Darwin's hypothesis. And an analogous argument applies in the case of Morgan.

Let it be granted (and Sidney Hook is invited to deny it *openly*—if that is his meaning) that so-called savage and barbarous societies do, in fact, represent a series of historical stages whereby civilisation came into being ; and let it be further granted that they are in themselves, and still more in their progression, intelligible only as modes of social organisation conditioned historically by the needs and results of *active production-practice* ; grant that, and the essence of the Morgan-Marx argument is conceded.

CHANGING THE WORLD

To summarise : In the tenth *Thesis* Marx effected a dialectical synthesis by eliminating the antagonism between " civil society " and savagery—and that between the " artificial " man of civilisation and the " natural " man in his—(according to one school, " unspoiled," and according to another " brutally uncouth ")—primitive stage. He saw that in all its forms, including that of " freely " competitive, commodity-production-based, bourgeois society, Human Society was *an association*, and an actively practical one; an association whose periodical transformations and re-transformations grew out of its practice and the resultants of that practice. And from the standpoint of this " associated humanity " he was able to envisage the future—a new society beyond its bourgeois form and the revolutionary mode of its coming to be.

Thus, the tenth *Thesis* led logically to the magnificently revolutionary eleventh *Thesis* : " The philosophers have only *interpreted* the world in various ways; the point, however, is to *change* it."

To understand the full force of this, it is necessary to remember the circumstances in which it was written—the fact that Marx and Engels were already engaged in the vanguard of the fight for Communism.

Not the least of the disservices which have been rendered to the cause of Marxism in the English-speaking world has been the dissemination, by its " popularisers," of the notion that Marx (and, in a lesser degree, Engels) were simply book-worms who, from the depths of armchairs, and the dust-and-cobweb-sanctified serenity of vast libraries, emitted a cloud of more or less luminous, theoretical " gas," which plain, " practical " men (in the every-day bourgeois sense) have had to reduce to terms of concrete application. It is this notion which makes it possible for the fool-friends of Leninism to argue that " Marx evolved the *theory*, but Lenin reduced it to *practice* ! " Which argument leads, in turn, to its elaboration by intellectual camp-followers of the proletarian struggle, into whole volumes of doctrine which have for their starting-point this notion of Marx as an embodiment of abstract-theory, virgin-pure from any contact with mere practice.

A classic example is provided by the publishers' note on the inside of the dust-wrapper issued with R. W. POSTGATE's *Karl Marx*. In this we are told that Marx "took some important part—*of a sedentary kind*—in working-class organisation."

Now, it is true that Marx spent a good deal of time, and that to superlatively good purpose, in the British Museum Library (as he did also, and earlier, in the *Bibliothèque Nationale* in Paris, and in the libraries of the Universities of Berlin, Heidelberg, and Bonn). It is also true that the British Museum is in Bloomsbury. But this no more converted Marx into a member of the Bloomsbury School of odd-job *literati*—an oracle of *Hobohemia*—than a cat's kittens, by being transferred to a pub, become pints of ale. It is necessary to emphasise, therefore, the fact that, if we take Marx's *Capital* (1867) as constituting the starting-point of the specifically Marxist movement, that this point was reached only after a long theoretical and practical struggle in the vanguard of the revolutionary movement of the day— a struggle in which Marx and Engels personally participated to a degree that occupied their whole time and brought them into practical and responsible contact with the revolutionary, democratic and proletarian movements alike in Germany, France, Belgium, and Britain.

Marx's name is for ever memorable as that of the man who (with his lifelong friend and collaborator, Engels) effected a new departure which opened a new epoch in the history of the proletarian class-struggle, and thereby in the history of the world. This as we have seen consisted in effecting a synthetic union between two historically developed forces which, till then, had existed, not only in separation, but in positive, objective, opposition—namely, the theoretical movement for Socialism and Communism ; and the spontaneous *practical* struggles of the proletariat. In terms of Stalin's celebrated aphorism "Theory without practice is sterile : Practice without theory is blind"— Marx (aided by Engels) rescued Socialist-Communist *theory* from its sterility, and proletarian revolutionary *practice* from its blindness.

The Bloomsbury-Greenwich Village notion is that Marx did this by first of all becoming pregnant in consequence of an enormous absorption of all the more repellantly indigestible volumes in the British Museum Library; then by extruding the results in the form of a huge theoretical egg; which, at long last, was finally hatched out by Lenin. (Bloomsbury's rôle, self-appointed, being to supply the concomitant cackling—*ex poste facto*—and in the process to "pinch" a double ration of the credit.)

The actual fact is that the Marxian theory was born in practical struggle and as a result of the practical struggle; that in form and in content it gained objective being, not in 1917, nor *after* 1867, but *before* 1848; that *Capital* instead of standing at the beginning of the history of Marxism, marks the *culmination* of its growth, and that on only one of its sides; that it continued to develop in struggle and by means of struggle, in which Marx and Engels directly, personally, and *responsibly* participated during the whole of their respective lifetimes; that it has, necessarily, continued so to develop ever since.

Not only in the revolutionary movement prior to the Year of Revolution, 1848, but in that revolutionary crisis itself Marx and Engels were in the forefront of the actual struggle— Engels in actual armed insurrection, Marx in the storm centre at Cologne, fighting the official censorship to such a tune that he was twice tried on a capital charge—"high treason." Marx and Engels helped to fire the opening shot of the campaign (the *Communist Manifesto*) and theirs was the last gun to be silenced (the *Neue Rheinische Zeitung*, last issued from Hamburg in 1850).

During the period from 1850 to 1864—the period in which Marx spent most time in the British Museum Library, and in which, therefore, by Bloomsbury standards, he was most " sedentary "—there was " nothing doing " in the way of actual, open, revolutionary struggle, anywhere in Europe. As Engels said : " only a literary struggle was possible "— and that struggle was waged more by Marx and Engels than by any men then living. An immense mass of journalistic work was done, of a value difficult to appraise since only a portion of it has, until recently, been resurrected from the files in which it has lain buried. What is known of it is sufficient to show that the developments after 1864 owe nine-tenths of their force to these " sedentary " but unremitting labours of Marx and, inspired by him, of Engels, and others of Marx's old revolutionary associates.

In 1864 Marx was in the open again, once more in a responsible post, at the head of the movement which, but for

him, would never have been born—the International Working
Men's Association. During the life of the I.W.M.A. Marx
performed herculean feats of drudging, detailed, labour on
its behalf. And after its fall (1872) he performed similar
labours on behalf of the various national Labour, Socialist,
and Social Democratic movements to which the
I.W.M.A. had given birth. After Marx's death, Engels
carried on the work single-handed, and died, literally, on
the job.

Marx and Engels wrote, in addition to a mass of articles,
and a volume of correspondence—all of a kind involving not
only an amazing range of theoretical research, but a direct
practical acquaintance with the actual movements of men
and circumstances then current—in addition to all this a
long string of books and pamphlets. Not one of these can
be cited which was not prompted by the theoretical and
practical needs of the revolutionary working-class struggle.
Even the most abstruse (and " sedentary " !) of them all,
Marx's Capital, was needed and that most urgently as a
guide to the elucidation of the tangled problems of practice
confronting that struggle. If Capital did not save the
degenerate epigoni of Social-Democracy from their decline
into the most banal, wretched, and cowardly opportunism,
the explanation must be sought otherwhere than in the
inspiring, revolutionary objectivity which glows from its
every page.

Sedentary !

From 1842 to 1883—forty-one years, and never fully
out of harness ; not even in the few odd months of nominal
holiday which were necessitated by his final illness ! Exiled
from Germany, France, Belgium, France again—! Twice
tried for his life. Twice the editor of a journal published
under the incubus of a special and particular censorship.
For ten years a principal contributor to the most advanced
journal then in being—the New York Tribune. The inspirer,
guide and leader of the mightiest, and most enduring popular
movement in history, the international movement of the
revolutionary proletariat ! The theoretician whose work
alone among the sociological speculations of the nineteenth
century stands valid to this day, more valid even than when
it was first promulgated—since facts on a world-wide earth-
shaking scale have verified it past all question, and experience
has deepened and widened its many-sided significance for
practical action !

Such was the " part " taken by Marx (aided by Engels) in working-class organisation. Bloomsbury concedes, graciously, that it was " important," but decides oracularly that it was " *sedentary* ! "

Over Marx's coffin Engels spoke a different and a far truer-sounding word : " Before all else Marx was a revolutionist. Fighting was his natural element. His name and his work will live on through the centuries."

THE BIRTH STRUGGLES OF MARXISM

That for which Marx and Engels stand clearly credited is the creation of the modern Socialist-Communist revolutionary-proletarian International *movement*.

But—" the educator must himself be educated "—and nothing, least of all a social movement, can be made *from* nothing. Before they could create this movement they had themselves first to be created as Socialist-Communist revolutionaries. And this could have happened to them only *in practical participation* in the Socialist and Communist theory and practice of their time. By actual, objective, participation in that movement they simultaneously transformed both themselves and it. They *lived* the revolutionary materialist *dialectic* it is their fame to be the first to have preached.

This dialectic is brilliantly exemplified by the fact that the *new* movement which Marx (aided by Engels) brought into being was not *only* one which brought into synthetic union two movements which had previously existed in separation : those of Socialist-Communist *theory* and spontaneous proletarian class *practice*. To achieve this " negation of the negation" between Theory and Practice involved as a concomitant the dissolution into antagonisms of previously existing unities—that between Socialist-Communist theory and bourgeois-humanitarian sentimentalism, and that between the spontaneous political movements of the proletariat and the traditional democratic-republicanism and revolutionary radicalism which simply continued the impetus of the Jacobin Revolution of 1789.

Up to the time of the Chartists (1836 onwards) the proletarians had made only sporadic appearances upon the political stage, and then only in their character of " swinish multitude," " disorderly rabble," " undisciplined, vulgar, mob," " Great Unwashed," or " sans culottes " [literally " without breeches ; in English, " backsides out ! "]. They had figured, and to a large extent still continued all through the Chartist period, to figure as a sort of poor relation of the bourgeoisie—the " great " Middle Class. A practical separation between the bourgeois and proletarian movements had been made in the trade unions and strike-combinations, which were usually short-lived, and were seldom attempted even in Britain on anything like a national scale. But until 1842, when the spontaneous movement of the factory workers in Lancashire and Yorkshire forced the hands of the Chartist leaders and led them to attempt the first political general strike in history, few people saw in the trade unions any political potentiality—beyond a negative, destructively disturbing one. Socialist theoreticians before Marx—with the notable exception of Robert Owen and his school—tended to condemn the unions out of hand. And even Owen saw no further than the possibility of using the unions to establish socialism—of converting them into societies for voluntary co-operative production and exchange.

The Socialists and Communists (the terms then were largely interchangeable) for their part were still at the " Utopian " stage ; as Marx and Engels called it. This does *not* mean, as critics eager to find any mud to fling at Marx have supposed, that Marx condemned *everything* they aimed at as absolutely foolish, or everything in their immediate proposals as incapable of practical application. On the contrary, as the life of Owen shows, some of their proposals *could* be put into practice quite easily ; the trouble was that they were not adequate as means to the Socialist-Communist end. That which constituted them " utopians " was that they still moved on the theoretical plane of Thomas More's *Utopia*. They still conceived society atomically, and therefore thought that their ideal schemes could be applied out of hand (without any sort of historical preparation). All that was necessary was that either (*a*) some powerful ruler should use his governmental authority to reorganise his kingdom on the lines of the new plan ; (*b*) some wealthy philanthropist should advance the capital to permit a sample " Utopia " to be set going ; or (*c*) that sufficient people should, by pooling their resources, be able so to begin. Attempts were made in the last of these three ways ; always with the result of demonstrating that within capitalist society men could so co-operate to produce only under the conditions of competitive capitalism—only as units in a capitalist whole.

The Socialist and Communist sects, *as such*, therefore tended to be both anti-political and opposed to any sustained

Trade Union struggle (as presupposing and perpetuating the
" competitive principle " they were out to eradicate). Thus,
Utopian Socialism was, in practice, a conservative force—and
as such had, and still has, a great attraction for avowed
Tories.

But, on the other hand, the critical propaganda levelled by
the Utopians against capitalist society supplied a powerful
stimulus to Radical, Republican, and revolutionary political
agitation. What the Utopians regarded as the *constructive*
side of their work proved in practice negative ; their *destructive* criticism, on the other hand, proved the most fruitful
work of their times. It led to the appearance of a tendency
within the general radical-democratic-republican movement
which increasingly modified its political outlook in an anti-
bourgeois pro-Socialist sense. There began to appear " Red "
republicans, " Socialist " democrats, and " Communist "
revolutionaries. These tendencies, however, did not effect a
new *synthesis* between Socialist-Communist criticism and the
outlook of Democracy-in-General. They proceeded wholly
upon the presupposition of the latter in its bourgeois form ;
and conceived it their business to recommence the Revolutionary movement of 1789 (which had already had one or
two, more or less abortive, recurrences in the 1830s) and
carry it through to the logical conclusion of its proclaimed
objectives—Liberty, Equality, and Fraternity. And the
Socialist-Communist sects who developed with them likewise
took their departure from bourgeois presuppositions. In
their case it was *not* the Revolution itself, whose " failure "
was by them deemed to have discredited all attempts at a
" mere " political revolution, which gave the point of departure but the theoretical principles worked out by the philosophers who had provided that Revolution with its *theory*.
Just as the *political* Socialists—the Socialist or " social "
democracy, " that section of the democracy which is more
or less tinged with Socialism "—developed the practical
side of the Great Revolution, and particularly the Constitution of 1793, to its logical conclusion, so the Utopians of
various grades developed the social *theory* of the eighteenth
century to its logical conclusions. The result on both sides,
super-added to the theoretical and practical confusion in the
wider bourgeois democratic-republican movement, was such
a chaos of discordant theory and practice—practice " blind "
because divorced from *theory* ; theory " sterile " because
divorced from *practice* ; and both the blindness and the

sterility made absolute because of the absoluteness of the rupture between theory and practice—such a chaos as has seldom been paralleled in history.

The writings of Marx and Engels from 1843 to 1847 demonstrate brilliantly the manner in which they brought order into this chaos. They negated the antagonism between Socialism and the proletarian struggle and, simultaneously, differentiated the unity of revolutionary Democracy-in-General into the dialectical antagonism of bourgeois and petit-bourgeois " democratic " theory and practice on the one side, and revolutionary proletarian-democratic Communism on the other.

These theoretical and practical turmoils all lie at the back of the concluding four theses on Feuerbach.

If ever there was a time when " mysteries "—of theory and practice—" seduced speculation into mysticism " it was precisely the time (early 1845) when the *Theses on Feuerbach* were written. Take, for example, the question of Materialism and Idealism as weapons of partisan struggle. In Germany critical Idealism had completely discredited eighteenth-century materialist *theory*, but had in turn become itself discredited practically from its official associations with the established order. Hence Idealism, interpreted in terms of rigid orthodoxy, became the weapon of the Reactionaries which drove the revolutionaries over to the materialistic *reinterpretation of philosophy*, which reached its zenith in Feuerbach. In Britain, on the contrary, eighteenth-century French materialism, checked for a time by the explosion of the French revolution, was spreading, particularly in connection with radical politics and Utopian speculations, and was countered from the side of reaction by simple dogmatic theology. In France, where the political issues were, in a sense, clearer, the theoretical issues were all the more confounded. Radical democratic and proletarian opponents of the exclusive domination of the bourgeoisie saw in German idealism a weapon against bourgeois " Voltaireanism." But simultaneously the aristocratic and clerical defenders of the restored Bourbon monarchy and of its Orleanist successor, the " July " Monarchy, established in 1830, saw in idealism allied to supernaturalism a weapon against the progressive bourgeoisie, and still more against the perennially insurgent proletariat, which the agitations of that progressive bourgeoisie were constantly stirring into activity. The materialist-minded proletarian revolutionaries thus found themselves, in their own despite, involved with, and to an extent compromised by association with, the theoretical standpoint of the bourgeoisie.

Since the theoretical warfare in each country reacted upon that in all the others, the result was chaos which took form as *eclecticism*—the political, social, and ethical doctrine of the " happy medium," the *juste milieu*—which doctrine was reduced to a system by VICTOR COUSIN (1792–1867). Speaking of the theoretical complexion of this time in both England and France, a contemporary writer (semi-materialist, semi-Comteist), GEORGE HENRY LEWES, (1817–1878) says :

> " Materialism is an *ugly* word, which connotes certain opinions of very questionable validity held by some writers and opinions, both silly and immoral, *which are wantonly attributed* to these writers by rash and reckless polemists. . . . The materialists have at least this important advantage, that they strive to get rid of all metaphysical entities, and seek an explanation of phenomena in *the laws* of phenomena. . . . If materialistic opinions are erroneous they are dangerous to the extent of their erroneousness ; whereas most men declare these opinions to be erroneous because they *believe them to be dangerous*. . . .
>
> The reaction against the philosophy of the Eighteenth Century was less a reaction against a doctrine proved to be incompetent than against a doctrine *believed to be the source of frightful immorality*. The reaction was vigorous, because it was animated by the horror which agitated Europe *at the excesses* (*!!*) *of the French Revolution* . . . the philosophical opinions of Condillac, Diderot, and Cabanis were held responsible for the *crimes of the Convention*. . . . Every opinion which had what was called ' a taint of materialism ' . . . was denounced as an opinion *necessarily leading to the destruction* of all Religion, Morality *and Government*. Every opinion which seemed to point in the direction of spiritualism [i.e., *idealism*] was eagerly welcomed, promulgated and lauded. . . . We can understand how indelible was *the association of Revolution with Materialism* in the minds of that generation."—LEWES : *History of Philosophy*, Vol. II, pp. 743–44.

And, speaking of the (eclectic supernaturalist-Royalist) school of Victor Cousin, he goes on to say :

> " Their main purpose is to defend morality and *order*,

which they [profess to] believe to be necessarily imperilled by the philosophy they attack. The appeals to the prejudices and sentiments are incessant. . . . The hearer . . . learns to associate all the nobler sentiments with spiritualistic doctrines, and all grovelling ideas with materialistic doctrines till the one school becomes inseparably linked in his mind with emotions of reverence . . . and the other with emotions of contempt for whatever is shallow and unworthy."—LEWES : *History of Philosophy*, Vol. II, p. 745.

Significantly paralleling this eclecticism, and the retreat to Idealism (and supernaturalism) which it both involves and masks, were the reactions produced by the impact of Utopian theory upon petit-bourgeois and proletarian democracy. To the Utopians (then as now) said Engels :

" . . . Socialism is the expression of absolute truth, justice, and reason, and has only to be discovered to conquer the world in virtue of its own power. And as absolute truth is independent of time, space, and the historical development of man, it is a mere accident when and where it is discovered. With all this *absolute* truth, reason and justice are different with each founder of a different school. And as each one's special kind of *absolute* truth, reason, and justice is again conditioned by his subjective understanding, his conditions of existence, the measure of his knowledge and his intellectual training, there is no other ending possible in this conflict of *absolute* truths than that they shall be mutually exclusive one of the other. Hence from this could come nothing but *a kind of eclectic, average Socialism* . . . a mish-mash of such critical statements, economic theories, pictures of future society . . . as excite the minimum of opposition ; a mish-mash the more easily brewed the more the sharp edges of the individual constituents are rubbed down in the stream of debate like pebbles in a brook."—ENGELS : *Socialism : Utopian and Scientific*, pp. 36–37 ; *Anti-Dühring*, pp. 25 26.

Mechanical metaphysical materialism led to Utopianism and the alternatives of fatalism and mystagogy ; idealism led to irrationalism and supernaturalism ; both led to Reaction. The attempt to amalgamate the two produced eclecticism and romantic sentimentalism—that is, Reaction disguised. What was the way of escape ?

One way—the philistine way, which is also the " typical

English " way—was to abandon all attempts to find a theoretical solution and fall back upon " practical common sense." This, however, simply reproduced eclecticism along with deliberately self-blinded opportunism.

Another way, the only way of escape from the tangle, was the way taken by Marx—the way of *practice, with its eyes wide open* ; of practice guided by a critical comprehension of the nature of the historical process of society and its positive objective outcome. The *real* content of the Critical Philosophy had been the *dialectic* method ; its Idealist systematisation had been merely the form under which this *real* content had been discovered. Similarly the *real* content of eighteenth-century materialism had been, not the metaphysical and mechanistic forms in which it had been systematised, but its affirmation of the *real* existence, the objective materiality, and the knowability of the external universe. A synthetic union of these basic materialistic affirmations with the dialectical method gave *Dialectical Materialism,* then as now, the only road of escape from the seductions of mysticism. And Dialectical Materialism, concretely applied to the antagonism dividing non-revolutionary, non-proletarian Utopianism from non-Socialist proletarian revolutionism, produced, in complete antithesis to all Eclecticism, a synthesis of the two forces : a Socialism or Communism which was proletarian and revolutionary, a proletarianism which was Communist and dialectic as well as revolutionary.

As against all and every speculative theory which approached the problem from the standpoint of the abstract *individual,* the standpoint was reached by which the problem could be approached from the *negation* of that standpoint and its negation in turn of the real objective relation between man and man in real, practical objective life.

" The standpoint of the *new* materialism [i.e., Dialectical Materialism] is *human* society—of socialised humanity "—in a word : COMMUNISM.

. . . . . .

It is an evidence of the amazingly keen penetration of Heinrich HEINE that he saw intuitively that this possibility was latent in the Hegelian dialectic as far back as 1834—years before Marx or Engels had left school :

" Our philosophical revolution is ended. Hegel completes the grand cyclus. We have seen since then only the development and perfectioning of the doctrine of the philosophy of Nature. . . .

K

"It seems to me that such a methodical race as ours must begin with the Reformation, then busy themselves with Philosophy, and only then, after finishing it, *pass on to political revolution*. I find this sequence thoroughly in order. The heads which philosophy has used for reflection a revolution may cut off, as shall hereafter suit its purposes. But Philosophy could have no earthly use for heads which a preceding revolution had decapitated.

"Let not your hearts be disquieted, ye German republicans! Your German revolution will be none the gentler or milder. . . . Thought goes before the deed as lightning precedes thunder. German thunder is, I grant, German, and in no sort of a hurry. It comes lumbering along awkwardly enough. But come it will, and when ye hear such a crash as naught ever crashed before in the whole history of the world, know ye then that *der deutsche Donner*, our own German thunder, has hit the mark at last. At that sound the eagles will drop dead from the sky and the lions in remotest African deserts will draw in their tails and slink into the depths of their royal caves.—HEINE : *Germany* (see Leland's trans., Vol. V, pp. 204–9).

Later, in 1847, after having met Marx and contracted a close friendship with him, Heine was more pointedly specific :

"I have been blamed for tearing away the veil from the German heaven, and laying bare to all that every deity of the old faith has vanished—that all that sits there now is an old virgin with leaden hands and a heavy heart—*Necessity!* Ah! I did but speak out what all now must be aware of. That which sounded then so strange is now re-echoed from every roof beyond the Rhine. And in what fanatic accents are these anti-religious sermons preached! We have fanatical monks of Atheism now who would burn Voltaire himself at the stake as an incorrigibly besotted Deist !

"I confess that this music does not please me. But, then, neither does it alarm me ; for I stood behind the great *maestro* [Hegel] when he composed it !—it is true, in characters so illegible and entangled that not everyone could decipher it. He loved me well, for he was quite sure I would not betray him. In truth—at times I thought him servile. And when, once, I broke out

impatiently at his saying, ' All that is *real* is rational,'
he smiled strangely and remarked : ' It might also be
said that all that is rational must become *real* ! ' He
looked round hurriedly ; but was at once at ease. Only
Henry Beer had heard him.

"Not till later did I understand such expressions. Then
I understood why in his *Philosophy of History* he had
declared that Christianity was a progress *because it taught
a god who died*, while the heathen gods had known no
death. What a step forward it is, therefore, if *God has
never existed at all* !

"With the overthrow of the old faith and doctrines,
that of the old morality is involved. . . . The destruction
of faith in heaven has in addition to a moral, *a political
force* ! The masses will no longer bear with Christian
patience their earthly sufferings : will yearn for the bless-
ings and joys of this life. The natural consequence of this
altered outlook is—*Communism*, which is spreading all
over Germany. And, indeed, it is only natural that the
proletariat should have, as leaders in its war against
existing institutions, the most advanced intellects, the
philosophers of the Great [Hegelian] School."—HEINE :
Letters on Germany (cf. Leland, V, 220–1).

Two incidental things are noteworthy in this powerful and
penetrating passage. The first is Heine's dexterous inversion
of Hegel's famous aphorism : " All that is Real is rational,"
etc. Engels, long after (1888), in his *Feuerbach*, worked out
the same dialectical inversion ; and the American Austin
Lewis, in the introduction referred to earlier, is so struck
with this part of Engels' essay that he specifies it as an outstanding example of the " great critical acumen " which
Engels displays " *now and then* " ! It is clear from the fact
that it appears in Heine as early as 1847, and from the connection in which it appears, that the " critical acumen " was
no product of Engels' elderly reflection. It was, in fact, the
practical point at issue which cleft the Hegelian school into
warring Right and Left wings.

Secondly, the whole passage bears other traces of the
influence upon Heine of his " deluded friend Marx." Particularly apparent is the influence of Marx's " opium for the
people " article in the Franco-German Year Book. The whole
passage illustrates very finely how Materialism, liberated from
its Egyptian bondage by the alchemy of history, returned to
the front rank of revolutionary struggle equipped with

weapons wrested from its one-time gaoler and taskmaster—Critical Idealism.

THE CRITICISM OF CRITICISM

Marxism was developed from the critical philosophy (as it left the hands of Feuerbach) on one side, and from materialist-utopianism on the other, in a series of polemic battles which began with the *Year Book* (1844) and culminated in the *Communist Manifesto* (1847–48). Its first front was formed against the feudal-clerical-monarchist Reaction from a standpoint which is in the main that of Feuerbach. The next was a front against the non-Socialist, anti-Communist Hegelian Left, as represented by Edgar and Bruno Bauer and Arnold Ruge. The third was against the sentimentalist-humanitarian, " no-class-war " Socialism which developed from the weaker side of Feuerbach's work. The fourth was against the egoistic-anarchist inversion of this " German or True " Socialism, which found expression in Max Stirner. The fifth was the fight against the petit-bourgeois perversion of Socialism which found its spokesman in PIERRE JOSEPH PROUDHON (1809–1865). Lastly came the battle all along the line in the *Communist Manifesto*. In each stage of this struggle a new aspect of Marxism was revealed. In each battle mysticism was defeated by an appeal to concrete, objective social *practice*. In every stage in turn the standpoint of " socialised humanity " was developed in opposition to that of the abstract individual in civil society, to that of the official representative of civil society—the State—and to that of abstract Humanity. Increasingly the battle slogan " Our business is to change the world " took on a specific concrete point until it emerged finally in the objective slogan : *Workers of the world—unite !*

We have room only for a few sample extracts to show the stages of this revolutionary progression. In the *Year Book* article above referred to Marx develops his attack upon the established order by means of an introduction to the Hegelian *Philosophy of Right*. Under that name was included by HEGEL : (1) Abstract Right : the absolute fundamentals of Law and Morals. (2) Subjective Morality (the so-called " moral law within "). (3) Objective Morals : (*a*) the family ; (*b*) civil society ; and (*c*) the State. And already, in 1843–44, Marx had reached the conviction that " right " and " wrong " in all the senses possible in that scheme, could neither be understood in themselves nor traced to any forms of law. All, he saw, were rooted in the primary fact from which civil society (which all the relations indicated presuppose) itself grew, namely, the economic constitution of society itself. In the *Year Book* article, however, this conviction only appears indirectly, allusively, since the whole is deliberately presented as an argument *ad hominem* (i.e., in terms of the standpoint adopted by the enemy).

It is agreed on all hands—his argument runs—that the *ancien regime* surviving in Germany must be overthrown. But from what standpoint ?

" Revolution needs a passive element, a material basis. Theory is realised in a people only in so far as it is the realisation of its needs. Will therefore the contradiction between bourgeois society and the State and the contradiction within itself be in accordance with the tremendous contradiction between the demands of German thought and the answers of German reality ? . . . Will the theoretical needs be immediately practical needs ? It is not enough that the idea should push forward to realisation ; reality itself must urge itself into thought. . . .

" In order that the revolution of a people may coincide with the emancipation of a particular class of bourgeois society, in order that one class may be regarded as the whole of society, there must be, on the other hand, another class in which all the deficiencies of society are concentrated. . . . The negative general significance of the French (1789) aristocracy and clergy conditioned the positive-general significance of the immediately contiguous and opposing class of the bourgeoisie. . . .

" In Germany, . . . where practical life is just as void of intellect as intellectual life is unpractical, no class in bourgeois society has the need and the capacity for general emancipation until it is compelled by its immediate situation, by material necessity, by its own chains, to take up this role.

" Where, then, is the positive possibility of German emancipation ?

" Answer : In the form of a class with radical chains ; a class of bourgeois society which is not a class of bourgeois society ; a class which is the dissolution of all classes ; a sphere which has a universal character only in virtue of the universality of its suffering ; a sphere which demands no particular right, because no particular wrong has been done to it, but *wrong as a whole and in general* ; a sphere which can appeal to no historical title but to a human title only . . . a class which is, in a word, the complete loss of humanity. . . . This dissolution of society as a special class is *the proletariat.*"— MARX : *Year Book* (see *Jewish Question*, Martin Lawrence, p. 26).

Hard indeed would it be to find a more striking example both of the many-sidedness of the dialectical method and of the penetrating quickness of Marx's grasp than this, that he should find the most truly *human* force in bourgeois society in the class which under the bourgeois regime and relatively thereto is most *dehumanised.* But precisely for that reason, once the *individual* point of view is abandoned for that of " socialised humanity " it " leaps to the eye "—as the French say—that *in its collective totality* the proletariat *is* humanity in *inverse form.* The other classes, having each their *special* interests, will of necessity, *as classes,* fight in defence of their speciality. But in so doing they will fight to preserve *that social division of labour upon which their speciality depends for its existence.* The proletariat, alone in its fight for emancipation, finds itself pitted in battle against that social division of labour itself. Other classes might, and did, fight against certain incidental effects of the system ; but the proletariat could not get into motion as a class without challenging at its very foundation that system itself.

Marx's view was immediately challenged, and from within the camp of the (Feuerbachian) Hegelian Left. The brothers EDGAR and BRUNO BAUER (who were, incidentally, blood relations of Marx) stood at the head of the School of " Critical Criticism," a school whose cardinal doctrine was that the Critical Philosophy (of the Feuerbach-Hegelian brand) should " queen it over the whole mob of the sciences "— including politics and law—each of which should be reconstructed in terms of a special Critique of its first principles. Hence the name Critical Criticism—the standpoint being that of the critical development of the principles of all criticism " pure " and applied.

Edgar and Bruno Bauer were men of established reputation —the latter, particularly, having acquired great notoriety from his rivalry and polemical battles with Strauss (on the question of Christian origins). When Arnold Ruge invited Marx to collaborate with him in the production of the *Franco-German Year Book* he also invited the Bauers. They refused, and instead founded a journal of their own, the *Universal*

Literary Gazette. Their programme was declared by the Bauers to be that of " exposing the shallow superficiality and inflated bombast of liberalism and radicalism," and to set up in opposition to " Socialism—that helpless gesture of philosophical incompetence " a return to the " true philosophy of self-consciousness of universality." In subsequent issues they categorically condemned the pro-proletarian attitude of the *Year Book* in the name of their critical universality, which stood above all partisan politics and all mere *class* considerations !

Naturally Marx and Engels were not the sort of men to let such an open challenge go by default. They replied in a volume (alas ! still-born, since the *Universal*, etc., had expired before it appeared) whose very title was a polemic in itself : *The Holy Family ; a Criticism of Critical Criticism ; against Bruno Bauer and Co.*

An amusing side-light is thrown upon this delightful satirical by-battle in the *Marx-Engels Correspondence* [see Martin Lawrence edition]. In the winter of 1855 (more than ten years later) Marx writes with huge chuckles describing to Engels visits from and to Edgar Bauer (who also had taken up permanent residence in London) and his brother Bruno (who had arrived on a visit) :

" Have seen Bruno again several times. Romanticism reveals itself more and more as the ' presupposition of the Critical Criticism.' In political economy he rhapsodises over the physiocrats (whom he misunderstands !) and believes in the beneficent effects of landed property. . . .

" As for our illusions about internal class struggles : (1) the workers have no ' hate ' ; (2) have never accomplished anything with such hate as they do possess ; (3) are a ' mob ' . . . which can only be tamed and led by force and cunning ; (4) give them a penny rise and everything is settled. No one, moreover, who does not belong to the ' descendants of the conquerors ' can play any part in world history—except in the theoretical field : etc. . . .

" Otherwise a pleasant old gentleman." . . .—MARX *to Engels*, January 18th, 1856.

What Bruno Bauer said openly in 1856 was in 1844 disguised under an elaborate philosophical argumentation which affected the loftiest disdain for any consideration but that of the " pure " critical intelligence which surveyed the Universe from a standpoint far superior to any mere " practical " consideration. Marx and Engels, bringing all their wit and sarcasm into play, punctured the solemn pretentiousness of this " universal standpoint " and revealed it as nothing else than the standpoint of the then dominant State and the established order.

Fighting the Bauers on their own Hegelian ground, Marx and Engels drove them logically from position after position:

"Proletariat and Wealth are opposites. As such they constitute a whole. They are two aspects of the world of private property. But that which concerns us here is the distinctive position each of them assumes respectively in this oppositional inter-relation. It does not dispose of the matter to say simply that they are aspects of one whole.

" Private property *as* private property (as *wealth*) is compelled to maintain its own existence. Thereby it maintains also its own negation—the *proletariat*. Wealth is thus the *positive* pole in the antithesis—private property satisfied with itself.

" The Proletariat, on the other hand, is compelled, *as* proletariat, to abolish itself, and in so doing to abolish likewise its conditioning opposite—the private property *for which* it is a proletariat. This is the *negative* pole of the antithesis—private property dissatisfied with itself, dissolved and dissolving itself.

" The possessing class and the proletariat present one identity—that of human self-alienation. But while the former feels at home and assured therein, and finds in the relation its own power and the semblance of a real human existence the proletariat finds in the relation its own nullity, a reflection of its own impotence, and feels in it all the reality of an *in*-human existence.

" Beyond question private property in its economic movement advances towards its own dissolution. But it does this only in consequence of an independent development of which it is not at all conscious—and which it undergoes quite without its own volition under the impulsion of the nature of things. It does it only inasmuch as it generates the proletariat *as* *proletariat*—only inasmuch as it creates a Poverty conscious of its own mental and physical poverty—only in that it creates a dehumanisation that becomes conscious of itself does it abolish itself."—MARX-ENGELS : *The Holy Family.*

Here with admirable dexterity, and while keeping within the strict rules of the Hegelian game, the argument of the Bauers—that, in so far as " Wealth " and its negation, the Proletariat, were *real,* they each carried their own negation *within themselves*—so that wealth constantly became not-wealth and not-wealth constantly wealth—this facile optimism, which incidentally excluded any *real* historical movement *as such,* is shown to be worthless even by strict Hegelian standards. As soon as we abandon the " contemplative " standpoint and cease to consider the *idea* of wealth in the abstract in contrast to an equally abstract *idea* of not-wealth (Proletariat)—as soon as we turn to the objective reality from which those ideas are abstracted and apply the criterion of objective practice, the pseudo-Critical sophistry is blown to shreds.

. . . .

Curiously enough, the first three paragraphs of the extract from the *Holy Family* given above are made the subject of a furious diatribe against Marx and his logical method by both MAX EASTMAN (*Marx, Lenin,* etc.) and RAYMOND POSTGATE (*Karl Marx*). The former cites it *as an example of the way Marx tried to explain himself to plain people* (like himself), and goes purple at the gills at the notion of being expected to find a meaning in such stuff. Raymond Postgate uses it to show how Marx himself was betrayed by the worthlessness of the Dialectic into talking nonsense in spite of himself. We shall hear more of these twain—the Castor and Pollux (or should one write Kastor and Polydeukes ?) of Freudian-Marxism—later. Here we offer a few observations for the benefit of the unfortunate Raymond Postgate.

We say " unfortunate " because, " though willing to wound " and not in the least " afraid to strike," he swings his critical chopper with such preposterous indexterity that he is always cutting his own feet from under himself. As thus :

> " In what useful sense can the proletariat, a large number of persons, be considered as forming a ' whole ' with private property a relation and an idea ? In what sense can they be its opposite ? They may be ' opposed ' in the conventional sense to the individual capitalists in the sense of wishing to do them an injury.

But the description as it stands is almost meaningless."
—POSTGATE, *loc. cit.*, p. 85.

Now much may be forgiven Raymond Postgate on the score
of his afflictions—an appallingly academic upbringing and
a congenitally enlarged spleen. Even so it is hard to forgive
any man who thinks he has described the proletariat adequately in the periphrasis " a large number of persons."
From a writer who sets out to teach " Marxism " *to Marx*
this is nearer to the incredible than any vision in the book of
Ezekiel. But even worse is Postgate's inability to conceive
" opposition " in any other form than that of a malignant
intent to inflict injury. This is not even the point of view of
bourgeois materialism, though it is that of the " single
individual." Whereas the former is that of " civil society,"
this is that of a most " uncivil " society. It is provisionally
to be classified as the *sub*-bourgeois-materialist point of view
—that of the *lumpen intelligentsia* or *Yahoo-bohemia* !

For Postgate's benefit let us point out that, if his jaundice
has abated sufficiently to permit him to re-read the passage,
he will perceive that the " opposition " discussed is the
logical opposition of a concept and its " opposite." Thus, for
instance, Raymond Postgate may be gratified to learn that
he has no fewer than *four* different pairs of " opposites " in
his own head ; i.e., (1) Top and Bottom ; (2) Back and
Front ; (3) Right and Left ; (4) Inside and Outside. In
charity we refrain from explaining why we do not include
another pair, the qualitative " opposition " of Enlightened
and its " Other."

In the passage in question it is perfectly clear to anyone
not reading it with intent to find fault that what is being
discussed is *not* the proletariat as a *concrete* fact, or the
private property *owners* as such. What is under discussion
is the logical categorical relation involved in the existence
of private property—its *positive* pole (wealth) and its *negative*
pole (*not*-wealth, or Proletariat). What is being discussed is
not the objective proletariat, *as such*—but the *proletarian
status*. That a classical scholar (as Postgate is) should permit
himself to forget, even in anger, that the proletariat becomes
such not in virtue of its *numbers*, but in virtue of its *status*,
its relation to the State as a whole, is lamentable even to
tears. Worst of all is the " howler " of treating the *Holy
Family* as a work of popular exposition instead of—what it
was—a satirical polemic in which the authors were forced
continually to use the terminology of the men they were

satirising. The explanation is simple and thoroughly discreditable to Postgate. He has followed Eastman's lead blindly and without " checking up " on his citations. The very next sentences following after the extract given above would have warned him that Eastman had no case :

" When the proletariat becomes victorious it will not thereby in any way become society in its absolute aspect. It will be victorious only to the extent that it abolishes *both* itself and its opposite. Then private property will disappear both *in the form of* the proletariat and in that of *its conditioning opposite.*"—MARX-ENGELS : *The Holy Family.*

The sense in which the *categories* Proletariat and " Wealth " (*non*-proletarianism) are contraposed in a Hegelian unity of opposites is plain here beyond any misconception. Later in the same work Marx and Engels speak in their own names and language. They are rebutting the charge that they " idealise " the proletariat :

" We are not concerned therefore with what this or that proletarian—or what the proletariat as a whole may *regard* as its *aim.* What we are concerned with is that which the proletariat *is* ; with what in accordance with this its *own being* the proletariat will be compelled historically *to do.* In the life-situation of the proletariat and its relation to the totality of bourgeois social-organisation, the *goal,* and likewise the *historical initiative,* of the proletariat are made irrevocably manifest."—MARX-ENGELS : *Holy Family.*

This is from the standpoint of the *Theses on Feuerbach* one of the most pregnant sayings in the whole literature of Marxism. It is notable for its traces of the Hegelian dialectic conception of History as a *becoming-process* in which " Necessity," arising directly from the *nature* of Absolute Being *as such,* arrives ultimately, after passing through a series of phases of self-antagonism, at unity with itself in the form of self-conscious, and therefore self-determined or " Free," Being. But it is still more notable in its dialectical negation of the Hegelian conception—its casting aside of the Hegelian mysticism, which, try as Hegel would, still made " history " and the " world of Nature " mystic absolutes whose connection with empirical reality in both departments was so elusive and tenuous that even a philosopher set upon achieving synthetic unity could not help but create the impression that the world of actuality was after all—*only the ghost of itself !*

Most notable of all is it in that, in casting aside all this mystery, Marx and Engels in this passage formulated a concept of class-struggle which so transcended all previous concepts thereof that its full profundity and scope eluded the comprehension of all the *epigoni* of Marxism without exception. Not until LENIN did there appear a Marxist who grasped the full richness and practical significance of the concept that the proletarian class-struggle arises, *not* from the *statistical average* of all its individual empirical relations to *the bourgeoisie* (likewise as a quantitative aggregate with a *statistical average* direction and force), but from its objective, categorical dynamic relation to the *organisation* of bourgeois society *as such*. In this paragraph—though it may be granted that a whole accumulation of historical experience makes it easier to see this to-day than ever before—in this paragraph can be found already the germ of the concept *The Dictatorship of the Proletariat*.

Let us note, in passing, that this passage emphasises and contrasts the dialectical distinction between what the proletariat *is*, and is bound *ultimately to do*, and what the proletariat at any given moment *thinks* itself to be, and at that moment *wants* to do. This is an illuminating example of the proposition of the tenth *Thesis*—which contrasts the standpoint of the *old* (mechanical) and the *new* (dialectical) Materialism, as that between the individual in civil society and that of *socialised humanity*. The old materialism, like the " very latest " eclecticism, invariably seeks to explain society from the *individual* and find a personal, and a subjective, origin for class conflicts. Dialectical materialism, on the contrary, explains the *individual* and the *class* from Society as an *objective*, dialectically developing, historical *fact*. Its explanation of class-struggles therefore includes an elucidation of the fact in impact with which all the Postgates, Eastmans, and Uncle Tom Cobleys of bourgeoisdom and eclecticism " skid " ingloriously into the solipsist ditch—the fact of divergence (even formal antagonism) between the subjectivity of an individual and the historical tendency of his class. Of this more in detail later ; for the moment take an example :—

Plekhanov cited this very paragraph in the course of his polemic with Lenin, who had contended (see LENIN : *What is to be Done*) that the proletariat in mass cannot acquire a revolutionary Socialist *consciousness* unless their social circumstances include the *theoretical* (as well as the *practical*) activity of a revolutionary Socialist Party. Plekhanov, in this instance, took the view of the *mechanical* vulgarisers of Marxism—that economic forces would engender Socialist theory in the heads of the proletariat *spontaneously* :

"The disputed question consists in this : Does there exist an economic necessity which calls forth in the proletariat a *demand for Socialism,* makes it *instinctively* socialistic, and impels it, even if left to its own resources, on the road to the social-revolution ? . . . Lenin denies this. . . . And in that consists his enormous mistake, his theoretical fall into sin."—PLEKHANOV : article in *Iskra,* August 1st, 1904.

Plekhanov was, up to a point, a most competent Marxist. Beyond that point he fell as far below the average of the Marxist writers of his day as, at his best, he rises above them. In this case it is amazing to find him blundering upon the very elements of dialectical materialism. If the passage from the *Holy Family* be compared with Plekhanov's comment the difference is glaringly apparent.

The very distinction Marx and Engels draw between the " spontaneous " desires and the subjective illusions entertained by the individuals composing a class *at any given moment,* and what the class, *as such,* will be *in the end* forced to *do,* derives its significance and its force from the fact that it is *in society,* in practical as well as intellectual intercourse, with their fellow-members of society that the notions, whims, and impulses of *individual* men and women become dialectically transmuted into *Theories* (such as Socialism), " become material forces by taking hold of the masses." Moreover, the very " economic necessity " to which Plekhanov appeals makes itself manifest in effect upon the social inter-relations of men, and not (as the *mechanical* materialists suppose) *solely* by conditioning their *interests as individuals.* Plekhanov, in fact, in this argument relapsed from the " standpoint of associated humanity " to that of " the single individual in civil society." He abandoned *dialectics* for *metaphysics.*

Eastman, with his genius for making the darkness opaque, cites Plekhanov's argument. He first of all accepts Plekhanov's version as the true Marxian view, then takes it as axiomatic that Lenin was right in practice, and concludes by arguing triumphantly that Leninist practice reaches its acme of admirability when it is most completely divorced from Marxist theory ! And he doesn't even stop there ! One rupture between theory and practice will not satisfy a glutton like Eastman. Since Lenin in his special theorising always supposed himself (wrongly " of course " !) to be a Marxist, this illusion must be shattered and the *ultra*-revolutionary, *super*-Leninist (read " Trotskyist ") practice advocated by Eastman must be linked with the *infra*-revolutionary theory of " scientific psychology " and the " instrumentalist-fictionalist-behaviourist-pragmatist-solipsist-any-old-ist" epistemology now taught in the universities of God's own country, the U.S.A. ! If he had remembered it he would have quoted :

" Where Life becomes a Spasm
And History a Whiz :
If that is not Sensation !—
I don't know what it is."
—Lewis Carrol.

The " Asses' Bridge " of Marxism

The concept of class-struggle is the *pons asinorum* of Marxism—even more than the *Theory of Value*, since your intellectual can abandon hope of understanding the latter and still retain his " face." The concept of class-struggle, on the other hand, seems so simple and obvious that every critical amateur imagines that he can explain it out of hand. It is therefore highly important to note that Marx and Engels themselves only reached a full grasp of it *by degrees*, and in the course of polemic battles arising out of their direct participation in the practical Socialist and revolutionary-democratic struggles of their time. They were notably influenced by a series of fierce proletarian uprisings (Lyons, 1832 ; England, 1842 ; Silesia, 1845) which arose spontaneously outside the influence of any theoretical revolutionary promptings.

Engels had a first-hand experience of the effects of the strike wave (and " plug " riots) of 1842, which forced the hand of the Chartist leaders and from its own momentum became an attempt at a general strike to secure the Charter. Engels contributed to the *Franco-German Year Book* an essay, *Outlines of a Critique of Political Economy*, which Marx described as " a work of genius." In that essay Engels compared and contrasted the movements of bourgeois Economy and those of Nature. In bourgeois Economy a general parity of prices was reached by means of the " higgling " of the market—that is to say, through the compensating cancellations of a whole series of *dis*-parities. A general concordance between supply and demand was attained by means of a whole process of local and general discordancies

—crises of glut alternating with or compensating crises of artificial dearth. In all these Engels saw an analogy with —and at the same time a contrast to—the dialectic of Nature, in which " a general law becomes apparent only through a series of seeming accidents." Engels drew the revolutionary conclusion that the economists were all at sea. So far as economic facts were expressions of a law of objective Nature, they were not simple, mechanical extensions of that law, since mechanically " automatic " laws do not exist in Nature. On the other hand, neither was bourgeois economy the expression of human plan, foresight, and contrivance, since the general objective results reached were never those which had been subjectively intended or desired. The laws of economy were therefore objective laws, not of " Nature " (in the limited sense), but of Society—laws which the political economists did not and could not by means of their methods manage to understand.

In the year (1844) in which this appeared, Engels wrote his classic study of the *Condition of the Working-Class in England*. In this he convinced himself, and all who chose to read his work, that it had in England, at any rate, ceased to be possible to treat the wage-workers as merely a sub-division of the " Third Estate "—the great " Common " People. He takes definitely the side of the proletariat, and cites in support of his standpoint, first Carlyle's view that " Chartism and the revolutionary activity of the working men arose out of the misery in which they live," and then *The Times*, which had said :

> " War to the palaces : peace to the hovels—that is
> the battle-cry of terror which may come to resound
> throughout our country. Let the wealthy beware ! "—
> Quoted by ENGELS from *Times*, June, 1844.

In his concluding summary Engels estimates the probable outcome of the conditions he has described.

If England retains its manufacturing monopoly, the factories will grow and the proletariat will grow still faster. Crises will recur and in consequence of the " deepening ruin of the lower middle-class " the proletariat will, sooner or later, be able to take advantage of the crisis, "overthrow" the existing power and begin a revolution. He expected the Charter would be enacted along with the repeal of the Corn Laws in 1846–7. [He was right as to the latter, but premature as to the former.] This would not, however, check the revolutionary movement :

> " If . . . the English bourgeoisie does not pause to

reflect . . . a revolution will follow with which none hitherto known can be compared. The proletarians, driven to despair, will seize the torch which Stephens has preached to them ; the vengeance of the people will come down with a wrath of which the rage of 1793 gives no true idea. *The war of the poor against the rich will be the bloodiest ever waged.*"—ENGELS : *Condition of the Working-Class in England*, p. 296.

Even if a part of the bourgeoisie should unite with the proletariat to institute a general reform, it would not help matters. The " more determined " of the bourgeoisie would only form a new " Gironde " which would sooner or later be swept aside by a newer and more terrible Jacobinism :

" The revolution must come ; it is already too late to bring about a peaceful solution, but it can be made more gentle than that prophesied in the foregoing pages. *This depends more upon the development of the proletariat than upon that of the bourgeoisie.* In proportion as the prole-tariat absorbs Socialistic and Communist elements, will the revolution *diminish* in bloodshed, ravage and savagery.

" Communism stands, *in principle, above the breach* between bourgeoisie and proletariat, recognises its historic significance *only for the present,* but not its justification for the future ; wishes indeed to bridge over this chasm, to do away with all class antagonisms. Hence it recognises as justified so long as the struggle lasts the exasperation of the proletariat towards its oppressors—as a necessity, as the most important lever for a labour movement just beginning ; but it goes beyond this exasperation because Communism is *a question of humanity and not of the workers alone.* . . . English Socialism, i.e., Communism, rests directly upon the *irresponsibility of the individual.* Thus the more the English workers absorb Communist ideas, the more superfluous becomes their present bitterness. . . ."— ENGELS, *ibid*, p. 297.

The concluding argument in the last given quotation which separates carefully the standpoint of Communism from that of the workers—is interesting evidence of the fact that Engels was not at this period *fully* " Marxist."

Engels himself draws attention to the discrepancy in a preface written in 1892—three years before his death. His book, he says, " represents one of the phases of the embryonic development " of " Modern international Socialism " :

" and as the human embryo . . . reproduces the gill arches of our fish ancestors, so this book exhibits everywhere traces of the descent of modern Socialism from one of its ancestors—German philosophy. . . . The dictum that Communism is not a mere party doctrine of the working class, but a theory compassing the emancipation of Society at large, including the Capitalist class, from its present narrow conditions . . . is true enough in the abstract, *but absolutely useless and sometimes worse in practice.* So long as the wealthy classes not only do not feel the need of any emancipation, but strenuously oppose the self-emancipation of the working-class, *so long the social revolution will have to be prepared and fought out by the working class alone.*"—ENGELS : *Condition,* p.x.

No more complete vindication of the standpoint of Lenin against that of Plekhanov could be wished for than that here given.

.   .   .   .

Marx himself in his *Year-Book* article, above-quoted, was likewise still showing the " gill-arches " of his theoretical pedigree. He envisages the Revolution as produced by an alliance between philosophy and the proletariat. It is, however, philosophy with a *difference*—which makes it no " philosophy." Likewise it is the proletariat, not in the *abstract*, nor in its empirical, statistical aggregation. It is the proletariat *in motion*, and therefore in process of dialectical transmutation, the proletariat as embodied social potentiality, to which philosophy (i.e., theory) will supply awareness and understanding, converting it from the proletariat *as such* (" a large number of persons !") and the proletariat *for itself* (a simple reflex-relation to the bourgeoisie) into the proletariat *in-and-for-itself*, a self-willed force negating the bourgeois *negative status* of the proletariat and all therein implied and thereby becoming the dynamic starting-point for a new development in which neither " philosophy " nor the proletariat existed *in form*—while the positive *content* of both was carried over in synthetic union in the new departure :

" Philosophy cannot be realised without the liquidation of the proletariat : the proletariat cannot liquidate itself without realising philosophy."—MARX : *Year Book*.

The Hegelian " gill-arches " are still visible—but already Marx had reached the dialectical unity of theory and practice and the revolutionary significance thereof. That he and

Engels should have reached this conclusion, and their practical
identification with the standpoint of revolutionary proletarian struggle by the Hegelian road, and not by that of a
simple extension of eighteenth-century materialism is profoundly significant for *dialectics*.

The Bauers, and their fellow Hegelian - Humanitarian
" Materialists " had, for instance, poured satirical scorn upon
the crude " idealism " of the Utopian Socialists and Communists.   Marx and Engels retorted with a " right-cross-
counter and a left-hook to the short ribs."   In so far as they
had moved no further than to the standpoint of Feuerbach,
the Bauers, themselves, were the " crude idealists ! "   On
the other hand, the real content of Socialism and Communism
was *materialist*.

Feuerbach's standpoint, adopted by the Bauers, was that
of *abstract Man*.   As Engels expressed it, later :

> " Feuerbach . . . takes his start from Man.   But
> there is absolutely no mention of the world in which
> this man lives : hence this man always remains the same
> *abstract* man. . . .   This man is not even born of woman ;
> he issues as from a chrysalis from the God of Mono-
> theistic religions.   He therefore does not live in the *real*
> world, historically created and historically determined.
> It is true he has intercourse with other men, but each
> one of them is *just as much an abstraction as he is himself*."
> —ENGELS : *Feuerbach*, p. 46.

That which Engels here summarises succinctly was the
point made in the *Holy Family* with overwhelming pungency
against the whole of the " critical " strictures of the Bauers.
As to Utopian Communist " idealism," whatever might be
its theoretical deficiency, the practical content of the Communist theory was materialist enough :

> " No great acumen is required to perceive the necessary
> connection of Materialism with Communism and
> Socialism—from the doctrines of Materialism concerning
> the original goodness and equal intellectual endowment
> of man ; the omnipotence of experience, habit, and
> upbringing ; the influence of external circumstances on
> man, the great importance of industry, the justification
> of enjoyment, etc.   If man constructs all his knowledge,
> perception, etc., from the world of sense, then it follows
> that it is a question of so arranging the empirical world
> that he experiences the truly human in it, that he be-
> comes accustomed to *experiencing himself as a human being*.

" If enlightened self-interest is the principle of all morality, it follows that the private interests of men must be made to coincide with *human* interests. If man is unfree in the material sense—i.e., *free*, not by reason of the *negative* power to avoid this or that, but by reason of the *positive* power to assert his true individuality—then one should not punish individuals for crimes but rather destroy the anti-social breeding places of crime, and give every person social room for the necessary assertion of his or her vitality. *If man is formed by circumstances, then the circumstances must be formed humanly.* If man is social by nature, then he develops his true nature only in society ; hence the power of his nature must be measured not by the power of a single individual, but by the power of society.

" *One finds these and similar propositions, almost word for word, in the oldest of the French materialists.*"—MARX-ENGELS : *Holy Family*, 1845.

This was not only a complete answer to the charge of " idealism " levelled by the Critical Criticism against Communism. It was an unanswerable counter-attack which stripped the " materialist " veil from the essentially idealistic standpoint of the Bauers. Most notably of all, it contains a complete rebuttal of the charge most commonly brought against Marxism—the charge of fatalism. Here, already, in the work written next after the *Theses on Feuerbach*—a work which was to a large extent their amplification—Marx and Engels concretely applying the standpoint of the last four of those *Theses*, point out and *credit in principle to the older* (revolutionary bourgeois) *materialists* the doctrine that, given a maladjustment between Man and Circumstances, there was a revolutionary alternative to a conservative, fatalistic, adaptation of Man to the conditions. *The circumstances could be and should be altered to suit Man.*

It is not Marxism—it was not the revolutionary Materialists of the eighteenth century who evolved the doctrine—that Man has no alternative to abject submission to circumstances, though such a gloss might be read into the eighteenth-century doctrine in consequence of the mechanical one-sidedness of its theoretical basis. It was the post-Darwinian, *reactionary* bourgeois and petty-bourgeois philosophers who evolved the doctrine that there was nothing to do but submit. And when the " up-to-date " critics of Marx, in repudiating this latter doctrine, imagine that they are thereby refuting both Marx *and* Materialism, they do but give a measure of their eclectic shallowness and general theoretical incompetence.

Marx and Engels note categorically the historical derivation of Communist theory from Materialist doctrines :

"FOURIER proceeds directly from the doctrines of French [eighteenth-century] materialism. The followers of BABOEUF were crude, uncivilised, materialists. *But even developed Communism derives directly from French materialism.* French materialism, in the form which Helvetius had given it, returns to its native home, England. Upon the morality of Helvetius, Bentham founds his system of enlightened self-interest, just as Owen, proceeding from Bentham, gave a basis to English communism. . . . The more scientific French Communists . . . develop, like Owen, the teachings of materialism as the doctrine of real humanism and as the logical basis of Communism."—MARX-ENGELS : *ibid.* [see the Appendix, Martin Lawrence edition, ENGELS : *Feuerbach.*]

In short, despite their parade of enormous critical superiority, the Critical Critics had crashed at the first practical problem they had tackled. Communism was not to be condemned for identifying itself with the proletariat : on the contrary, it was to be condemned in so far as, like the Bauers, it held itself aloof from " mere " politics, aloof from mere class considerations, and posed itself " above the battle " as superior to all but " universal " considerations. It was only in alliance with the practical dialectic of the revolutionary proletarian struggle that Utopian Socialism and Communism was able to shed its mechanical-metaphysical shell and emerge re-born as the dialectical-materialist theory of the objectively concrete (and therefore " materialist ") and practically dialectic, proletarian revolutionary struggle.

The standpoint of Marxism—of the union of Communist theory and revolutionary proletarian practice—of the conscious and purposeful proletarian class struggle—was attacked from several other angles. The Bauers had denounced the profanation involved in making the critical-dialectic an instrument of partisan political warfare. KARL HEINZEN, a leading (bourgeois) democratic-republican, attacked Marx, Engels, and their revolutionary Communism as a source of disruption in the united front of " the People " against the *ancien regime.* He attacked Engels for " failing to see " that all the friction between the capitalist employers and their workpeople arose from the fact that capital was deprived of its rightful power of self-expansion and self-adjustment by the constraining and oppressive power of the State. Set property and persons free from this oppression, make the State truly "political"—i.e. truly representative of the People as a whole—and all would be well. Heinzen was quite ready to agree to a law fixing maximum and minimum limits to the property any one individual was permitted by law to possess; but within those limits property should be, as men should be, "free." "I cannot imagine," he exclaims, "why Mr. Engels and the Communists are so blind as not to see that Force [i.e., of the State] also dominates property, and that the injustice in the property relations is only maintained by force. I call that person a fool and a coward who cherishes animosity towards a bourgeois because he is accumulating money, while leaving in peace a King who has accumulated power."

Marx replied to Heinzen in the *Vorwärts*, a journal published in Paris, after the failure of the *Year Book* (which never got beyond its first double issue). Marx, Engels, and Heine all contributed to *Vorwärts*, but withdrew their support when they found it was being conducted for no other purpose than that of getting German refugees in Paris to compromise themselves in the eyes of the Prussian Government. In his polemic against Heinzen, Marx demonstrated that here again "bluff commonsense" Humanitarianism, which could sing no other song in opposition to Communism than "Liberty (of Property), Equality (of all before the Law), and Fraternity (between Capital and Labour)" was simply a demand for the unqualified rule of the bourgeoisie:

> "It is typical of bluff commonsense that, where it manages to see differences, it does not see their unity; and where it sees unity it does not see difference. If it chances to note distinguishing qualities, it immediately petrifies them [into an *absolute* opposition]. . . . In stating that money and force, property and rule, money-making and power-acquiring are not the same, it is merely uttering a tautology."—MARX: *Vorwärts*, 1844.

> "'Force also dominates property' means only that property has not yet got political power into its own hands—on the contrary, is exasperated by arbitrary taxation, confiscation, privileges, the disturbing interference of the bureaucracy in industry and trade and the like. . . ."—MARX, *ibid.*

Since Capital is defined by the economists as " the command over labour," it is obvious that two sorts of power were in question : the economic power of the property owner and the political power of the State.

" In countries where the bourgeoisie has already conquered political power and where political rule is therefore nothing but the rule, not of individual bourgeois over their workers, but of the bourgeois class over the whole of society, Mr. Heinzen's dictum has lost its meaning. The propertyless are, of course, not affected by political rule so far as it relates directly to property."— MARX, *ibid.*

Again, it is fallacious to argue that the " injustice in the property relations " was " maintained solely by force." If Heinzen means only the " injustice " the bourgeoisie suffer he merely repeats what he has already said—that the bourgeoisie (in Germany) had not yet attained political power. If, on the other hand, he means the injustice complained of by the proletariat, then, since these property relations are " maintained " by the State power, in every place where the bourgeoisie rules and has organised this State power for the protection of its property and its relations :—

" The proletariat must overthrow the political power where it is concentrated in the hands of the bourgeoisie. They must themselves attain to power, to revolutionary power."—MARX, *ibid.*

Thus Heinzen had " only repeated unconsciously what Engels has said, and in the sincere conviction that he was saying the opposite. What he says he does not mean : what he means, he does not say ! " (MARX).

The delusion from which Heinzen suffered—that " force " in the shape of the State and its political power was the initiating cause and creator of the social relations " maintained " by it, is perennial to all bourgeois political thinking. At one pole it is found in the form of Die-Hard Toryism with its ceaseless clamour for the repression of " seditious," " blasphemous," and other doctrines " subversive " of the State ; at the other pole it is found in Anarchism with its demand that the State and its political power shall be abolished out of hand. Both views, and all the intervening shades of opinion which link them, fail utterly to see the concrete historical fact that :

" The ' injustice in the property relations,' conditioned as it is by the modern division of labour, the modern form of exchange, competition, concentration, etc., etc., does not in any way proceed from the political rule of the bourgeoisie. On the contrary, it is from these modern relations of production, which are proclaimed by bourgeois economists as eternal, necessary, laws, that the rule of the bourgeoisie proceeds."—MARX, *ibid.*

And this is so much the case that, if by any chance the proletariat should overthrow the political rule of the bourgeoisie before the material conditions necessitating that overthrow have been created in the course of historical development, then, in that event, the victory of the proletariat would be only temporary. It was for this reason that the Reign of Terror in the French Revolution, though it was, while it lasted, a rule imposed upon the bourgeoisie by the petty-bourgeoisie and proletariat in alliance, none the less did the work of the bourgeoisie in clearing away the last relics of feudalism from French soil by its hammer blows ; and did it better than the bourgeoisie would have done it :

" The timid and calculating bourgeoisie would have taken decades to carry out this task. The bloody action of the people thus cleared the way. Likewise the popular overthrow of the absolute monarchy would have been a mere affair of the moment had it not been for the fact that the economic prerequisites for the rule of the bourgeoisie had developed to the point of ripeness."—MARX, *ibid.*

In that spirit the Communists were rousing the workers to take an independent part in *the bourgeois revolution* then impending in Germany, not because they had any illusions about the bourgeoisie and its " eternal truths," but because they had no illusion about them :

" The workers know that . . . in the interests of its industry and commerce the bourgeoisie, even against its own will, must create the conditions for the unity of the workers, and the unity of the workers is the primary prerequisite of their victory. The workers know that the abolition of bourgeois property relations is not to be brought about by the maintenance of feudal property relations. . . . They can and must take part in the bourgeois revolution but as a preliminary condition for their own proletarian revolution. Not for a moment will they regard it as their goal."—MARX : *ibid.*

Heinzen and his fellow-republicans were, however, under an illusion with regard to the absolute Monarchy and its " force."

They supposed that princedom was the source of German society ; the truth is that German society was the source of princedom. Where in the case of property and its " injustices " Heinzen saw only the *difference* between property and the State power, in the case of the Communists and their concern for the " Social question " Heinzen saw only the unity of social and political questions—therefore " there is no more important question than that of monarchy versus republic." But, says Marx, while " the political relations of men are *also* social relations, since they are relations which bind man to man in society," at the same time social questions are political questions, but from a different angle :

> " The ' social questions ' which have been ' discussed in our time ' increase in importance in the degree that we emerge from the realm of absolute monarchy. Socialism and Communism did not originate in Germany, but in England, France, and North America. The first appearance of a really active communist party may be placed within the period of the bourgeois revolution, at the moment when constitutional monarchy *was abolished*. The most consistent republicans, the Levellers in England, Baboeuf, Buonarotti, etc., in France, were the first to proclaim these social questions. The *Conspiracy of Baboeuf*, written by his friend and comrade Buonarotti, shows how these republicans derived their social insight from the ' historical movement.' It also demonstrates that when the ' social question ' of Princedom versus Republic has been cleared away not a single social question of the kind that interests the proletariat has been solved."—MARX : *ibid.*

Moreover, the " social question," which is, in fact, the " property question," does not exist in the form in which the Heinzens envisage it, as a question of abstract right. It assumes different concrete forms at different stages of development, of industry in general, and of each country in particular :

> " The property question, which in ' our time ' is a world-historical question, has a meaning only in modern bourgeois society. The more developed this society is, the more therefore the bourgeoisie develops itself economically in a country, and the more, in consequence, that the State power has assumed a bourgeois expression, the more acutely does the property question obtrude itself—in France more acutely than in Germany, in

England more acutely than in France, in the constitutional monarchy more acutely than in the absolute monarchy, in the Republic more acutely than in the constitutional monarchy."—MARX : *ibid.*

Heinzen's " bluff common sense " was at fault at every point. It declared itself opposed to monarchy—but it could not explain how anything so opposed to common sense could have come into being, still less could have lasted so long. All it could offer as an explanation was that for centuries " bluff common sense and moral dignity " were, somehow, non-existent. Which is a left-handed way of admitting that for centuries the institutions of princedom corresponded to sense and morality instead of, as now, contradicting them :

> " In the same way that ' healthy common sense ' explains the rise and continuance of princedom as the work of unreason, so also religious ' healthy common sense ' explains heresy and unbelief as the work of the devil ; while irreligious ' healthy common sense ' explains religion, likewise, as the work of the *devil*—the parsons."—MARX : *ibid.*

Heinzen, with his " healthy common sense," was indignant at the " Communist narrow-mindedness which divides men into classes, or contraposes them according to their handicraft." He " left room for the ' possibility ' that ' humanity ' is not always determined by ' class ' or by the ' length of one's purse.' " To which Marx retorts :

> " Bluff common sense transforms class distinctions into ' length of purse,' and class antagonism into trade quarrels. The length of the purse is a purely quantitative distinction which may happen to antagonise two individuals of the same class. That the mediæval guilds quarrelled on the basis of handicraft is known. But equally well known is the fact that modern class distinctions are by no means based upon handicraft ; rather the division of labour produces widely differing modes of work within one and the same class.

> " Again, it is ' possible ' that particular individuals are not always influenced in their attitude by the class to which they belong. But this has as little effect upon the struggle between classes as the secession of a few nobles to the Third Estate had upon the French revolution. And, also, the nobles did at least join *a class*—the revolutionary class, the bourgeoisie. Mr. Heinzen, on

the other hand, sees all classes melt away before the solemn idea of ' Humanity.' "—MARX : *ibid.*

Heinzen's view, his championship of the " party of humanity," which refused to draw distinctions between bourgeoisie and proletariat, turns out after all to be a mere championing of the interests of the bourgeoisie under the name of " Humanity." His objection to the Communists, who saw *in addition to* the distinction between princes and subjects that also between classes, was the exact counterpart of the official attitude of the bourgeoisie wherever it had gained political power :

> " After the July Revolution [France, 1830] the victorious bourgeoisie (probably influenced by ' humanity ' !) made ' the incitement of class against class ' a crime, liable to punishment with fine and imprisonment. . . . English bourgeois newspapers could not denounce Chartist leaders and writers more effectively than by the reproach of ' setting class against class.' . . . In consequence of ' inciting class against class ' German writers are incarcerated in fortresses.   Mr. Heinzen talks the language of the French laws, the English bourgeois newspapers, and the German penal code."— MARX : *ibid.*

.   .   .   .   .

The concept of class-struggle, and the practical application thereof in the union of Communist theory with revolutionary proletarian practice—this deduction from the tenth *Thesis on Feuerbach*—involved Marx in two other polemics : with his one-time associate ARNOLD RUGE (whom Heine called the " grim doorkeeper of the Hegelian school "), and with PROUDHON.

The polemic against Ruge also appeared in *Vorwärts* and was occasioned by the revolt of the Silesian weavers in the summer of 1844.   The textile workers in this part of Silesia had for long suffered a number of grievances.   In addition to a fraudulent truck-system, and iniquitous robberies under the name of fines, etc., savage floggings and even hangings had been inflicted by the local State authorities on recalcitrant workers who had been provoked into personal assaults on factory bosses and foremen.   One of the workers, whose name is unknown, wrote a ballad in which the grievances of the weavers are voiced and the worst of the mill bosses pilloried by name.   A few stanzas will indicate its quality :

" You think potatoes for the poor
　　Suffice, while every glutton
Amongst you daily sits at your
　　Repast of beef or mutton.

The weaver bears his web to you,
　　You scrutinise it nearly,
And if there be one thread askew
　　You make him pay it dearly.

For half the sum of his poor wage
　　Pops back into your purses,
And if he murmur—in a rage,
　　You drive him forth with curses.

The wealth for which you damn your souls
　　Grim death from you will sever :
'Twill melt like fat upon the coals
　　Where you will roast for ever."

THE BLOODY ASSIZES : *Song of the Silesian Weavers*, 1844.

For singing this ballad inadvertently under the windows of one of the worst of the factory-lords, a street singer was seized and flung into the lock-up with threats of dire punishment to follow. An indignant crowd of weavers first rescued the ballad singer and then wrecked the police office—scattering the police to the winds in the process. Fully roused and mustered in strength, they proceeded to " make a job of it." Mill after mill was stormed. When the factory bosses or foremen could be caught, they were given a dose of their own medicine—a public flogging. The account books containing the record of the workers' alleged " indebtedness " for fines and truck were routed out and destroyed. In the cases of worse offenders the whole of their ledgers were burnt—" just to *learn* 'em." In the worst cases of all the whole mill was destroyed—first smashed in detail and then fired. The weavers meant, quite seriously, that, whatever else happened, *these* factory lords should be driven out of business. To make sure of this they went on to loot and destroy the banks, being careful to burn every ledger and security in the safes.

The revolt was general throughout the whole weaving district of Silesia. Troops were hurried up to crush it. After fierce fighting, in which the troops were more than once repulsed, the revolt was crushed. Executions and floggings followed, capped by a proclamation from the King of Prussia, in which the weavers were warned against evil courses and employers and employed were exhorted to show more Christian charity in their dealings with each other. A fund was opened for the relief of distress.

All this Arnold Ruge treated as a mere incident. It proved for Ruge only that the King of Prussia was a pious humbug and that poverty and distress, culminating in crime, could be cured only when the State had become " truly *political* " (i.e., bourgeois republican), and had carried out its programme of Reform. Meanwhile the incident proved that the King had no fears of, or reason to fear consequences from, the riotousness of a few weak weavers whom a couple of regiments were able to subdue.

The actual, practical, fact of workers' revolt and revolution is the acid test of every political theory. For Ruge the workers' revolt signified only that a few social reforms were needed—chiefly the removal of the feudal-absolutist régime and the setting up of a bourgeois republic. For Marx it meant something quite different. It signified that already, *before* the bourgeoisie had accomplished its revolution, the force was ripening which would *overthrow the bourgeois regime in its turn.* Ruge, it will be observed, argued exactly as the Mensheviks were later to argue in 1905 and (with the support of Karl Kautsky) 1917. *Marx argued as, later, Lenin argued.*

Marx argues in his article in *Vorwärts* thus (Ruge had written under the pseudonym, " A Prussian ") :

" The so-called Prussian [Ruge was, in fact, a Pomeranian] denies that the King's ' fears ' have any reality on the ground, among others, that a few soldiers sufficed to settle accounts with the weavers.

" It seems then, that, in a country where the longing of the entire liberal bourgeoisie for a free press and a liberal constitution—which longing was to be expressed at a festival with liberal toasts and liberal champagne froth—where all this was suppressed without the use of a single soldier by a simple Royal Cabinet Decree ;—in a country where the accepted order of the day is passive obedience ;—in such a country, then, the need to use armed force to crush " weak " weavers is an event of no moment, and nothing at all startling ?

" And, moreover, at the first encounter with the troops the weavers triumphed ! Only when the troops had been reinforced were they suppressed !

" Is the revolt of a mass of workers not " dangerous "
only because a whole army corps was not needed to
suppress it ? If the wise Prussian compares the revolt of
the Silesian weavers with the English workers' revolts,
the former will appear to him as distinctly *strong* weavers."
—MARX : Article on "*The King of Prussia and Social
Reform* " *Vorwärts*, Paris, 1844.

Marx analyses Ruge's suggestions as to the " reforms "
which the King of Prussia should have instituted. These
would have to wait until the liberal bourgeoisie were in
control of the State, but, said Ruge, they would then be
instituted and would put an end to grievances.

The grievance of the Silesian weavers, says Marx in reply,
is their condition of " pauperism "—the fact that they cannot
live on their unsupplemented wages. This *pauperism*, far
from being incompatible with a bourgeois régime, is one of
its fundamental requirements. For proof, Marx cites :
first the experience of England when pauperism on a large
scale appeared as one of the first results of the first (partial)
establishment of the bourgeois order after the Reformation.
He notes that the Poor Law of Queen Elizabeth—which treats
pauperism (*alias* " vagabondage ") as a *crime*—remained the
basis of English governmental policy down to 1834, and
despite " amending " Acts remained so in principle thereafter, *as it still does*, in a more hypocritical form.

With the experience of England is compared that of France
under the National Convention and under Napoleon. In
each case the attempt was made to abolish pauperism by
administrative measures : in each case the result was that
organised State " benevolence " became in fact a punitive
measure directed against the paupers as guilty of an offence
against the public. The " alms-house " of private benevolence
became the " poor-house," the " workhouse," which the
Chartists quite rightly regarded and treated as " *the Bastille
of the poor.*"

Malthus summed up the experience of the bourgeois order
in his Theory of Population :

" ' As the population unceasingly tends to overstep
the means of subsistence, benevolence is folly, *a public
encouragement to poverty*. The State can do nothing in
the face of this natural law but leave poverty to its fate.
At best it can make death easier for the poor ! '

" With this amiable theory the English Parliament
combines the opinion that pauperism is the sort of

poverty for which the worker himself is responsible, and which therefore must not be regarded as a misfortune but, rather, suppressed and punished as a crime.

" Thus arose the workhouse system . . . whose internal arrangements deter the poverty-stricken from seeking refuge from starvation. *In the workhouse are ingeniously combined benevolence and the revenge of the bourgeoisie upon such of the poor as appeal to its benevolence.*"—MARX : *ibid.*

England, says Marx, (1) first attempted to destroy pauperism by benevolence and administrative measures ; (2) then attributed the progressive increase in pauperism, not to the growth of modern industry, but to its own Poor Law ; (3) then, finally, after attempts in reforming the administration of public benevolence had failed to check the growth of pauperism, treated it as the fault of the poor, and punished it accordingly.

Nearly a century later we can read Marx's argument and marvel at his foresight. The treatment of the typically modern form of pauperism, mass unemployment, has followed historically exactly the same line. First, in the period 1885–1905, an attempt was made to destroy it by " benevolence and administrative measures " (Lord Mayor's Funds, Salvation Army and Church Army work depots and " Farm Colonies," and Labour Exchanges). Then an attempt was made to cure the defects of this system by the *organised State benevolence* of the Unemployment Insurance Acts and their careful administration. Finally, as the numbers of the unemployed continued to grow, an outcry was raised against " the dole " as the *cause* of unemployment, against the unemployed as " professional dole-drawers," against the " demoralisation of Poplarism," etc. And in consequence came the Means Test, and now the proposal for Concentration Camps in which the unemployed are to be " made employable." Hear Marx again :

" The general significance attained by pauperism in England consists precisely in the fact that *in spite of all administrative measures*, pauperism [read " unemployment] has, in the course of development, *grown into a national institution.* It has therefore become, inevitably, the subject of an extensive and ramified administration ; which administration, however, *no longer aims at extinguishing it, but only at disciplining it in perpetuity.* . . . Instead of going beyond administrative and charitable measures, the English State has *actually gone back to them*. It confines itself to " administering " that pauperism [unemployment] which is so desparing as to permit itself to be *captured and put under restraint*."—MARX, *ibid*.

Ruge's approach to the problem revealed yet one more example of the incurable insufficiency of theory divorced from practice—of the attempt to attain practical solutions from the point of view of the abstract individual by means of abstract notions of the State, rights, property, and all the rest of it. Accepting the illusory appearance of social relations—the deceptive appearance they were bound to assume when viewed from that individual standpoint—as objective *reality* Ruge fell into the mysticism and confusion of his whole school. Where a transformation of the objective relations of men in society was needed, Ruge proposed a transformation of the subjective attitude to those relations of the State on the one side and the workers on the other. All, of course, in the interests of humanity, harmony, and reform. Marx brings him back to earth :

" The State will never find the cause of social wrong in the ' State ' and ' the institutions of Society ' as ' Prussian ' requires of his King. Where there are political parties, each finds the cause of every evil in the fact that its opponent, instead of itself, is at the head of the State. Even the radical and revolutionary politicians seek the cause of the evil not in the *essence* of the State, but in a specific form of the State which they aim at replacing by another State form. . . .

" So far as the State recognises social evils, it attributes them either to natural laws which are amenable to no human powers, or to the defects of private life independent of the State, or to the futility of the administration which is dependent upon itself. Thus England finds poverty to be grounded in the natural law, according to which the population is always bound to overstep the means of subsistence. On another side, it explains pauperism from the sinful disposition of the poor, just as the King of Prussia explained it from the unchristian sentiments of the rich, and just as the Convention explained it from the suspicious, counter-revolutionary intrigues of the property owners. England therefore punishes the poor, the King of Prussia exhorts the rich, and the Convention decapitates the property owners."
—MARX, *ibid*.

Finally, in reply to all Ruge's strictures upon the " narrow-ness " of the Communists and their lack of " political soul "— (i.e., lack of concern for *absolute*, " universal " principles of government) :—

> " The workers in Lyons [1832] believed they were pursuing purely " political " aims and were only soldiers of the Republic, whereas they were, in truth, soldiers of Socialism. Their ' political understanding ' [in Ruge's sense] hid from them the roots of social distress . . . their ' political understanding ' deceived their social instinct. . . . However partial an industrial revolt may be [as in Silesia, 1844] it conceals within itself a *universal* soul ; ' political ' revolt may be never so universal but it hides a narrow-minded spirit under this universal form. . . .
>
> " Every revolution disowns the old society : in so far it is *social*. Every revolution overthrows the old power : in so far it is *political*. . . . The revolution as such—the overthrow of the existing power and the dissolution of the old conditions—is a *political* act. But without a revolution Socialism cannot be enforced. It requires this political act so far as it has need of the process of destruction and dissolution. But where its organising activity begins, where its proper aim, its " soul," emerges, then Socialism casts away its political shell."—Marx, *ibid.*

The Positive Outcome of Class Struggle

Arnold Ruge remained a republican democrat, cultivating in the depths of his " political soul " a philosophical contempt for *mere* politicians on the one hand, and *mere* Socialists and Communists on the other. But contemporary with him, and like him taking their rise from Feuerbach's Humanitarianism, were the " German or True Socialists," who are dealt with scathingly in the *Communist Manifesto*. Like Ruge, they distinguished sharply between the " social " and the " po-litical " movements ; but in the inverse sense. They opposed the Social movement to the political movement not in the relative, dialectical sense in which Marx contrasted them, conscious both of their unity *and* their opposition—but in Ruge's manner, starkly and absolutely. Hence they on the one side opposed all political movements for anything other than " Socialism," and on the other opposed the revolutionary proletarian Communism adhered to by Marx on the score of its " narrow one-sidedness " :

" French Socialist and Communist literature was completely emasculated. Since it ceased in the hands of the German [philosopher] to express the struggle of one class with the other he felt conscious of having overcome ' French one-sidedness ' and of representing not true requirements but the requirements of Truth ; not the interests of the proletariat but the interests of Human Nature, of Man-in-General, who belongs to no class, has no reality—exists only in the misty realm of philosophical phantasy."—MARX-ENGELS : *Communist Manifesto,* p. 32.

Practice revealed that this lofty exaltation above " narrowness " and prejudice was far from being as innocent as it seemed :

" The fight of the German . . . bourgeoisie against feudal aristocracy and absolute monarchy, in other words, the liberal movement, became more earnest.

" By this, the long-wished-for opportunity was offered to ' True ' Socialism of confronting the political movement with the Socialist demands, of hurling the traditional anathemas against liberalism, against representative government, against bourgeois competition, bourgeois freedom of the press, bourgeois legislation, bourgeois liberty and equality, and of preaching to the masses that they had nothing to gain from and everything to lose by, this bourgeois movement. German socialism forgot in the nick of time that the French criticism [i.e., of these *bourgeois* things], whose silly echo it was, presupposed the existence of modern bourgeois society, with its corresponding economic conditions of existence, and the political constitution adapted thereto, the very things whose attainment was the object of the pending struggle in Germany.

" To the absolute governments, with their following of parsons, professors, country squires, and officials, it served as a welcome scarecrow against the threatening bourgeoisie.

" This was a sweet finish after the bitter pills of floggings and bullets, with which those same governments, just at that time, dosed the German working-class risings."—MARX-ENGELS : *Com. Man.,* pp. 32–33.

The intense feeling packed into these scathing words has its roots in the passionate struggles of the time, and the anticipation of still more intense struggles to come. It is

M

impossible to read these words to-day without seeing that the
tribe of those who in 1840–48 made up the body of " German
or True Socialism " has far indeed from faded from the
earth.   As Marx and Engels were denounced as " wreckers "
and " impossibilists " from one side—that of Heinzen and
Ruge—so simultaneously they were denounced as " com-
promisers " and " one-sided moderates " from the other—
that of the " True " Socialism.   A like fate befel Lenin, and
has likewise befallen Stalin.   And in every case the " True "
Socialists, the Mensheviks and their Social-Democratic allies,
and the Trotskyites, have proved in practice to be the objective tools of Reaction, " welcome scarecrows " aiding Reaction
in its struggle against the rising tide of Revolution.

The enervating poison of " True " Socialism was not
confined within the frontiers of Germany.   In France the
tendency at whose head stood Proudhon counted in an
equivalent sense.   It encouraged the proletariat to struggle,
but *not as a class* ; it used the same abstract distinction,
that between the social and the political movements, and like it
opposed the social *to* the political movement.   This tendency :—

> " . . . sought to depreciate every revolutionary move-
> ment in the eyes of the working class, by showing that
> no mere political reform, but only a change in the
> material conditions of existence, in economical relations,
> could be of any advantage to them.   By changes in the
> material conditions of existence, this form of Socialism,
> however, by no means understands abolition of the
> bourgeois relations of production, *an abolition that can
> be effected only by a revolution*, but administrative reforms
> based on the continued existence of these relations ;
> reforms therefore that in no respect affect the relations
> between capital and labour, but, at the best, lessen the
> cost, and simplify the administrative work of bourgeois
> government."—MARX-ENGELS : *Com. Man.*, pp. 34–35.

Against this Proudhonian tendency Marx delivered a
shattering blow in his *Poverty of Philosophy*, which remains
a classic example of Marx's dialectical method, and one all
the more valuable in that Proudhon, in the work which Marx
subjected to a systematic analysis, had used what he imagined
to be the Hegelian method.   Owing to the point-by-point
manner in which Marx develops his critique it is more convenient to quote from the preliminary summary of Proudhon's
method Marx made in a letter to P. V. Annenkov (December
28th, 1846) :

" Why does M. Proudhon talk about God, about universal reason, about the impersonal reason of humanity which never errs, which remains the same throughout all the ages and of which one need only have the right consciousness in order to know truth ? Why does he produce feeble Hegelianism to give himself the appearance of a bold thinker ?

" He himself provides you with the clue to this enigma. M. Proudhon sees in history a certain series of social developments ; he finds progress realised in history ; finally he discovers that men, as individuals, did not know what they were doing and were mistaken about their own movement ; that is to say their social development seems at first glance to be distinct, separate, and independent from their individual development. He cannot explain these facts, and in a moment the hypothesis of the universal reason revealing itself is produced. Nothing is easier than to invent mystical causes, that is to say, phrases which lack common sense."—MARX to Annenkov, December 28th, 1846.

" What is society, whatever its form may be ? *The product of men's reciprocal activity.* Are men free to choose this or that form of society for themselves ? By no means. Assume a particular state of development in the productive forces of man and you will get a particular form of commerce and consumption. Assume particular stages of development in production, commerce, and consumption and you will have a corresponding social order, a corresponding organisation of the family and of the ranks and classes, in a word a corresponding civil society. Presuppose a particular civil society and you will get particular political conditions which are only the official expression of civil society. M. Proudhon will never understand this because he thinks he is doing something great in appealing from the State to society— that is to say from the official summary of society to official society.—MARX : *ibid.*

The specific parody of the " dialectic " used by Proudhon is worth notice, and is summarised by Marx thus :

" To throw light on [Proudhon's] system of antagonism let us take an example. *Monopoly* is a good thing, because (!) it is an economic category, and therefore an emanation of God. *Competition* is a good thing because it is also an economic category. But what is not good is the *reality* of monopoly and the *reality* of competition. What is still worse is the fact that competition and monopoly devour each other. What is to be done ? As these two eternal ideas of God contradict each other, it seems obvious to him that there is also a synthesis of them both within the heart of God, in which the evils of monopoly are balanced by competition and *vice versa*. As a result of the struggle between the two ideas only the good side will come into view. One must extract this secret idea from God and then apply it, and everything will be for the best. . . ."—MARX : *ibid.*

" Now I will give you an example of Proudhon's dialectic. *Freedom* and *slavery* constitute an antagonism. I need not speak of the good and bad sides of Freedom, nor of the bad side of slavery. The only thing to be explained is the good side of slavery. We are not dealing with indirect slavery, the slavery of the proletariat, but with direct slavery, the slavery of the black races in Surinam, in Brazil, in the Southern States of N. America.

" Direct slavery is as much the pivot of our industrialism to-day as machinery, credit, etc. Without slavery no cotton ; without cotton no modern industry. . . . Slavery is thus an economic category of the highest importance. Without slavery North America, the most progressive country, would be transformed into a patriarchal land. You have only to wipe North America off the map of nations and you get anarchy, the total decay of trade, and of modern civilisation. . . . After these observations what will be M. Proudhon's attitude towards slavery ? He will look for the synthesis between freedom and slavery, the golden mean of equilibrium between slavery and freedom.—MARX : *ibid.*

Such being the method of Proudhon, it was inevitable that he should oppose strikes and revolutionary political proletarian movements—the *actual waging* of class struggle as distinct from sentimentalising about its *idea*—and oppose them as " one-sided." Which draws from Marx the crushing retort :

" Every economic relation has its good and bad side : that is the single point upon which M. Proudhon does not contradict himself. The good side he sees explained by the economists ; the bad side he sees denounced by the Socialists. He borrows from the economists the necessity of eternal relations ; he borrows from the Socialists the illusion of seeing in poverty *only* poverty. He is in agreement with both in wishing to refer the matter to the authority of science. Science is for him reduced to the insignificant proportions of a scientific formula. It is thus that M. Proudhon flatters himself to have made a criticism of both political economy and of communism. He is below both the one and the other. Below the economists since as a philosopher who has under his hand a magic formula he believes himself able to do without entering into purely economic details ; below the Socialists since he has neither sufficient courage nor sufficient intelligence to raise himself, were it only speculatively, above the bourgeois horizon.

" He wished to be the synthesis : he is a composite error. He wished to soar as man of science above the bourgeoisie and the proletarians ; he is only the petty-bourgeois tossed about continually between capital and labour, between political economy and communism."— MARX : *Poverty of Philosophy*, Chap. II, sec. 1.

At the end of his *Poverty of Philosophy* Marx, having disposed of Proudhon, summed up his own position :

" Do not say that the social movement excludes the political movement. There never has been a political movement which was not at the same time social. It is only in an order of things in which there will be no longer classes or class antagonisms that *social evolutions* will cease to be *political revolutions*. Until then, on the eve of each general reconstruction of Society, the last word of Social science will be :

" Combat or death : bloody struggle or extinction ; Thus always the question is irresistibly put."

—MARX : *Poverty of Philosophy*, Chap. II, sec. 5.

Within a year of this the *Communist Manifesto* had been written and Marxism had passed from its critical-negative phase into its positively affirmative one. The two phases are connected by and conjoined in a developed world-conception to whose consideration we must now proceed.

CHAPTER V

THE DIALECTICS OF NATURE AND HISTORY

USING the *Theses on Feuerbach* as our point of departure, we have now completed a rough preliminary survey of the world-outlook and method from which Marxism arose. It is already becoming clear that neither of these can be understood apart from the other : the method is revealed in the outlook, and the outlook is implicit in the method. This unity-in-opposition is fundamental to the *dialectical* method, which derives its special distinguishing significance from the fact that—more radically and consistently than is possible by any other method—it develops the full implications of the philosophical postulate of the " identity " of Being and Thinking. A brief recapitulation will make it easier to pass to the next stage.

THE UNITY OF BEING AND THINKING

What does " identity " mean here ? That *Thinking* is the " same thing " as *existing* ? Saying this is, in the first place, the pitfall of Berkleyian solipsism ; in the second place, it is the grave (self-dug) of a whole school of pseudo-" Marxists "—the neo-Dietzgenian " Monists," of whom more later. . . .

It involves a fallacy which was exposed with subtlety and sufficiency at a classic tea-party :

" ' Then you should say what you mean,' the March Hare went on.

" ' I do,' Alice hastily replied ; ' at least—at least I mean what I say—that's the same thing, you know.'

" ' Not the same thing a bit ! ' said the Hatter. ' You might just as well say that " I see what I eat " is the same thing as " I eat what I see " ! '

" ' You might just as well say,' added the March Hare, ' that " I like what I get " is the same thing as " I get what I like " ! '

" ' You might just as well say,' added the Dormouse, who seemed to be talking in his sleep, ' that " I breathe when I sleep " is the same thing as " I sleep when I breathe " ! '

182

" ' It *is* the same thing with you,' said the Hatter. And here the conversation dropped."—LEWIS CARROLL : *Alice in Wonderland*, Chap. VII.

Thinking is an act performed by a human being, who must exist before he can think (" *Cogito, ergo sum* "—DESCARTES). All thinking implies existing—all existing does not imply thinking. Existing is presupposed in thinking : thinking is not presupposed in the fact of " Existing." Not *necessarily*. So far Thinking and Being are *different*. And when Thinking is distinguished *from* Being it is so far, and in that respect, placed *in opposition to* Being. But the opposition is not *absolute* : it is one of *relation*. Thinking and Being are *connected* in the very act of opposing the one concept to the other. Thinking is the act of an existing being who is endeavouring in his thought to reach a reliable conception (mind picture) of Being in one or other of its specific forms. Thought *as such*—the product of thinking as distinguished from the act of thinking—is the *reflection* of Being : Being is that which is reflected. Thus in their very opposition they are " identified " the one with the other as a mirror-image is " identified " with *that* of which it is the image or reflection.

The unity of Being and Thinking is therefore a union of interdependent opposites in which Being is the primary and originating, and Thinking the secondary and *derived*. Thinking can be treated as a *form of being*, as an activity of an existing being—as the means by which this being arrives at an *understanding* of the relations between himself and *the rest* of Being. Being, as such, *cannot* be treated as a form of Thinking—without confounding the objective fact of Being with the subjective *concept* " Being."

From this primary Materialist affirmation—of the *reality* of Objective Being, and of the *derived* and *reflex* nature of thinking, feeling, and willing—we pass to its second affirmation, the *unity* of the " opposites " *Theory* and *Practice*.

Thinking is an *activity* : to think is *to act*. The object, implicit or explicit, of this activity is to gain *knowledge*. What is knowledge ? A provisional definition—which is not so much a definition as a description—is : Knowledge is the consciousness of relations—objective and subjective ;—consciousness of the relations between ourselves as living human beings and the external universe, of the relations between the general and particular details in that external universe, and of the relations between the perceptions and conceptions (with all their concomitant subjective states) in which and by means of which we become *aware of existence*—alike that of ourselves and of the external universe. It is in our perceptions and conceptions that we become aware (" conscious ") of the simultaneous *likeness* and *difference* between ourselves and the external world. To be able to reproduce in a mind-picture the multifarious kinds and degrees of likeness and unlikeness in the external world of Natural Reality and in the internal world of Thought-activity and to arrange them all in their proper relations of co-existence and succession, action, reaction, interaction and causal interdependence—to be able to do this is to *know*.

Knowledge is consciousness of *relation*—more specifically consciousness of the relation between objective existences among themselves, subjective existences (percepts, concepts, etc.) among themselves, and of the relation between these two groups—the objective and subjective worlds. From another angle we might define " knowledge "—in its practical sense—as a justifiable and justified *certainty* of the correctness with which Thought (in any given instance) *reflects* objective Reality.

What is the ground upon which this *certainty*—that thinking has attained its object—a correct reproduction in Thought of the relations *produced* in the objective world—is based ?

One ground for certainty exists, and one ground only— that *Practice, objective* Practice, practice through *objects, verifies the correctness of the conception*—the reliability and usability of the mind-picture.

This gives us the second Materialist canon, the *certainty* of knowledge which is based upon a correct, objectively verified correspondence between Theory and Practice—upon their *unity* (one of indissoluble inter-action) based upon the *primacy of Practice*, which *practice* is the source, the object, and the final acid test of all knowledge.

The canon of the unity of Theory and Practice leads us from simple Materialism-in-general to *Dialectic* Materialism.

The *term* " dialectic " derives from the same root as *dia*-logue : a " speech " delivered by two persons alternatively in which the *opposition*, the statement and counter-statement of the two speakers, produces the " united " *progression* of the discussion.

It was used by the Greek philosophers, particularly by Plato, to denote the *art* of arriving at the truth by the confrontation and comparison of two opposite points of view. With Plato, also, it involved the doctrine that all *truth* for

Man was, even when it was most true *for* Man and Man's purposes, a *form of error*—Truth proper being possessed by the gods alone.

Stressing this latter conception to the exclusion of its converse, the Mediæval Schoolmen used the term " dialectic " to denote the art of demonstrating that no man could without self-contradiction claim to know the Truth *as God knows it*. With the Schoolmen dialectic degenerated into a technique of deluding an opponent into logical self-contradiction. It became, as with the post-Platonic *Sophists* (literally " knowers "), equivalent to sophistry, " the art of making the *worse* appear the *better* reason."

Kant revived the term (in his *Critique*) and restored it to its Platonic sense—somewhat modified. " Dialectic " with Kant is that branch of logic which treats of the validity of the results reached by analysis. With Kant it has only a negative importance—that of warning all reasoners that by the methods of the " Pure " critical reason (i.e., *purely* abstract reasoning) it was impossible to attain to Truth " as God knows it "—or, in Kant's terminology, the knowledge of *noumenal* (as distinct from *phe*-nomenal) Reality. This he proved by showing that a consistent process of " pure " reasoning reached exactly opposite, and therefore mutually destructive, conclusions about the *Ultimate* Nature of Things—*Things-in-themselves*. For instance, the logical proof that God exists was exactly as good (and therefore as bad) as the logical proof that God does not exist. One cannot by " pure " logic prove even one's own existence, since every endeavour to do so must start from some *empirical* (and therefore, to " pure " logic, inadmissible) affirmation.

Kant's successors, Fichte, Schelling, and Hegel, traversed Kant's position, Hegel being outstanding in the boldness with which he accepted Kant's challenge. Kant had rested in the conclusion that, since all reasoning about *ultimates* lands us in the self-stultification of absolute contradiction, no knowledge of ultimates is possible. Hegel started with the affirmation that ultimate existence is in essence Contradictory. Everything *is* and *is not*—all is *Becoming*. Thus Dialectics with Hegel became the logical technique of elucidating all Being as a process of *Becoming*—as a *unity* conceptually resolvable into progressively interacting *opposites*, whose opposition begot not *only* their mutual destruction *in themselves*, but *also* a new unity into which they dissolved, and from which a new development-producing opposition arose.

" Dialectic," then, is a term which has as its positive
content the conception of *development* consisting in the outcome of a union of interacting opposites—a process in which
unity is continually resolved into opposition, and opposition
(action and reaction) constantly resolved into unity again.
It has as its core the notion that all Things *act* and are *acted
upon*, that each thing is not only *What it Does*, but also *What
is Done to It* : that out of this perpetual interplay of opposites
old forms are constantly being destroyed and new forms are
as constantly being brought into being.

We have, in our survey, met with innumerable instances
of this *dialectical* progression. The Mechanical Materialism of
the eighteenth century grew out of the conflict between the
materialist and idealist metaphysicians, which in turn grew
out of the conflict between the Nominalist and Realist
Theologians (" Realist " here means the opposite of what it
means in current usage). Correspondingly the eighteenth-
century Materialist conflict with the Idealism of its time led
to a progress in Idealism—that of the Critical Philosophy and
the dialectical method. Out of their conflict in turn was
born the *new* Materialism—the Dialectical Materialism in
which *mechanical* materialism and Dialectical *Idealism* were
both destroyed as such—and both preserved, the one, as to
its dialectical *form*, the other as to its positive content.

The *truth* in eighteenth-century Materialism was its
Materialism. Its falsity lay in the *mechanical-metaphysical
form* in which that truth was presented. The truth in *Dialectical* Idealism lay in its dialectical form : its falsity lay
in its Idealist substance. *Dialectical Materialism* thus
develops from the oppositional interaction between non-
dialectical materialism and non-materialist dialectics.

This gives us the ground upon which the canon of the
Unity of Theory and Practice rests. *All* materialism is true
in so far as it affirms the *objective existence* of the external
world, its *materiality*, and its *knowability*. Its falsity, in its
pre-Marxian and non-dialectical forms, consists in its failure
to grasp the core of truth from which Idealism elaborates its
tissue of errors and delusions—namely, that *what* we know
we know *in* and *by means of* our brains—our thinking.

The *Idealist* is wrong in supposing that we extract Truth
wholly and solely from our brains—from the " Mind." The
materialist is wrong if he fails to see that Truth has to be
extracted *by means of our brains*—that the brain is *active* in
knowing. Both are wrong when they join hands to declare

that Thought existences are Real existences—that by any device of Thinking *as such* we can eliminate the primary *opposition* (antagonism, or contradiction) of Objective Existence and subjective reflection (consciousness) of that existence.

This is not " Monism." Monism* erects into the basic principle of its system the *error* common to both mechanical materialism and idealism, that of eliminating the ineradicable opposition—the opposition from which all thinking derives —between Subjective and Objective, between Material Existences and Thought " existences." Monism, in affirming that there *is no difference ultimately* between Thinking and Being, seeks eclectically to straddle *both* idealism *and* materialism. It is the Mr. Facing-both-ways of philosophy. It is in *absolute* opposition to Dialectical Materialism. That is why, as we shall see later, " Monism " is the philosophical uniform worn by the Revisionists, who seek to emasculate Marxism and turn it into an eclectic average between Liberalism and Toryism—something as far below both as revolutionary proletarian Communism (Leninist-Marxism) is above them.

The canon of the Unity of Theory and Practice leads us from subjective Dialectics to the objective Dialectics of Nature and History.

The unity of Theory and Practice is a unity of inter-relation. Theory, as such, is not Practice ; Practice, as such, is not Theory. So far they are opposites. But to *theorise* is to *act*. It involves subjective *practice* ; it cannot begin without, cannot be conceived as existing except as a subjective practice performed upon sense-materials supplied in and by means of objective practice. And the aim, object, and purpose of theorising is—newer and better practice. The unity of theory and practice is therefore created in their oppositional relation, their *interaction*. But out of interaction results come—changes in *both* terms of the oppositional unity. Practice changes Theory ; Theory changes Practice. The correspondence between Theory and Practice is constantly being destroyed and re-established in Practice. *The unity of Theory and Practice is based upon the primacy of Practice.*

What are the alternatives to this proposition ? There are three : (1) To assert that there is no *unity* ; which is a solipsist denial of all possibility of knowledge—even of our own mental states—a surrender to absolute supernaturalism. (2) To assert that *Theory* is primary ; which is the Idealist

* *Monism :* A completely consistent philosophy whether materialist or idealist, is, of course, " monistic " in the sense of anti-dualist. The text refers to that " Monism " which professes to " reconcile " them.

position all over again and leads ultimately to solipsism. (3) To assert that *neither* is primary. This is "Monism," and involves (*a*) a denial of the reality—the possibility even —of *practice*. Practice is objectively distinguishable from theory only in and by means of practice : as abstract concepts "Theory" and "Practice" are—*concepts only*, and as such are incapable of *practice*. (*b*) A denial of the reality of Thought, which is *real* in so far as it reflects what is revealed in *practice*. (*c*) In its negation of the objective *primacy* of practice, under a pretence of eclectically "uniting" material- ism and idealism, it involves a surrender of all defence against solipsism.

The unity of Theory and Practice—their *interaction*—is conceivable only on the Materialist basis of the *primacy of Practice*.

Marxism and Mechanistic Determinism

In the Dialectical Materialism of Marx, as we have seen repeatedly—though only incidentally—Nature and History constitute a "unity" of the *dialectical* kind. They are "one" and "not one"; they are connected yet opposed; the one (History) develops *from* the other (Nature), yet is the reverse of a simple *continuation* of Nature. History, which is "social- ised humanity" *in motion*, involves a continuous and develop- ment-producing interaction between Mankind (in its collective inter-relation) and Nature as a result of which both Mankind (collectively) and Nature are *altered*. History is the becoming process of human Society. It is the *unity*—the synthetic result of—the interaction between the opposites Mankind— as biological species—and the rest of Nature. History there- fore can no more be understood apart from Nature than it can be understood apart from Mankind.

So much would seem to be obvious—as indeed it is to all but "critical" revisers of Marx. All the world knows that one of the distinctive features of Marxism is its "Materialist Conception of History." And all the world knows, by now, that for most of the critics, revisers, and explainers of Marx this conception could with propriety be renamed : "The Mysterious Deception of History"! We saw earlier that Mr. G. D. H. Cole "explains" that it is not "Materialist" —not *really*! Another school of "Marxists"—the self- styled "uncompromising" school, whose slogan is that "ideas are BUT the reflex of material conditions"—contrives to exhaust it of all History by treating men as negligible, their thought-activity being of no perceptible importance. The academicians commonly treat it as a patent recipe for *rewriting* " history "—History being for them *not* the *objective process* whereby present-day society has come into a being, and whereby it will pass out of being again to give place to future society—not this, but so much of the incidental phenomena of this process as has managed to find its way into written or printed records. The futility and sterility of the academic approach is seen in the number of new names they have invented as substitutes for the " Materialist Conception of History " and " Dialectical Materialism." The " Materialist *Interpretation* of History," the " Economic Interpretation of History," the " Proletarian Monist Conception of History " (! ! !), " Economic Materialism," " Economic Determinism "—all these have been offered as substitutes for *Dialectical Materialism* and the *Materialist Conception of History* it implies.

A sample may be given of the sort of crime which has been perpetrated in the name of Marxism. To appreciate it rightly we must bear in mind the positive outcome of our examination of the *Theses on Feuerbach*, particularly the aphorisms " Men make their circumstances as much as circumstances make men," " Men transform themselves in the act of transforming their circumstances," and the Eleventh *Thesis* : " The philosophers have only *interpreted* the world in different ways : the point however is to *change* it." With those propositions in mind read this, from a work entitled *Karl Marx* :

" The materialist conception of history is sometimes referred to as ' economic determinism.' The phrase is less exact, but *it is not unjustified*. Marx continually insists that the developments which he anticipates, as well as those he describes, are ineluctable results of economic forces. The victory of the workers ' is inevitable ' ; *it is independent of our wishes*. Is it also independent of our actions ? There have been Marxian parties which seem to have thought so. . . . Their own task turned out to be only to await the revolution and to applaud. *Their attitude, though unreasonable, was quite probably strictly Marxian*. . . . Both Marx and Engels, in the end, always return to their original statement of the inevitability of the proletarian revolution."— POSTGATE : *Karl Marx*, p. 53.

Each of the three propositions we have italicised is false, and would have been known to be false by the writer had he been in the least qualified to write a " life " (however short) of Karl Marx. It is not merely *false* to say that Marx's conception is *mechanically* " determinist "; it is exactly the reverse of the truth as to Marx, and, at the same time, shows a complete ignorance of the position of the determinists to fasten upon them the assertion that historical events are " independent of our actions." It is false to say that Marx affirmed that " developments . . . are the ineluctable results of economic forces "—as false as it would be to accuse Marx of believing that a bird could fly with only one wing. It is false to assert that the workers' victory, when it comes, will be independent of their " wishes "—on the contrary, it will come (among other things) *because of* their wishes. It is false to assert that the " inevitability " of the workers' victory was the " original " statement made by Marx and Engels—on the contrary, they " originally " held (see ENGELS' *Condition*) that it was in the highest degree *desirable*—and " necessary " in the sense of indispensable for the establishment of Socialism, but only, *in the long run*, " necessary " in the sense of " inescapable " (or, as Postgate would say, " ineluctable "). Most of all is it false—and as false as hell—to assert that there is any warrant in any line written by Marx for the assertion that historical development is independent of men's acts, and that the " Marxist " party, which simply waits for the revolution to arrive (like a bus !), was " quite probably strictly Marxian." If Postgate does not *know* that this statement is false he knows less than nothing about Marx.

Let us take the last point first. We have seen already and demonstrated almost *ad nauseum* that for Marx and for Dialectical Materialism *Practice*, i.e., *what men do*, is the basis of all development in objective history, and in man's subjectivity likewise. Not only men's thoughts and men's sensations, but their very sense-organs, the primary sources of all consciousness, are generated in and by means of *practice* —by what men do. " In the beginning was the Deed," and to seek to interpret Marx so as to leave men's deeds out is as " rational " as it would be to attempt to isolate a bung-hole in order thereafter to build a barrel round it.

The problem is not whether what men do makes any difference, since it is self-evident that whatever happens in history does so because men have done the particular things they did do. The problem is, firstly, why they *wanted* to do the things they did do—or, alternatively, why they did them if they did not *wish* to. And, secondly, why the results of men's *doing* always turn out to be something they never quite intended—something which leads to other situations never imagined or desired. The problem, in short, is not one of " mechanism "—but one of *dialectical development*.

Postgate's use of the phrase " independent of our wishes " has been carefully chosen (from Marx)—and, then, as though of malice, completely misused. Postgate found it in the statement of his conception of history given by Marx in his *Critique of Political Economy* :

> " In making their livelihood together men enter into certain necessary, definite, relations, independent of their wills. . . ."—MARX : *Critique,* Introduction.

This, as can be seen at a glance, says the exact reverse of what Postgate imagines. It says no more than that man is born into a world and circumstances he had no say in choosing. It is as axiomative a statement as could well be imagined. It could only be mistaken by somebody suffering from a " complex,"—the victim of a subjective urge to read Marx " all arsy-varsity."

Again (leaving aside for separate treatment the question of the *absolute* inevitability of the victory of the proletariat), this same statement in the *Critique,* instead of affirming that a revolutionary crisis arises " independently of our wishes " affirms the exact opposite :

> " In considering such transformation [periods of social revolution] we must always distinguish between the material changes in the economic conditions of production . . . *and* the legal, political, religious, æsthetic, or philosophical . . . *forms* in which human beings *become conscious of the conflict and fight it to an issue*."— MARX : *ibid.*

Postgate is not only guilty of completely falsifying Marx's plain words ; he falls into the shallowest vulgarisation in regard to the " economic forces " of which developments are the " ineluctable " results. It is surely not asking too much to expect that a man setting out to write a life of Karl Marx should, at least, know that with Marx, *the human agents are included* in the sum total of " productive " or " economic " *forces*. For instance :

> " Of all the instruments of production, the greatest productive force is the revolutionary class itself."— MARX : *Poverty of Philosophy,* II, v,

Certainly Marx distinguishes between the *material* and the *human-social* agencies of production ; but never does he treat the former as in stark, *metaphysical*, antagonism to the latter. How could he, when his whole argument turned upon the historical outcome of mankind's *use* of the material productive forces ? How could he when his argument demanded that, as men's social organisation and knowledge developed, quantitatively and qualitatively, so the productive potentialities of the earth itself were not only *actualised* more fully but positively *increased*—(as by improvements in the breed of live-stock, cultivated plants, timber, etc.).

The plain truth is that Postgate—who scorns the dialectic —is self-imprisoned within the limitations of philistine " common sense," and is thereby rendered incapable of grasping a *dialectical* inter-relation. To him the practice of distinguishing differentiation and opposition in every unity and unity in every opposition, is simply an " old abusing of God's patience and the King's English ! " Still, he ought to have sufficient conscience to report Marx's words with some approximation to accuracy. The proletarian revolution *was* conceived by Marx to be " inevitable "; but the whole question turns upon *what* makes it so, and there can be no question that he expected it to arrive in the form of an historical process of *class-conflict* culminating in the victory of one of the contending classes. And if class-*conflict* and triumph therein does not involve both " wishing " and " action " (and plenty of it !), words have ceased to convey a meaning. Where is the possibility of reading a doctrine of *passivity*—of " waiting for the inevitable " in such passages as these :

> " The bourgeoisie cannot exist without constantly revolutionising the instruments of production, and thereby the relations of production, and with them the whole relations of society."—MARX-ENGELS : *Com. Man.*, p. 12.

> " The bourgeoisie during its rule of scarce one hundred years has *created* more massive and more collossal productive forces than have all preceding generations together. . . . What earlier century had even a presentiment that such productive forces slumbered in the lap of *social labour* ? "—*Ibid*, p. 14.

> " . . . we traced the more or less veiled *civil war*, raging within existing society, up to the point where that war *breaks out into open revolution*, and where the *violent*

overthrow of the bourgeoisie lays the foundation for the sway of the proletariat."—*Ibid*, p. 20.

" What the bourgeoisie *produces* is above all its own grave diggers. Its fall and the victory of the proletariat are equally inevitable."—*Ibid*, p. 20.

We draw attention to this final sentence because it is one of the few passages in which either Marx or Engels uses the phrase " inevitable " in connection with the triumph of the proletariat. Here it is clear, already, that the " inevitability " arises not *apart from*, or *despite* what men *do*, but on the contrary, *because of it*. It is because the bourgeoisie cannot help but *be active*, cannot be passive, that certain consequences are created, in face of which the proletariat cannot be passive, and so on. It might be argued, quite fairly (though inaccurately), that Marx's analysis of what the bourgeoisie would be *bound to do* is incorrect : it cannot be argued fairly that he excludes from his consideration what men wish, and (still less) what men do, and will do.

Postgate, however, presents to these considerations a shell like an armadillo :

" The certainty of this victory [i.e., of the proletariat] lies *outside the domain of our* control *or activity*. . . . Neither you, nor I, nor Lenin, nor Hitler, can alter it. Plekhanov . . . stated this brutally : ' It is not a question of what goal this or that proletarian sets himself at a given time, or even the whole proletariat. It is a question of what the class itself is, and of what, in view of this its being it is historically bound to accomplish ! ' "
—POSTGATE : *Karl Marx*, p. 53–4.

It will be observed that Postgate is so little familiar with the works of Marx and Engels that he is able to quote them without being aware of it. The passage he fathers upon Plekhanov is taken from the *Holy Family* of Marx and Engels ! We have discussed it above : here we need only observe that it says exactly the opposite of what Postgate imagines. It says that the nature and the situation of the proletariat will, in their conjunction, ensure that *the proletariat will do* thus and thus—that, in consequence of their doing this certain other situations will follow, and so on. If Postgate will dwell for a moment or two upon the significant *contrast* between " at a given time " and " historically," light may break in upon him. That he is in need of light he goes on to demonstrate :

" Marx himself allowed for no deviation from this

determinist (! !) attitude. There would, he admitted, be ' accidents.' The accidents which included the character of the leaders of the workers, might accelerate or retard the progress of history. But—lest we might think that free-will was creeping back into a determinist (! !) philosophy—he adds the *truly startling assertion* : ' These accidents fall quite naturally into the general course of development, and are compensated for by other accidents.' Such a statement is in Marx's own phrase ' mystical.' It is in its nature incapable of proof."—POSTGATE : *Karl Marx*, p. 54.

Postgate figures as a leading " authority " in the ranks of " British " Marxism (national mark brand ; as distinguished from " imported " varieties !). His case therefore calls for extra-special treatment. It will be necessary to instruct him (*a*) as to the bearings of the " free will " problem and its historical solution in Dialectical Materialism ; (*b*) as to the philosophical distinction between *essential* and *accidental* and the dialectical mode of resolving the antagonism between them ; (*c*) as to Marx's conception of the roles of Natural Law and Human Action in the historical movement. On all these questions Raymond Postgate is several degrees more ignorant than when he was born. *Then* he knew just nothing : now he will have to forget what he has mislearned steadily for twenty years before he gets back again to zero.

First, let us examine the " truly startling statement " of Marx's (which Postgate says is " incapable of proof "). It occurs in Marx's letter to Kugelmann, April 17, 1871 :—

" World history would, indeed, be very easy to make if the struggle was taken up only on condition of infallibly favourable chances. It would, on the other hand, be of a very mystical nature, if ' accidents ' played no part. These accidents themselves fall naturally into the general course of development and are compensated again by other accidents. But acceleration and delay are very dependent upon such ' accidents ' which include the ' accident ' of the character of those who at first stand at the head of the movement.

" The decisive unfavourable ' accident ' this time is by no means to be found in the general conditions of French society, but in the presence of the Prussians in France and their position right before Paris. . . ."— MARX *to Kugelmann*, 17th April, 1871.

It is proper to observe that the above quotation is taken

from the translation issued by Martin Lawrence. Postgate quotes the version made by Max Eastman whom he follows lovingly from bog-hole to ditch and back again. Happily the difference in the versions is not material for the moment.

What, now, is the force of Postgate's objection ? Marx says that, at best, the historical development of society can only be foreseen in its general direction, not in every incidental detail. These details which could not be foreseen play a part in determining the course of history *in detail*, they do not affect the general direction, *in itself*,—they affect it only in respect of accelerating or retarding the *time* taken to execute a given historical movement.

What is there hard to grasp in this argument ? Let us try an illustration. It can be predicted, with absolute confidence, that the rain which falls upon the earth will, if it be not absorbed into the earth, find its way into the rivers and so down to the sea. Rain falling upon a certain area in Europe will be determined by the lie of the land into the Rhine, and so into the North Sea. But, if the set of the wind changes before the storm breaks, a cloud drift of a few miles will cause that rain to fall on a slope which tilts it into the Danube and so into the Black Sea. Relative to the law governing the fall of rain and its flow to the sea *in general*, the interference of the wind, and the changes therein, are *accidents*. Thus, it is possible to predict with certainty that the rain will *fall*, and that (absorption ignored) it will *flow into the sea*. But *which* sea ? That cannot be predicted with certainty, because it depends upon " accidents "—that is upon circumstances not comprised within the determinants generalised in the scientific " law."

So, in the case discussed by Marx. The *general* need to struggle against the bourgeoisie arose from the general nature and tendency of society. But the specific *detail*, whether that struggle should pass from one form (general agitation) to another (armed revolt) is a matter which can only be decided provisionally, in terms of immediate circumstances, which again depend upon the interplay of (*relative*) " accidents." In the long run these " accidents " compensate each other : as, for example, to revert to the illustration above, the times when the wind diverts the rain to the Rhine are compensated by the times when it directs it to the Danube, so that in this case a statistical average gives an approximation which differs from the general law only to a negligible extent. It is an " accident " when a particular crisis compelling the proletariat to act in a revolutionary way coincides with the fact that they *then* and *there* possess leaders adequate to the occasion (or not adequate as the case may be). But over a whole historic epoch, the times when the proletariat is " in luck " will be pretty equally balanced by those in which its " luck is out "—with the important difference that a succession of failures will be a prime determining cause of the adoption of ways and means of developing adequate leadership—therefore of, in a sense, *creating* " good luck " *in advance*. Moreover, the " accident " of the coincidence of a crisis with adequate or inadequate leadership, operates on the side of the bourgeoisie as well as on that of the proletariat. And here again accident compensates accident, as in those many wars on record in which victory has been determined *not* by the " accident " of genius in the victorious general, but in the negative " accident " that the losing general was the bigger bungler.

But Messrs. Postgate and Eastman will have none of this. Their " communication " is indeed " Yea ! Yea ! and Nay ! Nay ! Whatsoever is more than this cometh of evil ! " Either a scientific law predicts everything down to the minutest detail ; or, there is no scientific law ! Either Marx's law of historical development enables predictions to be made—in which case all " accidents " should, they claim, be absolutely eliminated. Or, accidents will happen, in which case it is " mystical " to talk of any general law.

Such is the wretched philistine sophistry to which the Postgate-Eastman combination is reduced.

And moreover, when Marx says the course of history *can* be predicted in its *general* course and direction, Postgate and Eastman accuse him of " determinism " (which with them means " fatalism "). When Marx says that incidental details (" accidents ") cannot be predicted in advance, they accuse him of smuggling in " free will " by the back door ! They have not an inkling of the truth that the contradiction is not in Marx, but in their own individual and joint theoretical incompetence.

Let us dispose of the " accident " and so clear the way for the problem of " Free Will." This, in turn will lead us directly to the Marxian conception of the Law of Motion in Nature and in History.

.   .   .   .   .   .

" Every schoolboy knows " that the term " accident " is

used in current, everyday speech to indicate a happening that was not *intended*, or foreseen. If Postgate, through " incuriousness," quotes as " Plekhanov " something which is really " Marx," that is, in the circumstances, an " accident." So, if Eastman's cycle or car skids on a greasy road-surface and shoots him through a shop-front—that likewise is an " accident." In each case the result follows in natural sequence from its " cause "—inattention in the one case : greasy road-surface in the other. The result in each case was " inevitable " *in the given circumstances*, but that combination of circumstances was not foreseeable in advance, was not deducible as a " necessity " from the general nature either of Marx's or Plekhanov's writings, of Postgate, of Eastman, of cycles, cars, greasy roads, or the cosmic scheme at large. Therefore these particular results were " accidents " in the scientific sense of the term also.

Let us ask them a question. They take the lofty " scientific " ground that since everything is caused, nothing can happen " accidentally."

Very well then : suppose that Brother Eastman is knocked down by an automobile and breaks a leg, and Brother Postgate slips on the housemaid's soap and dislocates his elbow. Will either of them refrain from claiming on his " accident insurance policy " on the score that " *accidents do not happen* ? " And what will they say, and the judge, and the jury say if the insurance company refuses to pay on the score that " *accidents are scientifically inconceivable* ? "

There is, however, another sense of the term " accident "—a philosophical usage—with which both Postgate and Eastman ought to be familiar, but, clearly, are not. In philosophy " accident " is the logical opposite of " essence," " accidental " of " essential." That which is essential to a thing is that by means of which it is classifiable under a general category. For instance, whether a kettle is of tin, iron, or copper is *accidental* (relatively to its kettle-essence), as also is whether it has or lacks a lid, spout, or a hole in the bottom. That which is *essential* is that by means of which it is distinguished from common boiling-pots and pans on the one side, and tea and coffee pots on the other. The distinction is, observe, a relative one only, and dialectics cognises the fact that the accidental (as in the above instance, the *hole in the bottom* !) may become the *essential*. If the hole is sufficiently unstoppable (" quantitative alteration is qualitative change ") the kettle " essence " is abrogated and the hole becomes the essential fact.   What was a kettle with a hole becomes a hole surrounded by the (accidents) relics of a kettle!

A further illustration : it is *essential* to Postgate's human nature that he shall possess, among other distinguishing qualities, a spinal column surrounding a spinal cord whose uppermost end is a globiform mass of organised cerebral substance known to the vulgar as a brain, and inclosed in a bony enclosure—a skull.   That he should have a brain of some kind is *essential* to his human nature.   But that he should make the preposterous use he does of this equipment is not in the least " necessary " or " essential "—is, relative to his human nature, purely " accidental,"—though it is, no doubt, rigorously determined in the sense of being *caused,* and is, probably, *essential* to his being—Raymond Postgate.

BURIDAN'S ASS

With this we can pass to the question of Free Will and Determinism.   Postgate and Eastman formulate the dilemma in the traditional metaphysical form.   Either a man's will is " free," in which case his conduct is absolutely incalculable and a science of history thereby rendered impossible ; or, there is a science of history in which case man has no " freedom " and therefore can of his own volition do nothing.   If the will is " free " there can be no *science* : if there is no will, there can be no *history* !   How can this dilemma be escaped ?

The dilemma thus posed by Postgate and Eastman jointly and severally is typical of the metaphysical-absolutist approach which philosophy inherited from mediæval theology. It is in fact the old mediæval dilemma of Buridan's Ass, who starved to death from lack of ability to choose between two *absolutely* equidistant, and *absolutely* equally attractive bundles of hay.

Just as that dilemma was created by supposing the existence of things unattainable in practice—absolute equidistance, positive and relative, (absolute equality of sight in the two eyes of the ass being a condition of this), absolutely equal attractiveness, etc.—so, too, the metaphysical dilemma between " Freedom " and " Necessity " is created by the arbitrary abstract contrast of *absolute* " Freedom " and absolute " Necessity " as mutually exclusive *opposites*.   As soon as it is perceived that they are each dependent upon the other ; that each implies the other ; that each exists only relatively to the other ; that their opposition is a reciprocal relation which is constantly being established and resolved into a synthesis in practice—as soon as this is perceived the dilemma lapses into nothingness. Since, however, it has played a big part in history, and bears upon a vital aspect of Dialectical Materialism, we will examine it more in detail. But we cannot help making an observation by way of (temporary) adieu to Postgate and Eastman.

JEAN BURIDAN (whose name is eternally linked to this immortal ass, who is forever being dragged out to silence " determinists " with his braying) was Rector of Paris University in and around 1327. Moreover, he did not breed this ass for himself—he borrowed it from the stable of ARISTOTLE (approximately 384 to 322 B.C.), It is a fine comment upon those who assail Marx, because he is " not up to date," that they should thus have recourse to arguments which were born some 2200 years ago ! That the ass who brayed in Athens in 334 B.C. should be still braying in Bloomsbury in A.D. 1934 may be taken as an appropriate critical fanfare in honour of the " up-to-date " critics of Marx !

Dialectic method differs from the essentially metaphysical method of purely *formal* logic, in that it considers things in their *actual* connections, in their origin, in their ceasing to be, and in the movement which takes them from the one point to the other. That is what it means to treat them as *becoming* —rather than as *fixed*, separate, *kinds* of qualitative Being. And the proof of the superiority of the dialectic method lies in the *practical* fact that only when a problem can be approached thus " historically "—i.e., envisaged in its process of *becoming*—can it be at all satisfactorily solved.

This is illustrated in the present instance, the problem of Free-Will versus Necessity (of " Determinism " as it is customary, nowadays, to call it) by the fact that the problem arose originally in Theology and was in the first place a by-product of the doctrine of Future Rewards and Punishments. Theologically it involves the presupposition of the antagonism between the " gross " material body and the " ethereal " immortal soul. Only as a function of this " *soul* " in its absolute and irreconcilable antagonism to the " gross," " vile " *body* is the concept of a metaphysically " Free " (i.e., undetermined, uncaused, not-necessitated) Will even approximately intelligible. And, even then, it is explicable only as an hypothesis whereby to excuse the doctrine of

Eternal Damnation—the doctrine of God's Moral Government of the Universe by the mode of rewarding the Good with Heaven and punishing the Bad with Hell.

Even on that footing it raised more theoretical difficulties than it solved. For one thing, it raised sharply the problem whether God was not as responsible for his own Creation, and to his own creatures, as these creatures were responsible for their deeds, and answerable for them to their Creator. 'Tis a poor rule that works only one way. If man may rightly be condemned for being bad, why may not God be likewise called in question for *making bad men*?

There was only one way out of this difficulty (still, by the way, a problem all theologians confess they find rationally insoluble)—to affirm that God alone is Free : that in his Freedom he is answerable to nobody and for nothing. What he does, he does ; and that *He* chooses to do such and such is all the justification needed. Man is free only to realise the Will of God. That this involves that God foreknew that the majority of the human race would realise his Will only in the form of going to Hell, was a detail that only sentimentalists would boggle at. In this grim form Determinism (or Necessitarianism) was born as a theological doctrine— that which emerged as Calvinism, the creed aptly summarised by Burns :

> " Oh Thou, who in the heavens dost dwell,
>   Wha, as it pleases best Thysel',
> Sends *ane* to Heaven and *ten* to Hell,
>   A' for Thy glory !
> And no for ony guid or ill
>   They've done afore Ye !
>
> " When frae my mither's womb I fell,
>   Thou might'st hae plunged me in Hell,
> To gnash my gums, and weep an' wail,
>   In burnin' lake,
> Where damned devils roar an' yell,
>   Chained to a stake."
>
> " I bless and praise Thy matchless might,—
>   When thousands Thou hast left in night,—
> That I am here afore Thy sight,
>   For gifts and grace,
> A burning and a shining light
>   To a' this place !
>
>   BURNS : *Holy Willie's Prayer.*

Calvinistic Determinism arose as the doctrine of the revolutionary dictatorship of the Protestant-clerical leaders of the bourgeois revolt against the Catholic Church. It is interesting, dialectically, as the form in which the absolute authority claimed by the Catholic church passed over into its opposite absolute opposition to the claims of the Catholic church. And the growth of the counter-doctrine, of Free Will, was likewise connected with the emergence of the political need to effect a compromise which would exclude both the extremes—of revolutionary Calvinistic Republicanism, and of Catholic-clerical Absolutism. Thus the Free-Will doctrine was revived in connection with the Arminianism of Laud which, on the one side, relaxed the extreme terrors of Pre-destination to Eternal Hell and, on the other, exalted submission to the King, *his* Law, and *his* Church, into the first principle of politics.

Logically, as the Calvinists saw, Man's " freedom " could be *real* (as distinct from illusory) only as the negation of God's " freedom." The compromise doctrine which sought to include and harmonise both had to concede to man the power of, in practice, negating God's freedom, which, in theory, remained in abeyance for use when necessary to negate man's freedom.

Such a compromise was necessarily unstable ; hence, in the Puritan uprising against the Stuarts, the Left Wing was led, not by Calvinists (who became the *moderates* of the Left) but by the Independents who developed the doctrines of Free-Will to the revolutionary conclusion that God ruled only through and by means of the Free Will of his *Saints* ! (i.e., Corporal Zeal-of-the-Lord Busy ; and Sergeant Bind-their-kings-in-chains Jenkins, etc.). Hence it was as part of his counter-revolutionary attack upon the Puritan revolution that HOBBES returned to the Determinist doctrine —as SPINOZA, under similar provocation, though with a more revolutionary purpose, had done in Holland.

In philosophy the pedigree of the " Necessitarian " doctrine is impressive. It was a protest on two fronts : against the Theologian doctrine which made Free Will " the faculty whereby man contrives to get damned to Eternity " (VOLTAIRE) and against the virtual anarchism advocated by the *ultras* of Free-Will politics.

Absolute Freedom was repudiated unequivocally by SPINOZA (1632-77) :

" In no mind is there an absolute or free volition ; but

it is determined for willing this or that by a cause, which likewise has been determined by another, and this again by a third, and so on for ever."—SPINOZA : *Ethics*, Part II, prop. 48.

HOBBES was no less explicit :

" When the words ' free ' and ' liberty ' are applied to anything but bodies they are abused ; for that which is not subject to motion is not subject to impediment ; and therefore . . . from the use of the word ' free will ' no liberty can be inferred of the will, desire, or inclination, but the liberty of the man, which consisteth in this, that he find no stop in doing what he has the will, desire, or inclination to do."—HOBBES : *Leviathan*, Chap. 21.

LOCKE becomes, for once, contemptuous on the subject :

" Whether man's will be free or no ? . . . The question itself is altogether improper ; and it is as insignificant to ask whether man's will be free as to ask whether his sleep be swift, or his virtue square : liberty being as little applicable to the will as swiftness of motion is to sleep, or squareness to virtue."—LOCKE : *Human Understanding*, II, xxi, 14.

But for all that in their political speculations all of three grounded their theory of the natural origin of Government and the State in the existence of that very incalculable *in*determinateness of the Human Will which they denied. They fell back in their politics upon a doctrine indistinguishable from the Biblical cynicism—" the heart of man is deceitful above all things and desperately wicked." The State, they argued (as we have noted earlier), was necessary to keep the human atoms from flying asunder into chaos : alternatively it was necessary to keep the strong from preying upon the weak.

HOBBES (as usual) expresses this notion more bluntly and uncompromisingly than anybody :

" In the nature of man, we find three principal causes of quarrel. First, competition ; Secondly, diffidence ; Thirdly, glory. The first maketh men invade for Gain ; the second for Safety ; and the third for Reputation. . . . Hereby it is manifest that during the time men live without a common Power to keep them all in awe, they are in that condition which is called War ; and such a war as is of every man against every man. For War consisteth not in Battell only, or the act of fighting, but in a tract of time wherein the Will to contend by battell is sufficiently known. . . .

"Whatsoever therefore is consequent to a time of War, where every man is Enemy to every man, the same is consequent to the time wherein men live without other security than what their own strength and their own invention shall furnish them withal. In such condition there is no place for Industry, because the fruit thereof is uncertain, and consequently no Culture of the Earth, no Navigation, nor use of the commodities that may be imported by Sea; no commodious buildings; no Instruments of moving and removing such things as require much force; no Knowledge of the face of the Earth; no account of Time; no Arts; no Letters; no Society; and which is worst of all continual fear and danger of violent death. *And the life of Man, solitary, poor, nasty, brutish, and short.* . . .

"The Passions that encline men to Peace are fear of Death; desire of such things as are necessary to commodious living; and a hope by their Industry to obtain them. And Reason suggesteth convenient Articles of Peace upon which men may be drawn to agreement."— HOBBES : *Leviathan,* I, 13.

In short, clear and trenchant as Hobbes is (and what a joy it would be for students if all philosophers—including many Marxists !—contrived always to write as clearly and as pungently as Hobbes !) for all that he only makes the dilemma all the clearer. Man is, in the Hobbesian view, always the point of impact of two opposing forces—Desire and Impotence; Will and Constraint; Confidence and Fear; and so on. His conduct is a mechanical resultant of their interaction. Government is the one and only constraining force which keeps men's inflamed Passions and Greeds within such compass as permits escape from the " natural " condition of a life " solitary, poor, nasty, brutish, and short."

The view to which Hegel led the way was the opposite of this ; none the less it had, incidentally, curious affinities therewith. It saw as Hobbes saw, well and clearly, that Freedom was not so much a question of external constraint as one of positive *power to act.* But it saw also that this positive power in turn was generated from and by means of the external restraints. A thing (or a man) can be "Free" only in terms of its own specific nature ; and, since specification is a *limitation* as contrasted with absolute generality, the greater the specification the greater the *power* to act in that particular way *and none other*. The " freedom " was thus a *form* of the Necessity, while the necessity was the *substance* of the " Freedom."

With Hegel the Universal Existence was Absolute Spirit (" absolute in the sense that Hegel can tell us *absolutely* nothing about it "—ENGELS). From the necessity of its own being this Spirit was impelled to seek " freedom," and found it ultimately in the " universal consciousness " of Philosophy. How sorry this " freedom "—this " self-determination of Spirit "—was nobody demonstrated better than the " universally conscious " exponents of the Critical Criticism, and other adherents of the Hegelian Left.

Marx and Engels alone of the whole school of Young Hegelians were able to extract the real content of the concept which Hegel had presented in a mystically inverted form. It was not sufficient to do as Feuerbach had done (and with him the Bauers and others) and substitute the abstract consciousness of abstract Man for Hegel's Absolute Spirit : to do that preserved Hegel's basic fallacy while rejecting that which was fruitful in his method, its dialectic. The fruitful method was to start with the recognition that the " man " whose reasoning process provided the concrete fact from which the Hegelian Absolute was the final abstraction was Mankind in the *concrete*, Mankind in the totality of its *active* inter-relations, " socialised humanity "—the *ensemble* of objective social relations. Not in the abstract world of Theology, Metaphysics, or of Critical Criticism, but in the concrete world of Society in Motion—in History—was to be found this process which Hegel called " the Self-determination of Spirit."

In *absolute ignorance* (so far as such is conceivable) neither " freedom " nor " necessity " exist. In *absolute knowledge* (again as far as such is conceivable hypothetically) the antagonism between freedom and necessity disappears. And that which applies to the subjective *consciousness* of freedom and necessity applies to the objective relations of man from which that consciousness is derived. *Absolute impotence* plus consciousness equals absolute necessity ; but absolute impotence is absolutely inconceivable. Relatively absolute impotence can exist in relation to particular needs and desires. But these needs and desires exist in relation to society, which generates them and subjects them to perpetual transmutation. And that same society at the same time generates, develops, and perpetually transforms the power of satisfying needs and

desires, which power is the objective content of the concept
" freedom." " Freedom," said Hegel, " is the recognition of
Necessity." He who feels that he not only can but *must*
do so and so is " free "—to do *just that*, and *only* that—to
do it exactly in proportion as he is debarred by the specific
determination of his will from entertaining any notion of
doing anything else. He who desires to do so and so, but
cannot, is " free " only to desire, and to imagine ways and
means of gratifying his desires. Thus the conscious recognition of the subjective necessity of the desire and the objective
negative necessity of the lack of power to satisfy it together
provide the pre-condition in which the relative freedom of
reason and imagination is determined in the direction of
achieving a *power* (and thereby a *freedom*) of satisfying
desire which is adequate enough to override the obstacles
and is so far " free." The only freedom attainable by man is
therefore one which is created, magnified, enlarged, and
specifically developed in and by means of Society, the necessity
of its historical movement, and the necessity of the specific
inter-relation between the individual man and society. So
far as men in their social aggregation are conscious of and,
furthermore, *understand* the nature, scope, possibilities and
law of motion of the society into which they are, by their
practical life-activity, combined—so far as this *recognition*
of the Necessity impelling and confronting them exists, so
far men are capable of using their power with the maximum
of effect, and in so doing of progressively increasing it, and
with it their Freedom.

What applies to society in the aggregate applies likewise
to group combinations within society—to *classes*. So far as
they are *fully* aware of, and therefore understand, the necessities of their situation, so far they can make the most of such
possibilities as are available. So far as they do not possess
the subjective power of recognising the specific necessities of
their social being they are unfree—however much they may be
possessed of the illusion of freedom. And as with societies
and classes, so with individuals. " Power and freedom are
identical," and " power " is neither absolute nor abstract,
but concrete, and therefore specifically conditioned and
historically determined by the totality of the active inter-
relations between Society and Nature, and between Man and
Man within Society.

How does this bear upon the claim that Marxism is held
fast like Buridan's Ass ? It relegates that argument to where

it belongs—to theology and the abstract absolute and fixed, mutually exclusive antagonisms of metaphysics. Also it " places " this argument as belonging to the " crisis " which has arisen in all the bourgeois scientific camps as a result of the conflicts raised by the contradictions between the *dialectical* results obtained by scientific *practice* and the metaphysical mode of reasoning which the *scientists* have carried over from philosophy and its parent—*theology*.

The dilemma of those who cannot resolve the antagonism of Freedom and Necessity into the synthetic unity in opposition of Necessitated-Freedom and Freely-operating Necessity is that of the scientists who cannot distinguish between Cause and Effect, Essence and Accident, Form and Substance, Force and Matter, without rupturing their connection, and cannot connect them without abstracting away their concrete development-producing *difference*. It is the perennial dilemma of philistine " common sense."

But, to be charitable, there is this much of excuse for Postgate—he has taken his notion of the Dialectic from some true-blue " British " expounders thereof, who claim to understand it *better than Marx did* ! To anticipate somewhat the argument we will develop at length later, these " British " *super*-Marxians show their " dialectical " skill by taking care to *begin at the wrong end*. When they write books they solemnly write " The Beginning " *at the end* (see CASEY's *Thinking*) as an unconscious admission that their notion of the Dialectic is to proceed backside foremost ! First they postulate a closed (and therefore fixed) system of Nature, *into which* they proceed, as by a surgical operation, to *insert the dialectic* ! Then again they postulate a " closed " system of History, in which " Economics " is contraposed to Man, the Individual to the Class, the Class to Society, and each historic epoch—Feudalism, Capitalism, Communism—to those on either side of it. Upon this welter of fixed antagonisms they impose " the dialectic " which consists in affirming that, since " opposites are identical," therefore there are *no differences really*—and for the matter of that no *likenesses or connections* either. The result of this eclectic Irish stew—a statistical average of philosophical mutton, pork, beef, veal, peas, onions, carrots, and potatoes—is then decanted into three bowls in turn, labelled respectively Thesis, Antithesis, and Synthesis, and the contents of the third bowl are offered to believers as the Pure Marxian-Dietzgenian Balm of Gilead. To do him justice, Postgate's stomach revolts at the mess. And rightly so. But he ought to know better than to blame Marx, who was safely dead, and Engels with him, before this " bootleg Marxism " was ever invented.

Happily for our inquiry, Marx and Engels wrote, in the period between September, 1845, and August, 1846 (i.e., *after* the *Theses on Feuerbach* and the *Holy Family*, but *before* the *Poverty of Philosophy*), a work in which they themselves demonstrate how they approached the question of the *difference* between Nature and History and the *connection* between them. A glance at some relevant passages in this work (or so much of it as is pertinent to our purpose) will be invaluable at this juncture.

. . . . .

THE APPROACH TO THE PROBLEM

The work referred to was one in which Marx and Engels worked out in common the antithesis between their view —the Materialist Conception of History—and the ideological view of German philosophy :

> " The manuscript, two big octavo volumes, had long reached the place of publication in Westphalia, when we received news that altered circumstances [the fact that the Revolution of 1848–9 had come and gone, leaving Reaction behind] did not permit of its being printed.
>
> We abandoned the manuscript to the ' biting ' criticism of the mice all the more willingly since we had achieved our principal aim—our self-clarification."—ENGELS : *Feuerbach*, Foreword.

Years later Engels recovered the MS., and it passed with his papers to Bernstein. He published a few extracts, but the collective wisdom of the German Social-Democratic Party pronounced it as a whole " unsuited for publication ! " In 1930 Bernstein parted with the MS. to the Marx-Engels institute, and the whole work (except for a few chapters which have been lost) was published for the first time in 1932 under the name of *German Ideology*.

What makes this work—which it is hoped will soon be available in an English translation—so supremely valuable for us is that it is precisely this *clarification process* (which the German Social-Democrats regarded themselves as having outlived) which is needed by the Marxist movement in Britain to-day. [For the translation of the extracts given below the present author is responsible.]

. . . . .

" The hardest thing in the world to make is a beginning."

Do Marx and Engels begin by postulating a ready-made world-conception ?   A conception of Society ?   Of Man ?   Of Economics ?   Not a bit of it !

They begin with a FACT—*the fact of* PRACTICE :

> " The primary presupposition of all history is, of course—living, human, individual beings.   The facts which must first of all be investigated are, therefore, these individuals in *their bodily organisation,* and in the relation between this organisation and the rest of Nature. All historical investigation must start from these *natural foundations* and their *modification* in the course of human history by the *action of human beings.*—MARX-ENGELS : *German Ideology.*

Already we have made a breach in the metaphysical *impasse.* We do not begin by " supposing " an origin for history, or by *inventing* a connection between Man and Nature, and Man and Man.   We begin with the unquestioned and the unquestionable fact—real flesh-and-blood men, whose bodily appetites compel them to *act,* whose need to *act* is conditioned basically by their specific, concrete relationship to Nature, and by the scope, character, and quality of their physical powers.   Thus Mankind is the presupposition of all history ; and the Nature which produced Mankind as a biological fact, and which necessitates the dependence of Man upon the *active use* he can make of Nature, is the first presupposition of Mankind.   Mankind is, as biological species, the product of Nature.   That is the first, self-evident, *fact.* The second follows from it : Man's dependence upon Nature is not Abstract *Dependence-in-general,* it is specific and concrete.   Mankind needs Food and Shelter, and to get these he must *act*—if only to the extent of stretching out his arm to grasp Nature-produced food, or that of creeping into a hole to get out of the rain and cold.   Thus Man's specific dependence upon Nature compels him to *change* Nature, both as it is *for him* (e.g., by going in out of the wet) and as it is *in itself*—by learning the art of land-cultivation, etc.   But in thus modifying Nature Man modifies his own specific dependence upon Nature, and in modifying his *relation* to Nature he modifies *himself* both relatively and positively. Thus arises the second fact—Man the dependent product of Nature becomes *in action* Man the *producer* of non-" Natural " products.   He becomes the modifier, the changer of Nature, the producer of a *new* Nature, both external and (in so far as he *by action* modifies, changes, and develops his own powers and appetites) *in himself*. He becomes less *specifically* dependent upon Nature and more specifically dependent upon the products of his own progressively modifying and modified *activity*. Thus the starting-point of the Marxian *Dialectical Materialist* conception of History is no abstract hypothesis but a concrete practical *fact*—that of Mankind's " ineluctable " dependence upon its own *active* development-producing inter-relation with Nature.

It is of overwhelming importance for the subsequent development, and for the complete and utter confutation of the bourgeois critics (whose primary affectation is that their methods are " scientific "), that we should dwell upon the significance of this starting-point.

The English semi-materialist George Henry Lewes, husband of the translator of Strauss and Feuerbach (" George Eliot "), friend of Spencer, Huxley, and Tyndall, may well stand as representative of the " sturdy " English practical standpoint of the nineteenth century. In politics he was a Radical inclining towards Chartism. In questions of philosophy he was nominally a " Positivist," that is to say, he was " English " enough to repudiate the *name* of Materialism while quietly adopting its substance. His *Biographical History of Philosophy* —his best-known work—was one long and spirited manifesto against the " metaphysical " or *a priori* method, and in favour of the " positive " or scientific method. It was begun in 1846, at the time when Marx and Engels had barely completed their *German Ideology*. It contrasts the two methods thus :

> " This then is the difference between the methods of [metaphysical] Philosophy and Positive Science : the one proceeds from *a priori* axioms—that is, from axioms taken up without having undergone the laborious but indispensable process of previous verification ; the other proceeds from axioms which have been rigidly verified. *The one proceeds from an Assumption, the other from a Fact.*"—LEWES : *Biog. History of Philosophy*, p. xix.

Cavil might be raised over Lewes' terminology—as to whether the procedure of the positive scientist does not likewise involve the " assumption " that the " fact " is such as it is taken to be. But all verbalising apart, Lewes, in his appeal to the objective empirical test—" verification "— goes directly to that which is essential. In the same work Lewes defines the difference further :

> " [Metaphysical] philosophy aspires to a knowledge

o

of *Essences* and Causes, Positive Science aspires only to a knowledge of Laws. The one pretends to discover what things are in themselves, apart from their appearances to sense, and whence they came. The other only wishes to discover their *modus operandi* ; observing the constant co-existences and successions of phenomena among themselves and generalising them into some one Law."—LEWES : *ibid.*, p. xviii.

We have already seen that Marx and Engels, by means of the method of Dialectical Materialism and the criterion of *practice*, are able to go beyond this strictly negative repudiation of idealist presuppositions. None the less Lewes's definition decisively endorses the scientific character of the procedure of Marx and Engels. Again, in the prolegomena he wrote in 1867 for his larger *History of Philosophy*, Lewes reiterates his point of view :

"Correct reasoning is the ideal assemblage of objects in their true relations of co-existence and succession. *It is seeing with the mind's eye.* Bad reasoning results from over-looking either some of the objects, or their relations ; some links are dropped and the gap is filled up from another series. Thus the traveller *sees* a highwayman, where there is truly no more than a sign-post in the twilight ; and a philosopher, in the twilight of knowledge, *sees* a pestilence foreshadowed by an eclipse."
—LEWES : *History of Philosophy*, Vol. I, p. xxxvii.

Again, speaking of scientific procedure, he says :

"An infirmity . . . is the necessity we are under of dislocating the order of Nature by Analysis and Abstraction ; which artifice, since it leads to discovery, may be copiously used, on condition of our remembering that it is an artifice, and that the order we have dislocated must be finally restored, if the order in Thought is to correspond to the order in Things. . . . Abstraction is one of the necessary artifices of research. . . . Observation of [individual] cases, however patient and prolonged, will never suffice to disclose the Laws which are enveloped in the cases, and which form the real aim of Science. And what are Laws ? They are the *constants* of phenomena, and can only be separated from the *perturbations*, due to other Laws, by a process of abstraction which sets aside the variable *accidents* and individual peculiarities accompanying and determining each special case."—LEWES : *ibid.*, p. lxxxix.

It was necessary for Lewes in 1867 to emphasise the distinction between the *a posteriori* method of the positive sciences and the *a priori* method of idealistic speculation and Theology, because those were the days of the great Darwinian battle—when the supernaturalists and obscurantists of every shade were making their last open stand in defence of the right of " *Revealed Truth* " to dictate limits, methods, and conclusions *a priori* to all scientific investigators. Seven years later Professor Tyndall aroused a storm of protests from the reactionaries by his eloquent and courageous but carefully guarded Address to the British Association at Belfast, August 19th, 1874. He provoked a storm by his plain avowal :

> " The impregnable position of science may be described in a few words. *We claim, and we shall wrest from theology, the entire domain of cosmological theory.* All schemes and systems which thus infringe upon the domain of science must in so far as they do this submit to its control and relinquish all thought of controlling it. Acting otherwise proved always disastrous in the past, and it is simply fatuous to-day."—TYNDALL : *Belfast Address* (1874).

With the term " Dialectical Materialism " inserted in place of the euphemism " science " used by Tyndall, and idealism added along with theology, this affirmation could well stand as the Marxist challenge and defiance to-day.

. . . . . .

Marx and Engels began with living men and women and sought the *general law* of the interdependence between Men and *the rest of* Nature. That is to say, they sought to distinguish the respect in which Mankind as an animal species is *unlike* all other living and non-living things in Nature from those respects in which Mankind is *like* these other things. Also they sought in that which *connected* man with Nature, not only that concrete connection itself, but also the law of its *modification* by the *action* of human beings.

It is typical of the shallow sophistry and electicism into which bourgeois culture has degenerated in England since the " spacious days " of the great Darwinian battle that the critics who (like Postgate and Eastman) are incapable of making the elementary distinction between the " essential " and the " accidental " in all phenomena—which (like the distinction between *constants* and *variables*) is one which scientific investigation cannot progress one inch without

making—that they should in the very act of flouting Marx
and Engels for their (non-existent) " mysticism " and " metaphysics " parade their opinion that the conception of the
" evolution " of all things is, nowadays, a commonplace.
That the *word* is a commonplace cannot be doubted. But
that the conception is in any real sense of the word *grasped*
either realistically or scientifically may be more than doubted.
That the factors of whose interaction Human History is the
resultant are biological Mankind on the one side and the rest
of Nature on the other would be conceded by all Bloomsbury.
But how would they *envisage* this resultant progression ? Or
its determining causation ? Both would, in 999 cases out
of 1000, be confounded under the common *cliché*—" evolution."

As commonly used, this term merely states that a result
has appeared. As soon as the user of the term is pressed for
details, for some statement of the *law* of the progression,
we discover, in all but the odd case in a thousand, that he
has merely fallen into a fashion of speech made easy for him
by his total ignorance of the scientific and philosophical
issues involved. Lenin affirms that :

" Development [evolution] is ' struggle ' of opposites.
Two historically observed conceptions of development
(evolution) are : (1) Development as decrease and increase, as repetition, and (2) Development as a *unity*
of opposites and their reciprocal co-relation.

" The first conception is dead, poor, and dry ; the
second is vital. It is *only* this second conception which
offers the key to understanding the ' self-movement ' of
everything in existence . . . to understanding the destruction of the old and the appearance of the new."—
Lenin : *Materialism and Empirio-Criticism*, p. 324.

Since the first of these alternative conceptions of evolution
is the *non*-dialectical view commonly held, we will first
examine the *Marx-Engels* argument further and then contrast
with its progressive *constant*—its *law*—the conceptions established in certain relevant branches of Natural Science.

The Transition from Nature to History

The process whereby Mankind as a biological species came
into being is antecedent to all *human* history. It is part of
natural history and as such has been explored by the
biologists. But what biology *as such* cannot explain is the
subsequent development of mankind's group combinations—

their historical permutation ! It was at one time a favourite argument with the supernaturalists that, as there has been no ascertainable modification of the human species in any essentials in the period of recorded history, there is therefore no " proof " of the " evolution theory." The argument has lapsed more in consequence of the overwhelming mass of evidence as to the truth of natural transformation in other departments of biology than in consequence of the discovery of a few fossil remains classifiable as on the border-line between the Ape and Man.

That at some point or another the transition was made nobody nowadays doubts. But as to *how* it was made nobody *except Marx and Engels* ever offered anything more than a conjecture. Here is how Marx and Engels tackle the problem :

"We may distinguish human beings from animals by consciousness, by religion, by anything you please. They themselves *begin to* distinguish themselves from animals as soon as they begin *to produce* their own means of subsistence—a step necessitated by their own bodily organisation."—MARX-ENGELS : *German Ideology.*

All the greatest discoveries are marvellous from their simplicity—*once they are discovered.* And to Marx and Engels this discovery was so self-evident that they claimed credit for it only so far as it is included in the wider generalisation of the *Materialist Conception of History.* Yet so far is it from being self-evident that only a minority even of the nominal adherents of Marxism have ever grasped this *self-production of man* as its central, dynamic, pivotal point :

" Inasmuch as human beings produce their own means of subsistence they, indirectly, produce *their own material life.* The necessaries of life are, above all, food, drink, shelter, clothing and a few others. Hence the first historical *act* is the *production* of the means for the satisfaction of these needs, and thereby the production of *material life itself. This one historical fact is a fundamental determinant of all history.*"—MARX-ENGELS : *ibid.*

In this passage nine-tenths of the criticisms of Marxism, including all those which hinge on the alleged " mechanical " or " rigid " *determinism* of Marxism, are refuted at one blow. With it the supernaturalism which alleges that " *God* made man in his own image " meets its completest possible negation : Mankind not only made all the gods, but in all that appertains to man's specific and progressive differentiation from the Animal world *mankind has made, is making, and will continue to make itself likewise*. As Engels expressed it with an apt quotation from Goethe : " In the beginning was The Deed "— in the past " man converted himself from an Ape into a savage by the *act of production*." By the continuance of the act of production mankind converts natural material into human flesh and human force, maintaining its existence and at the same time progressively widening the difference between itself and the *rest of Nature*. And this basic *activity* determines not only the *static* fact that human society *persists*, but the dynamic fact that it persists through a definite and progressively complexifying series of transformations. This, *the* dynamically *active root*, the mainspring of the *movement* of History, is, most characteristically, the fact which all the critics of Marx and most of the " simplifiers " carefully leave out of account !

Let us attend to these critics for a moment.

A long and wearisome debate has raged on the fringes of Marxism as to the correct proportion of emphasis to be placed respectively on the " economic " and the " human factor " in History. And those who fight to relegate the " economic factor " to a subordinate position generally do so because of their anxiety to secure a " freer play " for ideas. Here is Postgate's version of this dispute :

> " Such aberrations as might be caused by . . . the play of the power of ideas, they [Marx and Engels] obviously regarded as trivial aberrations. The forces of history marched majestically and indifferently on. That this is really true seems very doubtful (!). . . . The theory of historical materialism is stated in two slightly varying forms by Marx, and in this variation lies the key to the truth. The more extreme form of the theory states that the ideas current in society are a *reflection* of social and economic relations ; the less extreme that they are *conditioned* by social and economic relations. . . . *Even though the first statement was professed by Marx, the second is more true*."—POSTGATE : *Karl Marx*, p. 55.

That " Man's capacity for self-delusion is simply infinite " —as Herbert Spencer lamented—is only too apparent. But even when forewarned of this human weakness it still comes as something of a shock to find that men professedly studying *History*—the science of the forms and conditions of the progressive development of human *society*—should so inveterately return, like the proverbial " hog to his wallowing in the mire," to the standpoint of the *single individual*, posed and contraposed to " society " as something with which he has only a spectator's interest. Postgate, who in this passage is typical of his kind—the whole brood of critics and would-be revisers of Marx—first of all detaches the *ideas* from the men in whose heads they are engendered ; secondly, he detaches the " process of history " from *both* the men and the ideas, and then, thirdly, proceeds to discuss learnedly whether the *ideas* are *reflections* of " social and economic relations," or whether they are only *conditioned* by these relations. He affirms that Marx would have " preferred " the former theory ; he himself votes for the latter.

Once again Postgate has made a discovery—a Mare sitting on her nest ! And he offers us—*one of the eggs* !

Does the affirmation that ideas *reflect* reality—material and social—contradict the affirmation that ideas are *conditioned* by social and economic relations ? Postgate says *yes*—and votes for the latter.

What does it mean to say that a thing or idea is *conditioned* ? In this conjunction the term is contraposed to *caused*. Thus, for instance, the oxygen in the air is a *condition* of the fire in the grate, and a *necessary* condition, since in the absence of oxygen the fire would be impossible. But it is not a *cause* of the fire, since the materials may be laid in the grate and the oxygen be present in unlimited quantity and yet no fire result.

Now apply that to the *causation* of ideas in the heads of individual men, and the *conditioning* of those ideas—their *development* by means of social intercourse. Postgate, it will be seen, has confounded two distinct problems—those of individual and of *social* development. *By treating them as one he has eliminated their History !* Marx and Engels affirm that ideas are *produced* in men by their practical activities, that actual physical impact between men's physical organism and their material surroundings begets, in addition to *objective* rearrangements of matter and its motions, that transformation of bodily energy of which we become *subjectively* aware as consciousness and thought. Thus the *cause* of ideas (which are " nothing else than the material world, reflected in the human brain and translated into forms of thought "—MARX) is found in the active interaction between men and material reality. So much is common ground between Marx and all Materialists. What now comes up for investigation is *what follows as a consequence* ? Does the process end there ? Or do these ideas, once begotten, operate (by influencing men's *social* conduct) as *forces conditioning* the development of ideas *in other men* as well as themselves being *conditioned* (modified, developed, etc.) in the heads in which they were engendered ? So far as he has a point, Postgate is labouring to assert that ideas do thus operate. What he is self-prevented from seeing is that it is precisely in their demonstration of how ideas became objectively *operative*, of how they were " conditioned " (by social-interaction) and developed from individual notions into " forms of social consciousness or public opinion," that Marx and Engels made their revolutionary advance.

Postgate will accept the " conditioning " of ideas by " socia l and economic relations "—a gesture in the direction of Materialism. But he will not agree that ideas *reflect* those relations, and so joins hands with the idealists ! Postgate's running-mate, Eastman, openly and idealistically denies that ideas reflect reality at all—for him they are " fictional substitutes for knowledge of reality." Eastman is (in unguarded moments) openly idealist ; Postgate, more cautious, tries to keep one leg in each camp !

Postgate's point is blunt—so far as he has one ! He is patently absurd in the alleged contradiction he seeks to father upon Marx—since it is obvious that from Marx's standpoint ideas *both* reflect social and economic conditions *and* are conditioned by them. He falls into inextricable self-contradiction, since he cannot separate in his head two different (though related) groups of phenomena—those of the *origin* of the ideas in the heads of *individuals* and those of the *development* of those ideas into forms of " public opinion " under the " conditioning " of *social* circumstance. Like all his kind—he loses the difference in the unity, and the unity in the difference. He alternatively dissolves Society into its component individuals, and drowns the individuals in Society.

Moreover he, again like all his kind, first abstracts from Society its " economic relations " and then opposes this abstraction to other abstractions : " social relations," " ideas," etc. If he will but remember that the economic relations of Society are its *active*, *production relations*, that they are *relations between men* as well as relations between Society and Nature, he will, with an effort, be able to compass the thought that *ideas* enter into production-relations as into all men's conscious activities.

But how ? That is just the point which Marx is investigating. And it will help Postgate and all other similar sufferers if they will but reflect that ideas can determine social conduct only if (1) they are in fact and reality *reflections,* and (relatively) reliable ones of actually existing reality, social and/or material ; and (2) become operative as *deeds,* and in consequence become *collectivised,* as a result of the conditioning of social intercourse, into " public opinions."

What Marx and Engels were investigating, what they did elucidate as no man before or since, was the general law of this conditioning of *individual* ideas into " forms of *social* consciousness or *public* opinion." To say therefore that they regarded the " power of ideas " as the cause of " trivial aberrations " in the course of history is to state the reverse of the truth. They were investigating *history,* the positive *movement* resulting from men's *activities,* from what men *do,* among other things *with their brains.* Their problem did not *end* with saying ideas were reflections of objective reality ; it *began* there. It was precisely the problem why " the road to hell is paved with good intentions, not with bad ones " (BERNARD SHAW), precisely why the planned purposeful activities of men produced results quite different from what was expected ; why even when men achieved that which they set out to achieve (in accordance with their ideas) the result was always both less and *more* than what was bargained for. In fact the problem, one of precisely an opposite order from that which Postgate supposes, was : Why, operating with fixed ideas, did *variable results* follow ? Why, if Nature is governed by *fixed* laws, do ideas so continually tend to *vary* ? This question could only be answered by an analysis of the *causes* and the *conditioning* of ideas in Society. Ideas had to be traced to their roots and a source found not only for their *persistence* but, much more significantly, for their *changes,* their growth and transformation. That this source should be found *outside* man's ideas, *as such*—in the concrete objective relations between man and man, and Mankind collectively and Nature—was not original with Marx and Engels. Others had treated history as the manifestation of Ideas ; others had treated it as the manifestation of immutable Natural Law.

Marx was the first to find a Law of History which, while it allowed full scope for the interplay of ideas and of Natural Law (each operating through Man as a physical, animal being and his *active inter-relation* with Nature), also, and at the same time *distinguished it from* both Natural Law and the Law of Mental operations, while it was also a dialectical connecting link between them.

Is it not marvellous ? Here were Marx and Engels, men
who spent their lives in a never-ceasing struggle, theoretical
and practical, to clarify their own ideas and those of other
men—all with a view to bettering their practice—whose whole
theory and practice was an eloquent demonstration of their
basic conception of the living unity of Theory and Practice ;
and now, getting on for a century after their struggle began,
we are smugly assured that their theory was—one of the
impotence of theory ! That their central idea was—that
practice is unaffected by Theory !

It is a positive relief to turn from these grotesque parodies
to the splendid simplicity and precision of Marx and Engels
themselves :

" As individuals express their lives so they are. Thus
what they are coincides with what they produce ; and
not only with *what* they produce but with *how* they
produce it. What individuals *are* depends, consequently,
upon the material conditions of production."

" Determinate [i.e., specifically *conditioned*] individuals,
productively active in a determinate way, enter, therefore, into *determinate* social and political relations."

" Class differentiations and forms of State are continually being produced in the life-process of determinate
individuals—not, however, by these individuals as they
seem to be, to themselves or to others, but as they, in
fact, *are*—that is to say, as they work, as they are
engaged in material production, as they are active under
determinate material limitations, presuppositions, and
conditions independent of their will."

" The production of ideas, conceptions, consciousness,
is directly bound up in the first place with the material
activity and the material intercourse of mankind, *with
the speech of actual life.* Conceptions, thought, and the
intellectual intercourse of men thus arise as a direct
product of men's material activity. The same is true of
mental production as it is expressed in the letters,
the politics, law, ethics, religion, and metaphysics of a
nation. *Human beings produce* their conceptions, ideas,
etc. ; but *real*, working human beings, determined by
a definite development of their productive powers, and
of the mode of intercourse, in all its ramifications, arising
therefrom."—MARX-ENGELS : *German Ideology.*

In earlier chapters we have from a number of different
avenues of approach reached by analysis just this fact—that

men's conceptions are *produced* by men's activity out of sensory perceptions of the phenomena of objective nature and the material facts of social life. It is a basic deduction from the facts of social life that the differentiation between men in society must present each and every man in a given society, at a given moment, with a *different* aggregation of material phenomena from that which confronts every other man. This is the fact with which the *solipsists* and " modernist " *empirio-monists* juggle. What they miss completely is the *practical* fact here brought out so illuminatingly by Marx and Engels—the fact, namely, that in the process of *consciously* producing their own collective means of existence men also, but unconsciously produce the objective grounds for the generalisation of *particular* experiences into theoretical concepts whose scope and validity far transcends the range of direct experience of any single individual.

Observe the shrewdness with which Marx and Engels contrast dialectically (i.e., combine in a unity of opposites) the material intercourse and speech of everyday life and the letters, politics, law, etc., the *mental production* of a *nation*.

That *ideas* are products—that conceptions are constructions for which sensations of practical contact with material reality are required—is getting to be a commonplace with even the noisier " psychological " schools. But even yet it is difficult to get a proper appreciation of the fact that the production of ideas involves in the first place *social intercourse* as the only means whereby the individual can transcend his limitations *as* an individual, and involves in the second place, and more pertinently, the use of a *technological instrument, an " invention," that of ordered speech.*

The Mental Outcome of Production-Practice.

Without words only rudimentary thought is possible—accurate or inaccurate. All the possibilities of dispute which the critics of Marx exploit to the full are created by our dependence upon speech both as an instrument of thought and as a medium of social intercommunication. I may perceive the fact of an apple, and another fact an onion. That they are different I can perceive likewise. But only when I have perceived a number of apples and a number of onions and have by practical handling learned to " abstract " the general likeness in the apples from their particular differences can I *name* this *generality* as " Apple." Similarly with the onions. But, to carry the process further and to reach the still more general conceptions of Fruit and Vegetables, Organic and Inorganic, and of their inter-relations and dependencies, not only needs on the one side an accumulation of perceptual experience beyond the possibility of any one man to compass, but also needs on the subjective side the development of the technique of using names as *symbols* for each generality comprised within each stage of the process of ratiocinnation. That this feat is accomplished, once learned, as unconsciously as is the act of digestion gives the idealist and the mystifier his chance. But what is completely left out of account by the mystifier is the fact that, unless we are to fall back upon the supernaturalist supposition that language, elaborated into all its functioning organisation of vocabulary and grammar, was " given " to Man, ready-made, at his Creation, language must be recognised as an instrument that has developed and could only develop *in practical use.*

And *language is of no use to a solitary individual.* It has a use only in social activity ; hence it is with language, as with other details of men's productive activity, that the actual practice of its use begets results over and beyond those immediately aimed at. The language-instrument itself acquires increasing complexity and precision as it is differentiated and integrated in use. Likewise the consciousness of the user of the instrument becomes increasingly developed— by differentiation and synthetic integration—in the process of, and also as a by-product of, using the language-instrument. Thus *speech* arising directly in the course of mankind's practical social activity begets possibilities of thought which simply do not exist until this activity has gone beyond a definite minimum degree of development. That these developments of thought react upon the speech which made them possible is no more to be wondered at than that children should react upon the parents who have brought them into being—again by *practical activity.*

Thus the fact that men do contrast their political and other ideas, and their language as such, with their practical everyday activities is not to be wondered at ; nor, if the distinction is made as a *relative* distinction, is it to be disallowed. What constitutes the difficulty which objectors to the Marxian conception cannot surmount is, firstly, their inability to see the *interconnection* between the political, religious, and other " ideal " activities and the more prosaic and " interested " activities of the *same human individuals* ; and secondly, their attempt to take *conventional conceptions* of mankind, as these conceptions may be current at any moment, as *substitutes* for the real living men and women in their actual material life-activities.

It was precisely this substitution of a *conception* of abstract " human nature," or " humanity," for the objective and concrete human beings in their actual real-life activities which was the ground of Marx's and Engels' fight against the *non*-dialectical materialists—the Owenites and the followers of Feuerbach—and it is still the ground of the fight between the Dialectical Materialists and the opponents thereof. The most pertinent fact of all is commonly left quite out of sight, namely, that it is in their common and mutual dependence upon *language* that mankind finds a most fruitful and perennial source of error. All those errors which arise from the variations worked in History on the theme " our Fathers have told us ! " would have been obviated, along with all the good that has come from the " socialisation of achievement," had language never been invented. The fact that, this notwithstanding, Mankind invented language because it was *necessary* to its existence emphasises the moral.

Marx and Engels in elaborating this point were tackling and solving what had seemed an insoluble riddle to the eighteenth-century philosophers. Rousseau, in his *Discourse on the Origin of Inequality*, discusses the question of the origin of language and its effects with animation :

" The first language of mankind, the most universal and vivid, in a word the only language man needed, was the simple cry of Nature. . . . When the ideas of men began to expand and multiply, and closer communication took place among them, they strove to invent more numerous signs and a more copious language . . . men at length bethought themselves of substituting for [gestures and imitative *sounds*] the articulate sounds of the voice which, without bearing the same relation to any particular ideas, are better calculated to express them all as conventional signs. Such an institution could only have been made by common consent, and must have been effected in a manner not very easy for men whose gross organs had not been accustomed to any such exercise. It is also in itself still more difficult to conceive, since such common agreement must have had motives, and speech seems to have been highly

necessary to establish the use of it. . . . For myself,
I am so aghast at the increasing difficulties which present
themselves, and so well convinced of the almost demonstrable impossibility that languages should owe their
original institution to merely human means, that I leave
to anyone who will undertake it the discussion of the
difficult problem, which was most necessary, the existence
of society to the invention of language, or the invention
of language to the establishment of society."—ROUSSEAU :
Origin of Inequality (1755).

The problem stated by Rousseau was a real problem, and
still is one for every standpoint except that of Dialectical
Materialism—of Marxism. Only if we recognise that *human*
Society begins in the *practical* modification of the " state of
Nature " by the mutual modification of humans in *combined
acts of production*—which at first may have been only inter-
mittent practices arising from special combinations of circumstances—do we realise that the origin of language (as cries
and gestures) and that of association are correlative facts,
both arising from the more primary fact of the *dialectic*
interaction of biological *near*-Men and Nature.

The dependence of all abstract thought upon the prior
existence of human society and *the Speech of actual life* was
recognised more or less clearly by all the English and French
Materialist School and their successors, the empirical-positivist
school of Spencer, Bain, Lewes, etc. The latter thus states
the case :

" If man is a social animal, *which is undeniable,* the
unit in a living whole, just as any one organ is the unit
of an organism, obviously his functions will be determined not only by his individual structure but also by
the structure of the Collective organism. The functions
of the liver, or of the kidneys, are determined partly by
their structure, and partly by influences from other
organs. Man's individual functions arise in relation to
the Cosmos ; his general functions arise in relation to
the Social Medium ; thence Moral Life emerges. All
the animal impulses become blended with *human*
Emotions. . . . Mind cannot be explained without constant recognition of the statico-dynamical relations of
Organism and Social Medium. . . . There is what may
be called an *a priori* condition in all Sensation, and in all
Ideation. But this is *historical,* not *transcendental* : it

is itself the product of experience, though not of the individual. . . . Man is no longer to be considered simply as an assemblage of organs, but also as an organ in a Collective Organism. From the former he derives his sensations, judgments, primary impulses ; from the latter *his conceptions, theories, and virtues.* This is very clear when we learn how the Intellect draws both its inspiration and *its instrument* from the social needs. All the materials of Intellect are images and symbols, all its processes are operations on images and symbols. *Language—which is wholly a social product for a social need*—is the chief vehicle of symbolical operation, and the only means whereby Abstraction is effected. *Without Language there can be no meditation ; no theory ; no Thought in the special meaning of that term.* A perception combines many feelings into one and is so far knowledge. A word—the symbol of a conception—condenses many perceptions into one ; and it is thus not only knowledge of a wider range, but is a knowledge which is *facultative,* and capable of transmission and preservation."— LEWES : *Problems of Life and Mind* (1874), Vol. I, pp. 159–67.

The earlier materialists were more acutely conscious of the social function of Language as the germinator of error, and as such they commonly opposed it to Thought as an obstacle rather than as its vehicle. Thus Hobbes in a famous passage says :

" In the right definition of names lies the first use of speech, which is the acquisition of science ; and in wrong or no definition lies the first abuse, from which proceeds all false and senseless tenets. Which makes those men that take their instruction from the authority of books, and not from their own meditations, to be as much below the condition of ignorant men, as men endued with true science are above it.

" For between true science and erroneous doctrine ignorance is in the middle. Natural sense and imagination are not subject to absurdity. Nature itself cannot err ; and as men abound in copiousness of language, so they become more wise, or *more mad* than ordinary. Nor is it possible without letters for any man to become either excellently wise, or . . . *excellently foolish.* For words are wise men's *counters* : they do but reckon by them.

But they are *the money of fools.* . . ."—THOMAS HOBBES :
Leviathan (1652), Chap. IV.

A century later the French Materialist, Helvetius (1715–71),
used the same fact with revolutionary intent to emphasise
the power of kings and governments to perpetuate delusions
favourable to their interests :—

" Languages owe their origin to necessity, not to
philosophers . . . it is with languages as with an
algebraic calculation. At first some errors creep into
it ; these are not perceived ; the calculation is continued
from step to step till we arrive at consequences absolutely
ridiculous. The absurdity is perceived ; but how shall
we find the place of the first error ? This requires the
repetition and the proofs of a great variety of calcula-
tions. Unhappily there are few capable of undertaking
it, and still fewer who will submit to the drudgery,
*especially when the authority of men in power opposes the
verification.*"—HELVETIUS : *On the Mind,* Essay I,
Chap. IV.

In sum : speech is a technological instrument developed in
practice under the impulsion of the needs of practice, is at
one and the same time a product and an instrument of
production. It is the dialectical link between the subjective
activities of the individual man and the ideological development of human society. It is an instrument for the production
of Truth—and for the production of error—and for the conduct
of the undying social conflict between them. It is the point
of transition from Practice to Theory, and from Theory back
to Practice again. It is the concrete refutation of every school
of solipsists and the objective proof of the Dialectical Materialist conclusion that—

" *Consciousness can never be anything other than
consciousness of existing : and men's existence is their
actual process of existing.*"

" We do not start from what men say, fancy, or
imagine to themselves ; still less from Man as he is said,
fancied, thought or represented to be in order from
thence and by that path to reach Man in the flesh. We
set out from real, active human beings ; and from their
actual life-processes we demonstrate the ideological
reflexes and echoes of this process of living."

" Even the phantasmagorias in men's brains are
necessary consequences, supplements, of their material,
empirically ascertainable living-process, a process con-

nected inseparably with its material presuppositions. Morals, religion, metaphysics, and other ideology, together with their accompanying forms of consciousness, therefore, no longer present an appearance of independence. They have no history, *no development of their own.* Human beings develop their material production and their material intercourse, and in so doing change their material environment, and, therewith, *change likewise, and by the same acts, their own thoughts, and the products of their thoughts.*"—MARX-ENGELS : *German Ideology.*

Here the challenge is driven right home. Not only does this *Dialectical* productive interaction between Man and Nature beget the *new result* of material products in which natural substance and *formative* human activity are dialectically united. But one and the same activity begets *also* the positive and relative transformation both of Mankind and of Nature. Moreover, the interaction of the men, dialectically linked in a *perpetual* process of mutual *self-transformation,* begets the further dialectical result of developing ideologies, whose development must in turn be understood *dialectically.* These ideologies, one and all, had in the hands of the bourgeoisie offered themselves as " explanations " of mankind's *material* activities in terms of " higher things." Marx and Engels meet them with the direct challenge—show that your ideology is capable of doing anything, except as an instrument for the material activities of actual living *Men.*

Moreover—and here came the acid test—all the non-materialist and non-dialectical ideologies had been patently unable to escape from the jaws of the Great Contradiction : either there was a *real historical movement,* an actual advance, or there was only an illusory semblance of progress. If the former was true, what became of the *fixed,* eternal, unchanging Verity which religion, law, orthodox politics, and transcendentalist moralists all postulated as the *Truth* " revealed " in their Systems ? If there was no real advance, and progress was only an illusion, why then had all these ideologies undergone a demonstrable historical *change* ? How could they *change* without admitting either that the historical process was *real,* and objectively dialectic, or, alternatively, that they themselves were inextricably part of the transient, illusory order ?

The challenge still stands. It has been answered only by silence, and by tacit acquiescence.

THE MATERIAL OUTCOME OF PRODUCTION ACTIVITY

So far we have considered the outcome of the interaction of Men and Nature with particular attention to its subjective side—to the outcome of the interaction in the modification of men and their thought-products. But there is another side altogether :

"In history at every stage there exists *a material outcome*, a sum of productive forces, a historically created relation to nature, and a historically created relation of individuals one to another, which outcome is handed down to each successive generation by its predecessor. Hence in each stage of history there is a mass of productive forces, *capitals*, which, while they are in fact *modified* by the new generation, also, and on the other hand, *prescribe* to the new generation its conditions of living, and thus give it its *definite* development, its *specific* character. *Thus circumstances make men as much as men make circumstances.*"—MARX-ENGELS : *German Ideology.*

Compare this, in all its limpid clarity, with the Postgatian version of the process of history "marching majestically on" (like the soul of John Brown), indifferent to ideas, to deaths, to births, to—anything ! To make the Postgate theory reasonably intelligible it needs to be carried to its logical conclusion—"the process of history marches majestically and indifferently on, regardless of whether there are any *men* left living in the world or not ! " And this, in point of fact, would be less absurd than the wretched eclectic bungle which Postgate is trying (in company with not a few others) to palm off as Marxism, which is nothing other than the old mechanical Natural Law Theory which saw in history only individual men, and nothing in men but their absolute dependence on Natural Law.

Postgate tries to save his face by arguing that Engels in his *Feuerbach* "makes observable ' deviations ' . . . from this rigidity." We will give two quotations ; one from Marx, one from Engels. The reader may then compare both with the extracts above written by Marx and Engels in collaboration. It will be seen that they all coincide ; that there is no difference between Engels' argument and Marx's ; and that the " rigidity " exists solely in the brain of the critic :

"*Man makes his own history*, but he does not make it out of the whole cloth. He makes it out of conditions, not such as he himself has chosen, but out of such as

lie ready to his hand. The traditions of all past generations weigh like an Alp [*alp* in German means both a
mountain and a *nightmare*] upon the brain of the living.
At the very time when men are absorbed in revolutionising *things and themselves*, in bringing about *what never
before was*—at such very epochs of revolutionary crisis
they anxiously conjure up and enlist in their service the
ghosts of the past, assume their names and their battle
cries and costumes that the new historic spectacle may
be enacted in time-honoured guise and with borrowed
language. Thus did Luther masquerade as the Apostle
Paul; thus did the Revolution of 1789 to 1814 deport
itself as Roman Republic and Roman Empire alternately.
—MARX: *Eighteenth Brumaire*, Chap. 1.

" *Men make their own history*, whatever its outcome
may be—in that each person follows *his own consciously
desired end*, and it is precisely *the resultant* of these many
wills operating in different directions and of their manifold effects upon the outer world *that constitutes history*.
Thus it is also a question of what the many individuals
desire. The will is determined by passion or deliberation.
But the levers which determine passion or deliberation
are of very different kinds. Partly they may be external
objects, partly ideal motives, ambition, ' enthusiasm for
truth and justice,' personal hatred, or *even purely individual whims of all kinds*. But, on the one hand, we
have seen that the many individual wills active in history
for the most part produce results quite other than those
they intended—often quite the opposite : their motives
therefore in relation to the total result are thus of only
secondary significance. On the other hand, the further
question arises : what driving forces in turn stand behind
these motives. What are the historical causes which
transform themselves into these motives in the brains
of these actors ? "—ENGELS : *Feuerbach*, pp. 49–50.
Engels goes on to say : " The old materialism never put
this question to itself." Postgate makes it a crime in Marx
that he did put this question, that he was not content, as
Postgate is, and as Eastman demands, to treat motives as
" ultimate " facts for which it is " determinist " to seek an
explanation—except in Freud ! What is worst of all, Marx
found the explanation—and years before Freud was born !
That is the sin for which Bloomsbury can never forgive him !
That the point may be cleared beyond all possible dispute

we will examine a few samples of the non-Marxian non-*historic* conceptions of "History"—and gain a further proof that Dialectical Materialism alone supplies a conception of history that will survive the experimental tests (*a*) of objective *visualisation*, and (*b*) of serving as a guide to practice.

And as a preliminary let us note here (that it may be compared with the extracts given above) a curious side-light on the Bloomsbury version of Marxism. Every tyro in politics has heard of Marx's " Labour " Theory of Value (which is, in point of fact, only Marx's theory to the extent of a radical modification which critics and simplifiers commonly ignore), but not one of these critics has ever noted that Marx's conception of history might with equal propriety be called the " Labour Theory of History ! " Yet these are Marx's words :

" Labour is, in the first place, a process in which *both* Man *and* Nature participate, and in which man *of his own accord* starts, regulates and controls the material reactions between himself and Nature. He *opposes* himself to Nature, *as one of her own forces*, setting in motion, arms and legs, head and hands, the natural forces of his body, in order to appropriate Nature's productions in a form adapted to his own wants. *By thus acting on the external world and changing it, he at the same time changes his own nature*."—MARX : *Capital*, Vol. I, pp. 156–57.

The Marxian conception of History is in fact the only conception of history which allows scope for the historical initiative of individuals and at the same time preserves the objective reality of the historical process as such.

The Theological conception—that Man was " created " by God and has no other choice but that between achieving, or failing to achieve, Heaven—or Hell, as the case may be—is a denial of any historical development at all. In *essence* Man on this theory remains to-day what he was on the day of his Creation. Incidents have happened to men : and incidental changes have taken place in the merely external trappings of men's existence. But fundamentals remain now as they ever have been.

Though the Theological conception is seldom advanced openly to-day—at any rate under that name—it is in essence carried over into the conception of the non-dialectical Materialists ; in which category can be included speculators so widely different as Hobbes, Rousseau, Herbert Spencer, Auguste Comte and H. T. Buckle. In all their cases History is merely the record of the external happenings which have occurred to Men. Society is merely a static inter-relation between men which is capable of a purely quantitative alteration only—a more or less perfect degree of division of labour. Their subject-matter is in fact *not History*, not *the objective development of the concrete material outcome of mankind's collective activity*, but the relative and subjective development of Man and his " civilisation." However much it may be camouflaged by the use of the term " evolution " (in the sense of simple unfolding), this conception remains (though it is as current as ever) fundamentally anti-historical in that only individual subjective progress is conceived as possible to man, and the only alteration possible in his circumstances that of simple increase and decrease in the consequences of his quantitative increase or decrease in knowledge.

Substantially the only distinction discoverable between the Sociology of Herbert Spencer and his school at the end of the nineteenth century and that of Thomas Hobbes in the middle of the seventeenth century is that the latter though frankly Tory and counter-revolutionary, is the less pessimistic from the proletarian point of view.

Here, for instance, is a characteristic passage from the *Leviathan* on the possibilities of revolutionary change which, as a Royalist, writing under the Commonwealth, Hobbes was not at all inclined to dismiss from consideration :

" Though nothing can be immortal which mortals make yet, if men had the use of Reason they pretend to, their commonwealths might be secured at least from perishing by internal diseases. . . . Therefore when they come to be dissolved, not by external violence but intestine disorder, the fault is not in men as they are the ' matter,' but as they are the makers and orderers of them. For men as they become at last weary of jostling and hewing one another, and desire with all their hearts to conform themselves into one firm and lasting edifice ; so for the want both of the art of making fit laws to square their actions by, and also of humility and patience to suffer the rude and cumbersome points of their present greatness to be taken off, they cannot without the help of a very able architect be compiled into any other than a crazy building, such as, hardly lasting out their own time, must assuredly fall upon the heads of their posterity."—HOBBES : *Leviathan* (1652), Chap. XXIX.

The old Tory has plainly a poor opinion of his neighbours, and of the luck likely to befall their bungling efforts at State-building. But, all the same, his argument concedes the possibility that the thing might very well come to pass, if only men " had the use of Reason they pretend to." Compare with that opinion of Hobbes's this more " modern " view:

" While this conception of societies as evolved . . . implies that in the slow course of things changes almost immeasurable in amount are possible, it also implies that but small amounts of such changes are possible within short periods.

" Thus the theory of progress disclosed by the study of sociology as a science is one which greatly moderates the hopes and the fears of extreme parties. After clearly seeing that the structures and actions throughout a society are determined by *the properties of its units,* and that (external differences apart) the society cannot be substantially and permanently changed without its units being permanently changed, it becomes easy to see that great alterations cannot suddenly be made to such purpose. . . . Evidently . . . the Doctrine of Evolution, in its social applications, is calculated to produce a steadying effect alike on thought and action."—HERBERT SPENCER : *Study of Sociology* (1878), Chap. XVI.

As between the old Tory and the modern Liberal there is more consolation in the old Tory ; and, what is more to the purpose, the fact is plain that the Spencerian conception has become under the influence of the Spencerised Fabians the official doctrine (" the inevitability of gradualness ") of the British Labour Party !

The " atomic " sociology thus held by both Hobbes and Spencer, and practically the whole of British academic orthodoxy, can be contrasted with the equally undialectical " unitary " conception of Auguste Comte. His admirer, F. J. Gould, thus summarises the programme given in Comte's *General View of Positivism* (1848):

" All departments of our knowledge are really component parts of one and the same Science—namely, the ' Science of Humanity.' . . .

" In social life Progress should be regarded as Order made manifest, as the object of Order, as the Development of Order. Order and Progress depend upon the co-operation of four social powers—womanhood, labour (working men), organising directors, and philosophers, considered not as fixed castes, but as moral and material agents. Otherwise . . . (1) Women, as representatives of Humanity ; (2) Working men as agents in the exploitation of natural resources ; (3) Organisers as ministers of the social capital and as political rulers ; (4) Thinkers, interpreters of history, counsellors in the present, forelookers to the future, educators."—F. J. GOULD : *Auguste Comte*, p. 81.

Comte thus presents the converse of the Hobbes-Spencer " atomic " theory of society. Whereas for Hobbes and Spencer men's integration into a society was purely " accidental " and of relative significance only (their *separation*, as units, being the *essential* and permanent fact), for Comte the reverse was the case. For him the integration was the essential, and the separation the non-essential. But in each case the relation of ruler and ruled, of owner and non-owner, of workers and director of work, was a fixed and inescapable feature. Comte furthermore goes to the length, under a sentimental pose of giving " recognition " to " women's place in society," of fixing the social *division* between the sexes even more absolutely and unchangeably than is the case in patriarchal-polygamous societies. Neither view includes the possibility of any radical *transformation* of society, of any truly revolutionary change. In each case " Society " is merely the sum of its separate parts—which is the acid test of a static, *non*-dialectical view.

HENRY THOMAS BUCKLE (1821–62) is remarkable as the first, and in the main the only, Englishman to attempt a scientific generalisation of the phenomena of history. His masterpiece, an *Introduction to the History of Civilisation in England* (1857–62), was never finished, but it remains a massive monument to his infinite patience, diligence, and inductive power. It is to be feared that despite the fact that it is regularly reprinted with each series of " popular classics " to appear, Buckle's work is seldom more than glanced at nowadays. For the bourgeoisie to-day, his methods are far too meticulously laborious ; his conclusions do not appear in any dramatic paradoxes or facile generalisations capable of homœopathic use ; to read him, in short, approximates much too closely to *work* for Buckle to be anything more than a name to the bourgeoisie. (He is far inferior, of course, to Hegel ; but Hegel is far harder to comprehend.)

For the proletariat and the proletarian intellectuals Buckle suffers the heavy disadvantage that his object was attained more effectively by other men working independently, who not only assembled evidence which demonstrated the truth of the propositions which he adopted only as tentative hypotheses, but transcended them by comprising them within generalisations which invalidated the primary assumptions of his method.   Between the publication of the first and second volumes—all that appeared—of his masterpiece there appeared two works which wholly superseded him : Darwin's *Origin of Species* and Marx's *Critique of Political Economy* These works simultaneously revolutionised the whole subject.

Buckle had patiently set out to find an inductive generalisation which would comprise both Man and Nature within the terms of a comprehensive Natural Law.   His method was to take the established conclusions of natural science so far as they bore upon Man and his civilisation, and then by the collation of the data recorded in literature and chronological narrative history to attempt to find the " Law " of civilisation.   For his purposes it was necessary to assume that Nature worked " according to fixed laws," and that the Nature of Man was, as part of Nature, fixed likewise and bound by *immutable* law.   Darwin's work demonstrated—though to this day few Darwinians realise it—that Nature proceeded not in a *mechanical* but in a *revolutionary* (i.e., a dialectical) way.   Marx demonstrated for his part that the " law " of human society, civilised and otherwise, was *revolutionary* likewise.   Between them they completed the work which the natural scientists had quite unwittingly begun that of completely revolutionising the scientific conception of Natural Law—by bringing Man and his Thought activity as well as his objective practice wholly within its scope.

THE TRANSFORMATION OF THE CONCEPT " NATURAL LAW "

The concept " Natural Law " has its history.   The concept Nature is—*not* " *natural*."   Primitive savages, as has been well said, " do not so much believe in the supernatural as *live* in it."   The concept Nature arises at first as the " other " of the concept of Supernatural Power.   The germ of the notion Natural Law appeared in the concept of a Necessity which set bounds to the arbitrary wilfulness of Gods and men The concept " law " had no existence with primitives, whose whole lives were bound by a custom it was unthinkable to depart from. But with the rise of the earliest civilizations and the radical revolutionising of primitive customs they entailed, the cosmological philosophers evolved the notion of a Natural Law imposed from somewhere outside of Nature to produce order out of chaos just as the law of the State produced " order " among men. This conception was carried over into Christian Theology on the collapse of the Roman Empire and formed the basis of its cosmology. For Necessity the Christian Theologians substituted Divine Omnipotence— insistence upon the *absolute* contrast between the power and the eternity of God and the impotence and perishability of the " world."

Theological insistence upon the mortality and finiteness of all mundane things begot an unperceived revolution in the conception of Nature. The insistence upon Divine Providence, Rule, and Design begot the conception of Nature as something whose very essence was impermanence, variation, mutability and decay—which only God's *will* could check. With the revival of learning and philosophy in the fifteenth century, and the beginnings of positive natural science in the sixteenth and seventeenth centuries, Necessity reappeared in the new guise of a " Power," " Force," or Natural " Law," which set bounds and limits to and imposed conditions upon these Divine interferences with the mutability of natural things. Natural Law was thus formulated as distinct from and even (though this was not admitted openly until a century later) opposed to the Law of God. Hobbes expresses the conception very finely :

" That when a thing lies still, unless somewhat else stir it, it will lie still for ever, is a truth no man doubts of. But that when a thing is in motion, it will eternally be in motion, unless somewhat else stay it, though the reason be the same, *namely, that nothing can change itself*, is not so easily assented to. For men measure, not only other men, but all other things by themselves. And because they find themselves subject after motion to pain and lassitude, think everything else grows weary of motion and seeks repose of its own accord . . . ascribing appetite and knowledge of what is good for their conservation (which is more than man has) to things inanimate, absurdly.

" When a body is once in motion, it moveth, unless something else hinder it, eternally."—HOBBES : *Leviathan*, Chapter II.

Natural Law thus became (as the Law of God grew less and less to be insisted upon as an explanation of the course of Nature) a conception of *Fixed* and *Necessary Limitations* to Change on the one side, and permanence on the other. Changes were interpreted as *interferences from outside* with natural persistences : persistence likewise was interpreted (when necessary, though shrewd old Hobbes had well and truly hit the mark when he said that men are more prone to attribute rest and inactivity to Natural things, than the reverse) as an interference from outside with a motion that would otherwise have been unable to " change itself."

This conception of the Natural Law as something *fixed,* outside of, and over-riding the concrete phenomena of Nature, was carried over from the eighteenth-century philosophers—who had completed the conception by adding as its counterpart a Moral Law governing the actions of Men— by the Natural-scientific and Moral philosophers of the nineteenth century. Though an accumulation of separate discoveries had undermined the conception it still stood to all appearances unshaken (as, for that matter, it still stands with all those " scientists " and " philosophers " who argue that it is not the business of science to " explain," since all that science can do is to " describe "—a conception which preserves the antithesis of an arbitrary and intrinsically inexplicable Law *imposed upon* things whose " behaviour " is fully explicable only as a consequence of this compulsion).

Darwin's discovery breached the *fixity* by demonstrating that in one immense and vitally important field of Nature (that of life forms, of living organisms) *the Law itself was subject to mutation.*

Natural philosophers had built up a body of organised knowledge which all rested upon the careful discrimination between species and individual varieties. The species themselves were neatly graded in an ascending scale of wider and wider generalisation, so that the Natural Order ranged from individual, through genera, species, family, order, etc., up to the Universal Order ; with everything as tidily in its place as the Brigade of Guards on the Horse Guards Parade, " Trooping the Colour " on the King's Birthday. No lawgiver since Procrustes ever demanded such implicit obedience as the pre-Darwinian natural philosophers demanded in the name of Natural Law (*alias* the Great Designer of the Universe, *alias* God) from the facts within their view.

And Charles Darwin quietly and patiently issued, after

long delay, a work written in a tone almost of apology, in which the whole of this order was as effectively shattered as the Trooping of the Colour would be if the Horse Guards' Parade suddenly became a volcano in full eruption.

Yet the cream of the joke, not yet realised by anybody but Dialectical Materialists, is that all Darwin had done was to explain *how exactly biological classification is objectively valid.*

Darwin explained that species are *real*, and not imaginary, distinctions which actually exist in Nature—that the distinction between a species and an individual variety is not one of conventional classification, but of reality. But it is not the same *kind* of difference. The older school of Naturalists had supposed that the *species* was a kind of blue-print held up by the Inscrutable Author of Natural Law to which the wayward individual variety conformed as best it might. If it conformed closely, it was " true to type." It got " good marks " from the Examiner ! If it varied widely it was an " impure " specimen, an " accidental " variation, to be disregarded. Thus for the older Naturalists the foundation of science lay in the absolute exclusion of any historical progression from Nature.

Darwin replied with the facts, which proved that the *mutability* of the variety was not at all the indefinite, haphazard thing the older science had supposed, that there was a *method in its madness*, and that nothing proved this better than the fact that it was *variation in a regular way which produced the species*, and not deviation in an irregular way which produced the variety !

DARWIN AS REVOLUTIONIST

This was a revolution whose profundity has not even to this day been fully appreciated by anybody but Dialectical Materialists.

For the bourgeoisie all it has meant has been that knowledge has been thereby " proved " to be not knowledge at all, but mere " opinion "—that Darwin " proved " that all the Naturalists had been talking nonsense—that later discoveries have " proved " that Darwin was talking nonsense—that it is therefore only the opinion of the moment that counts ; and that doesn't either—*not really* !

Raymond Postgate, for instance, observes :

" Marx is frequently compared to Darwin : the comparison is at no point more apt than in Economics. *We no longer* regard the *Origin of Species* as an *up-to-date*

biological textbook."—POSTGATE : *Karl Marx*, p. 78.
Up-to-date ! Charles Darwin worked an intellectual revolution. By the patient labour of more than forty years he
achieved a feat which won him the unstinted admiration of
the whole intellectual world, one which added so much of
new ground for patriotic pride to the countrymen of Francis
Bacon, John Locke, William Harvey, Isaac Newton, Robert
Boyle, John Dalton, Henry Cavendish, Joseph Priestley,
Michael Faraday and Charles Lyell, that most of their names
are forgotten while his is remembered. Yet all he really
accomplished was, it would seem, to provide the dilettanti
intelligentsia with an excuse for disregarding and contemning
every achievement of intellectual effort which is " *not up-to-
date* " !

The comparison between Marx and Darwin holds good for
reasons quite other than those of their limitations. They
achieved essentially similar feats ; they achieved them by
exactly parallel methods ; and their common achievement
made possible a higher synthesis of human knowledge than
was ever attained before. No two men ever worked a bigger
intellectual revolution. *They abolished the separation between
Natural Law and the facts of Nature.* They made it possible
for us to see the law *in* the facts, instead of postulating it
a priori as a goal towards which the facts " ought by rights "
to tend. They gave their quota of empirical proof towards
the establishment as a verified *law* of that Logical Unity of
Nature, History and the Thought Activity of Man which
Hegel had *guessed,* but which a whole century of positive
scientific discovery was needed to prove.

Hegel had *conceived* the Universe as a Unity in a perpetual
state of self-transformation—as perpetually undergoing a
process of revolutionary metamorphosis. Marx and Darwin
helped more than any two men to provide the proof of his
brilliant guess. It is well worth while to examine what it
was that Darwin did and compare it with Marx's achievement.

Before Darwin the accepted view was that the Universe
presented to our inspection a myriad array of different things,
whose essential qualities were fixed and unalterable, and
whose incidental (or " accidental ") variations were
" governed " by a Natural Law imposed upon them as it
were " against their will." Conceptually contraposed to this
Natural Universe was the world of Man, whose essential
Nature was *Freedom*—that of Man's Will and Man's Thought—

and whose conformity to Law, Natural, Human, and Divine—was incidental and " accidental " only. The contrast of Necessity in Nature and Freedom in Man, both as *absolutes* admitting of no qualification in themselves, but capable of an infinite variety of modes of application—this was the basic presupposition of the intellectual world which Marx and Darwin revolutionised.

The issue upon which Darwin joined battle was that of the fixity of species in organic Nature. The pre-Darwinian evolutionists of the Lamarck school had argued, *not* that species were capable of transmutation, but that variation was so much an absolute law of Nature that the *conception of species itself* was only subjectively valid.

It was on a wider scale, as though one should argue that because every blade of grass is different from every other blade therefore there is no such thing as *grass* ; except, of course, as a " convenient fiction."

The opponents of the Lamarckian evolutionists had replied with the masses of fact which proved persistencies in Nature of such a character as to destroy the theory of the *indefinite variability* of all living things. They said in effect—the " species " *grass* may make itself manifest in an infinite variety of blades, because it has *bladiness* as one of its properties. But, however much it varies, it still continues to be *grass*.

The issue was : which is " essential " and which " accidental," the *blades* or the *grass* ?

Darwin's answer was simple : Both are " necessary," and *both* are " accidental "—each in its place and degree. The *grass* cannot exist without exhibiting the quality of " bladiness " ; the blades, on the other hand, are *always becoming more or less* " grassy." The *species* lies not in the abstract quality of grassiness " one and indivisible," but in the concrete and specific *persistence* through a series of variations of the grassy character *in the blades*. In certain circumstances they may become blades of different *kinds* of grass—in time they may become seed-bearing grasses which, in certain circumstances, may become *not grass*, but grain-bearing plants. Wheat is not barley, nor barley oats ; neither is millet, or emmer ; yet the possibility—nay, the certainty—that wheat, oats, barley, etc., have a common ancestor in a variety of wild grass, and that all grasses likewise have a common ancestor, is plain for all folk to see if they will but look.

A field of wheat is, as it grows, first a field of *blades*, then of stalks, then of stalks with ears. The blades are not blades of *grass*—that we know from their after history. But check that growth before the stalk stage—and only experts could say but that the blades were those of *a variety of grass* ?

Shall we then say that wheat, oats, barley, etc., are *only* varieties of " grass " ? To say so would be to ignore the important fact that from wheat grains we grow wheat plants, from oats, oat plants, etc. Never do we sow wheat and reap oats. So far the orthodox are right. But on the other hand there is wheat *and* wheat, and it is, and has been, demonstrably possible to breed from wheat a whole number of different sub-species of wheat, all of which produce when sown not the parent variety, but the *new* daughter variety.

All of which proves, what ? That the *species* is not a *fixed* archetype to which varieties " conform " because they " must " or " ought "—but a regularly *periodical persistence* in variation. The fact that new species can be produced to-day makes irresistible the evidence pointing to the conclusion that they have been produced in the ordinary course of Nature in the past. Therefore the claim of the Lamarckians is justified so far, that *variability* is a primary fact in Nature. But it is not an *indefinite* variability, as the Lamarckians had assumed, not an *absolute* variability, such as would exclude all possibility of calculation in advance. It is a *definite* variability of a *periodical* kind ; though it is capable of indefinite extension and further variation in various ways, its variability remains *definite* and *periodical* and is governed not by the " caprice " of the organism, but by the cumulative interaction between the living thing and the conditions in which it lives.

The origin of species is to be sought in the *union in active opposition* of the organism and its environment—that is, the *dialectical* and revolutionary essence of Darwinism.

How is this different from the orthodox presentation of Darwinism ? How is Darwinism revolutionary ?

The stressing of the origin of species in a *union of opposites*— in an *active* inter-relation—differs from the orthodox presentation in that it stresses *both* the *opposition* and the *union* of organism and environment. In stressing these it stresses the fact that the *opposition persists* after the change has taken place and the new species have appeared. Orthodox Darwinians are concerned with evolution commonly as a " description " of the way in which the world has been filled with variety. Alternatively they are concerned to show that, since the difference between Man and Ape is formal and superficial only, all differences in Nature and real life are likewise only formal and superficial. In this way Darwinism becomes a doctrine of conservatism and reaction— a denial of *real objective progress*.

Herbert Spencer, for instance, pressed the aspect of the *union* forward in one part of his *Synthetic Philosophy* to the exclusion of the opposition. " Life is a continual process of adjusting internal to external changes." In this formulation the emphasis is laid first upon the continuity, then upon the completely mystical nature of the changes. External changes continually " happen." They are quite outside the scope of control by the organism, human or non-human, which can do no more than make the necessary " adjustment " in consequence of the " change." In other parts of his system it is true he insisted upon the struggle for existence. But in these cases no " adjustment " was possible or tolerable to Herbert Spencer. He could see in evolution movement in a straight line only—or, alternatively, on one plane only, in which ascent and descent, gain and loss, pleasure and pain, integration and dissipation, evolution and dissolution, were each the the necessary concomitants of the other. Thus he could see " progress " in human society only in division of labour, and the checking of the " struggle for existence " by law at those points where it threatened the institution of property. He could see nothing in Socialism but its authoritarian form, and as such, as a good Liberal, he fought it. He accepted the Darwinian concept not in the revolutionary sense that nothing is fixed, that everything can be, and sooner or later will be, *changed*, but in the conservative sense that changes are only relative and always gradual and slow. He used this as an argument against both revolutionaries and counter-revolutionaries, and was so far a " liberal " Conservative. But since in real life, on Spencer's own showing, changes of a kind were always necessary, and the practical question before men is always a question of *in which way* shall things be changed—the Spencerian argument counted in practice always on the side of opposition to every proposal of revolutionary change.

Darwinism, historically considered, had exactly the opposite significance. In the first place, it destroyed the old conception of fixed and insurmountable divisions in Nature. Darwin himself was compelled under pressure of theological challenge to extend his conception to include Man ; his followers have extended it to break down the barriers between animal, vegetable, and marine life ; and the chemists, working from their end, have effected the removal of the barrier between organic and inorganic substance. What was at one time supposed to be a *qualitative division* of matter into " living substance " and " dead substance "—substance incapable of Life—is now seen as a *quantitative* difference in the specific *movements* of one and the same basic *substance,* " Matter." And what is true of the division between living and non-living substance is now seen to be true of other divisions in Nature previously regarded as fixed. The different " Forces " of the speculative physicist have been long since resolved into different forms of " Energy," and Energy in turn has been resolved into the general *Activity* of matter, of which all particular kinds of movement, activity and change are specific varieties. The boundary-line between chemistry and physics has been completely eliminated and the unitary conception of an ever-active Nature has been experimentally established.

The accomplishment of this triumphant campaign was not the work of Darwin alone, or Marx, or even both together. But the breach they made between them in the defences of the old orthodoxy was so eminently practicable that the consummation of their victory was, after their work, a mere question of time.

There is yet another sense in which Darwin's work was revolutionary, and that is in the sense most pertinent to our occasion. His discovery was a confirmation of the Marxian proposition that *Men change themselves in the operation of changing Nature.*

All the other aspects of Darwinism we have examined merely establish the fact that the world is capable of change. That aspect which has the greatest significance for Man is Darwin's demonstration that *every species in the process of living changes itself and also by its active reactions changes Nature.* Here is a classic instance :

" Nearly all our orchidaceous plants absolutely require the visits of insects to remove their pollen masses and thus to fertilise them. . . . The visits of bees are necessary for the fertilisation of some kinds of clover. . . . Humble bees alone visit red clover. . . . The number of humble bees in any district depends in great measure on the number of field-mice, which destroy their combs and nests. . . . More than two-thirds of them are thus destroyed all over England. Now the number of mice is largely dependent, as everyone knows, on the number of cats . . . [Darwin cites direct testimony]. Hence it is quite credible that the presence of a feline animal in large numbers in a district might determine, through the intervention first of mice, and then of bees, the frequency of certain flowers in that district."—DARWIN : *Origin of Species*, Chap. VIII.

The cumulative effect of interactions of this kind is so vast as to be incalculable. Yet it is the side of Darwinism which has been lost sight of in the mechanical preoccupation of the pro and anti-Darwinists with the merely incidental question of whether the " arrival " or the " survival " of the " fittest " is the dominant " factor." Just as Marxism has suffered at the hands of pettifogging Philistines who have disrupted its organic unity into an aggregation of separate " factors " (all stone dead !), so in like manner Darwinism has by these same pettifoggers been debased into a mere abstract and sterile debate as to whether this factor or that is or is not the " chief " or the " only " factor. Once the Evolution process ceases to be regarded as a Dialectical Transformation—a *movement* which can only be interpreted as a two-fold process, a synthetically combined action and reaction which begets a *new* result from which a fresh action-reaction movement begins—once this view is departed from the whole concept is reduced to banality and camouflaged mysticism.

This much is certain : Darwin showed that the interaction between organism and environment all over the world is : (1) the outcome of the naturally *antagonistic* unity of organic and inorganic substance ; (2) the process whereby the whole world of Nature has been and is being perpetually transformed ; (3) an example to Man of the way in which he in turn has himself changed and can still further *change the world*.

THE PRIEST, THE PHILOSOPHER, THE SCIENTIST

Darwinism is explicable only on the basis of a Dialectically Materialist conception of the Universe ; and that fact is reinforced by the whole development of modern science and the transformation that has resulted in the relative status in the world of ideology of the Priest, the Philosopher, and the empirical Scientist.

We saw earlier how under priestly influence the conception

Q

of Law in Nature was identified with the conception of an overruling Providence ; and how, by degrees, this conception became transformed into its opposite, a *concept of Nature dictating Providence to its Over-Lord* !

This was not, of course, how it was phrased. The eighteenth-century philosophers were much too gentlemanly and much too pious as a rule to say such a thing. And, besides, it would not have been good politics ; hence, however badly battered the priests' doctrine might be, their revenues managed to survive with little loss throughout the whole process ! They even received augmentations as a consolation for yielding the intellectual hegemony to the Natural philosophers.

Heine's story of Immanuel Kant's resurrection of the God he had just decapitated is gorgeously apocryphal—though with their usual " genius for stupidity " the intellectual " flat-feet " have contrived to take it literally. In Chapter III we have quoted the passage in which Heine compares Kant to Robespierre as one who dealt as " justly " with God as Robespierre did with King Louis XVI. He goes on to describe how the theoretical proofs of the existence of God are demolished by Kant, and then continues :

" God since then has vanished from the realm of speculative reason. This obituary notice will perhaps take some centuries to get generally known ; but we here have long been in mourning on this account. *De profundis !* You think, perhaps, that there is nothing left but to go home ?

" Not yet, by my soul ! There is an after-piece to be enacted. After the Tragedy—on comes the Farce !

" Immanuel Kant has appeared hitherto as the philosopher, grim and inexorable. He has stormed heaven and put the whole garrison to the Sword. The Ruler of the Universe swims senseless in his own blood. Mercy is no more ! So likewise is Fatherly Goodness, and Future Reward for present privations. The Immortality of the Soul is at its last gasp ! The death-groan rattles in its throat ! And old Lampe stands by, his umbrella under his arm, a sorrowing spectator—the sweat of anguish bedewing his brow, and tears streaming down his cheeks.

" Then is Immanuel Kant moved to pity ; and to show himself as not only great among philosophers, but good among Men. He reflects : half good-naturedly, half ironically he decides :

" ' Old Lampe must have a God.   Otherwise the poor man could not be happy ; and people really *ought* to be happy in this world.   Practical common sense demands it.

" ' Well, let it be so for all I care !   Let Practical Reason guarantee the existence of some God or other ! '

" And, in consequence, Kant argues a distinction between the Theoretical and the Practical Reason, and by means of the latter brings again to life the Deity which Theoretical Reason had converted into a corpse."
—HEINE : *Germany*, Works, Vol. V.

As against Immanuel Kant, personally, this gorgeous burlesque proves, and was intended to prove, nothing. Heine was flying at higher game.   It is a fact, as he suggests, and as the records of the State Trials in Britain (as well as Germany) prove, that it always has been deemed by the State and by the Free-thinking ruling class as something particularly indecent when the lower orders not only lose their religion, but show themselves more than satisfied at the loss.

Newton's *Principia*, which worked out the mechanical laws of motion so as to include the movements of the whole Universe within an all-comprehensive Law of Gravitation, did, in fact, for all practical purposes, as an angry cleric said it did, " expel God from his own Creation."   Newton had supposed an initial " Divine " " push-off " for the " atoms " which were, so he said, " the bricks with which God had built the Universe."   But, given the " atoms " and them set rolling, there was nothing left for God to do but rest until it pleased him to " ring the bell for Gabriel " and order in the Day of Judgment !

Two centuries of subsequent discoveries have been able to transform radically the compact and ordered self-sufficiency of the Newtonian Physics.   But, all the same, this has been a development which has failed entirely to restore ideological predominance to the Priest.   Beaten out of the field by the Deistic philosophy which, in Diderot's phrase, " gave God his passport and conducted him politely to the frontier," the Priest enjoyed no restoration when that Philosophy was beaten out of the field in turn by the Empirical Scientists. Even though the scientists themselves may be, and often are, men who believe or affect to believe in the supernatural, the question of intellectual hegemony has long been settled. Even the Priests find it necessary, and fashionable, to make a parade of giving " scientific " reasons for their Faith.   Their intellectual destitution is revealed in the pathetic avidity with which they seize any scraps " science " may fling them.

This, however, does not mean that the age-long fight to win for Mankind in the Mass the right to use knowledge as a weapon of conquest in the struggle to change the world has been won.

We have, it is true, travelled far since Philosophers were tortured by Priests until they agreed to accommodate their conclusions to the creeds of the Church, and since experimental investigators into the secrets of Nature were rewarded with burning at the stake with their books and crucibles about them—as wizards, sold to the devil, " enemies to God and Man."

The Inquisition has gone—— ! But its place has been taken by a newer and even more implacable foe of rationality— the Fascism which in Germany has made holocausts of scientific works, and which has declared an even more unrelenting war against Marxists and Marxism, real and supposed, than even the Christian Church has ever waged against " heretic," Infidel, and Jew. Already in the sixteen years since the founding of the Communist International more Communists have been tortured, imprisoned, and done to death than fell victims to the Inquisition in all the years of its existence.

It is against this background that we must view the sinister fact that, after a century of unparalleled triumphs in empirical science and in the co-ordination of its results, the prevailing fashion in the intellectual world is one of surrender to the Priests and their one-time enemies but present allies the Philosophers ! Just at the point when victory positively touches their finger-tips the Experimental Scientists, instead of reiterating Tyndall's splendid defiance, with up-to-date extensions, retract and reverse it by issuing the word of command for a mass surrender of all faith in reasoning, for a general acceptance of obscurantisms which would have revolted the rational sense of a Mediæval Scholastic.

Thomas Aquinas did, it is true, accept *in terms* the " superiority " of the " Divine Reason " to the Human variety. But, having thus done his duty to God, he did his duty to his neighbour by showing a lively faith in the adequacy of the human reason to grapple with and solve the problems raised by practice for human understanding. The best advertised representatives of modern experimental science (particularly, in Britain) some who have received the " honour " of knight-

hood), raise their voices with one accord to avow that reasoning proves the inadequacy of reason, that experimental
science proves the inadequacy of experimental science, that
fullness of knowledge brings the knowledge that we know
not anything at all—save only the Inscrutable Mystery of
the Universe, before which we can but, " as sinners, believe
and tremble " !   The Jeans, Eddingtons, and their cogeners,
in short, by a somersault of logical self-stultification, place
themselves mentally, not merely *behind* the standpoint of
the Blessed Saint Thomas Aquinas—" the Angel of the
Schools "—but back at that of St. Simon Stylites on his
pillar in the Thebaid !   They offer us the high bliss of doing
likewise ; of mentally waiting, like him, " on one leg, forty
cubits high up in the air, lost in the contemplation of the
divine, while his excrements rose to his knees, and birds
built their nests in his hair ! "

.   .   .   .   .

Tyndall's challenge, abandoned by these " honoured "
scientists—perhaps as a price for their " honours," perhaps
as an acknowledgment thereof, anyway because they were
the sort of reasoners whom the bourgeois order in its days of
decadence was bound to honour—abandoned by these, the
maintenance of Tyndall's historic defiance and its elaboration
falls to the champions of the only standpoint from which
Tyndall's claim can be enlarged to include not cosmological
theory only, but the whole domain of Theory and its correlative Practice—*the standpoint of Dialectical Materialism.*
What are the root points at issue ?
Most loudly announced of all are the claims that " Matter
has been proved not to exist ! "—that " matter has broken
down into energy," while " energy has broken down into pure
mathematical formulæ ";   that space and time are shown
to be merely subjective-relative concepts ;   that Reason has
reached the end of its tether, and that there is therefore
nothing left to do but fall back upon Faith !   At which point
Sir Oliver Lodge invites all creation to listen-in to a mouth-
organ solo he proposes to render as soon as he reaches the
" *beyond* side of phenomena ! "
Let us take a look at these points.   And first as to *Faith.*
" Faith is the substance of things hoped for, the evidence
of things not seen."   Which of the great dialecticians it was
that Paul of Tarsus (or the clerical forger who, possibly,
invented " Paul ") drew upon for this definition, it is a fine

one and adequate for our purpose. *What* is hoped for ?
What is *evidenced* in " Faith " ?

It is impossible to say until we are told " *whose* Faith ? "

He who like Peter the Apostle " *lodges* " with one Simon,
a " *tanner* " (said Simon being a bookmaker), has as the substance of his hopes a belief in the possibility that a certain
quadruped will exhibit sufficient pedal dexterity to reach the
winning-post at least a " short head " in front of its nearest
competitor. It has as a second, but not at all secondary,
" substance " a belief in the ability and the willingness of
the said bookmaker to " pay out " at the stipulated rate of
odds. The *tanner* " lodged " is overt, and tangible, *evidence*
of this " Faith," which, being a subjective state of the
punter's consciousness, is " not seen," nor *see*able !

Now the Faith in this case may or may not be justified
by the event. And if the event gives the lie to the Faith, it
is therein proved to have been, so far, *un*reasonable. But
it was not an " irrational " Faith in itself. Horses *have* been
known to win races ; and bookmakers, in point of fact, pay
out on demand much more often than not. Hence the conclusion of the matter is that Faith, provided it be well based
in the actualities of material existence and well and truly
reasoned thencefrom, is not only *not* opposed to Reasoning,
but is, in fact, one of its implements. A scientific experiment
is, in its way, as much an act of Faith, in this sense of the
word, as is the " gamble " of the punter. (Observe : there
would be no gambling if the gambler were not always possessed
of the faith that his wager is *no gamble* !)

The experimenter creates a combination of circumstances
and observes the outcome. In most cases he has in mind an
expectation that the result will be of a particular kind. When
Galileo turned his telescope towards the planet Jupiter he
had " Faith " (*a*) that there was something to see, (*b*) that
he would be able to see it, (*c*) that it would be worth seeing.
Thus the experimenter proceeds on the primary supposition—
the Faith—that things happen in regular, measurable ways ;
that it is possible for human beings to observe happenings
with an approximation to accuracy ; and that it is possible
by reasoning to extract from these observations a *general
conclusion* which can be *used* practically for further observation, and for the attainment of wider conclusions.

What is true of the scientific experimenter, who works
with artificially created combinations of things and circumstances, is no less true of the actual practice of real life. Even

Sir James Jeans rises from his bed in the morning with the Faith that the integrity of his floor will remain unimpeachable —that his leap from his bed will not be a swift transition to the coal-cellar or the " fourth dimension." He dons his trousers sublime in his faith that their material reality and their physical properties (particularly their *opacity*) can be relied on *for all practical purposes*. He approaches his breakfast— egg, bacon, kipper, marmalade and toast—confidently filled with the " substance of the hope " that thereby he will be spatially filled and subjectively satisfied. Bacon may be in the Jeans *theory* an unintelligible congelation of " holes in a whirling field of electrical force "—none the less he likes it nicely fried, with another and a different " congelation " (called vulgarly an " egg "), fried with equal nicety, by its side. " Matter " may be in his theory a mere prejudice of the vulgar, but he will conform closely to vulgar prejudices as he champs his toast, and his bacon " he doth visibly and carnally press with his teeth " !

In a word, the actual practice of everyday life, and the actual practice of all men, alike those who live now and those who have lived in the past, is one long and overwhelmingly conclusive demonstration of the primary assumptions of Materialism—the objective existence of the material universe, the subjective-reflex character of knowledge, and that *reliability* of proved and tested knowledge which is the basis of the formula the *Unity of Theory and Practice*.

" Words are wise-men's counters, they do but reckon by them." If by the word " Faith " we mean no more than the belief based on experience that material reality will, other things being equal, continue to behave in the future as it has done in the past, then " faith " in this sense is none other than faith in the objective, knowable materiality and uniformity of the universe, in the parallel uniformity of knowledge, and in their synthetic combination in an inseparable Unity of Opposites—Theory and Practice.

But if by " Faith " is meant the *rejection* of this belief in the *Unity* of Theory and Practice, and the substitution therefor of a belief in their *absolute separation*, a belief in the unbelievability of knowledge, in the falsity of all evidence, and the absolute worthlessness of experience, rationally comprehended—if *this* is offered us as " Faith," we can but reply that he who argues thus carries his own refutation about with him. He would not argue at all unless he had " faith " (the *materialist* kind of " faith ") in the objective reality of sounds uttered with the lips, or of alphabetical characters on printed paper, " faith " in the adequacy of word-symbols to convey a meaning, " faith " in the force of *reasoning* to upset a theoretical conclusion reached by previous reasoning.

Thus the *practice* of the advocate of " Faith," as a negation of and the alternative to reasoning, is itself the complete negation of his *theory*, and he himself thus becomes an un-witting advocate of that which he denies.

" We learn men's beliefs," says Bernard Shaw, " not by the creeds which they recite with their lips, but from the assump-tion upon which they habitually *act*." Thus, to take a familiar illustration, when the Christians with great pomp and circumstance " consecrate " a cathedral, they thereby, *in theory*, convert it into the " house " of an Omnipotent, Omnipresent, Omniscient Ruler of the Universe. When, however, one observes that the cathedral has been most carefully equipped with a proper supply of *lightning conductors*, one observes the clear discrepancy between the " faith " recited and the faith actually acted upon. The *Theory* says, " This is the House of God " ; the *Practice* says," This House may be destroyed by lightning unless material precautions are taken to prevent such a happening." Thus Practice adds its ironic negation to all the affirmations of the Theory. The Theory affirms " God is omnipotent " ; Practice adds : " but we can at least prevent him from setting his own house on fire " ! Theory affirms : " God is Omnipresent " ; Practice replies : " Then we will use part of him to neutralise the possible damage done by the Rest of Him." Theory affirms : " God is Omniscient " ; Practice replies : " Then he knows that in this case there is something he will not be permitted to do ! " Theory affirms : " God is the Ruler of All Things " ; Practice replies : " We are not satisfied with his rule of the lightning ! Whether it be because of his indifference to having his own house burnt about his ears, or because he does not regard this as specially *his* house, or because his marks-manship is poor, makes no difference to the fact that this house may be struck by lightning, and that this calamity can be averted by the use of a lightning conductor ! "

Thus is the *Unity* of Theory and Practice vindicated on the basis of the *primacy of practice*, by the practice of its foes.

How does this fact bear upon the " crisis " in modern science ?

First of all it destroys, as we have demonstrated in other chapters, the spurious assertion that because knowledge is *relative* (is *human* only, a consciousness of *relation*) it is, therefore, *not knowledge*, not reliable so far as it goes. This, as we have seen, is the oldest of reactionary devices, one invented originally by priestcraft and mystery-mongering to create a demand for the " opium " they live by vending.

Secondly, it proves that the assertion that space and time are " purely " subjective is a sophisticator's juggle—a shuffling together of two totally different facts : time and space *as such*, and the *mode of their measurement by man*. The fact made so much of by the Jeans and Eddingtons that there are stars in space on which, if there are men like ourselves, they will only now be learning of the war of 1914–18, of the Defeat of the Spanish Armada, of the Discovery of America, of the assassination of Julius Cæsar, so that " absolutely " these events will all be " happening " simultaneously, is a juggle worthy of a parliamentary Under-secretary ! They will be " happening simultaneously " only in the consciousness of a number of *different* observers. And since *each* of these observers will experience that *sequence* of events in *exactly that order*, and none other, that order of events is thereby demonstrated to possess an objective validity. If it be argued that the " curvature " of space means that the news radiating from a given point of origin will reach every place *twice*, so that the one sequence will, coming " round the other way," overlap the other and create confusion for the observer who does not disentangle his time-sequences, we agree. But when that observer offers us *the tangle* as the *results of experiment* we reply that experienced *confusion* is itself proof of the existence of a *subjectively-created* disharmony between Theory and Practice which better Theory will enable men Practically to Disentangle.

" The proof of the pudding is in the eating." In real life, for practical reasons, the " punter " aforementioned often hears the result of the 3.30 (that being the " big 'un ") *before* he hears the result of the 1.30 and the 2 o'clock. He doesn't, not being Sir William Eddington, conclude thencefrom that space and time have all got jumbled up together, and are no longer usable as practical instruments. He puts the blame where it belongs, to the debit of his personal news-service.

How, in fact, has Mankind reached its conception of Space and Time ? Obviously, *in practice*. That we can repeatedly *move* ourselves from the *hither* side of a given object to the *beyond* side—that in the course of so doing we *pass* other objects and leave them *behind*—that all the things we scrutinise present themselves to our inspection before and behind, above and below, or side by side with each other—these are the *material* and *objective* facts from which Mankind generalises the conception of Space—the objective possibility of mechanical *movement*.

Similarly all the things we do, and all the things which are done to us, happen after or before each other, or simultaneously with each other. And in their simultaneous happening they endure for differing intervals. Day alternates with Night, and while either endures things happen *in* the light or in the dark. From this practically experienced *order* of sensations—of co-existencies and successions—an order that we can reconstruct imaginatively but cannot possibly construct in the first place ; from this objective experience we derive the concept Time—the general pre-requisite of all *movements of co-existence and succession, all development and all practical production.*

That space and time are *opposites* is self-evident. We *measure* the one from a practically given point in the other—even though it be a moving point, as when we reckon the space moved through in a *given time-interval* (i.e., a fixed *quantity* of time). That they are *united* is equally obvious, since nothing can happen " in " one which does not also happen " in " the other. That they are thus *a unity of opposites* need worry no one who has not pledged himself *a priori* to a desecration of the grave of Hegel, and a defilement of "every word that proceedeth out of the mouth of " Marx !

But when Bloomsbury in its " up-to-dateness," learning from the physicists that certain properties of bodies can be understood only if we take into reckoning along with their position in space (reckoned, of necessity, in the three " dimensions " of up-down, before-behind, side-to-side) *also* their position in the *time-sequence* of before and after—when Bloomsbury, learning this fact (which is *cardinal* to dialectic reasoning), proceeds to manufacture a space-time *unity* from which the *opposition* has been carefully excluded, Bloomsbury must be told that it is up to its old confidence trick of building mare's nests and offering them for sale as, and to, " flats " !

Water may exist as either a solid (ice), liquid (water) or gas (steam). It can in one condition *rest* on a slab, in another *flow*, in another *ascend* in the air. He who, however, seeks to " generalise " these phenomena by supposing a " solid-steam-flow resting in space-time," or a " red-hot icicle telling the time," or a " fistful of boiling snow supporting a professor," does thereby merely provide entertainment for the genial reader, and a cause of disgust for one less willing to " suffer fools gladly."

The assertions that " Matter has broken down into Energy " and that " Energy has broken down into mathematical symbols " are exactly of this kind. Certain *conceptions* of Matter have proved to be of provisional validity only, others to have no validity at all. Energy and Matter have been empirically demonstrated to be only two different ways of looking at one and the same fact. That is true. *But this is the very fact for which Materialism has been contending all along :*

" *Motion is the mode of existence of Matter.* Never anywhere has there been matter without motion, nor can there be. Motion in cosmic space, mechanical motion of smaller masses on the various celestial bodies, the motion of molecules as heat or as electrical or magnetic currents, chemical combination or disintegration, organic life—at each given moment each individual atom of matter in the world is in one or other of these forms of motion or in several of these forms at once. All rest, all equilibrium, is only relative, and only has meaning in relation to one or other definite form of motion."—ENGELS : *Anti-Dühring* (1878), p. 71.

No Matter without Motion : no Motion that is not Motion of Matter—such has been the battle-slogan of all Materialism from Democritus and Lucretius in the past to Marx, Engels, and Lenin in our own day. The empirical proof of their indissoluble connection is the final empirical proof of the truth of Materialism. The incapacity of the metaphysically-reasoning scientists to handle the fact when demonstrated is the final proof of the indispensability of the Dialectical mode of reasoning.

What in fact was " exploded " when the atom " yielded up the ghost" of *absolute* impenetrability, *absolute* sphericity, and *absolute* rigidity, was not Materialism at all, but the *anti*-Materialism which staked everything upon the conception of Matter as essentially *dead*, inert, and incapable of self-motion. All these *qualities* of the atom, which modern physics has experimentally done away with, were the qualities attributed to the atom by *the pious Sir Isaac Newton,* who

saw in these very qualities the proof that they were in very
deed " the bricks with which God had builded his Creation !"
What has gone, in the going of these *qualities*, is neither the
atom itself (which is livelier than ever for its release !) nor
Materialism (to which, in fact, these *qualities* were an obstruc-
tion)—but *God's bricks*, and the theory of *Design* built thereupon.   Modern physics has, in fact, killed the last excuse for
the argument for Design in the Universe.   The sheer completeness of the chaos which Jeans, Eddington and Co. offer
as a *theory* of the Universe is the last and most final proof
possible of the death of the " Great Architect of the Universe."

Finally, the assertion that " ultimate Reality " turns out
to be nothing but a set of " mathematical symbols " is one
that would have transported old Thomas Hobbes into an
ecstasy of derision : it is so perfect an example of that folly
which takes words as " money."   Dealing with the qualities
of matter, the physicist finds they can be dealt with rationally
only so far as they are reduced for comparison to terms of
quantity.   These quantities in turn, being quantities of things
in motion, must be compared as quantities of *motion*.   Motions
varying in quantity and in inter-relation simultaneously can
only be compared by means of mathematical equations in
which symbols stand as the representatives of varying
quantities of movement, and varying relations between
variable movements.   Thus *changing* relations can be expressed, but only in a complicated mathematical formula, and
when this is done with movements relatively universal like
the *changes* of movement-relation in the Universe as a whole
(as has been done by Einstein) the Jeans and Eddingtons
incontinently fall into a swoon of admiration ; and hurry to
offer, with trumpets also and shawms, incense and burnt
offerings on the altar of the Triune God of the Differential,
the Integral, and the Fluxional Calculus—Three in One, and
One in Three !

They have mistaken their altar.   If their desire is towards
only the extremity of irrationality in worship their place is
in the Temple of the Hyperboreans, who according to the
learned Doctor Smellfungus worshipped " a She-ass with
shaven buttocks ! "   If on the contrary they wish to do
reverence where reverence is due they should take their
offerings to an altar erected to the memory of *George Wilhelm
Frederick Hegel* !   He was the first to elaborate a logic upon
the basic fact that *all opposites*—particularly the opposites
Quality and Quantity—are linked in an identity, a fact of

which the modern history of physical science presents one long series of proofs, and he also, like Jeans and Eddington, was " standing on his head " and needed Materialism to put him right side up.

NEWTON, EINSTEIN AND DIALECTICAL MATERIALISM

Modern empirical investigation into the " properties " and movements of Matter has ended in Einstein's Revolution— in a " world turned upside down." That is the one thing upon which all scientific theorists are agreed. Upon everything else they disagree. Since, as we have claimed and maintain, the *practice* of empirical science confirms the theoretical premises drawn by Dialectical Materialism from practice, how do we square this outcome with our standpoint ? How do we escape the conclusion that Materialist practice destroys all confidence in Materialist Theory ?

Very simply. The practice of empirical science has destroyed utterly the theoretical bases of supernaturalism and idealism. What has collapsed is not, in the least, the *practice*, which the whole world-wide wonderment of electrical engineering, as also the radio industry, has vindicated in a way past all belief. What has collapsed has been the mechanical, *non*-dialectical, *anti*-historical *theory* which had survived not because of, but in spite of, the practice. To co-ordinate the practical achievements of empirical science we must eliminate the rupture between theory and practice. What is more, we must press home to its logical Materialist conclusion the primary basic fact which the whole historical development of science proves—that the unity of Theory and Practice is based upon *the primacy of practice*.

It is not to-day, any more than it has ever been, a question (as the Theologians, Supernaturalists, and Sophisticators allege) of Theory laying down " laws " for practice humbly to follow. The reverse is the case : unless *Theory takes its place in the team* and does its work as a *particular kind of practice* Theory is a delusion and a snare—a new and a worse mystification, a Chimæra, a Moloch, a Mumbo-Jumbo, a Quasheemaboo !

.   .   .   .

What is it, after all, that Bloomsbury has made such a coil about ?

Take the " atom." It was, as we have said, Newton who formulated the theory that all *substance*—all Matter—has *structure*, is, that is to say, built up of unit particles to which he attributed certain qualities. What Bloomsbury forgets, or, to be more offensively accurate, what Bloomsbury has never learned, is that this conception of Newton's, that Matter has *structure*, unified a previous contradiction and disclosed a contradiction in what before had been a unity. Before the Newtonian conception was adopted " Matter " was conceived as a mystical something-or-other that in a " pure " state was impenetrability absolute, but which became less and less solid under the influence of certain equally mysterious outside " forces." Thus a liquid was conceived as " partially *rarefied* matter," a gas as *absolutely rarefied* matter. By conceiving Matter as a *structure* Newton got rid of the mystical opposition of Matter and Forces and made the change from solid to liquid and gas a change intelligible in terms of the *relation* between the units of physical structure. Thus he got rid too of the alternative theory that solidity, liquidity, and gaseousness were absolute " states " having no interconnection " save in God."

Chemists working after Newton found that their practice produced results which demanded another unit of structure intermediate between the " atom " and the " mass," namely, the *molecule*, the unit of chemical combination. This molecule might be a single atom or a group of atoms, but chemical *changes* could be understood only on the supposition that the different *qualities* of material substance were differences of structural combination of unit groups (molecules) which were themselves *composites* in that they were groupings of different *kinds of atom*. Thus chemistry reached the conception of the chemical *element*.

It was perceived then that this destroyed the *unity* of the Newtonian system, which had supposed all atoms *absolutely alike* and supposed it possible to account for all changes as mechanical changes of relative position in these *uniform* units. Chemistry-practice was forced to postulate lack of unity in the units and a *sequence* in the structure of Matter. Already practice was beginning to prove that things can be understood only (*a*) in relation to each other, and (*b*) in their *historical* sequence of *movement*, their *process*.

By means of the conception of different kinds of atom (elements) distinguishable by their relative weight chemistry made immense progress. Most notably did the practice of chemical analysis prove that living bodies were composed of the same sort of matter as non-living bodies—that the difference between living things and non-living lay not in their substance, but in their *structure* and their concomitant differences of specific *movement*. This was supported from the biological side by the discovery of the *unit* of biological structure, which is not the atom, nor the molecule, nor the group of molecules (the *organic compound*), but the *cell*.

Continuing with non-living matter : not only was a unity proved to exist between the matter of the living and of the non-living world ; it was proved that this held good as between the earth and the sun, moon, and stars. The chemical elements were universal facts. They were therefore promoted by Theory, exhilarated by practical triumph, to the rank of *absolutes*.

Observe : the unity of the Universe, so far, rested on a basis of absolute *multiplicity*—the unchangeable and intrinsic *differences in quality* of the atoms of the various elements.

In the year 1869 a Russian chemist, Dmitry Mendelyeff, "threw the fat in the fire." He announced his belief (the world was ringing with Darwinism then) in the *evolution of the elements*. He did not, of course, put it as crudely as that, but that is what it came to. He showed that if the elements are arranged in the sequence of their atomic weights they form *an historical progression*, a series of groups inter-related in two ways—which we might express as " side by side," and " one above the other." All the elements within a group formed a quantitative progression ; each of the groups in turn reproduced the inter-relationships of the previous group on a higher scale !

There were gaps in the sequence. Mendelyeff predicted they would be filled by subsequently discovered elements of certain atomic weights and qualities. *And the elements were found as predicted.* What is more, after Mendelyeff's discovery of this Periodic Law, it was realised that the facts had been pointed out before by the German chemist, Lothar Meyer, who did not, however, draw the imaginative conclusions with which Mendelyeff forced the world to sit up and take notice.

What, now, was the logic of Mendelyeff's discovery ? Nothing less than this—that the qualitative differences between the chemical *elements*—the *different atoms*—pointed to *quantitative differences in their composition*. Few chemists took notice at the time of this " fanciful " conjecture—none the less the faith Mendelyeff held to the day of his death in 1907 was that all the chemical elements have qualitative differences, because they are quantitatively different combinations—structures—*of one unit substance*, i.e., *the ether of space*. What is most notable in Mendelyeff's discovery, viewed in its historic sequence, is its dialectical quality. It presents a partial return to the Newtonian conception, but on a higher plane. It perceives a whole series of stages—a discontinuous continuity, a dialectical progression, as the true " unity " of chemical substance—a unity revealed in a *sequence* of antagonistic contrasts, a sequence which is a continuous succession of revolutionary transitions. What is more, it made possible the discovery not only of the elements for which Mendelyeff had found places vacant (incidentally also the correction of the atomic weights of the elements which Mendelyeff had boldly " displaced " to fit the demands of this scheme), but also of several series of elements unknown to Mendelyeff, including one such series which, " periodic " in itself, refused to fit as a series into the " regular " periodicity of the sequence as a whole.

In 1912 an English chemist, HENRY MOSELEY (killed in Gallipoli !), revolutionised Mendelyeff's Periodic Law by a new mode of computation. Giving to the atoms each a number beginning with hydrogen as number One, he was able to bring the whole table of elements into an ascending scale from 1 to 92. A few gaps appeared in the Moseley table of atomic numbers. *These have since been filled exactly as the table demanded.* Moreover, of a whole mob of some seventy contenders for the sixteen gaps left in the Mendelyeff Table, Moseley was able to eliminate all but a few, and those sufficient. The rest were shown not to be elements.

Moseley's revision of the Periodic Law confirmed Mendelyeff's hypothesis as to its general content. The qualitative differences between the elements were proved to be expressions of the quantitative differences of their *composition*. And this proof was not merely theoretical, because in the meantime, and concurrently with Moseley, it had been found that elements existed which did in fact *change into other elements* ; and also that, in the case of other elements, a similar transmutation could be produced experimentally. Mendelyeff's " guess " was brilliantly confirmed ; the elements lost their absoluteness of qualitative *separation* and became united as different *quantities* of one and the same " stuff." Also they lost their absolute *immutability*—being proved to be transmutable.

But at the same time, in respect of the " stuff " of which they were all " quantities," Mendelyeff's " guess " was modified in a surprising fashion. This " stuff " was now conceived not in terms of unity, but as an *opposition*—an *antagonism.* The atom was resolved into a *relation* between a *nucleus* and an attendant *electron* (or *electrons*). The Periodic Scale now rested upon the quantitative differences in *both* the nuclei and the electrons. The nucleus (an enormously concentrated " core ") was charged with *positive* electricity : the *electron* (enormously smaller, but correspondingly more active) was a " particle " of negative electricity. The nucleus (now called a *proton*) had as many units of *positive* electrical charge as it had *negatively charged* units (the electrons) in attendance upon it. The simplest atom, that of hydrogen, had only one electron in attendance upon the nucleus, which had therefore one positive charge. A simple numerical progression, in units of positive charge in the nucleus and in units of negative charge in its attendant electrons, from 1 (hydrogen) up to 92 (uranium) gave the whole table of elements in a perfectly periodic series.

Two vitally important conclusions were thus established. The first and most obvious was that the atom was a structure, *but of electricity*. The second, not so obvious, was that the atom was a *unity of opposites*. The first conclusion pointed to a *contradiction* which threw the world of scientific theory into convulsions. In so far as electricity is a *form of energy*— a particular kind of wave-motion—it proved that " *matter is composed of energy.*" But in so far as it rested on the conception of a specific structural inter-relation of *unit-quantities* of " electricity " capable of precise measurement as to size and *weight*, that is to say having *mass*, it proved that electrical energy is a *form of matter* ! Thus " matter " is, really, *energy* ; while " energy " is really *matter* !

The second conclusion, that the atom is a unity of opposites, drew redoubled force from this contradiction, since it pointed to the conclusion that both energy and matter, to be understood, must be understood each by means of its opposite— that the fundamental reality is, *as dialectical materialism has all along supposed*, the material activity of active material, energy being the active aspect of " mass " (*i.e.*, matter), and matter (*i.e.*, mass) the inertial aspect of energy. Moreover, it pointed to the fact that the specific *movements* of objective reality were, in fact, not simple, mechanical continuations, but dialectical developments.

The force of this conclusion will be best seen from a brief examination of the progress of discovery between Mendelyeff and the present day ; it being understood that, since the theoretical revolution in the physical sciences is still in

R

progress, only tentative conclusions can be stated, and those only in their broadest non-technical outline.

.   .   .   .   .

The modern revolution in science began with the discovery which completed the scientific advance of the nineteenth century.

In 1886 HEINRICH RUDOLF HERZ succeeded in exciting electro-magnetic waves in the space surrounding an electrical apparatus (a transmitting and a receiving coil), and thereby laid the foundation for the development of " wireless " telegraphy, telephony, broadcasting, etc. The practical significance of the discovery has proved to be enormous ; but its theoretical significance was, if possible, greater still. First of all it established the fact that the objective difference between light, radiant heat, and electro-magnetic " impulses " or " oscillations " was *a relative difference* only, being one of the periodicity of their respective wave-lengths of propagation (which was also a difference of the " frequency " of impulsion—the shorter the wave-length the greater the frequency). Thus all the phenomena of energy seemed to be reducible to terms of wave-motion. Secondly, it provided a provisional proof of the existence of the (hypothetical) ether of space as the medium in which these wave-motions were propagated. Thirdly, it opened up the possibility of hitherto unknown forms of energy being discriminated by newer means of exciting either larger or shorter waves than any, till then, excited. This last conclusion was to prove true with a vengeance, since later discoveries brought the existence of the ether into question and established as a counter to the wave-theory of energy a return (again on a higher plane) to the abandoned Newtonian " emission " theory.

The crisis was brought to a head by the discovery in 1895, by Röntgen, of " X "-rays—rays of energy which proved able to pass through opaque materials impenetrable to normal " light." Crookes long before, in experimenting with electrical currents passed through a vacuum, and studying the curious luminous and other effects thereby produced, had found that a stream of " particles " passed from the cathode (or entry electrode) of the tube towards the anode (or exit electrode). These cathode particles raised a profound problem. Were they " particles " ? If so, of what ? Were they " waves " ? Again, if so, of what ? It was contrary to the then accepted belief to regard them as " particles " of *electricity*, since electricity as a form of energy must exist in the form of a *continuous* wave-motion. That they possessed electrical properties was soon proved. Articles subjected to their impact not only became raised to very high temperatures but became charged with negative electricity. But as against that the fact that their impact generated heat and caused motion in light bodies placed in their path proved that they possessed *mass*, and were, so far, particles of *matter*. Experiment proved that these particles were not ejected from the metal electrode—or, alternatively, that they were ejected from every kind of metal impartially. (To anticipate, somewhat, these " cathode particles " were eventually identified as what we now call " electrons.")

Röntgen discovered that when these " cathode particles " collided with the walls of the Crookes' tube or, better still, with a target placed within the tube, a new and highly penetrating form of radiant energy was engendered. The penetrating power of these X-rays is well known from the fact that they can be used to take photographs through materials completely opaque to ordinary light rays. Again, there was great perplexity as to the nature of these rays. The controversy was only settled in 1912 by the demonstration that they were electro-magnetic light rays of exceptionally short wave-length.

The Röntgen, or X-rays, because of their extraordinary penetrating power, gave scientists a means not previously possessed of attempting the disintegration of the atom ; and shortly after their discovery J. J. Thompson succeeded in knocking out of hydrogen atoms particles with a negative electrical charge which left the mass of the atoms intact, so far as could be ascertained, but changed electrically in that now it was a positively charged mass (an " ion "). Left to themselves, the electron and the positive " ion " (now called a *proton*) immediately recombined and so restored the original electrically neutral atom. There was only one conclusion possible : the experiment provided the proof of what had long been conjectured, namely, that each atom combined both forms of electricity—positive and negative. There was this difference, that, while the positively-charged particle, the *proton*, was enormously more dense, and so far seemed to retain all or nearly all of the *mass* of the atom, the negatively-charged particle, the *electron*, appeared to be composed of nothing but " electricity "—to be a " unit " of negative electricity. Thus while the experiment proved on the one side that the physical atom was composite, and that its

" nature " was basically electrical, it proved no less that *electricity itself has structure also* !

Discoveries followed, first of all along the lines of proving the composite character of the atom. BECQUEREL, in 1896, discovered that radio-activity such as could be excited artificially in a Crookes' tube existed as a natural characteristic of certain substances, such as the element Uranium, which, he found, emitted " rays " or " light corpuscles " without outside stimulus. Investigation following up this clue led to the discovery of several radio-active substances, and two newly revealed elements, both radio-active, polonium and radium. The properties of the latter were so astounding as to set the whole scientific world rocking. It was first of all an element, fitting properly into its place in the periodic table. But at the same time it was so highly radio-active that the " rays " or " corpuscles " emitted by it would (like X-rays) ionise the air—a proof that they were electromagnetic—liberate large quantities of heat, produce chemical changes and destroy minute organisms, or cellular tissues. At first glance it would seem that radium possessed the incredible property of *creating energy from nothing*—a flat contradiction of the law of the Conservation of Energy, the doctrine whose establishment constituted the highest and most comprehensive generalisation of Science. The only alternative was to accept the fact that the atomic structure of the radium was undergoing a natural disintegration and liberating electro-magnetic energy in the process. Since indications pointed to the fact that there was, concomitant with this disintegration of structure, an actual dissipation of *mass*, this seemed to imply that the doctrine of the Conservation of Energy was only saved at the expense of the correlative doctrine of the Conservation of Matter. The only way out of the impasse was to conclude that Conservation held good in general, but that, since matter could " break down into energy " (which implied that in Nature " matter had been organised from energy "), the two particular aspects of the General Law (*i.e.*, the specific Conservation of Matter and Energy in themselves) were of provisional and conditional value only.

There seemed to be a probability, however, that things had not gone so far in a revolutionary-dialectical direction as all that. It was possible that the " corpuscles " emitted by radium were in fact particles of *matter*—though of a sub-atomic level. To the investigation of these phenomena attention was therefore turned. Mainly by the work of RUTHERFORD and SODDY, the " emanations " given off by radium were found to be of three kinds : Alpha, Beta, and Gamma " rays," or " particles." (The whole future of science seemed to turn on the question whether they were " rays " —and therefore *energy*, or " particles," and therefore *matter* ! Nobody seems to have been prepared for the fact that they were *both* !)

The *Alpha-particles* gave the first surprise. These proved clearly to be particles, fourtimes as heavy as a hydrogen atom and moving with a velocity of round about 20,000 miles a second. They were thus the most powerful missiles till then known. Also they were clearly matter, but—and here came astonishment—spectrum analysis proved them to be " atoms " (more properly nuclei) of the element *helium* ! Nature had turned Alchemist and had done what all scientific doctrine had contended was impossible. It had produced one *element* from another ! Incidentally also, old Mendelyeff's " insane speculation " was proved to be no more than the sober truth !

The *Beta-particles* proved to be none other than the " cathode particles " such as were produced in the Crookes' tube ; that is to say, they were *electrons*, units of negative electricity, which were thus shown to enter as units into the structure of *matter* itself.

The *Gamma-particles* proved to be a higher and a more penetrating form of X-rays, produced by the impact of the *Beta*-particles (electrons)—whose velocity was enormously higher than anything till then achieved in the laboratory, ranging as it did from 60,000 to 180,000 miles per second— upon the surrounding matter.

The problems raised by this discovery were simply enormous in extent and complexity. It proved the inseparable con- nection between matter and energy. It proved that the transformation of matter from its atomic to its sub-atomic state involved the release of incredible quantities of energy. And it pointed clearly to the fact that energy itself has " structure " likewise. On the one side it proved that " matter " was composed of, and was therefore a *form* of, energy : on the other side it proved that energy, having structure, and being capable of disintegration into unit- particles whose size and mass could be measured, was only a *form of matter* ! These results were, by the older standards, absurdly self-contradictory. Yet they were the results reached by the most brilliantly accurate and most rigidly tested scientific methods then attainable. Further investigations only served to establish this contradiction (that "Matter" is *Energy*, and "Energy" *Matter*) the more irrevocably as the foundation truth of Nature and its objective dialectic.

Using the helium-nucleus (the *Alpha*-particle) as a missile, Rutherford proceeded to see how far it was possible to knock other atoms into the state of disintegration natural to radium. Investigation had proved that the elemental transmutation observed in the case of radium was a property of all the members of its group in the periodic table beginning with Uranium (No. 92) and ceasing with Lead (No. 82), so that Mendelyeff's "evolution of the elements" was established as a natural fact. (*But in regressive form!*) Rutherford and Soddy between them found that every atom had a kind of core or nucleus charged with positive electricity, surrounded by a number of attendant *electrons*. The positive charge in the nucleus was exactly proportioned to the number of the electrons and their negative charges. They found, too, that the atom, instead of being the "solid" particle of the Newtonian-Daltonian conception, must be conceived on the analogy of the solar system, with the nucleus occupying the place of the central sun, and the attendant electrons that of planets circling around it. Thus in measuring the atom, as has been done repeatedly with a close approximation to absolute precision, what was measured was the over-all space occupied within the outermost electron in the "planetary" system. Since these electrons move at an incredible speed they are, for all human practical purposes, *everywhere* (along the line of the orbits) *at once*, and so present the appearance of a body continuous over its whole orbital area. The mass of the total atom (nucleus plus electrons) is, however, packed almost entirely in the nucleus, which occupies *less than one-million-millionth* of the total space occupied by the atom. J. J. THOMPSON found that it was the nucleus (or rather the quantity of its positive charge) which determined the chemical character of the atom, since he discovered that nuclei of the same chemical *quality* existed with different weights.

These "isotopes"—variants of one and the same element—introduced a new and more bewildering variety into the question ; all the more so since in some cases, as with mercury, which has *seven* "isotopes"—the heavier varieties possess weights equal to the lighter varieties of elements with higher "atomic" weights. At the same time this clears up what had been a mystery to the older chemistry, that of different elements with identical weights. This discovery affected the general question only indirectly ; but it is worth noting that while on the one side, by means of the new conception of the atom, the multiple *qualities* of the various elements were reduced to terms of *quantitative* differences in their nucleus-electron composition, on the other side, by the multiplication of the 92 elements by their isotopes, the number of different nuclei was expanded to 223, and possibly more. Unity was reached only by concomitantly enlarging the multiplicity through which it found expression.

It was by means of the Rutherford-Thompson conception of the atom that Moseley made his revision of the Periodic Table. He *proved* (what Mendelyeff had guessed) that the electrical charge in the nucleus did not vary *continuously*, by imperceptible shades of difference, from nucleus to nucleus. On the contrary, it varied in a series of regular jumps, exactly expressible by the numerical sequence of 1, 2, 3, 4, etc., up to 92 (as above stated). This proved various things. Either it proved that electrical charge did vary in Nature by imperceptible shades of variation, but that these variations only became manifest after a certain quantitative minimum of variation had accumulated—in which case it proved that Nature did in fact move in a series of revolutionary leaps. Or it proved the same thing in another form—that the nucleus itself had a structure, being composed of units of positive electricity (the counterparts of the " electrons," the units of negative electricity). On this view the electrical units were themselves " particles "—*i.e.*, something analogous to the Newton-Dalton atom at a far more elementary level —while the Something-or-Other which provided their rays was an unknown territory yet to be explored.

Meanwhile other speculators had worked from the opposite pole of the problem and had considered the nature of Energy in itself—starting from the conception of a wave-movement (in the hypothetical " ether ") as its general form. It was concluded that energy itself has structure in that it is manifested not in a *continuous* succession of waves of an immutable character, but that the waves themselves have their *periodicity*, that energy is produced in Nature (or, rather, *transmuted* from one form into another), not by imperceptible variations, but in discrete *quanta*, in, so to speak, " *packets*." It was concluded that energy itself, though " ultimately " nothing but " pure movement," had a *structure* analogous to the complexification of structure observable in matter from the nucleus and the electron up to the most complex organic compounds, and that the qualitative differences in forms of energy could all be resolved into quantitative differences in its composition out of unit-quanta called provisionally " photons."

This conception of *quanta* was applied to the Thompson-Rutherford conception by NEILS BOHR, who elaborated the solar system conception of the atom—the point of Bohr's conception being his contention that the electron in its movement around the nucleus could not vary its distance from the nucleus indefinitely or in a *continuous* fashion. It could only circle in one of a succession of *periodical* intervals which bore a definite proportion to each other. Under the appropriate stimulus the electron would *leap* from an outer orbit to one closer to the atom, and in the act of leaping release the electro-magnetic energy which became apparent as radiation.

The War interrupted progress at this stage, and when it was possible to resume investigation on the close of the War it was the Bohr theory which gave the jumping-off point.

The Bohr theory had treated the atom as a " quantum "—a matter-energy packet—in which *leaps* from the one phase to its opposite were reduced to a regularly discontinuous-continuity. Progress was achieved in the direction of emphasising the discontinuity at the expense of the continuity. It was found that (apparently) the electron could, and did, vary in its orbit much more widely than Bohr had supposed. It could *leap* to outer orbits as well as inner and could on occasion leap outside the system altogether. In fact it was impossible to prove Bohr's theory because the electrons moved at such incredible speeds that for an electron to be here at one instant and the other side of the moon the next was well within its compass. None the less, in fact, the electrons did confine themselves to their respective atomic systems except in so far as the circumstances of their inter-relation were modified by the behaviour of adjacent systems. This is the celebrated " indeterminancy " or " uncertainty " principle of which so much nonsense has been talked by reactionaries in the interests of mysticism and clericalism. It is supposed by these reactionaries to destroy the objective foundation of the " determinism " upon which the very possibility of science depends. In fact, it does just the opposite, since the " indeterminancy " in question is, clearly, a specifically determined one. It is, for instance, because the electrons are moving so rapidly around their nuclei that it is impossible to see any one of them until it has been detached from its " natural " inter-relation, and therefore from its normal movement within that relation. It is only in the moment of their detachment, and not directly but in the reflex form of the electrical energy their detachment releases (manifest to us as a flash of light) that we can " see " them. Also it is the rapidity of their movement around a nucleus which makes the atom seem solid—since, as above noted, they are for all human practical purposes *everywhere-at-once* all over the sphere of their orbital movement around the nucleus. It is obviously impossible to say exactly *where* in this spherical area (or outside it) a given electron will be at any moment : firstly, because its speed makes concretely apparent the dialectical paradox involved in all motion (which involves that a body must both be, and *not* be, at a given point in a given instant of time) ; and secondly, because it is impossible to say in any one case in advance whether outside influences may or may not induce a given electron to leap from one path to another in the moment of its observation. At the same time, its general relations are sufficiently known to enable us to express as a statistical average with a high degree of accuracy the limits of its possible variation. It is much as it might be in the case of one searching for a given John Smith in the neighbourhood of his home on a Saturday night. The probability of his being out of town is not absolutely eliminated but small. The probability of his being in church is smaller still. The probability of his being " at the pictures " is higher, but not great. The probability of his being in a pub is greatest of all, up to as much as 95 per cent. But whether the pub. would be the " Cow and Cucumber," the " Bug and Glue-pot," or the " Pig and Pancake " would be almost impossible to determine off-hand.

This " uncertainty principle," therefore, far from being a negation of the determinism involved in Science, is simply its dialectical transmutation when applied in the concrete form of a developing universe as contrasted with its abstract universal form. It is in fact the exact counterpart of the Marx-Engels principle that accident plays its part in determining the concrete manifold of historical development. It is one more proof that the dialectic of Nature in its concrete-manifold phenomena can better be understood from the analogies provided by the historical movements of Society than by the undialectical methods of abstraction left over from metaphysical speculation.

These speculations, however, affected the problem more on the side of Energy and of the electrons in themselves than on that of the nature of the atomic nucleus—the *proton*.

It was known that the simplest element, *hydrogen*, consisted of a positively-charged nucleus (a " proton ") and one electron. Speculation took two alternative directions. Did the electron ever become absorbed into the *proton* ? And if so, what resulted ? Or, was the *proton* anything more than a unit of positive electricity, as the electron was a unit of negative electricity ? If *not*, why the enormous difference between its mass and that of its opposite, the electron ? If so, of what in addition to positive electricity did the proton-nucleus consist ?

In 1932 an answer was found. CHADWICK knocked out of the proton something unlike anything before discovered. It seemed to have weight—anyway, it could knock on another atom, like a hydrogen atom, and *break it up. But it had no electrical charge.* It did not attract or repel positively-charged protons or electrons. And, above all, its power of penetration was beyond anything known, since it passed through inches of lead without difficulty. This particle, the *neutron*, is now accepted as one of the basic constituents of the *atom. Experiment, in fact, seems to have got back to an " atom " at a lower level !*

Meanwhile BLACKETT had achieved the counterpart of this discovery : he found the *unit of positive electricity*—that all electronic particles are not negatively charged : some are positively charged ! So that now the term " electron " must be used to denote the *category* of electronic particles, which are divided into two classes, *positrons* and *negatrons,* units of positive and negative electrical charge respectively.

With the discovery of the *positron* (called sometimes the " anti-electron " as compared with the negative " electron ") an immense new vista was opened up. Its exploration should carry the revolution in physical science to its culmination. A few very tentative generalisations seem to have been provisionally established. The *proton* is now conceived to be a structure of *neutrons* and *positrons*. In their conjoined form they are converted into an " atom " by association with the appropriate number of *negatrons* (" electrons " in the older nomenclature).

Two alternative conceptions are offered in extension of this. The first is that, while the union of a neutron and a positron gives a positively charged proton, the addition to the combination of a negatron (*i.e.*, its incorporation into the proton as distinct from its external association) restores the neutron on a higher plane. The other is that the neutron represents a stage in the evolution of " matter " at which " electrical substance " in its positive and negative unit forms has not yet been differentiated. This view is based, largely, on the analogy of the biological growth of cellular tissues by the division of a " mother " cell at a certain stage of growth into two " daughter " cells, and so on ; and, also, on the formation of double stars by the subdivision of a " nova," a star at a certain stage of development. Another view, that of Dirac, is that the universe is full of electrons (negatrons), except that, owing to inequalities in the distribution of their total activity, there are throughout the Universe a number of " holes " which count practically as *anti-electrons* (positrons). Whichever of these views will prevail this much is certain : neither the neutron nor the positron remains long in isolation. The neutron becomes absorbed into some neighbouring atomic nucleus, and by doing so raises the weight of the nucleus by one unit—thereby converting an " element " into its isotope. The positron either becomes absorbed into an atomic nucleus likewise, in which case the " element " is shifted up one stage in the Periodic Table ; or, it pairs off with a negatron and both disappear in a " blaze of glory." This latter seems a clear case of the conversion of matter (the electron in either of its forms, in so far as it is a particle, cannot be denied the title of " matter ") into energy. But the process does not end there. The union of the positron and the negatron involves the conversion of their specific " radiation " into (apparently) a higher " mass." But the union of one pair of opposites produces at once the disruption of the union of an adjacent pair and the reappearance of the radiation ; which is followed by a fresh union, a fresh disruption, and so on indefinitely. This so far describes the phenomena of radio-activity quite well, and it is accounted for thus : the annihilation by union of the combined electrical charges of the negatron and positron (otherwise called the electron and the anti-electron) is really their transformation into two *quanta* of energy in another form, i.e., a *photon* and an *anti-photon*. The one becomes manifest as a flash of light ; the other serves to convert the union of an adjacent negatron-positron relation into their antagonistic differentiation.

It is clear that this process has simply infinite possibilities; and although, quite obviously, the phenomena present a perfect bewilderment of difficulties for a would-be generaliser, certain broad conclusions can safely be drawn.

It is clear, for one thing, that the much-trumpeted assertion that " science has proved that matter does not exist " is not only, as we saw earlier, absurd *a priori*, but also, on the evidence of the actual facts, totally without warrant. Even if the proof that matter is " composed of electricity " held good without qualification (as, for instance, by the case of the *neutron*), the evidence tells as much on the side of proving electricity to be a *form* or *state* of matter as it does on the side of proving matter to be " composed of energy." The proof that light, for instance, in common with all varieties of radiation, has *mass* at once places these phenomena in the category of *matter* for everybody who does not insist upon restricting the term " matter " to phenomena above the level at which the atom appears. That the hypothetical " ether " has been, apparently, eliminated from the universe seems, for some inexplicable reason, to give great joy to anti-materialists. They do not seem to realize that the re-establishment of the " emission " theory of light—as against the undulatory theory—tells more heavily in favour of materialism (and " mechanical " materialism at that) than against it. And at the same time the need to find a basis for Herzian " waves " as well as all the other varieties of radiation means, if the ether is eliminated as an exploded hypothesis, that these likewise must be accounted for in terms of an " emission " theory, and so be " waves " or " wave quanta " of, possibly, a form of material particle smaller than any yet discovered. That theory should rest content with the neutron and the electron as the ultimate limits of possible inquiry is unthinkable. Investigation into the " atoms " of Lucretius and the early Greek speculators gave rise to the discrimination between the molecule as the unit of chemical combination and the atom as the unit of physical substance. The atom, like the molecule, has been found to be composite. If we were to follow the fashion of the past we would shift the application of the term " atom " and apply it to the neutron. But as little as the original usage of the term prevented the advance from the Lucretian conception to the Newton-Dalton conception, and thence forward, would such a trick prevent, as seems *a priori* inevitable, the subsequent discovery that the neutron is no more " indivisible " than were its predecessors in the role of " ultimate " unit.

The philosophical error which the revolution in science has exposed lay exactly at that point—in the supposition of an " ultimate " of ideal simplicity out of which, with the aid of mechanical motion, the whole phenomena of the universe could be elaborated. Newton had a motive for making this supposition—the desire to find a function for God, even if it was limited to the simple and remote one of giving the atoms their initial " push off." Nineteenth-century mechanical materialism eliminated God, but onesidedly kept the rest of the Newtonian conception, with the result that under various disguises the need for some form or other of the God-hypothesis—the original " push off "—was constantly reappearing. When Jeans, Eddington and Co., therefore, faced with the crisis in modern science, try to get out of the difficulty by supposing a god who " designed " the Universe merely as an objective demonstration of the higher mathematics (their God having no other quality than that of being mathematically minded, but indifferent to every other consideration) they only make the confusion worse confounded. Apart from the obviously reactionary implications of the attempt, it involves the logical absurdity of attempting to revive Newton's primary postulate as an explanation of phenomena which, admittedly, have long since transcended all possibility of a Newtonian explanation.

The method of formal logic—that of discarding all differences to reach a category from which all difference has been eliminated, proves itself to be worse than useless in face of the facts we have been reviewing. Not by disregarding the differences between all forms of matter and all forms of Energy to reach an empty logical abstraction—the bare frame of the category " Universe " from which all specific content has been eliminated—do we reach a practically usable world-conception on the basis of such facts as these. The only unity into which the Universe can be conceptually resolved is that of a dialectically developing unity of mutually conditioning and mutually interpenetrating opposites—the developing unity in antagonism of active material and material activity. " Matter " exists, not in the abstract, but in the form of concrete and specific phenomena, each with its special distinguishing activity. " Energy " exists likewise, not in the abstract, but in the form of the concrete, specifically distinguishing activities of matter.

Energy is the active aspect of Mass (which is the essential characteristic of matter for all but sophisticators who seek to deny to sub-atomic substance the name of " matter ") : *Mass is the inertial aspect of Energy.* Only thus, dialectically, as a unity of opposites can the universe of objective Nature be conceived.

The pseudo-scientist, who in the interests of clericalism and reaction tells us that " Matter " has been proved to be " composed " of energy, rivals the fabled hero who made a sword out of " *pure* sharpness." He outdoes in absurdity the Connemara fisherman who defined a herring-net as " a lot of holes tied together with string." The *pseudo*-scientist *wants to keep the* HOLES *while denying the existence of the* STRING !

The *pseudo*-scientists suffer, in fact, from the same disease which afflicts the bringers-of-Marx-" up-to-date " — the *Bloomsbury disease*—which is an acute form of the malady chronic to Philistine " common sense " : a total inability to comprehend in one view *both* the difference *and* the likeness, the unity *and* the opposition, the essence *and* the appearance, the necessary *and* the accidental observable in all phenomena.

In the phenomena we have been surveying—those of the physical sciences, for instance—victims of the Bloomsbury disease can see that the old, hard-and-fast, immutable *qualitative* boundary lines have been shattered. And since for them science was wholly a matter of fixing such boundaries and establishing immutable permanencies, *for them* " Science has exploded " into something rarer than " gas " —which in Bloomsbury is neither rare, nor strange ! *Per contra* : hunted out of this ditch, they leap into the bog and declare that science is wholly and solely a matter of shattering boundaries and so proving that Nothing exists—*not really* !

The facts revealed by experimental science (as distinct from the interpretations placed on those facts by metaphysicians—who may happen also to be experimental scientists taking a " day off ") refute these victims from both sides. Science is a technique of fixing boundaries—but it is also a practice which destroys them. Most of all, it is a practice of unifying these two contradictory operations. And it is Science notwithstanding, since the *contradiction* is in Nature itself. Science does establish definite and specific boundaries—but they are not between *absolute Qualities*, they are between specific, developing, mutually transforming *relations of interaction.* It does *fix* boundaries—but since these are boundaries between quantities and qualities, forms and directions, of self-developing, interacting and counteracting *movements*, its fixing is of necessity provisional and conditional only. And since its subject-matter reveals itself as *Motion*, and since motion is rationally conceivable (in terms of " common sense ") only in the form of a contradiction, i.e., that a thing both is and is not in a given place at a given moment, necessarily the facts revealed by experimental science can be " conceived and rationally understood " only *dialectically*—" *only as revolutionising practice.*"

In the course of our survey we have touched upon several aspects of the work of Einstein. Since his *Theory of Relativity* (which in point of fact is no more than a mathematical generalisation of the facts above recited) is supposed by the less well-informed members of the intelligentsia to have destroyed the foundation for Materialism and Marxism, a glance at that theory will be in order here.

Einstein's Theory is expressed in complicated mathematical formulæ which are too abstruse to be discussed here. They are, in fact, formulæ produced to meet a need of physical laboratory practice—the need to treat complex combinations of variable movements as though they were single units in motion, and motions as though they were stationary quantities. To have conquered such a difficulty was a feat worthy the highest admiration. But to treat such formulæ as though they were literally film-photographs of the Cosmic Scheme is as rational as it would be to treat a cookery recipe as itself *a meal*.

For instance : Einstein's Special Law of Relativity *begins* with the fact that *absolute* motion cannot be conceived or measured in itself. Motions can only be conceived and measured relatively to a datum line or point. Bloomsbury has " gone *doolally* " over this " proof that motion is not real ! " and imagines that this is all Einstein has accomplished. That which has been proved is in fact the reverse : namely, that *nothing but motion* is " real " ; and of this proposition the " proof " was furnished over a century ago by GEORGE FREDERICK WILLIAM HEGEL in his *Phœnomenologie* and his *Encyclopædia of the Philosophic Sciences*. It is included in the primary assumption of his *Logic*—existence involves *relation*. It is true not only of motion but of everything which moves. The Quantity of anything can only be *measured* in some other thing. The *Quality* of a thing is *relative to* that upon which it acts, or against which it reacts.

The truth is that Einstein only *began* there. His problem was the practical problem of the astronomical laboratory— how to measure motion from a point which is itself in motion —and this complicated through several stages. For instance : suppose a chalk mark on the driving-wheel of an express locomotive. Suppose that locomotive to travel from London to Glasgow in a gale. Express as *absolute* motion the movement of that chalk mark watched by an observing telescopic eye situated *outside* " our " Universe. The wheel turns on its axis—hence the chalk-mark describes a series of circles. But as it turns it moves *forward*—so the circles are, from the " absolute " point of view, *not* circles, but loops. Then the wheel wobbles slightly on its hub. Then the engine rises and falls as the level of the road determines ; then it sways from side to side, bounces up and down, vibrates in reaction to the wind, and so on. Then the earth turns round on its axis, and also moves round the sun, which in turn moves towards a point in the Universe which is itself turning. Einstein found a formula for reducing all those motions to an abstract absolute relation.

What does this prove ? Whatever else it may prove, it certainly vindicates overwhelmingly the dialectical method which refuses to treat " absolutes " except as *relations*, and *abstractions* as anything but abstractions.

Again, Einstein fell foul, *not* of Newton's law of gravitation, as is often said—that law holds good within determinate limits —but with an assumption that Newton had included within the scope of his law. Newton had observed correctly that every particle in the Universe acted upon and was reacted against by every other particle—and that in a specific, quantitative way. Newton had supposed this as due to the interaction of (*a*) the inertia of bodies, and (*b*) the motion originally imparted by God. [Newton postulated as primary an *absolute* stillness (*inertia*) which it took a miracle, God's primal *motion*, to overcome.] Einstein leaves out God and substitutes an *active* for a *passive conception of inertia*. That is to say, when Newton began with the supposition that *nothing* can change *of itself* Einstein supposed the opposite— that everything *is* changing of itself and only confines its changes to particular directions, under pressure of the counter-changes in *everything else*.

Newton's " gravitation " was, in fact, the observed material phenomenon of *weight* raised to the scale of a universal phenomenon ; Einstein reminded us that *as in practical life* on earth *weight* is a fact of which we become aware, and which can only be measured in *relation*. We learn that bodies have weight by lifting them, by perceiving the relation of resistance between them and our muscles. We " weigh " them one against the other. Newton attributed this fact, *weight*, to a mysterious " attraction." Einstein is content with the fact that it is actual or potential motion and arises from the fact that Motion, Change, is the most fundamental fact about Matter we know.

Newton, to give things room to move—he knew they moved—supposed an Abstract Space for them to move in. Also, as things happened one after the other, he supposed a Mystical Abstract Time for these events to happen in. Einstein pointed out that, *looked at from the point of view of the Universe in itself*, Space and Time are *qualities* of the Universe, not its *pre*conditions.

Since the Universe *is* Everything-Everywhere, and that All-the-Time, there is for it no *where* to which to go, or from which to *come*. Also nothing can happen *to* it, since all that happens does so *in* it. As we in the world of actual practice mean by " space " room to move, and by " time " that which separates events in a succession, Space and Time *as we know them* cannot exist for the Universe as such ! All right ! Let the Universe worry about it. " It's *its* funeral, not ours." So long as we can still move about and still find a use for clocks, Time and Space, *for us*, carry on " business as usual."

What Einstein has proved herein is simply what the Dialectical Materialist has always contended—that human knowledge is knowledge of things *from the human point of view*, and that any pretension to absolute knowledge, to "final truths of the last instance," is only an *absolute pretence*. When Einstein goes on to prove that one of the *absolute* facts in the universe is the order of *succession* of events, which happen for every individual, without exception, in one and the same order of succession (or co-existence), Einstein vindicates the Materialist conception of Time and Space (which is that of the plain man in the workshop) as against the Bogey-bogey Absolute Time and Space of the meta-physicians.

What is the outcome of all this ? That in Nature there is one fact which is *absolute* (a *relational* absolute)—*the fact of Motion*—and one prime quality observable in the Motion of

Material Nature, and that is its dialectical quality of inter-action and the outcome thereof—a perpetually developing sequence of *new formations* linked *in a never-ending series by connecting revolutionary transitions.*

REVOLUTIONARY TRANSITIONS IN NATURE.

Marxism struggles, on its theoretical side, against a double weight of prejudice—the prejudice against Materialism in general, and the prejudice against the Dialectic in particular ; which latter prejudice is closely connected with belief in the permanence of the existing social order and a repugnance to the notion of revolutionary changes in theory and in practice.   A deeply ingrained prejudice has caused it to be generally believed that revolutionary theories are necessarily " unscientific " and " contrary to the natural order of evolu-tion."   It is necessary therefore to stress somewhat the fact that, as we have seen in the facts of physical science, evolu-tionary development in Nature invariably includes " explosion phenomena "—mutation leaps—stages of revolutionary tran-sition as connecting-links between the various formation stages in the evolutionary process as a whole.

This fact is important since, firstly, if it be true of Nature as a whole, it is true of the process whereby mankind has itself been produced ; and since, secondly, it is only in so far as mankind understands Nature that it can undertake the work of changing Nature with any prospect of success.

The central fact with which to begin is the fact that Nature, to be understood, must be studied *historically*.

Considered Quantitatively there is no question but that the Universe at any given moment is the Universe that was, in process of transformation into the Universe that will be. Only on the basis of this presupposition is the universe intelligible, and, therefore, practically usable at all.   Con-sidered Qualitatively it is equally self-evident that the universe is never for any two successive moments the same. So far the situation of things is substantially that envisaged in the ordinary " evolutionary " conception which has been a commonplace since the close of the battle of Evolution opened by Darwin's *Origin of Species*.   But, as we have seen, this conception needs to be considerably deepened and enriched before it becomes usable.   Particularly does it need to be deepened on the side of recognising that the continuous transformation of the Universe is not confined to surface forms only, but includes its fundamental structure and all the modes of motion which in their totality make up the activity of the Universe. Also it needs to be enriched by the recognition of degrees and orders of persistence which persist through all the infinite variety of the Universal Change.

This is most clearly apparent in the case of the phenomena of *Periodicity*, upon which, as we have seen, the modern crisis in Science principally turns. The nature and significance for Marxism of Natural periodicity can, perhaps, best be seen by means of an analogy.

Both *sound* and *light* are objectively forms of wavelike activity. In the case of sound the waves are propagated through the air ; in the case of light the activity involved is that of electro-magnetic waves. In each case qualitative difference—between varieties of colour in the case of light, and varieties of pitch in the case of sound—are objectively based upon differences of wave-length and frequency of vibration.

A tuning fork which makes 512 vibrations per second will excite air waves of two feet and more in length, and give out a note of a certain specific pitch. Another fork, making only half the number of vibrations per second (256), will give waves twice as long and emit a note of only half the pitch. Between these two points lies a whole octave of sound. The sound may be modified by imperceptible stages of flattening or sharpening by exciting wave-vibrations whose length and frequency varies in the requisite proportion from one or other of these extremes. Yet the qualitative difference to a musical ear in all these stages of gradual modification is not more certain and self-evident than is the parallelism between a key-note and its " octave."

In the case of colour the parallelism is very close indeed—though, of course, no suggestion of *identity* is implied. Between the upper limit of the spectrum (Red) and its lower limit (Violet) lies what we may fairly call an " octave " of colour. Here again the difference is objectively one of wave-length and frequency of vibration—Red having the higher limit of wave-length and the lower limit of frequency. The significant fact to grasp is that the " octave " of visible light is only one in the whole series of " octaves " of electro-magnetic wave activity which constitutes, as we have seen, one of the two most basic aspects of Nature. Colour in all its forms is as clearly distinguishable as a self-contained group (or *quanta*) as is an octave on the musical scale. The varieties within each group shade by imperceptible gradations the one into the other ; yet in each case we have the analogous quality of a return to the starting-point on a different level. In the case of the colour-spectrum the two limits of the spectrum are " octaves " of invisible light—infra-Red rays in the one case, and ultra-Violet in the other. Each of these varieties of invisible light are of immense importance to mankind both biologically and technologically.

The difference between the metaphysical non-dialectical conception of " evolution " and the dialectical conception of development is well illustrated here. The " evolutionist " (so-called) who clings to conceptions of the " inevitability of gradualism " order sees only the phenomena of infinitesimal changes : he is blind, or self-blinded to the *periodicity*, to the revolutionary " transformations of quantity into quality," to the qualitative *leaps*, and sudden transitions, which are illustrated by the movement of the scale from the key-note to its octave, and the emergence of the band of visible light from the whole range of invisible waves of radiation. The force of the difference will become the more apparent the more we proceed.

On the infra-red side of the band of waves which constitute visible light extends the band of " invisible " (infra-red) light rays, which covers (to use the spectrum band as a unit of measurement) eight octaves. The further we pass from the visible light band in this direction the more these waves grow *heating* in quality. Beyond the band of radiant heat lies the range of Hertzian waves (whose variety stretches from a wave-length of several kilometres to one of a few millimetres only, with a correlative inverse variation in frequency). On the ultra-Violet side of the spectrum band extend, firstly, the range of ultra-violet rays, then the " mitogenetic " rays given off by biological cells in the process of their natural division in growth, then the rays characteristic of " phosphorescence," then the X-rays, the Gamma rays, the electronic radiations, and finally the " Cosmic " rays, in which some observers are disposed to see the actual form in which " energy " becomes transmuted into mass.

Radiation cannot, it is clear, be understood simply as radiation-in-the-abstract. To attempt to arrive at the " true " nature of radiation by taking a statistical average either of its quantity or its quality would be, obviously, absurd. (Yet this, in fact, is what is quite ordinarily done in the case of human beings—*averaged* into " Humanity "—or aggregates of human beings averaged as " Society " or " the Community "). And, also, radiation, in addition to possessing other qualities besides those we have noted—velocity and force, for instance—must of necessity be a radiation of *something*. It must, that is to say, possess *Mass*—just as every specific Mass must possess some kind of *activity*—radiation being only one of an infinite number of possible activities, although possibly it is its most fundamental form, since the Einstein theory would seem to demand that simple mechanical motion must be conceived as proceeding in an undulatory or spiral fashion.

If now we turn to the consideration of Mass and its specific forms a similar *periodicity*, a similar inter-relation of quantitative and qualitative progression, a similar continuity in variation combined with variations in the continuity becomes apparent. At the lower end of the scale is the range of sub-atomic particles. Through the atom, the aggregation of atoms in the elementary molecule, the inter-relation of atoms in the compound molecule, the aggregation of molecules in inorganic substance, the structural inter-relation of molecules in the crystals, the functional inter-relation of molecules in the organic cell, the structural inter-relation of organic cells in living tissue, and the functional inter-relation of cells and tissues in the living organisms in all their variety, we have an ascending scale of periodic variation in which likeness in difference is not more important than difference in likeness. It will be seen that in the case of *Masses* the phenomena of progression is more clearly apparent, since the higher formation stages (the organic) clearly presuppose the inorganic ones, as these in turn presuppose the atomic and the sub-atomic formation stages. The law of motion of the living organism, as such, is not simply the law of motion of the cell quantitatively increased, any more than the law of motion of the cell is simply that of the molecule, the molecule that of the atom, or the atom that of its sub-atomic components. On the contrary, at each stage the law of motion of the preceding stage is *both included and added to*, and the quantitative alteration involves a complete qualitative change. Moreover, at the stage of the living organism it can most clearly be seen that the phenomena of masses and their specific movements are not those of abstract *units*, but those of aggregated and differentiated inter-relation, which inter-relation begets the progressive *movement* of the sequence as a whole, and of the periodical succession therein of stages of formation.

It must be clear now that the abstract conception of

" evolution " needs, as we have said, to be completely transformed before it is applicable to a process such as is here revealed. For one thing the interdependence and mutual conditioning of phenomena is expressed as a movement in space as well as in time. The higher stages of the sequence involve the *continuance* of the lower stages as much as their complete change of relation in the aggregate of interaction. The living organism cannot be understood solely from a study of electronic particles, or of atoms, or of any of the succeeding stages. Yet all are presupposed in the living organism and are necessary conditions for its existence. Electrons, neutrons, etc., could exist unchanged if there were no human beings. Human beings could not exist if the electrons, etc., were not in being. *The higher stages presuppose the lower, both in space and in time.*

This being clear the final step should be easy. Since the history of Nature is manifestly one of the progressive establishment of successive stages in a series of formations, each of which grows out of and at the same time involves a qualitative transformation of Nature considered in its totality, it is clear that the appearance of Mankind as a biological species constitutes in one aspect a quantitative continuation, and in another a revolutionary transformation of Nature.

Similarly : the scope and extent of this transformation can be understood only when the nature of the change has been grasped in both its aspects. In relation to Nature in its historical sequence, mankind, considered abstractly, is as much part of and yet distinct from Nature as the visible light spectrum is distinct from, and also part of, the whole range of radiation phenomena. Considered concretely, Mankind can no more be understood from the analysis of a single specimen than an organic cell or a positron can be understood in isolation. And just as the law of motion of electrons, atoms, and organic cells in their concrete objective associations are not simple multiples of the law of motion of the single specimen, so likewise the law of motion of Associated Man is of necessity something quantitatively and qualitatively distinct from the law of motion of Man-in-the-abstract.

As Nature, to be understood, must be understood in its developing totality, so Man to be understood must be studied in Mankind's *Historical Movement.*

And, since mutation leaps, stages of revolutionary transition, the objective transmutation of quantity into quality is, as we have seen, inseparably bound up with the whole development process of Nature, both in detail as well as in general, any conception of the historical development of Mankind-in-association, of human society, must of necessity include the conception of revolutionary changes as part of the total becoming process of Man, as an individual and collectively.

One such revolutionary transition is already implicit in the conception—the transition from the objective activity of Nature to man's subjective activity—to *Thought*! No one disputes the revolutionary quality of the difference between a universe in which Thought-activity has not yet been developed and a universe in which it exists. Considered abstractly, however, who can say that the difference involved is greater than that of any of the other transformations of quantity into quality we have been considering? That objective activity is the primary presupposition of subjective activity ; that subjective activity *is* a transmuted form of objective activity, must be clearly apparent, as is also the fact that subjective activity itself has its own special historical process in which formation stages linked by mutation leaps are necessarily to be traced. No less apparent is the fact that the reflex-oppositional relation of subjective activity (Thought) to objective activity (Nature) is itself merely an expression of the objectively antagonistic inter-relation between Man as a physical fact and Nature as alike his general presupposition and his particular conditioning environment. As we have seen, each phenomenon in Nature from the neutron to Man, or from the Herzian wave to the cosmic ray, must in the same way be understood from two opposite sides—those of its inner and its outer law of motion. The crowning point of Marxian Dialectical Materialism is therefore its revelation of the inner and the outer laws of motion of Human Society, and therefore of Man.

Before passing to a consideration of this the crowning aspect of Marxism, let us, both as a means of emphasis and of division, glance at a few illustrative quotations :—

First, here is Engels on the unitary connection between the three " universal " fields of dialectic development :

" We [Marx and Engels] comprehended the concepts in our heads materialistically—as *images of real things* instead of regarding real things as images of this or that stage in the development of the absolute concept. Thus dialectics reduced itself to *the science of the general laws of motion,* alike of the external world and of human thought—two sets of laws which are *identical in substance but which differ in their expression,* in so far as the human mind can apply them consciously, whereas in Nature, and also, up to now (for the most part), in human history these laws assert themselves unconsciously in the form of external necessity in the midst of an endless series of seeming accidents."—ENGELS : *Feuerbach,* p. 54.

Contrast with that, and in the light of the preceding discussion of the Dialectic in Nature, the following :

" So far as the dialectic, applied to material things, is merely a statement that nothing comes from nothing, that historical events, relations and institutions proceed out of each other, that they *frequently* (!) proceed by means of evoking an antagonism, and that . . . the ultimate result . . . *often* shares in the features of both antagonists—so far . . . it is *no more than a pale reflection of a consciousness of evolutionary process which is now common.*"—POSTGATE : *Karl Marx,* p. 87.

The best criticism on this is a *witness in agreement* :

" The Hegelian dialectic is unfitted to describe biological and social evolution. It describes superficial appearances rather than explains deep-seated causes. . . . It cannot be dissociated from the idea of catastrophe and revolution, of accumulated energy bursting through opposition, of a *simplicity* (!) of opposing forces which is never found in the actual world. . . . Biologically the ' negation of the existing state of things,' its ' inevitable breaking up,' its ' momentary existence,' is *impossible* (! ! !) . . . In one aspect the only fault one has to find with Marxian formulæ is but *verbal. But words suggest ideas.* . . . Biology alone was competent to give the clue to the proper understanding of the process of Evolution. . . . Hegel, not Darwin, was the intellectual father to Marx. . . ."—J. RAMSAY MACDONALD : *Socialism and Society,* pp. 112–118.

After a pause to congratulate Raymond Postgate on the company he has landed himself in, we can take (as an antidote) a sample of Hegel himself :

" Men like to try to make a change conceivable by means of the gradualness of transition ; but gradualness is precisely the merely indifferent change, the opposite of qualitative change. In gradualness the *connection* of the two realities—whether taken as states or as inde-

pendent things—is suspended . . . that which is needed
in order that change may be understood is eliminated. . . .

"In musical relations . . . while succeeding notes
appear progressively to move further from the keynote
. . . suddenly a *return*, a surprising concord emerges
which was not *qualitatively* led up to by what immediately preceded, but appears as an *actio in distans*, as a
relative to a distant entity. . . .

"Metal oxides (for instance, lead oxides) are formed
at certain quantitative points of oxidation, and differ in
colour as in other qualities. They do not gradually
merge into one another ; the relations which lie between
those *nodes* produce no neutral, and no specific determinate being. A specific combination appears which has not
passed through these intermediate steps, but is based
on a Measure-Relation and has qualities of its own. . . .

"All birth and death, instead of being a continued
graduality, are rather an *interruption* of this, and are the
jump from quantitative into qualitative change. . . .

"Ordinary imagination, when it has to conceive an
arising or a passing away, thinks it has conceived them
(as was mentioned) when it imagines them as *gradual*
emergence or disappearance. But . . . changes in Being
are in general not only a transition of one magnitude
into another, but a transition from the qualitative into
the quantitative, and conversely : a process of becoming
other which *breaks off graduality*. . . .

"Water on being cooled does not little by little
become hard, gradually reaching the consistency of ice
after having passed through the consistency of paste,
but is *suddenly* hard ; when it already has quite attained
freezing point it may (if it stands still) be wholly liquid,
and a slight shake brings it into the condition of hard-
ness."—HEGEL : *Science of Logic*, Vol. I, pp. 388–90.

Finally here is an exchange between Marx and Engels
which will round off this argument and clear the way
for a new aspect. On June 22nd, 1867, Marx writes to
Engels :

"You are quite right about Hoffman. You will also
see from the conclusion of my Chapter III [of *Capital*],
where the transformation of the handicraft-master into
a capitalist—as a result of purely *quantitative* changes—
is touched upon, that, *in the text* (at that time I was just
hearing Hoffmann's lectures), I refer to the law Hegel

discovered of *purely quantitative changes turning into qualitative changes*, as holding good alike in history and natural science. In a note I mention the *molecular theory. . . ."*—MARX *to Engels*, June 22nd, 1867.

This was in reply to a note from Engels which included the following, which in connection with the argument above may with propriety be described as *remarkable* :

"Have read Hoffmann. The more recent chemical theory, with all its faults, is a great advance on *the former atomic one.* The molecule as the smallest particle of matter capable of independent existence is a perfectly rational category, a ' node ' as Hegel puts it, in the infinite series of divisions, which does not conclude them but establishes a qualitative difference. *The atom—* formerly represented as the limit of possible division— *is now nothing more than a relation*, though Hoffmann himself falls back every other minute into the *old idea of indivisible atoms."*—ENGELS *to Marx*, June 16th, 1867.

It is not only the fact that one of Bloomsbury's " very latest " toys—the vanishing atom—was known to Marx and Engels as long ago as 1867, to which we here draw attention. Readers will note that this phenomenon was *rationally comprehended* by them as falling within the scope of the Hegelian Law (supported by Hegel with a wealth of illustrations, truly remarkable for his day). This in its wider application gave a conception of historical progression (or " evolution ") which was just as rich and all-sided as the conventional " biological " conception—which is all the MacDonalds and Postgates can rise to—is (as Lenin said) poor, flat, insipid, and sterile. As Hegel saw, the problem is—how is *real* change possible ? The " evolutionist " endeavour to reduce change to " alterations " so minute as to be negligible was not a solution of the fundamental problem. It was a roundabout way of denying that any *change* is *real*.

Such a view was impossible to men who had taken as their slogan : " our business is *to change the world."*

THE OBJECTIVE DIALECTIC OF HISTORY

The basic problem for Marx and Engels was—how is change in general *possible* in Human Society ? They did not seek a solution in a *pseudo-*" objectivist " conception of Natural Law. That the mechanical Materialists had done, only to reach the *impasse* that at the very moment when they were turning the world upside down they were explaining to each other that change, in itself, was intrinsically impossible. Neither did they seek a solution in the Absolute Idea, the omnipotence of the human reason and Will. That way Hegel had gone—to land himself in the impasse of declaring in one breath that history had reached finality in the State and Constitutional Government, and in another that finality was absolutely unthinkable.

They found a solution in the actual, practical *productive* inter-relation between living men and Nature. There under their eyes, and that of all men—had they but the wit to see it—lay the answer to the riddle ! Men did in fact—*produce*. New things were constantly being brought into being, and that as part of the basic life-process of Mankind, individually and collectively !

The far-reaching profundity of this discovery is easy to miss ; and all the critics of Marx, and 99.9 per cent. of the " simplifiers," miss it completely. Marx and Engels were seeking that which Hegel had sought before them, and HERBERT SPENCER was to seek after them—a means of bringing within the scope of a unitary conception the three great fields of philosophical survey : Nature and its Development ; Mankind and its History, individual and social ; and the Thought-Activity of Man, its genesis and significance. And already in 1845 (in the *Theses*) and in 1846 (the *German Ideology*) they had not only formulated on a positive, objective and *materialist* basis a conception of Universal Evolution, but also had solved the riddle which Herbert Spencer and his followers (the " shame-faced materialists " as Engels called them) continued to find insoluble to the end of the century.*

An admiring disciple (Hector Macpherson) thus formulates Spencer's claim to consideration :

" Spencer saw clearly that on the lines of the old Experience philosophy, the problem was insoluble. He saw that if the Mind cannot pass beyond particulars, as Mill said, it was hopeless to search for universal laws,

* Herbert Spencer's first formulation of the doctrine of Evolution was made in 1852 in an article, *The Development Hypothesis*, published in the *Westminster Review*. The prospectus of his *Synthetic Philosophy* was issued in 1860, and its first section (*First Principles*) began to appear in the same year. It was not concluded until 1896—a year after the death of Engels. The place of pioneer distinction occupied by Spencer in the history of the doctrine of Evolution makes the priority of Marx and Engels of first-rate significance.

hopeless to trace existence in its multifarious aspects to one dynamic process. What Spencer did was to start with two universal intuitions, *which cannot be proved*, and which must be accepted as necessities of thought— belief in personal identity, and belief in the permanent constitution of things which we call Nature. . . .

" Accepting as the data of philosophy, subject and object, self and not-self, Spencer deals with the general forms under which the not-self, the Cosmos, manifests itself to the self, the mind. These general forms . . . are space, time, matter, motion, and force. After a careful analysis . . . he comes to the conclusion that . . . all necessary data of intelligence are built up or extracted from experiences of force. Force persists. When we say that force persists we are simply saying that the sum total of matter and motion by which force manifests itself to us can neither be increased nor diminished. This, like personal identity, is an ultimate fact, an ultimate belief, which we must take with us as the basis of all reasoning. If force came into existence and went out of existence, the Universe would not be a cosmos but a chaos ; nay, more—scientific reasoning would be impossible. . . . Viewed thus, the Universe is one fact, the varying phenomena being but so many phases of the redistribution of matter and motion."—Quoted in DUNCAN, *Life and Letters of Herbert Spencer*, p. 517.

That Spencer was, on the showing of this admirer, not nearly so original as he (and his admirer) supposed—his complete ignorance of the whole Dialectical philosophy from Kant to Hegel is naively confessed in his *Autobiography*—that at best Spencer was doing substantially that which Feuerbach attempted in one way, and the post-Feuerbachian nature-materialists in another ; so much this extract makes abundantly clear.

No less clear is it that *Marx and Engels had transcended his conclusion before it was formulated.*

It was not at all sufficient to rest content with the fact that the Universe exhibited a " constant redistribution of Matter and Motion," with the self and not-self as *ultimates* (" which cannot be proved "), or with the fact that " the sum total of matter and motion cannot be destroyed." All these things are true, no doubt. But they are so only with a qualification which nullifies the significance they held for Herbert Spencer.

In the act and fact of *production* Marx and Engels saw, as

all men may, that Man himself not only can, but does, take a hand in the "cosmic" process of redistributing matter and motion. Thereby Man demonstrates his material "one-ness" with the cosmic process and material Nature—but also, and thereby, Man *alters* Nature, and that more or less completely in accordance with his own will and desire. This not only demonstrates man's "one-ness" *with* Nature, and Nature's processes of self-alteration. It demonstrates man's dialectical distinction *from* Nature, in the act and fact of his *productive* opposition of himself to Nature as one of Nature's own forces. More : it proved that Nature's production of change, alteration, and *new* formations was *no more* magical and mysterious than Man's production-activity ; and, also, that Man's power of production was *no less* "miraculous" than Nature's own. This applied to the celebrated "world-riddles"—the origin of life, of man, of thought—gave a conception so revolutionary that only now are we beginning to realise the immensity of its significance.

That the *sum* of the Matter and Motion in the Universe is a constant quantity is a fact, and one salutary to emphasise as against Supernaturalists, solipsists and other intellectual *nihilists*. But the indestructibility of matter and motion is only the conservative side of a truth which has another and a revolutionary side—the fact that *forms* of matter, and of motion—*including Mankind itself*—are *convertible*, capable of *radical transformation*, and that, given the necessary preconditions, by man.

The "one-ness" of the Cosmos is proved not by its abstract existence, but by this concrete and specific *convertibility*. The unity is not reached by ignoring the multiple differences : it is demonstrated by the *practice*—of both Nature and Man— which showed these differences to be *not* "ultimates" but mutable, conditional *products* of specific interaction. Not in the abstract evolutionism which first of all resolved all *change* into an infinity of alterations so minute that, like the nursemaid's baby, they could be ignored (as "only a little one") and so treated as non-existent ;—not thus, but as a process of active dialectical interaction, could Mankind, and its Thought-processes and their Historical progression, be brought within the scope of a unitary conception.

That the self and the not-self are "ultimates" in the sense that they and their oppositional relation are presupposed in all human experience is true. But equally true, and far more revolutionary in its significance, is the fact that every act of practice *produces* not only objective change, but the subjective alteration of " Experience."

And here lies the fact which shatters the whole of the elaborate " agnosticism " of the Spencerian system. Practice, and particularly social-co-operation in *production-practice*, is the generating source of the consciousness of self, and also of the inseparable inter-relation between the self and the not-self. Men do not need to " prove " by logic the existence of either ; both are *proved* simultaneously and in conjunction by the act and fact of practice—particularly production-practice.

Not that the Universe is " ultimately " *One*—but that all its immediate, concrete multiplicities show a capacity for being changed and transformed; not that mankind is, being material, *one with* the Universe, but that mankind, *because it is material in a material universe,* can participate in the universal process of transformation-begetting interaction, and in so doing can in social combinations *use* the Universe more or less in accordance with its will—this was the revolutionary fact upon which Marx and Engels based their sociology.

Observe : Marx and Engels did not fall into the " objectivist " (really : *contemplativist*) error of starting with biological Man and " tracing his evolution " thenceforward by means of a string of conjectures. Just as in his analysis of Capitalist Economy, Marx started with its *essential relation*—that of the *commodity*, and found therein, on analysis, all the basic relations of bourgeois society, so Marx and Engels found the logical starting-point for human society not by conjuring conjectures out of the past, but by examining the *present*.

Human beings (as biological specimens) can be " explained " —more or less—with the aid of the fact that men were evolved as a distinct species by Nature. *That of itself will not explain why they ever advanced beyond that stage.*

To find a ground upon which to base not only the Theory that Society could be changed, but a Practical technique for bringing that change to be, it was hopelessly irrelevant to look to the fact that what are now *men* were once (in the persons of their ancestors) *not yet men*. A cause adequate to change the present had to be found actually available *in the present*. A cause sufficient to account for the *existence* of society through all its stages had to be found operating in *all stages* of human history. Moreover, this had to be such a cause as would from its own nature undergo sufficient changes to account, as well as for the existence of human society, for the sequence of *changes*, in all their historical multiplicity, which society had undergone. Bourgeois speculators, then as now, failed utterly to grasp the need for this two-fold conception.

What fact is there which is actively operating *at all periods* of human history ? A fact sufficiently powerful to keep men in permanent inter-relation even when their differences of desire set them flying at each other's throats ? There is only one such fact—*the fact of common dependence upon production*.

But Marx and Engels were not concerned only with society as a simple *Continuity*. They were concerned, and that specifically and practically, with its *Dis-continuity*, its sudden jumps from one stage to another. These *jumps*, which so baffle the " evolutionist " and " gradualist " that he argues them out of existence, were not only the very things that had to be explained ; they were the outward and visible signs that *real* progress had in fact been achieved, that *new* forms of society could, and did, actually come into being—that the will to change the world had an objective justification.

That Marx and Engels found the Law of History in production and its dialectical consequences is well known. What is not so well known nor appreciated is the fact that they were aided in formulating their *dialectical* materialist conception of history—which is a law *both* of social evolution *and* of social revolution—by Hegel's brilliantly suggestive *law* of the transformation of Quantity into Quality. *This*, and not the " wooden trichotomy " of Thesis-Antithesis-Synthesis (which is only *one* of the *external forms* in which the Hegelian law is expressed) is the specific stimulus which Marx and Engels received from Hegel.

The Marxian Dialectical Materialist conception of History has in fact the reverse significance to that which is commonly attributed to it. It is only *incidentally* a conception of the law of social growth. It is *essentially* a conception of the *Law of Social Revolution*. We have seen the germinal forms of this above : " Men make their circumstances as much as circumstances make men." " The educator must himself be educated." " Social life is essentially practical." "The standpoint of the *new* materialism is *human* society." "The philosophers have only *interpreted* the world in various ways ; the point, however, is to *change* it." In their *German Ideology*, after a careful analysis, Marx and Engels draw their conclusions :

> " Finally we obtain the following results from the fully developed conception of history :

(1) In the course of their development the forces of production and the means of intercourse reach a stage at which, in the conditions then prevailing, these forces only do harm—they cease to be productive forces and become destructive (e.g., *machinery and money*).

In association with this we find that a class has been evolved which has to bear all the burdens of society while enjoying none of its advantages ;— a class which is forced out of society into the most marked contrast with all other classes ;—which comprises a majority of the members of society ;— and from which proceeds the consciousness of the need for a thoroughgoing revolution—a *communist revolution*—which consciousness can, of course, arise in the other classes also, but only where there is *a comprehension of the standpoint of this particular class.*

(2) The conditions within which specific forms of production can be operated are those of the social domination of a corresponding class in society ;— of a class whose social power (which arises from ownership) secures practical-theoretical expression in the then extant form of the State. In consequence every revolutionary struggle is directed against that class which, for the time being, is dominant.

(3) In all the revolutions which have taken place up till now the *kind* of production-activity has remained inviolate ; so that there has been nothing changed but the *distribution* of this activity—a re-allocation of the labour to different persons. *The communist revolution*, on the other hand, is directed against the *kind* of production-activity hitherto practised, and *will do away with* '*labour*' *as such*. It will make an end of class rule by abolishing classes—and will do this for the reason that this revolution is that of the class which no longer counts in Society *as a class*— is a class that expresses the *dissolution* of all the classes, nationalities, etc., within existing society.

(4) For the widespread generation of this *communist consciousness*, and for the carrying out of this communist revolution, an extensive *change in*

human beings is needed. This can only occur in the course of the *practical movement, in the course of the revolution.* Hence the revolution is necessary, not only because only thus can the ruling class be overthrown, but because, also, *only in a revolution can the uprising class free itself from its old trammels and become capable of founding a new society.* . . .

"For us Communism is not a condition of affairs which ' ought ' to be,—not an ' Ideal ' end in correspondence with which Reality is forced to shape itself. When we speak of Communism we mean the actual *movement* which makes an end of the existing order of things. The determinants of this movement arise directly from the conditions actually existing. . . .

"*Not criticism but revolution is the motive force of history.*"—MARX-ENGELS : *German Ideology.*

.   .   .   .   .

This magnificent passage is remarkable from a number of angles. Like *Hamlet,* it is "full of quotations." Not only can there be seen in it traces of the struggles we have already noted in the *Year-Book* articles and in the *Holy Family,* and also the Hegel-Feuerbach "gill-arches," but there are also new facets which give foregleams of the aspects of the Marxian system which were later to be more fully developed.

After the *German Ideology* and the parallel passages at the close of Marx's *Poverty of Philosophy* it was less than a stride to the standpoint of the first great classic in which Marxism took rank as an organised political movement—the *Communist Manifesto.*

In the spring of 1845 the *Theses on Feuerbach* closed with the classic avowal of the *need* to change the world—in the winter of 1847, and in the form of the *Communist Manifesto,* that *need* found living expression in a *deed* to whose echoes the world still rings.

T

CHAPTER VI

THE DIALECTIC OF REVOLUTION

In the Beginning was—The Deed.—*Goethe.*

OUR study of the formative period of Marxism, the period from 1844 to 1847, has presented Dialectical Materialism to us chiefly in its aspect of a critical-practical concept of *Theory* and its relation to *Practice* in general. Henceforward we shall be more concerned with its aspect as a practical-critical Theory of Practice in particular—the *Practice of Revolution*.

The transition was made, historically, in the *Communist Manifesto.* From that point (the end of 1847 and the beginning of 1848) Dialectical Materialism ceased to be merely the discovery of two gifted individual revolutionaries. Thenceforward " the word became flesh "—the theory and practice of two individuals became the developing Theory and Practice of a world-transforming movement, the revolutionary proletarian movement, against the Bourgeois Order and for a Communist Order.

We will consider this aspect of Dialectical Materialism with special reference to these heads :

(1) The *Communist Manifesto* as the " classic " formulation of the dialectic of proletarian revolution.

(2) The objective presupposition of that dialectic—*Capitalist Production* and the dialectic thereof.

(3) The proletarian *class struggle* as the objective-negative social *form* of that (capitalist dialectic.)

(4) The *Proletarian Revolution* as the " jump "—the transformation of bourgeois *Quantity* into proletarian-Communist *Quality*.

It will be remembered that, in keeping with our purpose, we will discuss these always in their theoretical aspects, in their logical connection with the Materialist *Dialectic* as such. The formulation of practical programmes lies outside our scope, though we shall, of course, be forced to consider the principles of such formulation in relation to Marx and Engels' practical-theoretical criticisms of the programmes of their day.

290

THE COMMUNIST MANIFESTO

Marxism as a theory of political practice received its classic formulation in the *Manifesto of the Communist Party*, written by Marx and Engels for the Communist League and adopted by that body at the end of 1847. It was published simultaneously in its original German and in a French translation early in 1848. It had hardly appeared before the revolution whose imminence formed the primary presupposition upon which its immediate policy was oriented broke out in France (the February Revolution, 1848) and in all the " Germanies " (including the Austrian territories and vassal States in Italy), beginning with the March risings in Berlin and Vienna, 1848. An English translation of the *Manifesto* first appeared in George Julian Harnay's Chartist-Communist journal, the *Red Republican*, in 1850.

Of the importance of the *Manifesto* in the practical politics of proletarian struggle it is superfluous to speak here. It remains unapproached and unapproachable : *the* classic of Marxism *par excellence*. No better tribute to its worth can be given than the well-authenticated story that its publication during the War in Constantinople in an abridged translation into Turkish excited the Sultan's police into issuing a warrant for the arrest of " certain seditious conspirators passing under the *alias* of ' Karl Marx and Frederick Engels.' "

Theoretically the interval between the *Communist Manifesto* and the *German Ideology* is imperceptible. The difference between them is wholly that of a transition from Theory to Practice. The Theory elaborated with minute care in the *Ideology* from the most carefully-tested practice-begotten materials is, in the *Manifesto*, made a starting-point for the elaboration of a general conception of the practical conduct of the revolutionary proletarian struggle.

In the *Ideology* " Communism " is defined as the real *movement* which makes an end of the existing order of things. The *Manifesto* begins with its classic mockery : " *A spectre is haunting Europe : the spectre of Communism !* " And it ends with its no less classic defiance :

" The Communists disdain to conceal their ends and aims. They openly declare that their ends can be attained only by the forcible overthrow of all existing social conditions. Let the ruling classes tremble at a Communist revolution. The proletarians have nothing to lose but their chains. They have a world to win.

" WORKING MEN OF ALL COUNTRIES, UNITE ! "—
MARX-ENGELS : *Communist Manifesto*, p. 39.

Here the aphorism in the *Ideology*, " not criticism but
revolution is the motive force of history," finds its objective
outcome and expression.

Similarly the sequence of the argument in the *Manifesto*
reproduces the ground-theory progressively elaborated in
manifold detail in the *Ideology* and in the whole polemic warfare which Marx and Engels began in the *Franco-German Year-
Book* and ended only with their lives. It would hardly be
saying too much to affirm that the *Communist Manifesto*
constitutes the logical central point in the theoretical life-
work of Marx and Engels. All that went before was a
preparation for the *Manifesto* ; all that followed after was
its vindication and elaboration. *The Communist Manifesto*
IS *Marxism in quintessence.*

Its logical sequence is decisive as to what Dialectical
Materialism meant to its authors. It begins with an affirmation of observed phenomenal facts—the concern of all the
State authorities of Europe at the growth of Communism ;
the unanimity with which all political parties condemned it,
and accused each other of it. This proved the importance of
Communism and the need for the Communists to declare
themselves.

The *Manifesto* proceeds to define objectively the conditions
in and from which Communism, as a movement, arises.
History—at any rate so much of it as is objectively operative
in the existing state of things—has been a history of class-
struggles in which a definite sequence of progressive development is observable. Out of the struggles of the past
has emerged as a positive outcome the bourgeois system of
production with a bourgeois social order to correspond. This
social order exhibits likewise its antagonisms ; not those of
the past, mechanically persisting, but *new* antagonisms,
peculiar and distinctive to the bourgeois system of objective
social relations. Relics of the past survive in the *forms* of the
State apparatus and in the traditions and illusions into which
reality translates itself in the heads of individuals. None the
less these survivals are " ancient " only as to their *forms* ; their
content is in every case that of existing bourgeois social relations.

The historically conditioned form of class-struggle distinctive of the bourgeois epoch is that between the bourgeoisie
and the proletariat. This struggle, though analogous to the
struggles distinctive of previous epochs, is one which could

not have arisen in any previous epoch. Once it arises all the other struggles within society, whether *vestigial* (such as the belated and anachronistic efforts of elements surviving from the feudal order of Society to recover their pre-bourgeois status) or *evanescent* and *transitional* (such as those of an innumerable series of strata, sections, and varieties of the petty-bourgeoisie—the class in which *both* bourgeois and proletariat are potential, and from which both were historically differentiated)—all these struggles are forced increasingly to become subsidiary to and variants upon the primary and basic struggle of bourgeois society, that of bourgeoisie and proletariat.

In the course of historical development bourgeois society —as a functioning objective whole—transforms the world in accordance with its impersonally collective will, and the objective result of that transformation is a *development* of both the bourgeoisie and the proletariat (within themselves), and of their mutually transforming antagonism and struggle. The more the bourgeoisie directs with concrete effectiveness the struggle of the social whole against Nature the more the concrete outcome of its triumph begets an increase in the volume, the intensity, and the degree of internal and external *development* of the revolutionary proletarian struggle against itself and its rule and order. The logical end of this process (which is in the long run inescapable) is the overthrow of the bourgeoisie and the triumph of the proletariat.

Only in relation to the general historical movement of the proletariat can the Communist movement be understood. It must be comprehended from two opposite sides : (1) as fundamentally at one with the developing struggle of the proletariat ; and (2) as a specific and distinct *form* taken by that struggle—its highest expression and most developed revolutionary phase.

The Communist movement is at one with the general proletarian struggle in that, firstly, " the Communists have no interests separate and apart from those of the proletariat as a whole " ; secondly, in that "the immediate aim of the Communists is the *formation of the proletariat into a class, overthrow of the bourgeois supremacy, conquest of political power by the proletariat* " ; and thirdly, in that " the theoretical conclusions of the Communists express in general terms the actual relations springing from the existing class struggle " (between the proletariat and the bourgeoisie), " from the historical movement going on under our very eyes."

On the other hand, the Communist movement is distinguish-able from the general movement of the proletariat in that (*a*) it is in practice the movement of " the most advanced and resolute section of the working class—the section which pushes forward all the others " ; while (*b*) it has, theoretically, " the immense advantage over the great mass of the prole-tariat of clearly understanding the line of march, the con-ditions, and the ultimate general results of the proletarian movement." Thus, in its specific consolidated form of the Communist Party, the Communist Movement stands to the general movement of the proletariat as conscious will and definite purpose does to impulsive reflex action in the indi-vidual. The Communist Party is not only the highest ex-pression of the revolutionary will of the proletariat ; it is its leading organ of revolutionary action, its chief means of transforming itself, in the course of and by means of struggle, from a mere aggregation of individuals united only by their possession of common needs and resentments into a definitely consolidated and organised revolutionary class force. Thus it is by the instrumentality of the Communist Party and the revolutionary struggle which it leads, theoretically as well as practically, that the proletariat becomes able ultimately to overthrow the bourgeois order and initiate a new historical epoch.

Such is the logical ground-theme of the *Communist Mani-festo*—upon which theme so many subsidiary developments are indicated and sketched out that every single paragraph in the *Manifesto*, nearly every sentence even, could with propriety and advantage be made the basis for a whole volume. Of all the political documents ever elaborated in the history of Mankind the *Communist Manifesto* is the greatest, the clearest, the most comprehensive, and the most historically pregnant by far.

.   .   .   .   .

As we shall see, the elaboration and vindication of the principles of the *Manifesto*—its conception of bourgeois society and of the dialectic thereof—its conception of history and the dialectic inter-relation between Nature and Human History—its conception of proletarian struggle and of the revolutionary objective thereof—the vindication and elabora-tion of these principles gave Marx and Engels work to do for the rest of their lives ; and that all the more so as, after the *Manifesto*, they were increasingly engaged in the practical conduct of the movement to which that *Manifesto* gave rise. How titanic these labours were can only be imagined, even, by those familiar with the literally enormous mass of their public and private correspondence as well as their literary output. And even those can imagine it only inadequately.

We shall therefore, precisely because of the immensity of the work they accomplished, be forced to confine our survey to a few only of the most salient points of their work. We will deal with their method—their logic, implicit and explicit —under the heads specified at the beginning of this chapter, beginning with Capitalist Production, the objective fact of which the class struggle between the bourgeoisie and the proletariat is the social, political, and ideological expression.

． ． ． ． ．

The Dialectic of Capitalist Production

Marx and Engels were both close students of economic science; Engels—in consequence of his first-hand acquaintance with " Manchester School " economists in their home town, and his actual commercial intercourse with them— was the first of the two to make a special study of the subject. Marx, however, after receiving the stimulus from Engels, soon outstripped his tutor and revealed a genius for which Engels could never sufficiently express his admiration :

"I cannot deny that both before and during my forty-years' collaboration with Marx I had a certain independent share in laying the foundations, and more particularly in elaborating the theory. But the greater part of its leading basic principles, particularly in the realm of economics and history, and above all its final clear formulation, belongs to Marx. . . . What Marx accomplished I would not have achieved. Marx stood higher, saw further, and took a wider and a quicker view than all of us. We others were at best talented : Marx was a genius."—Engels : *Feuerbach*, footnote, pp. 52–53.

All that Engels says is true ; yet, in his magnificent magnaminity, Engels brushes aside as of no account that which, *dialectically*, was of vital importance—the stimulating effect of his friendship and collaboration upon the development, the objective realisation, of Marx's unquestionable genius. But for Engels that genius would almost certainly have remained to a very great extent an unrealised potentiality. The Marx of history was the " natural " Marx *multiplied* in collaboration with Frederick Engels. Equally is it true, no doubt, that the Engels of history was the " natural " Engels multiplied by Marx. Thus the result is pretty much as Engels put it. Except that the world has gained in each of their cases, and that enormously, from one of the most inspiring instances of fruitful friendship ever known.

.   .   .   .   .

Marx's studies in economics are found in the following works :

(1) *Wage-Labour and Capital.* Delivered as a series of lectures to working men in Brussels, 1845 ; first published in the *Neue Rheinsche Zeitung* in 1849.

(2) *The Poverty of Philosophy.* A critique of Proudhon's Economic " utopia," published 1847. Is especially valuable as a demonstration of Marx's method of critically analysing the categories of economics.

(3) *Value, Price and Profit.* A lecture given to members of the I.W.M.A. in 1865. Uniquely valuable as written by Marx himself *in English.* Deals vividly and satisfyingly with the question of industrial struggle, which it vindicates triumphantly.

(4) *The Critique of Political Economy.* Published 1859. The first draft of what afterwards was rearranged and elaborated into—

(5) *Capital : A Critique of Political Economy:*
     Vol. I : *Capitalist Production* (1867) ;
     Vol. II : *Capitalist Circulation* ; and
     Vol. III : *Capitalist Production as a Whole.* These were finished by Engels after Marx's death.

(6) *Theories of Surplus Value.* A collection of materials intended for a fourth volume of *Capital,* which, after the death of Engels, passed into the hands of Kautsky and was issued by him in three volumes under this title.

The historical sequence of these works is highly instructive. It demonstrates in the teeth of all the critics that Marx did not " deduce " his theory of proletarian revolution from his " theory " of value—nor *vice versa.* It demonstrates that *both* theories are inseparably interconnected with each other ; and that they were developed under the stimulus of the needs of *practice*—that of the " actual movement to make an end of the existing state of things "—that of *changing the world.* The practical problems of the struggle created the need for a better, a more *usable,* more satisfactory, theory of capitalism. Marx and Engels overthrew the theoretical defences of the capitalist order, and particularly the economics in which it sought its chief vindication, as part of their struggle to overthrow that order.

This fact is of first-rate importance. It illustrates the canon of the Unity of Theory and Practice from yet another side ; and it, at once, rescues Marx and Engels from the stigma of having formulated *a priori* an *abstract theory* of immutable economic law.

All the works listed above were, it will be perceived, *polemics*—blows struck in battle. And the bigger they grow and the wider their scope, the more profoundly polemical they become. *Capital* is not in the least a " mere " exposition of an " original " theory of Value. It is a revolutionary critique of the logical category of value, and a revelation, under analysis, of the *objective* " *non*-economic " fact that " value is a relation between *persons* expressed as a relation between *things* ! " It is *not* a " system " of political economy— it is a critique of the basic categories from which *all* " systems " of political economy are deduced. It is *not* a presentation of immutable economic law—it is a demonstration that there is and can be *no such thing as an* " *immutable* " *economic law*. From the standpoint of classic political economy, for which economic laws were either immutable or not laws, *Capital* was the theoretical annihilation of all Political Economy. From the dialectical materialist standpoint it was a demonstration, as vivid as it was overwhelmingly convincing, that economics, to be a science, must take its place as an *aspect* of the wider science of History—the science of the Dialectical development of human society. Only as a study of one of the *momenta* of social development is economics possible as a science at all.

Does this fact, that Marx's economic studies were undertaken with a polemic purpose—the specific purpose of finding an impregnable theoretical basic from which to carry on a revolutionary struggle—does this " bias " vitiate Marx's conclusions ?

Not in the least. On the contrary, but for the fact that he was a revolutionary he would not have been sufficiently sceptical about the " immutable " categories of the classic economy to analyse them to their foundations and so revolutionise the science. There is " bias " and bias—there is a bias in favour of the truth as well as a bias against it, and the situation of a revolutionary who is always liable to be victimised by his neighbours or the public authorities is such as to ensure that he is either a reckless fool or a man of sufficient capacity to rise to such a comprehension of the truth as is of a higher order than that of his orthodox opponents. He has need to be *sure*; the reactionary is concerned only to be *safe*.

Marx's method is clearly apparent to anyone who will take the trouble to observe and reflect upon the sequence of the volumes of his *Capital*, and the sequence of the chapters therein. He does not begin with a ready-made table of economic categories : he *develops* the economic categories as he proceeds out of the concrete objective relations specific to capitalist society.

What is it which distinguishes Capitalist production from all alternative modes of production ? The fact (*a*) that it is one of the modes of commodity production ; and (*b*) that it is specifically *capitalist* commodity production—the production of commodities by the instrumentality of *wage-labour*.

In the classic world there had been commodity production by *slave*-labour ; in the medieval world by the labour of free craftsmen (the *serfs* only produced *commodities* indirectly—if at all) ; in each, as well as in the bourgeois epoch, there had been commodity production by independent small producers. But that which makes capitalist production distinguishable as a distinct and separate economic formation is that it is a system in which commodity production by wage-labour has become so dominant that all survivals of former systems become subsidiary agencies to itself as primary and dominant.

There is a dialectical movement here of a fascinating kind to which we will pay attention later, since it is a movement of *history*, and not that which we are now examining, the specific dialectic of capitalist economy in itself. Much confusion has resulted from the fact that critics cannot distinguish the general dialectical movement of *history* (including the bourgeois epoch) from the *inner* dialectic of specific capitalist economy. These are interlinked and they reciprocally interact (as the human anatomy is linked with human physiology and they, too, interact)—but their laws are quite distinct. [Marx himself uses this analogy and likens the economics of an epoch to its anatomy.]

Marx begins with the most central fact in capitalist economy in its most general aspect : *the Commodity*. A commodity is something produced. But not all things produced at all times are commodities. They are commodities only so far as they are *exchanged* ; and in their developed

form exchanged for money. They are capitalistically produced when the labour of production is that of wage-
labourers, hired (i.e., *bought*) in a (relatively) " open " or
" free " market. Capitalist production is therefore a system
of producing commodities *from* commodities (raw materials,
machinery, etc.) *by means of* commodities (the labour power
of wage labourers).

This universalisation of the commodity and all that it
implies is *the* distinguishing fact of capitalist economy.

. . . .

A methodological observation must be made here. Marx's
method in *Capital* is *based* on a conception of history. It has
history for its background and its subject matter fully
developed leads back to history again. For all that, it is not
the " historical " method, that of tracing the development of
economy through all its historical windings and turnings.
It is a logical-analytic method which develops the dialectical
consequences implicit in each of the relations revealed in an
analysis of the most general relation of all in capitalist society
—the Commodity relation.

For instance : Marx does not begin by describing with the
aid of anthropological research all the phenomena of those
primitive societies which produced solely for *use* ; and those
barbaric societies which had not risen above occasional
barter. He is content to analyse the relations which *exist*—
plain for all men to see if they wish to do so.

This fact has a big importance in this respect : many have
observed that *in the sequel* Marx presents the historical movement as one which, beginning in primitive societies—in which
property and property relations have not been established
and which are therefore (*and so far*) " communist " or
" communal "—proceeds through a whole series of *antagonistic*
(class-differentiated) societies, only to culminate in a return
to Communism on a higher plane. Uncritical friends of
Marxism have supposed from this fact that it is sufficient to
describe this cyclic process as proceeding " inevitably "—
in one continuous motion. This has given equally uncritical
enemies an excuse for saying that this " inevitability " is
mystical and unintelligible, and the whole panorama simply
one invented by Marx because he wanted Communism to come
and could find no better way of excusing his desire.

It is necessary to point out, therefore, that the " inevitability " of a process exists only in relation to its succession
of stages—only in relation to each stage taken in turn and

judged as a link between that which precedes and that which
follows from it.   There was no " necessity " in primitive
communism that would *of itself* cause history in the end to
return to communism again.   The inevitability in primitive
society was that it would *break up*.   Some primitive societies
broke up only to disappear.   Others were absorbed in detail
into new social formations—as primitives are absorbed into
capitalist society to this day.   But once *property* was established as a social fact (and it grew *inevitably* in consequence
of the development of production) each stage in the development of class-divided society followed inevitably in its turn
from the preceding formation.   Taking history as a whole
the inevitability of its process does not arise from Nature
as such, or from history *as such* :   it *arises from that which
forms the transition link between Nature and History, the fact
and practice of production.   The course of history is " inevitable " because men make it so—however little they may know
it.*

Moreover, though history as a whole is a continuous
progression, it is a progression through a series of stages,
each of which is continuous within itself, but discontinuous
with that which preceded and that which follows from it.
They are linked into a continuity by mutation *leaps* (periods
of revolutionary transition), which again have their distinct
laws.   To present such a process as a *simple continuity* is to
exhaust it of its dialectic and turn it into an " evolution "
of the single-track kind, which is not at all improved if it
be turned into a spiral escalator.

In the case we are concerned with, Marx's economic
analysis begins of necessity with those relations which are
general to all possible forms of capitalism—in fact, at first,
more than that, with relations general to all possible forms of
commodity production from the most occasional barter to the
most developed varieties of finance-capitalism.   Only by
progressive determinations of this generality into a series of
particularities and specialities does Marx reach the historical
movement of capitalist production as a whole.

For all that, though this logical method is the opposite of
the *formal* " historical " method, it is none the less *really*
historical ;   firstly, since its *real* content is that of actual
objective relations which have, in fact, developed historically ;
and, secondly, its method being *dialectical*, each category
established is treated (on the basis of *real* material) as linked
with, and the product of, the development of each preceding

categorical relation. The outcome is that Marx's method not only makes the categories of economics more rationally intelligible both in themselves and in their series than *any other economist* has ever succeeded in doing, but (applying the acid test of objective practice) he is able at every stage to illustrate the categorical movement from the movement of real objective history—of the world generally, and of Western Europe and England in particular.

Take the central " mystery " of the classic economy " Value."

As to this : it is hard to say who are in the deepest theoretical bog-hole, the " modern " economists, who reject the classic " Labour " theory of Value out of hand, or the " explainers " of Marx, who try to " save " it while accommodating themselves to the criticism of these moderns, before whom they stand, secretly, in awe.

One simple question puts the matter squarely on its feet : what is the *real*, objective fact which becomes apparent to economists, amateur and professional, empirical (housewives, say) and theoretical, as *Value* ?

As an economic category " Value " is a *generalisation*. Agreed ! But *of what* ?

Firstly, we challenge any of the " moderns " to (if they *must* reject Marx !) find a better answer than that given by the classic economists from WILLIAM PETTY and JOHN LOCKE down through ADAM SMITH to DAVID RICARDO—that value is a quality possessed by commodities which becomes evident either (*a*) in consumption, or (*b*) in exchange. The former expresses a relation between the " natural " qualities of the commodity and those of the (actual or prospective) *consumer* ; the latter expresses the relation subsisting between the *commodity owners* as a relation between the commodities themselves.

Whatever else may be said about it, this does give the term " Value " a meaning tangible and palpable to plain sense. Adam Smith's formulation of the matter could not be bettered from the standpoint of plain common sense :

> " Every man is rich or poor according to the degree in which he can afford to enjoy the necessaries, conveniencies and amusements of human life. But after the division of labour has once thoroughly taken place, it is but a very small part of these with which a man's own labour can supply him. The far greater part of them he

must derive from the labour of other people, and he must be rich or poor according to the quantity of that labour which he can command, or which he can afford to purchase.

"The *value* of any commodity, therefore, to the person who possesses it, and who means not to use or consume it himself, but to exchange it for other commodities, is *equal to the quantity of labour which it enables him to purchase or command.*

"Labour is, therefore, the real measure of the exchangeable value of all commodities.

"The real price of everything, what everything really costs to the man who wants to acquire it, is *the toil and trouble of acquiring it.*"—ADAM SMITH : *Wealth of Nations*, Book I, Chap. V.

Here is the "Labour" theory of value in all its splendid classic common-sense. Moreover, its splendid clarity makes plain its concrete social-historical concomitants :

"Every commodity, besides, is more frequently exchanged for, and thereby compared with, other commodities than with labour. It is more natural therefore to estimate its exchangeable value by the quantity of *some other commodity*, than by that of the labour which it can purchase. The greater part of people, too, understand better what is meant by a quantity of a particular commodity than by a quantity of labour. The one is a plain and palpable object, the other an abstract notion, which though it can be made sufficiently intelligible, is not altogether so natural and obvious."—ADAM SMITH : *loc. cit.*

So *natural and obvious* indeed !

Why is it that the eighteenth-century economists were not only, and from choice, as "natural and obvious" as they could contrive to be, but also managed to make their meaning crystal-clear—while their modern despisers regard themselves as profound in proportion to their impalpability and obscurity ? The answer is easy—and contains the whole secret of Marx and also of his critics. The eighteenth-century writers (and Marx with them) *had something to say : the "moderns" have something to conceal !*

Adam Smith and his contemporaries were fighting honestly and courageously to establish the bourgeois order ; Marx was fighting with equal honesty and courage to overthrow that order. The "moderns," without either honesty or courage, are fighting either to preserve a bourgeois order that has long since gone beyond any possibility of rational excuse, or fighting to excuse themselves for *not fighting* for the overthrow of that order. Which brings us to our second challenge.

We challenge any of the detractors and revisers of Marx to produce *any* critical refutation of the classic economists which will survive the objective practical test provided by history, except that which was effected by Marx.

They will not have the " Labour " theory of value either in its naïve classic form or in its critical-social form as presented by Marx. Very well. *What alternative theory have they ?* Simply this : with wearisome logomachy they reach at long last, and by a devious route, the conclusion that no *absolute* theory of Value is possible ! Alternatively : that society " makes up " its relative-absolute Value as it goes along !

The latter is the former turned into a bastard-solipsism ; the former is the Marxian doctrine that each stage in the economic formation of society has *its own specific* law of value, divorced from the historical relations in which it is true and demonstrable, and thus turned into a meaningless abstraction.

Let us test it.

Marx begins with the commodity-relation, the most general objective relation of capitalist economy. This, be it observed, is *not a " dogma "* [" the Marxian theory of value begins, in fact, with a dogma ! "—COLE], but an empirically evident fact. The commodity-relation, being a relation, has two sides—that of the two parties to *every* exchange of commodities. From the standpoint of each party *as buyer*, that which he buys is primarily a *use* value. From the standpoint of each party *as seller*, that which he sells is primarily an *exchange* value : each parts with that which it is not *worthwhile* for him to keep in exchange for something which it is *worthwhile* for him to get.

Thus, not dogmatically, but by objective analysis, is it established that the *substance*, the primary presupposition, of every exchange is *use-value*—the capacity possessed by commodities to satisfy human wants and desires. Unless this quality is present no exchange is conceivable.

Now observe. Use-value is presupposed in every exchange. But exchange is not in the least presupposed in use-value. And this is not only true *logically*. It is true *historically*. Men did, in fact, and to this day outside the sphere of Capitalist economy do, produce use-values (utilities) which, since they are never exchanged, never possess exchange value. Right at the very outset we see that the movement of dialectical analysis reproduces the movement of objective history.

Given exchange as a fact and practice, each " utility " entering thereinto becomes in so doing a *unity of opposites*— use-value and exchange-value. And since they are opposites-in-unity they establish a third term—their *unity*-relation— Value *per se*, which is the *general* of which all *particular* exchange values (each of which presupposes its *specific* use-value) are phenomenal forms.

Here again a connection with history is established. Exchange beginning as simple barter—the purely occasional exchange of This for That—does develop into systematised exchange, into buying and selling, which presupposes, logically *and* historically, an accepted *universal form of Value*, distinct from and opposable to all particular exchange values whatsoever. In a word, exchange begets—*Money*.

It is beyond question scandalous that Nature and History should so conspire to beget these Hegelianisms, these trinity relations of use-value (thesis), exchange-value (antithesis) and Value (synthesis), but, apart from moving a vote of censure on God or the processes of cosmic evolution; there seems nothing to do but accept the fact—as a fact !

Money begins as one commodity among many. Otherwise it cannot begin. A certain *quantitative* development of exchange is the presupposition of the *qualitative* discrimination of commodities in general into commodities in particular contraposed to their universal equivalent, *Money*. The germ of the money-relation exists as soon as we say " This is *worth* (i.e., equal to) That." But this germ can become ripe enough to walk about as an independent existence only when there is a sufficient *quantity* of commodities and *number* of exchanges to make it not only possible but necessary to find something of which we can say that *all things* are *worth* That (in greater or less *quantity*).

Observe the " *leap* from quantity to quality ! " Money, as money, is *qualitatively* different from commodities *as* commodities : yet it is born *of* commodities, *as* a commodity itself, and only under pressure of the quantities of commodities does it ascend from earth to the economic heaven to become not merely a *measure* of value and a *standard* of price, but also in virtue of its function of universal equivalent and exchange-medium, Value Incarnate, Money *as* Money.

Here, again and yet again, at every point the movement of dialectical analysis reproduces the actual historical movement. Money *did* grow out of barter. It was first simply one commodity among others which, for empirical reasons, was used to *measure* the values and *express* the prices of all the other commodities. It did thus become a *universal equivalent*, and, being therefore universally acceptable, it did become the universal medium of circulation. Various commodities were at various times selected by the " natural selection " of the practical exchange relations themselves to perform this function. Corn, wine, salt, cattle, hides, cowrie-shells, bronze, iron, and finally silver and gold—all have served historically to perform the functions of money. All have been in their day regarded as visible value *per se*—*qualitatively* superior, as such, to all the merely mundane commodities which only " have " value—while Money, it seems, *is* Value !

And not only does this historical-empirical illusion—the taking of the mirror-image of all particular values as the sole universal reality of Value—arise everywhere at a certain stage of development, the illusion takes on a concrete form and becomes the determinant of a new cycle of dialectical progression.

Money appears in the form of coin !

This seems at first no change at all ! Or at best merely a quantitative one. To cut a large weight of silver or gold into small pieces makes no difference to the worth of the whole or of the part. As value (money) they are what they were. Quite so ! And making the pieces round instead of square or rectangular makes no difference either.

But the point is that a *coin* is issued by a recognised authority, and bears a stamp to guarantee its weight and degree of fineness. It is accepted by a convention deriving its force from its immense practical convenience as *always what it says it is*, even though men know that in use it is bound to wear away.

Thus *money* comes in actual practice to function as an *Ideal Reality*, of which all specific and relative (exchange) values are the merely mundane reflections. And, being an Ideal reality whose earthly function (as coin in circulation) *is to represent itself*, other representations, *not commodities*, can be substituted for it. *Hence paper promises to pay money could and did take the place of and do the work of real money.*

Once again the dialectical analysis reproduces the movement of objective history !

U

Here again we can make a challenge. The classic economists
were quite unable to extract any development series from the
contradictions between use-value and exchange-value, and
between Value and Money. They could treat money only
empirically as a " given " fact. Its *connection* with the world
of commodities was obvious to them. So also was its empirical *opposition* to that world. What they could not do
was to establish the law of this unity in opposition, and
opposition in unity. They cut the knot by flatly *asserting*
the unity dogmatically. The " moderns," faced with the
same problem in an enormously more exasperated form, cut
the knot by dogmatically *denying* the unity. *Marx and Marx
alone—and this is our challenge*—in his chapters on money
in both his *Critique* and his *Capital*, grasps the unity in the
opposition and the opposition in the unity. *Marx explains*
the phenomena of *Money* (and the *Credit* which grows out of
its *ideal* functions)—while not one of his critics is able even to
attempt an explanation which does not make the confusion
worse than he found it.

.   .   .   .   .

G. D. H. Cole, in his *What Marx Really Meant*, begins his
chapter on the " Theory of Value " with a cry straight from
the heart :
> " Every theory of value I have ever heard of, with the
> single exception of the Marxian theory, has for its object
> an explanation of prices. But Marx's theory of value is
> so little a theory of prices that it is hard in the end to
> say whether it has any point of contact at all with prices.
> . . . If it does not seek to explain prices, what does it
> seek to explain ? The answer is easy. It is an attempt
> to explain how labour is exploited under the capitalist
> system ! "—COLE : *What Marx Really Meant*, p. 207.

Alas ! That one should have to be rude to one who is
trying so hard to be " good ! " And Cole *is* trying *so* hard to
struggle out of Oxford into daylight ! But how *else* is labour
exploited except through its *price* ? Or, more precisely,
through the contradiction between the exchange-value (and
price) of labour-power and its *real* objective social *use-
value* ? Cole's alibi for Marx breaks down in a way that
would shatter Bow Street with " laughter in court ! " It
embalms the very fallacy which Marx so thoroughly exposed
—the confusion between the act and fact of *labouring*, and the
human unit of *social labour force*.

Let us assist him. It is true that all economists except

Marx have tried to discover a law of exchange *equilibrium* by reference to which all prices could be treated as *variants*. Marx has the penetration to see that there is a prior question : *Why do things exchange at all* ? But this Adam Smith also saw. As we have shown above, he found the explanation in the *Division of Labour*. But that does not explain ; it only shifts the puzzle further back. How and why did this division of labour arise ? And whose labour is it that is " *divided* " ?

Just a moment's reflection is needed—and then the Great Light comes ! It is *Society's labour* which is divided, and the division arises from the empirical-historical fact that it is *in production* that society is created, and by means of production that society lives ! In the exchange-relation men express their relation as commodity-*owners* : behind that and prior to it is the social fact that the commodities have to be *produced*. As commodity *owners* men express their common dependence upon society and social production— and in their quantitative equivalent relation to each other commodities express their common relation to the social element in production—its productive force—the quantity of labour *society* has expended to produce them.

Not the fact that, as Adam Smith noted rightly, the exchange of commodities is exchange of equal quantities of *labour*—but the fact that this very empirical establishment of equivalence both created and revealed this " labour " as not an individual or personal, but a *social substance—this is the " Labour " theory of Marx*.

It is this fact—that Value in its most general and *social* sense expresses the relation between persons as a relation between things, and also the common dependence of persons and things upon production and upon the social force active in production—upon *social labour*—that makes possible the Ideal universal function of Money. That which it mirrors in its own *particular universal form* is the general universal *fact* of the dependence of society and all men in society, individually and collectively, upon historically conditioned and socially productive *Labour*.

Yet once again, from the most abstract and mysterious of all the categories of Economics, Marx's dialectic reproduces the most universal of all historical facts—the dependence of all men, at all times, and in all places, upon *productive activity* —*upon Labour*.

What does Cole *mean* when he talks of " explaining " prices ? The classic economists, who approached the question

from " the standpoint of the single individual," thought of
production as solely an individual matter—the correlative of
ownership. Their whole standpoint demanded that they
should prove that all incidental higgling apart, prices (the
money-names of values) would coincide with values, and not
only equilibrium but (and thereby) *equality between men* would
be established by freedom of competitive exchange.

That their theory has been falsified by the facts—that the
free play of prices secured by the freeing of the markets from
feudalistic restraints has brought *not* equality but the reverse
is true. But how does this affect the fact that prices *are* the
" money names of value " ? How does this affect the fact
that society lives and grows by production and, basically,
nothing but production ? How does this affect Marx ?

Cole, in his befuddled attempt to reconcile Marx with the
" modern " economists—whose standpoint, object, and
method are all in polar opposition to those of Marx—succeeds
in doing nothing beyond objectivising his own subjective
state of chaos upon the question. It is outside our scope to
analyse his confusion in detail, and we can herein indicate
only broadly the main dialectical *movements* of Capitalist
economy in general which Marx, in his *Critique* and the three
volumes of his *Capital,* analyses into their components in
an infinitely ramified series of interacting detail movements.
We must perforce content ourselves with affirming categorically that Cole's fallacy is one which he shares with all
the opponents of Marx : he seeks to reduce to terms of a
closed cycle that which Marx demonstrated to be the reverse
of closed, namely, a dialectically developing *progression.*

For instance : Money, the medium in which prices are
expressed, is evolved originally as one commodity among
many. So far its law of movement is identical with that of
commodities. That movement is one from production to
consumption, by way of *equivalent* exchange. Money, on the
contrary, progressively takes on an oppositional relation to
the commodities whose *quantity* it measures in its own ; and
develops a movement from (potential) consumers to (potential) producers. Ultimately money-economy emerges as
a process in which exchange (with this counter-movement of
commodities and money) becomes an inescapable intervening
stage between production and consumption, and becomes,
therefore, the primary pre-condition of existence for every
individual in a society dominated by money-economy. The
cycle of production-consumption is dialectically discriminated

into the antagonistic cycles of commodity movements and money movements.

This, again, is no *a priori* Hegelian construction. It is an actually observed and verifiable objective fact, and one which gives rise to and explains the actual movement of recorded history. From the simple movement of Money arises a developed function of money and a *new movement*—that of *Capital*.

Money makes possible a practice which would have been irrational in a "natural" (non-monetary) economy—the practice of *hoarding*. The fundamental irrationality of this practice—which will be perceived if one envisages the endeavour, in a primitive economy, to hoard flesh meats or fish —is as obvious as is the fact that it is the primary presupposition of Capitalist economy and also its governing objective. Here again the dialectical movement is apparent in that *negation* of "natural" economy by money-economy, which becomes objective in Capitalist economy.

Hoarding of money involves a breach in the cycle of commodities-money-commodities at the opposite point to that at which the commodity passes out of the cycle into consumption. Hoarding breaks the cycle to take the money out of the cycle. But this also involves the possibility that at a later stage the money may return to the field of exchange as *a new beginning*. Before, in the simple exchange-economy, the cycle began with the commodity and its production. Now the money appears, as it were, out of the clouds and offers itself in competition with the circulating money by means of which the exchange economy effects its cycle of equilibrium. Thus begins the development of the *quantitative* antagonism between Prices and Values. Thus begins the possibility of "buying cheap and selling dear." Thus arises that competitive endeavour to secure something for nothing which is the soul of "business" as the bourgeois understands it. Thus out of the very law of value itself arises the empirical fact of the falsification of that law in detail prices. For if economy is adjusted to the fact that values embodied in money can be "saved" from one cycle of production and thereafter brought into relation with the values engendered in a new cycle, the result must be a cumulative *dis*-equilibrium. First the balance between the volume of the money in circulation and that of the values it functions to circulate is constantly thrown out of gear. Secondly, and consequently, exchange becomes increasingly a competition to get more from an exchange than is given therein—the fact that somebody can only get something for nothing if somebody else gets nothing for something being hidden under the empirical opposition of money and commodities and the increasing complexity of the social relations of those engaged in the exchange. The equivalence involved in exchange is attained only ultimately—only as the average of a whole series of *unequal* exchanges. Hence arises the growth of the discrepancy between particular prices and the values they denote, which in turn reacts upon production. Producing with an eye to prices current involves a constant risk of producing in excess of requirements—and its concomitant under-production of other commodities. Thus the more complex the social division of labour, the wider the cycle of exchanges required to effect the equivalence which is the law of exchange. The *total* of the values exchanged is equalled by the *total* of prices : but *this equivalence is achieved only as the social outcome of a process in which in detail prices and values only rarely if ever coincide*. This is the Marxian law of prices—that especially in a capitalist economy an empirical law of prices (one reached by taking a statistical average of the prices current at any given moment) is impossible. And it is impossible because the *social* law of the equivalence of values and prices operates objectively only through a *process* which is the outcome of a whole series of personal practical exchanges in which the law is systematically falsified.

G. D. H. Cole finds it " hard to say " whether Marx's theory of value " has any point of contact at all with prices." We find it " hard to say " in view of Marx's analysis of value, of the objective exchange relation, and of the historical process which created the exchange relation and its historical outcome—the development of the categories of capital— where G. D. H. Cole's assertion has " any point of contact " with Marx.

.   .   .   .   .   .

When he set out to analyse the capitalist mode of production Marx was aiming at something far more comprehensive than " an attempt to explain how labour is exploited under the capitalist system." For one thing, this " explanation " had already been given, in principle, by the English Socialists (Bray, Hodgskin, Thompson, etc.), who had reached it as a deduction from Ricardo's labour theory of exchange value :—

" If the value in exchange of a product is equal to the labour-time it contains the value in exchange of a day's labour is equal to the product of that labour. In other words, wages must be equal to the product of labour. But the very opposite is the case. This objection against Ricardo by bourgeois economists was taken up later by the Socialists. Having assumed the correctness of the formula they charged the practice with inconsistency, and appealed to bourgeois society to realise in practice the conclusions which were supposed to follow from its theoretical principles. That was the sense in which some English Socialists at least turned Ricardo's formula of exchange-value against political economy."—Marx : *Critique of Pol. Econ.*, p. 71 and note.

But as Engels observes (Preface to Marx's *Poverty of Philosophy*), this application of Ricardo's theory to establish a " right " of the workers to " the totality of social production " on the ground that they are the only real producers, while it leads directly to Communism, is also, " as Marx shows, false in form, economically speaking, since it is simply an application of morality to economy " :—

" According to the laws of bourgeois economy the greater part of the product does not belong to the workers who have created it. If, then, we say ' this is unjust, it ought not to be,' that has nothing whatever to do with economy—it is only asserting that this economic fact is contrary to our moral sentiments. That is why Marx never based his Communist conclusions upon this, but, on the contrary, upon *the necessary overthrow, developing itself under our very eyes every day, of the Capitalist system of production*."—Engels : Preface to *Poverty of Philosophy*, p. 14.

It is, of course, true that Marx corrected the form of this Socialist deduction, and, at the same time, made a profoundly important correction of the Ricardian formula (by pointing out that what the capitalist buys *at its value* is not the worker's " labour," his *product*, but his " labour-power," his ability to produce). It is true, likewise, that this rectification did " explain how labour was exploited under the capitalist system," and that the basic relation of capitalist production thereby revealed played a fundamental part in Marx's conception of the " necessary overthrow " of the Capitalist system of production. But it is no less true that these, vastly important though they are, were incidental only to the more comprehensive scheme of laying bare " the special laws which regulate the origin, existence, development, and death " of the capitalist-social organism, " and its replacement by another and a higher " form of society. Marx's subject-matter was " the whole sphere of the conditions of life which environ mankind, and which, hitherto, have ruled Man," especially the forces and conditions of social production :

> " Active social forces work exactly like natural forces—blindly, forcibly, destructively—so long as we do not understand and reckon with them. But when once we understand them, when once we grasp their action, their direction, and their effects, it depends only upon ourselves to subject them more and more to our own will, and by means of them to reach our own ends. And this holds quite especially of the mighty production forces of to-day. As long as we obstinately refuse to understand the nature and the character of these social means of action—and this understanding goes against the grain of the capitalist mode of production and its defenders—so long these forces are at work in spite of us, in opposition to us ; so long they master us."—ENGELS : *Socialism*, p. 73.

In short, Marx was " attempting " to understand and to " lay bare the economic law of motion of modern Society "— " the natural laws of capitalist production "—" tendencies working with iron necessity towards inevitable results "— *not* with a view to providing the world with a brand-new " interpretation," but with a revolutionary intent to create the pre-conditions necessary for *changing the world*.

We saw above the manner in which Marx analysed the objective social relations implied in the Commodity. In its Value-form (which fully developed becomes the Money-form) the commodity—which is a specific, historically-conditioned form taken by the product of labour—is " the economic cell-form " of the whole organism of capitalist production. From its analysis Marx was able to develop the whole of the categories of political economy, and with their aid in turn he was able to outline the whole historical movement of capitalist society. That his method was not only materialist but dialectical we have already seen. A glance at the more salient features of the " law of motion " of Capitalist society will show that the objective movement of Capitalist production he revealed is *dialectic* likewise.

The characteristics of a *dialectical* movement are thus

described by Engels : " it does not move in the eternal one-ness of a perpetually recurring cycle, but goes through a real historical evolution." Elsewhere he distinguishes a dialectical movement (from one of simple continuation in one direction, cyclic or otherwise) by the following character-istics : it is (he says) a *process* which (*a*) is *antagonistic* in nature ; (*b*) involves a *contradiction* (from which arises a *whole series* of contradictions) ; (*c*) is, over all as well as in its details, a *transformation* of an extreme into its *opposite* ; and (*d*) has therefore as the kernel of its process the negation of the negation from which the whole movement arose. All these characteristics are found in the general law of motion of Capitalist production.

Capitalist production arose out of the pre-capitalist money-economy, which was, as we saw, a development from simple exchange-economy, as that was in turn a development from " natural " economy—the production of use-values for immediate consumption by individual or associated producers. Money economy, as we saw, created the possibility of *hoard-ing* : it also developed a use for these hoards. They could be borrowed (at interest) by potentates, etc., in need of an emergency supply of means of purchase or of payment. Also they could be lent to merchants enterprising enough to surmount the barriers between two or more markets. In these markets, as a consequence of natural differences in soils and climates, etc., the merchant could both buy cheap and sell dear. Thus both the usurer and the merchant could separately and in conjunction convert a given sum of money into *more money*. These " antediluvian " forms of Capital, as Marx called them, played a big part in both classic antiquity and in the Middle Ages. In each epoch they assisted the development of the then prevailing system, and, still more, contributed to its disintegration. But in neither case did they constitute the basis of the system of production.

This development—the transfer of production itself to a *capitalist* basis—arose as a development from certain specific historically-begotten pre-conditions which are revealed by the analysis of *industrial capitalism*—capitalism as a system of production. All Capitalism consists in converting a sum of money into *more money* by the direct or indirect exploita-tion of the prevailing social mode of production. The *usurer* of antiquity exploited the exploiters, or, alternatively, the producer as an individual. The *merchant* exploited the local

limitations of a number of scattered markets, and so contributed to the overcoming of those limitations. The industrial capitalist increasingly gains control of the whole
process of social production so that in the end production
becomes primarily *production of Capital*, and only secondarily
the production of the means of existence of the members of
society. It thus makes the *direct* exploitation of social
production for private advantage into a universally prevailing
system.

The economic *form* of this process is that a given quantity
of Value in money-form is exchanged for its equivalent in
(*a*) means of production, and (*b*) labour power. These in-
gredients are then *consumed* (productively) in the production-
process, with the result that a *new* use-value appears (the
product) which embodies an *enlarged* quantity of Value.
This being exchanged for money, the cycle is completed :
money has been converted into *more* money.

Viewed abstractly the process presents itself superficially
as a mystical *self-expansion* of Capital. Viewed concretely
the expansion is seen to consist in that transformation by
human labour of Nature-given *use-values*, which constitutes
production. If this concrete process is isolated from the
conditions which give it its specific form—if, that is to say,
we seek to treat the process as an expression of " natural
law "—which is what the bourgeois economists all sought to
do, we see nothing in the process beyond the *co-operation*
of the possessor of labour-power with the possessor of the
means of production. It is in this way that bourgeois apologists reach the comforting conclusion that " Capital and
Labour are brothers." But it is obvious that, since *every*
act of production, *everywhere*, and at *all* times, involves the
" co-operation " of labour-activity and the means of labour—
means of production—this reasoning eliminates from the
question everything which constitutes the problem, everything which distinguishes the *Capitalist* mode of production
from every alternative mode. To understand capitalist
production we must take into account just those very things
which the bourgeois economist pushes out of sight, beginning
with the fact that, *before* the " co-operation " of labour-
power and means of production *begins*, both have become the
property of the Capitalist producer. They co-operate only
as integral parts of the capital possessed by the Capitalist
initiator and controller of the process of production.

The capitalist *buys* the requisites of production : he *sells*

the product. So far he operates within the sphere of buying
and selling—of the developed monetary form of exchange—
and subject to its general laws. But the object of the capitalist (to turn money into *more* money) is one which is rendered
unattainable by the laws of exchange, which determine
that exchange cannot help but be, in the long run, the exchange of equivalents. The capitalist must find a way of
doing, within the scope of the laws of exchange, something
which those laws forbid—namely, of getting something for
nothing. He conquers the difficulty by finding on the market
a commodity which possesses the unique property of *expanding Value* in the process of its consumption. And such a
commodity exists when (but not till when) there appears on
the market the commodity *labour-power*. In the productive
consumption of labour-power a *new* and *expanded* value is
created, embodied in a product. Since the labour-power had
been *bought* (though only " on tick ") *before* it was consumed,
it was the property of the Capitalist when, by productive
consumption, it was converted, along with the raw materials,
into a product with an expanded value. That the *product*
is the property of the Capitalist follows as a matter of course
from the fact that the prerequisites for its production were
his property, and the act of production one performed at his
command. Thus the specially distinguishing character of
capitalist production consists in that it is production by
means of *labour-power bought in the market as a commodity*.

This fact must be considered from several distinct sides.
From the side of the labourer himself the operation consists
in the surrender of his bodily powers of production—unspeci-
fied in quantity—in return for a specifically limited quantity
of products. Before he can thus alienate the powers of his
own body the labourer must be their legal possessor. He must
be a " free " man. But before he will be willing thus to
alienate his own indeterminate potentialities he must be no
less " free " of the means of producing profitably on his own
account. He must be free *only* to sell the use of himself ;
free only to feel the full force of the necessity which constrains
him to submit himself to the exploitation of the Capitalist.
Thus the presuppositions of the operation on the labourer's
side are, firstly, his own personal liberty ; and secondly,
his lack of property, his *divorce from the means of production
and self-maintenance*.

From the side of the capitalist the operation has likewise
its presuppositions : Property in the means of production,

and the possibility of buying them, and also labour-power, as commodities on the market. What the Capitalist gives is determined by the state of the market—in the long run an equivalent value to that which he buys. But whereas the labourer gets in exchange for the use of his bodily powers only so much as will keep those powers in being, the capitalist gets in exchange for a specific quantity of value a commodity whose consumption *creates value*. He has only to prolong this productive consumption (to which he is, as lawful purchaser, legally entitled) beyond the point at which the purchase price has been reproduced, and all the additional values created during the stipulated period of service constitute a clear gain to him. That the capitalist is legally entitled to gain thus from prolonging the production process is as unquestionable as is the fact that the labourer's submission to the operation is necessitated by the social conditions in which the purchase and sale take place. That the capitalist at the end of the operation possesses *more* than when the operation began seems to the capitalist no more than justice. To the labourer it means the reverse—that more has been got from him than was returned to him—in a word, that he is " *exploited*."

In this fact, that under capitalist conditions the labourer produces not only values, but values in excess of, and *surplus* to, those received by him as his " share " of the product, is revealed not only the *origin* of the capitalist mode of production, but its essential nature and mode of maintaining itself in existence. The history of capitalist production is a history of the extraction of surplus value, of its realisation in money forms, and its reconversion into more Capital for the purpose of extracting more surplus value. Under each of those heads it undergoes a whole process of ramified development, of expansion, complication, and intensification ; but all through it remains in essence an historically conditioned process of the self-expansion and self-reproduction of Capital by means of the extraction, realisation, and capitalisation of surplus value. And in this, the basic antagonism from which it springs, and by which it lives and grows, can be found likewise in embryo the forces which in their full development will bring it to an end. In the *antagonistic* inter-relation imposed by capitalist conditions upon the two indispensables of all production (labour-power and the means of production) is found the germ from which arises the class conflict between the proletariat and the bourgeoisie which, in its full development, will end in the overthrow of the bourgeoisie and the victory of the proletariat. This overthrow of the bourgeoisie and its order will not arise *automatically*, since it will follow as the consequence of a developing struggle—a " more or less veiled civil war " which finally " breaks out into open revolution." It is " the violent overthrow of the bourgeoisie " which " lays the foundation for the sway of the proletariat." The struggle itself has its roots in the economic basis of capitalist society, and develops step by step with the development of capitalist production. None the less it is a falsification of Marx's argument to contend that he based his belief in the inevitable overthrow of the bourgeois order upon a notion that capitalist economy would in and of itself come to a dead-end. Marx's contention is that capitalist production in the end creates a situation so intolerable to (*a*) the proletariat, and (*b*) more or less to all the other strata of society intermediate between the proletariat and the topmost strata of the ruling bourgeoisie, that the volume and intensity of the revolutionary struggle will become too great for the bourgeoisie to be able any longer to resist. The rule of the proletariat following from this victory has its economic conditions likewise. The proletariat cannot get rid of the hateful consequences of capitalist production without abolishing the cause from which it (with its consequences) arises. The proletariat must therefore eliminate the divorce between the worker-producer and the means of production by making these the common property of society and vesting their control in " the State, that is, the proletariat organised as the ruling class." In this way the whole historical development of the epoch of capitalist production will culminate in the negation of the negation from which it arose.

We cannot here attempt to follow all the details of this historical dialectic process, which Marx traced through all its infinitely complex ramifications in the three volumes of his *Capital*. We will confine ourselves to a consideration of the culmination of the process—the dialectical development of the presuppositions involved in the " mutation leap " of the revolutionary transition from the capitalist to the Communist order of society. These presuppositions we shall consider from three aspects : (1) the general development within capitalist society of (*a*) the material bases for the Communist order, and (*b*) the development of the antagonism whose ripening will generate the force requisite for the overthrow of the bourgeois order ; (2) the particular development of these pre-requisites for revolutionary transition in the " highest phase of capitalism," its Imperialist epoch ; (3) their specific development in the period of General Crisis in which that epoch has culminated. In this way we shall be able to compare the general forecast made by Marx and Engels with the special analysis made by Lenin of the concrete historical developments which Marx and Engels did not live to witness. And with Lenin's analysis we shall compare the development of capitalist economy since his time.

. . . . .

Critics of Marx usually agree to accept his description of the historical development of capitalist society as " largely correct." But they raise cavils at his analysis of its causation, and thereby seek to escape his conclusion—that this *necessitated* process will have a *necessary* consequence. They admit, what they cannot very well deny, that great masses of capital have been accumulated, that a world-market has been created upon which all mankind is in greater or less degree dependent ; that capitalist production to this extent dominates the world. They admit likewise that the proletariat—" the class of those who live only so long as they find work, and find work only so long as their labour increases capital "—has grown both absolutely and relatively, and that the economic and political antagonism between the proletariat and the bourgeoisie has grown in scope and intensity until all the other issues of capitalist society become so interlinked with this more fundamental issue that none of them can be decided without taking it into consideration. But they see no objective causation for the antagonism, or, alternatively, see no developing *process* in the antagonism itself. The objective refutation of these critics is found in the *dialectical* character of the phenomena whose existence as phenomena they are forced to admit. Waiving, for the moment, the matter of the *antagonism* fundamental to capitalist production, let us consider its development in respect of two other dialectical characteristics : (1) the contradictions it progressively evolves, and (2) the examples it presents of " transformation of an extreme into its opposite." Two examples of the latter class will serve as preludes to the examination of the former.

Capitalist economy in its full development is pre-eminently the economy of " free competition." Even though in more recent times the ideal of Universal Free Trade has been abandoned in practice, even the advocates of Protection are careful to assure themselves and their opponents that their object is to secure " real " freedom of competition, or " free trade within the Empire." Taking this as a datum line, we can now contrast with it the state of things out of which capitalist production grew. In the mediæval epoch such a thing as " free competition " was unheard of, and would have been regarded as an unconscionable scandal. Only the excess of production over the immediate requirements of the producers (and their overlords) was exchanged at all, and in every market a fixed staple of qualities and prices was the rule enforced by properly constituted authorities. " Forestalling," i.e., buying goods before they had been placed on the " stall " and had had their prices fixed by authority (tantamount to " cornering "), and " regrating," selling a second time in the one market at a *new* and unauthorised price (tantamount to " selling dear after buying cheap ") were regarded as vile crimes, for which severe penalties were enforced. That capitalism and its free competition for the market, which in the end became as wide as the world, developed out of mediæval society is unquestionable. But so too is the fact that free competition is the *opposite* of the mediæval extreme. And, as we shall see later, free competition in turn is an " extreme " which subsequent development has turned into its opposite—oligarchical financial dictatorship.

The second example has already been given in another connection : the institution of property (the right to own and to alienate at will) in the land and the means of production, and with it the civil right of every citizen to property in his own person—-the legal negation of slavery and serfdom— were the preconditions from which has developed the propertyless condition of the majority of the population, and their consequent enslavement, in fact, to the owners of their means of living. Thus the institution of the universal " right " to property has been a means of making its possession a reality only for a privileged few, who thereby become the masters of Society, and the legal abolition of slavery has been the means of re-establishing it on a wider and more oppressive scale than ever. With these instances in mind we can turn to the consideration of the chief contradictions revealed in the evolution of capitalist society.

It is a commonplace that capitalist development has included an enormous technological advance, the development of the implements of production from simple tools such as a single handicraft worker could handle into immense masses of powerful and complicated machinery which require an army of men to operate them. This technological revolution has been forced upon the individual capitalists by competition which has, on the other side, eliminated in all the more advanced areas of the world every pre-capitalist alternative to the capitalist mode of production. Thus every member of civilized society has become dependent upon the market—upon finding in the market the requisites of personal consumption, after selling therein products or labour-power. To a greater extent than ever the whole of mankind has become either absolutely or relatively dependent upon the market and upon the social process of production which keeps it supplied both with commodities and with purchasers. But in direct and glaring contradiction to this fact of universal dependence upon the social process of production stands the fact that the products of *society's* production activity—which, in consequence of the technological advances aforementioned, grows increasingly to be an activity in which the whole working population directly and indirectly *co-operate*—are, when produced, *privately appropriated,* so that they reach the market as private possessions offered for sale for private advantage.

This contradiction grows more acute and more all embracing the more capitalism develops. The more technological advance makes possible an enlarged scale of production the more rapid is the elimination of the less well-equipped productive enterprises. Thus the more the numbers of the proletariat grow the more the social, co-operative character of the act of production is accentuated. Hence there grows too a more direct and imperative dependence of all members of society upon the market, alike as buyers (of means of consumption or means of production) or as sellers (of commodities or of labour-power). With all this increasing *socialisation* of the process of production, both in its technical and its social aspects, the private appropriation of the social product stands, by simple persistence, in ever-sharpening contrast. The need to make the mode of appropriation correspond to the increasingly *social* mode of production grows obvious to all —except the owners of capitalist property, and with them their dependants and their dupes.

From the relations from which this contradiction arises springs another : the contradiction between *the organisation of production* in the individual factory or enterprise and *the anarchy in social production as a whole.* This anarchy has a whole series of modes of manifestation. In the first place, every technological advance involves a displacement of labour. Skilled labourers find their skill obsolete ; semi-skilled and unskilled workers find themselves " redundant." In most cases this displacement is only temporary, but it almost invariably involves a transition from one occupation to another, and a concomitant loss of the market value of acquired skill and experience. For many the transition is, as Marx said, " one from life to death." Periodically this displacement of labour means the creation of an army of workers wholly unemployed ; over all it involves a steady increase in the numbers of the intermittently employed—the " reserve army of industry." The growth of the scale of production, of the scientific effectiveness of its organisation and equipment, and of the intensiveness of exploitation, combined with the general absence of plan in production as a whole (an inevitable consequence of its competitive character), all ensure that sooner or later in one branch of production, or in a number, production will exceed the capacity of the market. With the markets glutted, production is brought temporarily to a halt. Means of production stand idle or remain on the market unsold—as likewise does the labour-power of the unemployed. All the requisites of production exist, yet production is rendered impossible, because " the capitalist form of production prevents the productive forces from working and the products from circulating unless they are first turned into capital, which their very superabundance prevents " (ENGELS). The mode of production " rises in rebellion against the form of exchange." In these periodical crises " the bourgeoisie is convicted of incapacity further to manage the social forces it has called into being."

As a consequence of these crises, which are inseparable from the capitalist mode of production, a " partial recognition of the social character of the productive forces is forced upon the capitalists themselves." The more developed enterprises in production, as well as in the means of communication (railways, canals, telegraphs, telephones, cables, etc.), are taken over by joint stock companies, by Trusts, and (in some cases) by the State. The joint-stock company system, and with it the tendency towards trustification, becomes the general rule. Capitalist production does not thereby abate in the slightest its capitalist character, since the mode of appropriation remains as capitalistic as ever. But once

x

the *social* functions of the capitalist (as superintendent and director of production) are devolved upon salaried employees, and the capitalist becomes not a personal but a collective entity, the bourgeoisie is proved to be a superfluous class, an anachronism. This does not, of course, cause the bourgeoisie to withdraw itself voluntarily from the historical scene. Very much to the contrary. Aware of the precariousness of its position and of the growing hostility of the proletariat to itself and its order ; aware, no less, of the fact that every extension of the scale of production imposed upon it by its competitive character entails an absolute and relative increase in the numbers of the proletariat and of the intensity of its hostility against the capitalist social order, the bourgeoisie is driven into more and more flagrantly tyrannical and violent courses. The more superfluous the bourgeoisie becomes as a class, and the more consciously parasitic, the less grows the chance (if it ever existed) of a peaceful overthrow of the capitalist order.

Thus out of the antagonism basic to the capitalist mode of production which its development ripens to the explosion point of an irreconcilable class conflict, and out of the contradictions inherent in the capitalist social system, are developed both the forces making for revolution and the occasion for their passage from potentialities into actualities. And not only does the development of capitalism thus engender both the forces and the occasion for its own overthrow ; it engenders at the same time the basis for an alternative social order. In the socialisation of the technical process of production exists the basic developmental form for the communally co-operative production of a Communist order.

Similarly the collectivised condition into which capitalist ownership of the means and implements of production evolves, particularly in the higher stages of its development, makes it an easy matter for a victorious revolution to wrest their control from the present owners and develop collective ownership into public and common ownership. Co-operation to own the means and implements of production, and co-operation to use them productively, each develop within capitalist society, but in antagonistic separation—and in subordination to the general contradictions of capitalist society. The proletarian revolution, which will sweep away these conditions, will simultaneously solve the contradictions and eliminate the antagonism by making these means of production the common property of the workers who co-operate to use them and, vesting their control in their collective expression " the State, i.e., the workers organised as a ruling class." In this way the dialectic of capitalist production will produce both its negation and also the objective, material and social starting-point for a new era in the history of mankind.

These pre-requisites for the overthrow of capitalism and for the higher order of society which will succeed it develop into ripeness in the epoch which LENIN subjected to analysis in his *Imperialism : the highest Stage of Capitalism*. To this therefore we now turn.

.   .   .   .   .   .

Lenin's analysis starts from the concrete phenomena of the period in which he wrote (1916). The closing years of the nineteenth century and the opening years of the twentieth had seen the outbreak of a succession of wars and revolutions which had culminated in the World War of 1914, and was, although Lenin did not know it, to culminate in the two Russian Revolutions of 1917 and the wave of revolution which followed the close of the War. War had broken out between China and Japan in 1894, Greece and Turkey in 1897, Spain and the U.S.A. in 1898, Britain and the Boers in 1899, Japan and Russia in 1904, Italy and Turkey in 1911, the Balkan Allies and Turkey in 1912, the Balkan States among themselves in 1913, and World War had come in 1914. Revolutions had broken out in Russia in 1905, in Persia in 1906, in Portugal in 1907, in Turkey in 1908, and in China in 1911–12.

This ascending wave of wars and revolutions did not, *of itself*, make the epoch a *new* one, although it was significant that it came just when bourgeois Liberal optimism had convinced itself that " war is a wasteful anachronism " and that " revolutions have ceased to be possible." It is when we search for the cause of this series of outbreaks that we find the ground for discriminating an entirely new stage in the development of capitalism.

.   .   .   .   .   .

The Great War of 1914 brought starkly into view a significant quality that had marked, on a growing scale, the wars of this epoch. The Great War announced itself from the first as an *Imperialist* war, a war of annexations, a war for ruinous indemnities, " a war for the partition of the world, for the distribution and redistribution of colonies, of ' spheres of influence ' for finance capital, etc."—(LENIN).

The significance of this fact can be best judged in the light of Marx's comment upon the annexation of Alsace-Lorraine and the indemnity extorted by Prussia from France in 1871 :—

" Such is the lesson of all history. Thus with nations as with individuals. To deprive them of the power of offence you must deprive them of the means of defence. You must not only garotte, but murder. . . . History will measure its retribution, not by the extent of the square miles conquered from France, but by the intensity of the crime of reviving in the second half of the nineteenth century, *the policy of conquest*."—MARX : *Civil War in France*, p. 74.

By Versailles Treaty standards the extent of the territory and tribute extorted by Prussia in 1871 was indeed trifling. But it is not even the enormous difference in the territorial acquisitions aimed at by all the parties to the Great War, or the staggering difference in the indemnity finally demanded, which is in point here. By the common consent of all the combatants the Great War was fought, not as a national, but as an *international* issue—as a fight for the hegemony of the world and the control of its economic resources actual and potential. It constituted in itself concrete evidence that :—

" Capitalism has grown into a world system of colonial oppression and financial strangulation of the overwhelming majority of the people of the world by a handful of ' advanced ' countries. And this ' booty ' is shared by two or three world-dominating pirates armed to the teeth (America, England, Japan), who embroil the whole world in *their* war over the division of *their* booty."— LENIN : *Imperialism*, Preface (1920), p. 11.

Imperialism therefore is not to be explained as merely a change for the worse in the disposition of the governments of the " advanced " Powers. It has its roots in the facts and forces which have endowed these governments with their world-preponderance, and their countries with the character of being " advanced." It arises *not* from the *morals*, but from the *economics* of the epoch ; from the relation in which *all* the countries of the world stand to the specific forces of production which development has engendered, and to the world-market in which these forces realise, capitalistically, their potentialities.

Lenin noted five characteristics as distinguishing this *Imperialist* stage of capitalism :—

" (1) The *concentration* of production and capital has developed to such a high stage that it has created *monopolies* which play a decisive role in economic life.

(2) The *merging* of bank-capital with industrial capital and the creation, on the basis of this *Finance Capital*, of a *financial oligarchy*.

(3) The *export of capital* as distinguished from the export of commodities becomes of particularly great importance.

(4) *International monopoly combines* of capital are formed which *divide up the world*.

(5) The territorial division of the world by the greatest capitalist powers is completed.—LENIN : *Imperialism*, p. 81.

Each of these phenomena, taken separately, shows a difference of *degree* becoming a difference in *kind*. Thus, in their totality, they present a first-rate example of the " transformation of quantity into quality," which explains from the roots upward the complete change in the battle slogans of the bourgeoisie and the drastic reorientation of the immediate objects of capitalist production.

Taken as a whole, their central characteristic is the transformation of free competition into *monopoly*. " Imperialism is the monopolist stage of capitalism." This is not only a " transformation of an extreme [competition] into its opposite [monopoly]." As this transformation follows logically and historically from the previous transformation of (mediæval) monopoly into (capitalist) free competition it constitutes the completion of an antagonistic cycle—a *return to the starting-point on a higher plane*. As such it heralds a mutation-leap to a new synthesis—the point of departure for a new development. Or, to state the same thing more concretely, it indicates that the phenomena of imperialism are not to be dismissed as superficial or temporary aberrations, accidentally modifying the normal course of capitalism. They indicate that the *essential* relations of capitalism have developed all the potentialities latent within their primary antagonism, and that before further development is possible the antagonism itself must be eliminated. This can be seen most clearly if we examine in succession each of the five aspects distinguished by Lenin.

.   .   .   .   .

The concentration of capital and of production follows inevitably from the social conditions of capitalist production, among which the most general are (a) the social division of labour from which springs the differentiation of the various crafts and industries, and (b) private property in the land, and the instruments of production. Given these things and competition exists in its germinal form. Given the further development of (a) commodity production and (b) the appearance on the market of *labour power* as a commodity, and the conditions exist for the development of competition into its capitalist form. Capitalist production bursts the bounds which constrained competition and made it an essential and a universal condition of production. Competition imposed upon each capitalist the need to cheapen production. In other words, it made it imperative for each capitalist to produce on a *higher* scale, i.e., with larger masses of better organised and more thoroughly exploited labourers equipped with more effective and larger masses of machinery and means of production. In short : capitalism both extended and intensified competition, and with it the elimination of the less well-equipped producers. The logical end of this elimination could be none other than one solitary ultimate victor.

Concretely, however, certain difficulties must be overcome before this end can be attained. In concrete fact the field of direct competition is divided into a series of strata (different industries and branches of production) and a number of different centres (local and national markets which only in their aggregation constitute the world market). Thus before a lone survivor could be reached on a world scale lone survivors must first have been evolved in each of these strata, and each of these centres.

But the evolution of an absolute monopoly in any one industry (steel production, say) on a world-scale cuts across and conflicts with the evolution of a monopolist control of any local or national market, or economy. Thus the tendency towards monopoly, the more sure and certain it becomes, cannot realise itself *logically*, but must proceed *dialectically*, i.e., by the creation and progressive surmounting of a whole series of violent antagonisms. Moreover, since the rate of development, owing to climatic, physical, historical and political conditions, as well as economic ones, cannot help but vary from time to time, from industry to industry, and from country to country, the force and complexity of these antagonisms and their dialectical consequences cannot help but be multiplied beyond all reckoning. Hence, although the tendency towards monopoly must be recognised as an absolute law of capitalist production, it by no means gives grounds for the Utopian dream of a peaceful transition, through a regular process of " inevitable gradualness," from Capitalist competition to a world monopoly (or a number of national monopolies) which could be " taken over " by the State " on behalf of the people " without hitch, delay, or difficulty.

If the process is viewed not in its abstract *unity*, but in its concrete and multiform *totality*, it will be seen that the tendency towards monopoly is one that can only realise itself *approximately*, and never *absolutely*, since in its concrete forms each detail tendency engenders a resistance to itself which can only be transcended by engendering resistance on a higher plane, and so on, progressively, until a crisis either of war or of revolution (or of both) is precipitated.

In short, while the tendency towards monopoly does in fact involve the negation of competition within a number of spheres of production and exchange, it produces at the same time over the whole field of economy, and still more the whole field of society, an intensification of competitive antagonisms, so that the (approximate) attainment of monopoly, instead of eliminating competition (and antagonism) from society, *on the contrary raises them progressively to a higher and more destructive scale*.

This is seen most clearly if we remember that competition is of many kinds. There is, for instance, the general competition between those who buy and those to whom they sell, as well as the competition of the sellers and buyers among themselves. The elimination of competition among the sellers, instead of eliminating the competition among the buyers or between the buyers as a group and the sellers, only intensifies these latter forms of competition. When we remember that in the very basis of capitalist production is involved the antagonistic inter-relation of the buyers and sellers of the commodity labour-power—which itself springs from a relative *monopoly*, that of the means of living of the proletariat by the capitalists and the landlords in conjunction—the significance of the growth of monopoly combinations among the buyers of labour-power shows itself in all its revolutionary force.

We do not need here to prove that monopolist combinations are the rule in capitalist economy to-day, and not the exception. What concerns us is the *dialectic* nature of the development, and the objective proof it gives of the soundness both of Marx's analysis and of his method. Therefore we stress here only the fact that (a) monopoly appears as a result of the accumulation, concentration, and centralisation both of capital and of production which has been forced upon each capitalist by the *competition* which it was the historic mission of capitalist production to make universal ; and (b) the fact that while monopoly grows inevitably out of competition it constitutes (with the qualification above noted) its negation, and, therefore, also constitutes the objective basis for the general abandonment by the bourgeoisie of the Liberalism and Humanitarian-Internationalism typical of its ascendant phases. Monopoly capitalism is

" . . . no longer a competitive struggle between small and large, between technically developed and backward enterprises. We see the monopolies *throttling* those who do not submit to the monopoly, to its yoke, to its dictation. . . .

" Although commodity-production still reigns and is regarded as the basis of all economic life, it has in reality already been undermined, and the main profits go to the ' geniuses ' of financial manipulation. . . .

" A dominating position, and the pressure that goes with it—these are the typical features . . . this is what inevitably had to result, and has resulted, from the formation of all-powerful economic monopolies."—LENIN : *Imperialism*, pp. 26–27.

The tendency towards monopoly is concretised into a system with the emergence of a new category of capital, that of *Finance Capital*. This again gives an example of a " transformation of quantity into quality," of a *logical* continuation passing over into a *dialectical* development. As a giant capitalist enterprise (in steel production, for example) rises by simple expansion to a position of monopolist dominance in its specific industry it finds itself, as trade fluctuates, alternately possessed of more money captial (realised profits) than it needs for the expansion of its business and, contrariwise, faced with emergency needs for fresh money-capital. In the one phase it invests its surplus in Bank capital ; in the other it hypothecates a share in its capital to the Bank in exchange for a loan. A parallel process goes on with the Banks, and the two complementary processes end with a merging of the capital of an industrial monopoly and a banking monopoly to form a new type of monopoly which transcends the limitations of industry and banking each in themselves, and carries the process of *domination* to a higher and a more comprehensive scale. With the formation of Finance Capital begins the process of bringing the whole economy of the country of its origin under the complete control of a small group of financial oligarchs.

This process has another and even more far-reaching aspect. In so far as monopoly is attained it makes possible (if only temporarily) the stabilisation of prices and the limitation of production to the estimated needs of the monopoly-controlled market. As by doing this, relative excess of production is eliminated along with redundant managerial and sales staffs, the monopoly obtains an increased volume of profit in circumstances which preclude further investment of capital within its own sphere. Hence the export of capital takes on an ever-growing importance. The world becomes partitioned more and more, and in two distinct ways. Economically the export of capital facilitates the development both of horizontal and of vertical monopolies ; that is to say, the bringing of a given industry under the monopoly control of an *international* monopoly, and the establishment of a monopoly control of a *series of industries* which work up raw material from its point of natural origin to its final complete form. These processes intersect, collide, and also combine to beget higher forms of monopoly. Ultimately both of them converge on the two extreme points (*a*) control of the sources of origin of indispensable materials, naturally limited in quantity ; (*b*) control of markets in which to dispose of finished products. Both thus add impetus to the imperialist partitioning of much of the earth's territory as is still available for seizure by them. And, since this process of imperialist annexation had been completed (approximately) by the turn of the century—and the economic forces impelling the development still continued in accelerating operation—it followed of necessity that there must become manifest yet another transformation of " quantity into quality." The process of imperialist expansion brought each and every empire to the point at which further expansion could only be obtained at the expense of another Empire !

Already the penetrating power of Finance Capital had wrought a complete transformation of the relations between the " sovereign States " which make up what journalists and politicians love to call the " comity of nations." Whereas in diplomatic theory all sovereign States meet

and do business as equals (i.e., equally " sovereign " and
absolute within its territory), Finance Capital brings into
being a differentiation of States into debtors and creditors.
This inter-linking of States, the subordination of the host
of small States to the financial overlordship of a few great
Powers, supplements the open territorial partition of the
World. Its result was that by 1914 virtually every State in
the world outside of the few Imperial Powers (Britain,
Germany, France, the U.S.A., and Japan) was an economic
vassal of one or other of these " Empires." And, since all
of these Empires were impelled by the need to " expand "
still further, they could only expand at the expense of each
other. Thus the causation of the phenomena of Imperialism
and imperialist war was shown to be the development of
capitalism into a new and higher stage in which its antagonisms
were so much the more fully developed that their expression
in veiled or open imperialist war on the one hand, and in
potential or actual revolutionary uprisings on the other, was
inevitable.

.   .   .   .   .

It may be objected that, while Lenin showed, certainly,
that in monopolist-imperialism capitalism enters upon a new
and a higher stage of development, he did not and could not
show that this stage was the " highest " possible to capitalism
—which may conceivably reach yet another stage.

The answer to that objection is that it proceeds from the
assumption that the possibilities of development open to a
given historically-conditioned form of society are unlimited.
The whole of the facts and processes analysed by Marx, and
Lenin, show on the contrary that only a specifically limited
and conditioned development is possible to each historically
determined form of society :—

    " To the extent that the labour-process is a simple
    process between Man and Nature its simple elements
    remain the same in all social forms of development.
    But every definite historical stage of this process develops
    more and more its material foundations and its social
    forms. Wherever a certain maturity is reached one
    definite social form is discarded and displaced by a higher
    one. The time for the coming of such a crisis is announced
    by the depth and breadth of the contradictions and
    antagonisms which separate the conditions of pro-
    duction (and with them the conditions of distribution)
    in their definite historical forms, from the productive

forces, their productivity, and the development of their agencies. A conflict then arises between the material development of production and its social form."—MARX : *Capital*, Vol. III, p. 1030.

Two outstanding phenomena indicated by Engels as characteristic of the culminating phase of capitalism are shown by Lenin to have developed and be developing with extraordinary rapidity in the imperialist stage. These were (1) parasitism, and (2) the " partial recognition of the social character of production." Each separately, and still more both together, evidenced the fact that in the imperialist stage the contradictions and antagonisms inherent in capitalism were ripening to their maximum intensity.

Parasitism first becomes apparent when (by the formation of joint-stock companies, combines, etc.) all their social-productive functions are devolved by the bourgeoisie upon salaried employees, and the bourgeoisie becomes a purely parasitic class. In the stage of Finance Capital this parasitism develops and expands in all sorts of ways and directions. The process of bringing the whole economy of society under the direction of a tiny financial oligarchy includes objectively the launching and flotation of a host of speculative enterprises, development syndicates, holding companies, investment trusts, and so forth. The immense mass of capital required by each gigantic Finance-Capitalist monopoly is accumulated by every sort of device for collecting the spare cash of all, even to the very poorest, into a huge heap of money capital, which the financial oligarchs can turn into actual capital loaned or invested in enterprises in all the ends of the earth. At one time (Lenin notes) German capitalists envied British capitalists the freedom from legal restraints which made it possible for them to issue " one pound shares." Since then five-shilling and one-shilling shares have become far from uncommon, and the Post Office savings bank and " National " Savings Certificates compete with the Penny Banks and the gigantic " industrial " assurance companies to rake every pocket to provide the mass of money-capital with which the financial oligarchs fight for the mastery of the earth and for unlimited power to live parasitically at the expense of all mankind.

It is not only that the place once occupied by the industrial and commercial middle class is now occupied by a whole sub-strata of bourgeois society, *the rentier class*—the class whose sole occupation is clipping coupons from loan-stock, or presenting dividend warrants at the bank. In its upper strata this rentier class in fact includes a large proportion of the bourgeoisie proper and the bourgeois aristocracy, while its lower strata extend as far as to include stray members even of the proletariat. These phenomena (which, super-ficially observed and misunderstood, gave a ground for Revisionists and other apologists for Capitalism to talk of the " democratisation of Capital ") present collectively one side of the process, whose other side is the subjection of the colonial peoples to a double and treble exploitation, viz., that of the Imperialist overlord State, that of Finance Capital, and that of such native capitalism as is allowed to grow under the exploiting dominance of Finance Capital, pro-tected by the Imperial State. Thus the development of the resources of the colonial areas proceeds at an accelerating pace, but in subordination to and as part of the process of extending the dominion of monopoly capitalism.

Incidental to the development of parasitism into a uni-versally dominant system is the rise to general importance of reckless speculation and the swindling which invariably accompanies it. Gambling in " options," " futures " and speculative shares grows, with fraudulent company promoting, the " watering " of capital, engineered bankruptcies followed by reconstructions and so forth, into an accepted and usual way of getting rich. Whereas, on the plane of the exchange of commodities between (relatively) small producers, swindling and over-reaching in bargaining are phenomena only inci-dental to the process of production as a whole—since swindle is cancelled by counter-swindle in the final outcome—in the monopolist phase of capitalism swindling (dignified with the name of financial manipulation) is developed into a system and becomes a regular and usual mode of " original accumula-tion." This fact, that in its monopolist phase the first concern of capitalism is not so much the immediate extraction of surplus value (which, of course, is extracted in greater masses than ever) as the *diversion* of the already extracted surplus value into the grip of the dominant parasites is clear evidence that monopoly capitalism, despite the immense impetus it gives both to accumulation and to the development of the material means of production, is none the less *decadent*. Lenin cites the fact that as long ago as 1893 the income British *rentiers* derived from overseas investments was five times as great as Britain's income from foreign trade—from the export of commodities—as an example of decadent and parasitical development. While using its monopoly control of home production to reduce the volume of production to the level of ascertained market requirements, Finance Capital is impelled by its need and greed for ever-expanding profits to continually revolutionise the economy of the more backward areas of the world, while keeping them firmly in the grip of its monopolistic control. Thus Finance-Capital sums up within itself and develops with accelerating rapidity all the general contradictions of capitalism—particularly that between the increasing socialisation of the material process of production and the private appropriation of the product, from which arises as a consequence the increasing anarchy in social production as a whole. Finance-Capital from its nature is forced deliberately to strive for the attainment both of the *socialisation* and also, on a world-scale, the *anarchy*.

This raising of the contradictions immament in Capitalism to their highest power—and their extension to include the whole earth—finds expression in two distinct but related groups of phenomena : (*a*) those of war and revolutionary uprising, and (*b*) those of the fusion of the economic functions of Finance-Capital and the political functions of the State, whereby the financial oligarchy becomes the *de facto* wielder of State authority as well as the direct and indirect controller of the economic life of society and its members.

The tendency towards war is an inevitable result of the expansion of the various world-empires, which can only grow at each other's expense. The tendency towards revolutionary uprising is two-fold, being in part a reaction of the colonial masses against their subjection to and exploitation by their Imperialist overlords, and partly (as well as more basically) that general tendency of the proletariat to revolt which is potential in the most basic antagonism of capitalist production —that between the exploited proletariat and the exploiting bourgeoisie.

The tendency towards the fusion of the State and the financial oligarchy has a profound bearing upon the tendency to war (since war preparedness becomes then a matter of permanent necessity and therefore of deliberately settled policy). It has an even more profoundly dialectical reaction upon the developing tendency towards revolution.

Engels, in 1892, noted as instances of " partial recognition of the social character of the forces of production "—a recognition forced upon the bourgeoisie by the recurring crises inseparable from capitalist production—the " taking over of

the great institutions for production and communication
first by joint-stock companies, later on by trusts, then by
the State." In its full development such a process would
establish (as both Marx and Engels noted) a condition of
State capitalism—i.e., capitalist appropriation on a basis of
collectivised capitalist property within the form of State
ownership. This, of course, would not affect the basic
antagonism of capitalist society. On the contrary it would
make the divorce between the working-class and the means
of production *absolute*. For that reason Marx and Engels
(who envisaged its coming as a necessary logical outcome of
the law of motion of capitalist society) heralded its coming
as a prelude to *the proletarian revolution*, which would overthrow bourgeois society and eliminate the antagonism upon
which it was based.

Interpreting Marx and Engels (generally at second or third
hand) in a mechanically non-dialectical fashion, there grew
up (especially in Britain) a school of " Socialists " who saw
in State ownership *per se* the be-all and end-all of " Socialism."
Instead of seeing in the taking over of selected industries by
the State a concrete example to the proletariat of what it
could and should do, *if and when it became the ruling power in
the State*, this " spurious Socialism," which " here and there
degenerated into flunkeyism " (ENGELS), elaborated a whole
theory of the " gradual " transformation of capitalism into
" Socialism " by the piecemeal " nationalisation " of industry
after industry as each " became ripe for nationalisation."
This " socialism," which was especially prevalent in the
Fabianised strata of the British Labour Movement, received
its cruellest theoretical blow during the War, when the whole
of the land and industries of Great Britain were (in law, and
to a large extent in practice) taken over by the State, under
the Defence of the Realm Act, for the duration of the War.
Even the most purblind of Utopians could not delude himself
into regarding the result (with the rich crop of multi-
millionaire " profiteers " it included) as " Socialism." It
was, on the contrary, a concrete demonstration of the truth
of Engels' words :—

> " The conversion into either joint-stock companies
> or State property does not deprive the productive forces
> of their character as *capital*. In the case of joint-stock
> companies this is obvious. And the modern State, too,
> is only the organisation with which bourgeois Society
> provides itself in order to maintain the general external

conditions of the capitalist mode of production against encroachments either by the workers or by individual capitalists. The modern State, whatever its form, is an essentially capitalist machine ; it is the State of the capitalists, the ideal collective body of all capitalists. The more productive forces it takes over, the more it becomes the real collective body of all the capitalists, the more citizens it exploits. The workers remain wage-earners, proletarians. *The capitalist relationship is not abolished ; it is, rather, carried to its extreme.*"—ENGELS : *Anti-Dühring,* pp. 312–13.

But this concrete reduction to absurdity of the " Fabian " theory of " Socialism by instalments through nationalisation and municipalisation " by no means caused the theory to disappear. On the contrary : the actual impact of war, and of the wave of revolutions which arose with the close of the war, revealed that a parallel degeneration of " Socialism " from the " battle-philosophy of the revolutionary proletariat " into the most banal of opportunist Liberalism had become chronic among the leading cadres of the Parties of the Second International, and among those of their Trade Union allies. We do not need here to recite the record of prolonged and treacherous betrayal of the hopes and interests of the militant proletariat which constitutes the history of the Social-Democratic Party and its allies since August 4th, 1914. What concerns us is, firstly, the fact that this degeneration was proved by the outcome to have originated long before the War ; and secondly, the fact that it has its roots in the parasite nature of monopolist-imperialist Capitalism.

Because of its nature and situation monopolist capitalism can, and does, secure from the plunder of the colonies—achieved in a score of ways—an immense super-profit in addition to its gains from the exploitation of the workers at " home." To gain this above-the-average profit the im-perialist *ascendancy* of the home country and the corresponding colonial *subjection* of the area plundered are essential con-ditions—as is also the maintenance and consolidation of its monopoly grip at home. The maintenance of this relation has, however, its difficulties—all resting ultimately upon the danger of proletarian revolt at home and Nationalist revolt in the colonies. True to its innermost nature, the financial oligarchy soon realises that a little money spent in corruption can go a long way towards insuring it against immediate danger from either quarter. In the case of the home proletariat the means of corruption exist ready to hand. The influx of cheap foodstuffs, the material embodiment of the tribute wrung from the colonies, cheapened the cost of living for the proletariat at a time when the rapid expansion of industry made it inconvenient for the bourgeoisie to carry through a programme of reducing money-wages to correspond. On the basis of this " prosperity " grew up, alongside of and linked with the non-revolutionary " gradualist " theory of Socialism, the practice of Capitalist collaboration with the leaders of the Trade Unions covering the skilled trades and " key-position " workers, a practice which gave rise to a system of admitting this upper strata of the proletariat to a share in the super-exploitation of the colonies—the practice of conceding trifling wage advances or abstaining from imposing wage reductions. Combined with this a systematic policy of veiled and open corruption is resorted to. Actual cases of direct bribery (in the narrow sense) are rear and insignificant. But the indirect bribery which consists in flattery, in social patronage, in giving confidential " tips " from which big gains can be reaped, in aiding the economic and social advancement of sons, daughters and dependants, etc.— all these modes of-bribery have been employed systematically in all the Imperialist countries for the express purpose of winning the leaders of the proletariat—and through them their followers—over to a " more reasonable frame of mind." Thus the mentality which makes it possible for leaders of the Labour and Socialist movement to believe " sincerely " that " the country must come first," that " the Empire must be saved," that " the constitution provides a way of remedying all the legitimate grievances of the workers," that " violent revolution is against the interests of the workers," is a mentality which lingers on as a survival because it is fostered by the general and particular *corruption* spread by capitalism in its stage of parasitical monopolist-imperialist decadence.

.   .   .

Lenin's analysis of the " imperialist " stage in the evolution of capitalism may be summed up in his own words :

" From all that has been said above on the economic essence of imperialism it follows that it must be characterused as *capitalism in transition,* or, more precisely, as *dying capitalism.* It is very instructive in this connection to note that bourgeois economists, in describing the newest capitalism, currently employ terms like " interlocking," " absence of isolation," etc. . . . But the foundation of this interlocking, that which constitutes its base, is the changing social relations in production. When a big enterprise becomes a gigantic one and, working on the basis of exactly computed mass data, systematically organises the supply of primary raw materials to the extent of two-thirds or three-fourths of all that is necessary for tens of millions of people ; when these raw materials are transported to the most suitable places of production, sometimes hundreds of thousands of miles from each other, in a systematic and organised manner ; when one centre controls all the successive stages of working up the raw materials right up to the manufacture of numerous varieties of finished articles ; when these products are distributed according to a single plan among tens and hundreds of millions of consumers . . . then it becomes evident that we have socialisation of production going on right before our eyes and not mere " interlocking " ; that private business relations and private property relations consti- tute a mere shell which must inevitably begin to decay if its removal is postponed by artificial means ; a shell that may continue in being in a state of decay for a com- paratively long period (particularly if the cure of the opportunist abscess is protracted), but which will in- evitably be removed."—LENIN : *Imperialism*, pp. 114–15.

Thus by the use of Marx's method, and by its application to the historically concrete details of a stage of capitalist production which Marx and Engels foresaw in general, but did not live to observe and analyse in detail, Lenin vindicated triumphantly not only the validity of Marx's dialectical method, but also his conception of the " law of motion of capitalist society," his conception of its " origin, nature, development and inevitable end," a law of motion whose objectively *dialectical* character Lenin proved as no man, other than Marx or Engels, had proved before his time or since.

.   .   .   .   .

Lenin's description of monopoly capitalism as " dying capitalism " has been misinterpreted in Britain (more or less deliberately)—just as has been misinterpreted Marx's doctrine of the " inevitable collapse " and " necessary overthrow " of the capitalist system. The two conceptions are, in fact, identical ; the only difference being that Lenin, coming after Marx, was able to give the conception a richer, concrete

Y

content derived from the specific phenomena observable in his day. Subsequent developments have made it possible—with the aid of Marx and Lenin—to concretise the conception more sharply still, and in so doing to expose completely the fallacy and falsity of the misconceptions aforesaid, which consist in converting the conception of the " death," " collapse " and " overthrow " of capitalism into, alternatively, a conception of *automatic* mechanical breakdown (analogous to the wearing-out of a machine or the running-down of a clock), or of simple gradualist " evolution " (change into something-else *without* the dialectical development of antagonisms to their logical culmination in revolutionary crisis, and the violent elimination of the antagonism).

Lenin's description of the monopoly stage of capitalism as its *highest stage*—the stage which exhausts its possibilities of " evolutionary " as distinctive from revolutionary development—was, as we have seen, a faithful application (as well as elaboration) of the conception of Marx and Engels—that the complete *socialisation* of the labour-process involved the complete *separation* of the *productive function* of capital from the ownership of capital—a separation which becomes obvious when, in its parasitic *rentier* from, profit presents itself :

" . . . as a mere appropriation of the surplus labour of others, arising from the transformation of means of production into capital, that is, from their alienation from their actual producer, from their antagonism as another's property opposed to the individuals actually at work in production from the manager down to the last day labourer."—MARX : *Capital*, Vol. III, p. 517.

This alienation and antagonism are involved in capitalist production from the beginning. As we have seen it is the inner relation which constitutes the essential, and capitalist, nature of the mode of production of bourgeois society. When therefore, from being the inner relation connecting individual workers and individual capitalists in the production process, it becomes outwardly obvious as a fully-developed social antagonism—as a social and political *conflict* between the actual producers, *associated* by the production-process into a collective individuality on the one side, and the exploiting non-producers, equally associated by their ownership into a collective individuality *opposite* to theirs—it is obvious that (*a*) no further development is possible *within* this relationship ; (*b*) that the driving force of the antagonism, making development of some kind inescapable, will precipitate a transition to a new starting point for further development ; (c) that this new starting point has its material basis and its general form provided in the concrete forms of the positive and negative poles of the social antagonism itself, i.e., in associated production by associated owners for their common satisfaction.

" The result of the highest development of capitalist production is a necessary transition to the *reconversion* of capital [as means of production] into the property of the producers ; not, however, as the private property of individual producers, but as *the common property of associates*, as *social property* outright. At the same time it is a transition to the conversion of all the functions in the process of reproduction [of the social " Capital "] which still remain connected with capitalist private property, into simple functions of the associated producers, *into social functions.*"—MARX : *Capital*, Vol. III, p. 517.

That Lenin therefore, in his *Imperialism*, in so far as he treated the monopolist stage of capitalism as its " highest " stage, and, *therefore*, as the stage which led up to the revolutionary overthrow of capitalism, the stage of capitalism on its deathbed, was reiterating, reinforcing, in the act of conclusions of Marx and Engels, is proved to demonstration. That in identifying the phenomena of Imperialism, with all its concomitants, with precisely this " highest " stage of capitalism, Lenin deepened the concrete significance of the Marxian conception and extended the scope of its political application to include phenomena (particularly those of the dialectical inter-relation of monopolist industry and predominantly small-scale agriculture, those of the inter-relation of the colonial peoples and exploiting Imperialism, and those of the social-political consequences of parasitism) which Marx and Engels noted only in their germinal forms, is proved to demonstration likewise.

. . . . . .

If analysing the culmination of capitalism in monopolist imperialism involved the application of Marx's theory of the concentration of capital (and production), so the extension and deepening by Lenin of the Marxist conception of the revolutionary overthrow of capitalism (as distinct from and opposed to mechanistic theories of automatic collapse, or opportunist-idealist theories of its gradual " evolution ") involved the application of Marx's theory of *crises*—of the recurring crisis of glut which periodically interrupts the cyclic process of capitalist production as a whole, and of the General Crisis of Ripened Antagonisms in which Capitalism is fore-doomed historically to culminate. That the theory of the concentration of capital and its culmination in monopoly-capitalism is connected with the theory of crises and their culmination in general crisis is self-evident. What has to be noted is that their connection is a reciprocal interaction—concentration producing crises (not *as* concentration, but because of the antagonism between itself and the capitalist conditions in which it takes place), and crises in turn pro-ducing consequences which raise the scale upon which con-centration (with its concomitants) continues until it produces a further crisis, and so on. The ultimate outcome of this quantitative growth in the mass of concentration and the range of the recurring crises is a *qualitative* transformation of *both* : concentration becoming, as we have seen, monopolist-capitalism and Imperialism, and the recurrent cycle of alternating booms and crises being transmuted into an epoch of General Crisis.

The difference between this conception and that of either automatic collapse or gradualist evolution without " sudden leaps " or " violent transitions " should be too obvious to need labouring.

In considering the epoch of the General Crisis of Capitalism —the epoch whose opening became clearly manifest with the War crisis of 1914—we must remember that it is not merely a crisis of glut and is already more than a general economic crisis. It is a condition of crisis which becomes apparent in every department of social life—a condition in which economic, social, and political crises in each country separately, and in the capitalist world generally, succeed each other, act upon and react against each other, overlap each other and, finally, merge together in a universal condition of chronic crisis. As Lenin and, after him, Stalin, each found it necessary to emphasise, it is a mistake to suppose at any given stage in this process that there is, then and there, *absolutely* " no way out of the crisis " for the bourgeoisie. At the same time, since each and every one of the measures resorted to by the bourgeoisie (tariffs, currency manipulations, " new deals," wars and fascist counter-revolutions) only abate the crisis in one form or place, to intensify it in another form or elsewhere, it is correct to say that there is no final escape from the condition of general crisis possible to bourgeois society. The only way out for " associated humanity " is by the way of proletarian revolution.

. . . .

That the recurring crises (of over-production) which continue to be distinguishable as special phases in the epoch of General Crisis are not mere repetitions of previous crises may be seen from the amazing number and complexity of the subsidiary crises into which their total phenomena can be analysed. Of the " cyclic " crisis of 1929–33 VARGA, in his *Great Crisis* (p. 12), observes :

" Its course was greatly influenced by the *general crisis* of capitalism . . . by the increasingly monopolist character of post-war capitalism, by its intertwining with the *agrarian crisis* . . . by the extraordinary sharp *fall of prices*. . . . Other factors were the measures taken by monopoly capital and its state for the artificial solution of the crisis, which led to considerable delay in the outbreak of the *credit crisis*, and—in the long run— to the prolongation and deepening of the crisis as a whole.

" The final result is that the first *world crisis* in the era of the general crisis of capitalism has proved to be much deeper, of longer duration, and in every respect more devastating than any of the previous cyclic crises. This crisis also reveals some qualitatively new aspects : *currency depreciation* in almost all the capitalist countries, almost universal *non-payment of foreign debts*, and practically complete *cessation of capital export*. These are qualitatively new aspects which were not present in any of the previous crises."—VARGA : *Great Crisis*, pp. 12–13.

It is notorious that in addition to these qualitatively new aspects the old familiar phenomena of crises, masses of unsold commodities, of unemployed production plants and money capital, and of unemployed workers, existed on a *quantitatively* higher scale than ever. To cite an example only of the first (the most elementary) category :

" Tea is not gathered ; rubber trees are not tapped. Whole shiploads of oranges are dumped into the sea in London. Five million hogs were bought by the U.S. Government and destroyed in the autumn of 1933. In Denmark, 1,500 cows were slaughtered, weekly, and converted into fertilisers. In Argentine, hundreds of thousands of older sheep were killed and abandoned to make room for the young ; the cost of transportation to the slaughter-houses would have exceeded the money received for them. And so forth and so on. All this is happening at a time when millions upon millions of unemployed, and their families, are starving and are clad in rags. *Never before in the history of mankind has anything like this ever occurred.*"—VARGA : *Great Crisis*, p. 68.

These evidences of the *persistence* of crises of glut, as well as of the enlarged scale upon which, and the vastly more complicated and drastic character in which they recur are doubly significant. They confirm to the point of amazement the profundity of Marx's analysis of capitalist production and its law of motion ; also, their recurrence derives tenfold importance from the fact that the institution of all the various forms of capitalist monopoly, as also of the protective tariffs, which are, sooner or later, its complement, was impelled, in the first place, by no more urgent motive than the desire to obviate and escape from precisely this recurrance of commercial crises.

Events have proved that Marx and Engels were able to make general predictions which events have justified ; while their bourgeois and petty-bourgeois critics and detractors have been totally at fault. For instance : Engels in a foot-note to Vol. III of *Marx's Capital* (pub. 1894), wrote :

" A change has taken place in the character of com-mercial crises. . . . Since the last great universal crises of 1867, many profound changes have taken place. . . By means of these things ['colossal extension of means of communication,' 'infinitely more and more varied fields for investment of superfluous European capital '] the old breeding-ground of crises and opportunities for their growth have been stimulated or strongly reduced. At the same time competition in the internal market recedes before cartels and trusts, while it is restricted in the international market by protective tariffs, with which all great industrial countries, England excepted, surround themselves. But the protective tariffs are nothing but *preparations for the ultimate general industrial war, which shall decide the supremacy on the world market. Thus every element which works against a repetition of the old crises, carries the germ of a far more tremendous future crisis in itself.*"—ENGELS footnote ; *Capital*, Vol. III, p. 575.

This, at the time, was no more than a deduction, whose worth depended upon the validity of the analysis upon which it was based. That the proof was supplied, theoretically by Lenin, and practically by the phenomena of the world crisis of 1929–33, only the more serves to emphasise the soundness of Engel's deduction, and of Marx's analysis upon which it was based.

.   .   .   .   .

The commercial crisis (which, alternatively, may be called the crisis of glut) is to be understood, not so much as a force in itself, as a " trigger force " which releases an explosion of the contradictions and antagonisms which development in general has been piling up ready for release. The General Crisis of Capitalism must therefore be comprehended from two sides : (a) from the side of the accumulating *potentiality*, and (b) from the side of the concrete, social-historical actualisation of these contradictions and antagonisms.

> " The ultimate cause of all real crises is the poverty and restricted consumption of the masses as compared with the tendency of capitalist production to develop the productive forces in such a way that only the absolute consuming power of society would be their limit."—MARX : *Capital*, Vol. III, p. 568.

This discrepancy between the relatively diminishing power of consumption of the masses and the geometrically expanding social power of production, has, in turn, its ultimate root in the divorce between the actual producer and the means of production from which capitalist production takes historically its rise and which its development widens into an absolute antagonism which embraces directly or indirectly every single member of society. Moreover, since accumulation, (*i.e.*, the conversion of products into means of *Capitalist* production, into means for the purchase and the exploitation of labour-power, into *Capital*) is the law of life, and of growth for capitalist production, and accumulation implies a progressive increase in both the absolute numbers of the proletariat, and the proportion of the proletariat to the numbers included in society as a whole, it follows that this ultimate cause of crises—the limited consuming power of the proletariat and the unlimited expansion of the producing-power of society grows more glaringly obvious and irresistible in its effects with every advance of the productive technique of capitalist society. It does so, in fact, on an ever-expanding scale since every increase in productivity involves both an increase of exploitation—and, therefore, an increase in the (relative) restriction of consumption of the proletariat —and also a change in the organic composition of capital— the respective proportions of *constant* (that expended in means of production) to *variable* (that expended in wages) in the total capital—which, by reducing the volume of labour-power required in proportion to the volume of capital still further limits the consuming power of the masses ; becoming, in time, a tendency to *absolutely* decrease it.

Thus every advance of capitalism technically is a retro-gression socially, and a source of intensifying antagonisms for which crises of glut serve both as *expressions* and as *safety valves* ! Every crisis is a minor explosion which (by destroying a mass of relatively superfluous values and use-values,—as well as capital) relieves the strain upon capitalist production—at the expense of the members of society—and permits it to make a fresh start *on a higher level of production*.

The reasoning which sees in the general Crisis of Capitalism an analogous explosion of accumulated potentials of antag-onism raised to its highest power by the historical develop-ment to its highest power, likewise of the basis antagonism-relation from which the whole movement of capitalist society —economical and historical—takes its rise ; and which infers, therefore, that crisis on this universal scale must engender such a quantity and quality of destructive reactions in between the various strata, divisions, and classes of society as is bound to be followed by the transition of *society* to a new start on a higher plane, is therefore logically unimpeachable.

And this becomes all the more sure and certain the more the process of the *becoming* of the general crisis is observed in its concrete historical actuality.

The passage of capitalism into its monopolistic phase, for example, has entailed an increase in a geometrical ratio of the progressive relative and absolute reduction of the con-suming power of society which we saw to be implicit in capitalism from the start. Not only does monopoly capitalism make possible the depression of wages to their utmost economic limit, it creates, in the army of the unemployed and their dependants an increasing army of the pauperised whose level of consumption is forced down to below even physically-minimal limits. More than that, since monopoly capital makes possible a quasi-permanent buying (of raw materials, etc.) *below even their values*—especially in the case of agricultural and colonial produce—and simultaneously

a quasi-permanent *selling above their values* of its manufactures, monopoly capital extends its exploitation to, and
correspondingly depresses the consuming power of virtually
the whole of the not-yet proletarianised small producers,
whole strata of the middle and professional classes, and,
as well, the whole economy of colonial areas and all dependant
thereupon. Thus monopoly capitalism combines the maximum attainable productive power with the maximum
attainable reduction of the consuming power of the members
of society—and this in spite of the insane luxury spending it
makes possible for members of the exploiting financial
oligarchy and their beneficiaries and hangers-on.

It is self-evident that in these conditions crises such as
those of 1929–33 cannot be followed, as "normal" crises can,
by a depression which quickens into brisk trade rising to
a boom followed by a return of the crisis. The crisis of a
special kind cannot fail to be followed by a depression of
a special kind, and culminate in *a return of the crisis with no
period of boom intervening*, except in so far as a localised and
relative " boom " may be induced by recourse to war.

.   .   .   .   .

The inevitability of War is immanent in the imperialism
which is the political expression of monopoly-capitalism.
Equally inevitable is the latent or actual revolt of the
subjected and exploited colonial peoples. Still more inevitable is the revolt of the proletariat in each and every one
of its modes of manifestation from the " industrial mutiny "
of the strike to open revolutionary struggle in arms. That
these are no mere *a priori* deductions the history of the era
of the General Crisis has already proved. The World-war
of 1914 both saved capitalist society and commenced its
destruction. The uprising of the colonial peoples has been
manifested all round the world, but most of all in the undying
struggle of the Chinese workers and peasants which has
gathered force and volume, and ascended through a whole
historical series of transmutations to emerge finally as the
unconquered and unconquerable fight for a Soviet China.
The proletarian revolution has advanced from the realm of
prophecy and made itself manifest in the Bolshevik
Revolution, in the invincible U.S.S.R., and in the triumphant
accomplishment under the leadership of Lenin (the greatest
of all disciples of Marx and Engels) and of Stalin (the best
and greatest pupil of Lenin), of the transition from a shattered
bourgeois economy mixed with archaic survivals of pre-

bourgeois economy to a unified, consolidated, and swiftly expanding Socialist economy.

All these things add their quota to the intensification of the General Crisis with which capitalism is faced. As its need for fresh markets and wider areas of exploitation grows hourly nearer to desperation pitch the more it is brought concretely against the fact that the victory of the proletarian revolution in the U.S.S.R., the spread of the revolutionary struggle in China, and its development more and more into a specifically proletarian (as well as peasant) *Communist* revolutionary struggle ; each separately means, and still more both together, mean, that for Capitalism the world has shrunk just when it most needs that it should expand to twice its size. And with these struggles, too, grows throughout the whole area of capitalism the consolidation and intensification of the struggle of the increasingly revolutionary proletariat.

There is no need here, nor would it be part of our purpose to recite in all their multitudinous variety the proofs of the growing radicalisation of the proletariat extensively and intensively. It suffices for our purposes to cite the fact that the phenomena of Fascism are explicable on no other ground than the growing need confronting the financial oligarchy to proceed to ever more drastic methods to hold in check the rising tide of proletarian revolution.

Every day makes it clearer that the moving words with which Marx vindicated the heroic Commune of Paris in 1871, and hurled his devastating defiance against its exterminators, have an application far wider than that for which they were framed :

" After Whit Sunday, 1871, there can be neither peace nor truce possible between the working-men . . . and the appropriators of their produce. . . . The battle must break out again and again in ever-growing dimensions, and there can be no doubt as to who will be the victor in the end—the appropriating few, or the immense working majority . . .

" Whenever, in whatever shape, and under whatever conditions the class struggle obtains any consistency, it is but natural that members of our association should stand in the foreground. The soil out of which it grows is modern society itself. It cannot be stamped out by any amount of carnage. To stamp it out the Government would have to stamp out the despotism of Capital

over labour—the condition of their own parasitical
existence."—MARX : *Civil War in France*, p. 63.

.   .   .   .   .

Marx's analysis of capitalist-production is, as we have
shown, rigidly materialist in its *objectivity*, and scrupulously
dialectic in its consistent determination to see every fact in
its actual connections, and from every possible side—to see
every relation alike as it is in itself, and as a transitory phase
in the total development process of History, and, through
History, of Nature.   Marx's analysis of the relations of
capitalist-production, in themselves, reveals accordingly at
every stage, both the historical grounds from which each
relation arose, and the historical movement of which it constitutes a determinent.   Thus his analysis has the historical
movement of Society as its primary presupposition, continually reproduces the *movement* of history in the development of its categories and finally leads back to history as
the outcome of its own process.   A brief glance at the more
general aspects of Marx's celebrated—but almost invariably
mis-represented—" materialist conception of history " is
therefore necessary to complete our survey of his analysis of
the law of motion of capitalist society, since this, on Marx's
own showing, was a specific stage in the motion of history as
a whole.

.   .   .   .   .

THE LAW OF MOTION IN HISTORY.

In the introduction to his *Critique of Political Economy*
Marx gives the fullest formal statement he ever made of his
conception of history.   He explains that in the course of
his studies for his university diploma, and particularly in
consequence of his examination of Hegel's *Philosophy of Law*,
he came to the conclusion that :

> " legal relations and forms of the State can neither be
> understood in themselves, nor explained by the so-called
> general progress of the human mind.   They are rooted
> in the material life-conditions of what Hegel, after the
> fashion of the eighteenth century French and English
> philosophers, comprised under the name of ' civil
> society.' "—MARX : *Critique*, Intro.

He explains that the general conclusion at which he
arrived—and which his " friend Frederick Engels had also
reached independently "—a conclusion which " served as
a guiding clue " in all his studies in political economy was
" the following," which is set out as he gives it below.

[Readers will note the resemblances to parallel passages in the *Theses on Feuerbach*, the *German Ideology* and the *Communist Manifesto*. The paragraphs have been numbered for convenience of reference] :—

(1) " In the social production of their means of life, human beings enter into definite and necessary relation*s* which are independent of their will : production *relations* which correspond to a definite stage in the development of their productive *forces*. The *totality* of these production relations constitutes the *economic structure* of society. the *real basis* upon which a legal and political *superstructure* arises, and to which definite forms of *social consciousness* correspond.

(2) " The mode of production of the material means of life *determines*, in general, the social, political, and intellectual processes of life. It is not the consciousness of human beings which determines their existence, it is their social existence which determines their consciousness.

(3) " At a certain stage of their development the material productive forces of society *come into conflict with* the existing production relationships. Or, what is a legal expression for the same thing, with the property relationships within which they have hitherto moved. From forms of development of the productive forces those relationships turn into fetters upon them. *A period of social revolution then begins*.

(4) " With the change in the *economic foundation* the whole gigantic *superstructure* is more or less rapidly transformed. In considering such transformations we must always distinguish between the *material changes* in the economic conditions of production (changes which can be determined with the precision of natural science), and the legal, political, religious, æsthetic, or philosophic, in short, *ideological forms* in which human beings *become conscious of this conflict* and fight it out to an issue.

(5) " Just as little as we can judge an individual by what he thinks of himself, just so little can we appraise such a revolutionary epoch in accordance with its own consciousness of itself. On the contrary, we have to explain the consciousness as the outcome of the contradictions of material life, of the conflict existing between social productive forces and production relationships.

(6) " No social order is destroyed until all the pro-

duction forces for which it gives scope have been developed : new and higher production relations cannot appear until the material conditions for their existence have ripened within the womb of the old social order. Therefore mankind in general never sets itself problems it cannot solve : since, looked at more closely, we always find that the problem itself arises only when the material conditions for its solution exist, or at least, are already in process of formation.

(7) " We can, in broad outline, designate the Asiatic, the Classical, the Feudal, and the modern Bourgeois forms of production as progessive epochs in the economic formation of society.

(8) " The bourgeois production relations are the final antagonistic form in the development of social production—antagonistic, not in the sense of antagonism between individuals, but one inherent in the life conditions and social circumstances of the individuals, at the time when the productive forces developing in the womb of bourgeois society are creating the material conditions for the solution of that antagonism.

(9) " *This social formation, therefore, constitutes the closing chapter of the prehistoric stage of human society.—*MARX : *Critique of Political Economy*, Introduction.

In considering this, the fullest formal statement of their materialist conception of history made by Marx and Engels, the first fact to notice is its date. It was, Marx says, drawn up at about the time the *German Ideology* was written, namely, in 1845–6—*before* both the *Poverty of Philosophy* and the *Communist Manifesto*.

This fact is important from several points of view. In the first place it disposes completely of the notion that the Marxian theoretical system was born of prolonged burrowing in the British Museum—that it was wholly an academic construction derived from books. It was, in fact, begotten in the case of both Marx and Engels under pressure of the actual practical problems of the Socialist and Communist movements—as these again were special detail components of the revolutionary struggles of their time.

In the second place, the fact of its practical origin and purpose gives an entirely different perspective to this famous statement itself. Its *dialectical movement* leaps at once to the comprehension. It is not in the least (as is commonly supposed by critics and simplifiers) a *scheme* for writers of textbooks of Universal History. It is the statement of the *law of motion* of human society for *practical use*. The closing clause (9)—which is usually omitted in quotation—reveals the standpoint of the author in noon-day clarity. The whole period of human history, recorded and unrecorded, is treated as a *process of transition* from the Natural Animal Man to the fully developed Socialised Human Being of the classless, Communist society of the future ; which society, *because* it has eliminated its internal antagonisms, will be able to " command its fate " in a progressively increasing degree. Unless this basic *dialectical movement* is grasped, the whole conception is falsified.

Moreover, once this statement is viewed in this light its rigidly *scientific* method becomes clear : Marx deals with the *past* only so far as it is under a variety of historically begotten disguises *active* in the present. He indicates " broadly " the various economic " formations " which have preceded the present " bourgeois " formation as stages in the development of the " economic basis " of society, and it is in the sequence of these stages that the significance of the conception lies.

Marx's analysis begins with the concrete facts of present-day society. It finds in existence a fact of class conflict, and a body of revolutionary hopes and aspirations faced by a body of conservative and counter-revolutionary resistances thereto. These phenomena it traces to their common root in the *economic formation* of society. This, in turn, is traced to its historical causation in the previous economic formation —feudal society with its " civil " consequences ; and this, in turn, is seen to have likewise been an historical product.

The earlier periods—the " classic "—and the " Asiatic "— are included since, even in Marx's day, there was historical evidence sufficient to indicate that they had existed. But no special theory is formulated as to their historical transmutation in detail, nor is any theory indicated as to the formation stages in the period of history prior to historic record. It was later, *much* later, that the researches of Darwin and the anthropologists, Bachofen, Mannhardt, Morgan, Tylor, and Frazer, to name no more of a host, *provided the proof* of the Marxian thesis by proving that there had been a series of formation stages in the historical progression of human society from its most primitive beginnings up to the stage of " civilisation."

Marx's conception of history as formulated in his *Critique* is distinguished from all preceding and alternative conceptions of the historical *process*, by the qualities noted by Lenin (see his *Teachings of Karl Marx*, Works, Vol. XVIII). Firstly, it presents history as a definite *process* ; secondly, it considers the social activity of mankind as a *totality* of opposing tendencies ; thirdly, it traces these oppositions to their objective roots. It was thus " a consistent extension of Materialism to the domain of social phenomena " :—

> " At best, pre-Marxist ' sociology ' and historiography gave an accumulation of raw facts collected at random, and a description of separate sides of the historic process. . . . Discarding subjectivism and freewill in the choice and the interpretation of the various " dominant " ideas, demonstrating that all ideas and tendencies, without exception, have their roots in the . . . material forces of production, Marxism pointed the way to a comprehensive, and all-embracing, study of the rise, development, and decay of socio-economic *structures*."—LENIN, *loc. cit.*

It is self-evident that history as a *record* is a record of what men have done : of what has been done to men by men. It is also, so far as the facts are available, a record of what they have tried to accomplish—only too often without success. But if that is all history is, the ironical legend told by Anatole France becomes a most undeniable, as well as most melancholy, truth. Anatole France tells how an Oriental potentate caused his wise men to write the history of the whole world in 10,000 volumes. Then he ordered its compression successively into 1000, 100, then ten volumes, and then into one volume. Finally he ordered its compression into one sentence, and received in due course, this for his answer :—

> " They were born ; They suffered ; They died."

And, indeed, if the Dialectical Materialist conception of a *positive outcome* of the historical process itself be rejected, that is all that history has to teach. In bourgeois hands history is truly a " dismal science "—at best a chronicle of scandals, at worst a nightmare record of ghastly failures.

Marxism lifts the whole subject above this pessimism and futility. For one thing it gives a *reason* for the hopes and strivings of men. It faces the facts of oppression and crime ; but in doing so it gives a courage that enables the observer to see also their causes and above all their consequences ; and in these their cure—the foundation fact upon which a larger, saner, scientific optimism may rest secure.

The Marxian conception of history is notable, too, in that it is the first conception of history to give the mass of mankind the centre of the stage as the chief protagonist in the drama. All other conceptions bring in the " mob " merely as does a melodrama ; to provide an animated chorus of approval for, and a doltish, uncouth background to, the airs, graces, deeds, and posturings of the " star " performers— the " great " men. For Marxism history is what the *whole* of mankind has done, *not* only a few of them.

If it be examined carefully it will be seen that the Marxian conception of history pointedly discriminates two active sides in the structure of society—the *economic* structure, the " basis," and the *political* and *ideological* structure, the "superstructure." These in turn have *opposite* modes of movement, of advance. The economic basis grows by simple accretion, by the gradual addition of detailed alterations, which, infinitesimal in themselves, none the less, in time, become apparent as a *qualitative* change in the basis of society.

To take an illustration from the technological side of the economic basis of capitalism : Watt's steam engine was not so great an alteration of Newcomen's engine, or Trevithick's, as to call for any very great comment. Yet, at that time, and in the then existing circumstances, it made all the difference. The factory system was becoming more and more widespread. Machines driven by wind, water, horse, and man-power were coming more and more into use, and to make those machines coal was increasingly in demand. Coal-getting presented the problem of water in the pit and of its extraction. Watt's steam-engine was first invented as an *improved* variety of pumping engine. It needed little alteration to become a new source of motive power which qualitatively transformed a creeping advance into a break-neck industrial "revolution."

With regard to political, legal and moral changes quite a different process is to be observed. Here it is not a question of what any one man may change if he is so minded—as is the case with technological processes—it is a question of changes in codes and rules to which *all* must submit. Put thus it becomes obvious that questions of social change involving alterations in the *basic accepted* principles in government, law and morals—and also in the " minor morals " of etiquette and " taste "—cannot help but be fought out in the end as

" party questions," as questions of positive " Right "—as
questions in which it is self-delusion and " sentimentality to
imagine that quarter can be either given or taken." (BERNARD
SHAW.)

For instance : in Europe at the close of the Middle Ages
there arose the question of what, if any, were the proper
limits to the authority of the Papacy. This in the then prevailing state of Europe involved the practical question as to
which of *two* governments—that of the Church and that of
the State—had the prior claim to the obedience of the
individual. And, since this raised the further question—
what authority could decide between the rival claimants ?
there arose, in practice, though in a disguised form, the
claim of the individual to judge, not only as between Church
authority and State authority, but between all public
authority and the authority of the *individual* conscience.

It is a matter of history that this " Reformation " struggle
was fought out as a revolutionary struggle—with fierce
warfare, bloodshed, and savage coercion on both sides. It
is also a matter of history that it did not end until the whole
" ideological superstructure " of society had been changed.
That, as the struggle was actually fought out, the text of
the Bible and its interpretation became an immediate point
of contention, nobody denies. But *why* did the text of a
Bible whose canon was closed in the Fourth century become
suddenly a bone of contention on an all-European scale in
the Fifteenth and Sixteenth centuries ? Where had the
problem been in the intervening centuries ?

The questions raised in the Reformation struggle had been
raised, all of them, by different individuals as speculative
questions long before. Some of them had been raised by
heretical sects which had been crushed. So for the matter of
that had the steam-engine been invented *in principle*, many
times before Watt. Why did these questions raised in the
Reformation suddenly flare up into great party issues ?
Why were they not only fought out through a whole epoch
of revolution and counter-revolution, but so raised that
they culminated in the irony of " Counter-Reformation "—
the Catholic Church saving itself from destruction in those
lands where it retained its political dominance and temporal
power, by a voluntary self-criticism and purgation ?

No answer is possible except the one supplied by Marx's
materialist conception of history, which is revolutionary and
epoch-making precisely because it explains (what all alterna-

z

tive conceptions fail to explain) not only the continuity of history, but its discontinuity. Its dialectic quality lies in just this pivotal fact—*it explains the continuity from the discontinuity, and the discontinuity from the continuity*.

It is here more than anywhere that the " popular explainers " of Marxism in Britain have worked their worst mischief and given excuses for the whole brood of revisers, re-interpreters, and bringers-up-to-date. They have exhausted Marx's conception of its *dialectic*, and have turned it into either a simple continuation of the mechanical materialism of the eighteenth century or a dogmatic supplement to the eclectic nature-materialism of the nineteenth century.

The formulation of his conception of history given by Marx in the *Critique* is, in fact, their complete refutation in advance. It is nothing less than *classic* in its importance as a demonstration of the materialism in Marx's *dialectic*, and the dialectic in Marx's *Materialism*.

All materialism *begins* with the fact that men's ideas are *reflections*—are derived from objective material reality. That Marx's conception *includes* this elementary and basic form of Materialism is as obvious as is the fact that he gives a prominence never previously given to economic facts as the salient feature in that material Reality. But Marx's conception goes very far indeed beyond that elementary beginning. The " explainers " who see in it nothing beyond the fact that (in Ramsay MacDonald's phrase) " every department of life is *chained* to economics," not only thereby fail to grasp the real Marxism in the conception, but in practice debase it to the level of Ramsay MacDonald—than which no crime could be greater.

Marx's revolution in *Materialist doctrine* consisted in nothing less than an immense quantitative extension of (with its concomitant qualitative change in) the *material Reality* from which he explained men's ideas, and Thought-activity generally. The eighteenth-century materialists had taken into account only the phenomena of external and internal Nature, and those of personal association. The nature-materialists merely super-added (without homologating) the abstract conception of " evolution." *Marx saw that social relations were positive material facts which, developing in accordance with their own special law, not only operated as determinants in themselves, but radically transformed and re-transformed the operative significance of the phenomena of Nature and of association.*

This not only revolutionises the doctrine of Materialism : it provides a basis for the complete and final refutation of all Idealism. Most of all, in making Materialism *dialectic* it not only reduced the phenomena of social revolution to terms of the general law of social evolution, but also in providing an objective basis for the unification of Theory and Practice, it showed how the practice of revolutionary struggle could be rationally justified and scientifically guided. It is, in fact, here, in the classic formulation of his conception of history, that Marx's whole Theory and Practice, and those of the Marxism he and Engels between them inspired, are shown in their inseparable *unity*. Implicit in its compact formula is the whole of *Dialectical Materialism*, objective and subjective.

To realise its liberating force it must be viewed from a whole series of angles. Firstly, in its most general aspect it completely revolutionises the conception of the relation between the Individual and Society.

All previous materialists had conceived human society as a simple aggregation of human beings, and had, accordingly, seen in history nothing beyond a multiple of the phenomena of individual behaviour. On this view, which is substantially the view of all non-Marxist historians and sociologists, Society is the product of the aggregation of independently originating individuals : on Marx's view the individual is the *product* of Society, and not its raw material.

If the formulation quoted from the *Critique* (clause 1) be examined it will be perceived that Marx takes as his starting point production-*relations*. Men *enter* into these relations " independent of their will," and it is these *relations* which in their totality, constitute the *real* basis of society. It takes, perhaps, an effort to grasp the seeming paradox that relations *between* men must be conceived as logically and historically antecedent to the men themselves. But once it is seen that Marx is analysing *that which exists here and now*, and is reaching his conception of the Past by means of this analysis of the Present, it becomes obvious that to every man now living the social relations into which he enters in the course of " making his living " are most obviously things which pre-existed before him. If this analysis be carried back to its logical conclusion we reach the obvious " poser " : what about the *first* men ? As we saw earlier the answer is a dialectical one : *the first men were not men* ! Nature-evolved anthropoids, Not - Yet - Men, by their necessity - begotten struggle with Nature, converted themselves into men, and their inter-relation into a social one by *production-activity*. And this production-activity—this result-begetting, antagonistic inter-relation between Man and Nature—is the general source and origin of the whole movement of history, as it is also, in specific stages of formation, the *basis* of each and every historic epoch.

But Marx's conception is not limited to formulating the Law of Motion of human society in general—though, if the critics had perceived that what Marx formulated was a law of *motion* we might have been spared many follies. Marx discriminated this Law not only into its basic dialectical determinants, but also into its whole series of determined phases. Not the abstract law in general, but the specific, concrete law of the *transformation* of this motion, of the transition from epoch to epoch in history—the Law of Motion in detail, the specific Law of Social Revolution, is the outstanding feature of Marx's conception of history.

The key to the whole conception lies in the notion of distinct *formation-stages*—each with its own specific law of motion, its distinguishing dialectic. Marx distinguishes " broadly " (clause 7) four main stages : the Asiatic, the Classic, the Feudal, and the modern Bourgeois modes of production as " progressive epochs in the economic formation of society." And his minute analysis of the last of these stages gives us a clear understanding of his conception of what constituted a formation stage, and in what relation the stage stands in the sequence as a whole. As we have seen, capitalist production arises as a specifically determined form of commodity production and begets in its development the specific capitalist variety of money economy, which in turn is a special form of exchange economy. Each stage is linked to each ; each in its turn reacts upon and in time transforms the previously begotten stage ; all grow out of " natural " economy (the simple production of use-values for direct consumption), and all culminate in the complex hierarchy of cyclic movements of Capitalist economy as a whole. And this in turn completes its own self-expanding movement only to reach a situation in which it must be superseded by a return to Nature Economy on an enormously higher and more extensive scale.

With the aid of this conception it becomes possible to unriddle all the " mysteries "—of the rise and fall of nations, empires, etc.—which have baffled historical speculation.

Each formation stage in succession is relatively stable within itself. While its potentialities are being developed history in the *real* sense seems to have come to a stop. Yet this very stability is the chief promoting cause of the economic development which in the end breaks up the society and brings a new formation stage to birth.

In Marx's *Capital* the dialectical movement of the economic basis of capitalist society is analysed in detail and revealed in its totality ; and thereby a flood of light is thrown upon the root causation both of the stability of the preceding formation stages and of their instability. That Marx's conviction of the inevitability of a proletarian revolution had its roots in his Dialectic has more than once been urged as an objection against it. His reply, a complete and final one, would have been that the Dialectic is in the objective facts : that all he did was to bring it into the light of day. It was not Marx who decreed that it should be no more possible to explain Human Society in terms of a universal Law of Nature, than it is to explain biological phenomena in terms of chemistry or physical phenomena in terms of biology. It is the differences between phenomena which are the tangible and immediate facts with which objective practice has to deal : while their common resemblance and ultimate identity is only established after practice has revealed their mutual transformability in active interaction.

That Feudal Society was different from Bourgeois society was a fact of observation. That Bourgeois society had in fact grown out of Feudal society was a fact of record. That which was not apparent on the surface, nor given in the records was just the law of *the transformation* of the one into the other. The static view which conceived society as totally disintegrated by a revolution and restarted thereafter, and the purely abstract " evolutionary " view which affirmed solely that the new society was only the old society in a new shape were both refuted by Marx's conception. And they were refuted by being *synthetised*. The old society was broken up (as to its superstructure, its *conditions* of production), the old society was continued unbroken (as to its *forces of production*) in the new society. By discriminating the " unity " of the abstract concept " Society " into the concrete and specific antagonism of economic basis and legal and political superstructure (the *forces* of production and the *conditions* of production) Marx was able to formulate the law of social *movement*, transformation, and revolution. Marx's optimism in regard to the proletarian revolution was no *a priori* guess or sentimental projection. It rested and rests upon the objective validity of his analysis of the pre-requisites for and the consequent movement of capitalist production. Herein Marx revealed not only how and why capitalist production originated in the bourgeois production begotten *within* Feudal society ; but how and why Feudal society broke up to give place to bourgeois society. And in thus revealing the origin of bourgeois society Marx made its ending foreseeable and foreseen.

Marx's conception of history is indeed most notable on this, its most neglected side—its formulation of the Law of Revolution and the dialectic thereof. If the quotation from the *Critique* be examined it will be seen that out of nine clauses all but the first two deal with the revolutionary transformation of Society. Before Marx revolutions could be explained materialistically only as *interruptions* of the normal course of social development (or, alternatively, as returns to normality compelled by a deviation from Natural Law). Only idealistically could revolutions be brought within the compass of a general law—by treating them as products of the evolution of ideas. Marx was the first, and stands out as the only theorist who has adequately comprehended both the normal growth of society and its periodical revolutionary transformation within the compass of a single generalisation.

The consequences of this law for practice are simply enormous. On the one hand the need to treat society as a *process* (and not simply as a " structure ") cuts the ground from under the feet of all conservatism and all dogmatism *a priori.* Also it becomes impossible to treat society as a closed mechanism whose outcome is fore-ordained in the nature of its structural inter-relations. And it is no less impossible to treat society as a purely relative fact—a *mere* expression of private will and consciousness. Society—that which moves in history—is an objective fact, and it has structure, which must be understood before the individuals comprising society can be understood. But this structure is both the product of a dialectical process and the starting-point for a fresh development. That Society " evolves " from revolution to revolution is the first and most basic deduction from Marx's Law of Motion of Society.

But just precisely because Marx's conception destroys conservatism (the theory that society cannot fundamentally be altered) on the one side, and utopianism (the theory that Society can be revolutionised at will) on the other, it is the conception which vindicates a scientifically based revolutionary optimism to the full. Since a society (see clause 6) is never broken up until all the productive forces of which it is capable have been developed it follows that any general movement to revolutionise society is in itself evidence that the change can be made—that objective realities exist corresponding to the aspirations and hopes of the revolutionary class and party.

It is not, it will be perceived, Marx's notion that (for instance) the *idea of Socialism* will be begotten *automatically* in the heads of each and every individual proletarian. Ideas are engendered and develop necessarily in social intercourse, and therefore follow within limits their own law of development. But for the idea to arise in the first place, and to become general in the second place, an objective social reality must exist from which the idea has arisen. There must exist, and be felt to exist, a *social problem* for which a solution must be found—and it is under the promptings of the urgency of the problem as well as their cogency and applicability to the *needs* viewed in the light of practical everyday reality that ideas spread and develop into " forms of public opinion."

It was, in point of fact, as Engels notes, *not* the proletariat, but the intellectuals of the aristocracy and the bourgeoisie, who first formulated the general conception of Socialism as an alternative to the bourgeois order. Only *after* capitalist society had reached full maturity and had, therefore, revealed its inner contradictions in full force, did Socialism begin to spread among the proletariat. Conversely : although the idea of Socialism is by no means begotten *automatically* in the heads of the proletariat (and as soon as they become proletarians), there is borne in upon the proletarians—and that increasingly—the need to struggle first for immediate betterment, then ultimately for emancipation. Capitalism thus, while it does not automatically " put Socialism into the heads " of the proletariat, does, and that with ever-increasing urgency, create a series of problems for which a Socialist and Communist proletarian revolution is objectively the *only* final solution. And when the recognition of this fact (however vaguely and imperfectly as to details) becomes widespread among the proletariat it may be taken as proved that the objective possibility of the new social order exists.

THE CONCEPT OF " CLASS " IN MARXISM.

It is a noteworthy fact that in the formulation of the materialist conception of history quoted above Marx gives no " definition " of a *class*. This has been urged against the theory as a " weakness "—a " fatal omission." Such an objection would have left Marx himself speechless with amazement. He could but have pointed to the fact that in his formulation he had spoken of " property relationships," and had treated them as the reflex equivalents of " production relationships." Quite obviously, to anyone seriously bent upon grasping the conception, "class divisions" are *objectively* determined differentiations within a given social formation.

His conception of " class " and that of Engels is sufficiently indicated in their general argument :

" The history of all hitherto existing society [Engels adds : " all *written* history, that is "] is the history of class-struggles.

" Freeman and slave, patrician and plebeian, lord and serf, guildmaster and journeymen, in a word, oppressor and oppressed, stood in constant opposition to one another, carried on an uninterrupted, now hidden, now open fight, a fight that each time ended either in the revolutionary reconstruction of society at large, or *in the common ruin of the contending classes*."—MARX and ENGELS : *Communist Manifesto*, p. 10.

They go on to speak of the earlier epochs, in each of which there was a " manifold gradation of social rank." They add :

" Modern bourgeois society that has sprouted from the ruins of feudal society has not done away with class antagonisms. It has but established new classes, new conditions of oppression, new forms of struggle in place of the old ones."—MARX and ENGELS : *ibid.*

They note that in each of these epochs there existed in all classes " subordinate gradations," a fact which plays a big part (as we shall see) in the dialectic of class development.

The following extract (from Marx's *Eighteenth Brumaire*) leaves no room for doubt as to the basic meaning of the term " class " and its relation to the prevailing mode of production on the one side, and the conventional social stratification on the other. Marx is speaking of the French peasant proprietors :

"' Throughout the country, they live in almost identical conditions, but enter very little into relationships with each other. Their mode of production, instead of bringing them mutually into contact, *isolates them*. This isolation, moreover, is intensified by the inadequacy of the means of communication in France (1852), and by the peasants' own poverty. Their farms are so small that there is practically no room for division of labour, no chance for scientific agriculture. Among the peasantry therefore there is no possibility of manifoldness in development, no differentiation in talents, no wealth of social relationships. Each family is almost self-sufficing ; producing as it does the greater part of its requirements from its own plot of land, and thus providing itself with the necessaries of life through an intercourse with Nature rather than by means of social interchange. Here is one small plot of land, with one peasant farmer and his family ; there is another plot of land, and another peasant with a wife and children. A score or two of these atoms make up a village ; a few score villages make up a Department. In this way, by the simple addition of identical entities, the mass of the French nation is made up—much as a number of potatoes enclosed in a sack constitute a sack of potatoes.

" In so far as millions of families live in production relations which *distinguish their mode of life, their interests, and their culture* from those of other classes, and set them more or less in opposition to other classes, these peasant families *form a class*. But in so far as they are united by ties of simple propinquity and so far as their identity of interests has as yet failed to find expression in a national association, in a *community*, they do *not* form a class. Thus it is that they are unable to assert their class interests in their own name, whether through parliament or a congress. They cannot represent themselves : they must be represented."—MARX : *Eighteenth Brumaire*, Chap. VII.

This gives a description which will serve admirably for all the practical purposes of a definition—" production relations " which *separate* the interests, mode of life and *culture* of a " class " from those of the rest of society, also *unite* the members of the class together ; these are the positive and negative poles in the objective determination of a *class*.

It is here, precisely, that Marx and Engels made their advance upon all previous theories of society. Many had seen, indeed, it had been impossible not to see, the *negative*

or relative sense of the term " *class* of the community."
What had never before been grasped had been the historical,
objective basis alike of society itself and of the class inter-
relations within societies. From a purely relative descriptive
category (as with the libertarian bourgeois writers), and an
arbitrary legalistic category of fixed status (as with the feudal
legalists and their descendants, the bourgeois exponents of
absolute rights, legal and moral), Marx and Engels revolutionised the conception into one of *dynamic* and dialectically
developing relations of men to the basic production-process
which conditioned the activity, and therefore the development, alike of society as a whole, and of each individual and
sub-grouping within the social whole.

The difference this makes for practical understanding, and
for the practical use of concepts reached by the understanding,
is incalculable—it is " *revolutionary.*" It permits of the
concept that classes have a specific historical growth and
mode of self-development, of transmutation. It permits an
understanding of the historically developing transmutation of
the relation between the individual and society on the one
side, and the individual and the class on the other. It permits,
above all, of the concept of society developing *in consequence
of* class struggles—and not, as the bourgeois standpoint
demands, being *prevented from developing* by class antagonisms.

Above all, it permits of a solution of the riddle which has
baffled all the bourgeois legalists and moralists—the riddle
presented by the contradictions and disparities of the
whole arcana of " Rights " which philosophies of Law and
Morals seek to elucidate. That all " Right " is ultimately
one in essence, as is its reflex-opposite " Wrong," is a fact to
which language testifies, though, paradoxically, *only dumbly.*
The facts of actual life, on the contrary, present that bewilderment of contradictions between Public and Private right,
the rights of the State and of the Individual, the rights of
Property and the rights of those dispossessed of property,
the Right contemplated by Law, and the Right which is the
subject-matter of morals. All these, with the conflict between
the Right of secular conduct and the Righteousness of
Theology, form for bourgeois speculation an *imbroglio* of
mysteries before which speculation recoils baffled. Bourgeois
speculation either abandons the problem as beyond solution
—and hands it over to the mystics—or it seeks to deny its
existence, either by the brazen affirmation, falsified in the

very act of its assertion that " Everybody knows right from wrong ! "—or by the cynical " modernist " flippancy that " Each man makes his own morality for himself as he goes along."

.   .   .   .   .

The matter becomes simple when the Dialectical Materialist approach makes it so. Moral judgments are the application to social institutions and conduct of a standard of valuation derived from actual practical production technique. " Right " is conduct which does, and " wrong " is that which does not produce a result desired. Given a positive conception of society, and social conduct can be valued as to the desirability of the results likely to follow from a persistence therein ; can, that is to say, be valued as to its adequacy to produce a definitely desired end, from as many different points of view as there are differences of relation within society. That is the simple, positive and scientifically *usable* conception whereby Marx and Engels solved the " problem of Morals and Law " which had baffled, *and still baffles*, all speculation which operates from the bourgeois, or the supernaturalist standpoint.

Let it be observed, in passing, how utterly incapable of comprehending the essence of Marxism bourgeois critics are rendered by the myopia inseparable from their standpoint. The favourite " objection " raised by bourgeois critics to Marxism (Wickham Steed, ex-editor of *The Times*, is the latest) is that it "*does not allow for the moral sense in Man !* " In point of fact, it is the *only* conception of human society which both " allows " for and *explains* this Moral Sense, in such a way that it can be conceived as a practical fact and *used* for the ends of real life. Once it is perceived that the individual human being is not only a " unit " in a social aggregate, but an *active* detail in a *developing* plexus of activity—that in this development polar oppositions are inseparable and dynamically inter-related, so that the individual aforesaid is *also*, and more immediately, a unit in a sub-society, a " class," it becomes plain why in all class-divided society there is found, not only an inevitable variety of particular interpretations of general moral conceptions, but also the direct opposition of antagonised conceptions of basic moral principle—of moral standpoints. In a class-divided society there are, and must be, *as many positive moralities as there are classes*. That is why class struggles in their full development permit of no compromise : that is why they must be fought out to a finish. The *objective, social structure creates the antagonism*

DIALECTICS : THE LOGIC OF MARXISM

which the individuals and classes do but express. Only when that structure has been transmuted *as a whole* can the antagonism cease to find expression in one form or another.

The basic fact to begin with is that every particular society that has existed, or that can exist, is in its origin and essence *an economic creation*—not an inter-relation into which men enter because they *choose* to do so when " free " to do otherwise. It is a fact created by the physical, natural, inescapable *needs* of man in his bodily organisation, plus the further fact of practical experience, that once he has entered into active production inter-relations with his fellow human beings, a man becomes so *changed* in essential respects that he is thereafter incapable of returning to a " state of Nature," however much he may imagine himself able to do so.

It is not, as bourgeois theory supposed, that men " naturally free " agreed to part with a measure of their " natural liberties " to enjoy the advantages of association. The actual practical, demonstrable, historical fact is the reverse : animal-" Men," *forced* by Nature, associated because *not otherwise could they exist*. It is the *association* in a *production-relation*, an " economic " society, which *creates* all the *freedom* (i.e., from the " tyranny " of Nature) that Man as *Man* possesses.

Again : the range of moral choice practically achievable by a given individual at a given time is determined within two limits : (*a*) the power of control over Nature wielded by the society as a whole ; (*b*) the degree to which this power is at the personal disposal of the individual in question. Society exists, basically, as an association of men for the common purpose of *exploiting Nature*, and that fact persists, and must persist, as the basic fact of all human society whatsoever. But in a whole series of different stages in the development of the collective *exploitation of Nature* it has been possible, and is actually the case, that the " lion's share " of the result has gone to one section of society, with the further result that the remaining section has been in fact little if at all better off. Indeed, whole strata, in whole periods, have been relatively and positively *worse off* than if they had been animals. It is this fact (*a*) that the exploitation of Nature becomes historically transmuted into the exploitation of men by men in society and (*b*) that the exploited are at one and the same time physically, mentally, and psychologically incapable of living *apart from* society, and also at the same time *materially unable to live* in the given form of society, that provides the *positive basis* for " moral " indignation and for revolt against exploitation and oppression, and the fight for Freedom.

This gives at once the positive clue to the understanding of the whole dramatic series of struggles which, in their totality constitute the Bourgeois Revolution—in which we may distinguish as main phases the " Protestant " Revolution (Renaissance and Reformation) ; the " Puritan " and " Whig " Revolution in England, 1641–88 ; the American Revolution, 1776–82 ; the great French Revolution of 1789–1814 ; and the European and South American Revolutions of 1820 to 1848. In all these struggles the watchwords of " Liberty " and " natural right " played a dramatic role. We have seen already that they were fights to establish the legal-moral conditions for the bourgeois form of property, the distinctively bourgeois *mode of exploitation*, not only of Nature, but of Man by man. Let it stand as a challenge to all critics and would-be revisers of Marxism to explain objectively the vast process of the bourgeois revolution with all its amazing variety of phenomena and phases, those we have indicated and others subsidiary to them—and with them the aftermath of the bourgeois revolution in West and Central Europe and America, the whole series of more modern revolutions in Eastern Europe, Asia, and to a degree Africa (Egypt and South Africa). Let them show, if they can, how this vast panorama can be brought within the compass of a " law of motion " *by any method other than that of Marx and Engels*.

It is a safe challenge. A visit to any library will convince the most sceptical that the only modern historical research which has produced results of practical *usable* value is research which has been consciously or unconsciously informed by the method of Marxism.

A further challenge may be presented to the critics : by what method alternative to Marxism can it be explained how the heroic age-long struggle of the Bourgeoisie for Liberty, Equality and Fraternity has had as its positive outcome the creation of a state of Society in which all the battle cries of the Bourgeois Revolution are now rallying slogans for the revolutionary struggle of the Proletariat *against* the Bourgeois Order ? And, grim corollary thereupon, that, faced with the world-wide revolutionary challenge of the proletariat, the bourgeois ruling class is everywhere ostentatiously repenting itself of ever having given currency to such words as " Liberty " and " Democracy." Rather than concede to the proletariat " Liberty, Equality and Fraternity " *in their proletarian sense*, the bourgeoisie is beginning everywhere to deny that the words ever had any sense at all ! Marxism can explain this by its revolutionary conception of society. The bourgeoisie, rather than part with its actual social power, scraps all its theories, all its belief in the power of " right " and " reason," and falls back upon the frank, open and brutal assertion of the actual fact of *possession*. It is the supreme irony of ironies that only from the revolutionary proletarian standpoint can the work of the Bourgeois revolutionaries be either appraised adequately or historically vindicated.

The historical progression of the Bourgeois Revolution is thus described by Marx and Engels in the *Communist Manifesto* (1847) :

> " The modern bourgeoisie is itself the product of a long course of development, of a series of revolutions in the modes of production and exchange. Every step in the development of the bourgeoisie was accompanied by a corresponding political advance of that class. *An oppressed class* under the sway of the feudal nobility, an armed and self-governing association in the mediæval Commune—here independent urban republic (as in Italy and Germany), there taxable ' third estate ' of the monarchy (as in France) ; afterwards, in the period of manufacture proper, serving either the semi-feudal or the absolute monarchy as a counterpoise against the nobility [as in England under the Tudors], and, in fact, corner-stone of the great monarchies in general [cf. particularly the ' Grand ' Monarchies of Louis XIV in France, of Peter the ' Great ' in Russia, of Frederick the ' Great ' in Prussia, and of George III and George IV in England], the bourgeoisie has at last, *since the establishment of Modern Industry and of the world market*, conquered for itself, in the modern representative State, exclusive political sway.
>
> " *The executive of the modern State is but a committee for managing the common affairs of the whole bourgeoisie.*"

—MARX and ENGELS : *Communist Manifesto*, pp. 11-12.

This passage is decisive on several counts. Firstly, it disposes of the crudely mechanical notion, which interested ignorance has sought to fasten upon the Marxist conception of revolution—the Ramsay MacDonald notion—which is

common to ignorant enemies and fool-friends of Marxism—
that the essence of a Revolution lies in its *suddenness* and
destructiveness. " The biological view," says Ramsay Mac-
Donald, with an owlish sapience that awes criticism into
speechlessness from its sheer platitudinosity :

> " lays the very slightest emphasis on its ' critical and
> revolutionary ' (! !) side, because it is mainly constructive,
> and the idea of ' clearing before building ' is alien to its
> nature. *Street improvements are not biological pro-
> cesses* (! ! !)."—MacDonald : *Socialism and Society*, p.
> 114.

Street improvements ! It is quite in Dogberry's vein : " You
are thought here to be the most senseless and fit man for the
constable of the watch : therefore bear you the lantern ! "

Unfortunately—such has been the state of Marxist theory
in Britain—many have narrowed Marx's meaning to this
" clearing *before* building " sense. MacDonald's chickens may
be so well trained that they hatch *without breaking their shells*:
the *ultra*-" Left " smashes his eggs to give the chickens a
fair chance to grow ! The Marxist concept sees the smashing
of the shell as only the superficially destructive aspect of the
constructive growth of the *new* chicken !

To press the analogy further : *before* the " smash " (the
qualitative leap !) a whole process of quantitative growth—
increase in bulk, multiplication of organic sub-division—*must*
have taken place. Only when the requisite *quantity* has
appeared can the *qualitative* " leap " occur. Moreover, as
we may see from the standpoint of comparative biology in
the case of the chicken, and from the passage above cited
from the *Manifesto* in the case of the bourgeois Revolution—
the *quantitative* process itself can be discriminated into a
number of sub-stages each of which is connected with the
stages preceding and succeeding by a transitional " leap."
Embryology detects in the embryo a recapitulation of a whole
series of the mutation leaps whereby the species itself has in
nature-history come into being. A critical-historical view
detects in every revolutionary struggle relics of all the stages
of its becoming.

The passage from the *Manifesto* is decisive on another
point. Not only does it show that the bourgeois revolution
itself was achieved in a series of stages—each connected with
each by a *sub*-revolution, a minor mutation leap—but it
shows over all the general Nature of that revolution : *the
conquest of power by the bourgeoisie.*

To see in that conquest nothing but the conquest : to see in the progression nothing but the *progression* (and so treat the *conquest* as a negligible phase), each of these is a failure to grasp the process as a *whole*. The *continuity* must be found in the *sequence* of the dis-continuities. The *dis*-continuity must be seen *in the continuity*. In short : the transformation was objectively impelled by an economic development which (*a*) created the bourgeoisie as a class ; (*b*) pitted it in opposition to (1) the feudal order, then (2) to the post-feudal " Grand " monarchy ; and (*c*) consolidated it sufficiently to make it able to emerge completely victorious from the culminating crisis, and thereafter to impose its class will as the legal and moral standard of Right for all in society.

That the rule of the Bourgeoisie has begotten a general revolt against itself from the class which the bourgeoisie in its revolutionary days affected to regard as " one with us— *the People* ! "—needs no telling. That with which we are concerned here is that the historical Law of Motion of society which Marx set out in the Introduction to his *Critique*, and which in one form or another forms the actual overt or implied ground theme of all he wrote is a law which (*a*) was reached by the strictest of critical analysis—as we saw from the analysis of the *Theses on Feuerbach*—and (*b*) is confirmed by every objective test of historical record.

What is even more pertinent to our immediate purpose is that this Law both confirms and is confirmed by the analysis of the basic economic relations of Capitalist Production made by Marx in his economic writings, particularly in his *Capital*.

MARX'S HISTORICAL ECONOMIC CRITIQUE AS A WHOLE.

Let us consider what it is that the Law and the Analysis have in common—and what this means for Dialectical Materialism.

Firstly, they agree in the primary objective fact that it was in practical productive inter-relation with material objective Nature that human society *came* originally into existence, that it is by an unceasing continuance of this indispensable *practice* that society *maintains* itself in existence. By every test, theoretical and practical, this *production-activity* is shown to be the primary pre-requisite for all human existence whatsoever, individual and collective. It is the counterpart of the mutually-transforming interaction which is the objective, operative cause of *all* developmental processes traceable throughout all the Natural Universe. And it has its counterpart in that *active* inter-relation between Man as thinking *Subject* and external Reality as the *Object* of thought, from which active interaction sensations, perceptions and conceptions arise *as products*.

This latter fact is decisive, not only for Materialism in general, but also (and in a higher degree) for *Dialectical* Materialism. That which is " given " in the sensations which are the raw materials of all human brainwork (*Thinking*) is a *unity of opposites*—since sensation is and can be nothing other than the *felt* end (side, pole, aspect) of the *relation* between Object and Subject established by actual objective practical interaction. The Unity in Opposition and Opposition in Unity which forms the most universal category for all Dialectics is thus not " given " in the old automatic Hobbes-Lockeian sense, but is *given* in the Dialectical sense of being *the immediate unity of Object and Subject established in practice —practice through objects*.

Secondly each achieves the revolutionary result of a complete reversal of the relations between Theory and Practice posited by Speculative Theory and Idealism. This solves the problem that completely baffled even the revolutionary philosophers of the eighteenth century :

" Hitherto . . . the most useful discoveries have been made in the most barbarous times. One would conclude that the business of the most enlightened ages and the most learned bodies is *to argue and debate on things which were invented by ignorant people*. We know exactly the angle which the sail of a ship is to make with the keel, in order to its sailing better ; and yet Columbus discovered America without the least idea of the property of this angle. However, I am far from inferring that we are to confine ourselves merely to *a blind practice* ; but, happy it were, would naturalists and geometricians *unite, as much as possible, the practice with the theory*."— VOLTAIRE : *Letters Concerning the English Nation* (1729).

Finally, Theory and Practice, once Practice is recognised as *primary*, combine to demonstrate that things impossible to Man *as Man*—as an individual—are not only possible, but actually attainable by mankind—by " associated humanity." Society can, given the indispensable *quantitative* pre-requisites, make the *qualitative leap* " from the sphere of Necessity to the sphere of Freedom."

Compare with the concluding clause of Marx's statement of

his Conception of History—in which the bourgeois epoch is described scornfully but none the less critically as concluding the " *prehistoric* stage in human society "—the following from the Third Volume of *Capital* :

" In actuality, the realm of freedom does not begin until that point is passed where labour, under the compulsion of necessity and external utility, is required. In the very nature of things it lies beyond the sphere of material production in the strict sense of the term.

" Just as the savage must wrestle with Nature in order to satisfy his needs, and to maintain and reproduce his life ; so civilised man has to do, and must do in all forms of society and in possible modes of production.

" With Man's development this realm of necessity expands, since Man's wants increase. But at the same time the forces of production increase, by which these wants can be satisfied. Freedom in this field can consist of nothing beyond the fact that socialised man, the associated producers, govern rationally their interaction with Nature, and bring it under their common control, instead of being ruled by it as by some blind power ;— that they accomplish their task with the least expenditure of energy, and under conditions most adequate to their human nature, and most worthy of it. But all this is still a realm of necessity.

" Beyond it begins the development of human powers as an end in itself—the true realm of Freedom—which, however, can only flourish with that realm of Necessity as its basis.

" *The shortening of the working day is its fundamental premise.*"—MARX : *Capital*, Vol. III, pp. 954–55.

In one brilliant flash Marx brings us back to the problem of actuality—the need for and the power of the proletarian revolution. " The shortening of the working day." So simple ! So capable of being interpreted by the banal flatheads of petit-bourgeois reformism in terms of their own wretched opportunistic eclecticism. So magnificently revealing, *from the standpoint of* " *associated humanity*," when it is envisaged as the progressive reduction for *associated humanity* of their *collective* burden of *Necessary* Labour ; and thereby the creation of both the need and the power for Optional activity, for self-determination, for *freedom* !

And magnificently revealing too, retrospectively, as to the *human* aspect, of the whole series of struggles of the proletariat—for shorter hours, for better working conditions. Where the petit-bourgeoisie can see only the narrowest of utilitarian egoism—the "natural" laziness of the human animal—where the petit-bourgeois reformist and his twin, the *ultra*-"Left" can see only "Reformism" (as in the historic instance of the Ten Hours Bill) Marx could see, behind that superficial appearance, the reality of the "victory of a great principle" (See MARX: *Inaugural Address, I.W.M.A.*, 1864), a phase in *the becoming process* of the Revolution!

Marx's critical examination of Capitalist Economy in itself, and as a phase in the historical process, leads in each case to one and the same concrete fact : the overthrow of the bourgeois order by a proletarian revolution.

Out of what had been before he tackled it the self-confessed "dismal science"—the gospel of inexorable Necessity—Marx produced for "all who suffer and are oppressed" "the sure and certain hope" of a glorious deliverance : out of a "metaphysic" he produced a science. Out of an impregnable defence of the bourgeois order he produced an irresistible weapon of revolutionary proletarian war. No revolution in the history of theoretical progress at all equals the revolution worked by Marx. With a simple substitution of name for name we can apply, and that even more justly, to Marx's whole Critique of bourgeois economic science the lyrical apostrophe bestowed by Heine upon Kant's *Critique of Pure Reason* and the "Copernican revolution in thought" which it effected :—

> "To this sick old world, I also,—alas !—belong ;
> and it is with justice, indeed, that the poet says ' men
> walk no better for abusing their crutches.' In fact, I
> am the sickest of you all, and the most to be pitied since
> I know what it would mean to have health. Whereas
> ye —— !
>
> "Oh, men to be envied !—Ye are capable of dying
> stone-dead and being quite unaware of the fact ! Yes !
> Indeed, many of you died ever so long ago—and actually
> declare that for you real life is only now beginning !
> When I contradict such madmen they fly into rages and
> revile me abominably from every side. They spatter me
> with curses ! Horrible ! Yet worse, and far more
> revolting to me than any curses—they breathe out on
> me their loathsome charnel smell —— !
>
> "Avaunt ye spectres ! I pronounce the name of one

whose mere name is an exorcism.   I cry aloud :
' Immanuel Kant ! '

" It is said that night-wandering spirits are stricken
with terror should they chance to meet the headsman
and set eyes upon his executioner's sword. What a
terror must they feel if one holds out to them the
Critique of Pure Reason !

" *This is the sword with which Kant decapitated God !* "
—HEINE : *Germany* ; Works Vol. V.

Marx's *Capital* is the sword with which the whole theory of
bourgeois society was—not merely decapitated, but dis-
embowelled.

THE DIALECTIC OF PROLETARIAN CLASS STRUGGLE

The class struggle is an historically conditioned *relation* :
it is also an objectively developing *fact*—the antagonistic
existence of bourgeoisie and proletariat in their concrete
inter-relation. Out of this inter-relation develops a quantitative alteration and finally a qualitative change of the
struggle : it grows *less* sporadic in its manifestations ; it
includes *more* and *more* of the individuals and sections in
society as combatants on one side or the other ; it grows
more intense and *greater* in the volume of the impact of the
contenders ; finally it *reduces* all subsidiary issues of the
struggle to a *conscious one—which class shall rule* ?

Since, as we have seen, the outcome of the development
of the production process of Capitalist society with the concomitants of that process is to create a situation in which the
bourgeoisie can develop no further, this political crisis coincides, ultimately, with the economic crisis (of which it is
an expression). The consequence is that, in such an event,
the maximum of consolidation and momentum at the
proletarian pole coincides with the maximum disintegration
and loss of momentum at the bourgeois pole.

The outcome of such an inter-relation of forces—such a
dialectical antagonism—can only be a *revolution*—a mutation
leap to the starting-point of a new development.

Such is the general dialectic of the class struggle and its
logical outcome—revolution.

.   .   .   .   .

The Development of the Proletariat

We have seen that the historically conditioned economic
fact from which the proletariat arises is the fact that a class
is differentiated in bourgeois society consisting of an aggre-

gation of individuals, all of whom enter into the production process as *commodities*—units of productive force, purchased as are the inanimate means of production in the " free " market, and paid for at market rates. The primary fact about the proletariat is that its individual components thus stand in a doubly ambiguous and contradictory relation to the society in and through which they live. They are personally active agents in production ; in fact, the more capitalist production develops the more the proletariat becomes *the producing class par excellence*. But, as against that, they produce only as the purchased " property " of others, of the capitalist, with whose implements, and upon whose raw materials they perform, in " *his* " time, all their labour of production. Thus the proletariat produces, but only as part of another's " means of production," only as the animate manipulators, or attendants upon, the inanimate mechanism in which is embodied the *capital* which claims all the proceeds.

Secondly, the individual proletarian is in an ambiguous position in his private capacity, away from the work process. He is a man and a " free " man, as popular tradition and the politicians never tire of reminding him. It is in virtue of his freedom, his self-ownership, that he possesses the legal, as well as the moral right to dispose of himself to the best advantage he can—*in the labour market*! And this *best* he can do is to equate himself with all the other commodities in the market — ! And if he cannot find a purchaser, what then ——— ? Disguise it how he will, the proletarian who finds himself unsaleable, finds at the Labour Exchange, before the Means Test committee, before the Public Assistance Authority, that his true status, in the eyes of bourgeois society is that of a *misfit*—a parasitical dependant upon the actively productive mechanism of society.

In the sphere of economics the proletariat and the bourgeoisie meet, and struggle, as respectively the sellers and buyers of the commodity *labour power*. All the disguises, pretences, " ameliorative measures," " reforms," and whatnot, that leave that relation free to work out all its logic, leave in being the basic generating source of the class struggle between the proletariat and the bourgeoisie. Any " reform," or so-called " revolution " (like the Fascist " revolution " in Italy or Germany) which claims to " harmonise " this relationship while leaving it in being, does but mask temporarily the outward manifestations of the antagonism. In so doing, by penning an explosive force within a rigid container, it prepares inevitably for an explosion which will be all the more violent for having gathered its dynamic force in a confined space.

What was the law of motion of the proletariat as Marx envisaged it.

Firstly, by the development of capitalist industry individual proletarians are increasingly brought into personal contact with each other. This takes place within the sphere of work—in the actual labour process—in which, as industry develops, the number of labourers organised into a production unit grows ever larger and larger. But this also takes place within the sphere of private proletarian life. The rise of industrial towns, and proletarianised quarters in towns and countryside, creates areas of proletarian concentration of increasing number and extent. Finally the modern facility of rapid transit brings each of the workers of a country within the comprehension of every other worker in the land. Thus a community of feeling and a sense of class solidarity is created and developed by capitalist *production* despite all the capitalists individually and collectively can do to check and canalise its growth. This is true not only nationally, but internationally.

The feeling of international solidarity which was first of all generated in a religious disguise (in primitive Christianity) in opposition to the universal dominion of Imperial Rome) was perpetuated after the fall of the Roman Empire by the Catholic Church in the mystical form of a universal alternative to the dominion of the thrones, principalities and powers of this world. Brought back to earth and secularised by the revolutionary bourgeoisie in the days of the romantic enthusiasm generated in their struggle against feudalism and the post-feudal monarchy, it was, after the triumph of the bourgeoisie, vulgarised and deflated into the banal concept of the whole world " subdued " by the arts of trade and commerce and the seductive utilities of universal Free Trade. This having turned in the logic of events into a thing of mockery, a hissing and a reproach, the championship of the age-long fight for the solidarity of the Human Race passed over to a new and more radically revolutionary class, the international proletariat—for whom it expresses the universal need for liberation from the exploitation of the universally dominant bourgeois order, and the no less universal need of actual practical solidarity in the struggle for the overthrow of bourgeois rule.

Thus in its highest form—the revolutionary solidarity in struggle of the proletariat, nationally and internationally— appears, dialectically transmuted under the immediate conditioning of the bourgeois mode of production and its social order, an emotional impulse basic to the common humanity of the entire human race.

. . . .

Marx distinguishes broadly three phases in the historical development of the proletarian struggle. At first, while still an aggregation of individuals differentiated only from the craftsmen, small producers and peasantry of the post-feudal era by the seemingly personal and individual accident of misfortune, the proletariat riots and struggles as an impoverished " mob " to win back the status of small producers in town or country it has lost. During all the period of the Industrial revolution, and, in large measure supplying the mass support for Chartism, the proletarian struggle remained, largely, imprisoned within these small producers' illusions and aspirations. That is the first, or backward-looking phase, in the historical development of the proletarian struggle.

When, as happened in England in the days of economic expansion from 1850 to 1900, the proletariat in the main becomes forced by circumstances to face the fact that the Past will never come again, it settles down to " make the best of it." Its struggles take the form of endeavours to drive the best possible bargain with the bourgeoisie, partly through trade union combination, partly through pitting Radical politicians against Whig manufacturers, and both against Tory squires. Or, alternatively, using Tory squires against Whig manufacturers, Radicals against both, and generally trying to profit by divisions among their enemies.

It is to this period that the basic " conservative " traditions of the British Labour movement, both on its Trade Union and its Labour Party side, may be traced—traditions which are constantly reappearing in a new guise. It is therefore necessary to note particularly the two-sided (i.e., dialectical) character of this phase.

Its revolutionary side is seen in the dynamic aspect of the trade union struggle. This is how Marx and Engels summarised it in the *Communist Manifesto* :

" With the development of industry the proletariat not only increases in numbers ; it becomes concentrated in greater masses. *Its strength grows, and it feels that strength more.* The various interests and conditions in life within the ranks of the proletariat are more and more equalised in proportion as machinery obliterates all distinctions of labour, and nearly everywhere reduces wages to the same low level. The growing competition among the bourgeois, and the resulting commercial crises, make the wages of the workers ever more fluctuating. The unceasing improvement of machinery, ever more rapidly developing, makes their livelihood more and more precarious ; the collisions between individual workmen and individual bourgeois take more and more the character of collisions between two classes. Thereupon the workers . . . form combinations (trade unions) against the bourgeois ; they club together in order to keep up the rate of wages ; they found permanent associations in order to make provision beforehand for these occasional revolts. Here and there the contest breaks out into riots.

" Now and then the workers are victorious, but only for a time. The real fruit of their battles lies, not in the immediate result, but in *the ever-expanding union of the workers*. . . .

" Every class-struggle is a political struggle. . . . This organisation of the proletarians into a class, *and consequently into a political party*, is continually being upset again by the competition among the workers themselves. But it ever rises up again, stronger, firmer, mightier. . . ."

—MARX and ENGELS : *Communist Manifesto*, p. 18.

So vividly do many of the sentences in that passage apply to our own circumstances to-day that it is hard to believe they were written as long ago as 1847. And it is also notable that the whole passage would apply to recent developments in India, Japan and China. So far then its truth is abundantly attested.

What, however, we have to note as a set-off was the slackening off of the revolutionary tempo of the British workers after 1850. Broadly speaking, this was due to the circumstance of the strength of the Trade Unions (mostly confined to skilled workers at this period) on the one side, and to the undisputed hegemony of the economic world enjoyed by British manufacturers on the other. So great were the gains of the British bourgeoisie from the exploitation of the world market—the exploitation of India, the supplying of railway materials and machinery to America, Australia, and Europe generally—that it " paid " the British bourgeosie to concede a better wage standard to the skilled workers

than bed-rock economic necessity demanded, and so gain a
(relatively) continuous running of industry and an uninterrupted flow of profits. Cheap food, the produce of the
exploitation of India, North America and Australia as well as
Ireland, made things bearable for the unskilled workers,
and emigration provided a safety-valve for the surplus
population. The result was the appearance at the head of
the British Trade Unions and the political clubs of the workers
of a group of leaders who were firm in their faith that the
only rôle of workers' combination was to see to it that in the
cutting up of the " cake " (produced by the super-exploitation
of the world market made possible by Britain's enormous
economic superiority over the rest of the world) " organised
labour " should not be forgotten ! They were quite ready to
agree that only the " co-operation of capital and labour "
made it possible for the " cake " to exist, and they agreed
not to be exorbitant in their demands. They got their little
" crumbs " for the unskilled too. But however these " labour
lieutenants of capital " of the period 1860–1890 might contrive to glorify this policy of class-collaboration into (in their
own eyes) " practical wisdom " and " common-sense," it was
the bourgeoisie and its order that they served when they
induced the proletariat to be content to follow at the tail
of the " Great " Liberal Party and eschew all notion of
revolutionary struggle. Engels, noting the very beginning
of this process, remarked in sardonic exasperation (letter to
Marx, October 7th, 1858) : " this most bourgeois of nations
is apparently aiming ultimately at the possession of a bourgeois
aristocracy and a bourgeois proletariat *as well as* a bourgeoisie.
For a nation which exploits the whole world, this is, of course,
to a certain extent, justifiable ! "

Sooner or later, as Marx and Engels predicted as long ago
as 1848, the proletarian struggle was bound to move beyond
this conservative phase. As the rapidity of Britain's economic
world-expansion began to decline after 1875–85, and as at
the same time its hegemony of the world market began
increasingly to be challenged by Germany, France, and
the U.S.A., and as the fluid capital of Britain began to
be drained more and more from home expansion into overseas investments, so more and more the situation began to
change.

Britain began to show, as by 1867 the Continent generally
had begun to show, that the proletariat, or at any rate its
advanced guard, despairing of winning any permanent gains

within the fabric of capitalism, was beginning to aim *beyond* capitalism, at the establishment of a new order of society altogether.

The general development of the proletarian class struggle may thus be discriminated into the three phases (1) *insurrectionary immaturity* ; phase of *negative* or backward-looking revolutionism ; proletarians only a " class " politically in the comparative descriptive aggregate sense of " the *mob.*" (2) *Conservative phase ;* phase of consolidation of the proletariat in industry and its localities of dwelling, and a correlative consolidation of organisational forms, trade unions, benefit societies, co-operatives, etc. This consolidation in general has its dialectical negative counterpart in the *sharpening* of lines of demarcation *within* the class (between the skilled and unskilled workers, the trade unionists and the non-unionists, between trade unionism and politics, between union and union and craft and craft) and a corresponding blurring of *class* divisions through the empirical, opportunist character of trade union policy (" capital and labour are brothers "), and of the merging of " labour " politics as a detail in the general whole of petty-bourgeois liberalism and radicalism. (3) *The Revolutionary phase :* concomitantly with the growing mass, volume, and momentum of capitalist production itself the proletarian movement gains mass, volume, and momentum. It transcends progressively the petty local and sectional divisions within its own ranks of the middle period and correspondingly deepens and sharpens the cleavage between itself and the bourgeois order, its agents and its agencies. Increasingly the proletarian struggle becomes a conscious and deliberately purposeful struggle to win power sufficient to enable it to *compel* the introduction of a new order of society—one in which will be substituted for the presuppositions of the bourgeois order—those centring upon the *individualist* production of commodities for disposal in a freely competitive market—the presuppositions corresponding to the proletarian function in production, those of co-operative production of *utilities* (" use-values ") for social and personal consumption.

The Determinants of the Transition to Revolution

The general law of development of the proletarian class struggle holds good not only for the struggle as a whole in its historical sequence of stages, but also for the detailed sections and phases of the struggle taken separately—though here is to be observed the dialectical law that the transition from particular to general is made dialectically—as a movement countering an oppositional movement. Above we have taken the proletarian movement in Britain as typifying the proletarian movement in general; and, with allowance made for the differences in rate and quality of the development process of capitalist production in other areas outside Britain, a parallel process of development is to be observed in each main centre set up by capitalist production in turn. In each centre appears, more or less clearly defined, an insurrectionary beginning followed by a conservative and opportunist phase, which is succeeded by a positively revolutionary phase. The same sequence can be observed in detail *within* the component strata of the movement in each main sub-centre of capitalist production—areas which in the case of the " imperialist " Powers coincide with the sphere of action of the imperialist State and its correlative " nation."

Capitalist development involves the progressive *creation* of a proletariat, not only by the personal procreation of children born into the proletarian status, but by the *proletarianisation* of whole strata of peasants, artisan craftsmen, small producers, merchants, shopkeepers, professional intellectuals, and their offspring.

As each of these strata is destroyed—and their substitutes begotten by capitalist production in its dialectical progression also destroyed in turn—its members bring into the proletarian movement a recrudescence of the older phases of insurrectionism and conservatism. Thus in the proletarian struggle viewed as a whole—both in its international and its national phases—all its historically developed stages coexist as tendencies and counter-tendencies within the movement.

The mutual transformations begotten by the clash and interplay of these conflicting tendencies make up in their totality the positive outcome of the movement as a whole.

We may select then two concrete phases in the capitalist development process as being the ultimate determinants of the dynamic fact of social revolution :

(*a*) The actual, practical, *transformation* of separate human beings into a collective human being in the basic work-process of capitalist production as the center of generation of the *force of revolution* ;

(b) The objective, practical, persisting *resistance* to transmutation of the capitalist *conditions* of production—i.e., capitalist " property " in the instruments of production, and its concomitants in the capitalist State (the public, legal, political, and moral expressions of that " property " institution)—as the *force of counter-revolution*.

The nature of these two poles in the determination of proletarian social revolution is described vividly by Marx in the course of the development of his analysis of capitalist production. Dealing with the production of *relative* (i.e., *above the average*) surplus value, Marx explains its source in the *qualitative* superiority of the production force of a number of labourers working in co-operation as compared with the same men working in independent isolation. He observes the importance of this fact for the victory of the large Capital over the small in the course of competition, and then notes its social significance :

> " All combined labour on a large scale requires, more or less, a directing authority, in order to secure the harmonious working of the individual activities, and to perform the general functions that have their origin in the action of the combined organism, as distinguished from the action of its separate organs. A single violin player is his own conductor ; an orchestra requires a separate one. The work of superintending, directing and adjusting becomes one of the functions of capital from the moment that the labour under the control of capital becomes co-operative. Once a function of capital, it acquires special characteristics.
>
> " The directing motive, the end and aim of capitalist production, is to extract the greatest possible amount of surplus value, and consequently to exploit labour power to the greatest possible extent. As the number of the co-operating labourers increases, so too does their *resistance* to the domination of capital, and with it the *necessity* for capital to overcome this resistance *by counter-pressure*.
>
> The function of the capitalist being two-fold, *social* as director of a *social* labour-process and *individual* as actively exploiting, it is necessary to discriminate the two, and not confound them as bourgeois apologists do. It is not because he is a *leader of industry* that a man is a

capitalist; on the contrary, he is a leader of industry *because he is a capitalist.* The leadership of industry is an attribute of capital just as in feudal times the functions of general and judge were attributes of landed property."
—MARX : *Capital,* Vol. I, Chap. XIII, pp. 321-3.

Here the function of the capitalist labour process in generating a " collective consciousness " in the co-operating labourers and pitting this consciousness in ever-intensifying opposition to its repressive and exploiting aspect is stated with masterly precision. And the fact noted has its historical corollary in the Historical Law of Capitalist Accumulation.

Capitalist " property " has its two-fold aspect likewise. It is a " private " property which is, however, different from and historically destructive of previous historical forms of property, collective and private. The fights of the bourgeoisie against feudalism were fought out as fights for private right as against the arbitrary rights of social *status.* The capitalist, however, enjoys a *private* right, which rests upon a *social status*—which is all the more real the less its existence is admitted—that of monopolist of the means of living and of arbiter of the process of their production. In the exercise of their *right* the owners of capitalist property have enlarged their property at the expense of all previously existing " properties." The small proprietors and producers, the handicraftsman whose craft-skill is rendered obsolete almost overnight, the individual shopkeepers and bourgeois whom competition has stripped of their all, are none the less expropriated by reason of the fact that they cannot say where or to whom their " property " has gone. That which is certain is that they have been expropriated and turned into proletarians, and that this process of expropriation has been, and is, an inseparable concomitant of the development of capitalist property. All the screams of the bourgeois legalist and moralist against the proposal of the revolutionaries to expropriate them in their turn cannot conceal the fact that it is by expropriation on a colossal, a world-wide, and an ever-intensifying scale that capitalist property has grown and must grow.

Treating the general tendency of capitalist accumulation as an Historical progression, Marx notes the logic that Capitalist accumulation reaches the end of its *expansive* form when all alternative " property " has been absorbed by it; thereafter it can continue to accumulate only by an *intensive* magnification of its exploitation process which will defeat its own purpose by destroying all markets for its produce save its own process of self-expansion. It can continue to exist only by making all human existence impossible. Obviously capitalist property will thus create a categorically imperative need for its own expropriation in turn :

" Private property, as the antithesis to social, collective property, exists only where the means of labour and the external conditions of labour belong to private individuals. But according as these private individuals are labourers or not labourers, private property has a different character . . . [the annihilation of small producers' property] the transformation of the individualised and scattered means of production into socially concentrated ones, of the pigmy properties of the many into the huge property of the few, the expropriation of the great mass of the people from the soil, from the means of subsistence, and from the means of labour, this fearful and painful expropriation of the mass of the people forms the prelude to the history of capital. . . .

" What has now to be expropriated is no longer the labourer working on his own account, but the capitalist exploiting many labourers. . . . The capitalist mode of appropriation, the result of the capitalist mode of production, produces capitalist private property. This is the first negation of *individual* private property, as founded on the labour of the proprietor. But capitalist production begets with the inexorability of a law of Nature its own negation. *It is the negation of the negation.*

" This does not re-establish *private* property for the producer. It gives him *individual* property based on the acquisitions of the capitalist era : i.e., on *co-operation*, and the *possession in common* of the land and of the means of production."—MARX : *Capital*, Vol. I, Chap. XXXII, pp. 786–789.

Thus the law of movement of the proletarian struggle is that it is objectively that movement engendered by the process of capitalist production, which in the fullness of its development intensively and extensively will annihilate the capitalist mode of *appropriation* and liberate the historically developed *forces of production* from the trammels and obstructions of capitalist " property," so that these forces may become the positive basis from which a new historical epoch will take its point of departure.

So much for the revolutionary struggle considered in general. How is the theory to be applied in practice ?

As *practice* the proletarian struggle is one directed against the forms and consequences of capitalist production and the capitalist rule based thereupon. But its reactions to capitalism are not merely empirical reflexes of transitory and transitional details inherent therein—though these are the immediate materials with which it operates consciously and unconsciously. The proletarian struggle, in its consciously political, Socialist and Communist revolutionary forms, is increasingly governed by the general historical outcome of capitalism—the need to overthrow the rule of the bourgeoisie and to replace it by the rule of the proletariat, which cannot help but grow more and more set upon the attainment of Socialism.

The proletarian movement as a quantitative whole is not identical with the conscious and purposeful movement for Socialism and Communism. But the conscious movement for Socialism and Communism which derives from Marx, Engels and Lenin, is identical with the essential, general *movement* of the proletariat as an historically developing whole. It is to be differentiated from the quantitatively extended proletariat only as the essence of an historically conditioned movement is to be distinguished from its transitory immediate forms.

In general the role fulfilled by the Marxist movement within the aggregate proletarian movement is that of transforming the latter from an instinctive movement *away from* Capitalism into a concerted, organised, and consciously purposeful movement towards its revolutionary overthrow and replacement by Socialism and Communism.

Thus the role of the Marxist movement is that of transforming the proletarian struggle by participating therein, just as the proletarian struggle grown conscious is a movement to transform society—not by running away from it—but by participating in it and all its developing struggles.

It is thus that the Marxist movement realises Marx's aphorism—" The point, however, is *to change the world*."

THE DIALECTIC OF PROLETARIAN REVOLUTION

Socialism : and the U.S.S.R.

Were it not Utopian to expect any sort of Dialectical comprehension from the critics of Marx one might wonder at the failure of all but 1 per cent. of these critics to perceive in the victory of the Russian proletariat in November, 1917, and in the steady advance, despite all obstacles, of the development towards Socialism consequent upon that revolution in what is now the U.S.S.R., an overwhelmingly unanswerable confirmation of the Marxian Law of Social Growth in general, and its Law of class struggle and proletarian revolution in particular.

The bourgeois critics are, it must be conceded, not alone in this.   A whole section of the " Labour and Socialist International," including large sections of nominal " Marxists," are at one with the bourgeois critics herein.   Their excuses and their formulations vary.   They all agree, however, with the bourgeois critics in saying that what has happened in Russia from November, 1917, to date does not confirm objectively the truth of Marx's conception of proletarian revolution as the necessary historical outcome of the development of capitalist production.

There is, in fact, a section which seeks to deny that *any revolution has occurred in Russia at all* !   More general is the assertion that, whether the " Bolsheviks "—the Communists —wish it or do not, Socialism *cannot* be established in the U.S.S.R. because " only a bourgeois revolution was possible in 1917," and *therefore* (!) all that is established in the U.S.S.R. is a " sort of camouflaged capitalism."   Most general is the Kautskyite variation on this latter theme, namely—" Socialism *cannot* be established in the U.S.S.R. *in that way*—the way of Lenin and Stalin ! "

We will deal with these points so far as they present problems of Dialectical Materialist Theory.   We shall find that what is lacking is not Socialist potentialities in the U.S.S.R., but dialectical capacity in its critics.

First, as to the general form of Socialism, and the distinction between Socialism and Communism.

In the statement of the materialist conception of history given above (p. 303) Marx affirms [in par. 6] that " new and higher production relations cannot appear until the material conditions for their existence have ripened within the womb of the old social order."   In the quotation from *Capital* given above there is described the nature of the production relations which, developing *within* the bourgeois order, are such as can be developed *beyond* that order, and such therefore as provide *material conditions* for newer and higher production relations.   These are, as we saw above, (*a*) the technological equipment—machinery, power, plant, means of communication—which compels *co-operation* in its *use* ;   (*b*) the social legal *practice*, which, by means of joint-stock companies and their developments in stock, bond, and share-holding, makes actual *co-operation to own* the general form of capitalist *private* property ; (*c*) such a degree of ripening in the class antagonism between the proletariat (producers) and the bourgeois (owners) as will impel the former to burst its bonds and, as ruling class, set about the unification of social co-operation to produce with social co-operation to own.

A society in which the means of life are co-operatively owned by those who co-operate to employ them productively is a " Socialist " society. The Utopians thought it possible to remodel society at large by the piecemeal establishment of tiny " Socialist " societies of that kind. Marxism affirmed that the narrowest economic basis possible for such a society was that corresponding to the bourgeois political State. Given a political State in which the means of life—the land, means of production, and transportation, and with them the power of control—are all co-operatively owned by a co-operatively producing community of worker-owners and owning-workers —given this, Socialism is achieved, at any rate as to its starting point.

Before asking ourselves how far this has been achieved in the U.S.S.R. (the answer is well known, but we may as well both suit our convenience and give a crumb of consolation to the critics) let us dispose of the question of the difference between Socialism and Communism on this side.

It is wholly one of degree—except that, as in all things, quantitative difference is qualitative *change*. Obviously the amount of wealth available for each co-operating individual unit in a Socialist community depends ultimately upon the degree of productivity of the collective whole. From that, as a primary fact, follows the consequence that the *mode of allocation* of the produce of the collective activity will vary as varies the degree of productive efficiency attained in general and in detail. Certain deductions from the total produce on account of what bourgeois practice calls " overhead " charges are indispensable in any event. The proportion they bear to the total is, however, infinitely variable, since the " overheads " may be (in some respects) progressively diminished, while the total may be indefinitely magnified. The question arises as to the *principle* governing the allocation of the remainder when the requirements of future production, State functions, the sick, infants, aged, and emergencies have been met.

The older Socialist and Communist sects of the pre-Marxian era used to debate furiously the alternative merits of the "Socialist" formula "*To* each according to his *deeds*," and the "Communist" formula, "*From* each according to his *ability* : *to* each according to his *needs*." To discuss these as abstract principles would be idle. Both equally suppose a Co-operating community as the final judge both of *needs* and *deeds*, and the judgment of the community will obviously be determined in the last resort by the degree to which it possesses as a community means of consumption in excess of its more obvious and urgent *needs*. It is and can be a question only practical productive achievement can solve.

When production succeeds beyond a certain point, rigid rationing of products is a waste of time.. Up to that point it is an imperative necessity. Thus it depends upon the degree of productive development attained in each branch of production in a co-operating community how far it is possible to go beyond the *strict* Socialist formula of allocation in proportion to *deeds* and rise to the Communist formula of allocation according to *needs*. Also, only *after* the human individuals have been transformed in the process of revolutionary transformation will they have shed the habits and morals inseparable from a bourgeois environment sufficiently to enable the formula "*from* each according to his *ability*" to work spontaneously without the incentive of the Socialist formula (according to his *deeds*).

From all which it follows that, given the victory of the proletariat, the process of establishing Socialism in any country is a problem, first of all, of attaining the indispensable prerequisite *quantity and quality of production*.

In the *Communist Manifesto* Marx and Engels give the following as the general programme for the establishment of a Socialist State of Society :

"The proletariat will use its political supremacy to wrest, by degrees, all capital from the bourgeoisie, to centralise all instruments of production in the hands of the State, i.e., of the proletariat organised as the ruling class ; and to increase the total of productive forces as rapidly as possible.

"Of course in the beginning this cannot be effected except by means of despotic inroads on the rights of property, and on the conditions of bourgeois production ; by means of measures therefore which appear economically insufficient and untenable, but which, in the course of the movement, outstrip themselves, necessitate further inroads upon the old social order, and are unavoidable as a means of entirely revolutionising the mode of production."—MARX and ENGELS : *Communist Manifesto*.

Written though these words were as long ago as 1848, their general soundness and acumen is proved by the manner in which they sum up, as it were by a feat of prophecy, the course of development in Russia since November, 1917.

The proletarian State (" the proletariat *organised* as ruling class ") *has wrested*, and that *by degrees* (after the essential seizure of power) *all capital from the bourgeoisie*. It has " centralised " the main means of production into the hands of the State—and it is well on the road towards doing the same for the remainder. It *has* worked, and (in both Five Year Plans) triumphantly, to *increase as rapidly as possible the total of productive forces*. That this achievement is, so far, not only Socialistic, but such as would have been deemed so by Marx and Engels, cannot for one moment be questioned.

Those who contend that this end has been attained only through a series of partial failures, and after various alternatives have been tried, prove themselves, by this very contention incapable of comprehending such a *dialectical* process of development as is foreshadowed in the second paragraph of the quotation above. These critics see in the successive stages of the period of " military communism," and of the N.E.P., only the fact that each was abandoned as " unsatisfactory " ; they are unable to realise that each in turn was a provisional stage which served the purpose of directly and indirectly making it possible to *go beyond itself*. Neither stage was intended to be, by those who adopted and established them each in turn, anything other than a measure " economically insufficient and untenable," which was " unavoidable as a means of entirely revolutionising the mode of production." In fact, even more impressive (in some respects) than the triumph of the Revolution in the U.S.S.R. is the manner in which its actual practical course of development in face of particular circumstances and conditions which Marx and Engels could not possibly have foreseen, provides an objective proof of the manner in which Lenin and Stalin, by reason of the thoroughness of their Marxist grasp were able to use their theory as a guide to action.

That which has been attempted in the U.S.S.R. is often spoken of as " an experiment." The term is grotesquely inapplicable, since in a laboratory experiment all the conditions are deliberately contrived in advance to test the truth of a single proposition—all extraneous and disturbing influences being absolutely excluded. The practical handling of a practical situation stands on a different footing. None the less the term has its measure of application, and the " Russian experiment " has *proved* at any rate that, all difficulties notwithstanding, *Marxism provides a theory by means of which men can co-operate collectively to change the world.*

That which has been accomplished in the U.S.S.R. has been, firstly, to conquer triumphantly the enormous and innumerable difficulties attendant upon laying a foundation for a Socialist Society ; and secondly, to achieve a final and irrevocable victory in the work of constructing a Socialist Society. To have done this is to have gone as near to achieving a miracle as ever men want. No one who appreciates the extent of this accomplishment will be inclined to minimise it by belittling the number and intensity of either the difficulties which have had to be overcome, or of those which remain to be overcome.

It is these initial *a priori* difficulties which, undialectically isolated and so made insuperable, provide the theme for those who affirm either that (*a*) the Russian Revolution *contradicted* all the assumptions of Marxism ; or that (*b*) what happened in Russia *could not* have been a *proletarian* revolution, because economic conditions were not " ripe " for such a change. An examination of this argument—it is presented in two ways, but it is one and the same argument in essence—will lead directly to the heart of the problem of proletarian revolutionary practice.

Firstly, let us note how the argument is stated, and by whom.

Raymond Postgate puts the blame upon the Dialectic method, which he thinks can be and should be separated from *historical* materialism :

> " The dialectic appeared to indicate that the first proletarian revolution must occur in America or in Germany, the most highly-developed capitalist countries. When it occurred in Russia, Karl Kautsky proved on *strictly orthodox* (!) *Marxist* (! !) *lines*, that it had not

occurred there, and that Lenin was committing a
dialectical error in endeavouring to make it occur.
Lenin's reply was that ' revolutionary dialectic must
be infinitely flexible,' and that Kautsky was an old
fool."—POSTGATE : *Karl Marx*, p. 90.

Though we disagree, and fundamentally, with Postgate
as to the Dialectic (in the version of Lenin's reply given, for
instance, the sense would be better rendered thus : " the
dialectic *is* revolutionary *because* it is infinitely flexible "), he
gives a thoroughly correct version of Kautsky's attitude. He
would indeed have rendered the spirit of Lenin's retort to
Kautsky perfectly if he had inserted the term "*scoundrelly*"
in front of the words " old fool."

A whole-hog supporter of the Kautsky theory from a
different angle is Mr. J. Middleton Murry, late of the British
I.L.P. In the course of a lecture given in the Kings Weigh
House, London, afterwards reprinted as a pamphlet, *Christianity and Communism,* he affirmed :

" Russian Communism . . . is a very particular variety
of Communism, shaped by the particular circumstances
of that great but economically backward and *politically
barbarous* country. . . .

" In Marxist terms Russia was not even yet a bourgeois society when the [Bolshevik] revolution occurred.
It had no middle class. . . .

" Marxian Socialism is the economic organisation of
society which must, as Marx believed, necessarily follow,
by a process of revolution, on the economic and political
triumph of *the middle class*. . . .

" That is the Marxist prognosis of society. That I
believe to be fundamentally true. It follows that *a
Marxist* Socialist Revolution *was in theory impossible in
Russia*."—MIDDLETON MURRY : *Christianity and Communism*.

Mr. Murry, it is to be observed, approves of Marx mainly
because he conceives him as supplying a weapon against
Lenin and Leninism. Also by the simple historical illiteracy
of translating " bourgeois " as " middle class " (which blurs
over the fact that the bourgeoisie is *now* the *ruling* class)
he converts Marx into an apostle of the emancipation of his
own, the " middle " (and less than " middling " !) class.
Finally he prepares as above for his own gospel :

" I believe that in [Britain] *our* Communism will come
by the Christian way. I do not believe it will come by

the sheer revolutionary upsurge of the working classes."—
MIDDLETON MURRY : *ibid.*

From which we may learn why it was that in his *Necessity
of Communism* Mr. Murry was so insistent that " every country
gets the Communism it *deserves* ! " Russia, you must understand, being a *nasty* country, got a nasty sort of Communism :
Britain being, on the whole, a *nice* country, can if it likes
get a *nice* sort of Communism (Middleton Murry " Christian "
brand !), and it will serve as an antidote to the nasty Russian
variety ! Here is his historico-economic " explanation " :

> " The Russian Revolution *ought* to have been a bour-
> geois revolution, ideally speaking. That it wasn't was
> due, really, to the utter political and social backwardness
> of Russia. There *were* no bourgeois in Russia [! ! !].
> If there had been Lenin would have had no chance.
> (He would really have been in those circumstances the
> bourgeois leader, of course [! ! !]) . . . Russia will be the
> most backward State in the Communistic world. *It will
> have to learn the rudiments of civilisation still.* In other
> words, Russia had to have a proletarian revolution
> because it was incapable of a bourgeois revolution.
> Whatever naïve Communists may believe, a nation
> simply cannot omit a necessary stage in human develop-
> ment without paying for it. It has to pass through the
> *ethical* equivalent of that economic stage (! ! !)."—
> MIDDLETON MURRY : *Necessity of Communism*, p. 135.

We will examine the historical economics of this extract
later. Here we note only the logical beauty of the last
sentence. A " nation " can, it seems, in fact *omit a necessary*
(i.e., inevitable, inescapable, essential) *stage* in its *own* development—if, " of course," it *pays for it* " ethically." The
huckster turned evangelist never evolved a more perfect
professional self-exposure.

Professor Arnold Toynbee, who does not even pretend to
be a Socialist—a humanitarian Liberal with Labour sympa-
thies—stated the theory naïvely in a wireless talk in 1933, in
the form in which it circulates commonly among the non-
Marxian intelligentsia :

> " Russia has actually gone Socialist before any other
> country in the world, and this is an extraordinary thing—
> a thing which Karl Marx himself would assuredly never
> have predicted. . . . *According to Marx's theory*, you
> will see that *the United Kingdom ought to have been the
> first country in the world to go Socialist*, and Russia one

of the last, because in her industrial development Russia has been—and, I suppose, is still—one of the more backward countries."—ARNOLD TOYNBEE in the *Listener*, April 12th, 1933.

Finally Prof. John Macmurray (of London University), a Hegelian, in his *Philosophy of Communism*, affirms :

" It is often triumphantly pointed out that the Russian Revolution did not follow the lines mapped out by Marx for a Communist revolution, and that Lenin was compelled to develop a new theory which differs in important respects from that of Marx."—J. MACMURRAY : *Philosophy of Communism*.

Prof. Macmurray distinguishes himself from other critics, however, by affirming that this is no objection to either Marxism or Leninism, since the real question is whether Leninism is a " true dialectical development of Marxism."

The first assumption common to all these critics (their contradictions could have been multiplied by taking as many examples again) is the assumption that " according to Marx " each COUNTRY (*separately and in isolation*) goes through a mystical process called " economic development " which, though parallel in each case, moves in each country at different rates. It is also assumed that political phenomena are the *automatic results* of economic development—the origin of which is not inquired into but is supposed vaguely to have some mysterious connection with the " *country*."

The second assumption they share is that countries are " backward " or " forward " in economic development *in* themselves—*as* " *wholes*." The third assumption is that Russia's " backwardness " was *absolute*.

All these assumptions are false ; all are anti-Marxian, unhistorical, and anti-dialectical.

The first fact these critics fail to grasp is the world-wide *universality* of the economic life-process of Capitalism. Precisely because the production relations are *basic*, and the political and ideologic formations *secondary* strata in the formation of capitalist society, the bourgeois order presents, on a scale previously unprecedented in history, the phenomena of increasingly varied and multiplying disturbance and disparity as its *world-wide economic ramifications* cut the historical ground from under the feet of every local and national *exclusiveness*.

It is amazing that after a world war begotten by rivalries between the great imperialist Powers of the world in their life-and-death struggle for the hegemony of the *world market*, and control of the *world's* resources—of natural sources of motive power and raw materials—after this Titanic upheaval, which proved, if it proved nothing else, that the economic fate of every State and people in the capitalist world is inexorably inter-linked with that of every other—after all this men can still go on thinking and talking as though " backwardness " and its converse means *absolute independence of development*. As long ago as 1847, Marx and Engels wrote :

" The need of a constantly expanding market for its products chases the bourgeoisie over the whole surface of the globe. It must nestle everywhere, settle everywhere, establish connections everywhere.

" The bourgeoisie has through its exploitation of the world market given a *cosmopolitan* character to production and consumption in every country. To the great chagrin of reactionaries, it has drawn from under the feet of industry the national ground on which it stood. All old-established national industries have been destroyed or are daily being destroyed. They are dislodged by new industries, whose introduction becomes a life and death question for all civilised nations, by industries that no longer work up indigenous raw materials, but raw material drawn from the remotest zones : industries whose products are consumed, not only at home, but in every quarter of the globe. In place of the old local and national seclusion and self-sufficiency, we have intercourse in every direction, *universal interdependence of nations*.

" And as in material, so also in intellectual production. The intellectual creations of individual nations *become common property*. National one-sidedness and narrow-mindedness become more and more impossible, and from the numerous national and local literatures there arises a *world literature*.

" The bourgeoisie . . . draws all, *even the most* barbarous, nations into civilisation. . . . It compels all nations, on pain of extinction, *to adopt the bourgeois mode of production* ; it compels them to introduce what it calls civilisation into their midst, i.e., *to become bourgeois themselves*."—MARX-ENGELS : *Communist Manifesto*, p. 13.

That is what Marx and Engels wrote as long ago as 1847. And again we are forced to notice how pointedly every sentence reads, as though it were written for us to-day in the present situation of world crisis. Not only does it destroy utterly the stupid notion of the isolation of pre-Revolutionary Russia, and its " barbarism " ; it points directly to the fallacy underlying the whole argument.

Britain led the world in establishing the factory system and modern industry, especially in textiles : not until late in the nineteenth century did Japan set up a cotton-textile industry on any noteworthy scale. In 1935 British cotton manufacturers are in despair at Japanese competition, and at *the superiority in point of equipment of the Japanese* factories. And the cutting edge of the irony is that the machinery with which the Japanese factory industry was equipped came in the first place from England, *from Lanca-shire* !

So too it was with Germany, the United States, *and Russia*.

The very policy of absolutism maintained by the Tsars had as its corollary that, while the development of the native small producers and small manufacturers into big-scale bourgeois producers was checked and hampered, a welcome was extended to foreign capital willing to pay a price for the right to establish large-scale production in a land where labour-power could be bought more cheaply than almost anywhere in the world.

Mr. Middleton Murry's notion [which exhibits an ignorance and an insular narrowness that Marx and Engels would have regarded as incredible as long ago as 1847] that Russia " had *no middle class* " is the most grotesque of all possible inversions of the truth. The policy of Tsardom positively ensured that, *apart from the town proletariat* (admittedly a smaller propor-tion of the total population in Russia than in any State in Western Europe) there was in Russia little beyond the " middle class " (in the modern English sense of the word). The Court itself was " bourgeoisified " as every Court in Europe had to become, on pain of extinction, in the bourgeois epoch. It was, in fact, at one time the favourite theme of English schoolbooks of historical edification how " Peter *the Great* civilised " (i.e., bourgeoisified) the imperial Court of Russia. The Empress Catherine's patronage of the eighteenth-century French bourgeois philosophers, including Diderot, is (or ought to be) well-known. That Russia was of economic importance alike as a market and a producing centre as long ago as before the days of Queen Elizabeth the " Muscovy Company," established by Royal Charter in 1553, testifies. Earlier still one of the chief centres of the Hanseatic League was in Novgorod (Gorki).

That Russia's rate of economic development was retarded materially by the shift of the world economic centre of gravity from the Eastern Mediterranean to the Atlantic seaboard is unquestionable. That its slowness in developing its natural power resources caused it to lag behind the development of the centres which raced ahead on coal and steam power is undoubted again. But the merest tyro in economic history ought to be familiar with the fact that the cheap foodstuffs —particularly wheat, barley and rye—wrung from the poverty of the peasantry of Russia, particularly after their " emancipation " from serfdom in 1861 (a process which turned them into *petty*-bourgeois producers, and the land- lords into bourgeois landowners and " rent-eaters "), was an indispensable pre-requisite for the prosperity of British manufacturers during their period of world hegemony. So it was also indispensable to the manufacturers of the U.S.A. and Germany when gathering their strength to contest that hegemony with Britain.

It seems to be completely forgotten that, in a crisis in the American Civil War, President Lincoln astutely secured the diplomatic aid of Russia as a counterpoise against the pro- slavery policy of Napoleon III and the British Tories (by opening the negotiations which ended in 1867 in the *purchase* by the U.S.A. of Alaska from the Tsar), precisely because Russia's resources were sufficiently considerable to make its *economic* as well as military support decisive in a balance.

Finally it is curious that this " discovery " of Russia's *absolute* " backwardness " was made *only after* the War, into which Britain entered as an ally of Russia's ally, France ! And made, too, by men who had not a word to say of this " backwardness " until *after* the November revolution !

To sum up. That Russia was *relatively* " backward " cannot be denied. But what the argument of these critics requires is something far beyond this. It requires it to be proved that Russia was *so* backward as *not to have a proletariat at all*.

Given the undeniable fact that Russia most emphatically *had* a proletariat ; given the further fact that this proletariat was (*precisely because* the big capitalist enterprises in Russia were of the nature of " imperialist " on-thrusts into Russia from the most highly developed capitalism of Western Europe) more highly concentrated, in larger masses, and more intensely exploited than the proletariat in the West European bourgeois States, and these conditions insured that the class-consciousness reached by the Russian proletariat should be *more intense* and *more compactly organised* than was that of any other proletariat in the capitalist world.

It was in any event certain that the Socialist philosophy of Western Europe would find an entry into Russia—as had done the philosophy of the bourgeois revolutionaries of the eighteenth century. But, as though on purpose, the Tsardom, by sending all suspected revolutionaries into exile in the lands where this Socialism could be studied openly, ensured that the supply should be forthcoming a hundred times in excess of the power of the police to check it.

More still : the very " backwardness " of Russia, by which these critics mean the preponderance of small-scale agriculture in its total economy, was in the circumstances of 1917 an asset on the revolutionary side.

We have given above the process of reasoning by which Marx reaches the conclusion that the peasantry in the mass *must be represented by a power from outside their own ranks.* Given a situation in which the Tsardom could no longer carry on ; given a situation which, *the whole peasantry being one huge grievance,* was comparable to the situation in France in 1789–93, but on a more widespread and more intense scale —given further a proletariat compact, resolute, and well-led by the best Marxists in the world, and it followed that under the hegemony of the proletariat (led by the Bolsheviks, with Lenin at their head) *the whole peasantry of Russia supplied the mass and momentum* which made the Bolshevik Revolution irresistible.

To show how little such an eventuality would have " surprised " Marx we can produce *his own words*—an introduction written by Marx in 1882 for a Russian translation of the *Communist Manifesto.**

" Let us now turn to Russia. At the time of the revolutionary wave in 1848–49, the European bourgeoisie, no less than the monarchs, looked upon Russian intervention as their only salvation from the proletariat, which was for the first time becoming aware of its own strength. The Tsar was acclaimed as leader of the European reaction. To-day he sits in his palace at Gatchina, *a prisoner of war of the Revolution, and Russia*

---

* The MARX ENGELS *Correspondence* shows that as early as 1856 Marx was noting the development of capitalism in Russia and deducing revolutionary consequences. As early as 1859, Engels was noting that a revolution " by force " was " necessitated " in Russia.

forms the vanguard of the revolutionary movement in Europe.

" The *Communist Manifesto* was a proclamation wherein the inevitable disappearance of present-day bourgeois property relations was heralded. In Russia, alongside the growth of *the capitalist system* (*which is growing up with feverish haste*) and the *bourgeois* land-owning system (which is in its early stages of development) more than half the land is owned in common by the peasantry.

" The question we have to answer is : will the Russian peasant communes (a primitive form of communal ownership of land which is already on the downgrade) *become transformed into the superior form of communised ownership of land*, or will they have to pass through the same process of decay we have witnessed in the course of the historical evolution of the West.

" There is only one possible answer to this question. *If the Russian revolution sounds the signal for a workers' revolution in the West, so that each becomes the complement of the other, then the prevailing form of communal ownership of land in Russia may serve as the starting point for a Communist development.*"—MARX : Quoted in the Preface to German Edition 1890—given in Martin Lawrence edition, pp. 42–43.

Not only does this give the lie direct to all those who from Kautsky onwards have circulated the myth that Marx would have been " astonished " at the Russian Revolution, and that it " contradicted " his forecasts—it *does more.* It shows, firstly, that Marx personally would not have been " surprised " if the Proletarian Revolution had come in Russia *sooner than it did* ! Secondly, and even more trenchantly, it shows that Marx envisaged the *possibility* at any rate that the *most backward peasantry of Russia* would be able to *skip a whole epoch* and leap from *pre*-capitalist to *post*-capitalist conditions at a bound, always provided that they were aided thereto by a simultaneous and sympathetic proletarian revolution.

This " leap " was not it is true made, in the end, at just the point envisaged tentatively by Marx. Consequently the detailed development was not identically that which Marx indicated as a possibility. But *just such a transition as he envisaged is actually being made in the Soviet Republics in China.* And if the matter is examined closely it will be seen that the development of collectivised agriculture under the Five Year Plan in the U.S.S.R. has followed in principle just the very line to which Marx points by implication.

This introduction, which was one of the very last works written for publication by Marx, thus not only vindicates his foresight against all slurs and detractions, and vindicates his Theory in the teeth of all its critics. It also vindicates Lenin as the greatest, the most acute, and most universally competent theoretician among all Marxists since Marx and Engels ; and equally unequivocally it vindicates the line fought for by Stalin in the face of a sustained mass of calumny, slander, sabotage, and misunderstanding that would have broken the spirit of any lesser man—a line of advance which has brought the Russian Revolution through the successful accomplishment of the Five Year Plan on to the successful inauguration of the Second Plan, the definite beginning of *positive* Socialism in the U.S.S.R.

.   .   .   .

The " Russian " Revolution of November, 1917, can, in fact, only be comprehended theoretically (and its lessons *used* practically) if it be envisaged as only *relatively* " Russian." Only as a detail in the general, *world-wide* revolt of the proletariat—which *is world-wide* because its impelling *cause*, the capitalist mode of production, is likewise as *world-wide* as is that which it has created—*the world market*—only so can the November (" October " in Russian convention) Revolution *in* Russia be understood. On a world front proletariat and bourgeoisie are locked in a struggle which steadily intensifies in its essential force, but finds an infinite variety of phenomenal forms of expression according as the *incidentals* of local and national circumstance vary likewise. That which was victorious in Russia in November, 1917, was neither a local nor a national force—but *the revolutionary force of the world proletariat*, which broke through the bourgeois defences just exactly at that point because in that sector *the defences of the world-bourgeoisie were weakest.*

When therefore Mr. Middleton Murry asserts and argues that the revolution in Russia was an *entirely* and *intrinsically* ' Russian " revolution, he not only (in the traditional manner of bourgeois empiricism) takes the shadow for the substance, the *appearance* for the reality—he objectively falsifies the whole concept of Revolution, the whole concept of Communism. He concedes, in fact, with scarcely an attempt at disguise, the revealing truth that his basic objection to the revolution *in* Russia is that it reveals itself unmistakably as that (for him and his like) *ugly fact—a Proletarian Revolution.* Thus he reveals objectively that which an analysis of his argument proves to be true subjectively, namely, that *he is fighting* (and that in the *name* of " Socialism," " Communism," " revolution," and " *independent labour politics* ") *on the side of the White counter-revolutionaries all the world over,* not only against Proletarian Revolution in Russia, but against Proletarian Revolution everywhere, *especially in Britain.*

That is what it means to " believe," and act upon the " belief," that " Communism " will come in Britain " *in a Christian way* " !

And let there be no dubiety about it. Many " willing-to-be-Marxists " in Britain and the U.S.A. have adopted this myth, that the November Revolution " falsified the doctrine of Marxism " in one or other of its multiform varieties of application. The above analysis has demonstrated that they cannot entertain this theory without at some point or another being driven by the logic of their theory *into objectively Counter-Revolutionary " White " practices,* and that in direct hostility to the proletariat of their own respective lands.

· · · · ·

How did this myth that " Marx asserted " or that " Marxism premises " that the proletarian revolution *must* break out *at the place where* capitalism " reaches its highest point of development " gain currency ? As we have shown, it is an intrinsically *anti*-Marxian, *anti*-historical conception precisely because it is *anti*-dialectical and therefore mystically, or mechanically, *metaphysical.*

It involves the glaring fallacy of exhausting the Marxian conception of history of its dialectic by converting the dynamic *interaction* between the economic basis of society and its superstructure into a static mechanical correspondence—one in which the political ideological superstructure changes *automatically* in response to changes in the economic basis. More than that : it converts both basis and superstructure into *abstractions.* And, by thus eliminating the living human beings, whose active interrelation is expressed both in the basis of society and in the superstructure, *it eliminates the active, developing, and development-producing revolutionary struggle itself.* By treating each " country " as an absolute " isolate " it converts the Marxian concept into a grotesque metaphysical-idealist parody of itself. Its prevalence proves how Marxism stripped of its *materialism* relapses through bastard Hegelianism into idealist confusion, eclecticism, opportunism, sophistry, solipsism, and supernaturalism. Marxism stripped of its *dialectic* relapses through mechanical materialism into metaphysics, eclecticism, opportunism, sophistry, and supernaturalism likewise.

The historical originating cause of the myth in question is found (as its nature indicates) in the inter-penetration of the proletarian struggle by partially proletarianised sections of the petty-bourgeoisie (particularly lawyers, unfrocked priests, and other intellectuals) and the coalescence therewith of the " bourgeoisified " strata of the proletariat begotten, in the manner we have described above in the " conservative " or " middle " period (or phase) of development of the proletarian movement, particularly in imperialist countries. Kautsky is the outstanding representation of this degeneration of Marxism in Europe generally; but it is to the English-speaking world we must trace the ideologues responsible for promulgating the myth we are discussing in pre-war days in its " classic " dogmatic form. It was, in fact, *H. M. Hyndman* (and *not* Marx *or* Engels, or any *real* Marxist) who promulgated the dogma that the Revolution (which he prophesied *categorically* for 1889—then postponed like a Milleniarian, periodically for periods five or ten years ahead) *must break out in England, because* it was there that " Capitalism reached its highest point of development ! " This was typical of the eclectic mixture of Lassalleanism, Tory-Democracy, Jingoism and bombast which H. M. Hyndman was able in consequence of its appalling theoretical destitution to impose, as " Marxism," upon the revolutionary proletarian movement in Britain. Seventy-five per cent. of the *canards* which are stuck up only to be knocked down by the enemies of Marxism in Britain are not Marxian propositions at all, but relics of that *Hyndmania* which, more than any other single ideological force, is the cause of the theoretical backwardness and malformation of the Marxist and would-be-Marxist movement in Britain to-day.

In the U.S.A. the " onlie begetter " of the myth was Daniel De Leon, an altogether different character from the charlatan-adventurer H. M. Hyndman. De Leon was, in his way, a genius. But he suffered a curious limitation in that he was almost impervious to the Dialectic. He was shrewd enough to see that there was more of Lassalle in the German Social-Democracy than of Marx, and he reacted against it, only

(to use one of his favourite phrases) " to fly off the handle "
into a rigid, doctrinaire sectarianism.   Fundamentally his
materialism was mechanical.   Hence he was a victim to the
" patriotic illusion " in the form of supposing that " *the
Revolution must break out, etc.," in the U.S.A.* (and, of course,
be led by Daniel De Leon and his " fighting S.L.P.").   Curiously, too, still under the influence of mechanical thinking
and Americanism combined, he sought to make the sociology
of (the *American*) Lewis Henry Morgan an article of faith
along with that of Marx.   He wrote and spoke habitually of
the Marx-Morgan sociology.   But it is to be noted—and this
gives the clue to the weakness of De Leon's theoretical work
—he took the Morgan sociology *at its face value, in the rigid
mechanistic form* in which Morgan presented it—not in the
dialectical sense in which Marx and Engels interpreted, and
welcomed enthusiastically, Morgan's discoveries.

Morgan was a genius and a mighty discoverer ; after years
of boycott—during which his work has been secretly plundered
to provide a world reputation for shoals of men, pigmies by
comparison—Morgan's work and worth are coming, slowly,
to be more accurately (and therefore more highly) appraised.
But it must be confessed that, though De Leon, too, had talent
of a high order, De Leon's uncritical adulation of the Morgan
sociology told in effect more on the side of intensifying the
boycott and delaying the day of the just evaluation of Morgan's
work than in the opposite direction.

De Leon's total lack of the dialectic was revealed in the
articles of his dogmatic Marxist " faith " : (*a*) the reduction
of the distinction between a reformist policy and a revolutionary one to the formal question whether " Socialism " was or
was not made an " immediate " political " demand " ;
(*b*) the (virtually idealist) affirmation that the Social revolution would come *automatically* when, but not till when, *a
majority* " *understood* " *Socialism* ; (*c*) the disguised social-
pacifism that industrial unionism would permit the dis-
possession of the bourgeoisie *without recourse to insurrection.*

The belief that the proletarian revolution " must " break
out *in the state where* capitalism reaches its highest pitch of
development, derives directly from this mechanical conception that all that is involved is the growth of the *idea*
of Socialism in the heads of a sufficient number of *individuals,*
and that the growth of the idea is an *automatic* result of
abstract " economic development."   In Britain De Leon's

writings had a powerful effect in aiding the disintegration of Hyndmanism into doctrinaire sectarian " Left "-ism on the one side, and demagogic unprincipled opportunism on the other.

Marx and Engels saw with disgust and indignation the beginnings of the tendencies which De Leon and Hyndman fastened upon and fostered. Engels fought unceasingly against the absurdity of supposing it " Marxist "—

" simply to drill a theory in an abstract dogmatic way into a great nation, even if one has the best of theories developed out of their own conditions of life."—Engels *to Sorge*, December 7th, 1889.

" The American workers are coming along already, but, just like the English, they go their own way. One cannot drum the theory into them *a priori*. Their own experience and their own blunders and the evil consequences of them will soon bump their noses against theory—and then all right ! " — Engels to *Schlüter*, January 4th, 1890.

" In a country with such an old political and labour movement [as Britain] there is always a colossal heap of traditionally inherited rubbish which has to be got rid of by degrees. There are the prejudices of the skilled Unions . . . the petty jealousies of the particular trades . . . the mutually obstructive ambitions and intrigues of the leaders. . . . In short, there is friction upon friction. And among them all the Socialist League, which looks down on everything which is not directly revolutionary (*which means here in England, as with you, everything which does not limit itself to making phrases and otherwise doing nothing*), and the [S.D.] Federation, who still behave as if everyone except themselves were asses and bunglers, although it is only due to the new force of the movement that *they* have succeeded in getting some following again.

" In short, if one looks only at the surface one would say it was all confusion and personal quarrels, but *under* the surface the movement is going on. . . ."—Engels to *Sorge*, April 19th, 1890.

It is in the highest degree significant that the myth that " the Bolshevik revolution contradicted Marx " should thus be traceable to sectarian and opportunist groups which Marx and Engels themselves repudiated as *anti*-Marxian.

It is a negative proof of the indispensability of the

dialectical unity of Theory *and* Practice based on *the primacy of practice.* The actual practical achievements of the Bolshevik Revolution of 1917 and developments thereafter provide the positive proof of the value of the *Dialectical* Materialist method of Marx and Engels not only *as theory,* but as a *guide to Practice.*

The Dialectic of Revolutionary Practice

Dialectical Materialist Theory provides revolutionary political practice with a practical critical problem for its starting-point which may be formulated in the following contradiction :

    (1) A Revolutionary conquest of power *cannot* be planned in advance !

    (2) A Revolutionary conquest of power *must* be planned in advance !

The Marxist Dialectical Materialist Conception of History viewed abstractly—*solely* from the standpoint of its general *continuity*—gives the former : the same conception viewed, also abstractly, from the standpoint of its *discontinuity* in detail gives the latter. As soon as the conception is viewed *concretely,* and therefore dialectically, the contradiction is resolved into a unity :

    (1) A Revolution cannot be *made—until the necessary pre-conditions* have been evolved.

    (2) A Revolution can and *must be made—when* the necessary pre-conditions have been evolved.

Thus the problem for practice becomes a *dialectical* one : in the movements of the present do not forget the future ; in the aspiration towards the future do not forget the present. Which may be given a unitary formulation thus : use *every* movement, however local and momentary, as a means towards the end of creating the situation in which a transition to the open, positive revolutionary conquest of State power and authority will be not only *necessary* but practically feasible.

This revolutionary practical-critical procedure, which judges the practice of the present in the light of the end towards which it is designed to serve as a means—and, conversely, selects as the immediate end to be aimed at that which in the then and there existing circumstances best makes possible a further movement to another end more closely approximating to the (provisional) *ultimate end* of Revolution—this policy, illustrated by the whole life-practice, theoretical and practical, of Marx and Engels, finds its fullest and clearest expression in the theory and practice of *Leninism* ; which is—

> " the Marxism of the epoch of imperialism and of the proletarian revolution. To be more precise : Leninism is the theory and the tactic of the proletarian revolution in general, and the theory and the tactic of the dictatorship of the proletariat in particular."—STALIN : *Foundations of Leninism*.

In a later essay, *Problems of Leninism*, Stalin explained and vindicated this definition thus :

> " Is this definition correct ?
> " I think so. It is correct first of all because it gives an accurate demonstration of the historical roots of Leninism, which is described as Marxism *of the epoch of imperialism*—this being an answer to certain critics of Lenin who falsely supposed that Leninism did not originate until *after* the imperialist war. It is correct, in the second place, because it accurately indicates the *international* character of Leninism—this being an answer to the Social Democrats, who consider that Leninism is not applicable anywhere except in Russia. It is correct, in the third place, because it accurately shows the organic connection *between Leninism and the teaching of Marx*, describing Leninism as *Marxism* of the epoch of imperialism—this being an answer to certain critics of Lenin, who believe that Leninism is not a *further development* of Marxism, but merely a *revival* of Marxism, and an application of Marxism to Russian conditions."—
> STALIN : *Problems of Leninism* (in *Leninism*, Vol. I).

Stalin, it will be perceived, did not find it necessary to affirm that his definition also covered that particular imbecility with which we have been forced to deal—the allegation, namely, that Leninism *is not Marxism at all* ! This imbecility is possible only to those who contrive to envisage Marxism as a *closed* dogmatic system which excluded all possibility of further development. And that, in turn, has been possible to a far greater extent in Britain and the U.S.A. than anywhere else precisely because, from lack of—or even a positive repulsion from—the Dialectic Method, Marxism has, in those countries, been conceived either as a " *credo* to be swallowed whole " (ENGELS) or as a romantic mystification convenient for covering up an unprincipled demagogic *careerism*.

Taking Stalin's definition as a convenient starting point,

we can consider the dialectic of revolutionary practice under the following heads : (1) The general issue between a Revolutionary and a Reformist policy ; (2) the particular issue as between " Democracy " and the " Dictatorship of the Proletariat " ; (3) the special issue as between Proletarian Dictatorship and the Fascist Dictatorship.

The general issue between Reformism and Revolutionary Marxism is analogous to that between the philosophers and Dialectical Materialism. Whereas " the philosophers had changed only the interpretation of the world," dialectical materialism begins with the recognition that what has to be changed is the world itself. Similarly the Reformist, faced with the need for a change in fundamental social relations, confines himself in practice to attempting only such modifications of detail as leave in being those very social relations which it is, theoretically, his intention to transform entirely. Thus, for instance, the typical British reformist argues that while the Law and the Constitution need modification in certain respects and in ways favourable to the common people, these modifications would preserve and not in any way impair the *essentials* of the Law and Constitution. The typical Socialist-reformist argues that " we have solved the problem of production : now we have to solve the problem of distribution." As against both, Marxism envisages the becoming of a need for the overthrow of the Law and Constitution in their present forms and for a radical alteration of the mode of production (as well as the distribution which is a consequence of that mode) and of the whole social organisation based upon it.

But Marxism is not therefore to be confounded with the revolutionism *a priori* of the insurrectionary, Bakuninist, sectarian Left-ist schools. It does not confine its policy to an *abstract* opposition to capitalism in general, or an equally abstract advocacy of revolution in general. It subordinates all its endeavours to developing the historically conditioned force which alone is capable of overthrowing capitalism in the concrete—overthrowing the rule of the capitalist class.

Marxist political practice therefore discriminates itself clearly from both Reformism and Utopian-Revolutionism. That in Britain critics of Marxism usually confound it with one or other of these : or, alternatively, accuse it of being contradictory in that, superficially, it resembles both of them, is due partly to the incapacity of the critics and partly to the fact that both Reformism and abstract, doctrinaire, revolutionism were conjoined eclectically in Hyndmanism, the earliest (and noisiest) form of " Marxism," to maintain a separate party existence in Britain. In its decomposition Hyndmanism has left its relics in the shape of reformist and doctrinaire-revolutionist sects who are united only by their common hatred for the true Marxism (i.e., Leninism) of the Communist Party.

This fact is important from two sides. Doctrinaire (or " wall-eyed ") Marxism begins by conceptually separating the Theory (" Socialism ") from the Practice (the day-to-day struggle). It begins with a perverse assertion, namely, that the day-to-day struggle, as such, is a struggle only for the betterment " of Capitalism " ; hence it proceeds, having conceptually separated " Capitalism " from " Socialism " as *ideal absolutes*, to argue that the day-to-day struggle is " not for Socialism." Hence it is, it says, *Reformist*. The logic of this attitude, carried out in full consistency, is to argue that *therefore* the day-to-day struggle is " bad," and should be abandoned.

This it will be perceived is, under a disguise of " Marxist " *phrases*—which " on principle " must remain phrases lest they become sullied with " reformist " practice—nothing but a return to the standpoint of the Utopians, of the " German or ' True ' Socialists," and of the Proudhonian " Socialists," all of whom rejected as " bad " and denounced as " anti-social " and " reformist " the actual *practice* of day-to-day struggle as waged, particularly, in the form of strikes, and specifically-proletarian insurrections.

No better proof can be found of the anachronistic and reactionary character of this " Marxism " (which, significantly, exists only in the English-speaking world—and most of all among the Anglo-Saxons) than the fact that its actual practice is identical with, though its phrases are different from, those of the " True " Socialists and of the Proudhonian " Socialists " of 1844–50. Like the " True " Socialists, it seizes every opportunity to " confront the political movement [of the proletariat] with ' Socialist ' demands," and of preaching to the masses that they " had nothing to gain, and everything to lose, by this ' bourgeois ' movement." Like them it goes " to the extreme length of directly opposing the ' brutally destructive' tendency of Communism, and of proclaiming its supreme and impartial contempt of all class struggles " (save, of course, those waged by itself *on paper*). Similarly,

like the Proudhonians, it "seeks to depreciate every revolutionary movement in the eyes of the working class by showing
that no mere political reform [these "wall-eyed" Marxists
allege that the Bolshevik revolution was a "mere political
reform"!] but only a change in the material conditions of
existence, in economical relations, could be of any advantage
to them." (See *Communist Manifesto*, pp. 33, 34.)

This type of political "Utopianism"—these "wall-eyed"
Marxists are particularly prone to the ballot-box Utopia,
the notion that the capitalist class will "surrender un-
conditionally" as soon as a majority of *real* Socialists is
returned at a General Election—formulates the antithesis
between Reform and Revolution as that between making
"immediate demands" and "demanding Socialism, and
nothing less than Socialism"! The fact that the question is
thus formulated as a purely parliamentary question, as one in
which the bourgeoisie hold the initiative of giving or refusing
right up to the end—the fact that the process is conceived
as influenced by nothing but the quantitative increase or
decrease in the "revolutionary vote," proves that behind
these pseudo-"Marxist" and quasi-"revolutionary" phrases
is concealed an essentially abstract, anti-dialectical, anti-
historical, and therefore anti-Marxist standpoint.

The frankly Opportunist formulation of the antithesis
between Reform and Revolution equates the former to
"peaceful" and "gradual" progress, and the latter to
violent, catastrophic "sudden" changes. In its classic form
this opportunist formulation denies the possibility of "sudden"
or "violent" changes ; and as such opposes the concept o
"Evolution" to "Revolution." This, as we have seen in
discussing the concept of Evolution in connection with
Darwinism, is not only falsified by the actual dialectic of
biological evolution, but is an undialectical conception of
evolution as "simple increase and decrease"—a unilateral
movement from which all possibility of *qualitative* changes in
the form and direction of the movement have been excluded.
Theoretically it is based on the fallacy of seeing in the dialectical processes of the universe *only the continuity*. Practically
it is, therefore, the more sincere it is, the more forced to
conceive the bourgeois order as in principle the only social
order conceivable or attainable by Man. Its sophisticated
form—that which discriminates between Reform and Revolution by means of their relative "peacefulness" and "violence," slides over from *frank* Opportunism to Camouflaged

Opportunism, or Social-fascist resistance to proletarian revolution.

The eclectic formulation of the antithesis between Reform and Revolution makes the difference one of *formal* (as distinct from substantial) *principle*. The difference is, it is alleged, between alternative conceptions of *political method*. The " methods," be it noted, are conceived as being at all times equally available for practice, but they are conceived as leading, logically, to opposite results.

The theoretical worthlessness and practical opportunism of this formulation is seen from its now fashionable " up-to-date " form, which poses " Democracy " as in *absolute* and irreconcilable opposition to " Dictatorship." It will be perceived at once that no discrimination is made between bourgeois and proletarian democracy on the one side, or between proletarian and bourgeois dictatorships on the other. Thus this formulation cuts clean across the class-cleavage which is the real front line of struggle between the bourgeoisie and proletariat.

An inverse form of this eclectic formulation is the traditional Bakuninst contraposition of " Revolution " as always and at all times the " opposite " of political " Democracy " (called, in later derivations, " political action," which is contraposed to " direct action "). Not only does this formulation cut across the line of demarcation between the Bourgeoisie and the Proletariat (as in the case of its converse), but, in addition, it involves an opportunistic reduction of the conception of Revolution to the level of *one only* of its incidental phenomena —that of insurrectionary outbreak, upheaval, and riot. The conception of Revolution thus becomes a purely negative conception (as with opportunist Reformism of all shades)— all the positive and constructive elements in the conception being eliminated.

Against all these stands the Dialectical Materialist Conception of Revolution and the distinction between it and Reformism.

In its widest sense a Revolution comprises the *whole* historical process by means of which " the whole gigantic superstructure," legal and political, of a particular historically conditioned social formation is " more or less rapidly transformed "—conceived as a logical culmination of the ripening class-antagonisms developed within it under the impelling contradictions created by the development of " the material productive forces of society." From which it follows that a Revolution is *both* Theoretical *and* Practical ; Immediate *and* Ultimate ; political *and* anti-" political " ; parliamentary *and* anti-parliamentary ; gradual *and* sudden ; peaceful *and* violent ; constructive *and* destructive : in a word, it is a *dialectical* process of transition, a mutation *leap* which bridges over the gap between two distinct stages in the evolutionary progression of human society.

Viewed as practice, a policy is *Revolutionary* in proportion as it possesses *all* those characteristics, not *in separation*, but *in combination*. Thus it is folly to separate " immediate " from " ultimate " aims and treat one as opposed to the other. It is, for instance, folly and worse than folly to condemn the practice of formulating demands on behalf of the unemployed as " reformism." While it would be folly and the rankest of Reformism to treat anything conceded to the demands of the unemployed as an instalment of Socialism ; to refuse to recognise that the *extortion* of a concession stimulates the revolutionary class-struggle is merely *inverted reformism*. It is folly to treat Parliamentaty action, as such, as " reformist " or, conversely, " truly revolutionary." A revolutionary policy is " parliamentarian " in an *anti*-parliamentary way, and, vice versa, its anti-parliamentarian practice (outside the parliamentary sphere as well as inside) is " parliamentarian " in the sense of having a *political* objective—that of promoting the revolutionary proletariat to the position of ruling class. It is folly, and worse than folly, to treat " violence " as at all times and in all places " wrong," " bad," and " reactionary," and to conceive the practical choice to lie between a " peaceful " or a " non-peaceful " procedure .The revolutionary policy envisages both the possibility that " peaceful " practices may logically lead to situations in which " violence " *must* be resorted to, and its converse—that in certain situations it would be folly and worse to resort to violence. And so on.

The real issue as between a Revolutionary Policy and a Reformist one arises out of the objective nature of the proletarian struggle in general, and the dialectical *connection* between the essential and the " accidental " phases of the struggle. To separate conceptually the " accidental " from the " essential " (the " immediate " from the " mediated " or " ultimate "), and to proceed as though the " accidentals " were non-existent, and the " ultimate " the immediate objectives of the struggle, is to be self-blinded to the fact that the *essential* for practice is reached *through* the accidental, and the ultimate through the immediate. It is to falsify utterly the Marxian conception that the proletarian objective can be attained only in, through, and by means of " prolonged struggles transforming circumstances and men."

The Reformist view excludes all recognition of the *transforming power of the struggle as such*. It excludes all conception of the *constructive* aspect of destruction, and the destructive aspect of construction.

The governing objective of Revolutionary policy is the *conquest of* POWER *by the proletariat*. The pseudo-" Marxist " who narrows that conception down to the mere " capture of the political machinery of the State " becomes thereby indistinguishable from the open, liberalistic Reformist, who denies that any need exists for a *class* conquest of *power*. Both agree in thinking that all that is required can be done if only *the right sort of majority* is returned to Parliament ! As between the two the open Reformist is (because he is such openly) more respect-worthy and less dangerous than the concealed Reformist, who hides his real nature under a cloak of " Left " and " Revolutionary " phrases.

The issue can be made clear by an examination of the question of the Dictatorship of the Proletariat.

THE DICTATORSHIP OF THE PROLETARIAT AND ITS DIALECTIC

The dictatorship of the proletariat is in the first place the logical *continuation* of the proletarian class struggle. Since, however, it is the continuation of the class-struggle beyond the point of victory, it is a *complete* alteration of the struggle in the sense that what had been a revolutionary struggle against the ruling (bourgeois) class and state becomes in the new situation itself a new form of state and ruling-class actively engaged in repressing all resistance to its establishment of a new system of production and a new form of society. In the third place, since the dictatorship of the proletariat will succeed in its object only so far as it *abolishes the proletariat*, by abolishing all class-distinctions, it is its own negation—in that, obviously, its dictatorial function lapses along with all the resistance to itself which lapses in turn along with the objective class basis from which this resistance arose.

There is nothing peculiar or distinctive in the fact that the revolutionary rule of the proletariat will take on a dictatorial form. On the contrary, every revolutionary government must during its revolutionary period rule dictatorially since its historical ground of existence is the need to overthrow the forms of law and state which have till then prevailed. In such circumstances the revolutionary government is self-excluded from reinforcing its rule by the aid of the traditional precedents and sanctions which supported the rule of its predecessors. It must rule in virtue of its own inherent right, for which its own power of maintaining itself and enforcing its authority must be the guarantee. This was revealed over and over again at every stage in the development of the bourgeois revolution, and must be even more true in the case of the proletariat since—" the Communist revolution is the most radical rupture with traditional property-relations ; no wonder that its development involves the most radical rupture with traditional ideas " (*Communist Manifesto*).

Accordingly, the only thing even relatively new about the concept of the dictatorship of the proletariat is its name —which is only unfamiliar to British Marxists and critics of Marxism in proportion to their ignorance of the works of Marx and Engels. The Marxist concept of class-struggle,— that the great end to which all Marxist political practice must be subordinated as means is that of developing all proletarian struggles—local, national, and international ; industrial, political, and ideological—up to the point at which the revolutionary conquest of power by the proletariat becomes possible of attainment ;—this concept includes that of the dictatorship of the proletariat to anyone capable of envisaging the process involved concretely.

A familiar " democratic " juggle from the pseudo-" Socialist " and " democratic " camp falls under notice here. " Since the proletariat constitutes a majority in Britain, why cannot they win power *democratically* ? Where is the need for *dictatorship* ? " The juggle is a transparent one. Firstly, it confuses the *form* of " democratic " election with the reality of *democracy*—the rule of the common people. Secondly, it supposes (in the teeth of all evidence) that the winning of a parliamentary election, *of itself*, constitutes the " conquest of power." Thirdly, it supposes that the capitalist class (with its dependants and its dupes) will submit without a struggle to the verdict of a general election. Fourthly, it supposes that this " peaceful and democratic " procedure constitutes a *real* alternative to the revolutionary conquest, defeat, and immobilisation of the actual forces at the disposal of the bourgeoisie. Fifthly, it ignores calmly the fact demonstrated above, that *all* government in a class-divided society involves, of necessity, the dictatorial use of compulsion by one class at the expense of all other classes, and of the refractory members of its own class.

Had this been more clearly perceived we might have been spared—or might not have been spared—such affirmations as those of the Labour Party and Trade Union Congress in 1933, which declared an undying allegiance to " *democracy* " *in opposition to all forms of dictatorship whatsoever* ! We reply bluntly : " *democracy* " in the Labour Party sense *is itself a form of dictatorship* !

As long ago as 1903, before the Labour Party had fully emerged from its chrysalis stage of the Labour Representation Committee, and before the Russian Social-Democratic Labour Party had split into its Bolshevik (Leninist) and Menshevik (anti-Leninist) sections, at the time when the Fabian-led I.L.P. dominated working-class politics in Britain, the chief spokesman of the Fabians stated the position with inimitable force and clarity :

" Of course, if the nation adopted the Fabian policy, *it would be carried out by brute force exactly as the present property system is*. It would become the law ; and those who resisted it would be fined, sold up, knocked on the head by policemen, thrown into prison, and in the last resort ' executed,' just as they are when they break the present law. But as our proprietary class has no fear of that conversion taking place . . . the Fabian Society is patted on the back, just as the Christian Social Union is, while the Socialist who says that a Social revolution can be made only as all other revolutions have been made, by the people who want it killing, coercing, and intimidating the people who don't want it, is denounced as a misleader of the people, and imprisoned with hard labour *to show him how much sincerity there is in the objection of his captors to physical force*."—BERNARD SHAW : *Man and Superman*, pp. 203–4.

Several years before Shaw wrote this, William Morris, in 1889, in a lecture on *Communism* addressed *to the Fabian Society*, had put the same point with equal clarity and force, and in even finer words. Morris is criticising the notion of gaining Socialism by instalments of reform :

" We must not lose sight of the very obvious fact that these improvements in the life of the larger public can only be carried out at the expense of some portion of the *freedom* and fortunes of the proprietary classes. They are, *when genuine*, one and all attacks, I say, on the ' liberty ' and ' property ' of the non-working or useless classes, as some of these classes see clearly enough. And I admit that if the sum of them should become vast and deep-reaching enough to give to the useful or working classes intelligence enough to conceive of a life of equality and co-operation, courage enough to accept it and to bring the necessary skill to bear on working it ; and *power enough to force its acceptance* on the stupid and the interested, the war of classes would speedily end in the victory of the useful class, which would then become the new Society of Equality.

" Intelligence enough to conceive, courage enough to will, *power enough to compel.* If our ideas of a new Society are anything more than a dream, these three qualities must animate the due effective majority of the working people ; and then, I say, the thing will be done."
—WILLIAM MORRIS : *Communism* (Nonesuch " Morris," pp. 661–662).

And this in turn may be compared with a related passage from a polemic against the Anarchists written by Engels (who, it should be remembered, largely influenced William Morris) :

" Have these gentlemen ever seen a revolution ? Revolution is the most authoritarian thing possible. It is an act in which one section of the population imposes its will on the other by means of rifles, bayonets, cannon, i.e., by highly authoritarian means ; and the victorious party is inevitably forced to maintain its supremacy by means of that fear which its arms inspire in the reactionaries. Would the Paris Commune have lasted a single day had it not relied on the armed people against the bourgeoisie ? Are we not, on the contrary, entitled to blame the Commune for not having made sufficient use of this authority ?

" And so : either—or ! Either the anti-authoritarians do not know what they are talking about, in which case they merely sow confusion ; or they do know, *in which case they are betraying the cause of the proletariat.*"—
ENGELS : quoted by Lenin in *State and Revolution*, p. 49.

The reference to the Paris Commune reminds us that in the introduction he wrote in 1891 for a new German translation of Marx's *Civil War in France* Engels concluded with the pungent passage :

> " Of late the *Social-Democratic* * philistine has once more been filled with wholesome terror at the words : *Dictatorship of the Proletariat.* Well and good, gentlemen ; do you want to know what this dictatorship looks like ? Look at the Paris Commune. *That was the Dictatorship of the Proletariat !* "—ENGELS : Introduction to *The Civil War in France*, p. 19.

In a polemic against the Anarchists in 1873 Marx himself wrote to the same purpose :

> " When the political struggle of the working class assumes a revolutionary form ; when *the workers set up* in place of the dictatorship of the bourgeoisie *their own revolutionary dictatorship*, then they commit the terrible crime (!) of ' outraging principle,' for in order to satisfy their wretched, vulgar, everyday needs, in order to *break down the resistance of the bourgeoisie*, they give the State a revolutionary and transitional form, instead of laying down arms and abolishing the State."—MARX : quoted in *State and Revolution*, p. 47.

Marx, Engels, Lenin, William Morris, and Bernard Shaw, all at different times, and in different circumstances, turning their attention to the question of the proximate objective of the struggle for Socialism and Communism, all render the same verdict—the problem of " democracy," considered either from the working-class or from the bourgeois standpoint is, in concrete reality, a problem of how to achieve and how to exercise *the power to Dictate* !

It cannot for one moment be supposed that the British Labour and Trade Union chiefs (Walter Citrine, for example) are ignorant of the truth so pungently expressed by Bernard Shaw and so powerfully by William Morris (to cite none but " distinguished " British witnesses). That Governmental power is *power*—is necessarily *dictatorial*, though not necessarily arbitrary—they simply must know. Why, then, do they treat the demand for the vesting of Governmental power in *the proletariat as a class* as on all fours with the Fascists' demand that the proletarian struggle in all its forms shall be suppressed and dictatorial power be vested in the " corporate " state ?

---

* *Social-Democratic :* The term actually used by Engels. Altered by the Social-Democratic editors of the official edition to " *German* " ! (See edition published by Martin Lawrence, 1933, p. 19.)

Whatever their theoretical excuse, their objective attitude amounts to nothing less than this : that they fight for a state of society which, while it excludes Fascism (in form) on the one hand, excludes the reality of a Communist (i.e., a *proletarian*) revolution on the other.

What state of society is it which does this ?

Nothing less than the existing order of society—the *Dictatorship of the Bourgeoisie* camouflaged under " democratic " forms !

This ugly truth is never faced. Even when it is admitted to be true " in a measure," it is asserted as a set-off that this bourgeois dictatorship may be modified by constitutional means into the " democratic " rule of Labour. And this it is claimed is what Marx advocated.

The claim adds falsification to evasion. The points evaded are : (1) that all exercise of State power is necessarily dictatorial ; (2) that unless the rule of " Labour " means an *enforced* destruction of bourgeois rights and privileges, and a corresponding enlargement of those of the workers, it will be a mockery. As to Marx :

" The main point in the teaching of Marx is the class struggle. This has very often been said and written. *But this is not true.*

" Out of this error . . . springs an opportunist distortion of Marxism ; such a falsification of it as to make it acceptable to the bourgeoisie.

" The theory of the class struggle was *not* created by Marx, but by the bourgeoisie *before* Marx, and is, generally speaking, *acceptable* to the bourgeoisie. He who recognises *only* the class struggle is not yet a Marxist. . . .

" A Marxist is one who *extends* the acceptance of class struggle to the acceptance of the *dictatorship of the proletariat.* Herein lies the difference between a Marxist and an ordinary petty or big bourgeois."—LENIN : *State and Revolution*, p. 28.

Lenin's assertion has, in turn, been denied by Social-Democrats, English, American, and German. It has, however, direct documentary evidence. Witness the justly-celebrated letter from Marx to his friend Weydemeyer in 1852 :

" No credit is due to me for discovering the existence of classes in modern society, nor yet the struggle between them. Long before me bourgeois historians had described the historical development of this class struggle, and bourgeois economists the economic anatomy of the classes.

" What I did that was new was to prove :

(1) that the *existence of classes* is only bound up with *particular historic phases in the development of production* ;

(2) that the class struggle necessarily leads to the *dictatorship of the proletariat* ;

(3) that this dictatorship itself only constitutes the transition to the *abolition of all classes* and to a *classless society.*"—MARX : *Letter to Weydemeyer*, March 5th, 1852.

The unifying dialectic of this passage and its content in general have been, as will have been perceived, already demonstrated in the course of this essay. What is new here (or was to many British Marxists when Lenin first quoted this letter) is the phrase " dictatorship of the proletariat." Yet no one can deny that the *substance* of that phrase is to be found in every pronouncement of Marx we have examined, from his first essay in 1844 to his latest in 1882. Why then has there been so desperate an attempt in British (as well as German) " Marxist " circles to argue and explain away this phrase ? We will come later to the *objective* social and political explanation. Here we confine ourself to noting that this " British " attitude—which has been carried to the extravagant lengths of denying that Marx *ever* used the phrase *except in private* (!)—derives directly from Kautsky and his polemic against the Bolshevik Revolution.

Since Marx in his writings also refers constantly to *democracy*, it has been supposed in Britain that either Marx couldn't make up his mind, or else that he changed it as he grew older. Kautsky affirms categorically that Marx only intended by the term " dictatorship of the proletariat " to describe a political *condition*, and not a *form of government*. Whether this effort of Kautsky's is valid and whether it reveals anything more than a distinction without a difference can be proved by a few further citations from Marx and a consideration of their historic setting.

Firstly, to dispose of the question as to whether Marx " changed his mind " as he grew older, there is the passage given above from the introduction he wrote to the Russian edition of the *Communist Manifesto*. Marx speaks of the Tsar as a " prisoner of war of the Revolution " (it being then notorious that the Tsar dared not venture far abroad from fear of the terrorists), and of a Russian Revolution as giving the signal for world revolution. Nothing could have been further from his mind than " constitutional " revolution. And this was almost his last public utterance.

A little earlier, in February, 1881, Marx, when writing to the Christian Anarchist Domela Nieuwenhuis, had emphasised the fact that :

> " A socialist government does not come into power in a country unless conditions are so developed that *it can above all take the necessary measures for intimidating the mass of the bourgeoisie* "—MARX–ENGELS : *Correspondence*, p. 386.

In 1870, writing to Kugelmann upon the Paris Commune, then in being, Marx said :

> " If you look into the last chapter of my *Eighteenth Brumaire* you will find that I say that the next attempt of the French revolution will be no longer, as before, to transfer the bureaucratic-military machine from one hand to another, *but to smash it*, and that is essential for every real people's revolution on the Continent. And that is what our heroic Party comrades in Paris are attempting."—MARX : *Letters to Kugelmann*, 12th April, 1871.

Then too, as well as the polemic against the Anarchists quoted above, there is the famous passage in his letter of May, 1875, to the Social-Democratic chiefs in criticism of their Gotha " Unity " programme :

> " Between capitalist and communist society lies the period of the revolutionary transformation of the one into the other. There corresponds to this also a political transition period during which the State can be nothing else than the *revolutionary dictatorship of the proletariat*. The programme under consideration has nothing to say about this. Its political demands comprise nothing beyond the old familiar *democratic litany*. . . .
> " Even the most commonplace democracy, which sees *the millennium in the democratic republic* and has no suspicion that the class struggle has definitely to be fought to a finish *in this ultimate political form of bourgeois society*, towers mountain high over this kind of democracy which keeps within the boundaries of what is permitted, by the police, however logically impermissible this may be."—MARX : *Gotha Programme*, pp. 44–5, 47.

This passage is decisive both as regards the " dictatorship " and the " democracy." Quite explicitly the revolutionary dictatorship of the proletariat is postulated as the only State form possible during the transition from capitalism to communism. Equally definitely this dictatorship is envisaged as supervening upon and *replacing* the " democratic *republic*," which is categorically indicated as the political form of society in which the " class struggle has *definitely* to be fought *to a finish*." Kautsky's endeavour to quibble as between a " form of government " and a " political condition " is seen for the wretched quibble it is as soon as this fact is grasped. Obviously, if the dictatorship of the proletariat *follows upon* the " fight to a finish " which has taken place within the *form* of a *democratic republic*, it is *both* a " form of government " and a definite " political condition "—it is a condition both so far as the proletarian " dictators " are concerned, and also for the non-proletarian " subjects " dictated to. It is a form of government so far as it is a *state*, and has specific functions as the agency of a revolutionary transition, which, precisely because it is a *transition* and *revolutionary*, is a *continuation* of the class struggle in an altered form. Quite obviously the class struggle no more ends at the moment when the revolutionary class at last gets the upper hand, than it begins with the first attempt of the subject class at a revolutionary conquest of power.

Marx's conception thus, in that it envisages the very fact which the bourgeois and petty-bourgeois democrats refuse to envisage as a *positive* fact (the confrontation and antagonistic *struggle* of classes), and envisages too the process of transition *after* the conquest of power as continuous in substance with the process of struggle which has culminated in that conquest, is sharply opposed as a conception (as Lenin quite correctly notes) to that of any bourgeois or petty-bourgeois democracy whatsoever.

The issue is seen in its true bearings as soon as one contrasts Marx's words (and Lenin's interpretation thereof) with the "interpretation" offered by Kautsky in 1924. He quotes the sentence from the *Critique of the Gotha Programme* (included in the extract above), which includes the words " dictatorship of the proletariat," and then adds the comment :

" In the light of the experiences of recent years pertaining to questions of government, we might vary this sentence by saying :

" ' Between the time when the *democratic State* has a purely bourgeois *Government* and the time when it has a

2D

purely Labour Government extends a period when the one is being transformed into the other. To this a political period of transition also corresponds when the Government would generally assume the form of a Coalition."—KAUTSKY : *Labour Revolution*, pp. 53–4.

One reads this passage and marvels. Is it really possible that the man who could write *this* comment on *these* words of Marx could once have been regarded, and with some degree of plausibility, as the *leading* " *Marxist* " in Europe—in the *world ?* It gives a melancholy proof of the level to which Marxist theory had sunk between the death of Engels in 1895 and the rise of Lenin to world celebrity in 1917 that during the greater part of that period Kautsky should have held this repute almost unchallenged—except so far as Bernstein and the British I.L.P. regarded him as " too revolutionary ! "

A child could see through the " card-sharping " character of this Kautsky emendation of Marx's words. Marx envisages an historical process of transition *from* capitalism *to* communism—a process which grows less and less capitalistic in its *economy* and more and more Socialist. Contrasting with that is the political process of transition in which *no such simple alteration is possible.* Since it is, and cannot help but be, fundamentally a question of *which* of the two classes whose antagonism is basic in the bourgeois order shall *rule*, any notion of a *coalition of these classes* is ruled out. Coalitions of *parties* which more or less represent one specific pole in the class antagonism are not ruled out *absolutely*. But they are ruled out *relatively*, since in a revolutionary transition obviously that government is alone finally possible as the instrument of the dictatorship of the revolutionary *class*, which is most clearly and fully representative of its basic and general *revolutionary* will. Hence, disregarding incidental preliminary unions between the proletariat and other exploited classes, Marx goes directly to the *essence*—the fact that during the period in which the economy of society is being *purposefully* and *specifically transformed* from a capitalist into a socialist economy—a process bound to be sabotaged and obstructed, wilfully by conscious counter-revolutionaries, unconsciously and through ignorance and stupidity by the non-revolutionary elements of all classes—during such a period the State form " can be none other than the revolutionary dictatorship of the proletariat."

Such is Marx's reasoning: Kautsky replies by *ignoring* the vital part of the question, this *social* essence of the whole matter.

For Kautsky the whole question arises only within the walls
of Parliament ! It is solely a question of a " transition "
from the *time* when a *purely* bourgeois government holds
office to the *time* when there is a *purely* Labour Government,
and of the probable intervening stage of (presumably) compound " impurity " in which both lose their identity in a
" Coalition " ! It would seem incredible to an impartial
observer acquainted with the facts, but it is literally true that
Kautsky is believed by many in Britain (alleged " Marxists "
among them) to have *refuted Lenin* !

Kautsky claims to have based his " emendation " of Marx
upon the careful collation of experiences gained by the various
Labour and Socialist parties in their *participation in National
Coalition governments during and since the War* ! These were
truly strange conditions in which to look for a true perspective
of the facts of revolutionary class struggle ! On this basis he
offers a prophecy. He affirms that a *real* " proletarian revolution " took place in Germany in 1918, while only an " apparent " one took place in Russia in 1917. Thereupon he
affirms :

> " The bourgeois revolution ended in counter-revolution,
> the instrument of which is usually military dictatorship.
> . . . In the case of a real proletarian revolution, and not,
> as in Russia, an apparent one, all the conditions are
> lacking for such a development, which was an inevitable
> termination of the bourgeois revolution."—KAUTSKY :
> *ibid.*, p. 48.

The worth of this generalisation which derives its semblance
of historical truth (as to the bourgeois revolution) by arbitrarily selecting the moment when the bourgeois revolution
may be deemed to have ended, and (as to the proletarian
revolution) solely from Kautsky's personal " gifts " as a
prophet, has been revealed by the subsequent developments.
Kautsky (in 1922–24) affirmed :

> " In Austria there is a Christian Socialist Government,
> which would become impossible on the day the Socialists
> *decided to overthrow it* (p. 49).

> " In my judgment the working class is *stronger in
> Germany* than it is in Austria, although in the former case
> it does not control the militia . . . (p. 51).

> " [In] all countries where the conquest of political
> power by the proletariat is effected by means of
> democracy, which is the normal method *now that the
> military monarchies have collapsed* . . . (p. 54).

" Those who to-day reject the policy of coalition on principle are oblivious to the signs of the times, and incapable of rising to the height of their tasks (p. 54).

" A *real* counter-revolution is only to be found *in extremely backward countries* such as Hungary . . . (p. 46).

" Although the last political upheaval in Germany was not a proletarian revolution in the *proper* meaning of the word, as it only brought temporary power to the proletariat . . . the counter-revolution has not yet assumed the proportions usual in bourgeois revolutions, and *we may expect that the momentary reaction will soon reach its high-water mark* " (p. 46).—KAUTSKY : *The Labour Revolution* (English trans., 1924).

These extracts make grim reading to-day. They throw into lurid light the policy which, with Kautsky's approval, led the German workers to surrender the power they actually held for a time, in the hope that a coalition government would obviate the need for " violent " struggle and make possible a " peaceful " transition to Socialism. This policy too led the Austrian Social-Democrats through surrender after surrender, until the armed forces which they once controlled were used by the Christian " Socialist " Dolfuss to butcher the Austrian proletariat which, driven desperate, broke through the restraints of its incredibly treacherous Social-Democratic leadership to make a fight so heroic as to win the admiration of the whole world, and universal execration for that leadership and policy which had held back such magnificent fighting material until all chance of victory had gone.

Democracy AND " Democracy "

The real practical issue is one which the Kautskyite sophistry obscures under a cloud of pretentious ambiguities.

No revolutionary worker wants to be *dictated* to ; no revolutionary worker wants to dictate *personally* to anybody else. Every worker not absolutely degenerate in subservience feels he ought to have a say in the making of the rules he has to obey ; and every worker not absolutely degenerate knows that in real practical life co-operation involves plan, rule and regulation. When the ordinary worker calls himself a " democrat " he means that he feels in this way ; he affirms, that is, his right to a say in the government of his personal and his communal life.

If he be at all politically conscious he affirms in demanding " democracy " more than this. He affirms his " democratic " opposition to all the class privileges which place the worker in a position of subjection and subservience.

That is what " democracy " means to the average British worker : that is what it always meant to revolutionaries until Kautsky and his British imitators began to juggle with the word in order to find " democratic " excuses for their toadying to their Kings, Kaisers, Tsars and Presidents during the War, and for their hatred of Lenin and the Bolsheviks, who by daring, *and winning,* proved them to be the treacherous poltroons they were.

What is the difference between " Democracy," in the British working man's sense above, and the " *Dictatorship of the Proletariat* " as Marx, Engels and Lenin used the term ?

In essence : *no difference at all.* In fact, Lenin always claimed that the Dictatorship of the Proletariat was *democratic, real working-class democracy* ; while Marx quite often used the word " *Democracy* " *as synonymous with* " *Proletarian Dictatorship* " ; and never lost a chance to pour scorn on the petty-bourgeois parliamentarian charlatans who tried to fob off the workers with the parliamentary *form* of democracy instead of its revolutionary proletarian and Communist *substance.*

There is, it is clear, *Democracy* and " Democracy "—the reality and the humbug. Let us see if we can discover how to distinguish between them.

. . . . .

In their *Communist Manifesto* Marx and Engels describe the aims and objects of the Communist Party :

" The Communists . . . have no interests separate and apart from those of the proletariat as a whole. . . .

" The immediate aim of the Communists is the same as that of all the other proletarian parties : formation of the proletariat into a class, *overthrow of the bourgeois supremacy, conquest of political power by the proletariat. . . .*

" The Communists fight for the attainment of the immediate aims, for the *enforcement of the momentary interests* of the working class ; but in the movements of the present they also represent and take care of the future of that movement. . . .

" In short, the Communists everywhere support every revolutionary movement against the existing social and political order of things. . . .

" *Finally they labour everywhere for the union and agreement* of the *democratic parties* of all countries.

" The Communists disdain to conceal their views and aims.   They openly declare that their ends can be attained only by the *forcible overthrow* of all existing social conditions.

" Let the ruling classes tremble at a Communist revolution.   The proletarians have nothing to lose but their chains.   They have a world to win.

" Working men of all countries, unite ! "—Marx-Engels : *Communist Manifesto.*

If those clauses are carefully scrutinised it will be plain past all dispute that, without using the term, they envisage and describe what would be in fact a revolutionary dictatorship of the proletariat.   Also they use the term *democratic* as bearing a sense compatible with this " forcible overthrow " of the " bourgeois supremacy " and " *conquest* of political power by the proletariat."

They use the word " democracy " elsewhere in the same *Manifesto* in a sense even more unquestionably identical with the *fact* of proletarian dictatorships :

" The first step in the revolution by the working class is *to raise the proletariat to the position of ruling class, to win the battle of democracy.*"—Marx-Engels : *ibid.,* p. 27.

No words could possibly be plainer : to establish the proletariat as the *ruling class is to win the battle of democracy.* Obviously " democracy " to Marx and Engels was the fight to win ruling power for the workers and for the consolidation of that power—*because only thus could all class distinctions be abolished.*

It may be asked (it *has been* asked !)—might not " winning the battle of democracy " be understood as winning a majority at an election ?   Nowadays it might.   But in 1847, when *not a single worker in Europe had a vote*, it could not by any stretch of possibility be twisted to mean anything of the sort.

Besides !   Would Marx and Engels have invited the working men *of all countries* to " unite " *for a Parliamentary election* ?

Would they have bidden the ruling classes *of all countries* to " tremble " at the result of *a General Election* ?

Would this have been the " forcible overthrow of all existing social conditions " they " disdained " to conceal their intention to accomplish ?

It is clear past all possibility of dispute that in the *Communist Manifesto* Marx and Engels envisaged just such a revolution in essence as happened in Russia in November, 1917 ; and that they make perfectly clear by their description of the ultimate outcome they predict for such a revolution as they hope for :

> " Political power [which the revolution will conquer for the working class] properly so called is merely *the organised power of one class for oppressing another*. If the proletariat during its contest with the bourgeoisie is compelled by the force of circumstances to organise itself as a class ; if by means of a *revolution* it makes itself *the ruling class*, and as such *sweeps away by force* the old conditions of production, then it will, along with these conditions, have swept away the conditions for the existence of class antagonisms, and of classes generally, and *will* thereby have *abolished its own supremacy as a class*.
>
> " In place of the old bourgeois society, with its classes and class antagonisms, we shall have *an association* in which the *free development of each* is the condition for the free development of *all*."—MARX-ENGELS : *Communist Manifesto*, p. 28.

Of the many marvellously pregnant passages in this marvellous *Communist Manifesto* none is more pregnant than this. It proves quite beyond dispute that Marx and Engels envisaged the rule of the proletariat exactly as Marx himself described it three years later in the letter to Weydemeyer quoted above ; namely, as a *dictatorship of the proletariat*. It is also clear from this passage that they envisaged the conquest of power and the rule of the proletariat as occupying not two or three days of barricade turmoil, or of election bustle, but a " course of time," a " period of transition." And also in this very passage is indicated that very " withering away of the State " which the less instructed among critics imagine Lenin *to have invented* ! Here too and herewith is indicated the conception of a classless society for which the Second Five Year Plan in the U.S.S.R. is designed to pave the way.

No passage in the whole literature of Marxism links more closely together Marx and Engels and Lenin and Stalin than does this marvellous passage from the *Communist Manifesto*. And, what is directly to our immediate purpose, it demonstrates that the objective of them all has been, and is, just

exactly what the British working man means by " democracy "
(and just exactly what Kautsky and Walter Citrine do *not*
mean by that word), *namely*, the active and courageous
application of *every measure necessary to secure the final
extinction of all class distinctions whatsoever*.

What is the difference between the Communist idea of
democracy and the Social-Democratic notion thereof ? The
Communist wants to make democracy (i.e., the *rule of Demos*—
the common people) a *reality* for the workers in order that
these workers may by concerted and planned effort do what
is necessary to make it a reality for *everybody*. The Social-
Democrats are content, and want the workers to be content,
with the empty *form* of " democracy " while the capitalist
rulers alone enjoy its *reality and substance*.

.   .   .   .   .

At the core and heart of the word " democracy " in its old
historic, fighting sense (as distinct from its modern, humbugging, cowardly, parliamentary, swindling sense) is a *class*
demand—the demand for *class equality* ; for the abolition of
privileged classes. That is the sense in which the Fascists
hate democracy ; but that is not the sense in which the Social-
Democrats use it. They complain that the Bolsheviks
" violently " took away the privileges of the rich instead of
first of all asking their " Parliamentary " *consent* !

The Greeks, who invented the word " Democracy," always
gave it a *class* meaning. To them it meant, as we have said,
the *rule of Demos*, which meant the *loss of rule* by the
Aristocrats.

That was the sense which the word bore when it was revived
by the French Revolution of 1789.

EDMUND BURKE, who is regarded by the Universities as
one of the most profound political philosophers that Britain
has ever produced (and *he* was Irish !), fought the French
Revolution precisely because it was upsetting the " proper
subordination of classes " and giving power to " the swinish
multitude." He denounced Condorcet as a " fanatical atheist
and furious *democratic* republican." He refused to be seated
in the same coach with a " friend to the revolutionary doctrines of the French." France he called " Cannibal Castle," a
" republic of assassins " ; it was governed by " the dirtiest,
lowest, most fraudulent, most knavish of chicaners," its
people were " an allied army of Amazonian and male cannibal
Parisians," " the basest of mankind," " murderous atheists,"

" a gang of robbers," " prostitute outcasts of mankind," " a desperate gang of plunderers, murderers, tyrants, and atheists," " the scum of the earth."

There is no difficulty in detecting the class feeling here, or the identification of " democracy " with the destruction of aristocratic privilege. Nor can one fail to note that many a modern journalist at a loss for terms of abuse to hurl at the Bolsheviks seems to have turned to Burke for the loan of his vocabulary of denunciation of the Jacobins to use against their modern parallels.

George Canning, one of the most brilliant of the younger disciples of Burke, writing in the *Anti-Jacobin* in November, 1797, stated the issue clearly :

> " The poet in all ages has despised riches and grandeur. The Jacobin poet improves this sentiment into *hatred of the rich and the great* . . .
>
> " Another principle, no less devoutly entertained, and no less sedulously disseminated, is the natural and eternal *warfare of the poor and the rich.* In those orders and gradations of society which are the natural results of the original differences of talents and of industry among mankind the Jacobin sees nothing but a graduated scale of violence and cruelty. He considers every rich man as an oppressor, and every person in a lower situation as the victim of avarice, and the slave of aristocratical insolence and contempt. These truths he declares loudly, not to excite compassion or to soften the consciousness of superiority in the higher, but *for the purpose of aggravating discontent in the inferior orders.*"—CANNING : *Anti-Jacobin*, November 20th and 27th, 1797.

While Edmund Burke was raving at the French Republic a far better Irishman and far better man, THEOBALD WOLFE TONE, was in France seeking aid for the establishment of a United Irish Republic. Tone, too, was clear as to the existence of classes, and a better judge than Burke of their respective worth. He wrote in his diary in 1796 a famous passage :

> " Our [Irish] independence must be had at all hazards. If the men of property will not support us they must fall ; we can support ourselves by the aid of that numerous and respectable *class of the community, the men of no property.*"—TONE : *Autobiography*, O'Brien ed., Vol. I, p. 274.

Earlier than Tone another and better known " Democrat," JEAN PAUL MARAT, thus described the essential fact about the forces which scared Edmund Burke and his like out of their wits :

> " The Revolution was made only by the lower classes of Society, by the workers, artisans, petty traders, peasants, in short, by the entire *submerged class*, by those disinherited ones whom the rich call the *canaille*, and whom the Romans in their arrogance once termed the *proletariat*."—JEAN PAUL MARAT : *L'Ami du Peuple*, No. 667, July, 1792.

This passage is notable as giving what is probably the first modern use of the term *proletariat* in its revolutionary sense. It endorses the fact that all the " Democrats " of the period from 1792 to 1850 were men who fought for the abolition of the *subjection* of the " people "—who fought for the destruction of *class privileges* in order that the unprivileged mass might *rule* instead of the aristocrat or the plutocrat. Mere formal ballot-box " equality," which left monarchy, House of Lords, State Church, and plutocracy all in the actual enjoyment of power, would have seemed to them no " democracy " at all—nothing but a mockery of its name.

Marat, for instance, is famous both for his championship of the cause of the proletariat and for his share in achieving the Parisian revolt which brought to being the famous Constitution of 1793, which is thus described by Belfort Bax :

> " This celebrated Constitution of '93 . . . is probably the most thoroughgoing scheme of pure democracy ever devised. It not only formally recognised *the people* as the sole primary source of power, but it *delegated the exercise of that power directly to them*. Every measure was to be submitted to the primary assemblies of the " sections," of which there were forty-four thousand in all France. The magistrates were to be re-elected at the *shortest possible intervals* by simple majority, the central legislature was to be renewed annually, consisting of *delegates* from the primary assemblies, who were to be furnished with imperative mandates."—BAX : *French Revolution*, pp. 69–70.

This reveals a point about which British Labour Party " democrats " carefully keep silent. Formally " recognising " the " people " as the " ruling power " is very different from giving them the *actual power to rule*. The only constitution since 1793 to vest the *actual exercise* of power in the common people, and to make that exercise a day-to-day reality for them is that of the Soviet Republic which vests actual ruling power in the workers and peasants. Thus the proletarian dictatorship in the U.S.S.R. is the first real advance in democracy made since the overthrow (" Thermidor," 1795) of the Constitution of '93.

Out of the fights of the Parisian proletariat for the recovery of this truly *democratic* constitution, which virtually established the dictatorship of the Parisian proletariat (and was overthrown by the well-to-do bourgeoisie precisely because it did do so)—out of these fights came the first definite beginning of the *Communist* movement of modern times. This was made by the " Conspiracy of the Equals " headed by GRACCHUS BABOEUF (1796–97).

This Conspiracy is notable because it definitely identified *Democracy* with the demand of the proletariat for *real* as distinct from nominal and " legal " equality.

Their most common slogan was " Bread ! And the Constitution of '93 ! " They formulated their demands in placards posted up all over Paris by night, and they prepared to enforce their demands by an armed rising. The conspiracy was widespread ; but, betrayed by a spy, the ringleaders were captured and most of them executed.

Here is an extract from one of their placards :

" The object of society is to defend its equality, often attacked, in the state of Nature, by the strong and the wicked, and to augment by the co-operation of all the common means of enjoyment.

" Nature has imposed upon each one the obligation to work. No one can evade work without committing a crime.

" Labour and enjoyment ought to be common to all. . . .

" In a true society there ought to be neither rich nor poor.

" *The rich, who are unwilling to renounce their superfluity in favour of the indigent, are the enemies of the people.*"

It hardly needs to be added that the " Conspiracy " had a very clear idea of what was the proper treatment for these " enemies of the people," and it should be added that the Constitution of 1793 gave the people direct power to arrest, bring before the Revolutionary tribunal elected by the people, and demand instant judgment upon " enemies of the people." Clearly here the Constitution of '93 is passing by its own dialectic into the conscious Dictatorship of the

Proletariat.   This is made even clearer in the following
extract from a MS. pamphlet found in Babœuf's possession at
his arrest.   He has spoken of the Constitution of '93, and
of the " Revolution in Permanence " proclaimed by the
Jacobins in its defence.   He goes on :

> " What do we want more ?
>
> " Legislators, governors, rich property owners, listen
> in your turn !
>
> " We are all equal, are we not ?   This principle remains
> uncontested. . . .
>
> " Well ! we demand henceforth to live and die equal,
> as we have been born equal.   *We demand real equality
> or death !*   That is what we want.
>
> " And we shall have it, this real equality—it matters
> not at what price !   *Woe betide those who place themselves
> between us and it !   Woe betide him who offers resistance
> to a vow thus pronounced !*
>
> " The French Revolution is but the precursor of
> another, and a greater and more solemn revolution,
> *which will be the last* !
>
> " The People has marched over the bodies of kings
> and priests who coalesced against it ; it will be the same
> with the new tyrants, with the new political hypocrites,
> seated in the place of the old ones."—GRACCHUS
> BABOEUF : *Manifesto of the Equals*, 1797.

In this document we have what was probably the very
earliest formulation of that " Democracy " which is in substance also the Dictatorship of the Proletariat, and aimed at
establishing a Communist Equality.   The doctrine is still
in embryo, but it is already clear that the practical fact that
the Constitution of '93 did work out, in the then existing
conditions, into a *de facto* dictatorship of the Parisian proletariat receives its earliest theoretical recognition (though
only one-sidedly) in this *Manifesto of the Equals* of 1797.

Babœuf stresses the logic of the " equality " proclaimed as
an inalienable individual *right* by the revolutionary bourgeoisie of 1789.   For the proletariat this *equal right* is the
emptiest of mockeries, unless it includes the right of fair
access to " Bread "—to the means of living on a level of fair
" democratic equality."   Hence the demand for *equality in
work and enjoyment* ; hence the threat to treat as public
enemies the " rich," who are not willing to " renounce their
superfluity for the benefit of the indigent " (the bourgeois-
Christian formula for charity thus turned dialectically into a

revolutionary weapon against charity-mongering and dole-distribution). Hence too the threat of another revolution, a revolution of the *People*—i.e., the proletarian mass—which will be the *last* revolution, because it makes such a clean job of it.

The logical one-sidedness of the manifesto is seen in the fact that it ignores the *inequality* of using *equal rights* to enforce the demands of *one class only*—the proletariat. That, precisely, was the logical bourgeois reply to the demand of the " Equals." *Democracy*, they said, meant that *each individual* should be deemed " equal " to every other individual in the eyes of *the Law and the State*. To raise questions of " class " is logically impermissible. It is also indecent. In fact, bourgeois " democracy " demands that individuals shall be, by the Law, reduced to their common denominator as abstract *units* in the compound Humanity.

To which of course the proletariat had no " logical " reply —only the practical one : that at mealtimes it was anything but satisfactory to be an *abstract unit* ; at mealtimes a man is a concrete need for specific and concrete food. Therefore, argued the proletarian, the " democratic equality " which recognises my equality only in the abstract, and refuses to recognise it in the concrete because it has already " recognised " it " in Law "—this " democratic equality " is too " equalitarian " in its *democracy* and too " undemocratic " in its *equality*. As Anatole France expressed it :

" The Law in its majestic *equality* forbids rich and poor alike—to sleep under arches ; to beg in the streets ; and to steal *bread* ! "—ANATOLE FRANCE : *The Red Lily*.

JOHN HORNE TOOKE, the English lawyer-Jacobin, had the same opinion of " equality before the Law " : " The Law, like the London Tavern, is free to all—who can afford its charges ! " In a word : the assumptions of *bourgeois* " democracy " are based not on human, but on property relations. All *property* rights, recognised by the Law, are equally *rights* in the eyes of Bourgeois Law. It is only when one refuses to be persuaded that it is all-sufficient to endow a man with a " property right " in his own person, regardless of whether he possesses any means for maintaining that person in being, that the bladder of bourgeois equality-before-the-Law and its " democratic " expression " Equality before the ballot-box " is pricked.

The substance of the historical demand for *Democracy* has always been, on the lips of revolutionaries, a demand for the

abolition of classes. On the lips of conservatives and reactionaries the praise of " democracy " to-day is as it has been ever
since *Thermidor*, a praise of the Parlimentary pretence which
covers the fact of class subjection—the brutal negation of
all actual human equality.

Democratic Revolution and Dictatorship

Only the barest minimum of reflection is required to see
that all arguments as to " democracy " or " dictatorship "
in the abstract are worthless. " Words are the *money* of
fools ! " Only when we ask " *what kind* of democracy ? " or
" Dictatorship, *over whom* ? by *whom* ? and with what
alternative ? "—only thus, when the question is concretised
and it is made possible for us to examine it in its actual
practical connections, does the problem become one capable
of a rational solution.

For instance, to a Greek of the era of the City-States, in
which the term " democracy " was coined, it had, as we have
noted, a concrete meaning, and not at all an abstract one.
Either the function of making and administering laws was a
birth-right of the privileged *aristocracy*, or it was not. To an
aristocratic Greek democracy meant the loss of all his
privileges—an enforced subjection to the common level of
" equality." To him it meant exactly what a Communist
revolutionary proletarian dictatorship would mean in practice
to the aristocracy and bourgeoisie of to-day. A Greek, if
one could be brought back from the dead, would say of the
U.S.S.R., " There complete *democracy* reigns in all its tyranny
and horror ! " It is a historical fact that the first " tyrants "
to be so called (the Greeks again were the inventors of the
word) were *the* " *dictators* " set up by the victorious *democracy*
to rule as their agents in place of the aristocratic rulers who
had been chased away. To a Greek " democracy " involved
a " dictator " who was *ipso facto* a " tyrant."

Again, the Great French Revolution began in the decision
of the deputies representing the Third Estate (i.e., the
" Commons ") to demand and stick to the demand that
voting in the *States General* (i.e., the " Parliament ") should
be *individual*, and *not* by Estates. On a count of individuals
the Third Estate had a majority ; by *Estates* they were only
as One to Two ! The demand for " equality " for *individuals*
thus abolished the equality between *Estates*, and, moreover,
gave the Third Estate as *a class* virtually *dictatorial* power,
which they thereafter exercised on a cumulating scale.

Finally : In Britain to-day. All are *equally* " free " to stand as candidates for Parliament (*provided* they have each one hundred and fifty pounds to deposit !). All are equally " free " to persuade the electors to elect them (*provided* they have the means to hire halls, print and post bills, circulate handbills, and publish newspapers and pamphlets !). All are equally " free " to publish newspapers with a circulation of 2,000,000 daily (*provided* they have the odd £2,000,000 or so required for plant, printing, publicity, sales mechanism, etc., etc.). All are equally " free " to vote for the " best " man or party (*provided* they possess the means of knowing which and who *is* the " best " *for them* !).

Is it not perfectly clear that the *form* of democratic equality in Britain to-day, as everywhere else in the past, covers the reality that in a class-divided society only one class at a time can in fact *rule* ? Is it not clear beyond dispute that *equality* is a term whose meaning is absolute only in *relation* ? A quart pot and a gill are *equally* full only when they contain *unequal* quantities ; when they contain equal *quantities* their degree of fullness is grossly unequal.

It was the pressure of the historically experienced disparity between the legal and constitutional *form* of equality (political " Democracy ") and its *substantial reality* in the actual life-conditions of the proletariat which caused the slogans of the revolutionary proletarian democracy to change abruptly from the demand for " *real* Democracy " (that of the " Constitution of '93 " in France, that of " The Charter " in England) into one for the " Dictatorship of the Proletariat." It was made about the middle of 1848, when the course of the Revolution which broke out all over Europe in 1848 everywhere revealed the same sickening fact—that it was the bourgeois and the petty-bourgeois *democrats* who at every crisis surrendered to the counter-revolution even such " democratic equality " as they themselves enjoyed rather than yield a grain of " *real* democracy " to the proletariat. In that Year of Revolution the very words " democrat " and " democracy " became in the ears of the masses " a hissing and a reproach." A " democrat," in the light of the experience of that year, was a *poseur*, a pretender, a demagogic charlatan, brave only in words, generous only in promises, equalitarian only in the equal baseness revealed in every comparison between his words and his deeds.

In April, 1850, a meeting was held in London at which there was drawn up the " Articles of Agreement " for the formation of an *International Association of Revolutionary Communists*. These Articles were signed on behalf of the German Communist League by WILLICH, MARX, and ENGELS ; on behalf of the French Blanquists by ADAM and VIDAL ; and for the *English* Chartists by GEORGE JULIAN HARNEY. The first of these " Articles " reads :

> " The aim of the Association is the overthrow of all the privileged classes, and the subjection of these classes to the *Dictatorship of the Proletariat*, by the maintenance of the revolution in permanence *until the realisation of Communism*, which must be the final form of the organisation of the human community."—*See* RIAZANOV : *Labour Monthly*, August, 1928 [and *Marx Chronik*, 1934.]

The historical significance of this document, whose very existence had been forgotten until Bernstein parted with the papers he had inherited from Engels to the Marx–Engels Institute, is enormous. Its testimony to Marx's use of the slogan " Dictatorship of the Proletariat " is simply overwhelming.

We have already noted the close approximations to the slogan in Gracchus Babœuf on the one side, and the *Communist Manifesto* on the other. A historical connection is established as soon as it is remembered that the German *Communist League* was, when Marx and Engels joined it, the " League of the Just "—a secret society founded in Paris in 1836 on the Babœuvist model, and then headed by Wilhelm Weitling. A connection existed between the Weitlingian secret society and the French (Parisian) secret societies, led by Armand Barbès and August Blanqui respectively. Both Barbès and Blanqui had been members together of the " parent " society—the " Family "—founded in 1826 or thereabouts by Buonarotti, one of the original Society of the Equals founded by Babœuf. Thus the historical continuity through Marat, Babœuf, Buonarotti, Barbès, Blanqui and Weitling to Marx and Engels is complete.

Moreover, a comparison of the Article quoted above with the declaration of the objects of the Communist League, adopted at the same time (1847) as the famous *Manifesto*, reveals precisely the transition by which the slogan Dictatorship of the Proletariat was reached :

> " The aim of the League is the downfall of the bourgeoisie, *the rule of the proletariat*, the abolition of the old bourgeois society based on class antagonisms, and the establishment of a new society without either classes or

private property."—See RIAZANOV's Ed., *Com. Man.,* p. 340.

It will be seen that the chief change needed was to substitute the word "dictatorship" for the word "rule." The significance of this is revealed by the other verbal changes. The "downfall of the *bourgeoisie*" becomes that of "*all* privileged classes," and the reason is clear and double-barrelled. In the *Communist Manifesto* the immediate policy of the Communists was oriented upon the (hoped for) success of the bourgeois democratic and republican revolution then imminent in Germany. While "supporting every revolutionary movement against the existing order of things," even to fighting along with the bourgeoisie "whenever it acts in a revolutionary way, against the absolute monarchy, the feudal squirearchy, *and the petty bourgeoisie*," the Communists :

"never cease for a single instant to instil into the working class the clearest possible recognition of the hostile antagonism between the bourgeoisie and the proletariat in order that the German workers may straightway use, *as so many weapons against the bourgeoisie,* the social and political conditions that the bourgeoisie must necessarily introduce along with its supremacy, and in order that, after the fall of the reactionary classes in Germany, *the fight against the bourgeoisie itself may immediately begin.*"—MARX-ENGELS : *Com. Man.,* p. 38.

Thus, in the then conjunction of class forces, the initiative was with the bourgeoisie, and the policy of the proletariat, led by the Communists, was to participate in the bourgeois revolution to ensure (*a*) that the bourgeoisie did, in fact, clear the ground of reactionary institutions and forces, and so (*b*) leave the ring clear for a *second revolution,* that of the proletariat. Already in 1847 the two-faced rôle of the petit-bourgeoisie was foreseen. One section of it (the French "Social Democrats") was reckoned on as an asset on the side of revolution ; another section (in Germany) was expected to count on the reactionary side, against the revolutionary bourgeois.

The revolutionary explosion foretold in the *Manifesto* burst almost before the *Manifesto* itself saw the light of day. And up to a point every prediction of the *Manifesto* was fulfilled to the letter. Every party named in it behaved just as it was expected it would behave—*with a difference* ! The *Manifesto* had credited the bourgeoisie and the petit-bourgeoisie with such a revolutionary will as would make an end of the *ancien régime*, *before* the proletariat had gathered strength enough to begin its independent struggle against the bourgeoisie itself. Partly through its over-estimation of the courage and resolution of the bourgeoisie and the petit-bourgeois democratic republicans, but chiefly through its under-estimation of the disintegrating effect of their treacherous antics upon the proletariat, the expectation of the *Manifesto* was falsified. *For once the eagerness of Marx and Engels got in the way of their dialectic !* They had not reckoned on the effect on the quasi-revolutionary bourgeoisie of the genuinely revolutionary proletariat growing more consolidated with every day the revolution lasted !

As Engels expressed it years later in his notes on *The Dialectic of Nature and Natural Science* :

" In history it is in all the critical epochs of leading nations that movement through contradiction comes out really clearly. At such moments a nation has only the choice between the two horns of a dilemma : Either—Or ! And indeed the question is always put [by the logic of fact] in a totally different way from that desired by the amateurs of politics among the philistines of every period. Even the Liberal German philistine of 1848 found himself in 1849 suddenly, unexpectedly and against his own will faced by the question : Return to the old reaction in a more acute form, or, advance of the revolution to a republic, perhaps even to the one and indivisible republic with a socialistic background. He did not stop long to think and helped to create the Manteuffel-reaction as the fruit of German liberalism ! "— ENGELS : *Dialectic of Nature.*

It was the experience of this desertion of their own cause by the revolutionary bourgeoisie and petit-bourgeoisie that found expression in the new slogan " dictatorship of the proletariat," which was adopted, too, under the impulsion of the two greatest barricade battles of the Revolution—in each of which the proletariat, unaided in one case, and aided only by students in the other, put up a fight which shamed and disgraced the cowardly and treacherous bourgeoisie beyond redemption. In the days of June, in Paris in 1848, and in Vienna in May, 1849, the fate of the Revolution was, as became evident in the end, sealed. But before May, 1849, there seemed still a hope that all was not lost. Hence the defiant note, " maintenance in permanence of the revolution," sounded by Marx in the *Neue Rhenische Zeitung* at this period. Within a few days came the fall of Vienna ; and the corpses of the Viennese proletariat and their student allies were not cold before the *Neue Rhenische Zeitung* was suppressed and Marx was expelled from Cologne. Two months later the Baden Insurrection, in which Engels had served in arms, was finally defeated and the end of the revolution had come.

We have dwelt upon this tremendously important document, the *Articles of the International Association of Communists*, not only because it seems to indicate just when the slogan, " Dictatorship of the Proletariat " was substituted for that of the " rule of the proletariat," but because, also, it seems to settle the question of priority in its use as between Marx and Blanqui (who was at this time, as so often, in prison). Even more significantly it throws light upon a phrase in Marx's letter to Weydemeyer (given above), which seems to have received much less notice than it deserves.

In that letter Marx explains " what I did that was *new*." *Did, when ?*

The date of the letter is 1852. That is to say, it was *before* the *Critique*, before *Capital*, before even the *Eighteenth Brumaire*. It may mean (and to an extent no doubt does) the general sense and specific content of all Marx had written up to this point—in which case it is decisive as to Marx's use of the term " democracy " in the *Communist Manifesto*, *Poverty of Philosophy*, etc. But most of all it refers to the whole tone, policy, and concrete teaching of the *Neue Rhenische Zeitung*, which Marx edited from Cologne from June 1st, 1848, to September, 1848, when it was suppressed under martial law, and again from November, 1848, to May 19th, 1849, when it was finally suppressed and Marx expelled.

When Marx and Engels talked and wrote of Revolution they knew what they were talking about in the concrete, practical sense of the word as well as the theoretical. And it is trebly significant that it was thus, in the heat of actual revolutionary practice, that the slogan *Dictatorship of the Proletariat* was born.

Marx himself, in fact, seems to credit the coining of the phrase to the heroic Parisian proletariat of the Days of June, 1848 :

" The Paris proletariat was forced into the June insurrection by the bourgeoisic. In this lay its doom.

Neither its immediate admitted needs drove it to want
to win the forcible overthrow of the bourgeoisie, nor
was it equal to this task. The *Moniteur* had to inform it
officially that the time was past when the republic saw
any occasion to do honour to its illusions, and its defeat
first convinced it of the truth that the slightest improvement in its position remains a Utopia within the bourgeois republic, a Utopia that becomes a crime as soon as
it wants to realise it. In place of the demands, exuberant
in form, but petty and even still bourgeois in content,
the concession of which it wanted to wring from the
February republic, there appeared the bold slogan of
revolutionary struggle : *Overthrow of the bourgeoisie!
Dictatorship of the Working Class!* "—MARX : *Class
Struggles in France*, 1848–50, pp. 57–8.

This was written " in the winter of 1849–50." Taken in
conjunction with the other evidence and the fact that from
before Blanqui's arrest in May, 1848, until the autumn of
1850 (when Marx and Engels faced boldly the fact that a
reopening of the revolutionary struggle was no longer possible),
Marx and Engels had worked in close sympathy and contact
with the Blanquists on the one side, and the Chartist Communists on the other, it by no means excludes the possibility
that as early as June, 1848, the phrase had been coined by
Marx. If on the other hand it was the spontaneous invention
of the proletarian insurrection—so much the more credit to
Marx for accepting it as expressive of that at which his whole
policy was aimed.

Anyway, the dialectical transvaluation of the terms
" democrat " and " democracy " can be traced through each
of the three monographs in which Marx and Engels summed
up the experiences of the Year of Revolution, 1848–49. In
Marx's *Class Struggles in France* (1850), in Engels' *Revolution
and Counter-Revolution in Germany* (1850–51), and Marx's
Eighteenth Brumaire of Louis Napoleon (1852) a contempt
for the cynical self-seeking of the liberal bourgeoisie and
for the braggart cowardice and treachery of the " democratic " and " socialist " petty-bourgeoisie blazes at a white-
heat.

Engels, in a pungent chapter, deals faithfully with the
small-trader " democrats " :

" This class of petty tradesmen . . . may be considered as the leading class of the insurrection of May,
1849 [the crucial stage in the life of the German Re-

public]. . . . The German petty-bourgeoisie is capable of
nothing but ruining any movement that entrusts itself
to its hands.

" The petty-bourgeois, great in boasting, is very
impotent for action, and very shy of risking anything.
The *mesquin* character of its commercial transactions and
its credit operations is eminently apt to stamp its
character with a want of energy and enterprise. It is
only to be expected that similar qualities should mark
its political career. . . .

" Whenever an armed conflict had brought matters
to a serious crisis, there the shopkeepers stood aghast
at the dangerous situation created for them. . . .

" . . . In the case of defeat they risked the loss of
their capital. And in the case of victory were they not
sure to be immediately turned out of office, and to see
their entire policy subverted by the victorious proletarians
who formed the main body of their fighting army ? Thus
placed between opposing dangers . . . the petty-bourgeoisie . . . let everything take its chance, whereby,
of course, there was lost what little chance of succces
there might have been. . . .

" The petty-bourgeois rulers . . . not only abandoned
the insurrection to its own *uncentralised and therefore
ineffective* spontaneity ; they actually did everything
in their power to take the sting out of the movement, to
unman, to destroy it. And they succeeded, thanks to
the zealous support of that deep class of politicians, the
' *Democratic* ' heroes of the petty-bourgeois."—ENGELS :
Revolution and Counter-Revolution, pp. 104–6.

Marx, in addition to the passage cited above, thus contrasts
the Utopian (Proudhonian) and doctrinaire (Louis Blanc)
" socialism " of the petit-bourgeoisie with the fighting,
revolutionary Socialism of the proletariat :

" Under somewhat similar-sounding, general socialist
phrases . . . is concealed the Socialism of the *National*,
of the *Presse*, and the *Siècle*, which more or less consistently wants to overthrow the rule of the finance
aristocracy and to free industry and trade from their
hitherto existing fetters. . . .

" From this bourgeois socialism, to which as to every
variety of socialism a section of the workers and petty-
bourgeois naturally rallies, specific petty-bourgeois socialism, socialism *par excellence* is distinct. *Capital hounds*

this class chiefly as its creditors, so it demands credit institutions. . . . Since it dreams of the peaceful achievement of its socialism—allowing perhaps for a second February Revolution lasting a brief day—naturally the coming historical process appears to it as the application of systems. . . .

"While this utopian, doctrinaire socialism . . . above all, in fantasy does away with the revolutionary struggle of the classes and its necessities by small conjuring tricks or great sentimentalities . . . the proletariat rallies more and more round Communism, for which the bourgeoisie has itself found the name of *Blanqui*.

"This socialism is the declaration of the permanence of the revolution, the class-dictatorship of the revolution, *the class dictatorship of the proletariat* as the inevitable transit point to the abolition of class differences generally, to the abolition of the production relations on which they rest, to the abolition of all the relations that correspond to these relations of production, to the revolutionising of all the ideas that result from these social connections."— MARX : *Class Struggle in France*, pp. 125–6.

In his *Eighteenth Brumaire of Louis Buonaparte* Marx subjects the whole period of French history from February, 1848, to the *coup d'état* of December 2nd, 1851, to an analysis of a force superlative even for him. In the course of it he gives this description of the nature and origin of the social-democracy :

"To make a united front against the bourgeois forces, the petty-bourgeois and the proletariat had formed a coalition . . . the so-called Social-Democratic Party. . . . A joint programme was drafted, joint electoral committees were established, and joint candidatures arranged for. The revolutionary point of the socialist demands of the proletariat was blunted, and these demands were given a *democratic* gloss. Conversely, in the case of the democratic demands of the petty-bourgeoisie the purely political form was effaced, and they were made to seem as socialistic as possible. That was the origin of social-democracy. . . .

"The essential characteristic of Social-Democracy is this : democratic republican institutions are demanded as a means not for the abolition of the two extremes, Capital and Wage-Labour, but for the mitigation of their opposition, and for the transformation of their discord into a harmony. . . . The substance of the social-democratic aim is to transform society *by the democratic method*, the transformation being always kept within the petty-bourgeois orbit."—MARX : *Eighteenth Brumaire,* Chap. III.

What conclusions follow from this examination of the historical dialectic of the term " Democracy " and the revolutionary proletarian demand for it ?

Firstly, it has been clearly demonstrated that the *essence* of the demand for " democracy " was a demand for equality, which in the case of the proletariat took increasingly (and that necessarily) the practical significance of a demand for the abolition of class distinctions—which (and likewise necessarily) became under the pressure of historical development a demand for the overthrow of the Bourgeoisie, for the Dictatorship of the Proletariat, for Communism.

Secondly, it has been demonstrated beyond all possibility of question that Marx and Engels so understood, and so interpreted, the term " democracy," and that (whether Marx did or did not coin the phrase) Marx and Engels invariably substituted the phrase " Dictatorship of the Proletariat "— *or its equivalent*—after the events of 1848 had made the term " democracy " no longer usable as a rallying slogan for the revolutionary proletariat.

Thirdly, it has been demonstrated that the restriction of the significance of the term " democracy " to *one only* of its historically conditioned *forms*—that of (bourgeois) " constitutional parliamentarism " :

    (*a*) Falsifies completely and positively inverts the sense which the term bore with (for example) the Chartists and other champions of (proletarian) democracy.

    (*b*) Would have been and was scornfully repudiated by Marx and Engels as totally contrary to the plain sense of their economic, political, and theoretical teaching in general and in detail.

    (*c*) Is a treacherous and reactionary practice first invented by petit-bourgeois Utopians and eclectics to conceal their desertion of the proletariat and of all revolutionary struggles in favour of a huxtering endeavour to drive political bargains with the Reaction.

Fourthly, it has been demonstrated by events (not necessary to recite here) that—

(a) The attempt by Kautsky and the German Social-Democratic leaders to contrapose " democracy " *as an alternative proletarian objective to* the Dictatorship of the Proletariat, was in objective fact just such an endeavour to cover up a desertion of revolutionary proletarian struggle, and just such an attempt—this time *a brazenly open one*—to drive a huckster's political bargain with the Reaction, at the expense of the proletariat and its revolutionary struggle.

(b) The attempt by the British Labour Party and T.U.C. to erect " constitutional democracy " into a Party shibboleth—a dogmatic article of faith—and contrapose it " equally " to the Communist theory of Proletarian Dictatorship, and the Fascist theory of " leader " Dictatorship, is (1) a wilful persistence in the objectively treacherous course originally initiated by Kautsky and the German Social-Democratic chiefs (supported at the time by MacDonald and the British Labour Party under his leadership) ; (2) objectively, at the present time, a screen behind which the Social-Democratic chiefs seek shelter from the discredit history has heaped upon them.

Finally, the conclusion follows that, as we saw at the outset, the contraposition of " Democracy " to *any* sort of Dictatorship means, in practice, what all opportunism and eclecticism ends in, an objective co-operation with the bourgeoisie in *its* class-struggle against the proletariat. The denial of the class-struggle in theory is a waging of class-struggle *against* the revolutionary class in practice.

Here we reach, and from yet another angle, the vital importance *for practice* of the revolutionary dialectical method of Marxism. From any standpoint other than that of Dialectical Materialism it is impossible so to conceive Reality that measures adequate to the situation can be devised to *change* Reality. For that purpose all non-dialectical theories, since they are self-inhibited from attempting anything beyond *adaptation to* Reality, are not merely inadequate but positively obstructive. Non-dialectical Theory is, in itself, doomed of necessity to *non-dialectical practice*—to opportunism and all that opportunism implies.

.   .   .   .   .

Dialectically conceived, the Dictatorship of the Proletariat is the *realisation of Democracy* for the Proletariat. It is *that* precisely because, and to the extent that, it is the *negation*

THE DIALECTIC OF REVOLUTION   441

of Democracy for the bourgeoisie. For the proletariat, their Dictatorship collectively over their class enemies is simply the logical carrying out to its ultimate conclusion of the revolutionary class-struggle. Since its dictatorial aspect expresses only the quantity and quality of resistance to be overcome, the dictatorship of the proletariat ceases progressively to be a dictatorship as the objective fact of bourgeois resistance, actual or potential, ceases to exist likewise. When class divisions have ceased to be, the Proletariat as Dictator has nothing upon which to impose its will. The dictatorship lapses, leaving only—the Proletariat.

But the Proletariat is only a Proletariat relative to the conditions and relations of bourgeois society. From the moment it begins to exercise its Dictatorial power with effect, and to the extent that it is able to abolish the conditions and relations of bourgeois society and replace them with positive Socialist and Communist relations, from that moment and to that extent it ceases to be *a Proletariat*. When all class divisions have been eliminated there will remain only—*the associated humanity*—the Communist Society of *equal co-operators*.

In sum : the Dictatorship of the Proletariat can less than any historical epoch be understood other than *dialectically*. Since capitalist society is the final " antagonistic " formation stage in the development of human society—antagonistic in the two-fold sense that it is based, objectively, upon class-divisions, and based subjectively upon ignorance of the true relation between Nature and Human Society—its transmutation into a communist society involves " the most radical break with the past " it is possible to conceive, just because it is the most complete possible return, on a higher plane, to the spontaneous solidarity of the most primitive human society. The *form* of this process " can be none other than the dictatorship of the proletariat " precisely because its *content* is the negation of that negation from which all previous historical movement has sprung, namely, the negation of social solidarity by class-division, and, the condition for this, the negation of human self-determination or freedom by human impotence and human ignorance.

Some Criticisms of Marx's Theory of Revolution

In order that the force of this Dialectical and Materialist conception of the historical process of society may be the better appreciated we will compare with the process we have traced the variant view offered by G. D. H. Cole in *What Marx Really Meant*.

G. D. H. Cole, as we observed earlier, presents the tragic-comic spectacle of a Don "toiling upwards through the night"—the night in question being the inspissated gloom of Oxford University culture. That G. D. H. Cole is also, "by act of God," an inveterate liaison officer between everything mutually repellent, a living negation of the dialectic, makes his effort to find a golden mean between the Scylla of (say) Harry Pollitt and the Charybdis of (say) Arthur Henderson—and to do so in a manner suited to his reputation (with the higher command of the W.E.A.) as a decidedly incorruptible but not-too-*sea-green* Robespierre—a spectacle in expository acrobatics that has had no parallel since Blondin cracked eggs and fried an omelette on a portable stove on the tight-rope !

Cole begins well enough with the assertion that Marx's method is integral, not only to his conclusions, but to the entire basis of historical study on which his conclusions rest. But—who can command his Fate ? Cole has only the normal equipment in the matter of eyes, and the task of steering a straight course along this integral method while keeping one eye on Transport House, one on Sir Stafford Cripps, one on the Master of Balliol, and one on the corner around which Raymond Postgate may be lying in wait, would baffle the resources of the Great Beasts in *Revelation* (which were " full of eyes before and behind ! "). The resultant version of " what Marx *really* meant " would, had Marx been dead for anything less than fifty years, have caused him to burst out of his coffin and into vituperation in fourteen languages. Its general character is that of another mythical creation, whose taste was

> " . . . meagre and hollow, but crisp :
> Like a coat that is rather too tight in the waist;
> With a flavour of Will-o'-the-wisp."
> —LEWIS CARROLL.

Cole, for instance, supports unequivocally the Leninist interpretation of Marx's teaching on the State :

" Lenin, and not Kautsky, says what Marx said. Kautsky was only continuing to say what the German Social-Democrats so angered Marx by saying in the Gotha Programme of 1875. For Kautsky and the Social-Democrats as a party, had come to think in terms of the capture and democratisation of the Capitalist State, and not, like Marx, in terms of its overthrow and destruction."—COLE : *loc. cit.*, p. 181.

" It is well to be clear . . . that, despite all the casuistry that has been used in trying to represent Marx as holding a different view, there is no uncertainty at all about his own words, either in 1848 or, much later, in 1875. On this issue Marx was unquestionably a Communist, and not a Social-Democrat."—COLE : *loc. cit.*, p. 181.

So far, so good. But, after arguing the matter for more than a dozen pages, we get this :

" So far Marx was clearly right. But was he right in holding that [a genuinely Socialist] Government would have to *begin* by revolutionary measures designed to smash entirely the *bourgeois* State, and *then* at once to build up a new proletarian State of its own, before it could even begin upon its constructive Socialist policy ? The answer . . . is not clear. . . ."—COLE : *loc. cit.*, p. 195.

First you stir the mud up with a wooden spoon—then you observe that the mixture " is not clear ! " First you observe that the Social-Democrats were clearly in error because they envisaged their task as " capturing a machine." Then you explain that Marx's idea was not to " capture " the machine, but to *smash* it ! Then you explain that it might not be necessary to smash *all of it* at once ! And so you prepare your path to the sapient conclusion that some of the machine *may* have to be smashed—but some of it can be saved and used to smash the rest ! Finally you explain that this is not just ordinary reformism, because you do *smash* something ! On the contrary, it is " revolutionary constitutionalism." These are, of course, not Cole's exact words. But they quite fairly sum up his line of argument. Here are his conclusions in his own words :

" The case is different in the parliamentary countries as long as they remain parliamentary. For these States, while they retain their essentially *bourgeois* character, do embody considerable elements of *democratic service,* as well as of coercive capitalist authority, and have been ' liberalised ' to such an extent as to accord, *for the present,* considerable rights to the Opposition. If they *can be seized and controlled,* there are forces in operation within them that are *fully consistent with the purposes Socialists have in view.*"—COLE : *loc. cit.*, p. 204.

Parts of the curate's egg *were,* indeed, " excellent " !

" So long as they remain parliamentary ! " " Considerable *rights* to the Opposition " ! " If they *can be seized* and controlled " !

Is it not perfectly clear that the man who is so confident that Lenin and Marx were in agreement and, " so far, right," is also, and at the same time, completely at sea as to what they were agreed upon—and why ?

Who denies, for example, that the police among other duties control the traffic ? Do they, therefore, become any the less *police* ? Any the less an armed *force* ? Any the less part of the State power of coercion ? Does Cole aver that it is possible *without completely smashing the State machine,* as such, to separate the traffic-controlling function of the police from their bludgeoning and coercing function ? Would he split each policeman into three pieces, *abolish* one, *keep* one for " democratic service," and *remand* the other for inquiries ?

The whole essence of the question lies in what is the *essential function* of the State—not what *other* things it may *do* or *be* incidentally. Cole, like all the Social-Democrats, above whom he affects a superiority, seeks to exalt the " parliamentary," the law-making detail in the bourgeois State apparatus into an End in itself. But of what worth are laws unless they can be *enforced* ? The whole existence of any State, anywhere, at any time, depends primarily upon its power to *enforce its will*.

And that is, precisely, the issue—*does winning a majority in Parliament* ipso facto *ensure winning likewise the power to enforce, the power to compel* ?

Let us look at it in detail : so far as Britain is concerned Cole admits that the House of Commons is *not Parliament*—it is only one third of it ! If we must be " constitutional " let us stick to the facts—and they are that the " constitutional " sovereignty of Britain is wielded by " The King *in* Parliament," which means the Crown, the House of Lords, and the House of Commons *collectively*. Certainly the Parliament Act enables Bills to be passed " over the head " of the House of Lords. Certainly in that event the assent of the Crown is expected (not by Statute law but by " constitutional tradition ") to follow automatically. But this same Parliament Act ensures that *at least three years* must be consumed before this can be done ! *And in those three years ?*

Take it from another angle. The coercive power of the

State consists in a whole apparatus of force—army, navy, air force, police, coastguards, police reserves, special constables, judges, magistrates, gaolers, etc. Suppose it possible (as in the famous case of the Curragh " mutiny " in 1914) that these armed forces, or any considerable section of them, chose to flout the authority of the House of Commons—*what is the remedy Cole would propose* ? Can that *force* be overcome, save by a *superior force ?*

Do you say the rebels could not hold the field without supplies ? What *power* have you to *prevent them from helping themselves* ?

A mass resistance of the organised workers would do so if such were sufficiently roused. But Cole's policy is to refuse to rouse them until after the mischief is done, when it will be too late ! The *Vienna* policy erected into a system !

Take it from yet another angle. Even with the army, navy, etc., not actively hostile, how can any Government keep that army, etc., *fed* (and so on) from day to day without financial accommodations, or unless the Civil Service can be relied upon for its special function ? An organised sabotage from the banks or the civil service, or both, would make impossible the existence of any " Socialist " government *not already equipped with a backing of sufficient revolutionary force to crush both forms of resistance.*

Cole, like all Social-Democratic apologists, has stated to solve the problem from the wrong end. Unless the counter-revolutionary forces have *already been* demoralised and immobilised (if only for the time being) *before* the Governmental *authority* (not " machinery ") is seized (say, rather, " *conquered* ") by the Revolutionaries, the " seizure " will be the hollowest of mockeries—a death-trap.

Marx *does not* talk of *beginning* with the " smashing " of the machine—that occurs at the *end* of the first phase of the *prolonged* revolutionary struggle ; and it is done, if at all, because the revolution has acquired in consequence of, in the course of, and by means of *the struggle*, a " power sufficient to compel " obedience to its will. The smashing of the " machine," the complete reconstruction of the armed forces —(substitution of the *armed revolution* for the old standing army, police, etc., complete purging of the civil apparatus of the State)—all this is part of the *completion* of the uprising revolution, which also includes the smashing and dispersal of any counter-revolutionary armed bands who may be still in the field.

Cole, in short, by treating as negligible everything outside the parliamentary aspect of the struggle, shows that *he thinks the thermometer is the source of the heat*! He is therein the victim of what Engels called "*parliamentary cretinism* "—

> "That incurable malady *Parliamentary cretinism*, a disorder which penetrates its unfortunate victims with the solemn conviction that the whole world, its history and future, are governed and determined by a majority of votes in that particular representative body which has the honour to count them among its members."— Engels : *Revolution and Counter-Revolution.*

To Marx and Engels, on the contrary, Parliament could *at best* register decisions already arrived at in the country at large. That the winning of a Parliamentary majority might possibly (though in exceptional circumstances) express or accompany the culminating phase of the uprising revolutionary struggle for power Marx was quite prepared to admit —witness the famous (Engels') preface to *Capital* and the concession there that the *revolution* in Britain "might be made peacefully " :

> " . . . at least in Europe, England is the *only* country where the inevitable social revolution might be effected entirely by peaceful and legal means."—Engels : Preface to English translation, *Capital*, Vol. I.

Here, it will be noted (1) that the English situation is (or was) exceptional ; (2) that nothing is said about "parliament " or "constitutional " means ; and (3) that even in the other countries "peaceful" and "legal" means of struggle are *not excluded* as details in the whole process. And Engels is careful to add :

> " He [Marx] certainly never forgot to add that he hardly expected the English ruling class to submit, without a ' pro-slavery rebellion,' to this peaceful and legal revolution."—Engels : *ibid.*

That for normally constituted intelligences places the matter in its exact focus. Whether a parliamentary-constitutional triumph is or is not included as *one* of the many *phases* of the revolutionary *conquest of power*, it is this conquest which is the essence of the matter—as is *proved* by the inevitability of, at any rate, an attempt at a ' pro-slavery rebellion '—[a significant phrase recalling the outstanding event of that generation—the pro-slavery rebellion of the "Southern Confederacy " whose defeat by the

Federal Government of the U.S.A. was ensured by the mass enthusiasm with which the proletariat of the Northern States and the working farmers of the Middle-West rallied to its support.]

.   .   .   .   .

Intelligences are, however, not *normal* among the *intelligentsia* in the U.S.A. any more than in Britain.

Sidney Hook in his *Towards the Understanding of Karl Marx* has up to this point taken a line radically different from that of G. D. H. Cole. In fact, he falls over the edge through going to the opposite extreme. To him Marx is not insisting upon the need for *power*—the *word* " force " suggests to Hook only *one of its possible modes of manifestation*, namely " violence." And as Hook is positively bursting his braces through straining to be more revolutionary and more " Marxian " than Marx himself, he mentally translates as " violence " every reference Marx makes to " force." This causes him to observe on the sentence last quoted from Engels—a sentence which Hook characterises as " unconscious to the point of simplicity "—as follows :

> " As if it were not precisely the danger of a ' pro-slavery rebellion '—a counter revolution—which demanded that the revolution everywhere assure its victory by a *resort to force* ! "—HOOK : *loc. cit.*, p. 245.

You observe ! It is not, to Hook, a question of the revolutionary class *becoming a force*—it is a merely incidental question of *resorting to* " force " [read " violence "]. In the revolution as Sidney Hook sees it, the proletariat will refuse to accept victory as victory unless the bourgeoisie come out to be " beat up " good and proper ! And as though the above were not enough, Hook goes on to cap it :

> " As if the mandate for its legality (! !) were derived from the existing order, which always has a ' legal provision ' for changing the rules whenever they are working against it, and not from the power of the masses ! "—HOOK : *loc. cit.*, p. 245.

Here's a how-d'ye-do ! Who talks of " legality ? "

Engels certainly speaks of " legal " *means*, but legal means (i.e., means *not forbidden* by law) and " legality " (i.e., *by the force of* law) are as different as sucking-pigs and " pigs " of iron.

Political agitation, and organisation, trade unions, strikes, the publication of literature—all the work of the political parties and other organs of revolutionary class struggle are

" *legal means*," and the things obviously intended by Engels. Ballot-box struggles are also included, and *possibly* (though none too probably) a " constitutional " change. But, quite obviously, from the general sense of the whole passage, especially when read in the light of all the rest of Marx and Engels' work, the one sense which Engels' words exclude is the sense which Hook seeing not merely " red " but " infra-red "—seeing what is hidden from normal sight—reads into them, that of a *purely* " legalist " revolution in the bourgeois sense of legality.

Hook is no more safe to trust with words whose meaning has ossified for him (such as " force " and " legal ") than a baby is safe to trust with a box of matches.

.   .   .   .   .

Both Cole and Hook have no real excuse. Both can read German—and for both this acquirement has blunted their sensitivity of response to plain English. Still they both, as men who set out to " explain " Marx to the (presumably) unlettered and (by hypothesis) thick-witted, ought to have remembered that Marx on a certain memorable occasion put his doctrine into *one sentence in English:*

" The Emancipation of the Working Classes must be conquered by the Working Classes themselves."—Marx : *Statutes of the I.W.M.A.*, 1864.

It is true that this document is usually quoted at second-hand and incorrectly—(the state of Marxian knowledge in the English speaking world can be inferred from the fact that an American " Marxist " organisation, the S.L.P., went to the trouble of *translating* an edition of the *Address* to which these statutes are appended, in the belief that the German translation *was the original*, and a British " Marxist " body—the S.L.P.—solemnly *reprinted* this as a " new work of Marx, hitherto inaccessible to English readers " !)—but Cole should know of it, and Hook has quoted from a volume (Stekloff, *First International*) which includes it as an appendix !

Neither of them has the wit to see what 99 per cent. of *proletarian* propagandists have seen by instinct, that in this sentence the whole essence of Marxism is contained.

Examine it.

The question at issue is formulated *not* as one of forms of State, of " legality," of political systems, of morality, of ethical sanctions, or of " mandates," it is formulated simply, sufficiently and *fundamentally* as one of Emancipation.

It is not formulated as emancipation of the " people,"

or " the poor," or " the oppressed," and least of all " of the Nation." It is the emancipation of *the working classes*.

This emancipation, too, is *not* to be " obtained " or " brought about " or " made possible," or in any way conjured into being by any sort of " parliamentarian " or " anti-parliamentarian " hocus-pocus, and certainly *not* to be " captured." It *must be conquered*. Dwell on the *must be* : then dwell on the *conquered* by the *working classes themselves*. Then remember it was the Marx who wrote this as the first basic principle of the International which reopened the struggle which the Communist League had inaugurated in 1848 : it was *this* Marx who believed that this " conquest " might possibly be effected in England by " peaceful and legal " means.

Twist and turn as they will, Hook and Cole can make nothing out of these words but that which runs like a red thread through the whole lifework, theoretical and practical, of *both* Marx *and* Engels.

Consider the various slogans which we have in this essay noted as marking clear stages in the development of Marx's doctrine :

" Men make their circumstances as much as circumstances make men."

" The philosophers have only *interpreted* the world in various ways ; the point, however, is to change it."

" By Communism we mean the *real* movement which makes an end of the existing order of things."

" Not criticism but revolution is the motive force of history."

" Overthrow of the Bourgeoisie : Dictatorship of the Proletariat."

" The proletarians have nothing to lose but their chains. They have a world to win. Working men of all countries, Unite ! "

All these without exception are summed up—as the genuine fighters in the vanguard of the proletariat struggle have always (even when most unlettered) recognised—in the all-comprehending formula : " The emancipation of the working classes must be *conquered* by the working classes *themselves* ! "

That one word " *themselves* "—blasts all the sophistries of the Coles, Hooks, Kautskys, and all the rest into annihilation.

Is there any doubt ? Try for yourself. Read it over with a Cole-Hook-Kautsky tail on it :—" Emancipation . . . must

2F

be *conquered* by the working classes *themselves—through their Parliamentary representatives exclusively* ! "

.   .   .   .   .

Hook, to stick to his " Left "-ist point, proceeds to argue that Marx and Engels were wrong to admit even the *possibility* of a peaceful revolution in Britain, and therefore maintains his point against Lenin's explanation (in his *State and Revolution*) that in 1871 Britain was " without a military machine, and in large measure without a bureaucracy," while the conditions were such as to make conceivable a " people's revolution " (Lenin's phrase).

This Hook seeks to deny with a long string of historical " facts."   Upon these " facts " we make the following observations :

(1) Lenin's explanation " forced and unconvincing." England " no different " in 1871 from 1917.

Answer : Lenin refers to two points, military machine and civil service bureaucracy.   In 1870–1, Army in Britain : total strength 178,000 (62,000 of these in India); expenditure on all heads, £13,400,000.   In 1917 the War was on ; since then expenditure ten times that of 1871.   As to Bureaucracy : not until January 1st, 1870, did the modern civil service, recruited by public competitive examination come into force.   The civil service in 1870 cost 7 millions.   To-day it costs more than five times that amount.   Lenin's point is exactly correct.

(2) " Peaceful assemblage shot down at Peterloo." (they were not shot, incidentally, but *sabred* !).   What has this incident of 1819 to do with possibilities in 1871 ?

(3) " Marx witnessed . . . suppression of peaceful Chartist movement."—Chartist movement was *not* " peaceful," and for its final suppression the Government enrolled 150,000 special constables in London alone.   That is to say, its military and police force was so weak that the Government had to rely upon " popular " (in the bourgeois sense) support.   Lenin's point exactly.

(4) " At the very time Marx was making his exception in favour of England."   Hook has found a *mare's nest. Lenin* (see *State and Revolution*, pp. 30–1, *is not discussing the Engels preface of 1885 at all.*   He is discussing the letter to Kugelmann which does not name

England, but confines the argument to the "Continent." Lenin is explaining why.

(5) England had—in 1870—the "largest navy in the world."—Quite! Scattered all over the seven seas! The Naval Expenditure for 1870 was *under* ten millions—the lowest since before the Crimean War.

(6) England had "highly developed bureaucracy."—Nothing of the sort. See Answer 1 above. The English "bureaucracy" of the period had been the butt of every novelist—Dickens (Circumlocution Office), Disraeli, Trollope, all made mock at it.

(7) "In 1869, at a mass meeting in Hyde Park, Marx introduced a resolution which demanded political amnesty for Irish prisoners, etc."—Hook is in error—and irrelevant. Marx introduced his motion on the Council of the I.W.M.A. The Hyde Park meeting was organised (under I.W.M.A. inspiration) by the London Reform Union—the body which, in 1866, called the demonstration which tore up half-a-mile of the railings of Hyde Park. *And the Government submitted.*

(8) "Is this a country in which the revolution might be made peacefully?"—If Hook knew anything *really* of the strength of the Radical movement in the period 1864-1884—the period of Republicanism, Bradlaughism, and Chamberlain-Dilke Radicalism, which forced Gladstone to adopt the "Home Rule for Ireland" cry (from which in 1885 Chamberlain "ratted"), he would understand in what special conditions Marx made the reservation he did in favour of England. It *did then seem possible* that a "popular" democratic revolution might take place in Britain which would clear the way for and facilitate a proletarian revolution. It was the common belief of the time that Queen Victoria would be the last monarch to reign in Britain, and if she had died before 1887 *this would probably have proved true.* Marx's recognition of the "astuteness" of the British ruling class was based on (*a*) the skill with which they manœuvred their way out of the difficulties of this period, and (*b*) the incidental detail in this manœuvring of placating and winning over the leaders of the "great trade unions."

(9) Hook does not recognise that the epoch of Imperialism in Britain began *after* 1870 and not before.

(10) Hook should presumably know the history of the U.S.A.
better than that of Britain. But his question, " Was
it likely that in a country [the U.S.A.] in which feeble
and constitutional attempts to abolish chattel slavery
had called forth the most violent civil war of the nineteenth century, the abolition of wage-slavery could
be effected by moral suasion " shows the reverse.
It is a whole catalogue of historical misconception and
misrepresentation of Marx rolled into a sentence.
Marx's point was that at (about) the date in question
the total political and social correlation of class forces
in the U.S.A. was such that the proletariat which had
been drilled and trained to arms in a prolonged and
bloody civil war *might have*, and in alliance with the
industrial petty-bourgeoisie and the small farmer
class of the Middle-Western States *would have been able*
to effect a " people's revolution " (on the 1848,
European model, more or less) without meeting with
any serious resistance. Hook, with large scorn,
reminds us that at this time " the North was exercising a virtual dictatorship over the South." He
thinks this smashes Marx's conception. On the
contrary—*it proves it*. Precisely *because* the slave-
owners had been fought down and out and had been
annihilated as a political force, there existed no power
that could have resisted a *popular democratic* (not
Democrat in the U.S.A. party sense) *revolution*—out
of which the emergence of the proletariat as *de facto*
rulers and (ultimately) dictators, might conceivably
have proceeded, without any serious difficulty. *The
" dictatorship " of the North over the South could easily
have become* (had the circumstances favoured the
pre-requisite class consolidation of the proletariat)
*the dictatorship of the American proletariat over the
whole Federal Union.*

Observe ! Neither Marx nor Engels ever said it was
at all *likely* that this would happen either in Britain
or the U.S.A. All they said was that it was, then,
conceivable a priori—that there was nothing in the
nature of things to exclude it as a possibility.

(11) As a matter of fact, Hook, in the cases of both Britain
and the U.S.A. falls into the very fallacy which is also
that of Cole, and of all bourgeois pseudo-scientific
historians. He thinks it was *the same* Britain *before*

1832 as after ; the same *before* 1870 as after, and so on. He thinks that the U.S.A. was the same *before* and *after* the Civil War, and before and after the immense post-civil war expansion which opened the safety-valve for the potentially explosive force of the proletariat and petty-bourgeoisie in the industrial centres of the Eastern States of the U.S.A. He does not even seem to realise the immense difference between the U.S.A. before 1917 and the U.S.A. to-day. *The change in the official attitude towards mass immigration would give him a clue, were he really moving " towards the understanding of Marx."*

. . . . .

It is astounding but clearly evidenced by their arguments that neither Cole nor Hook has grasped the essential *core* of the Marxian conception of the proletarian revolution. Neither of them is able to rise above " the standpoint of the single individual in civil society." Neither of them even begins to grasp the concept of the proletariat (*not* as a simple aggregation of *separate* individuals, *but*) as an organic and developing totality which is in fact *itself the new society in process of becoming*.

Cole cannot see that Marx himself has indicated the *only* conjunction of circumstances in which could be realised his own pet plan of an alliance between the proletariat and the petty-bourgeoisie out of which the proletarian revolution *might* emerge without " nastiness " or " bother."

Hook, who, as a " Left," thinks always in terms of a mystical absolute " no compromise," thinks that " class consciousness " is not a dialectical *fact* but a moral aspiration ; thinks that proletarian revolution is only possible if the proletarians *as a personal moral discipline* keep themselves as *individuals* " pure and unspotted " from any " contaminating contact " with the bourgeoisie, big, little or middling ! It is not the proletariat as a concrete, historically conditioned, developing, social *fact* and *force* that he envisages, but an aggregate of individuals who merely happen to be proletarians ; and for whom a patent " technique " of revolution has to be " discovered " in the true Utopian fashion ! That is why Hook, to make a case for his Utopian-" Left-ist " misconception of Marx and Engels has to attempt to refute Lenin likewise. That is why Hook finally gives up the problem in despair :

" What led Marx and Engels into the error of qualifying their general position as they did . . . the author frankly confesses that he does not know."—HOOK, *loc. cit.*, p. 248.

. . . . .

Cole also " gives it up " ; but he is this much superior to Hook—he doesn't put the blame on Marx. He puts it to the credit of the *Ewigkeit* !

" We must conclude then that the extent to which a revolution needs to destroy the State, or even build upon it by a process of transformation rather than destruction, depends on the relation of *the aims* of the revolution to the essential character of the State *in which it conquers power*."—COLE : *loc. cit.*, p. 203.

" If the *structure of the State* is or becomes such as to exclude an advance towards Socialism by constitutional means, there remains for the Socialists no recourse save a resort to unconstitutional action."—COLE : *loc. cit.*, p. 205.

" Where this has been done [e.g., by Fascism] Marx's analysis unquestionably holds good, as it does wherever the State is of such a sort as to be beyond the reach of working-class or Socialist pressure. For there is under these conditions no alternative to a revolutionary method *as well as* a revolutionary objective."—COLE : *loc. cit.*, p. 206.

The rupture between Theory and Practice which can be traced through all these extracts is openly proclaimed in the last admission that, in certain circumstances, there is (alas !) " no alternative " to *squaring one's practice with one's theory* !

Cole, you see, is determined to be—*not* a " materialist," Oh no !—a *realist*. Such a conception as that of the *general nature* of the State—a nature traceable through each and every one of its specific *forms*, from the Temple States of ancient Asiatic civilisation, the city States of the Græco-Roman world, to the mediæval-feudal, and modern bourgeois States—such a conception is, of course, impossible to him. " Realism " forbids such " abstractions "—and in forbidding them cuts off the dialectic " at the main," and leaves the " Realist " with nothing but a bewilderment of separate and distinct " National States " which *because* they are all " different," cannot therefore be *in any respect* " alike." Then each National State is conceived not in respect of its *organic function* as an institution of Society, but as something separate and distinct from Society, something which movements within Society may or may not "destroy," "preserve," "build on," "reconstruct," or preserve from reconstruction.

Whether the one or the other is done depends, not upon the organic functional relation between the Society and its institution, the State, but wholly, solely and entirely upon the *subjective intentions* of the revolutionary Party (the *aims* of the revolution). Thus the whole question is removed from the sphere of an objective historical process and reduced to the " Realist " proportions of a game with a " Meccano " set, or a box of bricks—which can be built up, knocked down, added to, taken from, or " reconstructed " at will ; unless some nasty, spiteful Fascist has *glued the bricks together* !

Contrast with that the Marx-Engels conception. The State is an historically-conditioned phenomenon which appears at a certain specific stage in the historical development of Society, undergoes a whole series of permutations during the further development of Society, and finally disappears with the disappearance of the conditions which brought it into being :

" The State is therefore by no means a power forced on Society from the outside. Just as little is it " the realisation of the Moral Idea," " the reflection and the realisation of Reason," as Hegel asserted. It is the product of society at a certain stage of development. It is the admission that this society has become entangled in an insoluble contradiction with itself, that it is cleft with insoluble antagonisms which it is powerless to dispel. But in order that these antagonisms (classes with conflicting economic interests) may not consume themselves and society in sterile struggle, a power apparently standing above society becomes necessary, whose purpose is to control the conflict and keep it within the bounds of " order." And this power arising out of society, but assuming dominance over it, and increasingly separating itself from it, is *the State*."—ENGELS : *Origin of the Family*, chap. 9.

Cole, like all his kind, can only see the formal *separation* (indicated in the last sentence quoted) *to the exclusion of the connection and vice versa*. His argument amounts to this : the State is *the same as* Society in " constitutional, democratic States," it is absolutely *divorced* from Society in Fascist States. Marx was *wrong* as a sociological analyst. But he

might prove right *as a prophet*! This is the last word of
"Transport-House ' Marxism ' ! "

.   .   .   .   .

What are the *essential* characteristics of the State according
to the Marx–Engels–Lenin concept ?—the characteristics
which enable it to be distinguished from the Ancient Society
which preceded its appearance and the Socialist-Communist
Society which will follow upon its disappearance ?   There
are three :

(1) Organisation of the population on the basis of *territory*
    (as distinct from *kinship* in the ancient society, and
    by co-operative *function* in the Communist order).

(2) The existence of *a public power of coercion* no longer
    coincident and conterminous with the *armed people*.

(3) The power to levy taxes—which places the State and
    its personnel in an exploiting, parasitical relation to
    the productive activities of society.   In Ancient
    Society, as in the Communist Order, the administra-
    tive functions of such "government" as there was and
    will be form *directly part of* these productive activities.

Once the State is envisaged in this way it costs no effort
to see (*a*) why the State at any given time is *always*, and
especially in respect of its coercive and exploiting functions,
the *instrument* of the ruling class ; (*b*) why any given *form*
of State becomes *obsolete* as soon as that *ruling class* is
defeated in conflict (be that conflict bloody or unbloody)
with a revolutionary class, and (*c*) why the victorious
revolutionary class *must* organise *its own* State apparatus to
ensure the conditions in which alone it can reap at leisure the
fruits of its victory.

What is more : this conception enables us to understand
why the " democratic republic " (after the manner of the
constitution of 1793) was regarded by Marx and Engels
(*a*) as hypothetically attainable in their day—since the
big bourgeoisie had not then attained the enormous preponderance they possess in the period of Imperialism, and
the coercive and exploiting function of the State had not
then been developed correspondingly ; (*b*) as the form of
State in which alone the struggle between the bourgeoisie
and the proletariat could be fought out as an open, class,
fight for power without traditional illusions or anachronistic
obstructions.

This does not arise from any magic in the " democracy "
or the " republican " constitution.   It arises from the fact

that the balance of class *forces* will be so clearly seen that the proletariat may be able to *seize power* without serious resistance beforehand—as indeed the Bolsheviks did in November, 1917.

That this democratic republic nowhere exists to-day, that even petit-bourgeois " democrats " have ceased to clamour for its establishment (the British Labour Party, for instance, is not even officially *republican* !) is obvious. So, too, is it obvious that even in the " democratic republic " the issue would be decided (even if not a single actual blow were struck and the revolution were accomplished in the *form* of a process of " constitutional " change) by the interrelation of class *forces*.

Engels expressly makes the point that the official " constitutional " pretence that class divisions do not exist— the distinctive hall-mark of the " democratic-constitutional " State—is precisely the *form* behind which, in society, classantagonism ripens to its culminating explosion point:

> " The highest [bourgeois] form of State, the Democratic Republic, officially knows nothing of class distinctions. . . . In such a State wealth exerts its power indirectly *but all the more safely*. This is done partly by the mode of directly corrupting the State officials (after the fashion classical in the U.S.A.) or in the form of an alliance between Government and bankers which it establishes all the more easily when the public debt increases and when [joint stock] corporations have concentrated in their hands not only the means of transportation but those of production itself—using the Stock Exchange as a centre. . . .
>
> " *The possessing class rules directly through universal suffrage*. For so long as . . . the proletariat is not ripe for its economic emancipation, just so long will the majority regard the existing order of society as the only possible order, and, therefore, constitute themselves the tail, the extreme Left wing of the capitalist class. . . .
>
> " *Universal suffrage is the gauge of the maturity of the working class. It can and never will be anything other than that in the modern State*. But that is sufficient. On the day when the thermometer of Universal Suffrage reaches its boiling-point among the workers, *they as well as the capitalists will know what to do*."—ENGELS : *Origin of the Family*, chap. 9.

It is a remarkable fact (from several points of view) that

Cole begins his chief revisionist " improvement " upon Marx with precisely that very fact that Engels uses here as the proof that, and the explanation how, under the form of the " democratic State " the real ruler is *Wealth*.

To Engels (as to Marx) the joint-stock company was a device whereby all the spare cash of all classes was mobilised under the command of, and for the prime advantage of, Banking and Finance Capital. To Cole this " joint-stock " device is (*a*) something of which he conceives Marx to have known nothing (!), and (*b*) the historical means whereby an entirely *new* class—the rentier or coupon-clipping class—has come into existence. The coming of this new class, a new form of *petit-bourgeoisie*, Cole regards as radically altering Society from the form in which Marx envisaged it in the *Communist Manifesto* and later. Cole interprets Fascism as the seizure of power by this new middle-class independently of, and in opposition to, *both* the Big bourgeoisie *and* the proletariat. Therefore he argues that as a defence against Fascism the Socialist proletariat should seek an alliance with this new " middle class."

.   .   .   .   .

What constitutes a " class " in the Marxian sense ? Basically it is a specific relation to the mode of social production for the time being in operation. It is a social expression of that which, in base, is the social division of labour. Being a *social* expression—one in which the objective realities confronting Society are expressed through *individuals* and their *consciousness*—it expresses objective reality only in a more or less distorted and roundabout fashion. For instance : the *real* primacy of labour-activity in production is, in bourgeois society, expressed in the class subjection and the relative contempt with which that society regards the proletariat. Conversely, the *really* secondary and parasitical relation in production of the employer, as such (who only becomes a captain of industry because he is an exploiter of labour but seems, socially, to become an " employer " of labour *because* he is a captain of industry)—this derived, secondary, and parasitical relation becomes apparent in society as the supremacy, over-lordship, and class superiority of the bourgeoisie.

It is against the background of this primary antagonism of bourgeoisie and proletariat that the " middle class " or, more precisely, the petty-bourgeoisie is to be distinguished. As basically the bourgeoisie is the class which lives by the *buying* of the commodity labour power and the proletariat is the class that lives by *selling* the same commodity the fundamentality of their inter-relation in bourgeois society is made clear, and with it the secondary and dependent character (relative to this basic inter-relation) of all those strata whose means of living depend neither upon buying *nor* upon selling labour power.

The historical dialectic is apparent in the fact that the archetype of this class—the artisan master of a craft in the town and the independent freeholder farmer in the country—survives as an anachronism, a relic of the mediæval social strata from which both the proletariat *and* the bourgeoisie, *and* their inter-relation arose. The memory of this now superseded primacy survives as a tradition which, taken over by intermediate social strata later developed (strata which have no organic connection with this original but merely *resemble* it in so far as their social situation is likewise that of a grade intermediate between the upper and lower classes of society), helps these more modern strata to the consoling notion that " the Middle classes are the backbone of England ! "

But for purposes of social-political struggle the general situation of this " middle class " differs radically from that of either bourgeoisie proper or proletariat. These latter classes have a *positive* relation to the basic production process of society—a *positive* relation which not only persists, but is rendered sharper and more definite with the development of bourgeois society. The middle " class " on the other hand is only a " class " *relatively,* one only to be defined *negatively,* i.e., not by what it is so much as by what it is *not.*

For instance, to take a few examples : the shopkeeper, the lawyer, the fund-holder rentier, the small jobbing builder, the first grade Civil Servant, and the master mariner, are all members of the " middle class." They are so because they neither live by buying nor by selling labour power. In so far as they do buy labour power (shopkeeper, jobbing builder) they do so only incidentally, as a supplement to their primary function of selling *not* their ability to labour, but labour embodied in a *product,* the price of which product (and not that of the abstract ability to produce it as with the proletariat) constitutes their means of living.

It stands plain to sense that in the " middle class " we have not so much a " class " proper, as a whole welter of historically conditioned transitions between the two primary poles of bourgeois society. Every vicissitude of commercial,

industrial, and political development which for Society as
a whole means an equable progressive development, means
for the members of this class either sudden good fortune and
promotion to the " heaven " of the bourgeoisie or equally
sudden abasement to the " hell " of the proletariat. It is
for this class, earlier, and in more dramatic intensity than
for any class, or for bourgeois society as a whole, that " general
insecurity becomes the general law of existence."

How far is it possible for this class to constitute itself a
separate and distinct political force ?

If the reader will refer back to page 316 to the definition
quoted from Marx's *Eighteenth Brumaire*, he will find the
answer given in principle. " So far as individuals live under
conditions which separate their mode of life, their interests,
their traditions, and their culture from those of the rest of
society they constitute a class."

Tried by this test the welter of the " middle class " becomes
a chaos of incompatibles. They are separated; and at the
same time they are not separated. The rentier has not the
mode of life, nor the traditions, nor the culture of the big
bourgeois Finance Capitalist ; but his interest is at one
with his, except that he is wholly at the mercy of any
" wangle " (lawful or fraudulent) the Big Boss may choose
to put through. The shopkeeper has not the mode of life
of the proletarian ; but he may share his culture, and his
immediate interest may be, and is, to an extent bound up
with the prosperity, such as it is, of the proletariat. As it is
(as Marx showed in the case of the French allotment farmer)
with the peasantry so, to an even higher degree, it is with
the " middle class "—they do *not* constitute a class to exactly
the same extent that they *do* !

Hence it is that the middle class is *par excellence* the
breeding ground of the notion that classes do not exist, or
do so merely as relative-descriptive classifications of purely
provisional significance, categories above which men should
rise to the conception of the " Nation as a whole." Hence,
too, it is that the middle class is the breeding-ground of the
counter-notion that nothing exists but the *Individual*, that
the Nation, like the class, is a mere relative descriptive
category of no positive significance. Hence, too, the fact that
the specific politics of the middle class are always an eclectic
hodge-podge of *anti*-capitalism and *anti*-proletarianism—a
hodge-podge which, unrealisable as a policy in itself,
converts the middle-class politician and the middle-class

" mob " in general into agents or allies of one or the other of the primary protagonists, bourgeoisie and proletariat. Just as this class—which is no class—is doomed always to oscillate between the extremes of capitalism and proletarianism, so its politics, always in a state of inextricable confusion oscillate violently between the extremes of Revolution and Counter-Revolution. This is, however, not a mere oscillation only. Under the conditioning of the dialectic of objective history the more clear-sighted members of this class find themselves forced to choose the standpoint of one extreme or the other. Hence from this class come some of the outstanding exponents of revolutionary proletarian theory (Marx, Engels, Lenin, etc.) and at the same time the chief theoreticians of anti-proletarian counter-revolution.

And above all, since this class is not a " class," it (as Marx said of the French allotment farmer) cannot *represent* but must itself *be represented*. Hence it is this class which has served historically as the vehicle to carry into power every political Saviour, every " Great " Hero-Leader of modern times (Napoleon III, Gladstone, Disraeli, Bismarck, Lloyd George, Mussolini, Hitler). And it is this class which provides the *intelligentsia* which seeks to create both out of Marx and of Lenin, just such another " Great Man," and which, disappointed at failure from the intractability of the material, turns round for an alternative and finds it (since the *intelligentsia*, true to its petty-bourgeois type, must have its " Hero ") in—*Leon Trotsky* !

We can now, by contrast, approach the question as Cole wishes from the side of Fascism as a fact triumphant in Italy, Germany, Austria, and elsewhere.

Does the establishment of Fascism constitute any fundamental change in *basic* social relations ? Does it introduce any new mode of production ? Can it, even if it wishes to do so, find any mode of production which is at the same time *not* capitalist, and not Socialist-Communist ? Does it even propose to alter basic property relations ? *Or is it only a new and more ferocious method of preserving them* ?

Society rests upon a basis of *production*. Capitalist society rests upon *commodity* production by *wage* labour. Upon what does Fascism in practice and in theory propose to rest itself, if it be given full scope ? *Upon commodity production by wage labour* !

What is *the State* function in general ? To repress forcibly all revolutionary class struggles in the interests of the ruling class for the time being prevailing ! What is an invariable practical principle of Fascism ? That any and every attempt at revolutionary class struggle *by the proletariat* must be and shall be ruthlessly repressed.

Who are the ruling class in the Capitalist State ? The effective owners of the means of production—the dominant " aristocracy " of Capital. Who really rules in the Fascist State ? The effective owners—the " aristocracy " of Capital.

What is the difference, so far, between an ordinary pseudo " democratic " Capitalist State and a Fascist State ? This : that whereas a pseudo-" democratic " Capitalist State makes a pretence of yielding to the workers the possibility of peacefully changing the social system, in the Fascist State such a possibility is openly prohibited.

What is to be inferred from this difference ? That what are in the Capitalist State at a certain stage of its development useful safety valves through which the gathering force of discontent can vent itself harmlessly—(e.g., rights of free speech, of free press, free association, parliamentary opposition, etc.)—have become no longer effective as safeguards. *Fascism is the form in which Capitalism seeks to stave off Revolution by an anticipatory counter-revolution!*

Is Fascism then, *simply*, counter-revolution ? Not *simply*. It is counter-revolutionary in essence, but it is also a special historically conditioned form of counter-revolution—one that achieves its object by a demagogic exploitation of the illusions and disappointments left behind by the failure of the treacherous, class-collaborationist, opportunism into which Second International Social Democracy degenerated steadily during the years immediately before the War and thenceforward at breakneck speed.

Herein lies the crux of the whole matter. But for the particular quantity and quality of illusions (and disillusionment) spread by Social Democracy—and particularly, but for the refusal of the Social Democracy to follow the lead given by Lenin, first at the outbreak of war, then in the Bolshevik revolution of November, 1917—but for these things Fascism would never have been possible. Here are the proofs :

Fascism in Italy, Germany, Austria, Poland, etc., in each case originated in the Social Patriotism adopted and fostered by Social Democracy (as by the official British Labour Party) during the War. In each case the originators of the movement were able to exploit both patriotic and Socialistic sentiment and turn it against *revolutionary*

Socialism and Communism—in which work Social Democracy had prepared the way. In the case of Mussolini, he had been a leading Socialist journalist of syndicalist leanings, and his Fascism accordingly bears, emphatically, strong traces of syndicalist formulæ. The German Nazi Party, and the Austrian Christian-Socialists are both nominally " Socialist " Parties. The Party of Pilsudski in Poland is " Nationalist," but, likewise, owed its success among the workers (so far as it had any hold upon them) to the Socialist reputation of its leader. And so we might go on. The first point is that in the postulates of Fascism—nationality, the need for a union of *all* classes, the subordination of *mere* Parliamentarism to " public " needs, hostility to all *non*-Patriotic Socialism, and especially to Communism—on all *these* points Social Democracy had prepared the way for Fascism. The second point is that the need to maintain the established State and economic order against the attempt to overthrow it in favour of a Dictatorship of the Proletariat, was a " need " that, *before* any sort of Fascism had even begun, Social Democracy had maintained with all its force, even to the force of arms and the butcheries of Wels (the Butcher of Berlin) and Noske.

In Austria the case was glaring. Soviet Republics were established on each side of its territory in Bavaria and in Hungary. Austria, in which the Social Democrats controlled absolutely the armed forces and could (so they boasted) have overthrown the Government at any moment, needed only to link up with them to make of the Federal Union of all three a force too formidable to be overthrown. Instead, Austrian Social Democracy refused its co-operation and, actively as well as passively, assisted in the crushing of the Hungarian and Bavarian Soviet Republics. In Italy, when the workers had seized the factories, it was the Socialist (Social-Democratic) Party which refused to back the seizure with a revolutionary struggle and instead persuaded the workers to hand back the factories which they had successfully defended against armed forces, in return for employers' promises.

Everywhere it is the same—the ground was prepared for Fascism by the Social-Democratic betrayal of every principle vital to revolutionary Marxism and by the disgust and disillusionment spread among the workers as a consequence of this treachery.

Is, then, Fascism only another form of opportunist, class-collaborationist, Kautskyite Social Democracy ? No. There is a difference and a big one.

Social Democracy, despite all its " Marxist " theory, constrained its aspirations rigidly within certain limits of practice.
It refused to lead a revolutionary resistance to war; it
" opposed " war in the abstract—but supported it with all
its resources as soon as it became a concrete actuality.   It
refused to move against the Kaiser's government until that
government was *de facto* overthrown, when it put itself at
the head of the revolution avowedly to keep it within the
" bounds of moderation."   It deliberately prevented any
sort of expropriation of the capitalist class, and not merely
prevented the disarming of the bourgeoisie, but actually
itself armed special officers' corps to crush the Communist
rising.   By its *deeds* it preached nationalism, the negation of
all class struggles, especially *revolutionary* class struggles.
By its deeds it preached that the bourgeois order of society
was and is the only conceivable order, and any attempt at
its overthrow positively criminal.

All this placed the practice of Social Democracy in violent
opposition to its theory—which of itself could not fail to
spread confusion, demoralisation, and cynical disillusionment
on all sides.   Fascism thereupon emerged with a doctrine
which unified itself with the implications of the deeds of
Social Democracy and carried these implications to their
logical counter-revolutionary conclusions.

.   .   .   .   .

What part did the " middle class "—the petit-bourgeoisie—
play in all this ?   It played a big rôle, but one quite different
from that Cole supposes.   That the leaders of the Fascist
party in Italy, Germany, and Austria, are to a very large
extent petit-bourgeois is true.   But so, too, are the parliamentary leaders of *all* the political parties on the Continent,
and in Britain likewise.   The number of really big bourgeois
who play any part on the open political stage (before, that is
to say they are too old for the actual conduct of their business
enterprises) is remarkably few.   That the Fascist Party
played as much as possible upon the prejudices of the petit-
bourgeois in town and country is true likewise—but so also
does every non-revolutionary, every conservative and reactionary party when it is forced demagogically to mobilise
a political force.

What is certain is that Fascism was from the beginning
supplied with funds by Finance Capital and has, whenever
it has secured power, ruled scrupulously in the interests of
the economic force (Finance Capital) whose tool it is.

Apart from brutalities with little economic significance (the attack upon the Jews for instance, and upon the Socialist co-operatives) virtually nothing has been done specifically to benefit the petit-bourgeoisie except in so far as its interest is bound up (or deemed to be) with the interest of Finance Capital. The part played by the middle class was that of (a) demoralising force within the leadership and organisation of the Social-Democratic Party, and (b) duped and deluded leaders of a stampede of voting-cattle to the side of Fascism as soon as it looked like winning.

Mutatis mutandis (with change for change) the role of the " middle class " in the Revolution of the twentieth century has, so far, been so close a reproduction of the cowardly, treacherous role it played in the Revolution of 1848-9 as to be highly significant. The difference in the outcome—Fascism instead of simple return to arbitrary Monarchism—is a measure of the difference in degree of development and of revolutionary maturity in the proletariat. It is this which is the ultimate determining cause of Fascism.

Cole asserts, as Bernstein asserted more than thirty years before him (only to recant after he had been completely and irrecoverably refuted), that Marx's prediction of the " disappearance " of the " middle class " has been falsified. The old petit-bourgeoisie as Marx knew it, says Cole, has disappeared, it is true, but a new one has been evolved :

" Capitalism has found the art of diffusing industrial ownership while continuing to concentrate the effective control of economic policy in fewer and fewer hands, and has created a large and influential class of salaried and fee-taking professionals who form the nucleus of a new *petit-bourgeoisie* very different from the old, and infinitely superior in initiative driving power and power of resistance to the proletarians if it takes sides against them. To ignore or minimise the importance of these changes in the class system is to be guilty of wilful blindness ; and to recite in face of them an unrevised Marxian creed is to prefer a dogma to a workable policy of Socialist advance."—COLE : *loc. cit.*, p. 293.

" It is evident Marx was mistaken in supposing that the further advance of Capitalism would result in driving the entire intermediate element in Society down into the ranks of the proletariat, at any rate without an intervening phase in which this intermediate element would be powerful enough to make on its own behalf a bid for social and economic authority."—COLE : *loc. cit.*, pp. 293–4.

Let us test this theory by its conclusion. Suppose that this new petit-bourgeoisie does exist. What sort of economic system *can* it conceivably introduce, " on its own behalf," which is distinct in kind from Capitalism on the one hand or Socialist-Communism on the other ? The only conceivable economic system to correspond with these requirements would be a *return to post-mediæval petty industry*.

Now, let it be granted that the advocates of Fascism *often talk of doing this* ; than ask the question : how far is such an attempt objectively feasible ? And then the second question : wherein is this a *new* policy for the petit-bourgeois ?

As to feasibility : it is self-evident that a return to post-mediæval methods is feasible *only* with a population with post-mediæval tastes and requirements. Cole has only to envisage the attempt to (*a*) eradicate or (*b*) satisfy the demand for gramophone records and wireless sets in conditions of petty industry, to realise that of all possible Utopias he has hit upon the one most inconceivable historically.

As to *newness*, let us consult Marx and Engels :

" The mediæval burgesses and the small peasant proprietors were the precursors of the modern bourgeoisie. In those countries which are but little developed industrially and commercially, these two classes still vegetate side by side with the rising bourgeoisie.

" In countries where modern civilisation has become fully developed a *new class of petty bourgeois has been formed fluctuating between proletariat and bourgeoisie and ever renewing itself as a supplementary part of bourgeois society.*

" The *individual* members of this class, however, are constantly being hurled down into the proletariat by the action of competition, and as modern industry develops they even see the moment *approaching* when they will completely disappear as *an independent section* of modern society, to be replaced in manufactures, agriculture, and commerce, by overlookers, bailiffs and shopmen." [" Salaried and fee-taking professionals ! "]
—MARX–ENGELS : *Communist Manifesto*, pp. 30–1.

Here, written in 1847, is all that Cole is trying to say, said for him, and said properly, by Marx and Engels ! Observe :

nowhere is it asserted that the middle class *absolutely* disappears. Each particular *form* of petit-bourgeois social existence does disappear—sooner or later—and that with increasing rapidity. The fact that a *new* form is at the same time begotten no more destroys the fact that the old form has vanished than the existence of a grandchild proves that its grandfather is *not dead*! The whole of this " middle class " is increasingly threatened with extinction—but of a particular kind, i.e., as an *independent* section of society. It becomes increasingly a *dependent* section, one " *fluctuating* between the bourgeoisie and the proletariat."

It is as absurd to say *a priori* that " things *must* have changed radically since Marx's day," as it is to say *a priori* that they have *not* so changed. Both statements are equally invalidated by their *a priori*-ism. But it is a fair and valid challenge to those who assert that the *essential* relations of bourgeois society (as distinct from their incidental modes of manifestation) have changed, to invite them to show concretely wherein the situation of this " new *petit-bourgeoisie* " (a phase wherein for once Cole coincides, unwittingly, with Marx and Engels) is different from that envisaged in the extract given above. So little is Cole able to accept this challenge that Marx and Engels' words : " a new class . . . ever renewing itself . . . a *supplemental* part of modern society "—actually describe the class Cole has in mind better than he has described it for himself. Moreover, in noting its *essential* characteristic as " supplemental ", Marx and Engels refute by anticipation Cole's Utopian notion of the possibility of this " class "—which is only negatively a *class*, only a distinct class in the sense that its members *individually* are *not* really big bourgeois and *not*, positively, proletarian— could ever " seize " power except as the allies of, or agents acting on behalf of one or other of the parties to the primary and basic antithesis of proletariat and bourgeoisie.

The *Manifesto* supplies in this very section a concrete reply to Cole. It notes that the " *new* petit-bourgeoisie " has its own special brand of " Socialism " :

" This form of Socialism aspires either to restoring the old means of production and of exchange, and with them the old property relations and the old society, or to cramping the modern means of production and exchange within the framework of the old property relations that have been, and were bound to be, exploded by those means. In either case it is both reactionary and Utopian.

" Its last words are : Corporate guilds for manufacture ; patriarchal relations for agriculture."—MARX-
ENGELS : *loc. cit.*, p. 31.

Considering that this was written in 1847, it is nothing
less than marvellous—certainly in the highest degree significant—that this description more closely fits the demagogic
pretences of the Nazis, and Mussolini (and, in the main, the
outlook of the ex-Guild Socialist G. D. H. Cole also), than it
falls short of describing them.

Observe : no affirmation is made or is sought to be made
that Marxism provides solutions *ready-made* for every possible
concrete situation or contingency. On the contrary, it is the
essence of Marxism that no such ready-made solutions are
possible. At the same time, so acutely did Marx and Engels
observe and disentangle the essential (and, therefore, relatively
permanent) tendencies in bourgeois society from their accidental forms, and so often does objective development bring
a return of the old in a new and more developed form, that
it requires something like a Marx to discover wherein developments have changed *radically* beyond those that Marx foresaw.

The situation of the petit-bourgeois Socialism of the period
1830–48, compared with that of the " National-Socialism "
(Nazi-ism) of to-day, is superficially as different as it is
possible to conceive. That therefore there should be notwithstanding a *recognisable resemblance* amid all the differences is a fact of prime, concrete practical importance. It
does not prove Cole's point that Fascism, where it has been
victorious, is a *de facto* triumph of the petit-bourgeoisie, and
may lead to the establishment of an alternative form of
society different in principle from either Capitalism or
Socialism-Communism. On the contrary, it proves that, since
its programme is " both Utopian and reactionary," it cannot be realised in the illusory form it presents to its dupes
and to G. D. H. Cole. It can be realised only in so far as it
and these dupes serve the ends of the *real* originating force
of the reaction—the actual ruling power, Finance Capital.

.   .   .   .   .

Cole is so eager to find a " Marxist " warrant for his " real-
Marxism-up-to-date " (which, at its face value, cannot
easily be distinguished from simple Fabianised Liberalism)
that it is specially noteworthy that he makes no use of the
hackneyed quotations, beloved of Social-Democratic opportunists, wherein Marx admits the possibility of a " peaceful "
conquest of power by the proletariat. We have discussed

this matter above (page 446 and following) in connection with Engels' preface to Marx's *Capital*, and Hook's strictures thereupon. It is pertinent to cite here the passage which is usually relied upon by Revisionists, from Marx's speech at Amsterdam after the Hague Congress, 1872, of the I.W.M.A. :

"Some day the workers must *conquer* political supremacy in order to establish the new organisation of labour. They must *overthrow* the old political system whereby the old institutions are sustained. If they fail to do this they will suffer the fate of the early Christians, who neglected to overthrow the old system, and who *for that reason* never had a kingdom in this world. Of course I must not be supposed to imply that the means to this end will be everywhere the same. We know that special regard must be paid to the institutions, customs and traditions of various lands. And we do not deny that there are certain countries, such as the United States and England, in which the workers may hope to secure their ends by peaceful means. If I mistake not, Holland belongs to the same category. Even so, we have to recognise that in most Continental countries force will have to be the lever of the revolution. *It is to force that the workers will in due time have to appeal if, at long last, the dominion of labour is to be established.*"—MARX : *see* Stekloff, *First International*, pp. 240–1.

Why did Cole make no use of this passage ? *Because he simply dared not !* Cole's theory is that " the continued existence " of " the chance of a constitutional transition to Socialism " (which chance " still exists " in Britain)—

" depends on the persistence of conditions which do not drive the contending parties to the unrestrained extremism of despair. If a large part of the British proletariat were to go Communist, or a large part of the British middle-class Fascist, the possibility of getting Socialism by constitutional methods would disappear, and the serious development of extremism on either side would inevitably lead to a parallel growth on the other."—COLE : page 302.

Marx, you see, conceives that the *conquest* of power by the proletariat might be made peacefully, if and when its *force* (i.e., its " extremism " actual or potential) became *too great to be resisted.* Cole, on the other hand, conceives that a constitutional (i.e., a " peaceful ") transition (*not* " conquest ") might be made if and when the proletariat

lowered its *force* to the point at which it would need no
resistance ! And this is offered as an advance upon the
Fabian theory that Socialism might be smuggled in by
the back door when it would be kicked out at the front !
Similarly Cole when arguing for an alliance between the
proletariat and the petty-bourgeoisie simply dared not make
use of the words in which Lenin admitted the possibility of
such a course :

> " To carry on a war for the overthrow of the inter-
> national bourgeoisie, a war a hundred times more difficult,
> prolonged and complicated than the most stubborn of
> ordinary wars between countries, and to refuse beforehand
> to manœuvre, to utilise the conflict between one's
> enemies ; to refuse co-operation and compromise with
> possible (even though transient, unstable, vacillating
> and conditional) allies—is not this a laughable thing ? . . .
>
> " To overcome so powerful an enemy is possible only
> through the greatest effort and by dint of the obligatory,
> thorough, careful, attentive utilisation of every breach
> . . . every clash of interests . . . every possibility, how-
> ever small, of gaining an ally. . . . Who has not grasped
> this has failed to grasp one iota of Marxism."—LENIN :
> *Left-Wing Communism*, p. 52.

Here again the reason is obvious : with Lenin, as with
Marx, the basic presupposition is the revolutionary struggle
of the proletariat raised to its maximum of self-reliant
potentiality. With Cole it is this self-reliant revolutionary
class struggle which constitutes the *danger* to be avoided !
Marx and Lenin envisage the movement of the proletariat
as having become *de facto* Communist. To Cole this would
be " the end of all things ! "

Cole's contention, as against Marx, amounts to this :
two entirely new developments have radically changed the
inter-relation of class forces upon which Marx based his
theory of revolutionary struggle and the tactic appropriate
thereto. These new developments are (*a*) the coming of a
" new " middle-class of small investors ; and (*b*) as a consequence, the superseding of constitutional-democratic governments by Fascism. This, he claims, alters the situation
entirely, in that it opens up for Capitalism a new vista of
development capable of indefinite prolongation : the fact
that it is " development " *backwards* only the more emphasises
the fact that it is an alternative to the progressive develop-

ment of antagonisms from which Marx deduced the inevitable overthrow of the bourgeois order. Since Fascism is something of which Marx knew, and could know, nothing, it is obvious that Marx can give us little or no guidance in face of such an entirely new phenomenon.

Stated thus the trying-to-have-it-both-ways eclecticism of Cole's argument becomes as plain as a pike-staff. In the old, old style of the Fabian and the Bernstein-Revisionist, Cole uses Marx's argument in general to prove that Marx's argument in detail no longer applies. And it is notable that all (or most) of the off-shoots from the decomposition of the German Social-Democratic Party formulate their ground theme in substantially the same fashion. [See particularly *Socialism's New Start*, by " Miles,"—with its demand that, as a basis for " revolutionary unity," the U.S.S.R. should abandon the movement for the collectivisation of agriculture, and the production of means of machine-production which has made it possible and concentrate on the production of consumption goods instead.]

No long argument is needed to expose the fallacy upon which the whole case for this neo-Revisionism rests. That the passage of capitalism into its monopolist-imperialist phase presents phenomena unknown to Marx we have, ourselves, already noted—(*with the aid of Lenin !*). But in noting the fact, we noted likewise that instead of eliminating the relations, and the " law of motion " of capitalist society revealed by Marx, these new phenomena show these relations as *persisting* in intensified force and with a reinforced complication of contradictions, so that the law of motion revealed by Marx becomes even clearer in the phase he did not live to witness than in the phase he analysed in person.

For instance : Cole builds wholly upon the supposition that the historical change of capitalist property into stocks, shares, and bond-holdings has created, *not* a transformation of the Big bourgeoisie, but a new, " rentier " petty-bourgeoisie. This is doubly fallacious. It ignores the change in the *whole* bourgeoisie, and it forgets that so far as a petty-bourgeoisie is distinguished merely by the quantity of its property, it differs from the big bourgeoisie only in that being more needy it is more greedy. There is more, too.

What Cole is forced to blur over, in this connection, is the " other " of such *rentier*-differentiation as affects the " middle "-class ; namely, the transformation of the actually *working* sections of the technological and professional middle-

class increasingly into a " black-coated proletariat," a social
strata only relatively to be distinguished from the proletariat
proper, whose conditions in life, particularly in the period of
general crisis, become more and more assimilated to those of
the proletariat.   This fact, properly evaluated, reveals itself,
as we have shown, as one already anticipated in principle by
Marx; and, therefore, as one which demonstrates that his
main generalisations have gained rather than lost validity in
consequence of later developments.

   The contention that the victory of Fascism makes a *radical*
difference to the social-relations analysed by Marx is, as we
have shown, quite untenable.   On the contrary, the whole
aim and purpose of the " anticipatory counter-revolution "
which constitutes the essence of Fascism derives from the
existence of precisely the relations analysed by Marx, and
the need, in face of the rising tide of proletarian revolution
to resort to desperate " Emergency " measures, to stave off
the day of its inevitable victory.   Fascism, in fact, *proves*
the truth of Marxism by the frenzied ferocity with which it
seeks to stamp it out.

   That the mode of operation of the revolutionary proletariat,
and of the Communist Party, must differ *in form* under a
Fascist regime from that which it takes under a bourgeois-
constitutional regime needs no proving.   But this, instead of
calling for a modification of Marxist theory and practice is
a confirmation of their basic features, whether considered
separately or, still more, in their organic union.   Marxism,
which is the self-conscious revolutionary movement of the
proletariat and the toiling masses—which is Communism—
has always been " the *real* movement which makes an end of
the *existing* order of things."   That this existing order takes
on a Fascist form makes a big difference to the *form* which
that movement will take.   But it makes no difference at all
to its revolutionary essence.

   Thus, the contention that the emergence of Fascism has
invalidated the *essence* of Marxism—either in respect of its
theory or of its practice is shown to be false from every side.
In fact, it is a contention that could only have been raised by
those who had, beforehand, debased Marx's theory into a
conception of purely parliamentary-constitutionalist struggle
to achieve a " peaceful," gradualist, " revolution," which was
so little of a revolution, as ordinarily understood, that (in
Keir Hardie's words) " Socialism would come like a thief in
the night."   What the emergence of Fascism has shattered

has been, neither the theoretical postulates of Marxism, nor its basic canons of political revolutionary struggle. It has shattered the gradualist and social-pacifist perversions which had been substituted for genuine Marxism by the degenerate opportunism of *pseudo*- Marxist Social-Democracy and its offshoots.

To the proofs of this thesis given earlier in this work, it is hardly necessary to add anything. Yet, since, in Britain, ignorance of the actual writings of Marx is an invariable characteristic of his critics, we take the opportunity to remind them that, while Marx and Engels did not, it is true, live to witness counter-revolution in its Fascist form, they did witness it, *and fight it*, in several other forms—all of which bore a far closer resemblance to Fascism than these critics find it convenient to remember.

So far as the defeat and bloody repression of the pro-letariat, and of revolutionary Communism is concerned, Marx and Engels lived during the butcheries of the Days of June in Paris, 1848 ; and of the Paris Commune of 1871. So far as the abolition of " constitutional-democratic rights and safeguards " is concerned, they lived through the period of the *coup d'état* of Louis Napoleon, and the imperialist dictatorship thereby set up, and also (in the case of Engels) that of the Anti-Socialist Laws of Bismarck.

To argue, therefore, that Marx and Engels formulated their theory of political action on the supposition that the proletarian class-struggle, in itself, and in its revolutionary Communist expression, would always be permitted to operate on the plane of legality and constitutionalism, is to argue in the teeth, not only of their writings, but of the concrete historical circumstances within which, in fact, they lived and struggled.

How little they were, or would have been, inclined to alter their fundamental standpoint in consequence of a temporary triumph of reaction and of the replacement of a constitu-tional " democracy " by a Dictatorship, is shown particularly in Marx's classic analysis of the overthrow of the constitution of the Second French Republic by Louis Napoleon (Napoleon III) in his *Eighteenth Brumaire of Louis Napoleon*. We subjoin a few specimen extracts for the two-fold purpose of showing (1) that even in the act of noting that the phenomenon presented a superficial appearance of a simple repetition of past history, Marx is careful to show that the " return to the past " is made on a higher plane, with a radically new content, and, therefore, a new set of potentialities; and at the same time that (2) so far as the fundamental relations of society are concerned, and the antagonisms inherent therein, the " new " mode of government changed nothing but the forms in which those antagonisms inevitably become apparent. We select particularly passages bearing upon the relation between the revolutionary proletarian struggle and reformist Social Democracy :

" As one by one the leaders of the proletariat in the parliamentary and journalistic world fell victims to the courts of law, more and more dubious figures press to the front. The proletariat gets turned aside into doctrinaire experiments, into schemes of co-operative banking and labour exchanges. In other words, the proletariat abandoned the attempt to revolutionise the old order by its own united force, and associated itself with *a movement which staked its all upon the hope that emancipation might be obtained clandestinely behind the back of society, within the limits of the restricted life conditions of the prevailing order—an attempt foredoomed to failure.*"—MARX : *Eighteenth Brumaire*, Chap. I.

" The peculiar character of the Social-Democracy is summed up in this, that democratic-republican institutions are demanded not as a means to the end of abolishing the two extremes of Capital and Wage-slavery—but in order to abate their antagonism and transform them into an harmonious whole."—MARX : *ibid.*, Chap. I.

" Bourgeois revolutions, like those of the eighteenth century, rush on rapidly from success to success . . .

" Proletarian revolutions, on the contrary, like those of the nineteenth century, are constantly self-critical. Again and again they arrest themselves in the middle of their progress, and retrace their steps before making a fresh start. They are pitilessly and thoroughly scornful of the half-measures, the weaknesses and futilities of their earlier essays. . . . Repeatedly they recoil, appalled by the immensity of their own aims, and only at long last do they reach the situation from which all retreat is cut off and in which the conditions themselves cry out : ' *Hic Rhodus, hic salta !* ' " [i.e., " Here is Rhodes : *now* jump ! "*].—MARX : *Eighteenth Brumaire*, Chap. I.

* *Hic Rhodus, hic salta :* A Greek classic fable of a boaster who claimed to have jumped over the Colossus at Rhodes (equal to saying he had jumped over the Nelson column in Trafalgar Square). One of his hearers " called his bluff " by pointing to a nearby wall and saying : " All right, *here is Rhodes— now jump !* "

" The defeat of the June insurrection prepared and cleared the ground for the erection of the bourgeois republic. But this defeat also demonstrated that Europe has other problems to solve than those of simply : *either* Republic *or* Monarchy.

" It made clearly manifest the fact that . . . a bourgeois republic means the unbridled despotism of one class over all others. It proved that in all civilised countries where modern conditions of production prevail, where the formation of classes has reached an advanced stage of development, and where, after centuries of activity, all traditional ideas have been liquidated, the ' Republic ' can mean nothing but *the revolutionary or transitional* form of bourgeois society, as distinct from its *conservative* form of existence."—MARX : *ibid.*, Chap. 1.

" During the June days all the parties of all the other classes united against the proletariat under the name of the Party of Order. Stigmatising as the Party of Anarchy the party of the proletariat, of Socialism and Communism, the Party of Order announced itself as the Saviour of Society from these ' enemies of all society.'

" It took over from the old order the watchwords : Property, Religion, the Family, and Order, and made these into passwords for its armed forces. To its counter-revolutionary crusaders it cried ' *In hoc signo vinces* ' [" by this sign shalt thou conquer "]. Hence, when any one of the many parties which had united under those symbols against the June insurgents attempted, thereafter, a revolutionary struggle in its own interests, it was defeated in its turn to the accompaniment of the slogan : Property, Religion, the Family, and Order ! Society was ' saved ' again and yet again ; and with each salvation the circle of its rulers narrowed and a more exclusive interest was maintained against every more general one. . . .

" In the end the High Priests of Religion and Order were in their turn kicked off their tripods ; dragged from their beds in the dark of a foggy night, bundled into Black Marias and carted off to gaol or chased into exile— with their temple [i.e., Parliament] *razed to the ground*, their mouths stopped with dirt, their pens broken, and their Law torn up—all in the name of Religion, Property, the Family, and Order !

" *To crown all, the scum of bourgeois society became the Sacred Phalanx of Order, and the ' hero ' Crapulinsky entered the Tuileries as the Saviour of Society ! "*—MARX : *Eighteenth Brumaire*, Chap. I.

The parallel between this sequence of events and that which led up to the Hitlerite "revolution" in Germany is so close that it has led superficial observers into mistaking a resemblance for an identity. This is, of course, a serious error. None the less, the parallel is instructive.

The parallel holds good to a positively uncanny degree in respect of the " Sacred Phalanx of Order," the private army of the reactionary dictator. Those who, like G. D. H. Cole, see only the superficial, petit-bourgeois aspect of Hitlerite and Mussolini-ite Fascism miss the significant fact of the peculiar social composition of the innermost *cadres* of the Fascist fighting force—a composition which is, or was, the same with the original " fasci," the " S.A. troops " and with Mosley's " British Fascists "—*and in all cases was so far as more recent times are concerned imitated from one original*— the " *Black and Tans*." This social composition is that of (*a*) unemployed and more or less *declassed* ex-officers ; and (*b*) slum proletarians ; types produced in greatest number by, and especially fitted to be the cats-paws of Finance-Capitalism and its dictatorship.

All had their prototype in the private army—organised originally as a pseudo-revolutionary secret society—of Louis Napoleon, the " Society of December 10th " :

> " In these campaigns . . . [Louis Napoleon] was constantly attended by members of the ' Society of December 10th '—an association which dated from the year 1849.
> " Under the pretext of founding a charitable institution the Parisian slum proletariat had been organised into the ' sections ' of a secret society. Each section was under the leadership of Bonapartist agents, and the whole concern was under the command of a Bonapartist general.
> " Along with broken-down roués of questionable means of living and still more questionable antecedents, with decadent adventurers discarded from the ranks of the bourgeoisie, were to be found vagabonds, time-expired soldiers, prisoners who had served their terms, runaways from the galleys, cardsharpers, jugglers, pro-

fessional mendicants, pickpockets, sleight-of-hand men, gamesters, pimps, brothel-keepers, street porters, literary free-lances, organ-grinders, ragpickers, scissors-to-grind-men, tinkers—in short, all the elements of that nebulous. dissolute, down-at-heel, and out-at-elbows rabble whom the French comprise under the general name of ' Bohemia ! '

" It was of these kindred elements to himself that Bonaparte formed in substance the framework of the Society of December 10th—a ' charitable society ' in very deed, in that every one of its members was, like Bonaparte himself, inspired with a lively sense of the need to be charitable to himself at the expense of the producers of the nation ! "—MARX : *Eighteenth Brumaire*, Chap. V.

And since the parallel holds good so far, it is tempting to believe that it holds good with the necessary qualifications as to the probable outcome :

" Harassed by the contradictory demands of his situation—forced, like a conjurer, continually to keep the attention of the public riveted upon himself as a *substitute* for the first Napoleon—every day compelled to carry out some fresh *coup d'etat* on a small scale— Bonaparte throws the whole bourgeois social system into confusion. Laying sacrilegious hands on everything which the revolution of 1848 had spared as sacred, he makes some tolerant of revolution, and others eager for revolution. He produces Anarchy itself under the name of Order, by rubbing off from the machinery of Govern-ment every veneer of sanctity, by profaning it, by rendering it at once nauseating and ludicrous."—MARX : *Eighteenth Brumaire*, Chap. VII.

It would, as we have noted, be a fatal error, and one radically *anti*-Marxian, to suppose that because of the resemblances between the Mussolini and the Hitler *coups d'état* and that of Louis Napoleon, that there was nothing in the later phenomena beyond a repetition of the earlier. To reason in this way is to smuggle in again, by the back-door, the notion of society as an " edifice " capable of arbitrary construction, destruction, or reconstruction at will—irre-spective of historical and still more of economic circumstances —of which Marxism is the complete negation. Equally would it be an error to suppose that because the special implement employed by the Fascist dictators (in common with Louis

Napoleon) was a " private " army of a special social composition, that, therefore, the Fascist "revolution" consisted in essence, in a revolution effected by these classes *against* both the proletariat on the one side and the Big Bourgeoisie (the Financial oligarchy) on the other. Such a view fails to take into account the radically *contingent*, and *parasitical* character of the strata (ex-officers and lumpen-proletarians) in question considered in relation to the existing social mode of production. These social strata, singly and in combination, cannot *rule* except as the instruments of the class actually in control of production. The outward form of rule may be conceded to them (as is very largely the case in the Hitler-Reich), but every actual exercise of ruling-power reveals the fact that only the semblance of ruling authority is possessed by them,—the real power being that of the Financial Oligarchy from whom they draw their sustenance and for whom they do the " dirty work."

This conclusion is re-inforced by an examination of the special nature of the *coup d'etat* and rule of Louis Napoleon. Even in form the " private army "—the Society of December 10th, which " impersonated the proletariat much as Smug, the joiner, impersonated the lion "—played a rapidly diminishing part once the *coup d'état* had been accomplished. More and more the dictatorship of Louis Napoleon revealed itself as resting upon the Banks upon the one side and on the other upon the peasantry. Not, as Marx is careful to point out in a profound (and neglected) section of his *Eighteenth Brumaire*, upon the " revolutionary peasant "—the forward-pressing tendency of the main bulk of the peasantry which becomes increasingly apparent the more the peasantry and agriculture as a whole are subjected beneath the exploitation, direct and indirect, first of industrial, then of Financial Capitalism—but the " conservative peasant," the peasant who still remains hide-bound within the conditions of peasant production in itself.

A far closer parallel between the regime of Napoleon III and those of Hitler and of Mussolini can be found along this line than upon that of the superficial resemblance between their " private " armies and the social composition of these. But this parallel, too, breaks down as soon as it is examined closely, since it becomes apparent that while the Fascist *coup* is facilitated by exploiting demagogically the growing resentment of the peasantry at the exploitation imposed by Finance Capitalism—which Fascism " explains " as the consequence of " Marxism " and " materialism "—Fascism has, in fact, even less to give the peasantry (below the level of the "Kulak" class) than had the Bonapartist regime. It cannot help but prove, in practice, the utter falsity of its demagogic promises of relief, and of a " return of prosperity." It must intensify the exploitation of Finance Capitalism and of monopolist landlordism, not only as inflicted upon the proletariat and the urban middle-class, but also upon the working mass and majority of the peasantry. Thus the chief respect in which the Fascist *coups d'état* resemble that of Napoleon III is that, like it, they cannot rule without multiplying and intensifying social forces in antagonism to themselves and so making inevitable their revolutionary overthrow.

And in that, the chief, resemblance between the Fascist and the Napoleonic *coups*, we discover their most profound difference. As history proved, the Napoleonic Dictatorship could be replaced by a return to constitutional bourgeois rule. *Only a revolutionary alternative is thinkable under Fascism.* To call upon the workers to unite to prevent by mass struggle the effecting of a Fascist *coup* is one thing. To call upon the workers—struggling in conditions of illegality and under the naked brutality of a Fascist regime—to unite to *overthrow* the rule of Finance Capital in its Fascist form only to *restore* it in its humbugging bourgeois-constitutional " democratic " form would be to mock the workers in their misery and to insult their intelligence worse than Fascism does itself.

The victory of Fascism, everywhere, is not in the least *inevitable,* historically. In so far as Fascism is the last, desperate, effort of the bourgeois order to save itself from destruction at the hands of a proletarian revolution, it is, of course, *potential* in bourgeois society everywhere. But between the potential *will* to effect a Fascist counter-revolution, and its actual accomplishment, there is a great obstacle—that of an even higher potential, the proletarian revolution.

In so far as Social-Democracy in one or the other of its manifold disguises, lowers this revolutionary potentiality, either by checking its developemt or by diverting it into channels subordinate to the rule of the bourgeoisie, Social Democracy *does* help (as was the case in Italy, Germany, Poland and Austria) to make the triumph of Fascism possible—though, even then, only temporarily.

Thus we reach the conclusion of our survey, to find that in every essential the principles of theory and practice laid down by Marx and Engels as long ago as 1847, not merely hold good to-day, without subtraction or abatement, but have gained in multiformity of application, in force, and in urgency, in consequence of the culmination of the developments they were the first to foresee.

Rightly envisaged, the proletarian revolution *began* in the Days of June, 1848. It scored its first temporary triumph in the Commune of 1871, and its first permanent triumph in the Bolshevik revolution of November, 1917. Since the latter date bourgeois society has been definitely on the defensive. It may score temporary successes in counter-revolutionary raids (as in Fascism), but these only serve to prepare the way for more intense and more thoroughgoing revolutionary proletarian advances. In face of the challenge of Fascism the revolutionary proletariat purges away its half-heartednesses, its illusions, its sectarian prejudices. Ever nearer comes the day when the *Word* of the *Communist Manifesto* will take on real living flesh and blood and the workers of the world will, sweeping aside everything and everybody that seeks to obstruct them, *unite to win the whole world.*

" A spectre is haunting Europe : the spectre of Communism ! . . .

" The Communists have no interests separate and distinct from those of the proletariat as a whole. . . .

" The Communists disdain to conceal their views and aims. They openly declare that their ends can be attained only by the forcible overthrow of all existing social conditions. Let the ruling classes tremble at a Communist revolution. The proletarians have nothing to lose but their chains. They have a world to win.

" Working men of all countries, unite ! "

MARX-ENGELS : *Communist Manifesto.*

CHAPTER VII

THE DIALECTIC AND ITS CRITICS

In our survey of the theoretical practice of Marx and Engels we have sought to establish two facts :

(1) Dialectical Materialism as a logically united outlook and method must be accepted or rejected as a whole.

(2) The political practice of Marx, Engels, Lenin, and Stalin presents a continuous sequence logically consistent in itself, and with the theoretical requirements of Dialectical Materialism.

Neither of these facts has been accepted as proved over the whole field of (nominal) Marxism in the English-speaking world. Especially in Britain is it common to attempt an eclectic " revision " of Marxism (as distinct from an organic *development* such as Marx and Engels made in their own lifetime, and as Lenin and Stalin have made in our own day), a revision which takes the form of proposing the rejection of one of its integral phases and the retention of the remainder in conjunction with some alien theory supposed to be more " up to date."

We have made it abundantly clear that we do not champion a " dogmatic " Marxism—since Marxism is the most radical repudiation of all dogmatism conceivable.

Likewise we have made it clear that we do not fight for any " literalist " or " traditionalist " interpretation of the Marx-Engels " scriptures." We fight for Dialectical Materialism, which is the negation of all literalism and traditionalism, since its Dialectic is " above all things critical and revolutionary." There is no such thing as a *Marxian* " dogma."

To clarify completely the meaning of Dialectical Materialism and to promote its use as an instrument of theoretical practice, we have selected four representatives of typical trends within the distinctively " British " (and therefore *non*-Communist—in the Party sense) movement for Marxism. These we have (in order to elucidate, as well as vindicate, the Dialectic) submitted to separate critical examination.

This theoretical practice should provide " the proof of the pudding."

2H

All the four examples we select have, amid all their differences, one feature in common. All are, like the official British Labour Party, " equally opposed to Communism (i.e., to the Communist Party and International) and to Fascism."

We have proved already from the angle of objective practice that this attitude is simply a camouflage for a defence of the established bourgeois order. We propose to prove, by a critical examination of the theories of these exponents of anti-Communist Party " Marxism," that each of them leads logically to exactly the same point.

.   .   .   .   .

I.—" MARXISM " *minus* MARX !

Professor John Macmurray, of London University, celebrated the fiftieth anniversary of the death of Karl Marx by publishing a small work under the title of *The Philosophy of Communism*. For a British professor of philosophy, and in the main, he here showed a commendable change from the customary British " superior " detraction of Marx, and the usual eclectic discrimination of Marxism into an incompatible bundle of more or less obsolete " theories." Professor Macmurray, being a (modified) follower of Hegel, spares us that folly and rightly insists upon *the unity of theory and practice* as the basic essential in Marxism. He appreciates rightly the value of the Dialectic method—but he slides into the eclectic bog as soon as it becomes a question of *materialism*. He substitutes for the Marxian discrimination between Nature, History, and their reflection in the Thought processes of Man, one between the inorganic, organic, and super-organic processes in the Universe. This is obviously a relapse from Marxism into a species of modified Hegelianism. Marx and Engels discriminated an *infinite number* of stages of dialectic progression in the Universe. In the " inorganic " world, for instance, it is clear, especially in the light of modern physics, that the Law of Motion of physical Nature is different at the level of the atom from what it is at that of the electron, and different again at the level of the " element " and its molecular combinations, and at that of simple organic substance—the stage at which inorganic nature passes into the " organic " (a stage of revolutionary transition repeated continually in the physical life of living beings, in every act of breathing and digestion). Professor Macmurray's method makes the distinction between Nature and History, for instance, relatively absolute, and their connection, therefore, *mystical* !

It is by means of this " escape " from Materialism that Professor Macmurray introduces his proposals for a " dialectical " *revision* of Marxism :

> " What strikes me most forcibly about current communist propaganda is the absence in it of true dialectical thought. Instead we find a kind of Marxian fundamentalism which, while it takes its stand upon the teaching of Marx and his more prominent followers, denies *the essential revolutionary element* in Marxism. To be a dogmatic Marxist is to involve oneself in a practical contradiction and to fall back unawares into the very idealism which Marx repudiated. . . . *To insist on the acceptance of Marxian ideas is to value ideas above things.*"
> —MACMURRAY : *Philosophy of Communism*, p. 82.

And what according to Professor Macmurray is the true *revolutionary element* in Marxism ? He has told you : *it is the repudiation of Marxian ideas* in favour of Marxian " *things.*" And what are these " things " ? The magical, mystical, self-acting, " dialectical " processes of " reality " ! That is to say, after all the trouble Marx and Engels took to turn the Hegelian dialectic " right side up," along comes Professor Macmurray and *turns it all* " *arsy-varsy* " *again* ! Here is an example :

> " This orthodox fundamentalism reveals its non-dialectical character in its failure to recognise that the revolution which Marx prophesied *has already taken place*. That it happened in Russia and not elsewhere is a matter of considerable importance. It forces a *reinterpretation* in dialectical terms of *the forecasts* which Marx himself made."—MACMURRAY : *ibid.*, p. 82.

We have (in Chapter V) dealt with the allegation that the November Revolution falsified the " forecasts which Marx himself made," and we have there demonstrated that the exact reverse is the case—namely, that Marx *predicted* revolution in Russia, and a *communist* outcome thereof. Thus Professor Macmurray's basic assumption collapses and his argument with it. But it must be noted that for Professor Murray the whole process is so mystically Hegelian that a revolution has only to happen in one country to become instantaneously valid and actual for *all countries*.

Certainly the fact that the November Revolution in Russia had occurred *changed* both objective reality and men's subjective valuation thereof for all the world. But in the first place, *change* of itself is not *a revolutionary transforma-*

tion ; and in the second place, the change in men's subjective valuation of the world is not, as such, a change in their objective relations. That Professor Macmurray is at bottom an idealist is proved by his failure to make this vital discrimination. The reason for his failure becomes clearer the further we go :

> " That reinterpretation [of Marx] has been provided by Lenin. . . . The transference of communist fundamentalism to Leninism does not make it less dogmatic. . . . Communists still continue to expect that something like the Russian revolution will happen in the more highly industrialised countries of Western Europe. To expect this is to fail to think dialectically."—MACMURRAY : *ibid.*, pp. 82–83.

The first assertion in this passage is false : *Lenin did not " reinterpret " Marx's " forecasts."* Lenin, in his *Imperialism*, extended the application of Marx's own economic analysis to a group of phenomena which Marx did not live to investigate in person. To deny that Lenin in his *Imperialism* did so *extend* Marxism, and thus add greatly to its practical utility as a theory of action (as the ultra-Kautskyite *metaphysical* " Marxists " do), is to show an ignorance of the basic method of Marx and the unity therewith of the method of Lenin. But to assert that Lenin " reinterpreted " Marx is to commit identically the same Kautskyite error in its inverse form. The truth is that in all his basic work, and particularly in his theory of the State and of the revolutionary dictatorship of the proletariat (see LENIN : *State and Revolution*), as also in his policy on the questions of the peasantry, of agrarian problems generally, and of the colonial peoples and subject nationalities (basically peasant and agrarian in each case), Lenin achieved *a rediscovery, a systematic extension, and a revolutionary dialectical use of, the Marxism of Marx and Engels* which had been blurred over, vulgarised, and sophisticated into a miserable eclecticism by the officially " orthodox Marxism " of the Social-Democratic Second International. As Professor Macmurray (being a professor) probably gets his knowledge of Marxism in action at second-hand, from " British " sources, the quantity and quality of his misinformation can be guessed—though not, positively, conceived.

It is from these sources that Professor Macmurray draws the " information " that what Communists expect in the " more highly industrialised " (a rather curiously inexact phrase for a professor of philosophy—but he would be too polite to say " more advanced in bourgeois development ") countries of Western Europe is a *simple* replica of the November revolution. This is the favourite lie of the protagonists of the Second International. What Communists " expect " is that, sooner or later, the forces which precipitated the November Revolution *in* Russia will precipitate parallel explosions likewise *in each particular part of the political " superstructure " of world capitalism.* That the phenomenal forms of each of these revolutionary explosions will *necessarily* be different at each point, and time, of their manifestation is part of the very conception of their basic inter-connection and common causation. Professor Macmurray has been bamboozled by those " Marxists " who in one breath speak of a " world-crisis of capitalism " and in another of the *absolute* differences of nature and development of *each* " country " (i.e., State) in the world. This eclectic falsification —of the Marxism which forecasts a revolution as world-wide as the *economic formation* whose internal contradictions will beget it—is the basic juggle from which Social-Democratic opportunism develops its whole theoretical " justification."

Professor Macmurray shows how completely he has been blinded by the dust thrown by the Kautsky-ite school by this sort of argument :

" That the revolution which Marx foresaw happened in a largely *feudal* community like Czarist Russia. . . .

" The Marxian interpretation does work under feudal conditions in a world where industrialism has developed elsewhere. . . . It is more likely that the revolution should spread eastward to China, Japan, and India than it should spread westwards to the industrial countries of Europe and the United States of America."—MACMURRAY : *ibid.*, p. 83.

Here all the confusions are on parade in heavy marching order. The "largely feudal" nature of Tsarism is of a piece with the historical " understanding " which treats the *vestigial form* of the government of a State (Tsarist *absolutism* in this case) as the true index of its economy and social composition. The facts relevant are : that *Tsardom* was *post-feudal* when it was instituted ; that it *introduced* serfdom into Russia (at a time when it was being broken down in Western Europe) as a *reform* in aid of the merchants and usurers who were reverting to land exploitation in consequence of the shifting of trade routes ; that in its bureaucracy, its police, and the attempt at a rigid stratification of society the Tsarist policy was that of the Grand Monarchy of the post-feudal epoch *without any genuine aristocratic tradition to give it stability* (the place of this being supplied by the Greek Orthodox Church). Professor Macmurray could improve his comprehension of Marxism if he took a course of instruction from his colleague the Professor of Byzantine History.

Again, " the revolution will spread " (as something " contagious " presumably !). This is the Nesta* Webster conception of revolution *as a disease* ! That the revolution is the culmination of a *struggle*, whose basis is in turn the contradiction between the *forces* and the *conditions* of production—that, therefore, the revolution " spreads " to Eastern countries only *because*, and so far as, their traditional *forms* of political organisation, and social stratification, have been *undermined* and thrown into chaos by the introduction *into* them, and the impact upon them, of the Capitalist production of the Western world—all this is, it seems, concealed from Professor Macmurray. He is, therefore, self-incapacitated for perceiving that *the very spread of the revolution in the East* is precisely the " last straw " which will cut off the last hope from bourgeois society (" industrialised countries " as Professor Macmurray euphemises it !) of being able to stave off a like fate.

Professor Macmurray has a different version of the matter :

" An organic theory [as Marxism is according to the Professor] necessarily overlooks the superorganic [he means " spiritual," spontaneous, idealistic] elements which exist as forces of social development along with the organic forces. It therefore looks to mass action alone as revolutionary driving force, and, psychologically, mass action is blind action determined by the stimulus of environmental pressure."—MACMURRAY : *ibid.*, p. 84.

Lo ! the secret emerges ! The Professor of Philosophy doesn't like the idea of historical initiative resting with " mass action." And he knows so little of the masses, and of Marxism, that he repeats like a well-trained parrot the favourite lies of the intelligentsia, that "Marxism relies on mass action *alone*," and that mass action is " blind " and a mere reflex of environmental pressure. *That this is the exact reverse of Marxism* has been demonstrated over and over again in the course of this work, and that by citation after citation from the works of Marx, Engels, and Lenin.   But the Professor's ignorance of the whole teaching of Marxism in respect of class struggle and revolution is, incredible though this would seem, matched by his ignorance of capitalism itself !

> " The more highly industrialised a country becomes, the more the maintenance of its economic struggle depends upon a purposeful and a planned co-operation. *It is this, in fact, which impels all capitalist governments to institute universal compulsory education.*"—MACMURRAY : *ibid.*, p. 84.

It would be hard to find anywhere in the whole literature of the criticism of Marxism a more amazingly grotesque perversion of the actual facts. One has only to compare with this the analysis by Marx himself of the actual *co-operation* involved in capitalist production, *in contrast to its general anarchy in the world market,* to realise how hopelessly astray the learned gentleman is. The " purposeful " co-operation involved in capitalist industry is " purposeful " only so far as actual production in particular plants and branches of industry is concerned. Never did the capitalist world need planned control so much as now ; never was that need so widely recognised ; never were there so many plans and projects for the realisation of this needed control. And never was there so vast, complete, and unanimous a failure as that of every attempt to effect this planned control.

And, on the contrary, it is the masses whom the learned Professor so despises, who have in the U.S.S.R., in China, and in their revolutionary struggles throughout the world achieved a level of planned co-operation higher than anything the capitalist world has ever been able to attain. The very fact that the world to-day is still ringing with the repercussions of the heroic fight of the Viennese workers, and that despite all their terrorism the chiefs of the Hitlerite régime in Germany have to demand newer and more elaborate machinery for the " crushing " of the already three-times " crushed " Communist movement in Germany gives the proper answer to his suggestion that :

> " The effort to bring about a mass movement must involve, if it is to be successful, a reduction of the rational and deliberate consciousness of the *community* to the impulsive level."—MACMURRAY : *ibid.*, p. 184.

The scientific worth of the Marxian conception of history lies precisely in its clear demonstration of *how*, and *why*, the *purposeful* strivings of men (as individuals, in groups, in classes, and class-divided " communities ") produce by the sum of their total interaction a resultant historical movement of society which so transcends anything aimed at by individuals, groups, classes, or " communities " as to seem *relative to them*, a movement precisely at " the impulsive level." The planned co-operative control of society as a productive association which is impossible under conditions of capitalist production, will therefore be attainable *only after* the success of a mass revolutionary uprising which will impose *its revolutionary purpose and plan* upon the aggregate of social forces which the rule of the bourgeoisie has called into being, but proved itself totally unable to control. Professor Macmurray—being, as a specialist in philosophy, ignorant, as the etiquette of his profession demands that he should be, of history and economics—falls into the commonest of all petty-bourgeois fallacies, that of supposing that mass co-operation is *necessarily un-*reflective and *sub-*rational.

Social and class determinants operate to impel him into this pitfall. Bourgeois society provides objectively a ground for the opposition of the standpoint of the abstract individual to the aggregate of " society " or the State ; academic and professorial prepossessions impel him to equate this polar contrast with that of the " rational and deliberative " and the " impulsive and emotional " poles in the subjective processes of human consciousness. These again he equates (as bourgeois philosophers have done ever since the bourgeoisie became as a class conscious of itself and its social importance) with the contrast of " wise " ruler and intractable " mob." He does not seem to care that in so doing he has abandoned the last vestige of Marxism and reverted to the flattest of philistine superstitions.

As we shall see, the development of Professor Macmurray's argument demands this dialectical suicide. Here it should be noted, in passing, how uniformly the critics of Marx and Marxism prove themselves to be incapable of making that dialectical transition from the " standpoint of the single individual in bourgeois society " to that of " associated humanity " which is required for the rational comprehension and practical use of the method and concept of Dialectical Materialism.

Bourgeois-minded intellectuals visiting the U.S.S.R. to " see how the *experiment* (!) is working out " find among Communists a prevalent contempt for " idealism." Ignorant of the philosophical issues involved as between Materialism and Idealism (and even if they are not so ignorant, totally unable to conceive that plain workers have either a taste or a use for philosophy) these critics rush back to (bourgeois) " civilisation " to report either (a) that the Communists are " opposed to all *ideas* ! " or (b) that only sordid " material " motives are " recognised as valid by Communists ! "

Similiarly, another group of critics on learning that Dialectical Materialism involves the standpoint of " Associated Humanity," rush back to proclaim the news that " Communism is trying to produce a new *Mass-Man* ! " At once the journals of the intelligentsia become filled with elaborate scintillations in which the abstract " individual " of bourgeois speculation is turned inside out and the no less *abstract* individual so produced is held up for admiration or detestation as the " Mass-Man " of the Communist ideal ! Of the fact that the Communist revolution aims at producing the exact reverse of any sort of *abstract* man—namely concrete, actually developed, and actively functioning *human individuals*—this fact is totally beyond all petty-bourgeois reach or grasp.

Professor Macmurray, blinded by the same blinkers, says with fine force and accuracy :

> " The mechanisation of the mind, and the paralysis
> of the capacity for conscious reflection . . . would
> necessarily destroy the purposeful co-operation on which
> the working of a highly industrialised system depends."
> —MACMURRAY, *ibid.*, p. 84.

True ! But does Professor Macmurray draw the logical consequence from this fact ? Let him look at the actual state of the bourgeois world. Is the " popular " press, are the " fashionable " amusements financed and maintained by the bourgeoisie—novel, newspaper, cinema, and dance—Professor Macmurray can take his choice—are *these* anything but evidence of " mechanisation of mind " and " paralysis of the capacity for conscious reflection " on a more appalling scale than history can parallel ? Let him dig deeper. Let him contrast that sphere of world economics which is directly and exclusively under bourgeois control—world trade and finance (with its chaos of cross-purposes and colossal irrationality, its evidence of baffled bewilderment, etc.)—with the intelligent co-operation between workman and fellow workman in the actual work-process of production. If he will do that he will discover that the truth above quoted has exactly the opposite significance to that which he deduces. In the actual work process, particularly in a mass production factory where every worker must be constantly on the alert to synchronise his own movements with those of the fellow-workers whose operation precedes and follows his own, *every operation* (however monotonous and habitual it may grow through constant repetition) is one involving the *conscious, personal employment of means to secure an understood and preconceived end*. Every hitch and delay in the work process calls for the prompt exercise of *rational* faculties by the worker. It is only to *a spectator* that the work of production seems " irrational " ; and only to a spectator that the smooth-running of an industrial plant seems due to " directive ability " imposed from without upon a mass of purely " impulsive " agents of production. *The " Robot " is not a reality but a bourgeois ideal—one never realised, or even realisable in actual fact ; as a single day's experience in actual productive work in workshop, factory, mill, or mine, will convince any intellectual who tries it.* Any " paralysis of the power of reflection " to-day is the work of the bourgeoisie.

That which makes the bourgeois system of production intolerable to the worker is not that its work process makes for the " mechanisation of the mind " but that it makes for the *mechanisation of the Man*. To live and work the worker must possess a brain, however much bourgeois conditions of production subordinate him, *with his mind in full conscious working*, to the ends and purposes of a *Social* mechanism over which he, *the Man*, the worker (with his capacity for " conscious reflection " *stimulated and developed* by his actual work-activity) is denied all right and power of rational control. Forty years ago Engels pointed to the conflict between the (" rational ") *socialised* process of production, and the (blindly " irrational ") *individualised* mode of " distribution " in bourgeois society as the basic contradiction which would sooner or later precipitate a revolutionary crisis. But, though he writes learnedly and (according to his lights) sympathetically of Marxism and Communism, Professor Macmurray has learned nothing from Frederick Engels. And, let it be observed here, once and for all, that he who has not mastered that superlatively brilliant extract from Engels' *Anti-Dühring* which is published separately under the title of *Socialism : Utopian and Scientific*, has not mastered the most fundamental document in all Marxism, with the only possible exception (and that only partially one) of the *Communist Manifesto* itself. On the other hand, he who has really mastered both those documents can, try as he will, do no more in a Communist direction than set their manifold brilliance and profundity in a light in which they can be appraised at something near their inestimable worth.

Let us follow the Professor into his Serbonian bog :

> " The success of a mass movement by *endangering the economic mechanism* by which the *community* lives would produce . . . a *national* dictatorship in the interests of the maintenance of the *national* economic system. In other words it would produce a Fascist dictatorship."—
> MACMURRAY : *ibid, p. 85.*

One sees at a glance that by " economic mechanism " the Professor understands, *not* the process of *production*, the actual activity whereby natural materials are converted into *use*-values—but the purely bourgeois mechanism for the realisation of the *surplus values* embodied in those products by the imposed conditions of the bourgeois *mode of distribution*. That a " mass movement "—that is, a revolutionary proletarian one—*would* " endanger " that bourgeois *mode* of distribution goes without saying. That is what the mass movement is "*for.*" But in so doing it would be the reverse of " irrational," and " unreflective." It would do this *on purpose.* And only those who, like the Professor, confuse the *mode* of production with production itself—and therefore treat (as the bourgeoisie does, and must) the mode of " distribution," i.e., that of *realising* surplus values in their monetary forms, as the *only real* and important part of the progress of production as a whole—only those who reason in this bourgeois way can fall into the Professor's fallacy of supposing that the " endangering " of this " mechanism " (which said " mechanism " is and has been " endangering " itself into a chronic world crisis for the whole post-War period !) is the same thing as endangering the existence of human society—the " community." Substitute in the passage quoted the term " *bourgeois mode of appropriation* " for " economic mechanism," and the term " *bourgeois* " for the terms " community " and " national " and the Professor's words *come true.* A Fascist dictatorship is, as we have seen, one of the many uniforms the bourgeois State can, and will adopt, in the course of its historical struggle to maintain the bourgeois system of exploitation.

But, since it differs only in incidentals from the normal
dictatorship of the bourgeoisie, it is only the superficiality of
a petty-bourgeois idealist approach which can make this
incidental change into a difference *in kind*. It is petty-
bourgeois stupidity to glorify Fascist " dictatorship " (in
which the pseudo-" Dictators " are even more obviously
puppets than are the " democratic " figure-heads of Parliamentary *dictatorship*) into a Utopia : it is petty-bourgeois
cowardice to see in it the " End of All Things ! " And
nothing but petty-bourgeois ignorance which, with the
" wind up " at the prospect of Fascism, seeks excuses for its
opposition to revolutionary proletarian struggle (called
" mass movement ") in an imaginary *absolute* difference
between the " community " of Tsarist Russia and that of
" industrialised " Western Europe.

Professor Macmurray finding himself up to the knees in
the bog proceeds heroically to flounder in up to the neck :

> " Lenin worked on the hypothesis that the Bolshevik
> revolution . . . would be the final revolutionary move-
> ment and usher in the communisation of the economic
> life of the world. *But this has not happened.* (! ! ! !) "—
> MACMURRAY : *ibid.*, p. 85.

From the Reformation to the simultaneous founding of
the Third Republic in France and of the German Empire
in 1870–1 (at which latter point we can fix the culmination
of the political triumph of the bourgeoisie in the Western
World) is a period of over three and a half centuries. Since
the Bolshevik revolution in 1917 the whole political map of
the world has been made and re-made over and over again.
In addition to the Tsar, " Emperors " have gone from
Austria and Germany, the Sultan has gone from Turkey,
Kings have gone from the States of Germany and from Spain,
China has been involved in a deepening process of Nationalist
and Communist revolution, while the whole capitalist world
has been racked from end to end with the clash, impact
and recoil of the forces economic and political of revolution
and counter-revolution.   Proletarian revolutions have
occurred and been defeated in Hungary and Bavaria.
Revolutions, big and little, have been successful, only to be
betrayed, in Austria, Germany and various South American
States.   Proletarian risings have occurred four times in
Germany, once in Austria, and in Canton and Shanghai.
Communists have been executed in batches of a hundred at
a time in Japan. Fascist and semi-Fascist *coups d'état* have

occurred in half the States in Europe. And India, Egypt and Ireland have been racked from end to end with Nationalist movements which, in the case of Ireland have twice reached the pitch of actual open war. Nearly all this had happened between October, 1917, and the date of publication, October, 1933, of Professor Macmurray's book. Yet, in the light of these facts, he can say calmly " *this has not happened* ! " Should not the Professor " wait till the whistle blows " before saying " no score " ?

Lenin " expected "—*diagnosed* would be a better word—that the fall of Tsardom would open an epoch of revolutionary transition. He had openly advocated (as he claimed, and rightly, that the whole of the parties in the Second International should have advocated and would have done if they had been truly *Marxist*) the " turning of the imperalist war into a civil war against the bourgeoisie." Nobody pretends —Lenin never did—that this was, in fact, what happened universally. For one thing the parties of the Second International were too far gone upon the opposite course to turn back ; while the parties of the Left were neither strong enough, nor ideologically clear and coherent enough, to realise that Lenin, as always, not only meant what he said, but said precisely what he meant. But nobody who can remember the events of November, 1917, to November, 1919, can for one moment deny that the potentiality of a proletarian revolution was manifested in Western Europe in so high a degree as to make it seem, on reflection, next door to a miracle that the bourgeoisie was able to stave off the evil day. In Germany, Austria, and Italy in particular, the bourgeoisie was reduced to political impotence ; and only the creeping paralysis of Social-Democratic opportunism, aided in Italy by the crapulous romanticism of Anarchist utopianism, gave the bourgeoisie both the time and the opportunity to recover their political control. Similarly in Poland—it was the reinforcement of the bourgeoisie by the treacherous anti-Bolshevik malice of the Mensheviks and the Kautskyite Social-Democrats which made possible the Pilsudsky régime. Everywhere the coming of Fascism has been the price paid by the proletarian struggle, *not* for being revolutionary, but *for not being revolutionary enough, and at the right time*.

Even so, as we have proved, the coming of Fascism, far from making for the stabilisation of the bourgeois order, is itself a proof of the correctness of Lenin's diagnosis. It is in itself a proclamation of a permanent state of martial law, a permanent state of siege, a *counter-revolution in permanence* ! It is unintelligible except as the converse of its opposite, the proletarian revolution *likewise in a state of permanent development*. The very evidence to which Professor Macmurray appeals—that of the coming of Fascism—is the concrete evidence which refutes him.   Here, for proof, is what in fact Lenin " expected."   *Before* the revolution, as early as April, 1916, he drafted a resolution for the Kienthal conference, which affirmed :

" Imperialist war can only lead to an imperialist peace, that is, to the extension and augmentation of the oppression of small peoples and States by finance-capital, which not only made a gigantic upward swing before the War, but has continued to do so during the War."—LENIN : Works, vol. XX, Book 2, p. 388.

For the conference of the Bolshevik Party held in Petrograd (Leningrad), May 7th–12th, 1917—i.e., *between* the March and the November Revolutions—Lenin drafted a series of resolutions, from one of which, on the " present political situation," we take the following :

" The objective conditions for a Socialist revolution that undoubtedly existed before the war in the more developed and advanced countries have been, and are being, ripened with tremendous rapidity as a result of the war.   The crowding-out and ruin of small and medium-sized economic enterprises proceeds at an accelerated pace. . . .

" On the other hand, the forecast made by the Socialists of all the world, who in the Basle Manifesto of 1912 declared unanimously the inevitability of a proletarian revolution in connection with the imperialist war that was then approaching and is now raging—this forecast has been fully confirmed by the course of events.

" The Russian Revolution is *only the first stage of the first* of the proletarian revolutions that are inevitably being brought about by the war."—LENIN : *Works*, Vol. XX, Book 2, p. 408.

Finally, in 1919–20, Lenin wrote thus :

" The dictatorship of the proletariat is the fiercest and most merciless war of the *new* class against its more powerful enemy the bourgeoisie, *whose power of resistance increases* tenfold after its overthrow, even though overthrown only in one country.   The power of the bour-

geoisie rests not solely upon *international* capital, upon
its strong international connections. It rests also upon
the force of habit, on the force of small industry, *of
which there is plenty left,* and which daily and hourly
gives birth to capitalism and the bourgeoisie spontaneously and on a large scale. . . . Victory over the bourgeoisie is *impossible* without a *long,* persistent, desperate
life and death struggle, a struggle which requires persistence, discipline, firmness, inflexibility, and *concerted will-
power.*"—LENIN : *Left-Wing Communism,* p. 10.
From the cumulative force of these specimen extracts it is
clear that Lenin " expected " pretty much what has happened.
  Marx, Engels, and Lenin all make it abundantly clear in
their whole outlook that they envisage the proletarian
revolution as *an historical epoch* of " prolonged struggles."
That in the course of such an epoch there should be changes
of fortune on each side in varying parts of the whole field of
struggle follows necessarily from the nature of the conception.
That the bourgeoisie is *in fact,* at any rate for the time being,
stronger after the initial proletarian victory than before, *Lenin
himself points out.* Thus the peculiarity which so puzzles the
learned Professor, that the revolution gained successes, outside Russia, only in the East among peoples *only partially
bourgeoisified,* while in the West it received the set-back of
Fascist counter-revolution—this " peculiarity " is something
very easily explained in the actual conjunction of forces. *The
overthrow of the bourgeoisie naturally followed the line of its
weakness—not of its strength !* What is " peculiar," and that to
Professor Macmurray and his like, is the trick of dividing
historical processes into separate slabs *by the clock.* Because
the proletarian revolution did not produce itself automatically
—in style, in state, and *instanter*—like a packet of cigarettes
from a slot machine, he decides that " the machine is out
of order ! "
  " The point in history which makes it clear that it
[the Westward spread of the revolution] will not happen
is the acceptance by Russia of the task of creating a
communist society within Russia itself in isolation from
the rest of the world. The defeat of Trotsky on this
very point, and *the abandonment* (! ! !) by Russia of the
hope of an immediate world-revolution must be interpreted dialectically (!) as the assertion of the existing
régime in the Soviet Union, not as the final synthesis
of the historic process, but as the thesis of a new stage.

In accordance with the dialectical law this thesis must now produce its antithesis."—MACMURRAY : *ibid.*, pp. 85–6.

At first this passage seems only a sample of old-style Hegelian obscurity from which the reader can extract any meaning or none at will. On a closer scrutiny it becomes plain that a specific *innuendo* is conveyed by means of the elaborate artifice with which it is concealed. Quite plainly the passage is intended to suggest that when the Communist Party (indicated under the *alias* of " Russia ") adopted the plan of transforming the total economy of the U.S.S.R. from what it was into a Socialist economy (*alias* " creating a Communist society within Russia ") they therein and thereby put an end to the world-revolution and cut themselves off from participating in any future outbreak thereof ! That this is its *innuendo* is plain from the reference to Trotsky,— from the fact that his " defeat on *this* question " is treated as a first-rank turning-point in history. Under the seven-fold veil of Hegelian mysticism lurks, concealed, like Guy Fawkes in a coal-cellar, the Trotsky-cum-Kautsky attitude towards the U.S.S.R. and the policy of building a Socialist economy therein.

The *innuendo* is false and slanderous at every point. The defeat of Trotsky was not a " turning-point " (in Professor Macmurray sense) ; on the contrary, it was a refusal to turn back. It did not involve any " abandonment " of the world-revolution ; only in a secondary sense did it involve even a recognition that the wave of revolution which began in Russia in 1917 had in fact subsided. It did not involve any " isolation " of the U.S.S.R. from the " rest of the world " ; on the contrary, the plan expressly called for the importation into the U.S.S.R. of materials and *men* (technicians) and for the export from the U.S.S.R. of commodities in proportion. It did not involve any " isolation " of the Russian workers and peasants, led by the C.P.S.U., from the revolutionary struggle of the rest of the world. On the contrary, the only sense in which it was a " new " phase was one which revealed it as carrying the revolutionary struggle to a higher plane.

In short : all the assumptions upon which this passage is based are false. Once again Professor Macmurray has taken his " Marxism " and his " Leninism " at second- and third-hand. Only after they have passed through several stages of Kautskyite degeneration and Trotskyite perversion do they reach his deluded understanding.

This is all the more striking because involved in the adoption of the Fifteen Year Plan (in three Five Year stages) was the *objective dialectic* of social development as revealed by Marx and Lenin. That Professor Macmurray should examine *not* this objective, historical-economic dialectic, but a *subjective* dialectic, which he treats as its " real " essence, finally disposes of his claim to discuss, intelligently, any question of Marxism. We have only to consider, briefly, this objective dialectic, to have this proved for us beyond question.

.   .   .   .   .

The question of theory upon which Trotsky was defeated may be formulated succinctly thus :—Can a Socialist economy be built in one country alone ? Or, can it only be built on a world scale, or, at any rate, with the co-operation of all the technically most advanced countries in the world ? Trotsky, in substance, took the latter view ; and thereby gained the applause of all the mechanical and metaphysical " Marxists " in the world, all those who argued (and are still arguing) that the backwardness of Russia economically made it absolutely impossible for a genuine proletarian Socialist revolution to take place there.

The C.P. of the Soviet Union, led by Stalin, took a critically Marxist view. Whether the building of Socialism is possible, either on a world-scale or in one country alone, is not a question of *a priori* theory but of the concrete correlation of social and economic forces. Obviously, it depends upon (*a*) the economic potentialities—particularly as to raw materials, and mechanical power—of the territory won by the revolution ; and (*b*) the quantity and quality of the revolutionary *will* of the human beings directly concerned, taken in the aggregate. In the case of the U.S.S.R. the quantity and quality of economic resources were literally illimitable. From the start it was more than able to be self-sufficing in respect of food-stuffs ; its power resources in coal, wood, peat, oil, and water-power were, all told, second to none ; its mineral wealth was enormous. Only in a few cases —as in that of rubber—did it need to depend upon the outside world for supplies. True, many of these things were potentialities only, since they could only become actual when the country was equipped with a stock of machinery and a body of trained technicians it did not, at the outset, possess. None the less, all the material presuppositions for a Socialist economy existed, either actually or potentially within the frontiers of the U.S.S.R. That being so, the practical question resolved itself into a question whether the *will* to realise these potentialities existed (or could be aroused) in sufficient quantity and quality to make their realisation a certainty. And this, in turn, resolved itself into a question of " how can it be done ? "—a question of a concrete plan. Given a sound plan to work to, and the C.P. felt confident of its ability to rouse an adequate response from the workers and peasants who make up the overwhelming mass of the population of the Soviet Union.

Concretely, therefore, the issue upon which Trotsky was defeated was whether the workers and peasants of the U.S.S.R. should be appealed to along this line and for this end, or simply to hold on like a beleaguered garrison until the resurgent tide of world-revolution brought relief. Stated in this way the essentially negative and conservative attitude of Trotsky becomes plainly apparent ; and with it is revealed the reason why Trotsky and the Trotskyites have felt forced to cover up the bare bones of this skeleton in their cupboard by a flamboyantly theatrical pose of enthusiasm for the world-revolution (contraposed as an alternative to building Socialism in one country " alone ") and a never-ceasing campaign of slanders against the Plan, its design and its execution. So also becomes plain the radical rupture between Trotskyism and Marxism, which makes Trotsky a " hero " in the eyes of every petty bourgeois to whom hatred of Marx and Marxism is second nature.

Only a cursory glance at (for instance) the *Communist Manifesto* is needed to make plain that Marx and Engels always thought in terms of the building of Socialism (at any rate so far as its basis is concerned, which is all that is here in question) in *each* country separately. " Though not in substance, yet in form, the struggle of the proletariat with the bourgeoisie is, *at first*, a national struggle. The proletariat of *each* country must, *of course*, first of all settle matters with its own bourgeoisie." (*Com. Man.*, p. 20). The " first step in the revolution by the working-class is to raise the proletariat to the position of ruling class " which is, of necessity an operation which must be performed in each country separately. The programme sketched for the development of the revolution after the proletarian conquest of power (*Com. Man.*, pp. 27–28), while it is one that " will be pretty generally applicable " in all the " more advanced countries " is at the same time one which can only be applied concretely in each country *separately*. The notion of a spontaneous transition to world Socialism by all the countries in the world, simultaneously, is, instead of being Marxian, actually the antithesis of Marxism, which holds that " Communism is the *real* movement which makes an end of the existing order of things."

As that order in its specific, historical concrete forms, varies from country to country, *of necessity*, the movement can only reach its ultimate unity on a world scale through a whole manifold of different movements in each country separately.

Even the passages in the writings of Marx and Engels, which stress the need for international co-operation in the emancipation-process of the proletariat, support this conclusion and negate the Trotskyite one. In his *Principles of Communism* (1847) Engels certainly affirms that the revolution cannot " take place in one country alone "— that it will take place " at least in Great Britain, the United States, France and Germany, at one and the same time." But Engels goes on to affirm that in *each* of these countries the carrying out of the Communist revolution " will take a longer or shorter time to develop, according to whether industrial life has attained a high degree of evolution, has amassed great wealth, and *has a considerable quantity of the forces of production at its disposal*." Thus it is clear that as Marx and Engels envisaged it (and as practical common sense would expect), the Communist world-revolution would be attained by the converging development of a number of national proletarian revolutions, in each of which the transition to a Socialist economy would be made *separately*, by a concretely different process, and at a different rate. As the law of motion of Capitalist production made it certain that each country would develop at a different rate and in a different way, determined by the common relation of all to the world market, this conclusion has a far greater froce to-day than it had in 1847. Moreover, Engels and Marx agreed in emphasing the " quantity of the forces of production " available as determining the rate and course of the concrete transition to a Socialist economy. It is, therefore, perfectly clear that the decision to " build Socialism " in the U.S.S.R. " alone," and to begin the building by elaborating the " forces of production " quantitatively and qualitatively into such a form as was compatible with *Socialist* production (i.e., *social* production of means of social and individual satisfaction—of *use-values* as distinct from *exchange values*—by the associated labour of the associated owners of the means of production) was a decision exactly in line with the theory of Marx and Engels. In fact, it was the *only* available policy which was in line with Marxism. Trotsky's alternative policy was, it is equally clear, opposed to the line of Marx and Engels. Hence the defeat of Trotsky, far from constituting a defeat for Marxism and the Communist-proletarian world-revolution, was, in fact, the reverse, —a victory for them. This is clear, not only as a deduction from Marxist theory, but as a conclusion from the concrete facts.

Before the Bolshevik revolution, in August, 1915, Lenin argued thus :

" The United States of the World (not of Europe alone) is a State form of national unification and freedom which we connect with Socialism ; we think of it as becoming a reality only when the full victory of Communism will have brought about the total disappearance of any state, including its democratic form. As a separate slogan, however, the United States of the World would hardly be a correct one, first, because it coincides with Socialism, secondly, because it could be *erroneously interpreted to mean that the victory of Socialism in one country is impossible* ; it could also create misconceptions as to the relations of such a country to others. Unequal economic and political developmeut is an indispensable law of capitalism. It follows that the victory of Socialism is at the beginning, possible, in a few capitalist countries, *even in one taken separately.*"
—Lenin : *Works*, Vol. XVIII, pp. 271–2.

Later, in 1920, discussing the future development of Communism in Russia, he said :

" So long as we live in a small-peasant country, there will be a more solid economic basis in Russia for capitalism than for communism. Those who observe closely the life of the village in comparison with that of the town, know that we have not eradicated the roots of capitalism and that we have not undermined the base and support of our internal enemy. The latter is supported by petty economy, and there is only one way to undermine him, to transform the economic life of the country, *including agriculture*, on a new technical basis, the technical basis of modern large-scale production. . . . Only when the country is electrified, only when industry, agriculture, and transport are placed on the technical basis of modern large-scale production—only then will our victory be complete."—LENIN : quoted Stalin's *Leninism*, II, p. 61.

Thus, not only did Lenin envisage the possibility of " building Socialism in one country alone " and that before the War, he insisted that unless it was done as and when a political victory made it possible, that political victory itself would be unstable. In a word, instead of regarding the " acceptance of the task of creating a Communist society within Russia " as an entirely " new " start, as a turning-away from world revolution, Lenin regarded it as an indispensable *completion* of the political revolution and an inseparable part of the total process of world revolution.

Not only was Trotsky's attitude inconsistent with the theory of Marx and Engels, it was inconsistent with the concrete situation as understood by Lenin, both before and after the Bolshevik revolution. Most particularly was it in conflict with them in respect of the peasantry which, as Lenin saw, constituted the crux of the whole problem.

As the situation stood in 1925-7 (the period of preparation for the Plan : the period of Trotsky's bid for supreme power in the U.S.S.R., his defeat, and his expulsion) the capitalistic elements in the economic life of the U.S.S.R. out-numbered the socialistic elements. An attempt to " mark time " therefore would have involved a progressive growth in the capitalistic elements, a corresponding relative decline in the Socialistic elements and, over all, a progressive undermining of the dictatorship of the proletariat, leading in the end to its overthrow and the triumph of counter-revolution. To this process of degeneration and collapse, the only possible alternative was the policy of laying a foundation for Socialism by effecting the complete transformation of the national economy foreshadowed by Lenin.

The key to the alternatives of policy and their opposite outcome is found in the special situation of the peasantry, a class whose dialectical relation to the process of social development had received virtually no attention at all from " orthodox " Marxism in between the death of Engels and the rise of Lenin to world prominence in consequence of the Bolshevik revolution. To this " orthodox " exclusively-urbanised " Marxism " the peasantry constituted merely another kind of petty-bourgeois,—the most backward kind,— a homogeneous reactionary lump incapable of initiative and therefore to be disregarded, except in so far as it might be won over by opportunistic baits into an attitude of tolerance for the Social-Democratic Party.

Against this mechanical view Lenin prescribed a dialectical conception of the role of the peasantry in a proletarian revolution. Whereas the mechanical " Marxist " view (which Trotsky held, and still holds) merely discriminated the peasantry *relatively* into more or less " rich " and more or less " poor," Lenin saw that while the peasantry as a whole had a special function in relation to capitalist society, a relation based on the increasing relative exploitation of the agricultural producers by commercial, industrial, and finance capitalists, this function took on a special significance at a time of revolutionary crisis, particularly under a proletarian dictatorship.

The peasantry, in fact, presents a microcosm of society as a whole, in that its elements are in constant process of transition from the mean represented by the middle-peasantry —historically the original type—to the alternative extremes of wealthy peasant (a capitalist farmer in all but name) and impoverished peasant (a peasant already partly transformed into a proletarian). This three-fold division of the peasantry is of cardinal significance for the understanding of Leninist policy towards the peasant question ; and for the understanding, likewise, of the policy of building Socialism under the Plan.

Though the Bolshevik rdvolution was predominatly a proletarian revolution, it would have been impossible without the support of the mass of the peasantry. Hence the proletarian dictatorship rested on a two-fold basis—that of an alliance between the proletariat on the one side, and the poor and middle peasants on the other, the hegemony of the proletariat in this alliance being accepted by the peasants. This situation, be it noted, could never have arisen in the first place if the peasantry was everywhere and always a *reactionary* class ; nor could it have been maintained in the second place if the peasantry constituted in fact a *single* homogeneous mass. The alliance between the more revolutionary strata of the peasantry and the proletariat constituted, in fact, an extension of the class struggle into the ranks of the peasantry and the beginning of a struggle in which the poor peasants were pitted in ever-increasing antagonism against the rich peasants, with both sides seeking to win the middle peasants as allies in a decisive struggle.

The nature of Tsarist rule, intensified by the War, drove the whole body of the peasantry over to the side of the revolution : the failure of the Kerensky Government to deal with any of the questions vitally affecting the peasantry, drove the main bulk of the peasantry over to the side of the Bolsheviks. The land decrees of the Soviet Government won the peasantry in bulk over to its side during the Civil War, while the adoption of the N.E.P. (substantially a removal of most of the restrictions on internal trade) kept them on its side thereafter. But the N.E.P., in so far as it involved a return to bourgeois conditions of trading, involved a faster rate of economic differentiation between the rich peasants (who grew richer under the N.E.P.) and the poor peasants, who had suffered most, in proportion, during the Civil War, and the famine to which it contributed if it did not cause, and who therefore grew poorer relatively and absolutely under the N.E.P. These counter-tendencies affected the middle peasantry likewise, and hence, before the adoption of the Plan, there were clear signs of growing discontent among the peasantry. One of the chief objects of the Plan, therefore, was to create a new link, binding the peasantry to the pro-letariat and its dictatorship—that of the collective farm, equipped with better machinery, better agricultural appli-ances, and better technical knowledge than even the richest of rich peasants could command,—all of which means of higher and wider cultivation were made possible by the development of large-scale industry and the systematic application of the Plan.

The Plan therefore can, as Professor Macmurray observes, more wisely than he thinks, only be understood " dialec-tically." But the dialectic involved is not that of a trans-formation of the proletarian revolution into its " other," but that of the *development* of the proletarian revolution in the U.S.S.R. into a higher and *more revolutionary* phase. It was a process which involved the " solution of the peasant question," but not in isolation : it was solved by the develop-ment of large-scale industry as the basis of the national economy and the systematic transformation of agriculture from small-scale production by detached producers, into a large-scale, collective *industry* developing in co-ordination with industry as a whole. The peasantry in bulk (the poor and middle peasants) were transformed from peasants into collective farmers, into industrial workers whose work differed only incidentally from that of the industrial workers in the towns. Thus the age-long divorce (and antagonism) between the town and the country—an antagonism which Marx and Engels avowed it was the intention of the Communists to eliminate—has visibly received its death-blow from the adoption and carrying out of the Plan.

Incidentally, the carrying out of the Plan has eliminated from the economic and social life of the U.S.S.R. the main breeding-grounds of a bourgeois outlook—petty-production, petty-trading, and the " Kulak " or rich peasant class in agriculture—and so secured the dictatorship of the proletariat on a completely homologated basis. As a consequence, it has been possible, and necessary, now that the peasant *as such* occupies only a subordinate place in the national economy (controlling only some 10 per cent. of the total agricultural production)—the main bulk of the peasantry having been transformed into collective farmers, workers in the agricultural *industry*—to alter the electoral law of the U.S.S.R. in the direction of equalising the representation as between town and country workers, instead of giving the town workers the heavy preponderance given them heretofore.

This, of itself, is an indication that the U.S.S.R. has made a giant's stride in the direction of a classless society the condition precedent for the beginning of the positively Communist phase in the development of the U.S.S.R. as a whole.

.   .   .   .   .

Some of the developments we have noted above have become plainer since Professor Macmurray wrote. That is true, and necessary to state. But all of them were outlined in principle by the advocates of the Plan who secured its adoption—Stalin, of course, foremost among them—and all of them were scouted and derided *in principle* by Trotsky in his opposition to the Plan as proposed. What we have to note, therefore, is the fact that Professor Macmurray, in forming his estimate of the significance of the Plan, took as his guide neither the objective facts, nor the objective analysis presented by Stalin (and others) in support of the Plan, but the *ex parte* asservations of Trotsky who, it is notorious, had always been opposed to Lenin's view of the peasant question, and to his contention that Socialism *could* be victorious in *one country alone*. Why the Professor should thus, as though by instinct, prefer a *non*-Leninist, *non*-Marxist, *anti*-dialectical, subjective valuation of the facts, made by the defeated party in a polemic duel, in the

full tide of his defeat-begotten spleen, to the dialectic presented by the facts themselves, it is for Professor Macmurray
to explain. It is significant, however, that his adoption of
the mythical Trotskyite perversion of the facts enables him
to draw just the conclusion he wishes (as a good Labour Party
man) to draw:—

> " In accordance with dialectical law this thesis must
> now produce its antithesis. The development of fascism
> in Italy and Germany is quite obviously to any dialectical
> thinker the sign that bolshevism *has produced its own
> negation*, and that beyond both thesis and antithesis
> lies the final accomplishment of the synthesis through
> which alone a classless society can be achieved. It is
> through the negation of the negation that the final stage
> of the dialectic must be reached."—MACMURRAY : *ibid.*,
> pp. 85–6.

In the opening stage of his argument the Professor based
his case on the development of Russia *as* " Russia." Only
by postulating the development of Russia as proceeding
wholly and solely in consequence of its own *inner* causation
could he establish his conception of a contradiction between
the Bolshevik revolution and Marx's Dialectical Materialist
Conception of history. Now, when he wishes to produce an
antithesis to Bolshevism—to Communism in the U.S.S.R.—
this each-country-in-a-watertight-compartment theory is suddenly (and silently) replaced by its opposite—the theory that
there are no separate countries at all !—that revolutionary
struggle became obsolete *everywhere* after November, 1917 !

" Coming events cast their shadows before ! " Already we
can see that Professor Macmurray has set the stage in just the
only way possible to produce as his climax a Negation of the
Negation of Communism by Fascism ! Already we can hear
the premonitory minor chords from the orchestra which
prelude the appearance of Walter Citrine as the Fairy God-
mother—chasing away both the Black and the Red spectres
to replace them with their Negation—a Yellow spectre with
White Feathers in its Hair, and the star of a Knight's Grand
Cross of the Order of the British Empire on its distinguished
bosom !

And we are not mistaken. Fascism and Communism, we
learn, are linked into a " unity of opposites " by the fact that
both " believe in *force* " (which, of course, the British Labour
Party would never do—no ! not if it was *ever* so——!) :

" Fascism [says the Professor, brazening it out] is in

essence far more revolutionary than communism, and orthodox communism has no answer to it. For it was communism itself which chose to insist that economics was the determining factor in human life, and that politics was merely an expression of the economic organisation of Society. That is precisely what Fascism seeks to make of Society—a corporate, functional, economic organisation in which what has been politics becomes merely the administrative function of the economic organism."—MACMURRAY : *ibid.*, p. 93.

The reasoning is somewhat tortuous, but works out after this fashion : The Communists say that politics express the relations of the real objective economic life of Society. This is wrong. But it gives an excuse for the Fascists to say, " Very well, we will make politics correspond to economic actuality." And to this the Communists " have no answer ! "

What " answer " is called for ?

The Communists say that the politics of Capitalism express real relations in a *disguised* form. The *real* basic relation of bourgeois society is the day-to-day *dictatorship of capital*, which is the reality behind the disguise of " parliamentary constitutionalism and democracy." The Fascist says, " Very well. Since you have seen through the trick, we will drop the disguise and you shall have *the Dictatorship of Capital without disguise.*"

And Professor Macmurray, duped by mere phrases about the " Corporate State "—which means turning the State openly into what it is already in secret—a Capitalist Corporation run as a business for the profit of its shareholders, the owners of the land and the means of production !—Professor Macmurray regards this as " far more revolutionary than Communism ! "

Let him say that this is nearly as counter-revolutionary as Communism is revolutionary, and he will begin to see his way out of the fog in which he has lost his way.

.   .   .   .   .

What is Professor Macmurray's objection to the Communist affirmation that " it is not men's consciousness which determines their mode of life : it is their mode of life which determines their consciousness " ? This he repudiates categorically, naïvely disregarding the fact that in so doing he is repudiating Marx and Marxism *in toto.* He claims that the Negation of the Negation of Communism by Fascism is :

" . . . to insist that there are aspects of human life

which are of more importance than economics, and that freedom and equality must not be sacrificed to the demand for material power, whether that demand is made in the name of the capitalist class or of the working class. It is only as a demand for freedom and justice that the struggle of the oppressed classes for equality and freedom can in the nature of things be realised. Once subordinate politics to economics in theory, and the case for the emancipation of the worker . . . goes by the board."—MACMURRAY : *ibid.*, pp. 93–4.

Turn this about as you will you can make nothing of it but this—that the negation of the negation between the actual Dictatorship of Capital and the potential Dictatorship of the Proletariat is—to refuse by sheer force of intellect to recognise the existence of either !

Let us examine Professor Macmurray's propositions in detail.

" There are aspects of human life . . . more important than economics." There are things " more important " in individual life than the bowels and their functions, or any of the intestinal arrangements of man ! Quite true ! But until these intestinal arrangements are working and functioning in normal and adequate health no man can either fully or adequately realise these " more important " things.

" Freedom and equality must not be sacrificed to the demand for material power, whether that demand is made in the name of the capitalist class or of the working class." From which it appears that " freedom and equality " do, in fact, exist, but that their existence is threatened by the " demand for material power " made " in the name of the Capitalist class " (by Fascism) and " in the name of the working class " (by Communism). What " freedom " exists in bourgeois society to-day ? Such " freedom " as does not conflict with the " rights " of Capitalist property : namely, the " freedom " of the worker to live *by* labour, and the freedom of the capitalist to live *on* labour—the freedom of the worker *from* property *for* work : the freedom of the capitalist *from* work *for* the pursuit of property : the freedom of the capitalist to possess and to enlarge his possessions : the freedom of the worker to seek a " boss " and, having found him, to work for *his* benefit—alternatively the freedom of the worker to look for a boss and starve while he looks, " free " from all preoccupation with " material power." What " equality " exists to-day ? The equal right of all to live on their " property " and obey the law which forbids the acquisition of property save in the ways prescribed in the Book of Rules of the Game of Life as revised and brought up to date by the bourgeoisie !

These " freedoms " and this " equality " must " not be sacrificed " to any demand for " material power."

What " material power " is demanded by Fascism ? The power to prevent the worker claiming and exercising a " freedom " not included in the above list, since bourgeois society, officially, does not " recognise " it—namely the freedom of the proletariat to struggle for the overthrow of the material power exercised by the bourgeoisie to ensure that all the other " freedoms " shall be theirs !

What " material power " is demanded by Communism ? The material power of the proletariat to abolish " bourgeois freedom " and replace it with the real freedom of common ownership of the means of existence and enjoyment and common co-operation in their use for the common well-being.

Since Professor Macmurray is opposed " equally " to both, his Negation of the Negation means exactly—*The existing state of things, with no change, now and for evermore, Amen !*

Do you doubt it ? What, then, does it mean to say that " only as a demand for freedom and justice can the struggle of the oppressed classes for equality and freedom be realised. Once subordinate politics to economics in theory and the case for the emancipation of the worker goes by the board " ?

The struggle for freedom can only be realised *as a struggle for freedom.* That is to say, if the freedom be obtained the struggle stops. It loses its " reality " *as a struggle* ! The fact that it has *realised* (that is to say attained) the end for which it was adopted as a *means* makes apparently no difference ! For Professor Macmurray the end is nothing : the means everything. If the end were reached the means would no longer be *means.* If the oppressed ceased to be oppressed they could no longer struggle against oppression ! Therefore the oppression is " necessary " and the struggle is " necessary " in order that Professor Macmurray may negate the negation by depriving the struggle of its object and purpose and so turn it from a sordid, material struggle for power into a beautiful Ideal struggle, just for the fun of struggling !

Try it another way : politics must not be " subordinated " to economics. Therefore, the political programme of the workers must have a purely non-economic objective. But, since all objectives which have to do with the relations between classes turn upon the economic relations of which

those classes are the expression, politics must be purged of
all *class* objectives. They must cease to be *working-class
politics* [which incidentally is just what the Fascists demand !].

The State, for the control of which all politics are designed,
must correspondingly cease to be a *class* State. But if it is
not a *class* State, it will not be a State at all ! This cannot
be a Communist society since that, too, rests on the basis of
subordinating politics as means to the end of economic control.
What, then, can it mean ? It can have nothing to do with
flesh and blood, since this too is concerned with " economics "
and the realities of " material power." It can then only be
the Kingdom of Heaven, in which there is "neither marriage
nor giving in marriage," neither worker nor boss, neither
economics nor politics : only the Lamb and His Glory !

" Subordinate politics to economics in theory and the case
for workers' emancipation is gone." Why ? Because with
Professor Macmurray the Unity of Theory and Practice is
based *on the primacy of Theory* ! Once he admits that the
workers *are workers* because of material facts that are
primarily economic, that they struggle to win the material
power to shatter these economic constraints—once he admits
that and he will be forced to agree with Dialectical *Materialism*
—with " Russian " Communism—and all his beautifu
Hegelianism will go phut from a chronic paralysis of its
primary antithesis ! Therefore he goes the whole Hegelian
hog and affirms that Capitalism is begotten by the Idea of
Capitalism, the working class by the Idea of the working-
class, and struggle by the Idea of struggle ! All that is
required is that the workers should abandon the Idea that
they are workers, the capitalists shall abandon the Idea they
are bosses, and both shall abandon the Idea of struggle
and—lo ! the Negation of the Negation of Fascism and
Communism is complete ! " Citrine's in his Heaven ! All's
right with Transport House ! "

.   .   .   .

Professor Macmurray's whole argument is based upon
the commonest and most banal of logical fallacies—that
which the logicians indicate in the formula, *Post hoc : propter
hoc* [After *this*, caused by *this*]. He sees that *Fascism* arose
(*as Fascism*) only after Communism was victorious in Russia.
Therefore—Fascism was " caused by " Communism ! That
established, it is the simplest of feats for a Hegelian to treat
them as antitheses each of the other and to seek for a higher
synthesis in which both will be " reconciled."

But herein Professor Macmurray is glaringly and staringly guilty of false Dialectic. That Communism and Fascism shall constitute a true Hegelian " opposition " they must together constitute a *whole*, and be united by the " ground " they arise from in common. What common ground have Fascism and Communism ? There is one and one only— *the class struggle between bourgeoisie and proletariat*. That is the one and only presupposition common to both, which they interpret in opposite ways. Communism affirms that the struggle must be fought out to a finish : Fascism affirms that it must not and it shall not be fought out to a finish. Professor Macmurray negates this negation by affirming that the struggle must be fought—but *not to a finish* ! It must be carried on in permanence, " until the cows come home."

Put just like that, even a Professor recoils (as soon as he has slept off his overdose of Hegel). He finds a new " ground " for the antithesis. Fascism and Communism constitute a whole in that both " believe in force " :

> " The idea that it is necessary, if a classless society is to be brought into existence, to aim first at *capturing* (!) the *political organisation of the State* (! ! !) commits the Communist to the acceptance of the machinery of force for the creation of freedom. . . . It is this practical belief in the mechanism of the State which is the common ground of Fascism and Communism."—Macmurray : *ibid*., p. 89.

First of all, the formulation as against the Communists is false. Once again Professor Macmurray has taken his " Marxism " at second-hand, this time from that bastard Lassalleian Tory-democracy which H. M. Hyndman bluffed the British Labour movement into accepting as " Marxism." Only those whose " Marxism " is merely a veneer over a substratum of Lassalle (derived either direct through German Social-Democracy or in a sophisticated form through Hyndman) ever envisage the immediate objective of Socialism or Communism as " *capturing the political machinery* " (or " organisation ") of the State.

This is, in fact, as we have noted elsewhere, the complete reversal of the genuine Marxian doctrine of " *conquering* the political *power* " in the State. And the specific practical difference is (as Professor Macmurray may learn from the polemic between Lenin and Kautsky on the question) that in the one case the " captured " machinery or " organisation " is simply taken over as a going concern, whereas in the other the *power is conquered* by a process of historical *struggle*, in the course of and in consequence of which the old State machinery (or " organisation ") including especially the " public *power* of coercion " is shattered by the historically developed *force* of the revolutionary class and its struggle.

> " One thing especially was proved by the Commune, viz., that ' the working class cannot simply lay hold of the ready-made State machinery, and wield it for its own purposes.' "—MARX–ENGELS : Preface to German edition (1872) of *Communist Manifesto*.

This, while it makes no difference to Professor Macmurray's argument so far as Force in the *abstract* is concerned, completely shatters his conception of the *concrete* antithesis between Fascism and Communism. Once it is seen that their common " ground " is *the existing State* (i.e., the bourgeois State) which the Fascists fight to " capture " only in order to *preserve*, and the Communists fight *not to capture* but to *overthrow* and *destroy*, and their *real* antithetical relation is clear : Fascism is one (out of many) modes of defending the bourgeois order—an expression of the interests of the bourgeoisie struggling to preserve its ruling power. *Communism* is the highest of many, historically conditioned modes of expression of the proletarian class struggle against the bourgeois order and the conditions which give it ruling power.

Formulated thus the *real* content of each is seen, and their real mutual inter-conditioning. And with that is seen, too, the worse-than-worthlessness of Professor Macmurray's assertion that " Fascism is in essence far more revolutionary than Communism," and that " it is not without justice that Fascism claims to be a form of Socialism."

The *essence* of a thing is found in *what it does*—in its *real* movement. The *essence* of a Social movement is found likewise in what it does—in its specific *direction* of movement. Fascism is a movement *of* the bourgeoisie, *against* the revolutionary proletarian struggle, and *for* the making of the bourgeois State *absolute* and invincible against all such struggles. It is " Socialist " only to those who can conceive Socialism as consisting *in essence* in nothing but " making the State absolute," or to those who conceive Society as a mechanical *structure* incapable of movement, and Socialism as the arbitrary imposition of formal equality upon all on the basis of bourgeois commodity production. Both these " Socialisms " figure in Fascist demagogy. The former is a

recrudescence of the " German or True Socialism " which
facilitated the victory of the counter revolution in 1848.
The latter derives from Proudhon and was carried over by
Bakunin and popularised in the Latin countries (Italy and
Spain especially). Professor Macmurray correctly perceiving
that " Socialism " of a *sort* figures in Fascists' *promises* does
not perceive *what* sort—that it is the sort which is and was
" both Utopian and reactionary " as far back as 1848 !

And here we reach the kernel of the Hegelian *nut* ! In so
far as the one which was developed *after* the other, and in
opposition to it, is the *negation* of the former (and as such
is " higher " in form), it is *Communism* which, both as an
expression of the proletarian class struggle and as a more
developed form of Socialism, is the later born, and the
negation of all that Fascism is in essence—i.e., the class
struggle of the bourgeoisie camouflaged under a disguise of
Utopian, doctrinaire, and reactionary " Socialism." And
the Negation of their Negation is and can be nothing other
than the revolutionary dictatorship of the proletariat as the
transition—the mutation leap—to the classless society *and*
Communism of the future.

.   .   .   .   .

How stands the matter in respect of Professor Macmurray's
argument that " the mechanism of force " cannot be used
to secure " freedom."

Freedom of *what*, or *whom* ? From *what* ? For what ?

The Professor doesn't say ! He is concerned only with
Freedom in the abstract—the pure logical category of
" Freedom." As a formal logical category " Freedom "
excludes " Force " and " Force " excludes " Freedom."
Quite true !—*in the abstract* ! But what we are concerned
with in real life are not *abstract categories* but the objective
realities from which they are discriminated. And in real life
" power and freedom are identical."

Freedom is—the *power* to act, or to abstain from action.
Freedom is the *power to choose* between available alternatives.
Freedom has no meaning unless such a choice is backed by
the *power* of making it effective :—

  " Liberty or 'freedom' signifieth, properly, the
  absence of opposition ; by opposition I mean external
  impediments of motion ; and may be applied no less to
  irrational and inanimate creatures than to rational.
  For whatsoever that is so tied, or environed, as it cannot
  move but within a certain space, which space is deter-

mined by the opposition of some external body, we say
it hath not liberty to go further. . . . When the impediment of motion is in the constitution of the thing itself,
we use not to say it wants the liberty, but the *power* to
move ; as when a thing lieth still, or a man is fastened to
his bed by sickness.

" And according to this proper and generally received
meaning of the word, a ' freeman is he that, in those
things which he by his strength or wit is able to do, is
not hindered to do what he has a will to.' But when
the words ' free ' and ' liberty ' are applied to anything
but ' bodies ' they are abused ; for that which is not
subject to motion is not subject to impediment ; and
therefore when it is said, for example, the way is free,
no liberty of the way is signified, but of those that walk
in it without stop."—HOBBES : *Leviathan,* Chap. XXI.

How does this truth, so vivaciously stated by Hobbes,
apply in the present instance ? In the way we have indicated
elsewhere in this essay. The actual reality and force of an
individual's *individuality,* his " freedom " to do *this,* rather
than *that,* depends not upon his absolute nature—as Professor
Macmurray, being an idealist (and as such driven constantly
to take refuge in mysticism), supposes. It depends upon his
social situation, and upon the quantity and quality of *power
of command* over the forces of Nature with which the society
into which he is born is equipped.

The proletarians are as *individuals* so situated that they
are powerless to move outside the constraints imposed by
the necessities of their nature, of life—the primary needs
of food, clothing and shelter. To rise above this realm of
necessity they must acquire not merely " liberty " in the
sense of absence of external constraint, but positive power to
secure first these primary necessities and then the power and
the liberty to turn to other things. If the proletariat, therefore, in its fight for freedom, first of all creates the *power* of
class-solidarity in struggle as a means to the end of overcoming the constraints and compulsions of bourgeois rule,
it does what in the circumstances it *must* do to secure freedom.
If, victorious, the proletariat establishes this, its own class
solidarity, as a *ruling power* in its turn : it does so again as
the necessary means of securing the *real basis* upon which
alone can its collective and individual freedom be developed.

Professor Macmurray, yet another instance of inability to
rise above " the standpoint of the single individual in civil

2 K

society," envisages the "individual" and his "liberty" idealistically as mystical absolutes. He is therein at one with Fascism—whose conception of the individual, the State, and their interrelation is mystical-idealist all through !

.　　.　　.　　.　　.

The attempt to establish a dialectical unity of opposites out of Fascism and Communism on the basis of their common "belief in force" was a sorry one at best. That sort of dialectic we have learned to expect from Labour Party opportunists. We have a right to expect better from Professor Macmurray.

Where is there a political party that does not "believe in force ? " Even the Quakers believe in the *force* of Divine communication—the *force* of that which is "borne in upon the soul ! " Every party aiming at becoming a Government is therein aiming at becoming possessed of power sufficient to *enforce* its will as Law.

Does the Labour Party at the acme of its anti-Communist zeal ever propose to abolish the police force ?

The existing political parties are distinguished, not in accordance with their belief or non-belief in force, but in respect of the *kind* of force they aim at in consequence of the concrete particularity of their specific ends.

The Communists aim at creating the revolutionary force of the proletariat as a means to the end of attaining, through this force, wielded as a ruling power, the classless society in which the *force* of the whole society will be used by the whole society to win an ever greater freedom from Natural Necessity. Professor Macmurray does not agree with them. Neither do the Fascists, neither does the Labour Party. All these are agreed in condemning that which the Communists regard as vital—the generation in revolutionary class struggle of the proletarian class "*power enough to compel.*" Since these all agree in opposing the Communists on this point the true Hegelian opposition is that between the Communists and the revolutionary proletarian class struggle on the one side, and on the other *the counter class struggle of the bourgeoisie, expressed in various ways by the Fascists, the British Labour Party, and Professor Macmurray* ?

Let us call a witness whose credit Professor Macmurray dare not call in question—while Walter Citrine is listening !— Karl Kautsky :

" The contrast between reform and revolution does not consist in the application of force in the one case and not in the other. *Every* juridical and political measure is a *force* measure, which is carried through by the *force* of the State. Neither do any particular forms of the application of force, as for example, street fights or executions, constitute the essentials of revolution in contrast to reform. These arise from particular circumstances, are not necessarily connected with revolutions, and *may easily accompany reform movements.*"—KAUTSKY : *The Social Revolution* (1902).

" The conquest of governmental power by an hitherto oppressed class, in other words, a political revolution, is accordingly the essential characteristic of social revolution in . . . contrast to social reform. Those who repudiate political revolution as the principle means of social transformation . . . are social reformers no matter how much their social ideas may antagonise existing social forms."—KAUTSKY : *ibid.*

And also, most significantly, this :—

" Certain persons have maintained that Engels in his 'political testament ' [i.e., the preface to MARX's *Class Struggles in France*, which was the last thing Engels wrote and which the Social Democratic editors carefully ' bowdlerised '] denies his entire life's work and finally represents the revolutionary standpoint, which he had defended for two generations, as an error. These persons [i.e., Bernstein, and the Revisionists] inferred that Engels had now recognised that *Marx's doctrine—that force is the midwife of every new society*—was no longer tenable. . . .

" These people imagine that Socialism will conquer . . . . without any *violent convulsion* in the State, by peaceful means alone, through the friendly assistance of the Government. . . .

" He who knows Engels and judges him without bias, will know that it never entered his head to abjure his revolutionary ideas, and that the final passage in his introduction cannot therefore be interpreted in the sense indicated above."—KAUTSKY : *Foundations of Christianity* (1913), pp. 460–61.

And Kautsky had the best of all reasons for knowing that this was so, because he had been a party to the bowdlerisation which made possible the misinterpretation he rebukes.

These quotations from Kautsky do not of themselves
prove that Professor Macmurray is wrong on the general
question of *force in the abstract*. They do prove that he is
wrong to call himself a " Marxist " while absolutely repudiating the use of " force." And since we began with Professor
Macmurray's misconception of Marxism in the specific
instance of the Bolshevik Revolution, we may end with a
return to the beginning by means of yet another quotation
from Kautsky :

> " The English workers of to-day stand lower as a
> political factor than the workers of the most economically
> backward country in Europe—Russia. *It is the real
> revolutionary consciousness of these latter that gives them
> their great political power*. It is the renunciation of
> revolution, the narrowing of interest to the interests of
> the moment, to so-called practical politics that has made
> the former a cipher in actual politics."—KAUTSKY :
> *Social Revolution* (1902).

We can only echo Lenin's words : " How *well* Kautsky
wrote—in 1902 ! "

II—MODERNIST " MARXISM " :
RAYMOND POSTGATE AND MAX EASTMAN

Raymond Postgate also celebrated the fiftieth anniversary
of the death of Marx by writing a book—entitled *Karl Marx*,
to which we have several times referred in passing. It comes
up for special notice here, firstly because of its chapter on
the Dialectic, and secondly because of the connection between
it and an older work, Max Eastman's *Marx, Lenin, and the
Science of Revolution*, which Postgate describes as " the only
work . . . which deals with Marxism in a modern and
intelligent manner."

Max Eastman's book was published at a most unfortunate
time for its proper appreciation, namely, on the eve of the
General Strike, May, 1926. It has therefore never received
proper attention before, and may be treated as virtually a
new book, all the more so as its effects are only now beginning
to be apparent in curious ways and places.

Postgate has leaned heavily on Eastman, and has thereby
been betrayed into a whole brood of follies he might otherwise
have escaped. But as their two works stand they are linked
in (1) a common disparagement of Marx's work ; (2) a
common assertion that the Marxian philosophy is an

" economic determinism " ; (3) a common repudiation of this " economic determinism " in favour of " modern " *psychology* ; (4) a common and univocal detestation of the very name " Dialectic."

They have their differences, of course, each dealing an odd " backhander " or two at Marx which the other omits. But they agree in all the points listed above, and also in each still adopting the pose of being " Marxist."

We have already noted their joint onslaught on a passage from the *Holy Family* (which neither of them understands), and upon various other aspects of Marxism. Here we will deal with the basic issues raised in their critique.

On Modernity

Raymond Postgate commences his chapter on the Marxian Dialectic with these words :

" Every body of ideas, every philosophy, is, according to Marx, a reflection of existing economic circumstances. It is not truth, for there is no absolute truth while the present series of contradictions and class-struggles continues to unfold itself. As economic circumstances change, the philosophies change and disappear. Marxism, consequently, is itself but a reflection within the minds of the proletariat of its circumstances. As these circumstances change so Marxism becomes untrue. It is inconceivable that a system which was a true reflection of the social relations of 1847 and 1867 should be still valid to-day. Great portions of it must have, by its own standards, become obsolete."—POSTGATE : *ibid.*, p. 81.

It would amaze us were we not by now accustomed to the fact that every critic of Marx is a critic in exact proportion to his ignorance of the fundamentals of Marx, to find a passage such as that in a book purporting to " explain " Marx, and one written by an author with any sort of reputation, deserved or undeserved.

The first assertion made in this passage is false. Marx said that " ideas " individually and in their historical development were reflections of men's historically conditioned *social relations*. The words " existing economic circumstances " are doubly false in this connection : firstly, because there are other *material* and *social* circumstances than " economic " ones ; and secondly, because they exclude, among other things (what Marx never forgot), the influence upon men of subjective activity—of theory and *tradition,* " the inertia force of history " as Engels calls it.

The second assertion, that the *relativity* of knowledge is conditioned *solely* by class-divisions and antagonisms—so that, presumably, *absolute* knowledge will be automatically available for all in a communist society, makes absolute nonsense of the whole conception of the relativity of knowledge.

The third assertion, which implies that the coming and going of philosophies is a *mechanical* consequence of economic changes, flatly contradicts Marx's own materialist conception of history, in which the *differing mode of development* of the economic basis of society and of its ideological superstructure is the mainspring of the whole conception, and objective *practice* is conceived as the generating source of all knowledge.

The final assertion that a world-conception *must* be " out of date" because it was formulated earlier than yesterday is the most childishly uncritical affirmation it is possible to make. (It is, however, made by Max Eastman in almost identical words. It is, it would seem, a " hall-mark " of Bloomsbury and Greenwich Village.)

Taking this final assertion to begin with, let us ask a few questions :

Is the opinion that the Earth moves round the Sun *necessarily* false because it was held by some Greek astronomers 2000 years ago ? Or because it was rediscovered by Copernicus more than 400 years ago ? Is the fact that Napoleon was defeated at Waterloo on June 18th, 1815, any the less true to-day than when it happened ? Will it be any the less true if the whole World " goes Red " and a World Union of Socialist Soviet Republics is established ?

Raymond Postgate does not believe that either of these questions should be answered in the affirmative. But he tries to represent Marx's world-conception in such a light as to make it appear that Marx would have done so ! And he caps his work by the gratuitously absurd assertion that Marxism (as a world-conception) is fundamentally *only* a " reflection in the minds *of the proletariat.*"

The best answer to Postgate is a quotation from Engels :

" According to the Materialist Conception of history the determining element is, *ultimately*, production and reproduction in real life. More than this neither Marx nor I have ever asserted. If therefore someone twists **this** into the statement that the economic element is the *only* determining one, he transforms it into a meaningless, abstract, and absurd phrase. The economic situation is *the basis*, but the various elements of the superstructure —political forms of the class struggle and its consequences, constitutions established by the victorious class after a successful battle, etc.—forms of law—and then even the reflexes of all these actual struggles in the brains of the combatants : political, legal and philosophical theories, religious ideas and their further development into systems of dogma—also exercise their influence upon the course of the historical struggles, and *in* many cases preponderate in determining their *form*.

" There is an interaction of all these elements, in which, amid all the endless *host* of accidents (i.e., of things and events whose inner connection is so remote or so impossible to prove that we regard it as absent and negligible), the economic element finally asserts itself as the *necessary*.

" [Were it] otherwise the application of the theory to any period of history one chose would be easier than the solution of a simple equation of the first degree.

" *We make our own history* ; but in the first place under very definite presuppositions and conditions. Among these the economic ones are finally decisive. . . . *History makes itself* in such a way that the final result always arises from conflicts between many individual wills, of which each again has been made what it is by a host of particular conditions of life. Thus there are innumerable intersecting forces, an infinite series of parallelograms of forces, which give rise to one resultant— the historical event.

" This again may itself be viewed as the product of a power which, taken as a whole, works *unconsciously* and without volition. For what each individual wills is obstructed by everyone else, and what emerges is something no one willed. Thus past history proceeds in the manner of a natural process and is also essentially subject to the same laws of movement.

" But from the fact that individual wills . . . do not attain what they want, but are merged into a collective mean, a common resultant, it must not be concluded that their value equals zero. On the contrary, each contributes to the resultant and is to this degree involved in it."—ENGELS *to Bloch*, September 21st, 1890.

To those who have read the previous chapters of this work
there will be little new in this passage. Its essential content
is that which a careful student would have gathered from the
whole work of Marx and Engels, even in its absence. In fact,
the surprising thing about the letter is that Engels had the
patience to write it to an inquiring student. There is a
profound point in the quiet hint with which Engels continues :

" I would urge you to study the theory further in *its
original sources*, and not from second-hand ones. It is
really *much easier* ! Marx has, in fact, written nothing
in which some part of the theory cannot be found."—
ENGELS : *ibid.*

This neglect of the original sources—the works of Marx and
Engels themselves—is the chief cause of the wide spread of
the myth that Marxism is an " economic determinism."
Another is the fact that at the hands of vulgarisers and
opportunist manipulators the theory of Marx did—in the
absence of any easily accessible editions and translations of
the works of Marx and Engels—become an " economic
determinism." Engels himself repudiated its English variety
with scorn while living, but, this notwithstanding, it was
trumpeted abroad throughout the English-speaking world
(particularly by H. M. Hyndman) as the " genuine article "—
all the more so because the trumpeter (Hyndman, for instance)
thereby created an opportunity for himself to " correct "
Marx for having " carried the theory too far " !

Neglect of original sources and dependence upon an un-
verified tradition cannot, however, be pleaded as an excuse
for one who offers for public consumption what purports to
be a life of Marx by a Marxist, but is, in fact, a systematic
misrepresentation of Marxism and a belittlement of Marx
personally, for which the " life " serves as the merest camouflage.

Eastman herein differs from Postgate. Eastman is openly
and arrogantly contemptuous of Marx and Marx's Marxism.
He seeks without concealment to glorify Lenin as the " practical man " at the expense of Marx the mere theorist and
" ideologist." [Eastman's particular idiosyncrasy is to use
the term " ideologist " as Napoleon did—as a term of contempt.]

Eastman has a motive for lauding Lenin as the " scientific
engineer of Revolution "—and for seeking to establish his
thesis that every revolution must have its " engineer." When
he wrote his book Eastman was an earnest backer of the

claims of Trotsky to the post of " Chief Engineer of World Revolution " then rendered vacant by the death of Lenin ! Not only is Eastman largely responsible in the English-speaking world for the attempt to fasten the Fascist conception of the " leader principle " upon the Communist International ; he is the one who first gave currency to the myth that *Lenin had left this post to Trotsky in his will* !

It took a romantic poet-intellectual who had been swept loose from his intellectual moorings by the impact of the Bolshevik Revolution to evolve this *grotesquerie* that leadership in the Communist Party and in the revolutionary proletarian struggle is *a property to be bequeathed* like a slab of " real estate " or a chain of Kodak supply stores ! Now that the Trotskyite dawn which Eastman heralded so lyrically has revealed itself (as it soon did) as no dawn, but a phosphorescent miasma over a petty-bourgeois swamp, Max Eastman has faded from the political stage into an obscurity from which he emerges only as a sniper (at times under a pseudonym), persistently endeavouring to inflict such injury as he can by the circulation of his pet slanders at the expense of Marx's and Engels' Marxism, and Marxism-Leninism.

What has such as Max Eastman in common with Raymond Postgate ? Only this : that Postgate, like Eastman, has a grudge against the Communist Party (in each case mainly because the Party refused to take either at his own valuation). He is also of an age to be influenced by all the " modernist " " stunt " movements which have ruffled the waters of the intelligentsia since the War. Postgate " fell for " Eastman's malicious lampoon much as a callow youth " falls for " a vamp. Hence his " discovery " that Marx *must* be " out of date," and hence too his (belated) admiration for Sigmund Freud ! The fact that Postgate avows Eastman as the source of his inspiration is the best possible proof of his positively calf-like innocence in the matter.

.   .   .   .   .

A curious fact about this " it-must-be-obsolete-because-it-is-old " myth is that it is so " old-fashioned." Here, for instance, is an opinion dating from 1905, which is in substance identical with the view advanced by Max Eastman in 1926, and Raymond Postgate in 1933. The fact that it comes from no less an authority that *J. Ramsay MacDonald, M.P.*, will (surely ?) commend it to Postgate's admiration :

" His [Marx's] philosophy belonged to an old generation ; his logical view of the State was unreal ; the

words which he used together with the conceptions which
they expressed so accurately are inadequate in relation
to *modern thought* (! ! !) and misleading for practical
conduct ; in short, whilst fully accepting the collectivist
and Socialist conclusions of Marx, we must explain and
defend them with a different conception of Society in
our minds, different formulæ on our lips and different
guiding ideas for our activities.

"The place which Marx occupies is on the threshold
of scientific sociology, but not altogether over it."—
J. R. MacDonald : *Socialist and Society*, pp. 121–2.

Since MacDonald wrote, many things have happened—
including the Bolshevik Revolution. That despite all that
has happened it should be possible for Raymond Postgate,
who when MacDonald wrote these "modern" and "thought-
ful" words had reached nearly the age of *nine years*, to attain
as early as 1933 to the lofty pinnacle of critical observation
occupied by MacDonald in 1905, is a thing marvellous from
several points of view. Especially that of "modernity"!

Postgate puts his case categorically :

". . . resentment must be affronted, and the fact
that certain portions of the work of a *mid-Victorian*
philosopher and economist are sure to be *out of date* be
admitted. The out-of-date portion of Marxism then is
probably the dialectic, important though Marx and
even (!) Lenin considered it to be."—Postgate : *ibid.*,
p. 82.

Mid-Victorian . . .! "*Seen Greta Garbo's latest ?*"

.   .   .   .   .

In the teeth of Postgate's "probably" we have sought in
this work to demonstrate that it is the *method* of Marxism—
its dialectic—which gives the whole its living unity. If,
therefore, this method *is* obsolete the whole is not merely
obsolete but *dead* !

To affirm that Marx and Engels reached a number of
separate generalisations which still remain more or less valid,
but did so by means of a method which is so radically defective
that it is no longer even of provisional validity, is to affirm
that these generalisations are of doubtful value likewise. So
far as they are *true*, these generalisations are so in that case
not because of the radically defective method (if such it be)
by which they were reached, but in spite of it ; and they and
their truth can be better attested by other men and other
methods.

To say, therefore, that Marx's *Dialectic method* is " out of date " is to say nothing less than that Marx and Engels have nothing to teach us—except, through their failures, errors to avoid. Ramsay MacDonald says so with an unequivocal clarity which is, for him, almost unique. Eastman says so with as much plainness as is possible to a poet suffering from the spleen. Postgate prefers the pusilanimous method of suggesting that such is the case while ostensibly holding Marx up to admiration !

The Dialectic and Inevitability

The point at which both Postgate and Eastman level their chief attack is the doctrine of the " inevitability " of the triumph of the proletariat.

Herein they are nothing like so original as they imagine themselves to be ; and it is significant that they should choose a line of attack identical with that pursued by *all* idealism in opposition to every sort of Materialism. Always the Idealist cry has been that Materialism, in placing the *cause* for men's volitions *outside* the mystic and inscrutable nature of the *Will-in-Itself*, has, in thus treating each man's will as something *caused* and therefore *dependent* and *derived*, treated men as mere " conscious automata "—Robots afflicted with grandiose self-delusions !

The Idealist motive for this attack has been the logical need to find in the *inscrutable* nature of the Will-in-Itself a doorway through which to introduce *Absolute* categories (Eternal and Unchanging Moral Laws, absolutist conceptions of the State, the Soul, and God) into a universe which the development of the empirical sciences every day more and compels us to treat theoretically and practically as a completely interdependent whole, whose every particular aspect and specific movement is of necessity caused and determined by its interrelation in and to the *process* of the whole.

As we have seen in earlier chapters, this attack was not met, and could not be met, by the predominantly mechanical materialism of the eighteenth century. But it is met and refuted by the Dialectical Materialism, which, recognising that there are other modes of motion than simply mechanical ones, is able to recognise *both* the practical reality and efficacy of individual consciousness and will, and at the same time the causal inter-connection between these things and the objective material universe.

Mechanical Materialism sees only the *unity*, the *continuity*,

in the relation of Subject and Object, in consciousness. Idealism sees only the *dis*unity, the *opposition*, the apparent *break*
of continuity. Dialectical Materialism alone sees *both* the
unity and the *opposition*. It is from this basic fact that (as
we have seen) Dialectical Materialism derives its primary
canon—the Unity of Theory and Practice based on the
primacy of Practice.

Postgate and Eastman, most significantly, never once
mention this canon. Their case would have been shattered
from the outset if they had even admitted its existence.
Their whole polemic demands that they should treat Marxism
as a system of merely mechanical Materialism upon which, as
an afterthought, a mystical-idealist Hegelian logic has been
superimposed. For them the Dialectic is a purely abstract
metaphysical *interpretation*.

This double falsification enables them to attack as the
Prince Ruperts (or Jeb Stuarts) of ultra-modernity on two
fronts. Against the mechanical materialism which they
fraudulently substitute for Marxism they parade all the
arguments of all the Idealists. Against the spurious metaphysic they have substituted for the Dialectic they parade
all the arguments of all the mechanical materialists ! And
as positive virtuosos in theoretical inconsequentiality they
go on to reveal that their chief reason for opposing " determinism " as applied to the Will and the processes of conscious
thought is that they wish to open a doorway for Freudian
psychology and a solipsist epistemology.

.   .   .   .   .

Here are samples of Postgate's assault upon the Dialectic :

> " The theory of the inevitability of the victory of the
> proletariat is bound up with the dialectic. Indeed it
> arises solely from it : the moment the dialectic is seen
> not to be universally valid, at that moment the in-
> evitability of proletarian victory is destroyed. Socialism
> may be possible, it may be probable, but it cannot be
> inevitable."—POSTGATE : *Karl Marx*, p. 89.

> " A belief in the dialectic may be useful while it is
> *untrue*. Lenin, for example, clearly considered it useful
> and announced its validity in *very unmeasured terms* (! ! !).
> On the other hand it is at least arguable that its utility
> is less than has been imagined."—POSTGATE : *Karl Marx*,
> pp. 89–90.

From which we may discern that, in addition to the theoretical motives we have noted above, Postgate has a political motive for rejecting the conception of the inevitability of proletarian victory. If that victory is *in the long run* inevitable, the correct policy after every momentary setback is to *prepare for the next battle.* If on the other hand it is not inevitable, a setback may be taken to indicate that it was wrong to accept battle in the first case, and that what the proletariat should do is to " put away childish things " such as revolution, and, in plain English (*à la* G. D. H. Cole), " seek an alliance with the middle class." Anyway, it is certain, once the ultimate inevitability of victory is ruled out, that Lenin (fine fellow though he was—*for a Russian*!) was mistaken, and succeeded through luck more than judgment. And as the alternative to Leninism is Social-Democracy (whose whole policy nowadays may be summed up in Plekhanov's wail : " They should not have taken up arms ! "), and as the disgraced, discredited, disorganised and (after Vienna, and among proletarians) *universally execrated* Social-Democratic chiefs had no other shelter behind which to rally and reorganise than the British Labour Party—lo ! the mystery is cleared ! The attack on the doctrine of *inevitable* proletarian victory is a left-handed way of saying (as Transport House and degenerate German Social Democracy agree in saying) that the proletarian revolution is *only* inevitable if God and the middle class so will ! The trail of the Citrine is over it all ! Postgate has lined up with the modern British representatives of the old Irish parliamentary " revolutionists," who " *would make a revolution to-morrow, only the brutal police won't let 'em* ! "

Eastman moves outside this orbit. He is the Left wing of these Siamese twins of Modernist-Marxism. He states his case thus :

" In place of the assertion that the *instinctive* economic activities of men *automatically* produce social welfare, he [Marx] puts the assertion that *these same* activities *automatically* produce a Social revolution."—EASTMAN : *Marx, Lenin, etc.,* p. 98.

" His [Marx's] conception that when men enter into social relations, an ordered development arises which is *wholly independent* of their consciousness and their wills, was far more dependable for this purpose [i.e., of revolution] than the concept of the ' Economic Man.' . . . Marx abandoned the Economic Man *not because he wished to make a closer analysis of the concrete facts, but because he wished to stay further away from them. . . .* The Marxian ideology consists of fitting the abstractions of the Classical Political Economy, as amended *but not transcended* by Marx, into Hegel's *philosophy of the universe* as a dialectical evolution of *abstractions*—this also amended *but not transcended* by Marx—and thus arriving at a *mystical conviction of the ' iron necessity ' of the revolution* that he desired."—EASTMAN :   *ibid.*, pp. 98–99.

There is no need, after the evidence we have adduced in the earlier chapters of this work, to waste ceremony over these assertions.   Every word of Eastman's we have italicised is categorically false ;   and *must have been known to be* false by their writer if he possessed even an elementary grasp of Marx's dialectic.

Far from saying that men's consciousness and will play no part in producing the development of history, Marx's conception of history affirms categorically the opposite.   It is the *only* theory of history yet propounded which *simultaneously* allows for the activity of the human will and also for the conditions within which and by means of which that " will " operates to produce such results as are achieved.

One affirmation of Eastman's is sufficient to expose the shallow trickery involved in his malevolent burlesque of Marxism.   Marx asserts (in the statement of his conception of history, quoted above from the *Critique*, p. 303) that in their social life-activity men enter into certain necessary and definite relations with each other which are " independent of their wills."   The statement is axiomatic.   That men to produce at all must do so in definite social and material circumstances, at a particular time and in a particular place, and in an historically conditioned co-operation with certain other men and women—these facts, which constitute a plexus of " social relations "—obviously do not owe their existence to the " will " of the men born into them as a going concern, and do determine each man's prospects in life, the occupation he will follow, and the further relations into which he will enter.   Choose as he will between all the practically available alternatives, the fact remains that the range of his choice is limited by what exists " independently " of his will. At the same time his *need to choose* also arises from his physical constitution, which, *at his birth* at any rate, is " independent of his will."   And what is true of every individual is still more true of *all* individuals looked at in their collective interactions. That which is basic and forms the starting point is the physical constitution from which the *needs* of Man arise on the one side, and the constitution of Nature on the other. Together they make Man's *productive interrelation with Nature* a basic and inexorable *necessity*. But, however much this *necessity* may be imposed upon man " independently of his will," the fact remains self-evident that in *production* men do, and *must, use their wills*.

How does Eastman present these facts ? Quite simply. He asserts that Marx's conception was that " an *ordered* development " arose, which *development* was " *wholly* " independent of men's " consciousness " and " wills." One sentence from Marx shatters the whole of this impudent fabrication : " *Men produce their circumstances as much as circumstances produce the men* " (MARX-ENGELS : *German Ideology*). The classic phrase " Philosophers have only interpreted the world in various ways : the point however is to change it," blows the scattered ruins of the Eastman-Postgate into sub-atomic dust.

. . . . .

Postgate and Eastman both adopt an *a priori* psychological theory to " account for " Marx and for the popularity of the Dialectic with men like Lenin ; who, in particular, was *of course* (!) far more easily duped than are such practical men of affairs as Max Eastman and Raymond Postgate ! This theory is, as we have seen, the James-Dewey Pragmatist one that the dialectic may be " useful " even though it is *not true*.

Postgate does not explain what this means : Eastman does. It means just what Gibbon meant when he said of the mob of religions assembled in imperial Rome that " to the common people they were all equally true, to the philosopher they were all equally false, and to the magistrate they were all equally *convenient* " !

Men can accept false beliefs as true only so long as and so far as they do not attempt to test them in practice. A delusion widely spread is " useful " not to those deluded, but to those who are *not* deluded—to the cunning rogues who are able to practise upon popular delusions to their own special advantage.

Max Eastman seriously makes this into his theory of revolution. He argues (implicitly and explicitly) that, since the mass and majority of workers can never be anything but deluded, they *must be encouraged to cherish such delusions as will best enable them to be used by Great Geniuses of " Revolutionary Engineering."*

That this should be advanced as a " scientific explanation " of Lenin's successful leadership is nothing less than an insult when done in the name of revolutionary Socialism. That it should be endorsed (tacitly) by Postgate, and the work which propounds it recommended by him to the rank and file of the Socialist movement as the " only " work to expound Marxism in " a modern and scientific " manner, is trebly a scandal.

Eastman actually has the effrontery to claim the endorsement of Marx himself for his malevolently reactionary balderdash !

He gives as a " *quotation* " from Marx the following (from the *Theses on Feuerbach*) :

> " The materialist teaching that men are a product of environment and education—changed men therefore, the product of other environment and changed education—forgets that the environment is changed by men, and that the educator himself has to be educated."

So far Eastman's version does not differ materially from that given in Chapter I of this work (see *ante*, p. 30) ; but lo ! a sudden twist ! Eastman's version goes on :

> " It *becomes necessary* therefore to *divide society into two parts*, of which the one is *elevated above society*."—
> EASTMAN : *ibid.*, p. 125.

It is almost incredible, but there it is ! The very fallacy which Marx pointed out as the *logical dilemma* of mechanical materialist " determinism "—a choice of fatalism or the Great Man Theory—this very antithesis Max Eastman fastens upon and, by the aid of a mistranslation, advances as Marx's endorsement of his reactionary folly of a Great Man fatalism made while you wait !

Here is Eastman's elaboration of the point :

> " If this ' division of society ' had been kept in mind by Marx and Engels, and *made as much of* as the division of society into proletariat and bourgeoisie, scientific socialism would have a very different aspect from what it has. Instead of being described as " a union of science with the proletariat " it would be described as a union of scientists, or of *scientific idealists*—who may or may not be of proletarian origin—with the proletariat. Such a description . . . will be true . . . when socialism really becomes a science. . . .

" In order to teach the science of revolution . . . one should *begin*, it seems to me, with *an outline of the idea of a true society* ' as it has been developed by the *great Utopians from Plato to Kropotkin.*"—EASTMAN : *ibid.*, p. 125.

And it is this metaphysical, *a priori*, and fundamentally *fascist* conception—one which relegates the proletarian mass to the status of " boobs," " mutts," " poor fish " and general " Jimmy Higginses " to Great men " elevated above Society," the Eastmanite " Engineers of Revolution " !—it is this which Raymond Postgate, " Marxist," recommends to all and sundry as " the *only* . . . *modern* and *intelligent* manner " of interpreting Marxism.

And, lest there be any doubt, here is Eastman's description of what Lenin did, and how he did it :

" Lenin corrected the error of Marx, which was a mystic faith in the proletariat as such ; and he corrected the error of Blanqui, which was to trust all to the organisation of revolutionists. He saw that the organisation of revolutionists must be actually rooted in and welded together with the proletariat . . . so that they *not only assume* (! ! !) to represent the proletariat, but also, *when* a revolutionary period *arrives* (! ! !), actually do *represent* it. But he saw also that *they* must be *a distinct body of men who* ' *stand above society*,' and are *thus* able to understand it. And his arrant insistence upon centralised authority and military discipline in that body of men *smacks more of the tactics of Blanqui* than of the philosophy of Marx."—EASTMAN : *Marx, Lenin*, etc., pp. 144–5.

The arrogance of this is equal to its blatancy, and its blatancy to its offensive ignorance. To " understand " society one must stand *above* society ! If Eastman had been a Hegelian this might have been intelligible as an antithesis. But as Eastman repudiates Hegel with scorn and loathing it can only mean that Eastman out of the fullness of his contempt for the proletariat has " pinched " Nietzsche's notion of the Superman and " adapted " it.

.   .   .   .   .   .

Raymond Postgate does not follow in detail Max Eastman's neo-Nietzscheian-Freudian Great-Man theory of " revolutionary engineering." In fact, from internal evidence we must conclude that Postgate was too delighted with those parts of

Eastman's book which "jumped with his humour" (the disparagement of Marx generally, the accusation of "economic determinism," the repudiation of the dialectic) to be able to grasp its thesis as a whole.

But this doesn't prevent him from following Eastman blindly into an assault upon the Marxian *law of capitalist accumulation*.

Taking Eastman's word for it that Marx's method of *analysis* consisted simply in a mechanical application of the ready-made Hegelian formula : thesis, antithesis, synthesis (as grotesquely false an assertion as was ever made), Postgate follows Eastman into the illiterate attack upon a passage in the Marx-Engels *Holy Family* we have dealt with in an earlier chapter. Postgate also follows Eastman blindly into affirming that a celebrated passage in the chapter on the Historical Tendency of Capitalist Accumulation, in Vol. I of *Capital*, is likewise Hegelian, and *in the same way*, i.e., is a presentation *not* of a summary of the observed and critically analysed *historical process itself*, but (as was the passage in the *Holy Family*) an analysis of the dialectic implicit in the relations of *bourgeois property* considered *as such*. We must concede that, since grasping this distinction involves a fair measure of honest *brainwork*, it is perhaps unfair to expect intellectuals such as Eastman and his pupil Postgate to be able to achieve the feat. None the less we must affirm, for their admonition if not their instruction, that the logic implicit in a *social institution* (i.e., bourgeois property) considered *in situ*, as "given," and that explicit in its historical *becoming*, the origin and ending of that institution, is as different as is considering a house from the point of view of its desirability as a *dwelling*, and from the point of view of its artistic function in a landscape.

Here is, however, the passage from *Capital* upon which both Postgate and Eastman animadvert (Postgate, by the way, quotes not directly from the translation authorised by Engels, but from the extract from that translation made by Max Beer ! Why ? Is the authorised translation as inaccessible as all that ? Eastman makes his own translation— and a sorry mess it is !) :

> "The capitalist mode of appropriation, the result of the capitalist mode of production, produces capitalist private property. This is the first negation of individual private property as founded upon the labour of the proprietor.

" But capitalist production begets, with the inexorability of a law of Nature, its own negation. It is the negation of negation. This does not re-establish private-property for the producer, but gives him individual property based on the acquisition of the capitalist era : i.e., on co-operation and the possession in common of the land, and of the means of production."—MARX : *Capital*, Vol. I, p. 789.

Here is Postgate's comment :

" This is less surprising than the crude form given in the *Holy Family* [see *ante*, p. 152]. At least the categories are not mixed. All of them are forms of property relationship and so can be compared with each other. But in shifting the figures in the pattern the pattern has been changed. The proletariat is no longer the antithesis ; it has disappeared. *Instead Capitalism is the antithesis* to private property, and the synthesis has the unexpected shape of a synthesis of private property and *capitalism.* . . .—POSTGATE : *ibid.*, p. 86.

The assertion we have italicised is simply *false.* The antithesis to *individual* self-earned private property is *capitalist* property, the result of the exploitation not of Nature, but of Men. If Raymond Postgate has not yet learned the elementary Marxist conception that " to be a capitalist is to have not only a purely personal but a *social* status in production " (*Com. Manifesto* : see also *Wage-Labour and Capital, Poverty of Philosophy*, etc.), it is nothing less than an imposition for him to set up as an exponent *and critic* of Marx.

In the passage he criticises the *historical* sequence is not postulated by Marx *a priori.* It is taken from the actual facts in their historical order of succession and interconnection. Postgate dare not attempt to deny that the *self-earned* " property " of the small producer, the artisan-craftsman, the merchant-adventurer, the shopkeeper, etc., has been, is being and will continue to be *destroyed* hourly by the development of *capitalist property*, particularly in its modern developed form, that of *Finance Capital.* His own personal " property " as a writer is, for instance, *hourly* at the mercy of the currency manipulations of the Kings of Finance, and all the more so since that " debasing and defiling " of the currency for which men were *pressed to death* with public approval in the Middle Ages has become the world-wisdom in which the Old Lady of Threadneedle Street vies with the Federal Reserve Bank in Washington and—*Major Douglas* ! That capitalist *property* does negate " private " property based on the labour of the *individual* is a fact of universal notoriety.

Postgate cannot deny it, although he gives a half-hearted approval to Bernstein's attempt to prove that the process had begun to return upon itself ! (" Marx's prophecy has been *partly falsified.*"—POSTGATE, p. 79.) What therefore he follows Eastman in attempting to do is to imply that Marx's deduction from those facts is invalid ! Postgate's logical position is weaker here than Eastman's, since Eastman, who is an " instrumentalist-idealist " (and therefore an empirical-eclectic-solipsist !), *denies point blank that any science of history is possible* :

> " History is no one thing *or process*, except as it is made so by the interests of the historian ; it has *no cause* either within or without the consciousness of men, which explains it all."—EASTMAN : *ibid.*, p. 50.

Postgate wants to be a " Marxist," but he suffers all the time from the incurable Bloomsbury itch to switch the spotlight off " Old Man " Marx on to himself ! Hence he helps Eastman to shy his bricks, all unconscious of the fact that they all miss Marx and smash into his own cucumber frames !

What is the deduction that Marx makes ? In the chapter in question (which is the last but one in the volume) Marx summarises the whole process, whose general nature he has analysed in all its relations. He concludes that the development of the *forces* of capitalist production will, sooner or later, reach a point at which these forces *can no longer be used in a capitalist way.* He answers the implied question : what will follow from this ! Obviously a conflict in which every partial victory of the defenders of capitalist property only ensures a fresh battle with larger forces arrayed against it, a process which, ultimately, can have only one end, the defeat of the bourgeoisie and the destruction of " property " in its capitalist from. Thus the nature of capitalist property ensures its destruction by forces it itself engenders. The outcome lies on the face of the facts—*men will save production, and human society with it, by destroying the capitalist property limitations which have brought production to a deadlock* ! And if that be done what will society possess as its means of existence ? An accumulation of means and forces of production which, since they have ceased to be *private* property, have now become (there is no other alternative) *public* or *social* property. But this will make every man a

" proprietor " ? Exactly ! *Possession*, as a *fact*, will be restored. In the means of *production* this possession will be collective, *social* ; in the means of *consumption* it will, to an extent, be *individual*. In a Communist order " based upon the acquisitions of the capitalist era " the average actual possessions in means of consumption will, in fact, be far greater for the *individuals* composing that communist society than they have ever been for the average individual in any previous epoch in history.

Does Postgate see this, the obvious, meaning of the passage he has quoted ? All he can see is, by means of a bungling and irrational misreading [" Capital*ism* " (a *form* of society itself) for " Capitalist *property* " (a *relation* within society)], a chance to follow Eastman into asserting of Marx the logical inconsequentiality and incapacity which is his own.

Eastman, with the same passage before him, rather than surrender to its invincible logic—*deliberately jumbles up his translation to make the conclusion absurd.* Compare with the (authorised by Engels) translation above the following Eastman version :

> " This does not reinstate private property, but just individual *ownership* on the basis of the achievements of the capitalist era : co-operation and the common possession of the earth and the means of production which are themselves produced by labour."—Eastman, p. 102.

Eastman and his pupil Postgate may take their choice. If this is honestly the best Eastman can do in the way of translation, of what worth is his opinion of Marx and Marxism —a world-conception involving a grasp of a whole series of related problems in the objective development of Nature, of Human Society and its historical development, and of the theoretical and practical formulation and handling of those problems in their epistemological and logical forms ? That Marxism requires *knowledge* and *study* for its comprehension is self-evident. Every scientific conception does. That that study can only *begin* with the doctrine as formulated by Marx and Engels goes, likewise, without saying. Max Eastman, *from the fact of making his own translations, professes to know his Marx at first hand.* Since we have now detected him in two gross and undeniable falsifications of Marx's text, he must stand branded with one of two brands : either he is a *shallow-pated pretender* when he affirms that he has studied Marx himself ; or, knowing Marx's plain meaning, he has chosen deliberately to falsify it for malicious ends, in which case he is not only a *liar and a pretender*, but something difficult to describe in other than workshop language.

Postgate had the wit to see there was something wrong with Eastman's translation ; but he was not acute enough to see that *Eastman's conclusion required the false translation and was refuted by the correct one.*

It is in fact in this very chapter of Marx's *Capital*, and on this very page, and in this passage itself—*read in its proper context*—that Postgate can find the " proof " he and Eastman profess to be seeking of the "inevitability" of proletarian victory.

Postgate asserts (not having troubled to refer to *Capital* itself !) that from this passage " the proletariat has disappeared." If he really knew what he was talking about he would know offhand that the proletariat is *presupposed in capitalist property*, since the existence of a proletariat is one of the prime presuppositions of that property form. If he had troubled to look at *Capital* itself he would have found the proletariat *all over the page* :—

> " Along with the constantly diminishing number of the *magnates of capital* [will Postgate, and others, note that Marx does *not* say ' *of the capitalists* '] . . . grows *the revolt of the working class*, a class always increasing in numbers and disciplined by the very mechanism of the process of capitalist production itself. . . .
>
> " *The expropriators are expropriated.* . . ."
>
> " In the former case [i.e., rise of capitalism] we had the expropriation of the mass of the people by a few usurpers ; in the latter . . . the expropriation of a few usurpers *by the mass of the people*."—Marx : *Capital*, Vol. I, pp. 788–9.

And as a footnote to the last sentence just quoted Marx gives this :

> " The advance of industry, whose involuntary promoter is the bourgeoisie, replaces the isolation of the labourers due to competition by their revolutionary combination, due to association. The development of Modern Industry, therefore, cuts from under its feet the very foundation on which the bourgeoisie produces and appropriates products. What the bourgeoisie therefore produces, above all, are its own gravediggers. *Its fall and the victory of the proletariat are equally inevitable.*"—Marx-Engels : *Communist Manifesto*, p. 20.

Not only do these passages (all we can spare space for from

a chapter which must be read *as a whole* to be appreciated) prove Postgate's assertions to be stupid falsifications born of ignorance, and Eastman's assertions to be flagrant falsifications born of intentional malice, they shatter utterly the stupid myth that Marx ever predicted the " inevitability " of proletarian triumph in a *metaphysically absolute sense*.

The " fall " of the bourgeoisie is *historically* " *inevitable* "— not only because we may infer, *a priori*, that whatever has a *beginning* must sooner or later have an *end* ; but because the nature, mode and *direction* of its historical development is such as to exclude, *a posteriori*, all possible alternatives to its " fall." Its own system of production, which it cannot alter in fundamentals without committing suicide as a class, creates, develops, and ripens to explosion point the forces which will overthrow it. " Above all " it creates " its own grave-diggers." That is a deduction *from the facts*, and not from any preconceived notion.

Postgate implicitly, Eastman avowedly, *believes* the bourgeois system of production not only *capable of indefinite prolongation*, but (in Eastman's case) supposes bourgeois production—in its historically obsolete form of petty-bourgeois production—as the permanent basis for the society which will be built in future by the Eastmanite " scientific engineers of revolution." That is why Eastman, scorning the Marxian analysis of the objective historical development-process of society itself, proposes to *begin* with the construction of the " plan of an *ideal* society " to be derived from the study of the " great Utopians from Plato to Kropotkin " !—all of whom built their schemes on the postulate of *petty production*, in Plato's case *by slave-labour* !

Thus the *ultra*-" modernist " attack upon Marx and Marxism, which opened to the tune of " *it must be out of date* ! " ends to the tune of : " Back to petty-production, Plato, and slave-labour ! "

Once again the ultra-" modernist " assault upon Marx *ends on the plane of Hitlerite demagogy!* That this should have been achieved by a *free-lance pioneer of Trotskyism* is significant in the highest degree. That it should be applauded (even in ignorance) by Raymond Postgate from the standpoint of " British," *pro*-Social-Democratic, *anti*-Communist " Marxism " is, in its way, even more significant still !

Let us examine the *inevitability* of the victory of the proletariat from yet another angle.

In what sense does Marx use the term " inevitable." Quite obviously he does not (only a fool would suppose he did) use it in the fatalistic " Day of Judgment " sense. If any man says that it is *inevitable* that the sun will " rise " to-morrow, it is, of course, open to Postgate (or a Jesuit) to argue that the sun or the earth might have exploded before then, or that, for reasons not now operative, the earth may have gone off careering through the Universe ! Excluding fanciful suppositions and presupposing only the continuance of the natural processes now in actual operation, we may, *on that presupposition*, affirm unquestionably that the sun *will inevitably* " rise " to-morrow.

Marx's prediction of *inevitable victory* for the struggling proletariat had likewise its basis in verified facts—in the class struggle, its historical causation and its developing consequences. In its historically conditioned struggle with the bourgeoisie the proletariat acquires not only an " ever-expanding union " but also " *organisation into a class, and, consequently, into a political party.*" (MARX ENGELS : *Com. Man.*) This Party—the militant vanguard of the class is, in turn, *developed* theoretically and practically, in the course of struggles which bring an ever-increasing mass of the exploited into organised solidarity under its leadership. Thus the developing circumstances which spread a growing demoralisation in the camp of the bourgeoisie, improve its organisation and heightens the *morale* of the militant vanguard of the proletariat until it becomes a mass-backed *Communist Party*, steeled and tempered by struggle into an invincible instrument of Revolution. The same historical process which converts the optimistic faith in the future, once universal, in the bourgeois camp into its opposite—into desperate jingoisms, irrational egoism, anti-libertanianism, and general pessimism—transforms likewise the proletariat from a disunited mob of dependant individuals into a self-confident and united army led by a Party which " moves like one man " because it *thinks* and *feels* in a historically engendered unison. Thus Capitalism begets not only the *occasion* but the *instrument* for its own overthrow. Thus it is that the victory of the proletariat *becomes* " inevitable."

Neither in *Capital* nor in the *Communist Manifesto*, nor anywhere, does Marx or Engels or Lenin *ever even suggest* that this inevitability arises, except on the presupposition of this basic two-fold historical development : (1) of capitalist production ; (2) of the proletarian struggle. Nowhere do they suggest that the proletariat would be victorious *at* its *first effort*. On the contrary, *always* they insist that the victory will come only in consequence of *prolonged* struggles.

We have given evidence of this in earlier chapters almost *ad nauseum*. Still, in the hope that Raymond Postgate (and his friends) are still teachable, here are three relevant passages :

" Will it be possible to abolish private property at one blow ?

" No ! Such a thing would be just as impossible as at one blow to multiply the extant forces of production to the degree necessary for the inauguration of communal ownership in the means of production. For this reason the proletarian revolution, which undoubtedly will break out sooner or later, will only be able gradually to transform extant society.

" What is likely to be the course of this revolution ?

" In the first place there will be a *democratic constitution* drawn up, implying directly or indirectly the political rule of the proletariat. *In England,* for instance, where the proletariat is in a majority, *the rule of the proletariat will be direct.* [In countries with a predominance of petty-production and peasantry the rule of the proletariat will be *indirect.*]

" Perhaps this will entail a second fight, but it will inevitably result in the victory of the proletariat."— ENGELS : *Principles of Communism* (1847).

That is taken from the catechism drafted by Engels for the Communist League, which was replaced, with Engels' enthusiastic approval, by Marx's draft of the *Communist Manifesto*. Even in those days of revolutionary optimism the " inevitability " of the revolution is conceived as the positive outcome of an historical *process of struggle.* So here :—

" An oppressed class is the vital condition of every society based upon the antagonism of classes. The *emancipation* of the oppressed class therefore necessarily *implies* the creation of a new society. . . .

" The working class will *in the course of its development* substitute for the old order of civil society an association which will exclude classes and their antagonism. . . .

" In the meantime the antagonism between the proletariat and the bourgeoisie is a struggle between class and class which, *carried to its highest expression,* is a complete revolution. Would it be a matter for astonishment if a society, based upon the *antagonism* of classes, should, in addition, lead *ultimately* to a brutal *conflict*, to a hand to hand struggle, as its final *dénouement* ? . . .

" It is only in an order of things in which classes and class-antagonisms exist no longer that *social evolutions* will cease to be *political revolutions*."—MARX : *Poverty of Philosophy* (1846–47).

Again the citation is from an early work of the period of " youthful optimism." Again the revolution is envisaged as a prolonged process. Again it arises as a natural development of the class antagonism and struggle within society. What is more, the development is envisaged as going on after the revolution, after even the attainment of the classless society of the future ! Only wilful blindness through partisan spite or the invincible ignorance of bourgeois pedantry can class such a view as " fatalist."

Here is, however, an extract from a later work by Marx than *Capital*. It is from the Manifesto written by Marx for the International Working Men's Association on the occasion of the fall of the Paris Commune of 1871. Postgate ought to be familiar with it, because *he once edited a reprint of it* (from which, *of course*, he eliminated Engels' preface !) :

" The working men did not expect miracles from the Commune. They have no ready-made Utopias to introduce *par decret du peuple*. They know that in order to work out their own emancipation, and along with it that higher form to which present society is irresistibly tending, by its own economical agencies, *they will have to pass through long struggles, through a series of historic processes, transforming circumstances and men*. They have no ideas to realise but to set free the elements of the new society with which old collapsing bourgeois society itself is pregnant. In the full consciousness of their historic mission, and with the resolve to act up to it, the working class can afford to smile at the coarse invective of the gentleman's gentleman with pen and inkhorn, and at the didactic patronage of well-wishing bourgeois doctrinaires pouring forth their ignorant platitudes and sectarian crochets in the oracular tone of scientific infallibility."— MARX : *Civil War in France*, pp. 44–45.

The conclusion of this passage seems almost as though Marx had been gifted with *second sight* ! For comparison with Marx and Engels here is a passage from Lenin :

" The fundamental Law of Revolution—confirmed by

all revolutions, and particularly by all three Russian revolutions of the twentieth century—is as follows : It is not sufficient for the revolution that the exploited and oppressed masses *understand* the impossibility of living in the old way and *demand* changes. For the revolution it is necessary that the exploiters should *not be able* to live and rule as of old. Only when the masses *do not want* the old regime, and when the rulers *are unable* to govern as of old, then only can the revolution succeed."
—LENIN : *Left-Wing Communism* (1920).

Here likewise the presuppositions on the basis of which the *inevitability* of the proletarian revolution (and that on a world scale) is predicated are perfectly clear. They are in no sense of the word either arbitrary, *a priori*, dogmatic, mystical, or fatalist.

That which is premised is the *developing* interaction of men and circumstances in their specific, historically conditioned forms of, on the one side—a *proletarian mass* united and progressively transformed, individually, and still more collectively, in the revolutionary mass struggle which has equipped them with an adequate revolutionary leadership ; and on the other side—the *circumstance* of a crisis-racked, chaos-discredited, and by-internal-contradiction-transformed capitalist society.

Given that combination of men and circumstances and the result is—*scientifically inevitable*.

It is nothing less than a lie to say that this conception is fatalist. Fatalism says that, *despite* all that men do or do not do, the result is foredoomed. The Dialectical Materialist conception affirms that the result will follow *because of what Men are doing and will continue to do*. Marx's prediction of the " inevitable " victory of the proletariat is, it is true, " based on the dialectic "—not, however, on the purely *subjective* dialectic of the Postgate-Eastman imagination, but on the verifiable *objective* dialectic of Nature and History.

The Postgate-Eastman school says : Marx only *believed* a proletarian revolution was inevitable because he *wanted* it to be.

May we not reply to them : Very well, gentlemen ; may we take it that you do *not* believe it to be inevitable—*because you simply loathe the idea of its being really inevitable* ?

The Materialist Conception of Knowledge

Eastman's attack upon the Marxian Theoretical System is not only an attack upon its *dialectic*. It is an attack upon its Materialism. Postgate falls into the tactical error of trying to explain what he dislikes about the Dialectic. He wants to keep the " historical materialism " and, with reservations, the Marxian Economics. He does not see that, once their object-ive dialectical *movements* are abstracted, the processes of history and economics cease to be conceivable materialistically. With their *movement* gone they become lifeless and dead : history an unintelligibly arbitrary panorama of abstract sequences and successions ; economics a welter of contra-dictory metaphysical categories. As we have demonstrated above, the Dialectic of Thought is valid precisely because it has a material origin in the objective world of material practice, because it is in itself a subjective practice which *reflects* in its content and formal *movement* the corresponding movements in objective reality ; and, above all, because it is able to survive the acid test of objective *practice*.

It is this, probably, which rouses the resentment of all the literary josserini—all the *lumpen* intelligentsia who spend their days either in posing as more Marxist than Marx, more Leninist than Lenin, and more proletarian than the prole-tariat ; or, alternatively, in *nattering* at all three in the name of whatever-it-is which is the " Very Latest " ! Dialectical Materialism—the materialism of Marx, Engels, Lenin and Stalin—reduces thinking both in theory and in practice to brain-*work* ! The very mention of " work " is enough to scare out of its wits every coterie from Bloomsbury to Greenwich Village (and back again !). Beyond question, this is what has upset Max Eastman—who doesn't *discuss* the dialectic so much as spit every time its name is mentioned.

Be that as it may, the concrete fact from which we may begin is the fact that, on the admission of both Postgate and Eastman, Lenin (as well as Marx) *thought* he was using the Materialist Dialectic (*a*) when he built the Bolshevik Party ; (*b*) when he steered it through a whole series of struggles, practical and theoretical—against " petty bourgeois revolu-tionism " and " petty bourgeois degeneracy and oppor-tunism " ; and (*c*) when in the end he led the Party to the consummation of the victory of November, 1917, and to a successful outcome of the interventionist and civil wars which followed. Through all this Lenin " believed " himself to be using as his theoretical instrument the Dialectical Materialism of Marx and Engels.

The question now is : Was Lenin *deluded* therein ? Or did the success of his practice prove the *soundness of his* theory—his " belief " ?

Max Eastman is in a cleft stick. If he admits that Lenin's objective practical success proved the theoretical validity of his *brain-work,* his thinking, he must surrender to the logical implication of that admission. He must admit that Lenin (to say nothing of Marx, Engels, and the whole development of the Marxist movement) put Dialectical Materialism to the acid test of practice, and in so doing vindicated it past all possibility of cavil. To escape from this he must deny *absolutely* any necessary connection between Theory and Practice. And this, in fact, is exactly what he does !

He denies, as we have seen, that Marx did *think* either Dialectically or Materialistically—or, at least, ever *both* at the same time ! He contends, in fact and literally, that *all ideas are necessarily delusive* ! Thus for him any logical system—any developed series of related ideas—i.e., any *ideology,* is *ipso facto* a delusion and a snare. On the strength of this he " corrects " Engels ! In his *Ludwig Feuerbach,* Engels, discussing the development of religious theories, which he traces to their roots in a misinterpretation of the relations between Man and Reality, says :

" That the material life-conditions of the men in whose heads the thinking process goes on, determine, ultimately the course of this process, remains, necessarily, unknown to them. Otherwise the whole ideology would be at an end.—ENGELS : *Feuerbach,* Chap. IV.

Eastman quotes this, and then passes judgment, thus :

" It seems a very slight(! ! !) and obvious (! ! !) correction (! ! !) to say *material interests* here, instead of material conditions of life, but it is all the difference between science and mystical metaphysics (!) "—EAST-MAN : *ibid.,* p. 85.

A *slight* and *obvious* " correction " ! *Only* the difference between the objective *material* facts, and the *subjective,* individual, *valuation* of *some of* the facts ! *Only* that ! But " it seems obvious " that the man who by this " correction " prefers the subjective standpoint to the objective one, and some of the facts to their objective totality, and does so in the name of " science "—knows nothing whatever of science, facts, or the art of *telling the truth.* And, indeed, Eastman cannot complain of our saying so, because on his theory there is *no such thing as truth*! Not *really*! Men "make up" the "truth" for themselves as they go along!

Here is his view of the matter, or rather, here is the artistically embroidered "cod-piece" by which he conceals, while indicating, the indecency of his "theory of cognition":

> "The real inference to be drawn from the fact that our thoughts do not give us 'an exact representation of the universe,' is that we should cease putting up the pretence that they do. We should frankly acknowledge the *instrumental* character of all concepts, and face the fact that whatever generality and durability certain ones *may* attain, the only thing they can ultimately be relied upon to do is to solve special problems. . . . Not only is there no such thing as dialectic thinking, but there is no such super-intellectual knowledge of the "exact nature of the universe" as that to which an alleged dialectic thinking pretends to give access. . . .—EAST-MAN : *ibid.*, p. 111.

The last clause of this extract is not merely a piece of Eastman's impudence : it is an affirmation of his standpoint, and requires careful scrutiny.

What is "*super*-intellectual knowledge?" Dialectical Materialism claims that *real* knowledge is *attainable* by man ; that it is *real*, and *valid*, because it is *knowledge* of an objectively existing *material reality*, which is external to, and exists independently of man's consciousness or knowledge of it. Dialectical Materialism does not pretend that this knowledge when attained is more than *human* knowledge. "Knowledge,"—being in fact nothing other than consciousness of the *relations* between men as actively, *living* beings, and objectively *real*, material things, and their active interactions in turn,—can as little be *super*-human as corns and bunions can grow without feet to grow upon. At the same time, unless the things and active inter-relations, of which we became conscious, do in fact exist independently of our awareness of their existence, unless, that is to say, they are objectively "super-intellectual" as Eastman terms it, that which we regard as "knowledge" would be no such thing. It would be a mere mirage of "fictional presentations," a phantasmagoria of baseless *beliefs*.

Now, observe! Eastman does not merely deny the adequacy of Dialectical Materialism to reach a knowledge of the *exact nature of the universe*. He calls *real* knowledge

" super-intellectual " knowledge ! That is to say, he affirms that the only knowledge possible to man is *subjective knowledge*, knowledge of the " intellect " and its processes. That is to say, *Eastman denies the possibility, even, of any sort, kind, or description of knowledge of the objective, material world and of its attainment by any method whatsoever* ! Eastman affirms :

> " There is a value—not in dialectic thinking, for that does not exist—but in *believing that you think dialectically* [Eastman's italics]. . . . Believing in dialectic thinking is a method by which having made false intellectual assumptions about the nature of thought, you can escape from them, and win back your freedom to use thought as it was meant to be used."—EASTMAN : *ibid.*, p. 113.

And by whom was " thought " *meant to be used* in any particular way ? The only possible answer is " God ! " And that answer is in keeping with the whole passage which says nothing less than that, all thinking being *delusory*, one delusion can be used to negate another delusion and so produce the " illusion " that you " know " something (while, of course, all the time you don't !) That is to say, Eastman believes not in knowledge but in *belief* !

In his Appendix Eastman " goes the whole hog." He quotes the following as representative of his epistemological standpoint :

> " The object of the world of ideas as a whole is *not* the portrayal of *reality—this would be an impossible task* —but rather to provide us with an *instrument* for finding our way about the world more easily."—VAIHINGER : *Philosophy of " As If "* (quoted with approval by Eastman, p. 220).

Vaihinger's work was published in Germany in 1877. He was the leader of a school of avowed solipsist idealists, who returned via neo-Kantianism to a position barely distinguishable from that of Berkeley. Max Eastman is so philosophically illiterate as to seek to palm off this retreat into the sophistication and mystagogy of subjectivism, fictionalism, instrumentalism, pragmatism, empirio-scepticism (or by whatever other name he chooses to disguise his *irrationalist* anti-materialism) as a *scientific advance* !

And Postgate, sometime scholar of St. John's, Oxford— born in Cambridge, the son of a Don, educated and graduated at Oxford until he himself nearly became a Don likewise— this Raymond Postgate is so eager to be *up to date*, and so childlike in his eagerness, that he lets himself be led by the

nose back to George Berkeley and *the standpoint of* 1710 !
The "Very Latest"—in very deed ! Postgate scorns the
"mid-Victorian" Philosopher, and—deserts him for a
philosopher dating from the time when Queen Anne wasn't
even *dead* !

Postgate, it is true, does not go *consciously* all the way
back to Berkeley. But he has gone sufficiently far upon that
road with Eastman to be quite unashamed in his eclecticism.
We have seen above that Eastman denies the existence, or
possibility, of any *objective* historical process of social development ("revolutionary *engineering*," *à la* Eastman, is only
conceivable if human society is capable of being built up,
pulled down and altered in *this* way, *that* way, and *any* way
the mere *impulse* of the "revolutionary engineer" may
chance to direct !).

Postgate holds substantially the same conception of
history—without drawing, as Eastman does, the logical
counter-revolutionary conclusion :

> "it is not possible to say that history proceeds dialecti-
> cally *because* history, being an enormous mass of facts,
> is not a material which is capable of being so classified.
> *History* [Postgate says "in the sense in which Marx
> uses it "—but that is a bland tergiversation] . . . *is not
> the whole mass of past facts . . . but an excerpt from those
> facts made by the historian*."—POSTGATE : *Karl Marx*,
> p. 88.

This is, no doubt, what *the word* "history" means to an
Oxford Don or a Cambridge professor. It is this very thing
which makes these learned pundits so damnably exasperating
despite their gentlemanly futility, and their complacent
assurance that their work is perfectly useless and therefore
"disinterested." They are useful in spite of and not because
of themselves. History is no more a large heap of facts,
selected or otherwise, than a large heap of sawdust is a baulk
of timber. No science is a *mere* aggregation of facts. Still less
is it an arbitrary "*excerpt* from " the facts. History as a
science is a conception of *all* the facts ascertained *in the
totality* of their interactions, and, *therefore*, of the *movement*
resulting from that *total* of determining components. It is
because a science grasps the facts in their *active connections*,
and in their resultant *movement*, that it is possible for a science
to *grow*. Further and further reaches of *facts* as discovered
are traced by the analysis of their perceived movements into
their component interacting causes. Wider and wider

unifications of scientific knowledge are secured by the tracing out of the *connecting* action-reaction relations which in fact, and objectively, combine the facts surveyed by each of the sciences into the really-existent, objective Universe of Material Reality. The Postgate view—that " knowledge " in history, as in other sciences, is an *excerpt* from the facts—is, being an eclectic, passive *spectator* conception of knowledge, only a half-hearted camouflage for the solipsism which Eastman avows shamelessly. Eastman has the hardihood of his anti-materialist retreat to irrationalism—Postgate has the irrationalism without the hardihood !

This fact has a practical bearing of far-reaching importance. Postgate and Eastman are in the main stream of Social-Democratic tradition in one important respect. They suppose, as the vulgarised " Marxism " palmed-off as a substitute for the genuine article always supposed, that Marx and Engels held the view that the proletariat would attain to socialist or communist theory *automatically*.

We have given abundant evidence to the exactly contrary effect. The Dialectical Materialist conception of the Unity of Theory and Practice *excludes* at the very outset any possibility of any kind of conceptions being reached *automatically*. The development of conceptions from perceptions is achieved by *action*, by *practice*—the subjective as well as objective practice of objectively existing human beings in an objectively material world. No conception is *ever* reached, or can be reached (on a Dialectical Materialist view), except by *effort*, by activity, conscious or unconscious, as the case may be.

Marx and Engels contend that the *objective* nature of bourgeois society provides the material basis from which socialist and communist conclusions may be drawn, and that, if these material facts are viewed clearly, in the totality of their objective interactions, socialist and communist conclusions are the only *logical* ones which comprise all the facts in the totality of their objective interactions. Now it is true, as Marx and Engels insisted, that the practical, every-day participation of the proletariat in the actual *co-operative* work-process of capitalist production does give them a fuller and a more direct acquaintance with this *dynamic essence* of bourgeois society from which socialist and communist conclusions *can* be and are drawn than is given in the practical life-activity of any other class. And it is true, too, that their practical co-operation in struggles against the effects of capitalism does *prepare* them more thoroughly than any class for drawing the conclusion that the bourgeois order *can* be changed into a socialist and communist order of society by the revolutionary mass-action of the proletariat. But this practical experience does not *force* them of itself to *draw that conclusion*. On the contrary, the very *sectional* nature of their practical struggles and the very piecemeal view they are forced in practical life to take of their personal part in the production process, hinders them from drawing the revolutionary conclusion to which the facts with which they are familiar point *in their totality*. That is why the proletariat needs the aid of a revolutionary theory and revolutionary theoreticians before it is able to draw the logical revolutionary conclusions from the revolutionary facts which it handles—is indeed a *part of*—in everyday life.

The revolutionary theoretician becomes such as a consequence of placing himself theoretically at the standpoint the proletariat *as a whole* occupies in actual practice. The trained intellectual, if he is really " up to his job," can perceive and formluate in logically coherent concepts the *connections* between the facts and interactions which the proletariat deals with in its practical everyday life. Thus it is that the intellectual, provided he has the requisite skill at his speciality, *brainwork,* can and (when he has the capacity of a Marx, an Engels, a Lenin, or a Stalin) *does* bring to the proletarian struggle that theoretical comprehension of the struggle as a whole, its origin, development, and logical end, which is indispensable if that struggle is to rise above the level of blindly impulsive reactions against, and tentative, piecemeal efforts to gain relief from, the incidental effects of the capitalist mode of production and its inherent exploitation of the workers.

It is exactly in this way that the Communism (otherwise called the Scientific Socialism) of Marx and Engels was engendered. They were able by means of their discovery of the Law of Motion of Human Society to make possible a more understanding and a more objectively fruitful *practice* of the proletarian struggle. And this they did, not because they " selected " or " excerpted " *some* facts which suited their whim or their prepossessions *a priori*, but because they rigorously disciplined themselves to see *all the facts* available in the *totality* of their interconnections and resultant movements.

The need of the proletariat for *theory* is as ever-present as is their need to *practice* their class struggle against the exploiters. The actual leaders in that struggle cannot help but theorise as well as they are able. Here and there it is possible for individual workers and groups of workers to become specialists in the theory of the emancipation struggle of the proletariat and its concomitants. But in the nature of things this can happen only rarely. In fact the need for a political party of the proletariat arises as much from the need for a *theoretical* co-ordination of the experience, outlook, and standpoint of the proletariat as it does from the need to co-ordinate its local and sectional struggles into a general *practical* movement towards revolution.

It is for this reason that the theoretician and the intellectual has played such a big part, for good and for ill, in the development of the proletarian struggle. Since he is specially trained for the work of investigation and theoretical co-ordination, the intellectual from the middle or upper class, if he is conscientious as well as really competent, can give the proletariat invaluable aid. On the other hand, if he is in fact incompetent, or, being competent, has no conscience, and serves the proletariat merely as a hireling adventurer or soldier of fortune, always with his nose atilt sniffing for higher pay and bigger booty, he can do incalculable harm.

A sense of this harm and a deep resentment thereat is widespread among the more militant proletariat. Its general diffusion has produced (in combination with historically apposite circumstances) the phenomena, firstly, of a widespread belief that no intellectual is to be trusted ; and secondly, that of a practical endeavour, widespread and persisting over extensive sections and periods, to *do without all theory and theorists whatsoever*.

From its very nature this endeavour to dispense with theory has the result of limiting those who attempt it to the narrowest and most parochial forms of empirical opportunism —which in turn has resulted in the rise to leadership in the Anglo-American Trade Union and Labour movements of some of the most shameless opportunists on principle (who trade demagogically on the fact that they were *once* " working men like yourselves "), and a company of no-less-unashamed theorists who exploit these prejudices of the proletariat to the advantage of policies and programmes of petty-bourgeois and reformist eclecticism.

Reacting against this opportunism and eclecticism, sections of the proletariat, still obsessed with a deep-rooted distrust

of the intellectuals, fly off at the opposite tangent and formulate for themselves theoretical and practical systems of
inverted opportunism—systems whose implied presupposition
is that a " revolution " may be had at any moment if only
" the workers will it " !   Thus are born *un*critical and *anti*-
dialectical " Socialist " impossiblism, syndicalism, and anarchism.   And these in turn give scope for a whole brood of more
or less *de*classed (i.e., *lumpen*) intellectuals to give these
narrownesses and prejudices logical formulation.

Since both the eclectic-opportunist and the inopportunist
" revolutionary " *impulsive*-ist standpoints agree in denying
in practice—if not in theory—either the objective reality of
an historical dialectic process in Nature and Human Society,
or alternatively the knowability of such a process even if it
exists, both standpoints *agree* with the bourgeois standpoint
and maintain it consciously or unconsciously against the
revolutionary proletarian standpoint of Dialectical Materialism.   All the airs of affected " practicality " and of " scientific " superiority indulged in by the apostles of reformist
opportunism cannot conceal, and all the romantic " bluff "
and bluster of the " impossiblist " Utopians can do no more
than disguise, the fact that their theory and practice are, at
the final analysis, akin to those of the bourgeoisie and opposed
to those of Dialectical Materialism and revolutionary proletarian communism.

That the standpoint of Max Eastman is that of *impulsivism*
and " instrumentalism," and that this standpoint is identical
with that of Berkleyian solipsism is, as we have seen, avowed
by Eastman himself.   Postgate for his part has revealed
himself as an eclectic, especially in regard to history ; which
logically carried out leads him to Hume-ian scepticism and
agnosticism, a philosophical attitude which serves the same
function in philosophy as social-democratic reformism does
in politics.

Just as this reformism serves as a shield between the bourgeoisie and the blows of the proletariat, and at the same time
strengthens with its own force that of the bourgeoisie's
counter-blows upon the proletariat, so eclecticism and scepticism in philosophy stand as buffers between supernaturalism
and the blows of materialism, while also joining forces with
supernaturalism in its counter-blows upon materialism.

It is in this light—that of the affirmation by Dialectical
Materialism of the *knowability* of the dialectical development-
process of objective reality, and that of the denial of that

knowability by eclecticism and subjectivism represented respectively by Postgate and Eastman, that we can approach best the question of *Freudism*.

Postgate and Eastman are both eager to function (as bridesmaids ?) at the marriage of Marxism and Freudism. Let us see if we can discover what wish is " father " to this thought.

As to Freudianism

Eastman and Postgate are each of them scornful of Marxists because, so they allege, they " scorn psychology." Postgate, the more cautious, concludes his *Karl Marx* (and his attack upon the Dialectic) thus :

> " It is . . . probable, *as Max Eastman has argued* . . . that the abandonment of the dialectic will allow of the growth of a *more scientific and therefore* more practical revolutionary movement. . . . The nascent science of psychology can be taken hold of and used for revolutionary ends. . . . To those who like to use the names of great men as symbols, we may say that the next great task of revolutionary philosophy is the *reconciliation of Marx and Freud* ! "—Postgate : *ibid.*, pp. 90–91.

One Freudian (Otto Ruhle) has already written a " life " of Marx, in which Marx and his theories are all traced to the fact (*a*) that Marx suffered from a liver complaint in middle-life ; and (*b*) that, in consequence, he suffered from an " inferiority complex." How this accounts for theories which were not only drawn directly from the objective facts but also were (as we have shown in earlier chapters) all elaborated in their main outlines before Marx was 30 (between the ages of 25–29 to be exact) only a Freudian can tell. Another pleasing Freudian touch is the statement on the dust-jacket of Postgate's book that " Marx lived a happy, but *uneventful*, married life ! " Which means, to a Freudian, that he never once appeared in the divorce court either as petitioner, respondent, or co-respondent, and was thereby proved to be, by Bloomsbury standards, " slow ! "

Eastman with characteristic thoroughness in mendacity asserts that :

> " Among the extremer devotees of Dialectical Materialism in Russia, the very word psychology is denounced as bourgeois and counter-revolutionary."—Eastman : *ibid.*, p. 30.

The assertion as it stands is patently false. But if it be

translated to read that dialectical materialists have learned in pain and boredom that he who prates most of " psychology " is generally a bourgeois, and a counter-revolutionary at bottom, it would correspond with the experience of Dialectical Materialists much nearer the meridians of London and New York than that of Moscow. Dialecticial Materalism, obviously, does not *reject*—would be committing self-emasculation if it did reject—any scientific *knowledge* rightly so called. The *facts* revealed by the experiments of genuinely scientific psychologists all Dialectical Materialists welcome, And cannot help but welcome ; for the simple reason that *if emotional and conscious states, and their inter-related movements can be studied empirically and can be reduced to terms of objective law, that of itself will demonstrate them to be both dialectical and materialistic facts*—which will extend notably the world conception of Dialectical Materialism. What Dialectical Materialists are sceptical about is not " psychology " *as such*, but the claims of the individual, amateur, dilettanti, and introspectionist " psychologists." These they are sceptical about, *and with reason.*

For instance, we know now how little worth attaches *a priori* to any opinion offered by Eastman, or Postgate, about Marx, Engels, or Lenin. Is it likely we are going to " take their word for it " about Freud and psychology ? *Once bit. twice shy* !

It is in science as in other departments of life ; " fools rush in, where ' angels ' fear to tread ! " And it can be said categorically that nineteen-twentieths of the output of Bloomsbury on the subject of psychology has exactly the worth of its outpourings upon the subject of Marx and Marxism. It falls in fact within the formula of Alexander Pope :

" [Bloomsbury] still wanting, though [it] lives on theft ;
Steals much, spends little, yet has nothing left ;
[Bloomsbury which] now to sense, now nonsense leaning,
Means not, but blunders round about a meaning ! "
— POPE : *Epistle to Arbuthnot*, lines 183-6.

Or, one could fittingly press Dryden into service :

" The rest to some faint meaning make pretence
But [Bloomsbury] never deviates into sense.
Some beams of wit on other souls may fall,
Strike through and make a lucid interval ;
But [Bloomsbury's] genuine night admits no ray,
[Its] rising fogs prevail upon the day ! "
— DRYDEN : *Mac Flecknoe*, lines 19-24.

The first fact to face is that psychological phenomena constitute the subject-matter not of *one* science but of a number ; hence arises the practical difficulty of establishing even provisionally the frontiers marking off the territory of psychology from that of the sciences complementary thereto. Since the phenomena of psychology are those of the dialectical transitions from objective to subjective activity in the individual human being, it follows as a matter of practical inevitability that the objective study of psychological phenomena must at some point or another fall under the survey of *every* science which includes the objective activity of mankind within its purview. Even so far as the science of psychology, distinctively so called, has been (provisionally) established it is clear already that its experimental data fall for scrutiny and generalisation not into one science but into a whole series. At one end of the scale psychology is a sub-department of anatomy and physiology (normal and pathological). Eastman may rail against the fact until he is hoarse with railing, but that will not in the least alter the fact that the objective establishment of psychology as a positive science providing generalisations capable of experimental use has involved and must continue to involve the development of psychology as the empirical physiology of neural processes and reactions—the science of *conditioned reflexes*. At the opposite pole of its subject matter psychology passes without an ascertained break by way of the process of cognition into logic and dialectics which are, in turn, presupposed in all science—since all science involves the logical and dialectical *use* of human knowledge in order to reach higher and higher unifications of theory and practice. And here psychological phenomena presuppose and demand the recognition of the dialectical facts of society and its development, just as at the physiological pole they rest upon the dialectic of Nature.

In between the objective (physiological) and the subjective (logical) poles of the field of psychological phenomena lies the debatable land of emotional states and their resultant interactions. And it is here, on territory upon which from time out of mind spook-chasing, fortune-telling, soothsaying, wizardry, mystery-mongering, and priestly jiggery-pokery have all sought their Happy Hunting Ground, that Messrs. Eastman and Postgate set up their pulpit and call all Marxists (and other sinners) to repentance in the sacred name of the Herr Doctor Sigmund Freud.

We answer their call bluntly—a science of human psychology presupposes, and is possible only as a development from, a sound science of human society, such as is given in Dialectical Materialism, and Dialectical Materialism alone. The " psychology " which seeks to explain the individual without reference to the society—or which treats the individual as primary and society as secondary—damns itself as an unscientific mystification from the start.

What is Freudism ? In the first place it is not *one thing*, but four : (1) it is a practical technique of dealing with cases of neurosis, of mental pathology ; (2) it is a metaphysical *theory of mental processes* by which Sigmund Freud sought to generalise the results of his practical psycho-therapeutic technique ; (3) it is a metaphysical theory of the origin and nature of human society, and moral relations within society ; (4) implicit in the second and third of these is a theory of knowledge (an epistemology) and of the origin and nature of ideas.

We invite Messrs. Postgate and Eastman, and all Bloomsbury and Greenwich Village along with them, to take notice that only the first of these Freudisms falls properly within the frontiers of *science* at all ; and at most, only the first two can be called without a stretch of language primarily *psychological*. Again : the first, the real genuine Freudian psychotherapeutic *practice*, while it provides invaluable empirical data for scientific generalisation is *scientific* only in the empirical sense. Its data have yet to be homologated into a unified law capable of empirical verification, and capable also of assimilation into the general body of scientific knowledge as a whole. That Freud's own *metaphysical* generalisation is untenable is proved by two sets of concrete facts : (1) two other schools of psycho-therapeutics, deriving from Janet in France, and Maudsley in England, employ a substantially identical technique and produce thereby even more impressive results than any achieved by Sigmund Freud and do so while *totally repudiating the Freudian metaphysic*. (2) The Freudians themselves are split into three main subschools (those of Freud himself, Adler and Jung) while each of these has anything up to half a dozen sub-variants. These schools, be it noted, do not differ as do the various divisions in the camp of " Marxism " primarily on questions of the practical application of a body of theory accepted more or less in common. With Freudism the reverse is the case : here it is the *practice* upon which there is general agreement and the *theory* upon which the school flies asunder into a shoal of warring incompatibilities.

Our second concrete challenge to Messrs. Eastman, Postgate, and all, is therefore this : You talk of " reconciling " the theories of Marx and Freud. Now the theories of Marx we know and have stated herein. Now do *your* part—state, if you can, the *theory* of Freud, and point out, *if you can,* that which has to be " reconciled." Until this be done all your talk of the " science " of psychology, and of the " neglect " of it by Marxism is just so much " eye-wash "— pure Bloomsbury " bluff," " swank," and " baloney."

The plain truth is that it is not the *science* of Freud (whose actual therapeutical practice has rightly earned him a high place in the esteem of pathological practioners) which Bloomsbury cares one single rap about. It is with him as it is with Einstein : he has unwittingly given Bloomsbury a new toy, which Bloomsbury has devoted itself to with the same zeal and the same critical intelligence that it surrendered to the charms of Yo-Yo, Duke Ellington, and Mae West. Also, for the more politically conscious denizens of the jungle which has the British Museum for its central oasis, Freud's *metaphysic,* and his *metaphysical sociology,* and their implicit idealist and solipsist epistemology have provided a yearned-for way of escape from the grim fighting front of Dialectical Materialism and revolutionary proletarian Communism back into the camp of intellectualist-reaction, sophistry, subjectivisim, and, at the last, supernaturalism.

Psychologising—as distinct from the *bona fide* scientific study of the subject—became a " craze " with the War and as one of its direct consequences. The immense number of cases of neurosis (" shell shock ") and similar derangements calling for psychotherapeutical treatment made the intelligentsia aware, to its astonishment, of the existence of the science and its elaborated technique. As this technique became itself revolutionised in consequence of the enormous mass of experimental data provided by the War, and as, furthermore, Bloomsbury in the persons of its members gained a smattering of the subject from its experience in the hospitals, either as patients or as dilutee-" assistants " to the professional staff, Bloomsbury was primed to the brim for a " psychologising " craze as soon as the War ended. As, also, the War had shattered for Bloomsbury the repute of all its gods in the failure of all its theoretical lights, every bat in every belfry began to hold high revel.

Partly in consequence of the return to more or less " civil "
life of the swarms of dilutees ejected at the close of the War
from the industry of converting the by-products of the War
activity of " civilisation " into " triumphs of the healing art "
(or, alternatively, into " creatures that once were men ")—
partly, too, because all the sons and daughters of the upper
and lower strata of the petty bourgeoisie whom the War
had jolted clean out of their respectable ruts, were by the
close of the War so habituated to emotional drug-taking that
the satisfaction of their War-begotten excitement became an
imperative need—" psychology " became " all the go ! "
By the same rule that " where the carcase is there shall the
eagles be gathered," and along with the eagles the kites and
the carrion crows—just so the practical-critical crisis in the
science of healing brought into public view not only a number
of genuine and well qualified scientists, but also a whole
brood of sensation-seeking dilettanti who seized the chance
to swoop down on the field and set up as " psychological
experts " by the right of self-graduation.

In the kingdom of the blind the man with only one eye is
King ! But post-War Bloomsbury, deep in republican frenzy,
had no use for " kings." Any man with even one (mental)
eye left was urged by mass clamour to " join the revolution "
—one initiated by the man of Thessaly " who was so wondrous
wise he jumped into a holly-bush and scratched out both
his eyes ! " All Bloomsbury turned " psychologist " overnight ; and soon bookstalls were crashing right and left under
the super-imposed weight of the " easy outlines," " short
introductions," " new views of " and " modern conceptions
in " psychology, whereby Bloomsbury, true to type, sought
to make money out of its hobbies, and convert its internecine
pickings and stealings into a little ready cash and an intolerable deal of reputation. Almost before the " boom " had
arisen, Bloomsbury was racked end-to-end by the fratricidal
strife of some " two and seventy " warring sects of psychologists. Each claimed to be the " one and only " and each
demanded that all the other sciences should pay it its
full meed of reverence, toll, and tribute. Especially
tribute !

One of these post-war schools of the " New " Psychology
fought under the battle-name of " Behaviourists " ! It arose
as a violent reaction from its " opposite number," the Psycho-
Analytic School, and says " No ! " to every *Yes* this latter
school utters. The distinguishing mark of the Behaviourist

school is that it identifies mental and emotional phenomena so absolutely with physiological processes that it *denies* the existence of any sort of objective fact corresponding to the term " Mind." All mental phenomena whatsoever are treated as simple, untransmuted reflexes. In fact Men, like Animals, are but " conscious Automata." Thus the first school of " modern " psychologists is so *modern that it has just caught up with Lamettrie* !

If the Behaviourist school thus, in effect, denies the practical efficacy of the Mind and Consciousness, the Psycho-Analytic School counters by denying in practice the practical efficacy of the Body. Or, to be more precise, it reduces the body to a by-product of the *psyche*, or *pre*-Mind.

What gave this school its immense vogue among the intelligentsia and the middle class generally was its use of the concept the *Sub-consciousness*.

The older " Victorian " British school of physiological psychologists had established (especially at the hands of Henry Maudsley) the empirical fact that by far the greater part of the total stimulations of the sense organs received in the course of daily and hourly practical grappling with the material world disappeared from immediate consciousness unnoticed to become *latent*—" stored up "—in the brain and neural tissues. Though thus non-existent so far as the immediate consciousness was concerned, they remained potentials which at any moment might be called into functioning activity, just as the potential energy of gunpowder, or of a mixture of petrol vapour and the atmosphere, can be *actualised* by a spark.

Sigmund Freud (born 1867) opened a new chapter by treating this department of consciousness (which the older empirical-physiological school had treated as and called the *Secondary* Consciousness) as a separate entity which was always acting in opposition to the Consciousness proper, with which it was thus linked in an indissolubly antagonistic unity. He rechristened it " The Subconsciousness " and built a theory on the notion that desires, etc., recognised by the Consciousness as unseemly (or such as would be judged so by the public opinion of the social group to which the particular individual belonged) were ejected from Consciousness and banished to the lower regions of the Subconsciousness. But, like Satan expelled from Heaven, they took advantage of their exile to organise a war of reprisals against the Consciousness which had expelled them. And, just as Satan in mediæval legend constantly returned to earth to lure the innocent and respectable—the Fausts and the Marguerites—into every sort of deadly sin, so likewise the Freudian subconsciousness, seething and boiling in the " cellars " beneath consciousness, contrived by its agitations, upsurgings and splashings to determine ultimately the whole trend and shift of the ideological or intellectual consciousness.

Freud did not invent this theory " all out of his own head." Its ultimate derivation is from the Kantian dualism of Unknowable Reality and Subjective Presentation in Thought. Schopenhauer developed this (in opposition to Hegelianism) into a conception of the Universe as a Duality in antagonism of Absolute *Will* and Subjective *Idea*. Von Hartmann refined upon Schopenhauer by his *Philosophy of the Unconscious*, in which all the main positions of modern solipsism were maintained in the *inverse* form—a contention that rationality of every kind is a mirage illusion whereby the individual is goaded, lured, and deluded into fulfilling the purposes of the Unconscious Absolute. Shaw's " Life-Force," *metabiology*, is, like Bergson's *Elan Vital*, only Von Hartmann's " Unconscious " with an infusion of cheerfulness. All these are frankly idealist systems. And Freud, seeking a metaphysic with which to co-ordinate his empirically reached subjective duality of consciousness and subconsciousness, took over the Schopenhauer-Hartmann conception of a duality of *Desire* (or Appetite) and *Reason* (or Idea) virtually without alteration.

With Freud the *basis* of all subjective being is the general undifferentiated *Desire* which provides the " substance " of all thoughts, emotions, and ideas—all of which are specifically conditioned as *forms* by and in the Consciousness. But since his whole system pivoted in practice on his conception of a " censorship " exercised over these specifically determined *conscious forms* of desire by the " *Moral consciousness* " (taken straight over from Kant), the " censored " desires being driven back into the subconsciousness, where they at once started to ferment and proliferate themselves into a " complex," his followers soon modified the metaphysic into a conception of the subconsciousness as simply chock-a-block full of " censored " (i.e., mainly *sexual*) desires. In fact, Freud himself, in adopting the term *Libido* for his basic general undifferentiated " desire "—the ground theme or basis of all subjective states, as rational concepts and moral and artistic judgments were their superstructure—in choosing this name

Freud all but invited everyone to regard all states of consciousness as more or less camouflaged forms of sexual desire.

Already, as will be perceived, the Subconsciousness was, in
the Freudian mythology—which is being born under our very
noses—cast for precisely the same rôle as that played in
mediæval and modern Christian Theology by the concept of
Original Sin. Very soon it became apparent that every
effort to cover the stark, staring bones of Freud's patently
idealistic skeleton with good solid material flesh and blood
only resulted in making this basic *subliminal psyche*—this
general undifferentiated Desire (which with Freud himself
was, at first, quite a nice impersonal sort of " desire " for
anything-and-everything-all-at-once)—into something indistinguishable from the " soul " of Theological Dualism !

All the clamorous enthusiasm over Freud's " revolutionary
advance " turned out to be enthusiasm for a retreat not
merely *back to Kant*, but back further, behind Kant *to the
Middle Ages* !

Infuriated at this revelation of their own unimpeachable
respectability, the Freudian school launched out upon a
recklessly truculent anti-theological crusade. Freud himself
" discovered " a basis for the belief in God in the perennial
desire of *every* boy to strangle his father because he enjoys a
monopoly (so far as the boy knows) of carnal intercourse with
his mother ! The whole Freudian school rose in full cry and,
with whoops of triumph, achieved a feat of conceptual
audacity that had not been paralleled since the days of Old
Rome, and the ingenuity of the justly celebrated Menenius
Agrippa !

Turn to your Shakespeare, to *Coriolanus*, Act I, Scene 1,
and read there how this Menenius Agrippa blarneyed a
General Strike of the *plebs* into surrender by " telling the
tale " of the time " when all the body's members rebelled
against the belly." The belly, so ran the tale, admitted that
it got everything that went into the body, and that all the
body's members had to work to support it. " But," said the
belly, " all I get I give again, and nourish all in a way no other
member could do ! " Thus were the *plebs* persuaded to agree
that, though they might indeed starve the belly (the patricians),
they would themselves be the worse for it in the long run !
This demonstration applied to the social relation of exploiter
and exploited makes, as Marx said, every man *into a part
of his own body*. The Freudians achieved a world triumph by
means of a parallel feat. They substituted for the old battle-

slogan of the seventeenth-century Locke-ist sensationalist school—which school was of course much derided as being both materialist and " obsolete "—their own revised version.

Whereas John Locke had said, " There is nothing in the *intellect* which was not previously in the *senses*," the Freudians revised this to read : " There is nothing in the consciousness that was not previously in the sex organs " ! And at the mere sound of that *liberating word* Bloomsbury surrendered with enthusiasm, while Chelsea, Golders Green, Welwyn Garden City and all the other citadels of the Ideal welcomed the conquerors with wide-open arms and salvos of adulation.

Over the whole territory of Bourgeoisdom, yea, " from Dan unto Beersheba," strong men and maidens, young men and women not so young rose on their pinnacles of culture to bless the name of Sigmund Freud for that he had reconciled them to their fate at last ! He had compensated them for the drab, dreary, respectable monotony of their actual every-day lives, by the revelation that in the secret recesses of their very own pet and private subconsciousnesses they were in fact and deed Sinks of Sin and Havens of Festering Iniquity. They had only to let their imaginations loose and, in the sacred name of psycho-analysis, they could enjoy scandalous, lecherous, orgiastic, polygamous and polyandrous adventures to the full extent to which their anæmic imaginations could carry them on a diet of three French novels, half a dozen dirty Limericks, and the works of James Joyce (pirated edition, of course) ! And all this with not a penny to pay, and not a neighbour able to breathe a word of scandal ! If giving innocent pleasure to thousands of emotion-starved souls entitles anyone to a seat in Heaven, a front seat, with a cushion, should in fairness be reserved for Sigmund Freud !

For it was in his name that the Theological Dogma of Original Sin returned again to the bosoms which had yearned for him in secret while Agnosticism and Rationalism were " all the fashion," and returned like a super-Prodigal Son to the strains of the " Conquering Hero " and whole hecatombs of roast veal. All the co-respondents, actual and prospective, in each and every one of the respectable suburbs were provided with not merely an excuse but a positive encouragement to do as Byron did, " hate their neighbour and love their neigh-bour's wife."

In fact, that was just the fly in the ointment ! Freudianism waned in the end precisely because it took all the " kick " out of fornication by converting it from a Deadly Sin into a positively " scientific " virtue.

.   .   .   .   .

Viewed over-all the " Psychology " craze was a symptom. It represented, in sum, the impact upon the British intelligentsia of a new set of circumstances for which it was unprepared and against which it could but react in the best way it could manage. Not having a " reason " handy, it fell back upon " psychology " and became happy once again. But playing at psychologising had this as its Nemesis—it drove the addict sooner or later to choose between studying psychology proper—*real*, scientific, psychology, which leads straight to materialism and through materialism to revolutionary Marxism and Communism—or, as an alternative, to abandon even the pretence at psychologising in favour of a whole-hog descent into mysticism.

In several ways the post-War craze for " psychology " presented a curious parallel to the craze for the German Transcendental Philosophy which spread like an epidemic among the " cultured classes "—the forerunners of the modern intelligentsia—after the close of the Napoleonic wars. Each was a post-war " fashion," and each began as a left-handed recognition that in some more or less unintelligible way, the world had been changed. Each served the literary and artistic dilletante in the same way—as a brand new set of intellectual excuses for refusing to contemplate any radical change in social relations. And each defeated itself in so far as each in its different way led, at any rate a section of its adherents, to go forward from mysticism and reaction to materialism, revolution, and Communism.

Raymond Postgate is not of these favoured ones. For him " psychology " (*à la mode Bloomsbury* !) is a way of retreat *from* Marxism and materialism, back to something which is neither materialist nor Marxisn. For the moment he halts at the half-way house of asking for a new synthesis of Marx and Freud. There is no guarantee possible that his halt at this stage will be more than momentary. Already he shows-signs of subscribing to the doctrine of that sect of " psychologisers " which holds that as we cannot possibly " know " anything, *really*, nobody ever did, really, *know* anything at all ! Progress is, in fact, an illusion : " That which hath been *is* ; and that which *shall be* hath already *been*." That this, as of old time, leads straight to the conclusion : " Vanity of vanities ; all is Vanity ! " is too obvious to need labouring.

Each epoch in class-divided society has returned to this, the pessimism of *Ecclesiastes*, as each in its turn has neared the hour of its overthrow. It is a finely ironic comment on the ultra-" modernist " criticism of the Marxian Dialectic that the alternative offered is—the pessimism which was " up-to-date " when the Assyrio-Babylonian Empire was tottering to its fall !

Philosophically only two roads of escape from this pessimism are open. One is by way of the abandonment of all investigation, and all attempt at a rational comprehension of the Universe, and a surrender to supernaturalist illusion and fanaticism—the way of counter-revolution. The other leads by way of the Dialectical Materialist conception of the Universe as infinitely active, infinitely inter-connected, and perpetually developing, in definite and predictable ways, through a series of revolutionary transitions, into a future in which the process will continue beyond the power of human limitations to foretell. That is, *to the way of revolution*.

He who rejects Dialectical Materialism has therefore his choice : he can return to " the sheep of the priests, and the cattle who feed in the penfold of kings," or he can do as Bloomsbury does, recite daily the invocation : " Let us eat, drink, and be lecherous, for to-morrow we die : *and serve us bloody well right* ! "

III—NEO-DIETZGENIAN " MARXISM "

FRED CASEY

On one thing every " critical " interpreter and " explainer " of Marx from the non-Communist " Socialist " camp is agreed —Marxism, as Marx and Engels left it (or as Lenin extended it), is, like " patriotism " to Nurse Cavell—" *not enough* " ! In the course of this work we have seen that Sidney Hook, G. D. H. Cole, Middleton Murry, Professor Laski, J. Ramsay MacDonald, M.P., Professor Macmurray, Raymond Postgate, and Max Eastman all propose to amend Marxism at some point or another. It is true they do not agree in their amendments—true that what one would leave the other would reject. But all are agreed that in the name of " science " Marxism must be " revised up to date."

To their number we have now to add Fred Casey, High Priest in Britain (if not in the Universe) of Neo-Dietzgenian " Monist "-Marxism.

Casey's distinctive position is that, whereas all those named above either take the dialectic method of Marx " as read " or reject it out of hand, Casey claims to have done what Marx and Engels *neglected,* and what Lenin *failed to achieve,* namely, to reduce the Dialectical Materialist logical method to rule, regulation, and empirical practice. He claims nothing less than to have (with a little assistance from the late Joseph Dietzgen) finished the work which Marx and Engels left only partly done—and which Lenin attempted but bungled ! He claims categorically to be vending the *only genuine variety of Dialectical Materialism on the market* !

Fred Casey derives his importance from the fact that he is held in high esteem within the sphere of influence of the National Council of Labour Colleges as the leading exponent of " method in Thinking," upon which subject he has written two books, *Thinking* (1922) and *Method in Thinking* (1933). It is the latter of these works which we will take as the basis for our criticism.

To make Casey's standing clear it is important to remember that the N.C.L.C. claims to be, and is, the largest educational organisation promoting the study (nominally) of Marx and Marxism in the world. Casey's standpoint is not officially endorsed by the N.C.L.C. But his lecturing work is done in classes organised by that body, and his reputation has been made wholly in its movement. Caseyism is, in so far, accepted by the N.C.L.C. as at any rate a *permissible* variety of " Marxism " !

Caseyism offered to the world as Caseyism would not concern us for a moment : Caseyism offered, and widely accepted, as " Marxism," and as a *sort of* " *Marxism* " *superior* to any alternative brand, challenges the closest possible scrutiny.

Owing to the lamentable extent to which the Marxist movement in Britain suffers (as we have noted) from the traditional " British " vice, distrust for theory—which in practice means an inability to break away from the narrowest of empiricism and from the eclectic confusion and superficiality which goes with it—Casey, being an exponent of " pure " theory, acquires an enormously enhanced importance. Not only does he " like hills in Holland, derive his eminence from the flatness of the surrounding country " (Marx), but, owing to the general prevalence of fog in the mental atmosphere of the British " Marxist " and *near*-Marxist movement, he " looms large " as hills do, until, seen through the mist, he has come to pass as a sort of Mont Blanc, or Everest, of Marxist theory in Britain.

It is necessary to dissipate the fog, even if it takes an explosion to do it. Only then can Casey be judged in his true proportions.

.   .   .   .   .

Method in Thinking was published by a group of " voluntary tutors and others attached to the South-East Lancashire Labour College. They " feel honoured in undertaking its publication," because it is " a step in the direction of clearing up the confusion of thought and action existing in the Socialist Movement generally . . . pre-eminently war on confusion in the ranks of the workers."

Their " Caseyism " begins promptly :

" To defeat confusion requires *true understanding*, and to arrive at true understanding involves the application of methodical thinking, *because* confusion is often the *foster-child* of muddled thinking."—CASEY : *Method in Thinking*, Publisher's Preface.

Why " foster "-child ? Because the authors were too respectable to say " *bastard !* "—as their analogy requires. 'Tis a small point, but symptomatic.

There is theoretical confusion in the ranks of the workers, and this *does* manifest itself in a confused and self-contradictory practice. So far we can agree cordially. But is this confusion due wholly or even mainly to *lack of method in thinking* ? Is it not just as often—more often—in fact, almost universally due to *thinking methodically from the wrong standpoint, and within the limits of false assumptions* ?

Right at the outset we are brought face to face with an implication which cannot be allowed to pass without challenge. It is simply not true to say that the confusion in the ranks of the workers exists *solely* to the extent to which *lack of method in thinking* prevails. The thinking of all the critics of Marx and Marxism we have examined in this essay has been in each case thoroughly *methodical*. In each case the falsity of the criticism has been shown to consist, not in the *lack* of method, but in the falsity of the standpoint, of the primary assumptions made, of the objective observation of the facts called in evidence, and of *the method actually employed*. It is not a question of choice between *Method absolute* and absolute *absence of Method*. The question is a *practical* question—*which* of all the methods of thinking is the one which will lead to the fullest *understanding*.

And that, in point of fact, is what Casey's real claim is. It is a claim to possess the *correct* logical method, by comparison with which all others are worthless. That such a claim can (with due circumspection) be made for the standpoint and method of Dialectical Materialism as against all alternative standpoints and methods we agree. And the basis upon which that claim stands or falls is the claim that in Dialectical Materialism alone is achieved the indispensable unity of Theory and Practice. If it *could* be shown that Dialectical Materialism does not in fact effect a correspondence between the Subjective Thought-Activity of Men and the objective activity of the material Universe of Nature and Human Society, the claims of Dialectical Materialism would be refuted at their source.

Now that very statement of the claim of Dialectical Materialism to be superior to all alternative modes of conceiving reality carries with it (by necessary implication) a repudiation of any *absolute* superiority for Dialectical Materialism *a priori*. It is *in practice* that the superiority of Dialectical Materialism is manifest, not in any *a priori* superiority in its *inner* logical consistency. And this, in turn, carries with it the further implication that no claims can possibly be advanced *a priori* to the *absolute* finality of any opinion or conception, advanced or elaborated, by *any individual exponent* of Dialectical Materialism—not even for Marx, Engels, or Lenin. In this essay we have defended Marx, Engels, and Lenin against criticism ; but never on the ground that their method, considered *a priori*, was " correct," and all alternative methods, *a priori*, " incorrect." This very juxtaposition of " correct " and " incorrect " is a repudiation of the Dialectical standpoint, which recognises, for instance, that bourgeois philosophy and politics are " correct " within bourgeois limits.

The highest virtue of Dialectical Materialism lies precisely in the fact that it escapes on the one hand the scepticism, agnosticism, and ultimate solipsism which regards *truth* as *absolutely* and *wholly* dependent on the *point of view*—i.e., is *purely* a subjective creation ; and on the other hand the falsity of the dogmatism and mechanically metaphysical *absolutism* which refuses to perceive that all *particular* views and conceptions of Truth and Reality being synthetic unities of the objective and subjective aspects of that Reality which exists independently of perception and consciousness—are as such and in every individual case necessarily partial and limited.

When therefore we find at the outset that Casey's own pupils and admirers actually advance the claim on his behalf that he has presented " in a simple form the laws governing *correct* thinking," this very use of the word *correct* carries so heavy a load of dogmatic suggestion that our worst suspicions are aroused. And these suspicions are confirmed. The Publisher's Preface goes on :

> " This book is *unique* as a popular presentation of the much misunderstood and as often misrepresented Dialectical Materialism—an essential *part* of the theoretical system for which Karl Marx was *mainly* responsible."—CASEY : *Publisher's Preface.*

The word " *unique* " is the operative word here. It is as we shall see not used thoughtlessly or from lack of access to dictionaries. " Unique " is exactly the right term to describe the position claimed tacitly, not only *for*, but *by* Casey himself, for his distinctive standpoint and method. This *uniqueness* must be appraised in the light of the rest of the passage quoted.

Dialectical Materialism is, it must be noted, according to Casey only a *part* (though an " essential " one) of Marxism. And for Marxism, Marx was *only mainly* " responsible." If this latter were only a reminder that Engels and Lenin had also a share in the development of Marxist theory it could be passed with approval. We shall see that Casey means nothing of the sort. He includes them by implication in " Marx " and claims that all together were only responsible for constructing a " theoretical system " *which needed the addition of* " *Dialectical Materialism* " to make it really worth while ! For Casey the Marxism of Marx, Engels, and Lenin, is something in which Dialectical Materialism is only implicit. He claims to be the exponent of a technique which makes *explicit* that which Marx had, by accident or design, only guessed at without proving. This is the claim :

> " *Though* Dialectical Materialism is associated with Marx's name, and *though* the teaching of Marx is *the basis of revolutionary theory*, it should not be forgotten that Dialectical Materialism will remain an accepted principle when the revolution . . . has become a matter of old history."—CASEY : *Author's Preface.*

This says nothing less than that Marx's work is of purely temporary and provisional importance, while the really *permanent* and basic " Dialectical Materialism " was supplied

by *somebody else!* Who was that somebody? The publishers (and Casey) tell us :

> " Marx was *helped considerably* by Frederick Engels,
> but it was, however, *left to* Josef Dietzgen to apply and
> finally to work out the application of this system to
> human brain-work or thinking."—CASEY : *Publisher's
> Preface.*

The implications of this passage (whose substance is
repeated continually by Casey with variant amplifications)
are of fundamental importance. If, as this passage implies,
Marx (with or without the assistance of Engels) formulated
a " theoretical system " which *he himself* did not " apply " to
the process whereby men arrived at their thoughts, then
Marx must have built his system upon logical presuppositions
reached dogmatically *a priori*. His whole system must have
been a gigantic " castle in the air " resting on a basis of pure
and simple *supposition*. That this is identically the assertion
made in chorus by all the enemies, critics, and revisers of
Marx is, of all facts, the one we have most abundantly
demonstrated. Casey therefore begins his " unique " exposition of Dialectical Materialism by asserting (by implication),
firstly, that Marx constructed his theoretical system (his
sociology, economics, and politics) *without the aid of Dialectical
Materialism* ; secondly, that without the supporting under-
pinning of Dialectical Materialism " Marxism " (in the
historical-political sense) would collapse ; and, thirdly, that
the credit for Dialectical Materialism must be given—*not* to
Marx, *still less* to Engels, *least of all* to Lenin—to *Josef
Dietzgen* !

On one side this is a laboriously round-about way of
advancing the assertion that since the " essential " part of
" Marxism " is really Dietzgenism ; and since Dietzgen,
being dead, has no apostle or High Priest save only Casey,
he, the aforesaid Casey, is the Lord High King-Pin of
" Marxian " theory not only in Britain and the U.S.A., but
(if he had his " rights ") in the whole world ! This is its
comic side.

On the other side the Caseyite affirmation, since it reduces
Marxism to an *aggregation* of " theories " which are only
logically connected by implication, and which can only be
unified by means of a logical theory which neither Marx
himself, nor Engels, did in fact elaborate—this affirmation
is a complete surrender to the standpoint of the rejectors,
the critics, and the eclectic revisionists of " Marxism." This

is its tragic side, since it is, in substance and in effect a denial
of the dialectical unity of theory and practice which is the
starting point, the core, and essence of Dialectical Materialism
which is Marxism.

Dialectical Materialism is not *a part* of Marxism. Marxism
is *wholly* and *entirely* materialist and dialectical. To distinguish between Dialectical Materialism on the one side and
Marxism on the other—(except in the relative, practical
sense in which we can distinguish, provisionally, between
the Marxian method as such and particular forms and details
of its application)—is to do exactly as we have seen every
critic do. It is in fact to repudiate Marxism and to abandon
the Dialectical Materialist standpoint.

Let us see how Casey himself elaborates this basically
revisionist repudiation of Marxism and its Dialectic.

" So far as the Dialectics of the thought process was
involved they [Marx and Engels] certainly provided
enough material to work on as a base, had *anybody cared*
to elaborate it, and to abstract its laws, *but nobody did
until Josef Dietzgen . . .*"   —CASEY : *Method*, p. 193.

" Our work . . . is *no more* than a popular presentation of *Dietzgen's teaching* . . . we may truthfully
describe ourselves as being privileged to be *among the few*
who are as yet leading the members of our class to understand the nature of their own understanding *on the basis
of Dietzgen's work which is* . . . *the reduction to law of
that which Marx and Engels themselves used but never
completed in finished form.* It is . . . what Engels himself said *remained to be done*, the teaching of the laws of
the thinking process itself."—CASEY : *ibid*, p. 194.

" Our mission is to *render a service to humanity* . . .
by *bringing* scientific method into the general world of
thought."—CASEY : *ibid.*, p. 13.

Sorting out the various claims made in these extracts
we reach the following conclusions : (1) Marx and Engels in
their theoretical practice *used* a dialectical method but did
not " complete " the statement of its " laws " ; (2) Engels
(for self and Marx) admitted the existence of this gap in their
system ; (3) nobody filled this gap until Dietzgen did *after*
Marx and Engels ; (4) Dietzgen's work is presented *popularly*
(for the first time ?) by Casey ; (5) Casey in so doing is
" rendering a service to humanity," since he is doing what
was *never before done*, i.e., *bringing method* into the " general
world of thought ! "

Everyone is entitled to as good an opinion of himself as he can " get away with." And Casey certainly seems to have " got away with it " to no small extent. The trouble is that he feels his position of " unique " pre-eminence keenly ; and finds it necessary to dole out chastisement as often as if he were, *really*, Jehovah himself scattering storms and thunderings from the top of Mount Sinai.

In his *Method* all the small fry of Marxism are disposed of in the heavy-father manner. " Most Marxists " he tells us " fondle " the term Dialectical Materialism in a " slipshod " manner. In fact, " most Marxists," it would seem, fall into the category discovered by Casey of " wind instruments that ought to know better ! "

Engels himself does not escape : he was guilty of a " quite erroneous statement " (p. 122). And since the statement in question was quoted by Engels from Hegel and is also endorsed by Marx himself, it becomes clear that Casey's castigating rod is not witheld from those who might have been supposed to possess a high degree of competence in the use of the Dialectic method. In their turn, Plekhanov and Bukharin, " the Russian philosophers," " British Com- munists," certain " one-way Marxists," and " *other* muddled thinkers " all receive their castigation. But his largest and fullest vials of wrath are called into action for the benefit and reproof of *Lenin* ! That the general consensus of Marxist opinion (even among opponents) classes Lenin as the greatest of all followers of Marx and Engels makes no difference to Casey. Why should it, indeed, when Lenin :

" appears to miss the full understanding," p. 45 ;

" [was] not very clear in dialectical theory," p. 46 ;

" must have been muddled," p. 46 ;

" did not understand," p. 46 ;

" [suffered a] lack of dialectical clarity," p. 47 ;

" [was] astray on the question of mind and matter," p. 47 ;

" did not see . . . the central fact in the teaching of Dietzgen," p. 131 ;

" inconsistently left the door open to static idealism," p. 131 ;

" did not really understand," p. 131 ;

" contributed nothing new to the principles of dialectics," p. 190.

It is of course possible, *a priori*, that Casey may be right in all the instances we have cited. But to say that it is *a priori probable* that Casey is right in any of these cases would be to run very far indeed ahead of plain reason. On a worldly view it would seem, at first glance, to be long odds on the matter turning out to be quite contrariwise.

We need, happily, waste no ceremony over Casey since he wastes none on us. Thus we may blurt out at once the plain truth that what Casey offers as " Dialectical Materialism "—and browbeats all and sundry in the name of—is neither dialectical, nor materialist, nor Marxist, nor coherent logic, nor intelligible sense. It is protected heavily from criticism by the fact that Casey's understanding of understanding does not extend to the " laws " of grammar and syntax so that many of his sentences may mean anything or nothing or both. But what can be discerned at all clearly in the " encircling gloom " is categorically a muddle of half a dozen incompatible varieties of idealism and metaphysics all harnessed to the service of an eclectic " Centrist " social-democratic stand-point in the interest of which a clinging to the extreme Right is concealed under poses which out-brave the bravest of the " Left."

Casey, in a word, is playing in Britain to-day the part that Eugene Dietzgen (son of Josef) sought to play in the German Social Democratic Party during the battle between the Revolutionary rank-and-file and the Bernstein " revisionists " in the Party apparatus. Eugene Dietzgen thought his father's work (completely misunderstood and the misunderstanding systematised under the name of " Proletarian Monism ") would be " a means of reconciling both wings of the Party." He was unlucky ! The Right-wing didn't need him : the rank and file Left wouldn't have him ! The Right wing wanted nothing " proletarian " ; the revolutionary rank-and-file were not going to water down their materialism into any sort of two-faced " Monism " (which could be made to look like Materialism or Idealism according to taste !). Eugene Dietzgen therefore faded out of the picture in Germany ; but in the English speaking world where Marxist theory was in its infancy and the " genius for compromise " was regarded as an " Anglo-Saxon " virtue instead of the bourgeois vice it is, this neo-Dietzgenianism found disciples who in turn raised up among them a " prophet " whose name is Casey.

We will examine first the relation between Josef Dietzgen and Marxism, since the whole Caseyite claim pivots upon this point. We will then be able the better to appreciate the worth of the Casey version of " Dialectical Materialism."

JOSEF DIETZGEN AND THE MATERIALIST DIALECTIC

The point at issue, let it be remembered, is not the *worth* of Josef Dietzgen's work, *as such*, as a contribution to the literature of Dialectical Materialism. On the contrary, it is an integral part of the case against Caseyite *neo*-Dietzgenian " Monism " that in advancing baseless claims in the name of Dietzgen, this school is both falsifying his work in itself, and using him as a camouflage for an attack upon the very things he devoted his life to defending.

Let it be thoroughly well understood that in defending Marxism against Caseyism we are simultaneously rescuing Dietzgen himself from the bandits who have kidnapped him and who seek to use him for the ends of political blackmail.

The first point is : did Dietzgen, coming *after* Marx and Engels, *complete* the work they had left *unfinished* ?

The answer can be given in two ways. From the Marxian side we have demonstrated that the very essence and beginning of Marxism was historically the dialectical method itself. As we have shown in this essay by means of the relevant documents, Marxism began in the practical-critical problem, how can the world itself be changed ? The practical-critical development of the solution of this problem hinged philosophically upon the problem of the nature of knowledge, upon the relation of Thinking to Being, upon the objective criterion of Truth, upon the *unity* of Theory and Practice on *the basis of the primacy of practice. This is the logical essence of Marxism*, and we have proved that it was the actual, historical, starting-point for the whole development of Marxist Theory and Practice. There was, therefore, no such *gap* in the Marxian system as the *neo*-Dietzgenians allege that Dietzgen filled. Their whole fabric of allegation and inference is built upon a baseless assertion totally at variance with the facts. And, what is more, it is an assertion which could only be made *honestly* in total ignorance of the actual nature and scope of the Marxian world-conception. It can, of course, be made, *dishonestly*, with a full consciousness of hostility to Marxism as a *practice*—a hostility which it is not deemed expedient to avow.

From the side of Josef Dietzgen himself the assertion can be answered (1) by a comparison of dates ; (2) from Dietzgen's own works themselves.

Marx was born in 1818 ; Engels in 1820 ; Dietzgen in 1828. So far Dietzgen did, chronologically, " follow after "

Marx and Engels.   But, while Marx died in 1883, and Dietzgen in 1888, Engels lived on till 1895, working to the last.   The Caseyite suggestion—" nobody did . . . *until* Josef Dietzgen, etc."—which, if words have any meaning, implies a fairly prolonged interval between the *conclusion* of the labours of Marx and Engels and the *beginning* of those of Dietzgen, is already completely exploded.

The worse than worthlessness of the Caseyite myth is exposed to its roots as soon as the dates of the works of Josef Dietzgen are compared with those of the works of Marx and Engels.   Dietzgen's first work, *The Nature of Human Brain Work* (which contains substantially his whole contribution to the subject—his later work being merely a reaffirmation of its main positions), was published in 1867, in the same year as, but *before*, Marx's *Capital*.   Dietzgen's second and last work appeared in 1887—a few months before his death. That is to say that Dietzgen's main conclusions had been published *before* either of the better-known works of Marx and Engels (the *Communist Manifesto* excepted) had appeared. *Capital*, *The Civil War in France*, the *Critique of the Gotha Programme*, the *Anti-Dühring*, the essay on *Feuerbach*, the *Origin of the Family* and most of Engels' prefaces, all were written *not before*, but after the appearance of the work of Josef Dietzgen.

Thus it will be seen beyond all possibility of question that the Caseyite myth is the most complete of all possible fabrications.   On these dates a case might, if the Caseyites were audacious enough to attempt it, be made for the suggestion that Marx and Engels were " helped considerably " in their better-known work by Dietzgen !

But that claim has not been made, nor will it be.   Not because it would be baseless—that would be no deterrent to people with such a zest for building a convenient mythology out of their own imaginings—but because such a claim would tend to the exaltation of the work of Marx and Engels, as *the later and more fully developed*, over the earlier and more rudimentary work of Dietzgen.   The last thing in the world any neo-Dietzgenian " Monist " desires is to exalt the repute of Marx and Engels—*especially Engels* !   In fact, the whole mythology of " Dietzgen completing Marx-Engels' work " has been built up expressly with the revisionist intent of exalting a counter-reputation to that of Marx and Engels with a view to their disparagement and ultimate superseding.

Finally there is the witness of Dietzgen himself, who not

only called himself a " Marxist," but constantly in his journal-istic work referred to the work of Marx and Engels as ampli-fying and more fully elaborating the propositions advanced from his own special angle. In point of fact his first and most important work was actually submitted to Marx and Engels for approval in manuscript [MARX-ENGELS, *Correspondence*, pp. 251–3].

The plain truth is that Dietzgen himself should be held in high honour for exactly the opposite reason to that advanced by Casey and the neo-Dietzgenians. A self-taught working tanner, Dietzgen was able by his own unaided efforts, and *independently* of Marx and Engels, and *also* of Hegel, to elaborate a Critique of the primary assumptions made by the Kantians which negated those assumptions from a materialist standpoint. Dietzgen thus reached, in 1867, a standpoint substantially identical with that which Marx and Engels had reached (see quotation from the *German Ideology* above) in 1845–46. That Josef Dietzgen was able to do so much entitled him to high praise. And despite their faults—crudities of phrasing, occasional confusions of the argument by verbal acrobatics, wearisome repetitiveness—his works should certainly be read. They of themselves, read intelligently, will refute utterly the attempt made by the neo-Dietzgenians to establish a *cult* of Dietzgen at the expense of Marx and Marxism.

Casey's special contribution to this mythology is his repeated assertion that " Engels said " that " teaching the laws of the thinking process " *remained to be done*. Casey's assertion is simply false. What is more, it is quite unquestion-ably derived from a semi-literate misunderstanding of one sentence, *and one word in that sentence*, in an anything-but-good translation of Engels' essay on *Feuerbach* ! Here is the passage :

> " The Marxian philosophy . . . makes an end of philosophy in the realm of history, just as the dialectic philosophy of nature renders every philosophy of nature useless or impossible. Practically there is no further need to devise interrelations, but to discover them in facts rather. Instead of a philosophy forced from nature and history there remains then only the realm of pure thought—as far as any is left—the *teaching* of the laws of the thinking process itself, logic and the dialectic."— ENGELS : *Feuerbach* (Lewis' translation), p. 125.

Bad though this translation is, even judged on its face value, its meaning is clear enough to any normally con-

stituted reader. And particularly is this true of the word
we have italicised (*teaching*). Not one reader in a million
would fail to read this term as a *noun*—as the equivalent of
" science " or " theory " (as, for example, in *The Teaching of
Karl Marx*).

Casey manages the feat ! He reads it as a *verb*, and the
sentence as an injunction to him from Engels to *discover* and
to " teach " the " laws of the dialectic, etc." !

Engels does not say (even in the Lewis translation) that
anything " remained " to be *done*. He is describing how one
province after another has been captured from " philosophy "
(i.e., from *a priori* speculation) by the positive sciences. All
that " remains " *to philosophy* is " the realm of pure thought "
—*so far as there is any of that realm left*—the laws of the thinking process itself, logic and the dialectic. This *description*
of the " realm of pure thought " Casey, with simply incredible
stupidity, interprets as a confession of failure by Engels !

Both the badness of the Lewis translation and the absurdity
of the Casey interpretation are made clear by a comparison
of the sentence under discussion with the corresponding
passage in the translation approved by the Marx-Engels-
Lenin Institute :

> "For philosophy, which has been expelled from nature
> and history, there remains only the realm of pure thought
> (as far as it is left) : the *theory* of the laws of the thought-
> process itself, logic and dialectics."—ENGELS : *Feuerbach*,
> Martin Lawrence ed., p. 67.

A comparison with a parallel passage in Engel's *Socialism :
Utopian and Scientific*, of which the translation was revised
by Engels himself in 1892, excludes all possibility of doubt :

> " Modern materialism is essentially dialectic and no
> longer requires the assistance of that sort of philosophy
> which, queen-like, pretended to rule the remaining mob
> of the sciences. As soon as each special science is bound
> to clear its position in the great totality of things and of
> our knowledge of things, a special science dealing with
> this totality is unnecessary. *That which still survives of
> all earlier philosophy is the science of thought and its laws—
> formal logic and dialectic.* Everything else is subsumed
> in the Positive Science of Nature and History."—ENGELS :
> *Socialism : Utopian and Scientific*, pp. 39–40.

Thus sinks without a trace the neo-Dietzgenian myth of
the jerry-built theoretical system of Marx and Engels pulled
together into an enduring whole by the Dietzgenian theory of

understanding ! At the very best Dietzgen was a *pre*-Marxian *Marxist* : at the worst, in his bungles (which are the parts of his writings the neo-Dietzgenians batten upon), he keeps alive the delusion of the existence of a " realm of pure thought " into which *positive* science could not enter, the mystic key of entry being a magical " method " of " pure " introspective logic. This neo-Dietzgenian perversion of Dietzgen's own teaching is not only on all-fours with the introspectivism *a priori* of the solipsists and Freudians, *but it is also* the bastard " Marxism " taught by Fred Casey.

THE POINT AT ISSUE

Casey is very fond of " quoting " Engels—much in the same way as the devil is said to be fond of quoting Scripture—with intent to deceive. He says :

" Frederick Engels . . . worked along with Karl Marx in founding scientific socialism . . . and he told us in that work dialectics was their ' best tool and sharpest weapon.' "—CASEY : *ibid.*, p. 12.

Here for comparison is what Engels actually said :

" We [Marx and Engels as against Hegel] comprehended the concepts in our heads once more materialistically—as images of *real* things, instead of regarding the real things as *images* of this or that stage of development of the Absolute Concept. Thus dialectics reduced itself to *the science of the general laws of motion*—both of the external world and of human thought—two sets of laws which are identical in substance, but differ in their expression in so far as the human mind can apply them consciously while in nature, and also up to now for the most part in human history, these laws assert themselves unconsciously, in the form of external necessity in the midst of an endless series of seeming accidents. Thereby the dialectic of the concept itself became merely the conscious reflex of the dialectical motion of the real world and the dialectic of Hegel was placed upon its head, or, rather, turned off its head (on which it was standing before) and placed upon its feet again.

" And this materialist dialectic, which for years has been our best tool and sharpest weapon, was, remarkably enough, discovered, not only by us, but also, independently of us, and even of Hegel, by a German worker, Josef Dietzgen."—ENGELS : *Feuerbach*, p. 54.

For Engels the dialectic is—*the law of motion* in its two-fold aspect, objective and subjective. The distinction (in *mode of expression*) between these two aspects—one which derives from the reflex-oppositional relation of the subjective movement to the movement of the objective world of which it is the reflex (and " reflection ")—is as important as is their *connection*. Of primary importance is the fact that this connection is established only *in practice and by means of practice*. In fact it is clear on the face of Engels' description (even if it were not abundantly clear from every line Marx and Engels ever wrote) that but for *objective practice* there would, and could, be no subjective reflection of the external world at all.

This, and nothing else but *this*, is the " best tool and sharpest weapon "—the *objective* dialectic—for the simultaneous discovery of which Engels, with characteristic generosity, gives Dietzgen all (and, by inference, *more than all*) the credit he deserves. It is characteristic of the neo-Dietzgenian monomania that Engels' generosity should be twisted into an excuse for robbing him (and Marx) of all the credit due to him, and, further, that it should be made the starting-point for the elaborate mystification and misrepresentation of substituting for the Marx-Engels objectively dialectical *world-conception* a subjectivist, *a priori*, logical technique !

As we have seen, Dialectical Materialism does not *begin with* an *a priori* affirmation : it begins with the *fact* that men exist and *must* (as their everyday practice proves) *do* certain things in order to continue in existence. Materialism reinforced by the Dialectic method differs from the older, mechanical materialism in two basic respects : (1) as just stated, it begins with the concrete fact of actual material *human* existence ; and rejects the metaphysical method of beginning with an *a priori* postulate about the Universe—as, for instance, whether it is " One " or " Many," whether it is Continuous or Discontinuous, and so on ; (2) in emphasising the reflectional character of all perceptions, conceptions, etc., it emphasises the objectively *practical* character of all mental activity. Thoughts are thus not at all *passive* reflections : they are the resultants in actively interacting subjective states and processes of the active practical interconnection between living human beings and the interconnected totality of an incessantly active, and *therefore* developing, material reality. Whereas mechanical materialism treats the universe as a *closed* system analogous to a machine, dialectical materialism treats it as infinitely creative *process*.

Thus Dialectical Materialism distinguishes itself and its point of view from *Idealism* by its affirmation, on the basis of actual, everyday *human practice*, (*a*) of the reality and knowability of the world of material reality ; and (*b*) of the inseparable *connection* (unity in opposition) between the subjective activity of Man and the objective material activity, the reality, which it *reflects*—as well as grows out of—and is therefore inseparably linked with. From " mechanical " and " metaphysical " materialism it distinguishes itself, as we have seen, by affirming the Dialectic character of the *unity* of Being and Thinking : i.e., it affirms the *oppositional* nature of that unity as well as the primacy of Being therein ; and it affirms no less the *active* aspect of Being, *its Becoming*, as the primary, practical basis out of which this developing *unity* of Theory and Practice arises *on the basis of practice.*

Let us see what Casey (who claims, let us remember, to be " unique " as its wielder and exponent) makes of this " best tool and sharpest weapon " of revolutionary proletarian struggle.

The " proof of the pudding is in the eating." Casey " corrects " Bukharin in regard to the unity of Theory and Practice, Engels in regard to Freedom and Necessity, and Lenin both in regard to Mind and Matter, and also as to the Dialectical Unity of Opposites. If Casey can " get away with it " on these basic points he will be indeed " unique."

.   .   .   .   .

Let us begin by seeing how Casey, in contrast with Engels, discriminates between Idealism and Materialism :

" For the Purpose of describing the nature of *Material-ism*, the Material is *all thoughts*, and the General is all that class of thought which has . . . the general character of accepting the objective existence of matter and of contending that matter as distinguished from thought is the dominant factor in determining thought. These thoughts . . . constitute Materialism.

" For the purpose of describing the nature of *Idealism*, the Material is again all thoughts, but the General is all that class of thought which teaches that all so-called material things are really mental, or at least that Mind is the primary and dominant factor in connection with them. . . .

" For the purpose of understanding how *Materialism* and *Idealism* are one even though they are two, the Material is still again all thoughts, and the General is just the simple objective fact that all thoughts are the result of a physical process wherein brains produce thoughts with the aid of sense-perceived objects."— CASEY : *ibid.*, p. 150.

What is obvious here, right at the start, is the purely subjective, passive *spectator's* point of view. Idealism and Materialism are not compared as alternative methods of subjective *practice*, as alternative and mutually exclusive modes of approach to Reality, but merely as two different kinds of one and the same thing, namely, abstract theoretical systems. It is in this respect that they are " *one*, even though they are *two*." Whether one thinks idealistically or materialistically one is in each case " thinking," and in this purely relative-descriptive sense Idealism and Materialism do fall into line as parts of the total Thought-Activity of Mankind, whether that Totality is taken at any one moment, or in its historical sequence considered as a whole.

But as soon as either of those " wholes " is considered, as Engels said, in its actual existence (" as it presents itself to each one of us ") what we see is the mutually exclusive *antagonism* of Idealism and Materialism as *rival* Theories of Reality, between which in real life a man must choose, however hard he may try to escape the necessity of choice. It is, for instance, only from the standpoint of the most wretched petty-bourgeois opportunism that " Marxism " becomes *only* another kind of Liberalism, or " Communism " *only* another kind of Religion. Food and poison are " alike " in the same way, in that they are both natural *products* and both (usually) *organic* substances. In addition they both *exist*, and thus form part of the " One " of Universal Existence. But in practical life poison *as such* is no substitute for Food *as such* ; all the instances in which poisons may be used as food, and food may become poisonous notwithstanding. The proposition that " Materialism and Idealism are One " thus requires, in practice, the significant qualification—*only in those respects and circumstances which make it possible to ignore their character of mutually repellent opposites, a character immediately apparent in practice.*

Does Casey add this vitally important qualification ? He does the opposite ! He scoffs and jeers at those (including by inference Marx and Engels) who make it :

" Our method enables us to see that Idealism and Materialism are opposed as two contradictory systems *only* because they are two generalisations *within* . . .

one physical process of thinking."—CASEY : *ibid.*, p. 151.

" Those *who do not understand* the dialectics of the thought-process *think* Materialism and Idealism are two *opposed* systems of thought that cannot in any circumstances be reconciled. But we, *with our knowledge of dialectics*, can see quite easily that while they are two systems . . . their similarity *or reconciliation* consists in recognising that they are *just* two parts of *one* thought-process which is itself *one* part of a material universe."— CASEY : *ibid.*, p. 151.

" Of course, if we still like to use the words Idealism and Materialism, by way of *accommodating our language* to the needs of those who as yet do not understand dialectics [Marx, Engels, and Lenin, for instance], all well and good, provided we do not forget that in this connection Materialism will mean those thoughts that fit the *generality* of things while idealism will mean those which do not. *Therefore*, materialism will signify true understanding and idealism will mean misunderstanding." —CASEY : *ibid.*, p. 152.

We have here a fine example of the " unique " way in which Casey carries out his " mission " of " service to humanity," that of " bringing scientific method into the general world of thought." The *method* consists, it will be perceived, in affirming on the slightest provocation, or none at all, that everything is all one *because*, at some point or another, everything is connected with everything else ! In the above passages, for example, Idealism and Materialism are " reconciled " by the simple trick of abstracting from each its specifically distinguishing character and presenting the result as simple, abstract (but *not* " socially necessary ") human brain activity. But Casey calmly ignores the fact that this *one* " physical process of thinking," in which *all* possible systems of Idealism and Materialism coexist, is not that of any *real* human being, living, dead, or yet to be. It is an *abstract* process, which has taken place not in actual but in *abstract* brains, in an *abstract* world which exists only in the *abstract* ; that is to say, not at all ! Casey is not concerned with the *real* world of material practice at all, but with the world of empty categories—a world as purely subjective as the world of Dreams.

The whole practical point of Dialectical Materialism, its break from the world of " pure " subjective abstractions into the world of practical concrete, material, reality, its

rejection of all " idealistic balderdash," and its appeal to
practice as the acid test of all thinking—all this Casey dis-
misses with contempt ! Casey, in fact, sets out a diagram
(p. 149) in which " Abstract and Concrete," " Subjective and
Objective," Matter and Mind, Heat and Cold, Contraction
and Expansion, Materialism and Idealism, are in each case
carefully bracketed together under the general title of One.
In one conceivable set of circumstances only can these pairs
of reflex-opposites become " all one "—and that is when they
form parts of a *Table of Logical Classifications.* Something
and Nothing, as general categories, as abstract classifications,
each imply the other—as when we say Casey's argument
either means Something or it means Nothing ! But to say
that the *particular* " Something " which Casey argues for is
" Nothing," without adding the qualification " nothing
sensible," nothing *usable*, nothing *to the purpose*, or nothing
in the least resembling genuine Dialectical Materialism, would
be to do that which Casey does systematically (and calls it
his " Method ")—namely, commit mental suicide by trying
to palm off the logical category under which a given thing
may be classified, as a substitute for *the thing itself*.

In Casey's " understanding " of Materialism and Idealism,
the difference between them is that Materialism is *true*
understanding and Idealism a *mis*understanding. This, if it
means anything, means that *every* misunderstanding is
" idealism " and *every* true understanding is Materialism.
Since every man must in real life be constantly guilty of misunderstanding, every man must be more or less an " idealist."
And since the biggest fool that ever lived is bound in practice
to understand truly something, sometimes, if it is only the
way to his own mouth, every man is bound to be more or less
a materialist. That is to say that Idealism and Materialism
coexist necessarily in *every* individual and their difference is
purely relative, a mere matter of " the way you look at it."
For Casey, they are not rival conceptions of the relation
between Thinking and Being, historical Party names denoting
significant divisions and struggles between real men in a
real world. The difference between Idealism and Materialism
is for Casey simply the subjective empirical difference of the
degree to which men do, or do not, employ Casey's Patent
" Method " in thinking !

That this is not merely *subjectivism* (and therefore Idealism
at its worst) but also egoism inflamed to the bursting point,
must already be apparent. It is, in fact, *solipsism*, since for

Casey (all his talk about " brains," " physical processes " and the rest of it, notwithstanding) nothing exists except as an abstract logical category, and abstract categories can " exist " only in a world of abstract mentality.

.   .   .   .

Two facts, revealed in the extracts given above, are characteristic of Casey's " Method : (1) Casey never employs the criterion of objective *practice* as the test of Truth : always for Casey Truth is the " general." Since, in actual life practice, it is the *differences* between things, and the inter-actions from which those differences arise which are the things with which we are primarily concerned, it follows that the method of reducing everything to an abstract generality is not only the negation of all Materialism and all Dialectics, but also the negation of any possibility of reaching a con-cretely objective and usable Truth. (2) Casey's method being as we have seen wholly subjective (when he speaks of " brains," etc., he means only the *idea*, or *category*, not the concrete thing) it is in practice indistinguishable from the " fictionalist instrumentalism " of Eastman and Co. The best proof of this is that he arrives at the same political standpoint —that of a systematically contemptuous disparagement of the Communist Party, and a glorification of the individual " revolutionist in his own right." Max Eastman, the avowed neo-Utopian, neo-Bakuninist, Trotskyite, *super*-Leninist, and solipsist scorner of the Dialectic finds a common platform *both in theory and in practice* with Fred Casey the " unique " *super*-Marxist, apostle of neo-Dietzgenianism. Truly " mis-fortune " doth make strange bedfellows ! All the foxes who have lost their tails naturally gravitate together to form an *anti-Tail* party !

CASEY AND THE UNITY OF THEORY AND PRACTICE

Casey, as we have seen, derives his " Method " from the *Unity* of all Being. This unity he postulates *a priori*. It is for him something " given "—as it is with Berkeley and all idealists, who in the name of unity deny the existence of matter.

Casey quarrels with Bukharin for asserting that the *unity* of Theory and Practice is " based on the *primacy* of Practice." For Casey there can be no *primacy* ; otherwise the *unity* (in which the difference is lost, and the question of *primacy* along with it) would not be a " true," that is to say, not an *absolute*

unity. Similarly, he quarrels with Engels for saying that
" Freedom is the recognition of Necessity," since this bases
Freedom on the *primacy* of Necessity ; and quarrels with
Lenin, first of all for asserting that the *unity* of Mind and
Matter is based on the primacy of Matter, and secondly for
affirming that in the Universal Totality of Things—the
Universe considered as a Unity of Opposites—the *unity* is
relative while the opposition, struggle, development and
movement are absolute (i.e., *primary*).

In all these cases the method of Casey can be submitted to
the acid test of objective *practice*.

Casey categorically falls foul of Bukharin's proposition,
" the interaction between Theory and Practice, their unity
develops on the basis of the *primacy of practice*." He comments thus :

> " This is after telling us that ' both theory and practice
> are steps in the joint process of the reproduction of
> social life.' He might just as well have said that the
> chariot of social life is drawn by the two horses Theory
> and Practice, both of which run together but Practice is
> always first."—CASEY : *ibid.*, p. 136.

All the beauties of the Casey " Method " are here, including
the special Casey brand of humour. Casey is so incapable of
objective visualisation that even when he attempts it he
squints. He cannot even rise to the height of conceiving two
horses harnessed *tandem fashion* ! He is so determined not
to " put the cart before the horse " that he *carries the horse
alongside in a side-car* !

The most obvious fact of all—that the *unity* referred to
by Bukharin is neither more nor less than an *inter-action*—
and the no less significant fact that this is a *developing* interaction—which, *because* it is a development, a movement, a
process of simultaneous coming-to-be and going-out-of being,
is a fact requiring the discrimination of the relatively constant
and variable, primary and secondary components of that
movement—of the comprehension of all this Casey is as
incapable as is the babe unborn. What he needs for his
" Method " is an *abstract* " Theory " resting in peace and
amity side by side with an *abstract* " Practice," so that the
two in their harmony may make up the " Unity " of the
Abstract One of his logical adoration.

It is true that Casey is not always consistent in this—
a fact not surprising in a logically " unique " " missionary "
whose notion of being dialectical is to achieve, by hook or

by crook, a state of permanent and irreducible self-contradiction. In his preface he had said :

"Dialectics should *leaven* the whole of revolutionary
theory and practice, and while the latter is at the moment
very pressing, the former is the more permanent, because
the revolution will pass."—CASEY : *Author's Preface.*

The statement, apart from its worth as an affirmation, is
not free from ambiguity—therein being truly "methodical"
in the Casey manner. If the terms "former" and "latter"
refer to *theory* and *practice* respectively we get the result that
with Casey theory and practice are "united" only as are
man and wife—and *one of them is looking eagerly forward to
a divorce*! If, on the other hand, these terms contrapose
"Dialectics" and "whole" (theory *plus* practice) we get
the result that Casey's theory and practice are only incidentally "dialectical"—that "Dialectics" is a purely subjective
affair which has no necessary connection with objective
changes in nature and human society. As we shall see, this
is (with the inevitable succession of blunderings into the
opposite opinion—that there is nothing which is not dialectical)
the more permanent mood of the Casey "method." For him
"dialectics" is a logical trick of the trade of which he holds
the patent rights. He reproves Bukharin thus :

"If Bukharin wanted to tell us that in capitalist
countries, Theory, in the person of the Professor, is
divorced from Practice in the person of the worker, but
that in Russia, dialectical materialism is expressing
itself by remarrying Theory and Practice in the heads
of millions and thus producing the *vigorous twins* (!)
of a new Science and a new Culture, all well and good.
He might have done it, however, without trying to make
us a present of the ancient materialist's walking-stick
that . . . has only one end, for he wants the unity of
theory and practice to be all due to one of them—the
practice. Practice and Theory lose their distinctions
when under the name of 'social life' but considered as
practice, and as theory, the one is no more primary than
the other."—CASEY : *ibid.,* pp. 136–7.

The first observation which occurs to the reader of this
passage is a remembrance that its author is *self-described* as
one with a "mission" to "defeat confusion" by "*bringing
scientific method into the general world of thought.*" It is
certainly a "unique" method, and "unique" impudence to
call it "scientific." "If" Bukharin had "wanted to tell"

anything of the sort he would have been unfitted for the post
of Poetry Editor to a wall newspaper in a crèche for mentally
deficient infants. He was, in fact, when he used the words
Casey objects to, heading a delegation of U.S.S.R. *scientists*
to a World Congress on Scientific Method and Technology.
As for walking-sticks which have " only one end," they are
the sort in common use : the other " end " is a *handle*.
Otherwise they would be like Casey's " method "—they
could not be " grasped." Theory and Practice can only
" lose their distinctions " in " social life " if that is considered *in the abstract* as a logical category emptied of content.
And only when Theory and Practice are similarly reduced
to Abstract categories, and considered in abstraction, does
the question of primacy cease to arise. From all this it is
clear that (so far as his native genius for bungling, his in-
sensitiveness to the need for precision in the use of terms, and
his general literary incompetence will let him be) Casey is
persistantly *anti*-materialist in his method, and simply
incapable of grasping the first elements of any sort of
dialectics. For proof, contrast Casey's strictures on Bukharin
with a few passages from the paper upon which Casey comments :

" Both theory and practice are the *activity* of social
man. If we examine theory not as petrified ' systems '
and practice not as finished products . . . but *in action*,
we shall have before us two forms of labour activity,
the *bifurcation* of labour into intellectual and physical
labour. . . . *Theory is accumulated and condensed
practice*."—BUKHARIN : *Theory and Practice from the
Standpoint of Dialectical Materialism*, p. 3–4.

" In *Marx* we find the *materialistic* (and simultaneously
dialectical) teaching of the unity of theory and practice,
of the *primacy* of practice, and of the *practical criterion
of truth* in the theory of cognition. In this way Marx
gave a striking philosophical synthesis, in face of which
the laboured efforts of modern pragmatism . . . seem
but childish babble."—BUKHARIN : *ibid.*, p. 5.

" The interaction between theory and practice, their
unity, develops on the basis of the *primacy of practice*.
(1) Historically : the sciences ' grow ' out of practice,
the ' production of ideas ' differentiates out of the
' production of things.' (2) *Sociologically* : ' social being
determines social consciousness.' The practice of material
labour is the constant *force matrice* [moulding or mother

force] of the whole of social development ; (3) *Epistem-ologically* : the practice of influence on the outside world is the primary ' given quality.' "—BUKHARIN : *ibid.*, p. 5.

"Practice is an active break-through into reality, egress beyond the limits of the subject, penetration into the object, the ' humanising ' of nature, its alteration . . . the objective world is changed through practice, and according to practice, *which includes theory* ; this means that practice verifies the truth of theory."—BUKHARIN : *ibid.*, p. 7.

Here again the contrast with the Caseyite conception is glaring and obvious. So also is the transparently childish cunning with which Casey has selected an odd sentence to serve as the basis for his diatribe. So also is the fact that Casey in selecting this sentence must have been aware that Bukharin, in affirming the primacy of practice in the *develop-ment* of the interaction between theory and practice, does so with the fullest possible support from Marx himself. That Casey thus deliberately opposes his " method " to that of Marx is a fact he discreetly conceals from the pupils who come to him to learn " Marxism " and the " Dialectical Materialism " of Marx. Not otherwise could he hope to palm off upon them his spurious substitute.

The specific points of difference are these : Casey conceives " unity " as absolute one-ness ; Bukharin, as a materialist dialectician, conceives it as the *interaction* which " unites " the interacting things into a *developing* whole. Casey's conception is not only abstract but exclusive of all real movement and development. He can only superadd an abstract category Development to his pile of abstractions and assert that the result is a " unity "—because he says it is.

Casey and his friends can take their choice : either he is a bungling incompetent to whom the barest elements of philosophical reasoning are so much " Greek "—in which case his claims to expound anything, let alone Dialectical Materialism, become disgustingly farcical ; or he knows that he is affirming, in principle, all the time a metaphysical conception of an Absolute Existence, relative to whose fixed unchangeability all movement, change, and development are only " appearances " of the *mind's own making*. That his " method " is consistent with the latter conception (that of pragmatism, instrumentalism, and all modern solipsist ideal-ism) is proved at every point. That he should call such a method either " dialectical " or " materialist," let alone

both, and still more that he should claim that it is " Marxist,"
is either incredible ignorance or *wilful Jesuitry.*

.   .   .   .   .

Casey's solipsist idealism is all but openly avowed in such
passages as this :

> " A dialectician, a proper one we mean, would realise
> that objective truth *needs no search* because it is already
> given in the material universe existing all around us
> and in us. He would see that this objective reality is
> itself always changing, and therefore that *each new theory*
> is just a more or less correct way of looking at the
> universe, or of some part of it for the time being. He
> would accordingly recognise that each new theory as
> it came was merely *a new outlook to enable the facts* of the
> *period* to be more consistently understood, and that a
> future period, with a *different grouping of facts,* will bring
> forward a different understanding."—CASEY, p. 40.

It *may* of course be true that a thing has only to exist for
Casey to become possessed at once of the " truth " about it ;
but if so that will prove that Casey is, like God, *omniscient.*
Ordinary mortals have to acquire " truth " by practical
activity. The probabilities are, however, that he is simply
stealing a phrase from Bukharin, and spoiling it in the
stealing. Bukharin says (following Marx and Engels) :

> " Practically—and consequently epistemologically—
> the external world is ' given ' as the object of active
> influence on the part of social, historically developing
> man. The external world has its history. The relations
> growing up between subject and object are historical.
> The forms of these relations are historical. . . . The
> question of the *existence* of the external world is cate-
> gorically superfluous, since the reply is already evident,
> since the external world is ' given,' just as practice itself
> is ' given.' "—BUKHARIN : *ibid.,* p. 6.

Casey converts the " given " knowledge of the *existence* of
the external world into an automatic and instantaneous
" knowledge " of all its detailed inter-relations and interactions, and their consequent developments ! If this is
merely folly, it is the greatest feat in that direction since the
Wise Men of Gotham raked the horse-pond for the moon !
If it is not folly it is solipsism.

Of more practical significance is the fact that Casey, even

when he blunders near to the borderline of materialism, holds back in time to keep within the subjectivist camp. That truth grows " out of date " (as all Bloomsbury proclaims) is not due simply to the fact that the material world changes *in itself*. It is due even more to the fact that the world is constantly *being changed by the practical activities of Men,* who change themselves in the active practice of changing the world. Thus theories must be changed not because Truth as such has *qualitatively* altered, but because there is *quantitatively more and more to know*. When Casey denies that it is possible to discover " the truth " piecemeal, or (pp. 39–40) that " there can be any bits or portions of such truth," he denies the whole basis of the materialist theory of cognition— the affirmation of the *knowability* of the external world. If the external world is knowable it can be such only through its changes, and knowledge of it in general and in detail *can* only be gained bit by bit and in *progressive practice*. The alternative view is the idealist view, *that Truth and the connection between the separate facts of the external world is wholly and solely a mystical creation of the Mind*.

And this Casey actually affirms :

> " Facts, however, can be understood only when they are related to each other, so we *invent* theories or generalisations to *make them* intelligible and *consistent as a whole*. In *this way* we form at any one time a body of knowledge."
> —CASEY : *ibid.*, p. 39.

This says nothing less than that " knowledge " is *wholly an invention* ; which may be true of Casey's own " knowledge " but is patently false in every other respect.

It must be conceded of course that Casey is here repeating in a left-handed and bungling way that which the " instrumentalists " assert : namely, that " Reality " is in a constant state of flux, and " Mind," being permanent and unchangeable in essence, cannot *know* this Reality in itself, but can " know of it " in the subjective sense of " adapting itself " more or less adequately to the transient *effects* in Mind of this ever-changing Reality. This is the theory lurking behind Casey's " Method." We repeat : if it has been reached by an ignorant bungle, its author must be very ignorant and very bungling. If it has been achieved consciously and understandingly, by what term is it possible to describe a man who offers as " Dialectical Materialism " what he knows to be its complete and entire negation ?

MIND AND MATTER

The radically *anti*-Materialist standpoint taken by Casey comes out in his every discussion of the relations of Mind and Matter. He reaches the question first when he is talking (in the accents of the pot calling the kettle " smutty face ") of *tautologies* :

> " There are many variations on this theme ; some even worked up into imposing compositions, rendered . . . mainly by ' *wind* ' *instruments who ought to know better* !
>
> " Here is one : ' Matter is the mother of mind ; mind is not the mother of matter.' Now matter *is the whole*, and mind is a part, so in this sense matter is equally the mother of treacle, and potatoes and all other things. But *since these things actually constitute the matter*, then according to the statement matter must be the mother of matter, the mother of itself."—CASEY, pp. 56–7.

The Jesuitry here is transparent. The proposition " Matter is the mother," etc., affirms that Matter and Mind stand in the relation of antecedent and consequent in a *process of causation*. In addition it is denied that the converse holds good.

Casey dare not affirm openly that Mind is the *cause* of Matter ; but he does the next best thing—he seeks to jeer the converse out of court by means of an intentionally offensive prelude, and a reference to " potatoes " and " treacle." Finally he affirms that " Mind " is a *part*, while " Matter " is the " whole," and so seeks to reduce the proposition to the absurdity (as he thinks it) " Matter is the mother of itself." Whether the term " mother " (used here by analogy) is a fitting one is not in question. The real issue is that of *causal interconnection*—of interdependence in sequence. The proposition maintained by materialism against clericalism and supernaturalism is that the Material Universe is *self-caused* and does not necessitate the supposition of a *Mind* as " *first* cause." Casey either knows that this proposition is the one which Jesuits of every denomination constantly seek to ridicule ; or he does not. It is hardly likely that he does not ; but in either case he must again take his choice between being branded as incredibly ignorant or convicted of *employing the methods of a Jesuit*. If the universe of material phenomena at any given moment (including *treacle*, and *potatoes*, tomcats, and Casey) is to be conceived intelligently it must be conceived as in constant activity and development in consequence. In which case the Material Universe *as it was* must be postulated as the " cause " of the Material Universe that *is* ; and that which *is* as the " cause " of that which will be. Therefore the proposition " Matter is the mother of itself " has nothing at all intrinsically objectionable in it. On the contrary, Casey's own objection to the proposition is a tacit denial that the Material Universe is capable of *Development*. That is, of course, a denial of the bare possibility even of any objective dialectics ; and this, as we shall see, is the implicit standpoint of Casey (the " dialectician " !) :

> " The correct view, *of course* (! ! !), is that matter is not ' the mother of ' these things, but, as said, actually is the things *because* (! ! !) the parts constitute the whole. The tautology will come out *clearly* (! ! !) if we remember that the *word* ' matter ' is a general *name,* while all others are *only* (! ! !) special names for *the same thing* " (! ! !).— CASEY, p. 57.

Here Casey in set terms denies that the " whole " of the universe is anything other than the sum of its parts. He does in fact cite the axiom " the whole is greater than the part " as a tautology, which it is. But if he had quoted the axiom *correctly* and had affirmed that " the whole is not *greater* than the *sum* of its parts," he would have affirmed, as he does in the passages above quoted, the direct negation of all dialectics —as well as of practical experience.

One can have *all* the parts of a watch or a machine, and yet not have the watch or the machine *as a whole.* The whole is created not by the simple aggregation (in *any* fashion) of the parts, but by their specific interrelation, in which case the whole is *qualitatively* " greater " than all the parts in separation. In social life this fact plays a big part, as Marx shows in his *Capital.* It is the force created, *over and above the simple sum* of their individual productive forces, by the co-operation of labourers in the process of production which gives capitalist production its superiority over small production, and the bigger Capital its superiority over the smaller. But for the practical significance of the law that the " whole " is *greater* than *the sum* of its parts, none of these things could happen. Yet it is this law, vital to dialectics (the law of the transformation of quantity into quality) that Casey denies with scorn and jeering. Is it an accident only that his jeering grows most loud and most self-conscious at just this point ? Has he some sort of an inkling that the transmutation of objective activity into the subjective activity of consciousness and thought (generalised as " Mind ") is another example of the same " leap " in Nature from quantity to quality ?   Is he putting up a " bluff " here because he knows that *here* genuine Dialectical Materialism scores most heavily ?

Whatever his motive, he " bluffs " :

> " A favourite wording of the same idea takes this form : ' Matter is a condition for the existence of mind, but mind is not a condition for the existence of matter.' *So say the big boys who are profoundly educated and thus know all about such things."*—CASEY : *ibid.*, p. 57.

> " The statement on the surface (! ! !) means that matter is a condition for the existence of any and every one of its parts . . . that matter is a condition for the existence of itself.

> " The argument you will notice is coming from the same brain as in the former case *though it is now showing over a more flashy collar and tie."*—CASEY : *ibid.*, p. 57.

Casey is right in saying the argument is substantially the same : that he should use the same reply was inevitable, and we need not labour to repeat the refutation.   What is interesting is to inquire who are these " big boys " with " *flashy* collars and ties " whom Casey scorns ?   Here are a few :

> " Matter is not a product of mind, but mind itself is only the highest product of matter."—ENGELS : (summarising *Feuerbach*).

> " *Mind is a product of matter*, but matter is more than a product of mind, being perceived *also* through the five senses and thus brought to our notice."—DIETZGEN *Positive Outcome*, p. 95.

> " Matter is that which, acting upon our sense-organs *produces* sensations.   Matter is the objective-reality given to us in sensation."—LENIN : *Materialism*, p. 116

> " Matter is a philosophical category which refers to the objective-reality given to man in his sensations— *a reality which is copied, photographed*, and *reflected* by our sensations but which exists independently of them.' —LENIN : *Materialism*, p.102.

It will be observed that among the culprits who describe and treat Mind as a *product* is the very Josef Dietzgen whose philosophy Casey claims to be expounding !   His brow beating manner is therefore to be explained either as the arrogance of an almost perfect ignorance or as the malice of one " caught with the goods on him ! "

Casey returns to the point later and makes it the ground for a direct attack upon Lenin :

> " Many people (including Lenin . . .) say that thought is *real but not material*. Very well. Do they mean that the universe is made of two things, Matter and Mind, Matter on the one hand and Thought on the other ? Two things so different that each can never be the other in any circumstances whatsoever ? *If so, what do they mean by talking of a Universe at all,* since the Universe, *as the word itself tells us,* is one thing as well as being many. It is just as bad as saying that the universe is composed of matter and gravity or matter and nonsense. (! ! !)

> " Had Lenin really understood . . . ? "—CASEY : p. 131.

As the word " tells " us ! Well indeed did Thomas Hobbes observe that " words are wise men's counters, they do but reckon by them ; they are the *money* of fools ! "

The question is not as to the appropriateness or otherwise of the term " Universe "—or, for that matter, of Casey's use of the word " composed." Nobody would deny that the Universe *includes* both gravity *and* nonsense—at any rate while Casey is still living. (He will supply the " nonsense " and induce the " *gravity* " in his victims !) What is in question is whether " Mind " (a subjective generalisation) can ever " become " Matter—objective, material reality. All Casey's bluff cannot conceal the fact that his argument *implies that it can* ! As thus :

> " Had Lenin *really* understood (!) that ' the division of the One and the knowledge of its contradictory parts *is* the essence of dialectics ' . . . then he ought to have known . . . that while mind and matter are for some purposes *considered as* being two contradictory parts or poles, they are *taken as* being One and not two in *speaking of* the universe."—CASEY : p. 131.

Quite apart from the fact that the whole passage is a ludicrous shuffle, the concluding assertion is simply a brazen lie. When " speaking of " the Universe men simply do not " take " mind and matter as " being one "—*unless they are idealists*. A man can only speak of the Universe as it appears from the human standpoint and the relation of object and subject, the interaction of Matter and Mind, and therefore their *difference* is presupposed in all such discourse. Casey has simply concluded a shuffle with a downright falsehood.

To show the extent of his shuffling here is the passage from
Lenin to which he refers :

" ' Thinking is *a function* of the brain ' says Dietzgen
[*Positive Outcome*]. ' My desk as a picture in my mind
is identical with my idea of it. But my desk outside of
my brain *is a separate object and distinct* from my idea.'

" These very clear materialist propositions Dietzgen
however completes thus : ' We distinguish between the
object of sense perception and its mental image. Nevertheless the intangible idea is *also material* and real
(*ibid.*).' . . . Here is an obvious untruth. That thought
and matter are ' real '—that they exist is true. But to
call thought material is to make an erroneous slip, is to
confuse materialism and idealism. But, in truth, it is
only an inexact expression of Dietzgen's who elsewhere
speaks quite correctly."—LENIN : *Materialism*, p. 205.

It is in the highest degree significant that it is Dietzgen's
" obvious untruths " which Casey selects to defend at the
expense of his " clear materialist propositions."

But it is essential to Casey's " Method " that he should do
this very thing. The passages in which Dietzgen, through
over-eagerness to rout the supernaturalists and metaphysical
Dualists, fell into the use of ambiguous phrases, could all be
removed from Dietzgen's writings, or re-worded, and the
sound materialism and dialectic quality of his work would
only stand out all the clearer. But if the corresponding
passages were deleted from Casey's work the *whole would be
gone* ! His very " method " itself rests on a foundation
composed of nothing else than this " mare's nest " that Mind
and Matter, *as such*, are *One* :

" The expression ' matter ' is simply a general *name*
employed when we are not using the special names for
its parts. It is therefore only another name for existence.
Both are general names for the same thing."—CASEY :
ibid., p. 57.

" Since ' matter ' and ' existence ' have both the same
meaning, the statement [Matter is a condition for the
existence of Mind, etc.] may be rendered in these words,
' existence is a condition for the existence of one of the
parts of existence, but one of the parts of existence is
not a condition for the existence of existence. . . .
Since existence at any moment is composed of all its
parts taken together . . . the statement amounts to
no more than the lovely sentence : ' Existence is a con-

condition for the existence of existence."—CASEY : *ibid.*, p. 57.

By now the reader will have become as exhausted and as exasperated as we are with this three-card trick logomachy. Duty, however, compels us to go on to the end. And we are within a hand's turn of Casey's secret.

Let us accept Casey's conclusion provisionally and see what comes of it.

Existence and Matter are two names for the same thing. Existence has as its " parts " anything and everything which has the quality of " existing." Therefore, *every* image in every brain (including the dreams of poets, and the frenzied fancies of the victims of insanity and *delirium tremens*) things which most certainly " exist "—must form " parts " of " existence." Therefore, since they undoubtedly " exist," the purple turkeys with straw hats, the red rats, the green cobras, and the pink elephants with yellow-spotted wings cavorting in the brains of a dipsomaniac in the last stages of alcoholic insanity are all " material " and therefore " *parts* " *of Matter* !

We can now see why Casey is so eager to insist that it is wrong to say that " matter is a condition for the existence of Mind." " Matter " for him, and " Existence " likewise, are *mental facts*. What is more, there are no " facts " for Casey which are not *mental*. The differences between " Mind," "Matter" and "Existence" are therefore to Casey of no greater urgency than those between Rough and Smooth, Sweet and Sour, Hot and Cold, and so on. They are merely arbitrary " pragmatic " distinctions between figments of the imagination made at the whim of the " reasoner."

All this is, of course, very good and " up-to-date " pragmatism, instrumentalism, empiro-monism, or whatever " modernist " name you choose to give it. *It is, however, the negation of Materialism and the reverse of Dialectics.*

It is the negation of Materialism because it begins by repudiating the reflex-oppositional relation between the objective material world and the subjective world of thought which is the presupposition of all Materialism. If Thought does not *derive* its reality and force from the *primary* reality of the material universe, only one possibility remains as an alternative—the Mind itself must be the *primary* reality and the very existence of the material world sinks to the rank of a hypothesis, and the status of a figment in a delirium. In contesting the *primacy* of Matter Casey repudiates Materialism.

Likewise, in affirming the equal claims of Theory and Mind to " primacy " as against Practice and Matter, he not only makes " primacy " itself a *purely* subjective " valuation." He, in effect, denies the *reality* of *objective development*. In effect he affirms that *no new thing can ever come into existence*. He admits " change " of a relative kind. He denies that *Development* is absolute, i.e., objective and real.

This forms the basis for his attack upon Engels.

FREEDOM AND NECESSITY

Casey's notion of the dialectic is limited to one phrase, " opposites are identical." He repeatedly quotes a phrase from Lenin, and smacks his lips every time he quotes it :

> " The Division of the One and the knowledge of its contradictory parts *is* the essence of Dialectics."— LENIN : *Materialism*, p. 321.

But when Casey quotes it the accent is on the " *One*," and the " division " is treated as like the servant girl's baby, " only a little one," and therefore negligible. What Casey is concerned with is not at all how *new* things come into being while old things pass out of existence as parts of the same process. Such a skipping into and out of existence would seem to him a trifling with the virgin honour of his unblemished " Existence " (which is also " Universe," " Matter," " Mind," " Motion," " Old Uncle Tom Cobley and all ! "). Casey is, in fact, all the time insisting that " Truth " consists in uniting in one concept every possible aspect of a thing and then extracting the *general* quality of the aggregation. Since things exist for him, only *as conceived*, things which can be differently conceived are handled in his " Method " as all these things at once. Since a bun can be at different stages both possessed and eaten, Casey, in the name of logic eliminates the stages (as " relationships ") and so achieves a " dialectical " bun which is simultaneously possessed and eaten ! His book is, of course, full of assertions to the contrary. It has minor materialisms breaking out on every page like pimples on measly pork ; but the general continuity of the " Method " is this affirmation, that the primary source, origin, and end of all dialectics is the Oneness of Universal Existence. He has not the remotest suspicion that Oneness, Universality, and Existence are already " one " because he has made them so by abstracting everything but their purely logical " being." They are, as he says (without understanding the force of the saying), *only names* for *abstract generality* from which all concrete, particular, and distinguishing qualities have been removed with meticulous care.

His attack upon Engels is a classic proof that his " method " requires that no sordid question of " primacy " shall arise as between Theory and Practice, Mind and Matter, or Freedom and Necessity.

Casey states his case thus :

> " Man's activity is free when *considered* in the relationships where the free aspect is more General than the compulsory ones, and it is compelled when in those relationships when the aspect of compulsion is more General than those of freedom, *because* in each case thought is made to fit the more of things rather than the less."—CASEY : *ibid.*, p. 122.

If this means anything at all, it means that men are " free " exactly to the extent to which they can persuade themselves that they are so. And from this the conclusion follows (which every bourgeois politician will endorse with enthusiasm) that to make people " really " free all that is necessary is to *persuade* them that they *actually* are so in fact ! " Rule Britannia ! " for breakfast, dinner, and tea in perpetuity should make us (as indeed we are already according to the politicians) the " freest people in the world," because we would never *consider* anything except from that standpoint from which the " free aspect is more General than the compulsory." Anyway, " free " or " compelled," the difference is only in the way you " regard " the matter ! Casey goes on to point out that the statement to which he objects—that "Freedom is the recognition of Necessity"—derives from Hegel " and may be found " endorsed by Engels " [in his *Anti-Dühring*], and then continues :

> " This sentence means that the only freedom man has lies in the knowledge that he has none at all, because all things are necessary, and consequently that his passage towards the future will be all the more easy in proportion as he discovers and obeys (!) the laws of nature and likewise those of social development, or economic development, willingly, instead of otherwise."—CASEY : *ibid.*, p. 122.

Once again Casey's ignorance equals his arrogance of assertion. Like all the revisionists he leaps at every chance to assert that Engels was (and Marx also) a " mechanical determinist," and to " correct " him by a counter-affirmation

of the " freedom " of the human will. He has neither knowledge nor acuteness enough to perceive that Engels (and
Hegel) state here the only grounds upon which a *real* objective
conception of freedom (as distinct from the subjective *illusion*
thereof) can be reached. What all these revisionists and
critics (Casey among them) leave out is the fact that the world
can be changed by the purposive action of men, but on condition
that men attempt only such things as in the nature of the
circumstances then existing are *possible*. Man is not " free "
to achieve impossibilities. But he is free to achieve possibilities, and free likewise (within limits) to develop his own
individual and social power to achieve possibilities. Consequently the better his knowledge of his own and Nature's
powers, *and* limitations, the better can he employ his actual
known powers to achieve ends that positively and relatively
increase his power (*freedom*) to achieve the ends set himself
by his understanding (as distinct from a blindly ignorant)
will. We have discussed the point several times above, and
we recommend to Casey—and his admirers—the quotation
from Thomas Hobbes given on pages 465–6.

This conception that a thing or Man is " free " in proportion to its or his *power to act* in accordance with its or *his*
nature—that its or his freedom is *a mode of the existence of its
or his Necessity*—this Casey will have none of. For him
Freedom is either *absolute*, " pure " freedom or no freedom
at all :

  " ' While this particular idea comes to us through
  Engels, and therefore through a materialistic (!) medium,
  it is the same in its inner meaning as that of the idealistic
  Catholic priest who in a discussion of ' free will ' defined
  ' liberty ' as ' consonance with law.'

  " Of course the priest meant consonance with or
  obedience to God's laws, and he illustrated his contention
  with the idea (!) that a tram-car is freer to move while it
  is controlled by the rails than it would be if it ran off the
  rails.

  " So far as our argument is concerned the phrase we
  are discussing simply (!) puts in place of the God-made
  law of the priest the laws of the materialists (!), and in
  the case of the Marxists the economic laws in addition (!).
  But each is no more than *a lame attempt* to define ' Freedom ' while in reality admitting or claiming that there
  is no such thing. In this respect both materialists and
  idealists agree in being ' one-enders,' and moreover in

being both at the same end on this occasion."—CASEY,
pp. 122-3.

Once again " they are all out of step but our Jock " !

Casey's qualifications as a " bringer of scientific method
into the general world of thought " are all paraded here.
Because a Catholic priest is *ex officio* an " idealist " he cannot
(*qua* Casey) use any argument which does not *ipso facto*
become an " idealist " argument !

If Casey doubts the truth of the priest's assertion about the
tram-car he might persuade the Bury Town Council to lend
him one of their trams, so that he can try the experiment of
" releasing " the tram from the " bonds " of rails and setting
it " free " to career over the asphalt and the cobble-stones !
The result should educate him ! It might even " free " him
from an illusion. If he " borrowed " the car without permission
it might even " free " him from his " liberty " !

Casey's inveterate subjectivism is revealed in his character-
isation of a formula endorsed by Marx himself (who uses
it more than once, and who read every line of the *Anti-Dühring*
before publication), as well as Engels and Hegel (and the
" Catholic priest ") as a *lame attempt* which denies freedom in
the act of affirming it. His stricture can have only one
meaning : that " freedom " is an absolute, and is attainable
as such. The only sense in which this is even conceivable is
that of " Freedom " as an *abstract logical category*, exhausted
of all concrete particularity. Since the world for Casey is a
world of logical abstractions (of which the world we ordinary
mortals live in is, at best, a poor and muddled-up copy), he
feels as direct a personal grudge against Engels, Marx, and
the materialists as the evangelicals do against the Atheist
who casts doubts upon the reality of the " mansion " awaiting
them in the skies. Like them, he feels that he is being robbed
of a valuable " property " :

> " The sort of Marxists who quote this phrase [" Free-
> dom is the recognition of Necessity "] are just those
> [Marx, Engels, Lenin, etc.] who make much of being
> materialists, so let us look at it a little more closely.

> " They teach, quite correctly, that there is no ' pure '
> thought, that is, thought by itself ; for every thought
> must have an object as its base, and, therefore, that
> thought is always secondary in this respect.

> " But if thought must have an object, without which
> it cannot occur (!) at all, how does the thought of freedom
> arise when there is no such object ?

" According to the quotation ' necessity ' is taken as an objective fact from which the thought of necessity arises. So far the statement is correct and clear enough. But then it tells us that the same (! ! !) thought is also a thought of freedom, or *actually is freedom,* while in the latter case there is no objective freedom, no proper (!) or real (!) freedom to act as the objective base of the thought.

" Now if there is no objective freedom, it would seem impossible to have a thought of it. And yet there is a thought of it. So the phrase betrays *either a lack of dialectical knowledge,* or else it is *a very serious theoretical slip.*"—CASEY, p. 123.

This passage, with its cavalier dismissal of Hegel, Marx, and Engels as " lacking in dialectical knowledge," provides a crucial test of Casey's Materialism.

Unless the mind is subjected to the *necessity* of choosing it can be " free " only in the sense of " free from all power of action." Action cannot be Action-in-General : to be *real* (as distinct from a logical category) action must be of something upon something. It must therefore be subject to the *necessary* limitations imposed by the nature of the acting things, which limitations include the *necessary* pre-conditions. None the less, so far as a man *can* choose, and make his choice effective, he is, *so far, free.* And the materialist needs to go no further than this concrete fact of which all men are aware in practice and the understanding of practice, that men can *act* and do produce specific results which they have set themselves to produce, to find the objective reality from which the concept " freedom " is derived.

But Casey cannot accept this ! Why ? Because it entails admitting that the unity of Theory and Practice—their interaction—is established on the basis of the *primacy of practice*. It entails admitting that it is from the practical experience that we can do some things and cannot do others that men derive the concepts of both Freedom and Necessity. It entails admitting the primacy of Matter over Mind and of material practice, of practice through objects, as the generating source of men's conceptions both of Mind and of Matter, and of their active interrelation—through bodily practice.

Since Casey denies all this, he must deny likewise that men *can, if* (in and through practice) *they have learned how*, change objective reality progressively in such a way that their actual personal power of self-disposal will be multiplied out of all recognition ; that positively and relatively they will become increasingly *free* the more they attain to a *real* power of command over the forces of Nature.

That this can be done only in, through, and by means of Society is the basis of the materialist case for the proletarian fight for " emancipation," i.e., for freedom. But, since this conception makes the attainment of freedom by the workers contingent upon the " knowledge," the practical " recognition " of the necessary conditions in which alone this freedom can be attained, it will be, according to Casey, " no freedom at all " ！

Thus Casey's " method " not only *begins* by repudiating the standpoint of Marx ; it ends by repudiating his revolutionary conclusion—repudiating not only all possibility of, but all desire for such a *necessitated* process as a proletarian revolution !

This logical outcome of Casey's " Method " is seen exemplified further in his attack upon Lenin's handling of the concept " Unity of Opposites."

UNITY AND OPPOSITION

The Dialectical concept of the Unity of Opposites is an extension to logic of the homely proverb " it takes two to make a quarrel." For an opposition to arise, in objective reality, the things opposed must have some ground in common ; and they are, moreover, " united "—in the sense of *combined* in an action-reaction relation—in the fact and act of opposition. This, however, is far too rational for Casey. He wants an " opposition " which is *not really* an opposition, and a " unity " which is *not really* a unity—" the glory equal, and the majesty co-eternal." Constantly he reiterates : " Existence is one thing which is at the same time two (or many) things ! "

Since this bears a superficial resemblance to the famous Hegelian formula, " Contraries are Identical," quite a number of unfortunate victims have been deluded by Casey into supposing that this mystical rigmarole is the true genuine " dialectics." We have seen how Casey has brazened it out against Bukharin, Lenin, Engels, and by implication also against Marx and Hegel, all of whom, according to Casey, were " bad " dialecticians. And we agree—if Casey's " dialectic " is " good," *bad* they are, in truth and deed ! *Per contra*—if the Dialectic employed in common by all these (and for the matter of that by Dietzgen, Plekhanov, and a host of others) should prove to be *good*, it follows that Casey's dialectic is very, very much the reverse.

A curious fact arises : Finding an " opposition " to exist between his " dialectic " and that of Lenin, Engels, etc., it never occurs to Casey to attempt to " reconcile " them ! On his " method " the *good* dialectics must be also, and *because* it is good, the *bad* ; and this must apply conversely to the " bad " dialectics. And on his " method " they can be " reconciled " quite easily. Their *general* nature is Dialectics, they are " only " good or bad in relation to each other ; *therefore*, if one overlooks the trifling fact that they contradict each other at every point, the " good " dialectics and the " bad " dialectics, being " parts," form the " whole " of Dialectics, which is neither good nor bad because it is both, or either as you please ! In a word : " there's nothing either good or bad "—or for that matter fat or lean, real or unreal, up or down, round or square, etc., etc.—" but *thinking* makes it so " !

That is the sole *positive outcome* of Casey's *Method in Thinking* !

But Casey does not draw this eminently practical conclusion. On the contrary, as we have seen, he rails and jeers, scoffs and sneers, and tries every trick he knows to *destroy* the Lenin-Engels' " bad " dialectic by means of his own. Why ? Because facts are stronger than Casey's " method," and as soon as he lands in a *real* struggle he finds that it is, as Lenin says, *absolute* ! Casey, struggling like fury to convince all creation that struggle is " only *relative* " (i.e., *not real*), is reminiscent of the old Irish Nationalist Parliamentary Party, which spent its lifetime " Fighting like devils for conciliation, and hating each other for the Love of God " !

The phrase of Lenin's against which Casey rails off and on through his whole book is this :

" The unity . . . of opposites is conditional, temporary, and relative. The struggle of the mutually exclusive opposites is *absolute, as movement and evolution are*."— LENIN : *Materialism*, p. 324.

Casey is so obsessed with his " unity " *a priori*, and the consequent *relativity* of all " disunity," that he fails to see that the force and significance of this passage depends primarily upon that of the term " *opposites*." There are, though Casey on his " method " is debarred from rising to the comprehension of the fact, two radically different kinds of " opposition " contemplated in Dialectics. One is the opposition of things in *objective* nature, which do in actual fact, *act upon and react against each other.* Two billiard balls in collision upon a billiard table are visibly and obviously *at the moment of contact both opposed and in union.* Their subsequent opposite movement is (as every billiard player knows) the *consequence* of their having been *in union.* Quite another kind of " opposition " is that of the categories in logic, in which unity is premised as that into which " opposites " can be reconciled. For example : the One and the Many as " opposites " lose their opposition in the general category of Number, as Number and Magnitude lose their " opposition " in the category of Quantity, and Quantity and Quality in turn become " reconciled " in the higher category of Essence, which with its opposite " Form " (or " Accident ") is reconciled in *Being* or Existence.

Not only does Casey fail to perceive the radical distinction between these two kinds of " opposition "—the one *created* by the logician for his purposes (and therefore purely provisional, arbitrary and contingent), and the other objective and *real,* and therefore *primary* and, for practice, *absolute,* as Lenin (who is talking of *objective* dialectics) says ; but his " Method " compels him to deny (in effect) all reality to the objective and absolute form of *opposition.* He knows, and can know, only purely *logical* relations—pure formalities of *relative* discrimination. And his " dialectic " consists in this, that he takes *the categories of formal logic* in their most abstract inter-relations as constituting the General Nature of Reality. Since all logic consists in classification, in grouping phenomena according to their degrees of likeness and unlikeness and bringing all phenomena within the compass of the most all-embracing classification, all formal logic consists in finding the degree and kind of likeness in all differences. All particular men are different—but they are all alike men. All cats are different ; but they are all alike *cats* ! A mouse is very unlike an elephant ; but they are both alike *animals.* A boil on the neck, a sunset, a plate of fish and chips, and Ramsay Mac-Donald have each and all their notable *differences,* but they are all *alike* in this—that they all *Exist* !

A preliminary sorting has to be done in order that these points of resemblance may be logically detected. The men must be sorted from the cats, the cows, and the cabbages (by means of their common quality of " humanity ") before their unity with the cats and the cows, etc., can be found

(in their common animality) and a union with the cabbages
attained in virtue of their common (or general) quality of
living organisms. Thus logic involves a simultaneous process
of analysis and synthesis (separation and combination), and
an ascending series of discriminations of likenesses in unlikeness, and unlikenesses in likeness. It is this *practice* of reducing
phenomena to *order*, system, and unity which is the basis
of all logic. And it is in this sense that Logic is a technique
of " reconciling all differences." In analysing phenomena
the logical procedure is to break up a " general " group or
class by means of a series of stages at each of which an
" opposition " or " contradiction " is established. Thus we
may take the General group, class, or " category " Dwelling-
House and divide it into : Brick Houses, and not Brick.
These two new " generals " or categories are, it will be
perceived, *unities* within their own frontiers, and " opposites "
or contradictories (in that the one is what the other is *not*)
in contrast to each other. The analysis proceeds further and,
taking the category Not-Brick Houses, divides it into Stone
and *not*-Stone houses ! And so it proceeds until all the logical
" material " has been used up. In this way we shall have
discriminated the General category Dwelling-House into a
whole series of sub-general categories, and these in turn into
their sub-classes, and so on until each particular house has
been assigned its place in the whole scheme. In doing this
we shall have established a harmonious series of ordered
gradation in which each *particular* forms " part " of every
general, up to the category itself which is a *particular category*
in the General world of Categories.

All this is simple and easy, and the indispensable practical
basis of all logic—provided always that one remembers that
the classification, the analysis and the synthesis, the discrimination and the combination, is all a process *which we
ourselves have performed*. It is a systematised judgment which
we have passed upon the facts, and must not in the least be
mistaken for the facts themselves.

It is precisely *here*, at the very first fence, that Casey comes
down with a *crash*. His whole " Method " consists in substituting his classification of the facts for the facts themselves !

In reaching our classification we proceeded to establish a
whole series of purely comparative " oppositions "—as, for
instance, Brick Houses and *not* Brick Houses. Here obviously
the opposition is purely logical and formal. A Brick House
does not in real life " oppose " or " contradict " a Stone

House ; nor do they " unite " to commit assault and battery upon, or even run candidates in opposition to, wooden shacks, tin bungalows, caravans, and tents. All repose in harmony under their communal umbrella—the category of Dwelling-House ! Their " opposition " is purely relative, provisional, and contingent upon the point of view and " purpose " of the one who is passing the judgment. But the same is true of their general agreement and harmony, called in logic their " unity " or " identity." So far as a tent is a dwelling-house, it is *logically* identical with (falls into *one* and the same general category as) Buckingham Palace or the Waldorf-Astoria Hotel. But that does not mean that the owner of either of the latter would or should be willing to accept a tent as an equitable exchange of dwelling ! Thus the general likeness, unity and identity is no less provisional, relative, and contingent than the particular differences, oppositions, and disparities. Hence on the plane of formal logical judgments unity and struggle are each equally absolute and equally relative, *which is what Casey is fighting for all the time* !

But, as we saw above, what is true of the relations between the categories in formal logic, is *the reverse of true* of the relations between things in the objective world. Casey, in fighting for the *Universal Truth of this abstract categorical relation* is adopting the point of view of pre-Kantian *a priori* dogmatism, the point of view of the Schoolmen, who claimed that the categories of Logic existed objectively, and had rested from all eternity in the impersonal bosom of God.

As soon as the abstract Categories are given an Objective Reality—as soon, for instance, as the assumption is made that the universal category *Existence* (derived by abstraction from the fact that all particular things *exist*) is the substance and Reality of the Objective Universe, logic itself is turned into its own negation, and the more logically one proceeds from this illogical starting point, the more intense grows the absurdity of the result. Hence the paradox that Casey is saved by his own incompetence as a practitioner of logic from the consequences of his own incompetence as a theorist of logic. By reasoning illogically from illogical premises Casey performs the equivalent of the mathematical operation of reaching a positive result by the negation of a negative. He blunders into assertions which have the astonishing quality of being reasonable. It is true that Casey generally recovers his " logical " faculty in time to achieve the irrationality his false premises require. None the less, it must be conceded that he does occasionally reach the truth—if only by deviating through incompetence from his true line of error.

What, however, he cannot escape is the fact that by treating the categories of formal logic as objective realities he renders himself incapable of one single inch of Dialectic *Movement*.

Return for a moment to the fact that the method of formal logic reduces all phenomena—whether of likeness or unlikeness, connection of disconnection, or, what you will—to the status of judgments passed by the logician, to that of degrees and kinds of " relationship ' in a logical unity. One may accept this result naïvely (as Casey does) as a revelation of the " One-ness " of the Universe, or one may deduce from it two opposite critical conclusions.

(1) One may argue, as do the various schools of " pragmatists " :—Things are what they are *only* because I *judge* them to be so. That this judgment is only " partial " we know, because to reach the concept of general likeness we have had to discard all the innumerable particular differences between actual things ; and to reach the concept of particular difference we have had to discard all their varieties of special, general, and universal likeness. This means, to a Pragmatist, that logical conclusions are reached by the systematic " falsification of Reality " ; and, if it be true, as it is, that men do, in fact, reach results by the aid of logic, this in turn can only mean that a fictional substitute for Reality *serves men's purposes quite as well as if it were the genuine article*. This can only be the case if true Reality consists not in the chaos of phenomena (which is *unknowable* because it is a chaos), but in so much of Order as the Logical mind itself establishes as it goes along. *This, the Pragmatist conclusion, is as we have seen the one into which Casey is continually blundering*.

(2) One may take the opposite conclusion and argue thus :
Things in formal logic are what *logic* makes them to be. But this is not the fault of the things, it is due to the limitations of the *formal logical standpoint* and method. Formal logic assumes that each thing or phenomenon is complete in itself, and therefore, that it must be known either wholly or not at all. Once it is perceived that logic is a technique of classifying, *not things per se*, but things, and the interactions between things, as viewed from the standpoint of (and classified in respect of their relation to) *Men*, and all the

difficulties drop away. The categories of formal logic express correctly the relations between men as thinking subjects on the one side and things in their active interconnections in the objective world on the other. Logic, therefore, has as its basic subject-matter *a fixed inter-relation* between two *mutually exclusive,* actively inter-acting and developing " wholes," the subjective " whole " of consciousness and the objective " whole " of material things in their aggregate totality of inter-action. From which it follows that the fixed classifications, etc., of formal logic have their objective truth in the fixed relation between thinking *Subject* and the *Object* of its thought. This relation, be it observed, is an *absolute* relation which is presupposed in all thinking what-soever, and which cannot *wholly* be transcended by any art or artifice.

It *can* be transcended relatively by any and every individual man in so far as by social intercourse he can make the experience of others available as experience for himself : in this way a body of knowledge transcending individual attainment is in fact achieved, and this, of itself, refutes the pragmatist. And, as we have seen, the gulf between the subject and object can be bridged in the relative sense that men can, do, and must act upon the external world, and in so doing build up for themselves a *real* knowledge of the *changes* it is possible to produce in the external world, and which the external world, can, does, and will produce, in the consciousness of man. In all this the reflex-oppositional relation between thinking *subject* and material *object* of thought forms the constant, persisting, permanent, absolute element giving continuity to all thought, while the develop-ment (i) of the objective world in itself (ii) of the practical interaction between men as living material things and that objective world and (iii) of the subjective activity of men, stimulated by and reflecting this objective practical inter-action, supplies a totality of ever-changing material in-separably interwoven with the ground theme of the un-changing basic *fixed* relation.

This recognition—that the *fixity* of logical categorisation, though a formality of the subjective judgment is, none the less, *not* an absolutely arbitrary formality, *not* a mere prag-matic assertion of a transcendental mind, spirit, or judgment, but a *necessary* conclusion from an objective relation is the first distinguishing quality of the dialectic method of reason-ing. Its second and no less important distinguishing quality is that (as against Casey, the Platonists, the mediæval school-men, and the like) it affirms that this objective fixity which gives reality to the process of logical categorisation is not a Quality mystically immanent in the Absolute and Universal Whole, but *a relation*, an *absolute* relation, between the sub-jective activity of men, as such, and the objective activity of the material universe.

Where Casey (and the mediævalists) find the Absolute, Dialectics finds the Relative and vice versa. For Casey the Truth of Logic is the Truth of the Universe, which since the Universe has the unfortunate habit of being always " on the run " has to be " made up as we go along." For Dialectics the Truth is the Truth *of the relation* between Men and Things, which relation is as permanent in *substance* as it is pri-gressively changeable in *form*. Therefore for Dialectics Truth remains valid and usable, *because* it is not only always growing, but always, through all its growth, *consistent with itself*.

So, too, with " struggle " and antagonism. The primary presupposition of all knowledge is the antagonistic juxta-position and the relation of inescapable *struggle* between Man and Nature. That Man is " one " with Nature is an affirma-tion that has its degree of truth. But that Man as thinking subject, and as an historically developing being, is so *opposed* to Nature that his whole being as thinker, and as historically conditioned and specific Man, derives from that *opposition* and its concomitant *struggle* ; and that, therefore, his " unity " with Nature is such as to *compel* the struggle, and not in the least to prevent it—the struggle growing in force, volume and intensity the more it begets results—all these facts are obvious as soon as stated. Thus for Man the struggle with Nature is *absolute*, as his (and Nature's) movement and evolution are. Man's " unity " with Nature is, as Lenin said, " conditional, temporary, relative."

.   .   .   .   .

Movement, development, and struggle are basic and primary postulates for the Dialectic (and in that sense *absolute*) precisely because the Dialectic differs from *formal* logic in that, while formal logic is adequate for all purposes where the phenomena to be classified can be treated as fixed and " given " once and for all, Dialectics, as Engels says :

" comprehends things and their representations (ideas) in their essential *connection*, concatenation, motion, origin, and ending . . . Dialectics [pays] constant regard to the innumerable actions and reactions of life and death, of progressive or retrogressive *changes*."—ENGELS : *Socialism*, pp. 34–5.

Casey, in fighting against the conception of struggle and motion as absolute, is fighting against the very basis of dialectics. The logic which Casey employs is, in fact, nothing but formal logic turned upside down !

So great is the mystification which the neo-Dietzgenians have spread that it is necessary to observe here that the Dialectic is neither a *substitute for* formal logic nor the *same thing* under another name. (Casey makes both assertions impartially !) There are not *two logics,* one " bad " and one " good." Still less is it correct to identify absolutely and mechanically the " bad " logic with the bourgeoisie and the " good " logic with the proletariat.

Both formal logic *and* the Dialectic are necessary procedures in scientific investigation. To rupture their *connection,* to regard the " dialectic " as *new,* and formal logic as *old* and *dead,* is to make nonsense out of their *difference.* To assert, as Casey does (p. 16), that " that which is ordinarily called Logic " may also be called, *more correctly,* " Dialectical Materialism," is to make absolute nonsense out of their *connection,* and tell a plain lie into the bargain.

The Dialectic is no more a substitute for plain, every-day *formal* logic than algebra or the calculus is a substitute for simple arithmetic. Just as the higher mathematical operations are designed to achieve an arithmetical result in circumstances which transcend the scope of ordinary arithmetic—dealing as they do with unknown and variable quantities and relations between quantities which cannot be expressed as simple units or multiples of simple units—so Dialectics is a technique of bringing within the scope of formal logical treatment progressive relations and processes which from their nature contradict the assumptions of fixity and definiteness with which formal logic begins its work. Dialectic logic does this by taking as its starting-point the very fact that formal logic is forced to exclude—that *nothing* can be *understood by means of itself alone* : everything must be understood as (*a*) coming *from* something else, (*b*) moving *to* something else, and (*c*) moving under the impulsion of an active interaction between itself and its circumstances. Therefore Dialectics treats each and every thing as the embodied *movement* resulting from the interaction between other things. Without opposition, contradiction and struggle, *resulting* in movement (change, development, etc.), dialectics would be impossible. Given movement and its transformation as the subject of study and Dialectics is indispensable. On the other hand, where the persistencies of form, substance, and inter-relation are relatively constant, formal logic is the technique of reasoning required.

In affirming as Casey does (every time he refers to " one-enders ") that Dialectics is a universal *substitute* for formal logic he volunteers for the post once filled with distinction by Sir Hudibras :

> " For he by Logarithmic Scale
> Could take the size of pots of Ale ;
> And tell by *sines* and *tangents* straight
> If bread or butter wanted weight,
> And wisely tell what Hour of the Day
> The clock doth strike—by *Algebra* ! "
> —BUTLER : *Hudibras*, Part I, canto 1, lines 121-6.

The indispensable worth of the Dialectic in contrast with Formal Logic lies in the fact that, while the latter deals only with that which *is* (i.e., with things and qualities treated as fixed, unchangeable, and *absolute*), Dialectics deals with things as *fluid*, as perpetually coming into being and going out of being. From the standpoint of Dialectics the *existence* of any particular thing, or relation between things, is therefore the *persistent* element in a movement distinguished as a variable constant from the components which, as constant variables, beget in their interaction the *developing* " existence " of the thing *as a resultant movement*.

For instance, if at a cinema a film were projected on to the screen as a *continuous* succession of pictures, all the spectators would see would be a *continuous blur*. By the device of an intervening shutter which separates each picture in the film sharply from its neighbour—so that what is projected is a *discontinuous* succession—the eye can detect and the brain can comprehend the developing *succession* of stages. The discontinuity is visibly that which creates the continuity of development—the elimination of the discontinuity would beget the negation of development, the undifferentiated sameness of the blur. So it is in the objective world. Development is development because it consists in the creation and destruction of a whole series of stages in a sequence. The sequence *results* from the stages and the antagonistic contrast between them. The sequence is the positive outcome of the stages, *is* the stages in process of transition, just as each stage is a relatively stationary phase in the movement considered as a whole. Each stage again is created by a specific " opposition," " struggle," or action-reaction relation ; thus finally the *struggle* is *absolute* and constant, while the sequence considered as " one " *whole,* as a " unity," is " conditional," temporary, interrupted, changing, in a word *relative.*

   .   .   .   .

We need only give a few examples of Casey's " reasoning " to convict him of his inveterate and incurable formalism, subjectivism, and incapacity for Dialectic reasoning :

> " The basis of methodical thinking lies in knowing that the universe is one thing at the same time that it is millions of things. It is one *and* many, singular and plural, general *and* particular, etc., etc."—CASEY : *ibid.,* p. 34.

This, as we have shown, is that which Formal Logic takes as its basic assumption. Casey does not treat it as an assumption *to be tested* and proved subject to qualifications (as, for example, that the " one " thing which is the " Universe " changes every second ; so that it is such with the qualification that it is never twice the *same* " One "). Casey treats it as a dogmatic axiom to be swallowed *a priori,* and so converts it into a metaphysic.

Similarly he affirms that :

> " if the whole is absolute then every part is absolute *because* the whole *is* the parts, and the parts *are* the whole. We are talking of *one* thing, the universe, which is at the same time *two* things, or millions of things, for each single thing may be treated in the same way."—CASEY : *ibid.,* p. 35.

Here he gives a splendid example of how to blunder upon a truth by deviating from error. The " whole " and the " part " are each absolutes in *relation to the other as relative.* Absoluteness is itself a *relation* ; relativity is itself relative. For Dialectics the relative includes the absolute and vice versa, since they are as inter-related as the inside and the outside of a pot. But Casey's argument demands that the " absolute " should *exclude* the " relative," and vice versa. Hence he achieves the absurdity that the parts are *absolute* only because they *are* the whole. In fact the whole is as much created by its parts as the parts by the whole. According to Casey, *all* that is true of the " whole " must likewise be true of the " part " : *therefore, qua* Casey, the spare wheel of a car will carry you to London as well as the " whole " car would !

The sheer madness of Casey's " Method " is proved by the fact that a bedevilment of the most commonplace technical procedure of elementary formal logic passes always with Casey for " Dialectics " :

> " We can see that the old saying ' Nothing is, everything is becoming,' is a one-ended doctrine [alas ! poor Hegel !] that really ought to be ' Everything is, *and* everything is becoming,' because everything exists even while it changes, for how could a thing change if it did not exist ? . . . This composite or double character of things is called Dialectics."—CASEY : *ibid.*, p. 38.

The bemuddlement is Absolute ! Hegel affirmed (reiterating the axiom of Heraclitus) that the existence of any given thing could only be understood as a *becoming*, as a transition from one state of being to another. That it was in *substance* the same did not in the least alter the fact that it was *in form* never the same for two moments in succession. His affirmation was therefore that Being *is* Becoming : that only in *transition* do things exist, that the *Absoluteness* of things consisted in their *fluidity*, that only *relatively* were they fixed as forms of existence, as existences or entities. This is all too easy for Casey. He needs not one Absolute, but two— absolute Being *plus* absolute Becoming—only thus can he achieve his logical feat of " uniting " these two absolutes into One—the composite absurdity of a Being (which cannot *become*) plus a Becoming (which cannot *be*).

CASEY AND EDUCATION FOR EMANCIPATION

Casey's book, as we have seen, is offered us as " preeminently war upon confusion in the ranks of the workers." We have sampled its quality, and can conclude that Casey is a homœopath who believes in curing a disease by *itself* !

We pass over without detailed notice Casey's criticisms of and objurgations against the Communist Party. After all, that Casey with his " Method " should disagree with the Communist Party (along with Hegel, Marx, Engels, Lenin, and others) is decidedly a compliment to that Party. If he had *praised* it—that would indeed have been a serious blow.

What is more to our purpose is Casey's Theory of independent working-class education. This is important because of his standing in the N.C.L.C., which has always prided itself on standing four-square for the self-education of the workers expressly as a means to the end of their own class emancipation by means of revolutionary struggle.

How does Casey conceive the revolutionary struggle ; and what part does he conceive education will play in this struggle ?

The question is an acid test for the Marxian Dialectic. It raises concretely the question of the mutual relations between the individual, the class, the masses, Society and the State ; and also that of the concrete relation of Theory to Practice in the revolutionary proletarian struggle. Upon this question as a test one we can decide objectively the worth of Casey's claim to be the teacher of a " Method " of Thinking indispensable for the emancipation struggle of the workers.

Both questions are linked by Casey himself. In discussing the relation of Might and Right he raises the question whether it is " right " to use " force " to abolish Capitalism. His basic proposition is :

> " The Nature of morality, therefore, consists in nothing beyond the upholding of the general interests over the particular, and if force is necessary to do that it is justified even to the extent of war."—CASEY : *ibid.*, p. 164.

And what is the *general* interests ? *The interest of the majority !*

> " If the Purpose is to serve the workers' interests, a study of the Material will show that of the 47,000,000 of our population, approximately 7,000,000 may be described very roughly as the capitalist class, and the remaining 40,000,000 as the working class. *Therefore* the position becomes clear at a glance, for that Might will be right which serves the General interests. Consequently capitalists' Might and the authority *which rests on it are wrong*."—CASEY : *ibid.*, p. 163.

Two things are clear from these extracts : (1) that morality is a fixed abstraction—the serving of the General *interest* ; (2) that this *general* interest is *not* that of society considered as an objective whole, but that of the *general average of individuals* considered as such. That is to say, Casey's " Morality " is that of bourgeois individualism, and leaves him not a leg upon which to stand in opposition to the Jingo who proclaims a " patriotic " war as just and " right " *because* it has the support of the immense majority ! Again, on Casey's view the workers form a " class " only in the relative descriptive sense in which one might make a " class " of " red-headed

men, or men born of a Tuesday " (to quote Patrick Pearse) !
To say that " interests " are involved without considering
whether these " interests " are those of the individuals *as
such* (which may be gratified at each other's expense), or
those of their *class needs and aspirations* (which unite them
as a class in antagonism to other classes), is to cut off at the
outset all basis for a positive scientific discussion of the
question. Casey decides the matter as one of *Abstract* morality
affectingonly individuals in the *abstract*.

He goes on to discuss whether we could not " say, by
education " bring about " the social revolution in a *peaceful*
manner."

Does Casey go straight to the obvious point of this question
and discuss the possibility of " educating " the bourgeoisie
up to the point of realising the need for their class surrender ?
Not in the least ! He launches out upon a discourse upon
economics and surplus value and concludes :

> " There are many variations, crossings, and over-
> lappings in this theme of *one gaining at another's expense*,
> and while there are also many intricate points which
> cannot be treated here, the same general argument will
> apply in all cases. It is a matter of each group struggling
> to secure an advantage over the others. But since no
> reform can give the advantage *to everybody*, it follows
> that no reform can do away with the system.

> " The capitalists, to be sure . . . do not as a class
> want to abolish surplus value as a whole, *because in that
> event they would have to work for their living* just as other
> people do."

> " From all this it would seem that no agreement is
> possible, and that the only General feature that can come
> out of such Material for the Purpose of building a new
> society is a revolutionary situation that will have to be
> settled by force."—CASEY, p. 168–9.

The whole question is postulated on the basis of the
existence of the surplus value " cake," and the " impossibility " of any reform " giving an advantage " to *everybody*.
Since the surplus value *and* the competitive scramble are
" given " in the supposition itself, it is not surprising that a
" reform " leaves both in existence. But to conclude from
those premises that a revolution is necessary because " no
agreement is possible " is to argue in the teeth of the very
supposition made. In terms of the case the surplus-value
" cake " has been scrambled for as long as capitalist produc-

tion has been in existence, and the fact that those capitalists who gain often do so at the expense of each other (in which case the losers are stripped of their share of the common capitalist gains made at the expense of the proletariat) has made not the least difference to the generally prevailing belief in the need to maintain the scramble, and the production of surplus value which provides the prizes. If the production of surplus value can go on indefinitely there is no reason to suppose that the scramble would not continue indefinitely likewise—and this all the more because, from the point of view of the *individual as such*, there is a sporting chance that he, too, might pick up something in the scramble ! This, in fact, is the very basis upon which the policy of Labour reformism proceeds, that of providing guarantees for the *continuance* of the production of surplus value in return for a concession to some section of " workers " of a few crumbs from the surplus-value cake—said crumbs being extracted by them in alliance with the big bourgeoisie from the landlords, the Church, the " foreigner," the colonies, or the " unorganised " workers, as the case may be. Casey says nothing to challenge the basis of this " blackmail " theory of Labour politics ; on the contrary, by treating class questions as fundamentally *individual* questions he deprives himself of all grounds for rejecting it !

Casey, however, produces from nowhere a " revolutionary situation." Since he postulates as its premise only the *normal* relations of Capitalist production, we are left with only two choices : Either (1) Capitalism is *always* in a " revolutionary situation " (as ladies who " love their lords " are always, more or less, in an " interesting condition ")—in which case the coming of the revolution depends, *à la* Eastman, on the quite inexplicable advent of a heaven-sent Scientific Engineer of Social Revolution, or, alternatively, (2) the " revolutionary situation " must come as an interference *from without* with these *normal* relations of capitalist production. Neither view is Marxist : both conceptions stand in fatalistic antagonism to a dialectical conception of development, since the abstract *normality* they postulate excludes the conception of *self-contradictory* development culminating in a *crisis* of class-conflict, from which it is possible to find a revolutionary way out. Of the dialectic in capitalist production, of the role of the crisis in creating a revolutionary situation, of the role of the class-struggle to maintain the standard of life of the proletariat at a human level in transforming the proletariat from an aggregation of *inbividuals* into an objectively *real* organic entity, the *revolutionary class* ; of the part played by political parties and their propaganda in facilitating this development and creating the *force* which will be competent to convert the potentiality of a revolutionary situation into the actuality of a proletarian revolution—of all this Casey says not one word, and is debarred from saying one word by the very abstract, metaphysical and anti-dialectical " method " he employs.

His only reason for supposing a " revolutionary situation " is that the workers (for reasons which he does not state) will wish to " abolish surplus value "—which in point of fact makes the coming of the " revolutionary situation " wholly and solely contingent upon a *subjective* logical fact—the acceptance by the proletariat in mass of the categories of Marxian economics. Conversely, the Caseyite " reason " for revolution is that the capitalists as individuals "do not want to work "—a piece of demagogy in the first place, and in the second a characteristic reversion to a *subjective* explanation of objective phenomena.

Casey concludes his discussion of the rôle of education in society thus :

> " No educational agreement is possible, *because* education is always for some Purpose, *consequently* each type of education will tend to serve the purposes of the group whose interests it represents."—Casey, p. 169.

Education, says Casey, always *tends* to serve the purposes of the group whose interests it serves : it does this because education is always for some " purpose," and consequently it serves some interests, and therefore it serves some purpose, and—but there is no need to go on ! In Casey's " logic " there is no such thing as an objective practical criterion of truth, and no objective social standpoint from which that criterion is to be used. In fact, strictly speaking, there is in the Casey logic *no objective world* and no objective *fact*, " society," at all. " Education " for Casey is merely an impartation of " prejudices "—unless it is supplied by him, in which case it is the impartation of " true understanding." When Casey says " interests " he means it to be inferred— " what the silly mutts believe to be their interests " ! And behind all is the unspoken implication that if the bourgeoisie as well as the proletariat could only be forced to acquire the Casey " Method in Thinking," all would be over in no time !

Do you suppose this merely a fantastic assumption born

of spleen, uncharitableness, and party malice ? Put it to the test ! Here is the next paragraph but one :

" Before leaving . . . education, we may refer to the vague notion prevalent among workers to the effect that education is good for them. The idea taken in this broad way contains very little sense, for no relationships are stated.

" . . . If Independent working-class education is good for workers, *this is because* it is bad for capitalists. The latter . . . give support to an education supposed to be free from undesirable class feeling, while all the time this very freedom from class issues is actually a class issue in itself, because it tends to keep the workers from *studying class issues*. Therefore such boasted impartiality is really very partial to the capitalists."—CASEY, pp. 169–170.

To be believed this needs to be studied carefully. Firstly, note the contemptuous reference to the " vague notion prevalent among workers " which " contains very little sense." Then notice that education is *only* " good for " workers (as *individuals*) *because* it is " bad for " capitalists— which if it means anything at all is the Max Eastman notion that the workers can *at best* be tools in the hands of the super-revolutionist, as an alternative to being tools in the hands of the capitalists.

Thirdly, notice that the capitalists (being *also* mutts !) are fools enough to support an education *because they suppose* it to be *free from* " class feeling "—which is, of course, something the capitalists never allow themselves to indulge in ! Fourthly, Casey (expert in logic !) makes *in the same sentence* a dexterous substitution of " class *issues* " for " class *feelings*," and (finally) complains of capitalist-supported education that it " tends to keep the workers from studying class issues " ! The passage begins with " education " treated as a mere matter of personal whim or preference. It ends with a suggestion of the workers as a purely passive mob of " nit-wits " waiting to be instructed in " class issues " before they will even be aware that such things exist !

We challenge Casey's whole standpoint and outlook in general and in detail.

The workers have not a " vague notion " that education is (like Guinness, cod-liver oil, or Epsom salts) " good for them." They have a passionate conviction, born of bitter and humiliating experiences, that they *need knowledge and theoretical training* even more, almost, than they need bread—not to teach them that there are such things as working-class " issues," but to teach them how best to deal practically with the issues raised concretely in their everyday life and practice. The workers do not want Casey or any other body to tell them what " issues " they shall study, or what " issues " they should leave alone as " none of their business." Such a teacher, who starts with the presupposition that the workers are little better than cretins, while he is their heaven-sent " instructor," has only one ground of quarrel with the most bourgeois of deliberate misleaders of the workers—*that he constitutes a trade rival* ! What the workers *need,* and what in increasing numbers they are coming to know they need, is to *make for themselves an " issue "* out of their right to know as much as they can assimilate of all that there is to know, and all that shall hereafter be made available for knowing.

To get the taste of Casey's petty-bourgeois snobbery out of our mouths, let us see how real revolutionary fighters handle the question of education :

> " Without philosophy . . . scientific socialism would never have come into existence. Without their sense for theory scientific socialism would never have become blood and tissue of the workers. . . .

> " . . . The struggle should be so conducted that its three sides, the theoretical, the political, and the practical-economic (opposition to the capitalists) form *one harmonious and well-planned entity.* . . .

> " It is the specific *duty of the leaders* to gain an ever-clearer understanding of the theoretical problems, to free themselves more and more from the influence of traditional phrases inherited from old conceptions of the world, and to keep constantly in mind that *Socialism, having become a science,* demands the same treatment as every other science—*it must be studied.*"—ENGELS : *Peasants' War,* Preface, pp. 27–29.

Here is the case for independent working-class education, stated as nobody could state it better. " Socialism "—the science of the workers' revolutionary emancipation struggle— " must, like every science, *be studied* " !

Here is another extract of like quality :

> " This does not mean, of course, that the workers have no part in creating [their independent *class*] ideology. But they take part *not as workers,* but as Socialist theoreticians . . . ; in other words, they take

part only to the extent to which they are able, more or less, *to acquire the knowledge of their age and advance that knowledge.* And in order that working men *may be able to do this more often*, efforts must be made to raise the level of the consciousness of the workers generally ; care must be taken that the workers do not confine themselves to the artificially restricted limits of *literature for workers*, but study *general literature* to an increasing degree.

" It would be even more true to say ' were not confined ' instead of ' not confine themselves,' because the workers themselves wish to read, and do read all that is written for the intelligentsia, and it is only a few (bad) intellectuals who believe that it is sufficient " for the workers " to tell them a few things about factory conditions and to repeat over and over again what has long been known."
—LENIN : *What is to be Done*, Works, Vol. IV., Book 2, p. 123, footnote.

Against all the quackeries and pretences of the vendors of patent " methods in thinking," Lenin delivers his challenge. The workers need *theory* ; that is the first point. To acquire that theory they must learn to claim, and to assert, their right, and duty, to range the *whole field of knowledge* so far as their capacity for study and assimilation will take them. Not on the puny basis of a wretchedly petty and jerry-built " method of thinking "—a method born of opportunist conceit out of petty bourgeois ignorance—a method masquerading under the doubly-fraudulent labels of " Dietzgen " and " Dialectical Materialism "—upon both of which it is a travesty and an outrage—not on this basis, but on a basis as broad as the total accumulation of the hard-won, historically acquired, culture of the entire human race does the theory of proletarian revolutionary struggle rest as on an unshakeable rock.

.   .   .   .   .   .

CASEY'S " METHOD "—AND DIETZGEN'S

Casey's much trumpeted " Method " is expressed in the formula : Purpose ; Material ; General. With Casey this becomes literally a " Holy Trinity " surrounded with all the mystery and all the terrors of the creed of the Blessed Saint Athanasius. As with the latter, " unity in trinity and trinity in unity " is to be worshipped. Likewise we are warned against " confounding the persons " and " dividing the

substance." The " majesty " is equal : and the " glory "
co-eternal ! Purpose does duty for the Creative Will of the
" Father " ; the " Material " is the incarnate Divinity from
whom all Salvation proceeds ; and the " General," like the
Holy Ghost, " proceeds " from *both* the Father-Purpose and
the Material-Son ! Also Casey is as convinced as Athanasius
that he who doth not think thus rightly of the Trinity,
" without doubt he shall perish everlastingly ! "

What does all this hocus-pocus mean ? Here is Casey's
version :

(1) " That you must have some definite PURPOSE
in mind if you want to think with good effect.

(2) " That you must not allow yourself to guess, or
to dream as to how you intend to realise that
purpose, but must consider all the available
MATERIAL relating to that purpose.

(3) " That you must not base your conclusions on
little bits of the material, that is on special cases,
but must fit your thought to the GENERAL
nature of the material, of course within the
limits covered by your purpose."

—CASEY : p. 25.

One needs only to scrutinise this formula once (after a few
samples of Casey's use of it) to spot the fallacy which stares
one directly in the face.   Casey has taken Dietzgen's *terms*
and totally miscomprehended their *meaning* !   " The hands
are the hands of Esau (Dietzgen) but the voice is the voice of
Jacob (Casey)."

*Casey's secret is that he does not in the least know the meaning
of the term " general " as used by logicians, including Dietzgen.*

Casey uses the term in its vernacular sense—that in which
we say " it *generally* rains when I take a holiday," or " Jones
is *generally* drunk on Friday night," or " the 7.53 from
Clapham Junction is *generally* ten minutes late."   For Casey
it means " *true on the average of cases* "—that is to say, *not true*
in *some* cases.

For a logician—and whatever else Dietzgen was he was
certainly a logician—the term *general* has a *specific* and not
a " general " meaning in the vernacular sense.   A *General*
quality in logic is that which permits the establishment of
a classification.   A quality possessed in common by *all* the
examples under survey (which examples, *each* of them, differ
in *other* respects) is their *general* or distinguishing quality as
a group or class : likewise the qualities they possess *in*

addition are their *particular* differences, and enable them to be distinguished as *particulars* from the *general* category as such.

Dietzgen's whole point—and it was of immense importance and merit—that he should have made it especially as against the Kantians was that " understanding " consisted in nothing more mysterious than this simple *practical* discrimination between the particular *and* the general in all *concrete* and *objective* phenomena, *including concepts themselves treated as phenomena for objective investigation.*

To appreciate the point fully one should remember the vogue of Kant and the central point in all the Kantian logic. Kant started with the problem, How are synthetic judgments possible *a priori* ?   That is to say : I affirm " John Jones *is* a man."   Here I assert that the *particular* object of my immediate contemplation (" John Jones ") possesses the " general " quality of belonging to a class, group, or category which includes *many* individuals.   It is thus not only an assertion about "John Jones," it is an assertion that there exists a *class* of objects which are *all* distinguishable by the possession in common of the quality of " humanity."   Now this, says Kant, is asserting something far beyond the power of any individual to know from experience.   It is a judgment *a priori* (in advance of experience) ; it is a synthetic judgment in that it affirms the existence in John Jones of *two* contrasted (" opposite ") qualities, particularity and generality in combination.   If all knowledge were derived from actual experience, such a judgment would be impossible.   *Therefore* : the Reason in man is a Transcendental faculty whereby the particulars of experience are endowed with logical *forms* which permit synthetic judgments to be passed upon them.

It is this Kantian assertion that all we can possibly gain from the world of experience is knowledge of separate, distinct, and unconnected particulars—and, consequently, that all conceptions of generality, universality, cause, effect, sequence and consequence, quality, quantity, time, space, etc., are wholly *creations of the subjective understanding* that Dietzgen is battling against.

Dietzgen accepts in common with Kant (that which constituted Kant's chief contribution to philosophy) the discrimination between objective reality and the subjective form in which we become conscious of its existence.   But he denied flatly the Kantian assertion that this objective

Reality was unknowable *in itself*. He affirmed—and therein took the materialist standpoint—that the thing as it is *for us*, is also the thing as it *is* " in itself." To talk about the " thing *for* itself " was to talk animistic nonsense. It is true, as Kant said, that we first become aware that a paving-stone exists by reason of what it does to us ; but in knowing what a thing *does* we know at any rate that much about it, and by going on to find *all* the things it *could* do to us, and to other things, and all the things we could do to it we can learn progressively all that the paving-stone *is* " *in itself.*" To ask what the paving-stone is *for* itself is to ask *what it feels like to be a paving-stone* ! Whether paving-stones have feelings is, so far, beyond our powers of ascertainment. To that extent the paving-stone remains " unknown." But " unknown " and " unknowable " are very different things—even when the difficulties of discovery (as in the case of the *other* side of the moon) are so great that the unknown is, for all we can see, likely to remain such indefinitely.

As to the question of " synthetic judgments *a priori* " Dietzgen, by the same materialist method, exploded the Kantian " mystery."   These judgments were, he demonstrated, neither *synthetic* nor *a priori* : they were analytic and *a posteriori*.

Even the very first experience of a human being—that of being born—of passing from a pre-natal to a post-natal state —gives in the differing quality of two states experienced in succession the basis for the concepts of likeness and difference, continuity and discontinuity, succession and non-successive continuance, of being, non-being, and their immediate unity, *beginning to be*.   All these are discoverable *a posteriori* by analysis as " given " in the experience.   Similarly, in judging that " John Jones is a man " we discover analytically in the objective fact John Jones that, in addition to being uniquely " John," and particularly " Jones," he is generally one of a class with all the other specimens comprisable under the category Man.

From all which it follows that while it is true, as Kant says, that all reasoning consists in synthetically comprehending a group of particulars by means of their generality, or conversely in discriminating a general category into its component particulars, all this is done (despite Kant) on the basis of and by means of objective practice—practice through objects. Admittedly the universe presents itself to inspection *at first glance* as a bewilderment of totally distinct and *unique* particulars. But equally true it is that on a second, third, fourth and forty-millionth glance we shall have perceived, along with those particularities, generalities of a wider and wider range up to and including the most universal category of all Existence. In every unique thing (*this* table, say, or *that* chair) there coexists along with its uniqueness all grades of particularity and generality up to the most universal (the fact that it *exists*).

Universal qualities, about which Kant made all the mystery, were thus objectively experienced *facts*, and as much " phenomenal " as any facts. They only became " forms " of the logical understanding when, in subjective *practice*, a human being, in classifying his experiences, distinguished *in thought* between the *generals* and the *particulars* of concrete objective experience.

For Dietzgen therefore the terms : Purpose, Material, and General, had specific and materialist meanings. His concern was with *concepts* and their materialist origin, significance, and importance. Since all our concepts arise as modifications in *our* consciousness, and are distinguishable from each other as *particulars* in the " general " or " *universal* " of consciousness, all concepts whatsoever had that nature in common. All were thus inextricably united in the universal *whole* of consciousness. Likewise, since we are conscious only of existing in a *specific* relation to the external world (only in active interaction with which do we *become* conscious at all), the *content* of all our particular and general states of consciousness is this *common, unvarying, universal* fact of practical interrelation between ourselves (as thinking *subjects*) and the external world and its changes (as the *objects* of our thought). For Dietzgen, therefore, the process of distinguishing *between* the " general " and the " particular " in any given case was one of *practical* discrimination between qualities which co-existed in concrete experience. Their co-existence was the basis from which their separate " existence " *in thought* was derived, and the fact of their objective co-existence was, to him, of even more urgent importance (as against Kantian mysticism) than the fact that they could be separated, *by abstraction*, in thought. Thus, that a *general* category " man " was a *particular* in relation to the *more* general category " Animal," while being at the same time *general* in relation to particular " men," was sufficient to explode the Kantian " mystery " alleged of the " synthetic union of the *opposites* particular and general."

Curiously enough, though Dietzgen did not know it—
(and this is a striking testimony to the soundness of Dietzgen's
reasoning in general)—*this was the very line taken by Hegel*
from the purely logical side, in his assault upon the Kantian
system of rigidly antithetical categories.   Those who are
mystified at the terminology of Hegelianism—especially the
" identity of contraries "—should, in justice, remember that
they owe it nearly all, not to Hegel, but to Immanuel Kant.

Dietzgen's term, " purpose," was identical in meaning
with the more usual term " point of view."   For Dietzgen
the term " material " was used in a twofold sense : (1) as with
Kant, as denoting the objectively given *content* in any
concept under analysis ;   (2) as denoting the objective
material world itself and its phenomena.   These senses were
with Dietzgen necessary correlatives—the former being only
the subjective *aspect* of the latter.   But in his eagerness to
smash Kantian mysticism he sometimes confounded the two
senses—as when he treated the *concept* of a desk as " material "
in the same objective sense as was the desk itself.   But even
here the slip was verbal only—it was never in doubt that
Dietzgen conceived thought as a *reflection* of an actual,
objectively existing material world.   Likewise, for Dietzgen,
the process of understanding was that of tracing " general "
concepts back to their concrete *originals* ; as much as it
was one of " deriving the *general* from the concrete."   To
distinguish the " general " was for Dietzgen likewise to
distinguish the " particular."   Always Dietzgen insisted upon
the objectivity of *observation* as the indispensable prec-
requisite of the subjective *practice* of understanding.

Now turn to Casey and observe the difference.   Not only
does he never insist upon objectivity of observation, he never
notices that in distinguishing the General one also, and by
the same act, distinguishes the Particular.   His " general "
as we have seen, is a *general average*—a something-more-or-
less which is distinguished, *not* by its *objective* existence, but
by a subjective " magic " called " method."   " Material "
for Casey is, *as with Kant*, a wholly subjective, *logical*,
" material," never the objective material of *objective reality*.

Casey has borrowed everything from Dietzgen—*except the
materialism of his method* !

.   .   .   .   .

It may seem surprising that Casey should be guilty of so
glaring a bungle.   It may even seem, to those less practised
in logical discrimination, as though the difference between

the technical-logical and the vernacular-descriptive senses of the term " General " has been made too much of. An illustration or two will make the issue clear. Socialism as a concept can be defined in one of two ways : (1) one can distinguish it as a *particular* " ism " from *all* other " isms "—from the *General* category of " *isms* " ; or (2) one can define it as the opinion generally (i.e., on the average) prevailing among " Socialists." In the former case one must then proceed to state that which *all* varieties of " Socialism " possess as their essential *common* characteristic—i.e., the aim or object of attaining a form of social organisation based upon the " socialisation " of production, of the ownership of the means of production, and of the means of consumption and enjoyment resulting—and proceed to evaluate Socialist bodies, movements, and individuals by the degree to which they do, or do not, subordinate all their endeavours, as *means*, to the attainment of this end. In the latter case one takes the average opinion current among " Socialists " as *normal* (or " general "), and evaluates all particular " socialisms " as extreme or moderate according to whether they go beyond or fall short of this average. The practical difference this makes is enormous. On the former view the " true " Socialism, the one most closely corresponding to the *general* logical concept as defined, is the militant Marxism of the Communist International. On the second view the " true " Socialism in Britain is that of the British Labour Party ! On the former view the Nazis are *excluded* ; on the latter they are included because they *call* themselves " Socialists." As we have seen, Casey takes the second view !

Again, in considering that which is " general " to the human race one is faced with the fact that there are White, Black, Brown, " Red," and Yellow races—each of which has other distinguishing peculiarities besides colour. On the objective-logical view taken by Dietzgen and all Dialectical Materialists all these differences would be disregarded, since their common humanity would consist in those morphological and physiological characteristics which they possessed *in common*, and which at the same time are not possessed by organisms other than men. On Casey's view the *general* would be a general *average* in between White, Black, Brown, Red, and Yellow men ! Something like the result of an accident at a dye-works !

The Dietzgenian view uses the concept *general* as a means of distinguishing—a means of *separation*, between particular

" generals." Casey sees nothing in it but its *unity*. Hence while for Dietzgen the distinction between particular and general is created by the single logical act which places them in *opposition*, Casey pleads tearfully for their equal right to *coexist* in permanent union, all unconscious of the fact that thereby he negates entirely Dietzgen's whole critical refutation of Kant !

In a word, Casey's idealistic bemuddlement is *Absolute*.

CASEY'S HUMOUR

It would be unfair to take leave of Casey without acknowledging his most remarkable and pleasing side—his sense of humour, and his comforting assurance that humour is still permitted to those addicted to his " Method." Here is a sample—or, at least, it is difficult to believe that this can, even by Casey, be intended seriously :

> " Our opponents *cannot* think *as we do* (! ! !) we mean, not in general, and *this* (! ! !) *is why they will fight*. It is not just simply that all history tells us it will be so, rather is it the *physical* nature of *thinking itself* explains how it is that history has that particular tale to tell."— CASEY, p. 173.

This goes one better than those who make all history a matter of psychology—this turns psychology in turn into *phrenology* ! Now see how Casey explains dialectics :

> " To say for instance that ' yes ' and ' no ' can be reconciled and *become the same thing* seems, on the surface, like (!) talking nonsense, and yet it is easily explained (! ! !). Suppose we ask ' is the parcel light ? ' and the answer is ' Yes,' and then we ask ' is it heavy ? ' and the answer is ' No.' We have here two equally correct but completely contradictory (! ! ! !) forms of the same thing *because* (! ! !) the same answer is given by a positive in one case and a negative in the other, so in these relationships the *two* of positive and negative are *one* (!)."—CASEY, p. 35.

Casey " reconciles " the opposites of positive and negative —by changing the *verbal* form in which one and the same fact is stated ! No wonder he dislikes the Marx-Engels-Lenin-Hegel kind of dialectic ! His exemplar and master must be Tom Hood :

> " So they went and told the Sexton,
> And the Sexton tolled the bell ! "

Here is Casey showing how every proposition must be valued in relation to the purpose in view, and being playful withal :

> " Looking at the formula now from another angle we may possibly get a little fun out of it (! ! !) at times. If, for instance, a workman on a high building were to shout down to a fellow-workman on the ground, ' Dick, what time is it ? ' and Dick shouted back, ' What's the purpose in view ? ' this *may raise a laugh* (! ! !)."

In " general " (as Casey would say) it would be more likely to start a fight. But, be that as it may, Casey makes haste to warn us :

> " But if such joking were to become general it would *tend to lower the dignity of the science* (! ! !). Therefore, *as a rule*, this attitude should be avoided (! ! !)."—Casey, p. 61.

Sancta simplicitas ! Casey promised to be simple, and " simple " he is in very deed !

A fair exchange is no robbery ! In return for Casey's " little fun," and in gratitude for his assurance that " even a little humour is permissible if it be not overdone," we offer him two samples, both illustrative of logical operations, and both sufficiently ancient not to constitute a precedent for those likely to " lower the dignity of the science." The first is pertinent to the question whether " mind " is or is not " part " of Matter :

> " The Verdict and Arbitrament of Seiny Jhon
>
> " At Paris, in the Roast-meat Cookery of the Petit Chastelet, before the Cook-shop of one of the roast-meat sellers of that lane, a certain hungry Porter was eating his bread, after he had by parcels kept it awhile above the reek and steam of a fat Goose on the spit . . . and found it so besmoaked with the vapour as to be savoury. . . . After having ravined his penny loaf he was about discamping and going away ; but, by your leave . . . the Master Cook laid hold upon him by the Gorget, demanding payment for the Smoak of his Roast meat. . . .
>
> " The altercation waxed hot in words, which moved the gaping Hoydens of sottish Parisians to run from all parts to see what the issue would be of that babbling Strife and Contention.
>
> " In the interim of this Dispute, to very good purpose, Seiny Jhon the Fool and Citizen of Paris happened

there, whom the Cook perceiving, said to the Porter,
Wilt thou refer and submit unto the noble Seiny Jhon
the decision of the Difference and Controversie which is
betwixt us ? Yea, by the blood of a Goose, answered
the Porter, I am content. . . .

" Seiny Jhon, the Fool . . . commanded the Porter
to draw out of the Fob of his belt a piece of Money, if
he had it. . . . This Seiny Jhon took and [after making
sure it was good money] in a profound silence of the
whole doltish people who were the Spectators of this
Pageantry . . . he finally caused the Porter to make it
sound several times on the stall of the Cook's shop.
Then, with a Presidential majesty . . . he first, with all
the force of his lungs, coughed three times and then
with an audible voice pronounced the following sentence :

" The Court declareth, That the Porter who ate his
Bread at the Smoak of the Roast, hath civilly paid the
Cook with the sound of his Money."

—Rabelais (1483–1553) : *Gargantua and Pantagruel* ;
   Book III., ch. 37.

The second illustrates no less appositely the difference
between the " logical " and the *real* union of opposites

" How the Skoler of Oxford proved by souphestry
ii chekyns were iii

" The father, the mother, and the young scholar
sitting at supper having before them no more meat but
only a couple of chickens, the father said on this wise :
Son, so it is that I have spent much money on thee to
sende thee to school. Wherefore I have great desire to
know about what thou hast learned.

" To which the son answered and said : Father, I have
studied sophistry and by that science I can prove that
these two chickens in the dish be three chickens.

" Marry, said the father, that would I fain see.

" The scholar took one of the chickens in his hand and
said : Lo ! here is one chicken ! And incontinent he
took both the chickens in his hand jointly and said :
Here is two chickens and one and two maketh three !
Ergo here is three chickens.

" Then the father took one of the chickens to himself
and gave another to his wife and said thus : Lo ! I will
have one of the chickens to my part and thy mother

shall have another. And because of thy good argument *thou shalt have the third to thy supper*—for thou gettest no more meat here at this time."

—THE HUNDRED MERRY TALES, *circa* 1400.

From which instructive narrative we learn, beyond a peradventure, that the Casey "method" in "thinking" was practised, *and also found out,* more than five hundred years ago!

EPILOGUE

SURVEYED as a whole the life-work of Marx and Engels is, whether considered in respect of their Theory of Practice or their Practice of their Theory all of a piece. It is a whole, a living, developing, self-expanding, self-rectifying Unity of Theory and Practice, which derives its living force, its quickening power, and its ever-widening and deepening significance from the fact that this unity is based on the primacy of Practice.

Its conception of the inter-relation of Theory and Practice, is the vital essence of Marxism and is that one aspect in its many-faceted unity in which the significance of Dialectical Materialism is most clearly seen and most easily grasped. This *unity* is a unity of inter-relation : it is *Materialist* in that it is based on the primacy of practice, and *Dialectical* in its postulation of the indispensable precondition for both the practice and the unity, namely, the reflex-interactive relation of the Subjective World of Thinking, Feeling, and Willing to the really-existent, and material Objective World, from which it is derived and in relation to which alone it possesses reality, significance and meaning.

Its world-conception is *Materialist* alike in its Objectivity and in its Activity—in that the world is conceived as a totality, and by means of its inseparably connected and never-ceasing interacting *movements*.

And it is *Dialectical* in that these inter-acting movements are recognised as begetting, of necessity, a perpetual self-transformation of the Universe as a whole—a universally inter-connected series of processes in which old forms, formations, and inter-relations are constantly being destroyed and replaced by new forms—the *resultants* of the universally interactive movements, and processes of movement.

So, too, is its Theory of Knowledge *Materialist* in respect of its objectivist-Realism, its affirmation of the Knowability of this objective, material, reality, and its repudiation of all subjectivism. It is also, and at the same time, *Dialectical* in its recognition of the Relativism involved in the reflex character of knowledge, and of the primacy of objective practice, practice through objects, in generating that knowledge. It is *Dialectical-Materialist* above all in its recognition that the process of cognition is an activity—a subjective *practice*—and that the movement of Thought resulting from this practice reflects the objective movement of dialectically developing Reality as a whole.

Its essence, for Practice, is summed up in the inspiriting slogan : *The philosophers have only* INTERPRETED *the world in various ways : the point, however, is to* CHANGE *it.*

.   .   .   .   .

We began our inquiry with the observation of a fact—that all the critics of Marx, those ostensibly friendly even more than those avowedly hostile, begin by disrupting this living unity of Theory and Practice into a jumble of theoretical oddments from which, along with the unity, the *life*—the vitalising, unifying, practice—had been eliminated as irrelevant. We have ended our inquiry with a survey of criticisms and projects for the revision of Marxism, all of which proceed on fundamentally the same assumption—that Practice in Marxist Theory plays a neglible and subordinate role, and can be disregarded : that the Theory of Marxism is not a whole but a mechanical aggregate from which parts can be removed at will and replaced by new and " more up-to-date " substitutes.

We claim to have proved in detail, as well as in general, concretely as well as inferentially, that Marxism, being a living whole, must be accepted or rejected as a whole—that it needs no " revision " from the outside, since it provides within itself its own means of organic self-revision ; that those who aim at " revising " the *theory* of Marx aim, consciously or unconsciously, at revising its Practice, at turning it into something other than " the real movement to make an end of things as they are "—the revolutionary proletarian class struggle for the overthrow of the bourgeois order, for the Dictatorship of the Proletariat, for the objectively dialectical transformation of society from capitalism into the classless Order of Socialism and Communism.

.   .   .   .   .

That which distinguishes the Revisionist is that while the open Counter-Revolutionary fights to destroy Marxism frankly, as a living whole, the Revisionist seeks to convert Marxism into a dead aggregate of abstract theories—only mechanically inter-connected and capable of every sort of eclectic substitution and replacement—and does so under cover of an " acceptance " of Marxism and in the name of bringing it up-to-date. In either case, it is the *living movement* of Marxism which is aimed at : in each case the end envisaged is the same, the conversion of Marxism into a *corpse*, of interest only to anatomists and museum curators. The whole history of Marxism has been one of battle against these two groups of foes.

In its first period, that of the crisis of 1844–50, Marxism was itself a *minority movement* aiming at the complete and objectively revolutionary transformation of the " demo-cratic " proletarian struggle. Marxism did not offer itself as a *revision* of Utopianism, democratic-republicanism, or socialist-democracy. It offered itself frankly as their revolu-tionary alternative. It was conscious of the fact, and " scorned " any attempt at its concealment, that however much it might agree in incidentals with such proletarian and socialist or communist movements as had preceded it, it was radically different from them in that it combined those incidentals in an entirely *new* synthesis—that of a revolu-tionary, dialectical theory and a dialectically revolutionary practice.

In its second period Marxism, more or less dominant in the First International (1864–72), faced the systematic endeavour to *revise* it, which was headed by Michael Bakunin.

That which Bakunin attacked directly was the Marxian Dialectical conception of historical development upon which was based the Marxian conception of a dialectically-developing revolutionary *class* struggle. The most cursory inspection of Bakuninism is sufficient to reveal the truth of Marx's saying : " Bakunin never assimilated *Materialism* : he was only *adulterated* by it ! " Bakunin's whole conception was *anti*-dialectical. His conception of society was the " atomic " conception of all bourgeois political speculation ; his conception of " classes " was the reflex-relative bourgeois conception of rich *versus* poor—(and, hence, in the Bakuninist theory, the *poorer*, the more " revolutionary.") His con-ception of revolution was the purely negative-political conception of the negation of " authority "—of the State *in the abstract*. Because Bakunin was quite prepared to " accept " many of the incidentals of Marxism his quarrel with Marx is (by critics whose standpoint is equally non-Marxian) commonly regarded as one of " mere " *personalities*. Because Bakunin invariably in his propaganda exalted these incidentals (Atheism for instance) into ends in themselves, he is by the more stupidly uncritical type of critic regarded as " far more revolutionary " than Marx. What is missed by all these critics is the fact that Bakunin rejected *in toto* that which is basic and *essential* in Marxism—*its unifying logic*, its dialectical synthesis of Theory and Practice. They do not see that Bakunin was a typical " Left " *revisionist*.

During the rise and progress of the Social Democratic Parties and of the Second International, the fights waged by Marx and Engels, and those who most closely adhered to their standpoint (among whom the only one at all comparable to their stature was Lenin) were all fights which centred on the same basic question—Marxism as a living *unity* of Theory and Practice as against Marxism as a fortuitous aggregation of abstract doctrines, any one of which was detachable and might be replaced without disturbing the vital, organic *unity* of the conception as a whole.

Thus it was that Marx and Engels warred against Lassalle —with his undialectical, abstract, metaphysical dogmas of the " Iron Law of Wages " and the " Right to the whole Produce of Labour," and his totally unhistorical conception of the " free " Social and Democratic State—against Dühring and his *anti*-dialectical, abstract, pseudo-" Scientific," dogmatic system of Socialism ; against the anarchists to the " Left " and the compromising concessions of Liebknecht and Bebel to the Lasselleans to the Right. In every one of these cases it was the living *unity* of Marxist Theory and Practice—its Dialectical Materialism—which was defended against attempts to kill it by " revision."

This became patent and obvious in the effort made by Bernstein, after Engels' death, to secure a *revision* of the Social-Democratic Party programme. In Britain, owing on the one hand to the theoretical incompetence of Hyndman (the nominal spokesman of " Marxism ") and to the petty bourgeois eclecticism of the Fabians on the other, Bernstein's effort has never been understood or described with any sort of critical appreciation. It is known, of course, that he claimed that the law of the concentration of Capital as formulated by Marx was being falsified by events. This was trumpeted abroad by the British Fabians as " proof " of their wisdom in having rejected Marx's economics altogether. The fact of the concentration of Capital is now so obvious that the Fabians have discreetly forgotten their " wisdom " along with its " proof " and now try the new method of " accepting " Marx—with variations !

All the time there has been discreetly pushed out of sight the essential fact, namely, that Bernstein proposed a revision of Marxism *all along the line*, and proposed to abandon, not only the economics of Marx but the *whole* of its fundamental Dialectical Materialism. Bernstein frankly rejected both the Materialism *and* the Dialectic, and along with it the Dialectical concept of Revolution. He frankly proposed a return to *Kant*—and an accommodation of the Social-Democratic programme to the standpoint of the abstract individual in bourgeois society. He was, in fact, an *inverted Bakunin*. And the most profound criticism of Bernsteinism was that passed (in private) by his friend Auer, the arch-opportunist : " My dear Ned ; you are an ass ! One *does* these things : one does not *say* them ! " Bernstein, in fact, was asking for no more than the open acknowledgment that the line and direction of the Social Democracy had become (as the events of the War and the post-War period have made it impossible to deny) the *reverse* of that of Marx and Engels. It had abandoned the standpoint of the proletariat in deeds, and maintained it only in words. In *practice*, it stood upon the standpoint of bourgeois society ; in *theory* it stood upon that of the proletariat. In the end the logic of its own contradiction brought it to the pass of openly attempting, not only through the mouthpiece of Kautsky but officially, as a party, to achieve the " emancipation " of the proletariat within the framework of the bourgeois social order. As soon as it had ceased to be able to delude even itself into believing that this was possible, it was swept aside contemptuously by the Hitlerite Fascists for whose coming it had prepared.

Concurrently with the fight against Bernsteinism, Lenin carried on his classic struggle against its Russian counter-part, Menshevism, and as part of that struggle he fought his battle against the philosophical Revisionism which cropped up even within the Bolshevik party in the period of depression after the defeat of the revolution of 1905–6. Lenin's *Materialism and Empirio-Criticism* stands exactly on all fours with Engels' *Anti-Duhring*, and Marx's *Poverty of Philosophy* as a titanic blow struck in defence of the living essential of Marxism, that which makes it an organic unity, its Dialectical Materialism.

Thus has the objective dialectic of history also demonstrated beyond any possibility of question that Marx and Engels themselves, and following them Lenin and Stalin, manifest invariably in practice that unity of theory and practice which constituted Marxism's theoretical point of departure, and which constitutes the goal at which the whole theoretical practice of Marx and Engels was aimed. Marxism, which to-day is also Leninism, must be accepted or rejected *as a whole*. And as a whole it is, as is affirmed in the *Programme of the Communist International,* a " revolutionary mode of conceiving Reality with a view to effecting a revolutionary change in that Reality." This, and neither less nor more than this, is Dialectical Materialism.

With our primary purpose thus accomplished we may fittingly conclude with a few leading suggestions for the guidance of those whom this all-too-protracted " essay in exploration " may have inspired with a desire to explore further.

In no respect has Marxism been more falsified than in that it has been presented as a doctrine which denied all worth and reality to the *individual,* and his (or her) subjective activity. The doctrine of the Unity of Theory and Practice negates this falsification from the root upward. Dialectical Materialism, far from being a system of *fatalism,* is the direct and positive negation of every sort of fatalistic theory which denies reality and force to the *activity* of mankind, whether that activity be overt and objective or merely subjective. Certainly it emphasises the fact that each specific activity can have only the effect of its nature and natural scope. But in so doing it affirms the *objective* reality of that effect within its natural limits. Moreover, Dialectical Materialism, by its conception of the compound cumulativeness of the force acquired by the *individual* in collective and co-operative practice, negates all mystical and fatalistic pessimism by its demonstration of the *real* possibility of transcending in collective co-operation the subjective limitations of the individual *in isolation.* Dialectical Materialism stands triumphant in its demonstration that men can and will *change* the world of Reality both subjectively and objectively. In its demonstration of the unity of theory and practice Dialectical Materialism includes the demonstration of the practical importance of theory and the significance, therefore, of every individual addition to the sum total of theoretical understanding attained through *subjective* as well as objective practice.

Dialectical Materialism thus negates the spurious

" individualism " of bourgeois *subjectivism*—of theory radically divorced from practice, and practice arbitrarily subordinated to dogmatic theories *a priori*—in all its varieties, up to and including all the " anarchisms " which are, as we have proved, merely transmission belts conveying speculation which has lost its grip upon reality back to the logical goal of all *anti*-rationalism, namely, solipsism and supernaturalism. But Dialectical Materialism negates this spurious " individualism " by affirming on objectively intelligible grounds, the *real* and indispensable worth of objective and subjective *individuality*. That this individuality is converted from a dream vision into a realised fact only in objective, social, co-operative *practice*, makes it the negation of the " individualism " of bourgeois and " bohemian " posturing. In this lies a measure of the transcendental superiority of the individuality conceived and attained by Dialectical Materialism, and by its world conception and method, its united theory and practice, alone.

Dialectical Materialism is the negation of any and every variety of dogmatism—of superficial *a priori*-ism. The criticism of the *method* of his *Capital* quoted with approval by Marx himself from a Russian economist is a classic repudiation in advance of all who would substitute for a genuine objective analysis any sort of arbitrary attempt to " fit thoughts to things " :

" Marx only troubles himself about one thing : to show, by rigid scientific investigation, the necessity of successive determinate orders of social conditions, and to establish as impartially as possible the facts that serve him for fundamental starting-points. For this it is quite enough if he proves, at one and the same time, both the necessity of the present order of things, and the necessity of another order into which the first must inevitably pass over ; and this all the same whether men believe or do not believe it—whether they are conscious or unconscious of it. . . .

" Such an inquiry will confine itself to the confrontation and the comparison of a fact, not with ideas, but with another fact. For this inquiry, the one thing of moment is, that both facts be investigated *as accurately as possibly* and that they *actually form* each with respect to the other different *momenta of an evolution*.

" But, it will be said, the general laws of economic life are one and the same, no matter whether they are applied to the present or the past. *This Marx directly denies. According to him, such abstract laws do not exist. . .*

" The scientific value of such an inquiry lies in the disclosing of the special laws that regulate the origin, existence, development, death, of a given social organism and its replacement by another and a higher one. *And it is this value that, in point of fact, Marx's work lies.*"
—Quoted in MARX : *Capital,* Vol. I, preface, p.xxvii–xxviii.

Commenting on this, Marx asks : " What is he picturing but the *dialectic method* ? " So much has been said by open opponents and deluded or incompetent expounders to represent the dialectical method as either a dogmatic mysticism or a ready-made recipe to be applied as mechanically as a slot-machine is worked, that it is before all things imperative to insist, as this passage does, upon the strict objectivity of observation and the scientific precision of analysis employed in the method of Marx. This is before all things indispensable in the use of Dialectical Materialism as a method.

Marx himself observes upon this matter :

" *Of course the method of presentation must differ from that of inquiry.* The latter has to appropriate the material in detail, to *analyse* its different *forms of development,* to trace out their inner connection. Only after this work is done, can the actual *movement* be adequately described. If this is done successfully, if the life of the subject-matter is ideally reflected as in a mirror, then it may appear as if we had before us a mere *a priori* construction.

" My dialectic method is not only different from the Hegelian, *but is its direct opposite.* . . . With me . . . the ideal is nothing else than *the material world* reflected by the human mind and *translated* into forms of thought.

" The mystifying side of Hegelian dialectic I criticised nearly thirty years ago, at a time when it was still the fashion. . . . In its mystified form dialectic became the fashion in Germany because it seemed to transfigure and to glorify the existing state of things. In its rational form [i.e., the Marxian] it is a scandal and an abomination to bourgeoisdom and its doctrinare professors. because it includes in its comprehension and its affirmative recognition of the existing state of things, the recognition at the same time also, of the negation of that state, of its inevitable breaking-up ; *because it lets nothing impose upon it, and is in its essence critical and revolutionary.*"—MARX : *Capital*, Vol. I, preface, pp. xxx–xxxi.

Objectivity of observation, the affirmative recognition of what *is*, the simultaneous recognition that " things have just this worth—that they are *transitory* " (HEGEL), this method which " lets nothing impose upon it," which is *essentially* " critical and revolutionary "—*this* is the method of Dialectical Materialism.

As a supplement to these descriptions of Marx's own method can be taken the classic description of the Dialectical Materialist world-conception given by Engels in his *Socialism : Utopian and Scientific* :

" When we consider and reflect upon nature at large, or the history of mankind, or our own intellectual activity, at first we see the picture of an endless entanglement of relations and reactions, permutations and combinations, in which nothing remains what, where, and as it was, but everything moves, changes, comes into being, and passes away.

" We see, therefore, at first, *the picture as a whole,* with its individual parts still more or less kept in the background ; *we observe the movements, transitions, connections, rather than the things that move, combine, and are connected.* . . .

" But this conception correctly as it expresses the general character of the picture of appearances as a whole, does not suffice to explain the details of which this picture is made up, and so long as we do not understand these we have not a clear idea of the whole picture. *In order to understand these details we must detach them from their natural or historical connection and examine each one separately,* its nature, special causes, effects, etc. This is primarily the task of natural science and historical research. . . .

" But this method of work has also left us as legacy the habit of observing natural objects and processes in isolation, apart from their connection with the vast whole ; of observing them in repose, not in motion ; as constants, not as variables ; in their death, not in their life. . . .

" [This] metaphysical mode of thought, *justifiable and necessary as it is* . . . sooner or later reaches a limit beyond which it becomes one-sided, restricted, abstract, lost in *insoluble* contradictions.

" In the contemplation of individual things, it forgets the *connection* between them ; in the contemplation of their existence it forgets the *beginning* and *end* of that existence ; of their repose, it forgets their *motion. It cannot see the wood for the trees.. . . .*

" Dialectics, on the other hand, *comprehends things and their representations* (ideas) *in their essential connection, concatenation, motion, origin, and ending. . . .*

" Nature is the proof of dialectics, and it must be said for modern science that it has furnished this proof . . . and shown that, in the last resort, Nature works dialectically and not metaphysically ; that she does *not* move in the *eternal one-ness* of a perpetually recurring cycle, but goes through a *real, historical, evolution.*"

—ENGELS : *Socialism,* pp. 29–34.

Supplementing this classic description of the contrast between the petty rigidity and narrowness of the metaphysical mode of reasoning—(and of all its empiricist, eclectic, and subjectivist derivatives)—and the magnificent sweep and infinite *flexibility* and *variety* of the Dialectical Materialist world - conception, we may cite a practical illustration. Among Lenin's notebooks there was found a set of notes on Hegel's *Science of Logic.* Included in them is the following table of the " Elements of Dialectics " :

" ELEMENTS OF DIALECTICS.

(1) *Objectivity* of observation. Not ' examples,' not unrepresentative forms. The thing in itself.

(2) *Totality* of the manifold *relations* of the things to others.

(3) *The Development* of the thing (or of the phenomenon). Its own movement, own life.

(4) *The inner* contradictory *tendencies* (*and* sides) in the thing.

(5) The thing (appearance) as *sum and unity of opposites.*

(6) The *struggle* or unfolding of the opposites.

(7) The union of *analysis* and *synthesis.* The splitting up into the separate parts and the totality, summation of these parts together.

(8) The *relations* (of the thing or appearance) not only manifold but *general, universal.* Everything (appearance, process, etc.) is connected with *every other.*

(10) An *infinite process* of revealing of *new* sides, relations, etc.

(11) An infinite process of *deepening of knowledge* of the thing, appearance, process, etc., by men ; *from appearance to essence* and from less deep to deeper essence.

(12) From *co-existence to causality* and from one form of connection and reciprocal dependence to another deeper and more general.

(13) The *repetition of* certain features, properties, etc., of *the lower stage in the higher*.

(14) Apparent return to the old (*negation of the negation*).

(15) The *struggle of content with form* and *vice versa*. The throwing off of the form, transformation of the content.

(16) *Passing* of quantity into quality and *vice versa*.
    (15 and 16 are examples of 9)."

This table gives us not only an objective proof of the scrupulous and unremitting care with which Lenin reached his conclusions ; but also an instrument of simply incalculable value for all students seeking to acquire a practical facility in the use of Dialectical Materialism as a method. We can say of this, but with far better reason, what Kant himself said of his own dialectical method—" He who has once sampled the Critical method will have done for ever with all dogmatic twaddle."

.   .   .   .   .

Precisely because it is, both in its Materialism and in its Dialectical method, above all things *critical and revolutionary*, Dialectical Materialism provides a practical critical weapon both of defence and offence against the whole of the Cultural Reaction which is general and symptomatic of the decadence and collapse of the bourgeois order. That order is visibly collapsing culturally and morally even before its economic and political collapse has become sufficiently advanced to beget more than the preliminary symptoms of the culminating crisis—such as the various local triumphs of Fascism. Against this cultural reaction—above all in philosophy, art, and morals—only Dialectical Materialism makes or can make any serious headway. As the crisis deepens so increasingly will it become necessary that the upholders of the standpoint of the revolutionary proletarian struggle should be

able by means of the Dialectical Materialist world conception
and its practical critical method to meet and defeat cultural
reaction on cultural grounds and with cultural weapons.
Thus alone will it be possible to carry the revolutionary
banner into the field of culture and rally to its side all the
elements of the intelligentsia and of the cultured strata of
the bourgeoisie who are not too demoralised by the decadence
of the bourgeois order to be able intellectually to place
themselves at the standpoint of the proletariat.   The defence
of the *positive* objective method of all scientific investigation,
and of the *unitary* world conception thence resulting, thus
passes, by the dialectic of history (which induces the desertion
to mysticism and supernaturalism of whole strata of the
intelligentsia), over to the revolutionary proletariat and
Dialectical Materialism.   Here another classic passage from
Engels illustrates and emphasises the reason why.   Answering
the *pseudo*-" scientific " Eugene Dühring who postulated
the " unity " of the universe as an *a priori* presumption from
which its rationality and natural laws were to be *deduced,*
Engels says :

" In the first place, thought consists in the decomposition of objects of consciousness into their elements as
well as the bringing of mutually connected elements into
a unity.   *There can be no synthesis without analysis.*

" In the second place, thought can without error only
bring those elements of consciousness into a unity in
which, or in the actual prototypes of which, this unity
already existed beforehand.

" *If I comprehend a shoe-brush under the class mammal,
it does not thereby become a milk-giver.* . . . If his entire
method of proof were really correct, Herr Dühring
would not have gained a single point over the spiritists.
The spiritists would curtly reply, ' The universe is a
unity from our standpoint also.   The division into the
hither and the beyond only exists from our special
earthly original sin standpoint.   In its essence (*that is,
God*) the entire universe is a unity.' . . .

" If we speak of existence and merely of existence,
the unity can only consist in this : that all that we are
concerned with about all objects is that they *exist.* . . .
For as soon as we take a step beyond the simple fact that
existence is common to all things, the *distinctions betweem
these separate things* engage our attention, and if these
differences consist in this, that some are black, some

white, some alive, others not alive, some hither and some beyond, we cannot conclude therefrom that *the same existence* can be imputed to all of them alike.

" The unity of the universe does not consist in its existence . . . since it must first exist before it can be a unit. Existence beyond the boundary line of our horizon is an open question. *The real unity of the Universe consists in its materiality and this is established, not by juggling phrases, but by means of a long and difficult development of philosophy and natural science.*"

—ENGELS : *Anti-Dühring.*

Here, by that serenely poised practicality which identifies the philosophical conclusions of Dialectical Materialism with the " naïve realism " of the plain, everyday working mass and majority of mankind, Engels shows how all sophistication and obscurantism can be met and defeated. Not only was Dialectical Materialism first attained by Marx and Engels as a synthesis of practical critical dialectics with the practical standpoint of revolutionary proletarian struggle. The defence of that struggle, and its carrying forward to an objectively triumphant conclusion involves the maintaining of that synthetic unity, and the maintaining therefore of the theoretical outlook, standpoint, and method by means of which all the virile elements left in the various strata of the bourgeoisie can pass over to the standpoint of the revolution and play their part in defeating the reaction and in changing the world.

It may be supposed that this implies that very adulteration of the revolutionary proletarian struggle with alien elements to which we have traced the rise and development of the social-democratic degeneration of Marxism. It implies nothing of the sort ; since the Dialectical Materialist objection to petty bourgeois intellectuals, etc., is not that they are *objectively* members of classes other than that of the proletariat, but that they may bring, have brought, and (unless safeguards are adopted) will continue to bring into the proletarian struggle *an alien class standpoint* and a theoretical system to match. Marx expresses the matter thus :

" The substantial aim of the social democracy is to transform society by *the democratic method*, the transformation being kept always within the petty bourgeois orbit.

" Do not run away with the idea that the deliberate

purpose of the petty bourgeois class is to enforce its own selfish class interest. The petty bourgeois believes that the special conditions required for his own liberation are likewise the general conditions requisite for the salvation of the whole of modern society. He thinks that in no other way can society be saved and the class war *averted*.

" Nor must it be supposed that the representatives of the democracy are all shopkeepers or enthusiastic champions of the lower middle class.

" What makes them politically representative of the petty bourgeoisie is this : They fail utterly to transcend intellectually those boundaries which in real life constitute the material limiting conditions of petty bourgeois existence. Consequently they are impelled in their theoretical practice towards precisely the same aspirations and the solution of the same problems as those which in material life are raised by the material interests and the social situation of the petty bourgeoisie."
—MARX : *Eighteenth Brumaire*, chap. III.

In the real life practice of society the petty bourgeoisie of every grade finds itself in the social scale always at a point " above " that occupied by the proletariat and below that occupied by the bourgeoisie proper. Is it to be wondered at,therefore, that in its political theorising the petty bourgeoisie should constantly reveal its class limitations by formulating policies, programmes and solutions, all of which turn upon the need to secure the " golden mean," the exact middle course, the perfect " General Average " in between the " extremes " of proletarian revolution and bourgeois counter-revolution ? This was the naïvely paraded " virtue " of petty bourgeois Liberalism and Radicalism. As the last relics of the Liberal Party drop below the Parliamentary horizon its watchwords pass by " divine right," as it were, to Transport House, which proclaims as its crowning virtue that it stands " equally " opposed to *both* Communism *and* Fascism ! It recalls, thereby, Bernard Shaw's classic aphorism :

" A moderately honest man, with a moderately faithful wife, moderate drinkers, both, in a moderately healthy house : that is the true middle-class unit."—BERNARD SHAW : *Man and Superman*, p. 238.

The solution of any difficulty likely to arise from the influx into the ranks of the revolutionary proletarian struggle is indicated in the Dialectical Materialist conception of the theory and practice of revolutionary proletarian struggle. The practice of systematic self criticism by the revolutionary proletarian Party is the guarantee—and the only conceivable guarantee—that its unity of theory and practice will be maintained at the requisite level. Self-criticism by the revolutionary proletarian Party implies both the objective activity and the theoretical understanding of that activity. It implies that the activity subjected to criticism shall be the objective activity of the Party, as such, co-ordinated and directed to a specific end. It implies that the criticism shall be made from an objectively practical critical standpoint. At each point it involves a Dialectical Materialist outlook whereby the objective activity has been directed, and a Dialectical Materialist method of criticism whereby alone concrete conclusions can be drawn. The self-discipline of the Party is implicit in the canon of " unity of theory and practice." This discipline is at one and the same time a guarantee against the sophistication of the Party by alien elements ; and a safeguard against the spurious, Eastman-Trotskyite conception of the Party as a flock of sheep driven by super-Bakuninist " engineers of revolution." The cure for this latter petty bourgeois nonsense is not its *sub*-social-democratic inversion, the conception of the Party as a few noble-natured, high-minded " leaders " *driven* by the Party flock of sheep ! The " sheep " must be eliminated from the conception altogether. The Party must be conceived as an actively organic whole in which *all* are equally active and functioning parts of the whole—the said whole being the totality and outcome of *all party activities*. These activities, in turn, must be conceived as deriving their whole and sole justification from the extent to which they serve to promote the growth, consolidation, progression, and triumph of the revolutionary struggle of the proletariat in mass :

" Upon what rests the discipline of the revolutionary Party of the proletariat ? How is it controlled ? How is it strengthened ?

" First, by the *class consciousness* of the proletarian vanguard and by its *devotion* to the Revolution, by its steadiness, spirit of self-sacrifice, and heroism.

" Secondly, by its *ability to mix* with the toiling masses, to become intimate with, and to a certain extent, if you will, to fuse itself with the non-proletarian toilers.

" Thirdly, by the *soundness* of the political leadership, carried out by the vanguard, and by its *correct* political strategy and tactics *based on the idea that the workers from their own experience must convince themselves* of the soundness of this political leadership, strategy, and tactics.

" Without all these conditions, discipline in a revolutionary party, really capable of being a party of the foremost class, whose object is to overthrow the bourgeoisie and transform society, is impossible of realisation. Without these conditions all attempts to create discipline result in empty phrases, in mere contortions."

—LENIN : *Left Wing Communism*, p. 11.

Thus, on the objective and subjective sides of both theory and practice—the side of the practical rectification of theory as well as that of the theoretical rectification of practice, Dialectical Materialism, *and its continual development* is an indispensable pre-requisite for the growth of the revolutionary proletarian struggle ; as that in turn is indispensable for any practically effective struggle against cultural reaction.

Finally, as a warning against the neglect of Theory in general and against conceiving Theory in too narrowly empirical and " practical " a fashion—against, that is to say, any conception of Theory which in any way or degree minimises the infinite many-sidedness and comprehensiveness of Dialectical Materialism, we add a final quotation :

" It must be borne in mind that the sharp change which modern natural science is at present undergoing gives rise to reactionary philosophical schools and trends. It is extremely important, therefore, to study the questions which the latest revolution in the field of natural science has brought to the front. . . .

" Unless this is done militant Materialism will be neither militant nor Materialist. . . . The overwhelming mass of representatives of the bourgeois intelligentsia have fastened upon Einstein's theory, although Einstein himself does not actively oppose Materialism. . . .

" But in order to avoid reacting to such a phenomenon unintelligently we must understand that no natural science, no Materialism whatever, can hold out in the struggle against the onslaught of bourgeois ideas, and the restoration of bourgeois philosophy, without a *solid philosophical basis*. In order to give aid to this struggle and help to carry it to its successful conclusion, the natural scientist must be a *modern* Materialist—a conscious adherent of that materialism which Marx

2S

represents ; that is, he must be a *dialectical* Materialist.

" To achieve this [we] must organise a systematic study . . . of the dialectics which Marx applied concretely in his *Capital*, and used in his historical and political works with such success that to-day . . . the awakening of new peoples and new classes to life confirms the correctness of Marxism daily more and more.

" Basing ourselves on the manner in which Marx applied the Materialist conception of Hegelian dialectics, we can and must work out these dialectics, from all sides. . . . Modern natural scientists will find . . . in the Materialist interpretation of Hegelian dialectics a number of answers to those philosophical questions which the revolution in natural science has brought to the front, and which cause the intellectual admirers of bourgeois fashions to *slip* into the reactionary camp. . . .

" Unless we set ourselves this task and carry it out systematically, materialism will never be militant Materialism. It will remain . . . *not a fighter, but one who is fought.*"—LENIN : *On Religion*, pp. 40–41.

It was the acceptance by the present writer of this stirring call for more and better *practice* in the theoretical field as a personal admonition that gave rise to this essay. In the existing concatenation of circumstances in the revolutionary proletarian struggle in Britain, it was absolutely imperative that something of the kind should be attempted by somebody, however poorly qualified. If the result is to cause in any degree a renewal of attention to the writings of Marx and Engels themselves, and a correspondingly improved appreciation of their practical, as well as their theoretical worth—and with this a fuller appreciation of the vital and inseparable unity and continuity of the theory and practice of Lenin and Stalin with that of Marx and Engels—the object of the work will have been amply attained.

" HERE I STAND : TO ME NOUGHT ELSE IS POSSIBLE."

INDEX